Let Her Speak for Herself

Frontispiece from Naomi *by Chara Broughton Conant*
(American Tract Society, 1898)

Let Her Speak for Herself

Nineteenth-Century Women Writing on the Women of Genesis

MARION ANN TAYLOR AND
HEATHER E. WEIR

Editors

B

Baylor University Press
Waco, Texas

Cover Design by Stephanie Blumenthal
Book Design by Diane Smith

Library of Congress Cataloging-in-Publication Data

Let her speak for herself : nineteenth-century women writing on women in
Genesis / Marion A. Taylor and Heather Weir, editors.
    p. cm.
Includes bibliographical references and indexes.
ISBN-13: 978-1-932792-53-9 (pbk. : alk. paper)
1. Bible. O.T. Genesis--Feminist criticism. 2. Women in the Bible. I.
Taylor, Marion Ann. II. Weir, Heather.

BS1235.52.L48 2006
222'.110922082--dc22
                              2006019739

To our foremothers in faith,
known and unknown,
who read, interpreted, and taught the Bible before us.

Contents

Part 6: Lot's Wife and Daughters, Dinah, Tamar, Potiphar's Wife—The Other Women of Genesis   399

Lot's Wife and Daughters

Dinah

PREFACE ˙

The headless woman on the cover reminds us that history has forgotten women who interpreted the Bible. This book is part of the long process of recovering the voice of women interpreters. The idea for the book began with a question.

A few years ago, when Marion Taylor was teaching a class on the History of Old Testament scholarship, a student asked if she could do her term paper on a significant woman in the field of Old Testament studies. Taylor's initial response was to suggest a number of twentieth-century women who had made a significant contribution to the field. The focus of the course, however, was biblical studies in the nineteenth century, and Taylor was left wondering about women interpreters before the second half of the twentieth century. Donald K. McKim's *Historical Handbook of Major Biblical Interpreters* did not help in her quest.[1] Of the 101 individuals covered in McKim's book only two twentieth-century women (Elisabeth Schüssler Fiorenza and Phyllis Trible) were included. McKim recognized the omission of women and non-Western interpreters in his introduction and invited others to supplement his volume by producing additionally needed resources.

Taylor's search for women interpreters continued. She was convinced that women had read and interpreted the Scriptures throughout history and that some records of women's interpretations must exist, although women's voices were never included in any courses or readings she had done as an Old Testament scholar, specializing in the history of interpretation. She found that other women had recognized the gap in knowledge of women interpreters of scripture. Patricia Demers examined women interpreters as an English scholar.[3] However, Demers's book is quite short and her own engagement

[1] Downers Grove, Ill.: InterVarsity, 1998.
[2] McKim, x.

with feminist hermeneutics effectively shifts the focus of the book away from recovering voices of women interpreters from the past to engaging contemporary issues. Similarly, Marla Selvidge's book, *Notorious Voices: Feminist Biblical Interpretation, 1500–1920*,[4] focuses narrowly on the "notorious voices" of proto-feminists.

A number of books written by church historians pointed to the names and writings of women throughout history. Internet resources on English literature, including "A Celebration of Women Writers" suggested countless names of women to be investigated.[5] With the help of Renata Koke, the possibility of mounting a course on women biblical interpreters became a reality. Heather Weir took the first course on women interpreters and began to work on the search for more interpreters.

As the project grew, the decision was made to focus research on the nineteenth century, a period of great interest to biblical scholars in terms of the development of new approaches to the study of the Bible and in terms of women's history. A Lilly theological research grant allowed Taylor to spend a sabbatical year doing research on women interpreters of the nineteenth century.

The task of finding women interpreters of the Bible has been difficult. Techniques of a detective are needed. Weir unearthed the names of many women by entering "Mrs." as author and "Bible" as subject in various library search engines. She also tried entering popular Victorian girls' names (e.g., Sarah, Elizabeth, or Mary) and "Bible." Searching the inventory lists of used booksellers and searching various publishers advertising lists uncovered still more names and books. Through our extensive research, we unearthed the titles of more than a thousand books written by nineteenth-century women on the Bible.

Once we had the titles, the task of finding the actual works also proved to be challenging. Many books written by women are now very hard to find. Some are available through interlibrary loan; the interlibrary loan staff at the University of Toronto assisted us immensely in our search for these hard-to-find treasures. The writings of many British writers are only found in British Libraries. Happily, an increasing number of primary and rare materials, particularly writings of Canadian women, is being published on the Internet. Thanks to the generous support of the Louisville Institute, we have been able to find many of the interpretive works of American women. A Lilly Research

---

[3] Patricia Demers, *Women as Interpreters of the Bible* (New York: Paulist Press, 1992).

[4] New York: Continuum, 1996.

[5] Mary Mark, "A Celebration of Women Writers." http://digital.library.upenn.edu/women/ (accessed Nov. 7, 2005).

Expense Grant opened up the possibility of seeing the works of women that are now found only in British libraries. We have often felt overwhelmed at the amount of material we have found, and are still finding. We also felt compelled to make this material available so that wider scholarly discussion and analysis of these works might begin.

As we have worked on this project, the excitement of recovering lost voices of foremothers of faith has energized us and given purpose to this work. As we have shared our discoveries with colleagues, students, friends, and family, they have responded with surprise and excitement. Their positive response to the material has encouraged us to continue with our work. This work could not have been completed without the generous and gracious support of the whole Taylor family as we worked all summer by the lake—thank you all.

We would like to thank the faculty, staff, and students at Wycliffe College for their encouragement. We especially thank Isa Hauser for her unflagging zeal in searching online catalogues for women interpreters, Wendy Amos Binks for her help in finding biographical information, Kari Reed for scanning documents, Jasmine Shantz for scanning and editing many works, and Beth Ranson for copy editing scanned documents. Tom Power was an invaluable help in finding biographical and secondary resources. The students of "Bad Boys and Bad Girls of the Bible," "Women in the Old Testament," and "Women As Interpreters of the Bible" all used this material in class and gave valuable feedback. Glen Taylor used some of this material in his course on Genesis and provided encouragement throughout the project. He also thought up the title of the book and spent many hours proofreading it. Claire Alexander edited many chapters and contributed to their clarity. We also acknowledge the invaluable contribution of Meredith Donaldson to this work, especially in biographical research and organization of material.

Other colleagues and friends who have assisted us include Diane D'Amico, David Kent, Cynthia Scheinberg, Peter Erb, Jonathan Slater, Christiana DeGroot, Tim Larson, Renée James, Heather House, Wanda Malcolm, Donelle Ruwe, Gillian Mitchell, Leslie McLean, Lorraine Hudson, and Sarah Baum. Carey C. Newman at Baylor University Press has encouraged our work on this project from the beginning and pushed us to be bold in our writing.

Note: our notes appear as footnotes and the nineteenth-century author's notes appear as endnotes. Scripture references and comments in square brackets are ours.

INTRODUCTION

All writers must go from *now* to *once upon a time;* all must go from here to there; all must descend to where the stories are kept; all must take care not to be captured and held immobile by the past. And all must commit acts of larceny, or else of reclamation, depending how you look at it. The dead may guard the treasure, but it's useless treasure unless it can be brought back into the land of the living and allowed to enter time once more–which means to enter the realm of the audience, the realm of the readers, the realm of change.

~Margaret Atwood[1]

Biblical scholars must bring out hidden treasure from interpreters long ignored and forgotten by the academy. A significant number of English-speaking women published works of biblical interpretation in the nineteenth century. Most of these women's writings have been forgotten; their voices are no longer heard. Until now, these important texts have been overlooked by most academic reconsiderations of the religious life and theological education of nineteenth-century Britons and Americans. The time has come to let these women reenter time and speak for themselves.

The recovery of women's lost writings is important because these works invite us to reconsider both the roles women played in the religious life of their communities and the influence such women had both on other women and men through their roles as educators and scriptural interpreters. These writings shed light on women's culture in the nineteenth century and provide important data on women's roles in society and in the church. They give witness to the variety of approaches and literary genres used by women interpreters. They contain lost exegetical traditions and insights of women and offer remarkable examples of gendered exegesis as women read the Bible through

---

[1] Margaret Atwood, *Negotiating with the Dead: A Writer on Writing* (Cambridge: Cambridge University Press, 2002), 178–79.

the distinctive lens of their culture and gender identity. The writings, then, raise a number of important questions about how culture affects interpretation, how women interpret differently than men, and gendered exegesis.

The writings also show how the scriptures functioned in the lives of women devotionally and practically. They show women's involvement in the religious education of children, young people, and adults. The collection unearths a lost witness to the impact of changes in biblical studies on lay women and men (for example, the rise of historicism, travel, archaeology, evolution). The writings suggest that the scope or definition of what is generally considered to be the genre of biblical interpretation be expanded to include the writings of those who stood outside the academy. Finally, these voices call us to search the records further to recover other lost voices of women who interpreted the Bible, who provide important, empowering models for readers today who are faced with the task of interpreting the scriptures.

There are many challenges for the modern reader in reading and understanding these nineteenth-century interpretations of the Bible and allowing the women writers to speak for themselves. We need to consider them in their social, religious, and cultural contexts, as well as to understand our own world and the way we read and react to these texts.

The World of Women in Nineteenth-Century Britain and America

Home and family were the center of most women's lives in the nineteenth century. Scholars often use the terms "the cult of domesticity" and "true womanhood" to describe the collection of attitudes that developed in the late eighteenth and early nineteenth centuries regarding women's roles in the family and society and women's virtues.[2] These attitudes developed as industrialization and urbanization moved the center of men's work from the home to the factory, and from the country to the city. The increasingly separate spheres of men's and women's lives are also associated with the privatization of faith and feminization of Christian piety.[3] Despite the feminization

[2] For a discussion of these terms see Barbara Welter, "The Cult of True Womanhood: 1820–1860," *American Quarterly* 18 (1966): 151–74.

[3] Callum G. Brown. *The Death of Christian Britain: Understanding Secularization 1800–2000* (London: Routledge, 2001), 35; Barbara Welter, "The Feminization of American Religion: 1800–1860," in *Clio's Consciousness Raised: New Perspectives on the History of Women*, ed. Mary S. Hartman and Lois Banner (New York: Harper & Row, 1974), 137–57; Darrel M. Robertson, "The Feminization of American Religion: An Examination of Recent Interpretations of Women and Religion in Victorian America," *Christian Scholars' Review* 8, 3 (1978): 238–46.

of the church, almost all women were barred from ecclesiastical positions of power in the church; they could not fill traditional clergy roles. The exceptions to this rule were usually found in newer movements, like the Holiness Movement, or groups located outside of the mainstream denominations, such as the Quakers, or on the foreign mission field.[4]

Nineteenth-century women's magazines, gift books, and religious writings emphasized the importance of the four attitudes or qualities every woman was expected to display: piety (or religion), purity, submissiveness, and domesticity.[5] The very high value that Elizabeth Rundle Charles (1821–1889), a popular British writer, placed on true womanhood reflects the views of many women and men of this period. She regarded piety as a feminine virtue and divinized the feminine virtue of service. The true life of women is equated to God, and Jesus' life of service and sacrifice becomes the ideal woman's life.

> Christianity has exalted the ideal of womanhood, not by changing it but by showing that the true life of woman, which is love, is the very essential being of God; for it is written that "God is Love." . . .
>
> Our Lord Jesus Christ has exalted the mission of women, which is sacrifice and service, not by changing it, but by making it His own, in that He came "not to be ministered unto, but to minister, and to give His life as a ransom for many."[6]

This exalted view of women's piety, purity, and vocation of self-sacrifice and ministry affected how some women read stories about women in the Bible. For example, when some nineteenth-century female readers read Genesis, they looked for examples of how the women displayed the feminine virtues advocated by nineteenth-century culture. Women interpreters, internalizing the divinization of female virtue, often placed the responsibility for family problems or successes on the woman's shoulders. Female characters in the Bible were often judged as being either saints or sinners on

---

[4] See Beverly Zink-Sawyer, *From Preachers to Suffragists: Women's Rights and Religious Conviction in the Lives of Three Nineteenth-Century American Clergywomen* (Louisville: Westminster John Knox, 2003), 69–122. See also, Catherine A. Brekus, *Strangers & Pilgrims: Female Preaching in America 1740–1845* (Chapel Hill: University of North Carolina Press, 1998). For British women, see Christine L. Krueger, *The Reader's Repentance: Women Preachers, Women Writers, and Nineteenth-Century Social Discourse* (Chicago: University of Chicago Press, 1992). Also see Timothy Larsen, *Contested Christianity: The Political and Social Contexts of Victorian Theology* (Waco, Tex.: Baylor University Press, 2004). On women in foreign missions, see Barbara Welter, "She Hath Done What She Could: Protestant Women's Missionary Careers in Nineteenth-century America," *American Quarterly* 30 (1978): 624–38.

[5] Welter, "The Cult of True Womanhood."

[6] Elizabeth Rundle Charles, *Sketches of the Women of Christendom* (New York: Dodd, Mead, n.d), 2.

the basis of how well they fit into the nineteenth-century's understanding of true womanhood.

The cult of domesticity restricted women's lives to the private sphere. Depending on their social class and wealth, the work that women actually accomplished in the home setting varied. Although some women had domestic help, either servants or slaves, many women performed a variety of tasks associated with running a household and raising a family.[7] Harriet Beecher Stowe (1811–1896), for example, wrote to supplement her husband's meager salary, but found it difficult to balance her domestic responsibilities as mother and wife with her writing. She describes her life of juggling her many responsibilities in the following letter:

> Since I began this note, I have been called off at least a dozen times; once for the fish-man, to buy a codfish; once to see a man who had brought me some barrels of apples; once to see a book agent; then to Mrs. Uphams to see about a drawing I promised to make for her; then to nurse the baby; then into the kitchen to make a chowder for dinner; and now I am at it again, for nothing but deadly determination enables me ever to write; it is rowing against wind and tide.[8]

Stowe's "deadly determination" was fueled by the need to provide for her family as well as a sense of vocation. Susan Warner (1819–1885), Christina Rossetti (1830–1894), and Grace Aguilar (1816–1847) are all examples of single women who supported not only themselves but also their families through their writings. Similarly, Clara Lucas Balfour (1808–1878) lectured and wrote to supplement her family's income as her husband's early alcohol abuse had left the family in poverty.

Other women wrote simply out of a desire to serve others through their work. Often they wrote for their own families and friends. For example, Lady Eliza Verney (d. 1857/58) wrote her book on Isaiah as devotional material for her family; later it was published for the benefit of others. Her husband inscribed the book to the author's memory as follows:

---

[7] The American author, editor, and abolitionist, Lydia Maria Child (1802–1880), for example, summarized her year's work in her diary in 1864. Her extensive list included the writing of 53 articles and correcting proofs for a new book, the cooking of 360 dinners and 362 breakfasts, sweeping and dusting the sitting-room and kitchen 350 times, filling lamps 362 times, caring for sick friends and family members, making 83 items of clothing and assorted linens, preserving two pecks of fruit, mending clothes and carrying out other many other jobs too small to note. See Jeanne Bodyston, "Cult of True Womanhood," located online at http://www.pbs.org/stantonanthony/resources/index.html?body=culthood.html (last accessed April 21, 2005).

[8] Edward Wagenknecht, *Harriet Beecher Stowe: The Known and the Unknown* (New York: Oxford University Press, 1965), 167–68.

To the memory of one who, richly endowed with intellectual gifts, devoted them all to the glory of God and the highest welfare of every one connected with her. This fragment, written by her for the devotional exercise of her family, and used during the last two months of her life, while mourning the loss of a beloved daughter, is sorrowfully inscribed by her bereaved husband.[9]

Although women's writing took place in the private sphere, their writings often brought them into the more public world of the academy, the church, and the government. Barred from the pulpit, they used their pens to preach.[10] They gained a voice without a body. Objections to women speaking in public were overcome as writing "allows a faceless, disembodied utterance to go forth without a timbre or tone, unaccompanied by braids or bosoms or other enticements to male desire."[11]

Many women who took up their pens produced books used in the academy and church by scholars, ministers, and theological students. These included translations of scholarly books, such as Sophia Taylor's (fl. 1864–1900) translations of numerous German commentaries and works of theology[12] and Elizabeth Palmer Peabody's (1804–1894) translation of Guillaume Oegger's *The True Messiah* (1829) from French in 1842. Other women translated ancient texts: Helen Spurrell (fl. 1885) translated the Old Testament from Hebrew,[13] Agnes Smith Lewis (1843–1926) worked on Arabic and Syriac manuscripts,[14] and Julia Evelina Smith (1792–1886) translated the

---

[9] Eliza, Lady Verney, *Practical Thoughts on the First Forty Chapters of the Book of the Prophet, Isaiah* (London: James Nisbet, 1858), iii.

[10] Many women, including Harriet Beecher Stowe, included sermons in their novels, or modeled their novels after sermons. See Gayle Kimball, *The Religious Ideas of Harriet Beecher Stowe: Her Gospel of Womanhood* (New York: Mellen Press, 1982).

[11] L. Robert Stevens, "Intertextual Construction of Faith: Julia Wedgwood (1833–1913)," in *Women's Theology in Nineteenth-Century Britain*, ed. Julie Melnyk (New York: Garland, 1998), 84.

[12] For example, Franz Delitzsch, *A New Commentary on Genesis*, 5th ed., trans. Sophia Taylor, Clark's Foreign Theological Library 2 (Edinburgh: T&T Clark, 1888–1894); Isaac August Dorner, *History of Protestant Theology: Particularly in Germany: Viewed According to Its Fundamental Movement: And in Connection with the Religious, Moral, and Intellectual Life*, trans. George Robson and Sophia Taylor, 2 vols. (Edinburgh: T&T Clark, 1871); C. F. Keil, *The Book of Ezra, Nehemiah, and Esther*, trans. Sophia Taylor (Edinburgh: T&T Clark, 1873); Gustav Friedrich Oehler, *Theology of the Old Testament*, trans. E. D. Smith and Sophia Taylor, 2 vols. (Edinburgh: T&T Clark, 1880); Ernst Wilhelm Christian, Sartorius, *The Doctrine of Divine Love: Or, Outlines of the Moral Theology of the Evangelical Church*, trans. Sophia Taylor (Edinburgh: T&T Clark, 1884).

[13] Helen Spurrell, *A Translation of the Old Testament Scriptures from the Original Hebrew* (London: James Nisbet, 1885).

[14] For an account of Lewis's travel and acquisition of manuscripts, see Agnes Smith Lewis, *In the Shadow of Sinai: a Story of Travel and Research from 1895 to 1897* (Cambridge: Macmillan & Bowes, 1898).

entire Bible from the original languages.[15] Specialty books like Julia Greswell's
(fl. 1873) *Grammatical Analysis of the Hebrew Psalter*,[16] and Elizabeth Smith's
(1776–1806) *A Vocabulary, Hebrew, Arabic, and Persian*[17] also became part
of the world of the academy. Fanny Corbaux (1812–1883) and Antoinette
Brown Blackwell (1825–1921) published articles in scholarly journals.[18]

Many women of faith wrote educational materials in the form of cat-
echisms, children's Bibles, story books, study guides, books of prayers, and
devotional guides. These educational books often began as stories or teaching
materials for the author's children. Sarah Trimmer (1741–1810), for example,
educated her twelve children at home, then wrote books to assist others in
educating children. For many women, their role as educators was both a moral
responsibility and an extension of their position in the domestic sphere. In
the preface to a book written in 1899 for young women who had finished
their formal education, Charlotte Laurie (fl. 1899), the Assistant Mistress at
the Ladies' College, Cheltenham, argued:

> That there is great ignorance of the Bible in the present day is admitted on all
> sides. The remedy for this lies largely with the women of England, who in one
> way or another are often called to teach scripture—it may be as teachers in day
> and Sunday schools—as elder sisters; above all, as mothers.[19]

Women's self-understanding of their responsibility as "priests of the home"
was extended beyond the home to correcting the faithlessness of society. This
self-understanding was encouraged by their society's idealization of a true
woman as the moral guardian first of her family, then of society as a whole.

Women's domestic, religious, and maternal ministering roles were often
extended to include those outside their own family, such as the poor, the
uneducated, the sick, the prisoner, and the unchurched, both near and far.
Women wrote books based on their experiences in these ministries of service.
Adult educational writing by women, including studies for mother's meet-

---

[15] Julia E. Smith, *The Holy Bible Containing the Old and New Testaments. Translated Literally from the Original Tongues* (Hartford, Conn.: American Publishing, 1885).

[16] Julia Greswell, *Grammatical Analysis of the Hebrew Psalter* (Oxford: James Parker, 1873). Greswell's book contains two letters of endorsement from two male scholars addressed to her father. The letters commend the use of the grammar by students preparing for divinity studies at Oxford.

[17] Elizabeth Smith, *A Vocabulary, Hebrew, Arabic, and Persian* (London, 1814). This vocabulary was edited and prefaced by J. F. Usko.

[18] Fanny Corbaux, "The Rephaim, and their Connexion with Egyptian History," *Journal of Sacred Literature* n.s. 1 (1851): 151–72; Antoinette Brown Blackwell, "Exegesis of 1 Corinthians, XIV., 34, 35; and I Timothy II., 11, 12," *Oberlin Quarterly Review* 4 (1849): 358–73.

[19] Charlotte L. Laurie, *On the Study of the Bible* (London: Society for Promoting Christian Knowledge, 1899), 3.

ings, commentaries, studies for the College by Post,[20] and devotional guides, often had many of these service ministries as a background. Ministries that grew out of an ethic of service and self-sacrifice allowed women to move into more public and political roles associated with various reform movements, such as slavery, suffrage, temperance, and women's rights.[21] Many women wrote and sometimes spoke publicly about these issues, and so stepped into a public controversy. For example, Elizabeth Cady Stanton (1815–1902), Angelina Grimké (later Weld, 1805–1879) and her sister, Sarah Grimké (1792–1873), were all vocal abolitionists in the United States.[22] Stepping into the public sphere on the issue of slavery led the Grimkés to become advocates for women's rights;[23] Stanton also moved into this field from her earlier abolition and temperance work. In England, Annie Besant wrote polemically on the issue of women's rights and roles in society.[24] Victorians often referrred to such discussions as the Woman Question.

Many of the published women came from privileged families and had received the best education available to them at that time. Some knew Greek, Latin, and Hebrew and many learned French and German.[25] Many women

[20] Mary Louisa Georgina Petrie, *Clews to Holy Writ or, The Chronological Scripture Cycle* (London: Hodder & Stoughton, 1894).

[21] In an article called "Ministering Angels," Anne Summers writes:
And 'women's mission' was largely expected to be its own reward; duties, rather than rights were proclaimed as the motor principle of women's actions outside the home. It is possible to admire self-abnegation without acquiring a taste for it; . . . The ethic of female service and self-sacrifice permeated initiatives from which many have benefited, but which cannot properly be heralded as emancipatory. Not only nursing, but teaching, social work and even the feminist movement itself possess a large and dubious inheritance from the value system of the sisterhoods and ladies bountiful of the nineteenth century (*History Today* 39 [1989]: 37).

[22] For a summary of the Grimké's work see Dorothy C. Bass, "'In Christian Firmness and Christian Meekness': Feminism and Pacifism in Antebellum America," in *Immaculate & Powerful: The Female in Sacred Image and Social Reality*, ed. Clarissa W. Atkinson, Constance H. Buchanan, and Margaret R. Miles (Boston: Beacon Press, 1985), 201–25. Also see Elizabeth A. Clark and Herbert Richardson, *Women and Religion* (New York: Harper, 1996), 237–64; Elizabeth Cady Stanton, *The Slave's Appeal* (Albany: Weed, Parsons, 1860).

[23] See especially Sarah Grimké, *Letters on the Equality of the Sexes and the Condition of Women* (Boston, 1838).

[24] Annie Besant (1847–1933) wrote many works against Christian morals and argued that the Bible could not be the basis of a moral society. One of her key works that addresses women and marriage is *God's Views on Marriage as Revealed in the Old Testament* (London: Freethought Publishing, 1881).

[25] For example, Florence Nightingale's facility with languages enabled her to read the Bible in Greek, Latin, German, and Hebrew at a rudimentary level, to wrestle with issues of translation, to keep up to date on recent critical theories, and to incorporate into her own devotional reading her favorite German, Italian, and French writers. See *The Collected Works of Florence Nightingale*, vol. 2 of *Florence Nightingale's Spiritual Journey: Biblical Annotations, Sermons and Journal Notes*, ed. Lynn McDonald (Waterloo, Ontario: Wilfred Laurier University Press,

writers were the daughters, sisters, or wives of clergymen. Their relatives gave them access to the finest theological libraries, an ear to the latest controversies and developments in biblical studies and theology, and connections to both the publishing world and the world of the academy. Others received only a basic education at home, then continued their own education by reading. Some, like Clara Balfour, were almost entirely self-educated. A visitor to the Balfour home described it as being filled with books: "I perceived that a great space of the walls was covered with shelves, & well filled with Books: it was like a regular student's library."[26] Julia Smith asked her father to buy her a Latin Grammar when he visited Hartford. When he arrived home without it, she saddled a horse and rode into Hartford herself to buy the book.[27] The women who wrote on the Bible valued education, both for themselves, and for others.

Although British and American women's cultures shared many common elements, there were clear differences between the cultures that affected their writing. With London as the major publishing centre for the English-speaking world, British women were building on a well-established literary tradition. Elizabeth Montague (1720–1800), Elizabeth Carter (1717–1806), Hannah More (1745–1833), Anna Barbauld (1743–1825), Mary Wollestonecraft (1759–1797), and other eighteenth-century women provided examples of scholarship for British women to follow.[28] While some American women, such as Sarah Hall (1761–1830) and Catherine Putnam (1792–1861), who lived in cities like Philadelphia and New York, had access to libraries and publishers, North American women did not have a strong literary and cultural tradition to build upon.[29] The few Canadian women such as Mary L. T. Witter (fl.

2001), 34, 94. Julia Evelina Smith knew Greek and taught herself Hebrew so that she could translate the Old Testament from the Hebrew original; see Marla J. Selvidge, *Notorious Voices: Feminist Biblical Interpretation, 1500–1920* (New York: Continuum, 1996), 215. For a full treatment of Julia Smith and her family, see Susan J. Shaw, *A Religious History of Julia Evelina Smith's 1876 Translation of the Holy Bible: Doing More Than Any Man Has Ever Done* (San Francisco: Mellen Research University Press, 1993).

[26] John Dunlop, *Autobiography of John Dunlop* (London: Spottiswoode, Ballantyne, 1931), 153–54.

[27] Selvidge, *Notorious Voices*, 215.

[28] See Sylvia Harstock Myers, *The Bluestocking Circle: Women, Friendship, and the Life of the Mind in Eighteenth-century England* (Oxford: Clarendon, 1990). Women like Mary Astell (1666–1731) and Margaret Askew Fell (1614–1701) could also be cited as literary foremothers for British women. However, it is not clear that these earlier women scholars and authors were known to the later eighteenth-century bluestocking circle. On discontinuity between generations of women scholars, see Gerda Lerner, *The Creation of Feminist Consciousness: From the Middle Ages to Eighteen-Seventy* (New York: Oxford University Press, 1993), 165–66.

[29] Hannah Adams (1755–1831) was considered the first professional American writer. She began publishing around 1784. See Sarah Pelmas, "Hannah Adams," in *The Cambridge Guide to Women's Writing in English*, ed. Lorna Sage (Cambridge: Cambridge University Press, 1999), 4. Also see Thomas A. Tweed, "An American Pioneer in the Study of Religion: Hannah

1870–1900) that wrote in this time period had even fewer resources and were influenced by both American and British writers.

There were differences in the religious culture of Britain and North America. In England, there was an established episcopal church, surrounded by dissenting churches, which gradually gained rights during the nineteenth century. In the United States, religion tended to be democratized; a distrust of educated clergy, along with the democratic ideals of the new republic led to many populist religious movements in the United States during the first half of the nineteenth century.[30] The Canadian church reflected characteristics of both the United States and Britain but was distinct from both.

British women could travel more easily to the rest of Europe and to the Holy Land than could North American women, which allowed them to address issues of theological controversy, new scientific discoveries, and archeological finds in their writings. British women also had access to the archeological finds displayed at the British Museum, which were often incorporated into their books. Their travel and access to artifacts gave them a better sense of the historical and cultural context of the biblical texts. American women did not have this easy access to cultural artifacts, though they read travel journals and saw pictures of artifacts. Harriet Beecher Stowe wrote about being overcome with emotion when she was in Europe and able to see the great paintings, which she had only ever seen in prints.

In the United States, the civil war, the slavery issue, and the expansion of the west were the focus of many women's and men's energies during the nineteenth century; energy which might have been given to biblical scholarship and writing was spent elsewhere. These factors, along with the lack of literary tradition and education, may account for some of the differences in genre[31] and content[32] between North American and British women's writings on the Bible.

Adams (1755–1831) and her "Dictionary of All Religions," *Journal of the American Academy of Religion* 60, 3 (1992): 437–64.

[30] See Nathan O. Hatch, *The Democratization of American Christianity* (New Haven: Yale University Press, 1989), especially his introduction. Hatch writes, "Increasingly assertive common people wanted their leaders unpretentious, their doctrines self-evident and down-to-earth, their music lively and singable, and their church in local hands" (9).

[31] For example, many British women wrote commentaries but, to our knowledge, no American woman did; in fact, American women called for commentaries written by women. See Carolyn De Swarte Gifford, "American Women and the Bible: The Nature of Woman as a Hermeneutical Issue," in *Feminist Perspectives on Biblical Scholarship*, ed. Adela Yarbro Collins (Atlanta: Scholars Press, 1985), 25.

[32] The British educational writer Charlotte Tucker (see part 1, "Eve—The Mother of Us All") wrote a work drawing on the idea of a Bible Museum and a knowledge of artifacts that she had from the British Museum. The American educational writer Susan Warner (see part 3, "Hagar—the Wanderer") wrote a work set deep in the American woods.

However, although different sociological factors influenced British and North American women, there was a certain degree of transatlantic cross-pollination which meant that both groups read and were influenced by one another's works. The American evangelist and writer Phoebe Palmer (1807–1874) took her revival to Canada and Britain, where Catherine Booth (1829–1890) heard her preach. Palmer influenced Booth to take up a preaching career of her own.[33] The writings of Grace Aguilar, a British Jew, influenced a number of Christian and Jewish writers on both sides of the Atlantic. She was published in American journals and Sophia G. Ashton (fl. 1855) boldly plagiarized Aguilar's *Women of Israel* in her work *The Mothers of the Bible*.[34] Harriet Beecher Stowe went on a speaking tour in Britain and later corresponded with a number of prominent British authors. She also introduced the American edition of Charlotte Elizabeth Tonna's (1790–1846) *Collected Works*. Numerous books were published on both sides of the Atlantic, with or without the author's knowledge and permission. H. Hasting Weld's (1811–1888) collection of American writings on women of the Bible included three pieces by British writer, Clara Lucas Balfour.[35] This trans-Atlantic web of influence meant these women were not working alone, their work was shared among peers, and together they worked to understand the Bible outside the male academy.

Women and Biblical Interpretation in the Nineteenth Century

Accounts of the history of biblical interpretation in the nineteenth century have focused almost exclusively on the rise of criticism and on the lives and publications of key men associated with European, British, and American universities. Women who were scholars and whose lives were touched by the academy and higher criticism have been ignored and thus forgotten.

Historians depict the nineteenth century as one of change and turmoil as a number of developments challenged the traditional approach to reading the Bible as God's inspired, infallible, and historically and scientifically accurate Word. At the beginning of the century, few lay people were aware of biblical criticism; by the end of the century most lay people knew biblical criticism existed, even if they did not all accept it.

[33] Harold E. Raser, *Phoebe Palmer: Her Thought and Life* (Lewiston: Mellen Press, 1987), 135.

[34] See Aguilar and Ashton's works in part 2, "Sarah—The First Mother of Israel."

[35] See Rev. H. Hastings Weld, ed., *The Women of the Old and New Testaments* (Philadelphia: Lindsay & Blakiston, 1848). In Weld's preface, he notes that all the works except Mrs. Balfour's were written expressly for the collection. He is unapologetic about his inclusion of Balfour, saying "for the republication of her articles, no one who reads them will require an apology" (v).

The first challenge arose as the Enlightenment dictum "interpret the scripture like any other book,"[36] was taken seriously, and the attention of scholars focused not only on the language of the Bible (lower criticism), but also on reconstructing the pre-history of the biblical texts (higher or historical criticism). Much scholarly attention was given to the book of Genesis, in particular. The traditionally accepted notion of the Mosaic authorship of the first five books of the Pentateuch was challenged as various theories about sources were proposed. Great debates took place around the number, dating, and ordering of the proposed sources that stood behind the present shape of the book of Genesis.[37] The British and American public became aware of scholarly debates about the pre-history of biblical texts through newspaper reports of clergymen's unorthodox views and various British and American heresy trials,[38] through controversial publications,[39] as well as through church newspapers, book reviews, and even novels.[40]

A second development that challenged the traditional understanding of scripture and undermined confidence in the text was related to the project of revising the King James Version of the Bible in light of new understandings of the Hebrew and Greek languages and, in the case of the New Testament, new manuscript evidence. While women were not directly involved in this revision, some women were concerned about possible theological and gender biases in translations produced by men.[41] Issues surrounding translations and

---

[36] Benjamin Jowett, "On the Interpretation of Scripture," in *Essays and Reviews* (London: Parker & Sons, 1860), 377.

[37] During the last quarter of the nineteenth century, the German scholar Julius Wellhausen (1844–1918) presented a synthesis of the views of many other scholars that became known as the JEDP theory in his book, *Geschichte Israels* (Berlin: G. Reimer, 1878). Wellhausen's views were popularized in England by S. R. Driver (1846–1914) in *An Introduction to the Literature of the Old Testament* (New York: Charles Scribner, 1891).

[38] For example, people read about the unorthodox views of Bishop Colenso and the heresy trials of William Robertson Smith and Charles Briggs. On Colenso, see W. Neil, "The Criticism and Theological Use of the Bible, 1700–1950," in *The Cambridge History of the Bible: The West from the Reformation to the Present Day*, ed. S. L. Greenslade (Cambridge: Cambridge University Press, 1963), 281–83, 286. On Smith, see Warner M. Bailey, "William Robertson Smith and American Biblical Studies," *Journal of Presbyterian History* 51 (1973): 285–308; Richard Allan Riesen, *Criticism and Faith in Late Victorian Scotland: A.B. Davidson, William Robertson Smith and George Adam Smith* (Lanham, Md.: University Press of America, 1985). On Briggs, see Ira V. Brown. "The Higher Criticism Comes to America, 1880–1900," *Journal of the Presbyterian Historical Society* 38, 4 (1960): 193–212.

[39] For example, *Essays and Reviews*.

[40] For example, Mrs. Humphrey Ward's novel *Robert Elsmere* (London, 1888).

[41] On the gender bias of translators, earlier in the century Sarah Grimké wrote:
    In examining this important subject, I shall depend solely on the Bible to designate the sphere of woman, because I believe almost every thing that has been written on this subject, has been the result of a misconception of the simple truths revealed in

manuscript evidence increasingly affected women who studied the Bible as the century progressed.

A third development came from science, as geological evidence and theories pointed to an older earth than that postulated by Bishop James Ussher's (1581–1656) dating system, which placed creation at 4004 B.C., so the historicity of the seven-day account of creation was called into question. Darwin's theory of evolution synthesized several movements in scientific thought and provided a different model for thinking about the natural world. The developmental paradigm associated with evolution (earlier periods in history were more primitive than the present) affected the way people interpreted the Bible. Harriet Beecher Stowe, for example, explained some of the behaviour of Abraham, Sarah, and Hagar as coming from a more primitive time in the world's history.

A fourth challenge came from historians and archaeologists and even world travellers, as new data became available which encouraged readers of scripture to look at the world of the Bible in new and different ways. Biblical scholars adopted a scientific and historical approach to the text and rejected more traditional theological methods of interpretation. Benjamin Jowett (1817–1893), for example, argued that the traditional layered interpretation of scripture[42] should be set aside and only the original meaning considered.[43]

These developments in the academy affected both male and female readers of the Bible in several ways. Some became skeptical and, like the hero of the Mrs. Humphrey Ward's novel, *Robert Elsmere*, lost their faith. Others reexamined their faith and either modified their views of the nature of the Bible and its inspiration or reaffirmed a traditional understanding of the Bible. Many began to incorporate scholars' insights into their work and were drawn to a more literal, rationalistic, historical, and culturally sensitive reading of the Bible. Still, in 1880, Albert Cave claimed that 99% of scholars in

---

the scriptures, in consequence of the false translation of many passages of Holy Writ. My mind is entirely delivered from the superstitious reverence which is attached to the English version of the Bible. King James's translators certainly were not inspired. I therefore claim the original as my standard, believing that to have been inspired, and I also claim to judge for myself what is the meaning of the inspired writers, because I believe it to be the solemn duty of every individual to search the scriptures for themselves, with the aid of the Holy Spirit, and not be governed by the views of any man, or set of men. ("Letter 1: On the Original Equality of Woman," in *Letters on the Equality of the Sexes, and the Condition of Woman* [Boston: I. Knapp, 1838]).

Also see Selvidge, *Notorious Voices*, 146, 213.

[42] Historically the scriptures were interpreted in multiple, layered senses. The most common medieval scheme was the four-fold interpretation of scripture, which included the historical, allegorical, moral, and analogical meanings of the text.

[43] Jowett, "On the Interpretation of Scripture," 419.

England, Scotland, and the United States still believed in the Mosaic author-ship of Genesis.[44] It was only the last two decades of the nineteenth century that witnessed an increasing openness to the conclusions of critical scholars among academics, clergy, and educated lay women and men in both Britain and America.

Popular articles and books like those of Julia Wedgwood (1833–1913), a cousin of Charles Darwin and friend of Robert Browning, attempted "to bring the results of recent criticism" to readers of the Bible. She thought criticism was "fitted to restore to us our Bible with the freshness of a new Reformation and the preciousness of an ancient faith."

> The test by which Biblical criticism must stand or fall is its power to render the moral purport of the Old Testament intelligible. If under its analysis the history and literature of the most remarkable people of antiquity ceases to be an abracadabra from which here and there we derive edification, and becomes a coherent and rememberable [sic] chapter in the history of thought, then the Newer Criticism will mould our Bible, and in teaching us to read it will vindicate whatever is destructive in its work.[45]

Wedgwood then proceeded to reevaluate traditional views of inspiration and to set forth the critical views of prominent German and British scholars.[46] She tried to be sensitive to the problems that criticism raised for readers. Regarding the late dating of the Psalms, for example, she wrote:

> When devout readers of the Psalms are told that words which have expressed for them what they never could have expressed for themselves, are in fact not individual utterance, but the typical expression of a race, they are conscious of a deadly chill. The feeling is almost that of the Magdalen beside the tomb of the risen Christ. The critics seem to have taken away their most intimate companion and interpreter, and they know not where he has been laid.[47]

Wedgwood was one of a number of highly educated women whose lives were touched by the resources of the academy (men, ideas, and books) and who became involved in criticism in hitherto unrecognized ways. Women

---

[44] W. Glover, *Evangelical Nonconformists and Higher Criticism in the Nineteenth Century* (London: Independent Press, 1954), 36.

[45] Julia Wedgwood, *The Message of Israel in the Light of Modern Criticism* (London: Isbister, 1894), 5, 28–29. She wrote this book as a supplement to *The Moral Idea: a Historic Study* (London: Trübner, 1888).

[46] Wellhausen and Driver were two scholars that Wedgwood used.

[47] Wedgwood, *Message of Israel*, 40.

were consumers, practitioners, popularizers, and in some cases critics of higher criticism.[48]

The developments in the academy, however, did not affect all readers of the Bible. The choir of women interpreters associated with the academy and higher criticism are joined by an even greater chorus of women's and men's voices from the world of popular belief and unbelief, who have been ignored in the histories of biblical interpretation.[49] The voices of these more traditional non-critical interpreters, as Gerald Bray suggests, "remained influential in the churches, and at the popular level generally."[50] Indeed, a non-critical approach to the Bible, which was in continuity with the history of how the Bible had been interpreted, flourished in Britain and America.

Most of the books on the Bible written by nineteenth-century women are part of this *vox populi*.[51] Most practiced non-critical exegesis, which retained the distinction between the literal and spiritual senses of the text. While many women writers emphasized the importance of the literal sense of the text, and used insights from history and geography to aid their reading, they were not willing to dispense with spiritual and theological understandings of the text.[52] They continued to use traditional methods of discerning God's voice in the book that they continued to regard as much more than "any other book."[53]

Popular writers of the nineteenth century continued to read the Old Testament and New Testament together, so they made intertextual connections between the two. They often used an associative approach, letting texts resonate with each other. These interpreters were firmly rooted in their commitment to the scriptures as being for the church and synagogue. By continu-

---

[48] Both Christina Rossetti and Harriet Beecher Stowe were critics of higher criticism. For Rossetti's criticism, see *The Face of the Deep: A Devotional Commentary on the Apocalypse*, 2nd ed. (London: SPCK, 1893); and for Stowe, see *Footsteps of the Master* (New York: J. B. Ford, 1877).

[49] Timothy Larsen speaks of the importance of listening to other voices in his recent work, *Contested Christianity* (Waco, Tex.: Baylor University Press, 2004)

[50] Gerald Bray, *Biblical Interpretation: Past and Present* (Downers Grove, Ill.: InterVarsity, 1996), 306.

[51] Most of their exegetical writings were practical and popular in nature and grew out of ministry-based projects. Mrs. Lucas Shadwell, for example, published the notes she prepared for a study group of working class men and women whom she welcomed weekly for years. Her intent was "to render the happy evenings profitable as well as interesting, by plain and practical personal application of the great lessons to be learnt in that Word, so rich in interest, as well as alone able, through the Holy Spirit's teaching, to make wise unto salvation" (*Bible Exercises, for the Family Reading, for the Cottage Meeting, and the Temperance Bible Class* [London, (1869–1872)], i).

[52] Bray, *Biblical Interpretation*, 306.

[53] Thus many women would have argued against Benjamin Jowett's famous dictum that the Bible should be interpreted "like any other book" ("On the Interpretation of Scripture," in *Essays and Reviews*, 377).

ing to read the Bible with sensitivity to its theological nature, and not strictly its historical context, women continued to explore the richness of the text's witness of faith. To use Christina Rossetti's metaphor from *The Face of the Deep*, they continued to dive for pearls and collect amber that some academics had set aside in their search for other treasures.[54]

Women's Approaches to Interpretation

Women interpreters used a variety of approaches to the text. Most women exegetes of the nineteenth century interpreted scripture along traditional lines in accordance with long-established theological presuppositions about the nature of the Bible as God's Word. They used various techniques to find the spiritual and moral lessons for themselves and their readers. Many believed that the Holy Spirit enlightened them and taught them through the scriptures, the living word of God. Their encounters with the Divine in reading scripture became the basis for their authority in teaching others. They looked for connections between their lives and experiences and the biblical characters' lives. They looked for spiritual analogies of historical reality; they imitated Bible characters; they sought timeless and universal truths in the text; they drew moral inferences from the text. They used various types of figurative readings including typology, symbolism, and allegory. They used an associative approach that connected images from various parts of scripture.

---

[54] See the prefatory note to Rossetti, *The Face of the Deep*, vii. Rossetti was highly critical of scholars who missed the spiritual, theological or moral meanings of the text. She writes:

It is, I suppose, a genuine though not a glaring breach of the Second Commandment, when instead of learning the lesson plainly set down for us in Holy Writ we protrude mental feelers in all directions above, beneath, around it, grasping, clinging to every imaginable particular except the main point. Take the history of the Fall. The question of mortal sin shrinks into the background while we moot such points as the primitive status of the serpent: did he stand somehow upright? did he fly? what did he originally eat? how did he articulate? Or again, man's overwhelming loss ceases to be the chief concern, when at the gate of Paradise our eye lights upon the flaming sword. How about that sword? was it a sword as we understand a sword? was it a blade flashing and swaying towards each point of the compass, or was it rather a blazing disk to be flung with rotary motion against the foe? . . . At every turn such questions arise. What was the precise architecture of Noah's ark? Were the Cherubim of the Tabernacle, of the first temple, and of the second Temple, of similar or of diverse aspects? Clear up the astronomy of Joshua's miracle. Fix the botany of Jonah's gourd. Must a pedestal be included within the measurement of Nebuchadnezzar's 'golden image'? In the same vein we reach at last the conjecture which I have heard quoted: In which version was the Ethiopian Eunuch studying Isaiah's prophecy when Philip the Deacon met him? 'By there, my son, be admonished: of making many books there is not end' (Eccles. xii.12). (*Letter and Spirit. Notes on the Commandments* [London: Society for Promoting Christian Knowledge, 1883], 85–87.)

They read Old Testament stories in light of the full canon of scripture. The New Testament was often used as a lens for interpretation of Old Testament narratives.

Many women were readers and writers of novels and stories, which drew them to the narratives of scripture. They saw subtle nuances and gaps in the narratives. They often used their story-telling abilities to embellish the texts. Some saw the bigger picture of salvation history. Some imported meaning into the text whereby some texts became prooftexts for their own ideas. Many who looked for the deeper meaning of the text were also aware of its literal and historical meaning.

Many women were self-aware in the process of interpretation and wrote about the process to help others learn how to interpret the scripture.[55] In a tract called *Eyes and No Eyes; or, How to Read the Bible Aright*,[56] Mrs. Mary Martha Sherwood (1775–1851) told a story about a boy who liked to read the Bible for the "pretty stories" it contained. He knew the contents of the stories but not the lessons to be learned from them. "He had never prayed to God the Holy Spirit to open his understanding like Lydia's when she listened to Paul. Acts 16:14."[57] His uncle told him the Bible did not consist of "pretty stories" written only for our amusement.

> [His uncle] tried to explain to him that holy men of old had written the scriptures as taught or directed by the Holy Spirit for our instruction; and that by the blessing of God upon our reading, they are able to make us wise unto salvation, through faith which is in Christ Jesus. That the accounts they give us of Abraham, Jacob, David, Moses, the Israelites, and others, are written to show us the evil consequences of forgetting the will of God and sinning against him.[58]

His uncle suggested that those who now read the Bible in a careless, inattentive manner, may also be said to "have eyes but see not."[59] The tract contains a cluster of scripture texts on how to read the Bible that includes 1

---

[55] Mary L. G. Petrie (Mrs. Ashley Carus-Wilson) wrote a popular handbook on hermeneutics, *Unseal the Book: Practical Words for Plain Readers of Scripture* (London: The Religious Tract Society, 1899), in which she sets out principles for reading the Bible in its historical and cultural context using all the available tools of the academy. She included the traditional Christian practices of praying before reading scripture, memorizing scripture, and practicing the principles of the faith.

[56] New York: American Tract Society, n.d.

[57] [Mrs. Sherwood], *Eyes and No Eyes; or, How to Read the Bible Aright* (New York: American Tract Society, n.d.), 9. Note that no author is given on the title page of the tract, but this tract is bound together with one of Mrs. Sherwood's tracts.

[58] [Mrs. Sherwood], *Eyes and No Eyes*, 9–10.

[59] [Mrs. Sherwood], *Eyes and No Eyes*, 11.

Corinthians 10:11, the Old Testament stories were written as an example for instruction; 2 Timothy 3:16, scripture was written for teaching, reproof, correction, and training in righteousness; John 5:39, scripture testifies about Jesus; and Acts 10:43, the scriptures testify to salvation through Jesus.[60] The author of the tract then admonished readers to read the Bible carefully and prayerfully for its spiritual message of salvation.

> Pray earnestly every day that, like young Samuel and Timothy and Josiah and other holy youths mentioned in the Bible, you may be taught of God to know him and to love him, to feel the evil and burden of sin, to sorrow over it, and to repent of it; to see the value of the Saviour, and to believe on and love him. Then your heart will be changed, you will find pleasure in following him and seeking to do his will.[61]

Although many women presented their work with humility in their introductions, they clearly felt competent to do the work of biblical interpretation. They were aware that, as women, their interpretive work took them into a realm that was traditionally reserved for males. They recognized that they had neither the formal education nor the same tools to do the kind of work male scholars and clergy did. Still, they confidently interpreted scripture, and used scripture as a means to discuss issues important to them. They appropriated the message of the text, applied it to their own lives, and shared their insights with others.

Women's writings show the influence of scripture on daily life. They allow us a new entry point into the private and public lives of nineteenth-century women. Their experiences as women in a culture, which emphasized differences between sexes, races, classes, and religions, affected how they read and interpreted the Bible.

Challenges in Reading Nineteenth-Century Writers

Readers need to be aware that reading these nineteenth-century interpreters is not always easy, as we cannot expect them to conform to modern assumptions. Readers may initially react negatively to some of these texts. Readers will certainly be surprised by what they encounter; they may have difficulty believing that women wrote some of these pieces. One contemporary reader working with the texts found that she appreciated them more and more as she reread them. She got past her initial culture shock and began to appreciate what the writers were doing with the biblical text. So we suggest that

[60] [Mrs. Sherwood], *Eyes and No Eyes*, 13–14.
[61] [Mrs. Sherwood], *Eyes and No Eyes*, 15.

the texts be read sympathetically, for upon entering the mind of nineteenth-century women, the text will seem quite different. Readers should be sensitive to the language and tone of each selection. The following questions provide a guide for reading:

1. What sort of literature is this? Is it a narrative retelling of a biblical story, a commentary on the biblical text, a poem, a sermon, a devotional reflection, or some other form? Who was the intended audience of this reading? Do authors write differently for adults and children?

2. Who is the author? What is known about her? What is her religious background? What does she bring to the text from her theology and experience? How does her theology and experience affect her reading of the biblical text?

3. What was the author's purpose in writing this piece? What moral lessons does the author draw from the text? What was her agenda in writing?

4. What methods of interpretation was she using? Does she use typology, allegory, symbolism, association, prooftexting, or other methods? Is she re-telling the biblical story? How faithful is she to the text? When and how does she embellish the text? What kind of dance partner is she with the text? Does she lead or does the text lead?

5. What barriers between her own culture and language, and the culture and language of the biblical text does the author see and address?

6. Does this work reflect or challenge the "cult of true womanhood"?

7. Is there a feminist message in the readings? How does the author (as a woman) read the Bible? What does she see that a man might not see?

8. To get the most of these readings, readers should ask themselves:
    • What does the biblical text say?
    • What do these women interpreters say the biblical text says?
    • What presuppositions do I bring the reading of the biblical text and its nineteenth-century interpretations?

Why Genesis?

Women's writings on women in Genesis have been selected for a number of reasons. Genesis features many prominent and active female characters, and nineteenth-century women, like women readers throughout history, are drawn to female figures in scripture. Many important issues relating to women have traditionally been associated with Genesis. The interpretation of the creation and fall accounts in Genesis 1–3 is important for understanding women's roles in family and church. Sarah was often mentioned in Anglican marriage ceremonies as an example for wives. Examining the accounts of women in Genesis allowed women interpreters to talk about issues in their lives: marriage, procreation, children, barrenness, and family relationships. Genesis is well represented in the interpretive works of nineteenth-century women, and, therefore, it is a good place to begin listening to the voices of these women interpreters.

Part 1

EVE—THE MOTHER OF US ALL

Introduction

Eve stands as a pivotal figure for women interpreters of the Bible not only because the biblical creation story presents her as the first woman in history, but also because historically she was the best known woman of the Old Testament. When nineteenth-century women wrote about Eve, they faced a complex history of interpretation that included Christian art, theology, and literature. In telling the story of Eve, these women were not simply retelling the story found in Genesis 2, 3, and 4. They had a pre-understanding of the text based on the history of interpretation and their own experiences. They interacted with the traditional understandings of these texts, either by reinforcing, challenging, or overturning them.

The creation account in Genesis 1:26-29 describes the creation of human beings, both male and female. Genesis 2 focuses specifically on the creation of Adam and Eve. In Genesis 2:20-25, Adam named all the creatures, but no helper was found for him. So God created a woman out of his rib and brought her to him. Adam identified her as "bone of my bones and flesh of my flesh" and named her woman. Genesis 3 recounts the temptation story and Adam and Eve's expulsion from the Garden of Eden. The serpent approached Eve and asked "Yea, hath God said, Ye shall not eat of every tree of the garden?" Eve entered into dialogue with the serpent and when she "saw that the tree was good for food, and that it was pleasant to the eyes, and a tree to be desired to make one wise, she took of the fruit thereof, and did eat, and gave also unto her husband with her; and he did eat." God appeared in the Garden, and addressed, then judged the man, woman, and serpent. Following upon God's judgment, Adam named his wife Eve, "the mother of all the living." God then expelled them from the Garden of Eden. Genesis 4 contains the story of Eve's children, Cain, Abel, and Seth. After Seth's birth, Eve disappears from the Genesis account.

The portrait of Eve found in Genesis is cryptic; her character is not fully developed, the dialogue is brief, and neither her feelings nor her motivations are mentioned. The gaps and silences of the text invite theological reflection and embellishment, an invitation taken up by many interpreters, including nineteenth-century women. The authors reflected on significant details and unanswered questions, such as: what was the significance of the creation of Eve from Adam's rib? Who told Eve about the prohibition on the fruit? Was Adam present when the serpent approached Eve? Why did Eve speak to the serpent? Women writers also invented dialogue, unveiled emotions, and imagined Eve's life in more detail than presented in the biblical narrative. They grappled with the implications of Eve's story for the discussion of women's nature, character, and role in society.

Nineteenth-century women used other canonical and deuterocanonical literature to inform their interpretation of the story of Eve in Genesis. In the New Testament, Eve is mentioned in 2 Corinthians 11:3 and 1 Timothy 2:13-14, texts which discuss the place of women in the church. She is also mentioned in the Apocryphal literature in Tobit 8:6, Sirach 25:24, 40:1, 42:13, and 4 Maccabees 18:7. Other Scriptures were also used to interpret the story of Eve. The women writers used some rather unexpected texts to illuminate Eve: for example, the story of Herodias (Mark 6:21-29), the marriage of the sons of god to the daughters of men (Gen. 6:1-4), and Eve's association with the virtuous woman in Proverbs 31:10-31. Extra-biblical works, including John Milton's (1608–1674) epic poem, *Paradise Lost* (1667), informed the imaginations of many of the women interpreters.

Nineteenth-century women wrote about Eve for a variety of reasons. Their purpose in writing determined what aspects of Eve's story they highlighted. Most writers addressed the implications of this story for the roles of women and men in family and society. Some readings are traditional; others move in quite different directions. Traditional interpretations emphasize women's subordination at creation, her propensity to evil or weakness making her vulnerable to temptation, her responsibility for "the fall," and a negative understanding of the word "helpmeet." Most female interpreters explored ways to push beyond the barriers very traditional interpretations of Eve imposed upon women.

It is important to realize that the answers these women give to the Woman Question were very complex. The very act of writing and publishing put female writers into the more masculine public sphere. In many of these works a tension exists between respecting tradition, both cultural and religious, and giving women a chance. Sojourner Truth said, "I have heard the Bible and have learned that Eve caused man to sin. Well, if woman upset the world, do give her a chance to set it right side up again."[1] Most nineteenth-century women writers attempted to give Eve, and women, a chance.

The nineteenth-century women writing on Eve had religious, moral, or ideological lessons to teach readers. Many of them moved from the story of Eve to the theological problem of temptation, its nature and the question of how to resist it. Many also moved quickly to the New Testament. Others raised the theological issues of the image of God, the nature of the curse, the origin of evil, the nature of sin and the way of salvation, and the providence and foreknowledge of God. Some writers focused on selfishness as Eve's besetting sin, others on pride. A number of women focused on Eve as a woman, wife, or mother. Some used the story of Eve as a platform for ideological issues: for example the place of women in home and society, and the question of the authority of Scripture.

The hermeneutical approach of the women writers also shaped their readings of the text. Most read the plain sense of the text as having some historical reference. Some raised the question of whether the text should be read as myth, parable, or allegory. Several followed a traditional typological reading of the text, where Adam is a type of Christ and Eve is a type of the Church. Some women, who were aware of the scholarly debates about the literary sources behind the present text of the book of Genesis, and other creation stories from the ancient world, brought the resources of the academy to their interpretation of Eve.

These selections on Eve include a variety of genres: letters, essays, stories, poetry, and lessons for both children and adults. This variety of genres reflects the variety of purpose behind the works. Points of theology were argued in letters or essays. The story of Eve was retold as a positive or negative moral example. Poetry expanded on the feelings of characters in the text, or spoke briefly but eloquently on a single issue.

The intended audience of these writers also influenced their treatment of Eve. Some women wrote for children, and so substantially simplified the story and the issues it raised. Others wrote for teenagers and young adults and used Eve's story to shape the moral thinking and behaviour of their audience. Most wrote for an adult audience, and many may have anticipated a primarily female audience. Some of the more polemical works were intended for a mixed audience.

---

[1] Margaret Washington, ed., *Narrative of Sojourner Truth* (New York: Random House, 1993), 118, cited in Karen Baker-Fletcher, "Anna Julia Cooper and Sojourner Truth: Two Nineteenth-Century Black Feminist Interpreters of Scripture," in *Searching the Scriptures*, ed. Elisabeth Schüssler Fiorenza (New York: Crossroad, 1995), 41–51.

This diverse collection of writings on Eve shows that women of the nineteenth century did not speak with one voice on "the mother of us all." Their interpretations range from Eve as the crown of creation to Eve as the victim of power; from a woman to be pitied to a woman to be praised; from the "protoplast of womanhood" to the slave of men; from the companion of man to man's seducer to evil. Women found the texts on Eve to be theologically and ideologically problematic. While a few wanted to cast off the weight of tradition and overturn the authority of the Bible entirely, most attempted to redeem the story by reshaping the way the text was heard.

§1 Hannah Mather Crocker
(1752–1847)

Hannah Crocker, the granddaughter of Cotton Mather, and seventh child of Rev. Samuel and Hannah (Hutchinson) Mather, was born in Boston. As a member of a prominent, scholarly New England family, Crocker had access to the extensive Mather family library of more than 1500 volumes. Her husband, Rev. Joseph Crocker of Tauton, Massachusetts, was a graduate of Harvard and a captain in the Revolutionary War. The Crockers had ten children.

Crocker's literary career began after her husband died in 1797. She wrote a series of letters in 1810 defending the Society of Free Masons against charges of excessive revelry in Boston pubs; these letters were published in 1815 as *A Series of Letters on Free Masonry*, by a Lady of Boston. In 1816, she published a temperance homily for sailors called *The School of Reform, or Seaman's Safe Pilot, to the Cape of Good Hope* and a biography of Madam Knight, Benjamin Franklin's teacher.

In *Observations on the Real Rights of Women, with Their Appropriate Duties, Agreeable to Scripture, Reason and Common Sense* (1818), Crocker interacted with British women educators and thinkers, especially Hannah More (1745–1833)[2] (to whom the work is dedicated), and Mary Wollstonecraft (1759–1797).[3] Crocker's work was the first book on the rights of women written and published by an American.

[2] More was a prolific evangelical writer and scholar whose works included *Strictures on the Modern System of Female Education* (1799).

[3] Wollstonecraft was a feminist writer who wrote the controversial *Vindication on the Rights of Woman* (1792).

Crocker saw the biblical story of the creation and fall in Genesis 1–3 as the foundation of her argument for women's rights. She interpreted the biblical story of the creation and fall and contrasted women's roles under the Jewish and Christian dispensations. She argued that women and men were equal before the fall, and that the fall brought about the subjection of women. The gospel redeemed women, so they are no longer subject to men. While she argued that men and women have different "natural" roles in society, she insisted that they were in all ways equal, especially in their ability to think.[4]

From Hannah Mather Crocker, *Observations on the Real Rights of Women, with their Appropriate Duties, Agreeable to Scripture, Reason and Common Sense* (Boston, 1818), 7–14.

Chap. 1
Of the creation and fall of our first parents.

THE foundation stone of the present work must be laid in the first creation of the human race. When the great Jehovah had created the earth, and all things therein, he created man; male and female created he them, in his own image, so far as he endowed him with intellectual powers and faculties, and gave him an immortal and rational soul, and powers of mind capable of reasoning on the nature of things. And the Lord God said, it is not good for man to be alone; I will make him an help meet for him: And the Lord God caused a deep sleep to fall upon Adam, and he slept and he took one of his ribs, and closed up the flesh instead thereof. And the rib, which the Lord God had taken from man, made he a woman: and brought her unto the man, and Adam said, this is now bone of my bone, and flesh of my flesh: she shall be called woman, because she was taken out of man; as she partakes of my original nature, she shall therefore partake of my name; therefore shall a man leave his father and his mother, and shall cleave onto his wife, and they shall be one flesh: See Gen. ii. 24.

It seems, says an able commentator,* to have been the Creator's design to have inculcated the lesson of perfect love and union, by forming the woman out of the man's body, and from a part of it so near the heart, as well as to make woman of a more refined and delicate nature, by thus causing the original clay to pass, as it were, twice through his refining hand. Now it is consistent to say, if they become one flesh, there should be but one and the same spirit operating equally upon them both, for their mutual happiness. Adam, having given her a name, and placed himself as her guardian, became in some measure, responsible for her conduct, as the rightful protector of her innocence. It should be recollected, as a small palliative for Eve, that the command, respecting the tree of knowledge and forbidden fruit, was [given] before the woman was made: see Gen. ii. 16 and 17. And the Lord God commanded the man, saying, of every tree of the garden thou mayest freely eat; but of the tree of knowledge, of good and evil thou shalt not eat, for in the day thou eatest thereof, thou shalt surely die. She must therefore have received her information from Adam, if she knew of any command; as she probably had heard of it, by her answer to the serpent. Perhaps Adam communicated it to her as the injunction of their Maker, but possibly with such mildness and indifference, that she was not fully impressed with, the importance of the command.

It seems, that, in an unfortunate hour, these then pure and happy beings, were separated. Oh, fatal hour! Oh, inconsiderate Adam! How couldst thou leave the friend of thy affection to wander in the garden, unaided by the support and strength of thy arm, and the pleasure of thy conversation. Didst thou for one moment feel the supreme dignity and full consequence of being placed lord of the lower creation? Didst thou walk forth to survey the animals created for thy use, and subjected to thy dominion? No, no; we say pride had not then polluted the human heart. Thou wast not then puffed up with the idea of knowing good and evil; but thou might have had tenderness enough for thy 'rib, that was taken from thy side', to have kept near enough to her to protect her innocence from the wiles of the tempter. Nothing can justify Eve's imprudence in parlying with the serpent at all; and she is condemnable for holding any converse, or supposing knowledge was ever desirable, that must be obtained in any clandestine or dishonorable manner.[5] No one can approve of the asperity of Adam's answer to his maker, when called on to answer how he knew that he was naked. He answered evidently with a very indignant air: The woman thou gavest to be with me, gave me of the fruit of the tree, and I did eat. It does not appear, from his own account, that Adam withstood the temptation with more fortitude than Eve did; for she presented the fruit, and he received it without hesitation; but it is plain she did not yield immediately, though the most subtle agent of the devil told her that her eyes should be

[5] Most of the women writing on Eve, including Crocker, understood the serpent in Genesis 3 to be Satan. This understanding came from reading other parts of scripture, as well as from Christian tradition and art. Revelation 12:9 identifies Satan as "that old serpent." Mary Cornwallis also used Jude 6 and 2 Corinthians 11:3 to argue for the identification of the serpent as Satan. (*Observations, Critical, Explanatory, and Practical, on the Canonical Scriptures*, vol. 1, 2nd ed. [London: Baldwin, Cradock, & Joy, 1820], 13.)

opened, and that she should be like a God. When indeed she saw that the tree was good for food, and that it was pleasant to the eyes, and a tree to be desired to make one wise, she took of the fruit thereof, and did eat. It appears her desire was to obtain knowledge, which might be laudable, though her reason was indeed deceived.

And reason is quickly deceived, says the eloquent Saurin,[6] when the senses have been seduced. It was already yeilding to the temptation, to hearken so long to the tempter.

By the joint transgression of our first parents, sin, misery and death were introduced into this present world. They appear equally culpable; yet God, who is ever wise and just in his dealings, passed the most severe sentence on the woman, as she was told her sorrows should be multiplied. And a still harder fate attended her. She was reduced, from a state of honorable equality, to the mortifying state of subjection. Thy desire shall be to thy husband, and he shall rule over thee. Heaven never intended she should be ruled with a rod of iron; but drawn by the cords of the man, in the bonds of love. It is however evident, Adam was placed over her as her lord and master, for a certain period, and by the express will of his maker, and was taught to appreciate his own judgment as every creature was brought to him to give them names; and whatsoever names he gave them, they were called. And he gave his rib the name of woman, and displayed some judgment in the reason given for calling her woman. For she is bone of my bone, and flesh of my flesh, and therefore she shall be my equal. She shall have equal right to think, reason and act for herself, with my advice corroborating. He should therefore have resisted the temptation with manly fortitude, and, not only by precept, but by example, strengthened her resolution to resist the evil spirit: but he fell a prey to his own credulity, and sunk his posterity in depravity.

However strange their conduct may appear to the human understanding, we fully believe, in the great scale of divine providence, it was perfectly just they should be left to commit sin and folly, to convince the human race of their insufficiency, when left to act for themselves; and, from their example, shew to their posterity, the propriety of placing their dependence on Him, who alone is able to keep us from falling.

There is a very beautiful description of our primeval parent's first, interview, in Miss Akin's [1781–1864] *Epistles on Women*.[7] We give the extract in her own style:

---

[6] Probably Jacques Saurin (1677–1730), a French priest and later prominent minister in the Reformed Church of France, and known as an eloquent preacher. His sermons were translated into English.

[7] Lucy Aikin, *Epistles on Women, Exemplifying their Character and Condition in Various Ages and Nations* (London: J. Johnson, 1810).

"See where the world's new master roams along,
Vainly intelligent, and idly strong;
Mark his long listless steps and turpid air,
His brow of densest gloom, and fix'd infantile stare.
No mother's voice has touch'd that slumb'ring ear,
Nor glist'ning eye beguiled him with a tear.
Love nurs'd not him with sweet endearing wiles,
Nor woman taught the sympathy of smiles.
Ah! hapless world, that such a wretch obeys,
Ah! joyless Adam, though a world he sways.
But see they meet, they gaze, the new born pair,
Mark now the youth, and now the wond'ring fair
Sure a new soul that moping idiot warms,
Dilates his stature, and his mein[8] informs.
A brighter crimson tints his gloomy cheeks,
His broad eye kindles, and his glances speaks."

From this description, there appears to commence a sympathy of nature, or mutual affection, inherent in nature, which perhaps might operate on Adam's sensibility, and cause him insensibly to partake of the forbidden fruit that proved their fatal fall, and her deepest humiliation; as she is placed under subjection to the man: And the command was put full force, under the old Jewish dispensation, as they bought and sold their wives and daughters, and their cattle. But, blessed be God, the bonds are dissolved, the snare is broken, and woman has escaped by the blessing of the gospel.

* Lord Coke [Bishop Thomas Coke (1747–1814), British Methodist, appointed superintendent of American Methodism by John Wesley, and styled "bishop" in America. He wrote a multivolume commentary on the Bible.]

Chap. II

Woman is restored to her original rights of equality under the christian dispensation.

HERE, indeed, is the love of God manifested to the disobedient children of men. Though by the fall of our first parents misery and death was the consequence; yet the promise is made good to man, that the seed of the woman should bruise the serpent's head, and that in her seed, all mankind should be restored to peace and happiness. And at the appointed time Jehovah was pleased to over-shadow the espoused wife of Joseph: and there was more than a common presence of the divine eradiator attending at his birth [Matt.

[8] *his mein* means "his demeanor."

1:18-25]. The wise men or astrologers of the east had calculated a new star that would appear about that time, and it forboded some great event to take place. Agreeably to their calculation, at the very time they were gazing for the stranger, behold it did appear agreeable to their expectation, and by the bright and effulgent light of this new and till now unknown star, the wise men of the east were directed till the star reflected on the menial place of the birth of our Saviour. And here was the degraded woman found; exalted to the highest honour of embracing in her maternal arms the Son of God himself in human nature [Matt. 2:1, 9-11]. What an interesting scene it must have been to the wise men that had been looking for some great event to take place! What a scene it must have been to the man of sensibility! The amiable, the devout Mary, apparently degraded, is now exalted to the highest honour among men; and life and immortality are brought to light, by the divine influence of the gospel, under the dispensation of grace. She, who was condemned to servitude, is now, by the blessing of the dispensation, restored to her original privileges: As the woman was first in the transgression, and, in some measure, the cause of their fall, she is now, by divine goodness, made the instrument of bringing life and future happiness to mankind.

The prophecy is accomplished, that in her seed all nations shall be blessed: Herein she is exalted and fully restored to her original dignity, by being the mother of our blessed Lord and Saviour Jesus Christ, according to his human nature. This, surely, must place her equal with man, under the christian system. Since the christian era, she is no longer commanded to be the slave to man, and he is no longer commanded to rule over her.

§2 Lucy Barton
(1808–1898)

Lucy Barton was the daughter of Quakers, Lucy Jesup (1781–1808) and Bernard Barton (1784–1849). The Bartons lived in the coastal town of Woodbridge, England. When her mother died giving birth, her father left his job as a coal and corn merchant and became a tutor and later a bank clerk and poet, writing about eight volumes of verse and a number of occasional pieces. Lucy Barton worked as a governess and wrote a number of books for children. Her father encouraged her as an author and wrote prefaces and introductions to her books. They coauthored *The Reliquary*, published in 1836. Lucy Barton also published a selection of her father's letters and poems after his death. After her father's death, Edward Fitzgerald (1809–1883), writer, translator, and family friend, who had promised to care for Lucy, married her. Their disastrous marriage ended within a year: Barton and Fitzgerald were incompatible in terms of character, lifestyle, and faith. Lucy Barton's works on the Bible include: *Bible Letters for Children*, 1831; *The Gospel History of our Lord and Saviour Jesus Christ*, 1837; *The Life of Christ: a Gospel History for the Use of Children*, 1857; *Natural History of the Holy Land, and Other Places Mentioned in the Bible*, 1856.[9]

The extract below is from Barton's *Bible Letters for Children*. Unlike the American Crocker, who used Genesis as a platform for women's rights, Barton wrote to instruct children. She carefully explained terms that children might not understand. She quickly passed over the details of the creation of the world to the fall. She discussed the fault of both Adam and Eve. Barton did not distinguish between the results of the fall for man and woman: both Adam and Eve were seen as having to work for food. She asked her readers to empathize with Adam and Eve rather than blaming them or thinking them foolish for their sin. Neither Crocker nor Barton read the text in a completely traditional way. Barton subtly revised the traditional focus on the guilt of Eve and asked readers not to judge Eve and Adam harshly.

Barton's tone was familiar and gentle until the last two paragraphs, where she made an evangelistic appeal. She ended her letter with an altar call for her readers, and stated that God's love was conditional upon their repentance.

From Lucy Barton, *Bible Letters for Children* (London: John Souter, 1831). [Text taken from the American Edition (Philadelphia, 1832), 10–13.]

Letter I
Creation of the World—Expulsion of Adam and Eve from Paradise

MY DEAR CHILDREN,

A GREAT while ago this pleasant world was not made, and there was no sun, or moon, or stars, and we never could have found out who made all these things, if the Bible did not tell us: and all that the Bible says is true, for it is God's word. I suppose you know that it is there said, that "in the beginning God created the heaven and the earth." When the earth was first made, it was very dark, and it had nothing beautiful upon it; but God said, "let there be light and there was light." He made the grass to grow, and the flowers to bloom, and he created all the animals that live.

[9] Sources: A. H. Bullen, Rev. James Edgar Barcus, Jr., "Barton, Bernard," in *The Oxford Dictionary of National Biography*, ed. H. C. G. Matthew and Brian Harrison, vol. 4 (Oxford: Oxford University Press, 2004), 191–92; Sheldon Goldfarb, "Fitzgerald, Edward," in *The Oxford Dictionary of National Biography* 19:786–89.

To create, means to make something out of nothing; now this great and powerful Maker, from whose hands came all this pleasant earth, made us, and from him nothing can be hid.

You know that Adam was the first man who ever lived in this world, and that God placed him in a delightful spot, called the garden of Eden, and gave him a woman, named Eve, to be his wife. Now in this garden was a tree, called "the tree of the knowledge of good and evil," of which the Lord told Adam he was not to eat. But Satan, who makes it his business to tempt us all, took upon himself the form of a serpent and tempted Eve to eat some of the fruit of this tree; and she did eat and gave some to Adam, and he did eat.

Then they were ashamed, and tried to hide themselves among the trees in the garden. "And the Lord God called unto Adam, and said, where art thou?" He said, "I heard thy voice in the garden, and was ashamed, and went and hid myself." Now if Adam had not felt that he had done wrong, he would not have been afraid, or ashamed, to have met his kind Creator, who had given him so many good things: and, in trying to save himself from punishment, he laid the blame on Eve, saying, "The woman whom thou gavest to be with me, she gave me of the tree, and I did eat." And the Lord God said unto the woman, "What is this thou hast done?" and the woman said, "The serpent beguiled (or tempted) me, and I did eat."

Then was the Almighty much displeased with them, and turned them out of the garden into the wide world, where they were obliged to till the ground; that is, to work hard to get bread to eat.

Now, perhaps, some of my young friends may think, how silly it was of Eve to take this fruit, and of Adam to be tempted by his wife; and it was very wrong in them to disobey the commands of the Great God. But I would have you think a moment, and you will find this thought may proceed from pride. You think you would have done better: that had you been Eve, you would not have taken the fruit.

But are there not many things in which you are just as much to blame? Have you not often disobeyed the commands of your parents, when they have wished you to deny yourselves any thing not proper for you? and you must, if you hope to be happy here, learn to deny yourselves much. Have you not said in your hearts, "Where can be the harm of this little thing!" Now, this is a temptation of Satan's, who will tempt even little children to do wrong; and the more you strive to resist him, and obey the commands of your parents, the more strength will be given you by your Heavenly Father as you grow in years, and place your entire dependence upon Him, to grow in grace and find favour in his sight.

God sees us even in the darkest places, and knows all we do, and say, and think. He loves little children, and has said, "Suffer little children to come unto me and forbid them not" [Mark 10:14]. Here, then you are asked to come to God; to tell him your wants; to confess to him your sins, and to ask him to pardon you, and take care of you.

But God will not love you unless you repent of your sins, that is, feel sorry for them, and believe on the Lord Jesus Christ.

Yours, affectionately.

§3 Esther Hewlett Copley
(1786–1851)

Esther Copley was born in London, the youngest daughter of a wealthy silk manufacturer, Peter (Pierre) Beuzeville and his wife, Mary (Marie) Meredith, both of French Huguenot descent. In April 1809, she married James Hewlett, an Anglican curate in Oxford. They had three sons and two daughters. She married William Copley, a Baptist minister in Oxford in 1827, after the death of her first husband. Esther Copley had previously become a member of the Baptist church. William later became an alcoholic while a minister in Eythorne, Kent. During this time Copley wrote his sermons for him and saw that the congregation ran well despite her husband's handicap. He left both his wife and the church at Eythorne in 1843. She stayed in the village until her death in 1851. Two of her sons became priests in the Anglican Church, but she remained a Baptist.

Copley was a prolific author. Her household management manual, *Cottage Comforts*, published in 1825, was very popular, reaching its twenty-fourth edition by 1864. It was filled with practical advice for the working classes. Copley wrote *A History of Slavery and its Abolition* (1836) for children, from the viewpoint that slavery is a result of human sinfulness; this work is presently considered her most significant. Her other books for youth included *Scripture Natural History for Youth* (1828), *Scripture History for Youth* (1829), and *Scripture Biography* (1836).[10] The money she earned from writing supported her family. In a letter to her husband William, written around 1829, she listed what she had earned from her publications, and wrote that she hoped these earnings would "contribute to your comfort and that of our dear children."[11]

[10] Source: Rosemary Mitchell, "Copley, Esther," in *The Oxford Dictionary of National Biography* 13:343–44.

[11] See Hewlett-Beuzeville-Roussel, "Writings: Esther Hewlett/Copley," http://www.witness.com.au/esther%20writings.htm (accessed May 5, 2005).

The following excerpts on Eve are from *Scripture History for Youth* and *Scripture Biography*. These volumes were meant to complement each other; *Scripture History* gave the meta-narrative of the biblical story and *Scripture Biography* the details of biblical characters' lives. Unlike Barton, who addressed young children in her work, Copley wrote for an older audience, especially young women. Like Crocker, Copley discussed her theology of marriage and the roles of men and women using the story of Eve. Copley advised her female readers to cultivate true female attractions, rather than external beauty. Copley gave women a lot of power in her definition of helpmeet. Her own life experiences as mother, wife, and widow, and particularly her enabling relationship with her alcoholic husband, were the lenses through which she read the text. In the extract from *Scripture Biography*, Copley argued that the influence of the gospel had moderated the curse; women became the means of redemption through bearing children. Like Crocker, she saw women and men as equals under the gospel. Copley portrayed Eve and all women positively.

From Esther Hewlett Copley, *Scripture History for Youth* (London: H. Fisher, Son & P. Jackson, 1833), 16–20.

In the creation of Eve as a companion for Adam there are several things observable and interesting—other creatures were created, both male and female, of every kind—but Adam was first formed, and afterwards Eve.

"The Lord God said, 'It is not good that the man should be alone; I will make a help meet for him.'" The wise and tender Parent of the universe knows perfectly well the circumstances and necessities of all his creatures, and often prepares for their supply before the need is perceived by themselves;— Adam had made no complaint of solitude, when God declared his purpose of providing him a companion. But observe again, when God designs to bestow a mercy, he generally makes the individual sensible of his need of that mercy: before Eve was created, Adam seems to have discovered that among all the creatures who passed before him, and received from him their names, while each was formed for society, and all were provided with suitable companions, for him no companion was found—none of erect form—none possessed of a reasonable soul—none endued with the faculty of intelligibly communicating ideas. Adam was the creation of the sixth day; and it is probable that on the same evening the creatures were named by him, after which, during a deep sleep which the Lord caused to fall upon Adam, a rib was taken from Adam, and moulded into a female form, which, on his awaking, was presented to him, as the intelligent and affectionate companion of his existence. If this supposition be correct, the first happy pair joined in the grateful devotions of the first sabbath—perhaps, the *only* sabbath that dawned on man in a state of innocence.

From the circumstances related of the creation of Eve, we gather what is the proper sphere which woman is destined to fill—which she is fitted to adorn and bless, and in which she finds her own true dignity and happiness. Without revelation, the most grievous mistakes have been made on this, as well as on almost every other subject. In some countries, women have forsaken the gentle duties of their sex, and engaged in warlike pursuits, or in the affairs of state—in our own country, before the introduction of the gospel, women used to conduct all great affairs, whether of government or battle, and the men sunk into inglorious repose and submission. But a contrary error has much more commonly prevailed: woman has been degraded below her level; in some instances treated as a slave, compelled to perform the severest labour, to undergo the greatest hardships, and utterly deprived of all rational intercourse with the lords of creation. In other cases, (it is so in Eastern countries to the present day,) woman is regarded only as an animated toy, formed for the amusement and gratification of man; all her cares and concerns are directed to the decoration of her person; she is totally denied every kind of moral and intellectual culture, and, to justify this worst kind of barbarity, it is asserted that she has no soul, and, therefore, is incapable of rational converse or improvement. Revelation alone places woman in her proper sphere; and on this account, among many others, females are bound to especial gratitude, whose privilege it is to find their place in society where God's holy book has assigned it.

Woman was made out of man—hence she has a claim to be treated with affection and respect, as part of himself—but hence, too, she should learn, that a respectful and rational submission becomes her. She was created after man, from man, and for man. She was taken (observes Mr. Henry[12]) not from the head, to rule; neither was she taken from the feet to be trampled upon; but from the side, to be equal with man; from under his arm, to be protected; and from near his heart, to be beloved by him.

She was designed to be a help meet for man—that is, 1. a suitable companion, capable of holding rational and spiritual communion with him; and, 2. a willing and active assistant to him in all his cares and enterprises; the sweetener of his toil, and (since sorrow, through sin, has become man's sad inheritance) the soother of his sorrows. At a very early age, the consciousness of being intended as the companion of man awakens in the female bosom, and gives rise to a thousand devices for cultivating attractions. Thus we learn what to consider the truest attractions, and such as are really worth

---

[12] Matthew Henry (1662–1714) was an English nonconformist minister and Bible commentator. Henry's *Commentary on the Whole Bible* (1706) is still a widely used reference work. This famous quote on Eve is from his commentary on Genesis 2.

cultivating. A fair face, broidered hair, costly array, and mere exterior accomplishment, have little to do in forming a helpmeet for man; too often they completely disqualify the possessor for filling that destined character; they are frequently accompanied by a disinclination to the duties which such a character supposes and requires; often to pride and extravagance, which render the individual a waster and destroyer, instead of a helpmeet; and sometimes to vice, by which she becomes a blot to her husband, instead of a crown.[13] But whatever tends to the cultivation of her intellectual powers, qualifies her to become the intelligent and interesting companion of her future husband, and the able instructress of his children. Whatever induces habits of industry, prudence, forethought, and a host of every-day virtues, fits her for domestic management, on the due arrangement of which so much of the welfare and happiness of families depend. Whatever promotes self-government, and tends to enrobe the female soul in humility, and deck it with the ornament of a meek and quiet spirit, proves a valuable preparative for her becoming the helpmeet of man in those various scenes of trial, perplexity, and vexation, from which the happiest lot on earth has no exemption; and above all whatever tends to promote the prevailing influence of genuine religion, is in the highest degree valuable, as rendering her a helpmeet indeed; not merely a pleasing companion in the joyous hours of gaiety and prosperity, but a faithful monitor, a sympathizing friend, a Christian counselor; a ministering spirit in the hour of adversity, sickness, and death. Oh that young women in general were disposed to cultivate these truly valuable female attractions!

From Esther Copley, *Scripture Biography: Comprehending all the names Mentioned in the Old and New Testaments* (London: Fisher, Fisher, & Jackson, 1835), 220–22.

–Eve–

LIVING, or, ENLIVENING. The name given to the first woman, as the mother of the whole human race. When the benign Creator had brought into existence the earth, and all the various forms and orders of beings that inhabit it, and had placed in its most favoured spot man, as the delegated governor of all, He was pleased to say of this last and most noble produce of creating skill, "It is not good that he should be alone, I will make an help meet for him." This partner and companion for Adam was not, like the other creatures, formed immediately from the dust of the earth, but was taken from Adam himself. "For the Lord God caused a deep sleep to fall upon Adam,

---

[13] In his commentary on Genesis 2:21-25, Matthew Henry calls woman "a crown to her husband, the crown of the visible creation."

and, during its influence, He took one of his ribs, and closed up the flesh instead thereof; and the rib which the Lord God had taken from man, made he woman, (or female man,) and brought her unto man."

Our great poet Milton has beautifully expressed the joy and transport of Adam, on beholding and receiving this inestimable gift at the hands of his beneficent Creator. He very happily supposes him, during the sleep of which he had been the subject, to have had some glimpse of a lovely creature of his own aspect and complexion, and fitted to be his companion; and that then he was awakened to somewhat like a sense of deficiency, in that all other creatures were formed in pairs, while he alone was solitary; but, almost before the consciousness of desire could be felt, the want was supplied. The lovely image of his dream was presented to him in waking reality, by the great Father of the universe, who Himself solemnized their marriage union, and pronounced upon it His holy benediction. Adam at once understood that this was the lovely companion of his future existence, the partaker of his nature and his flesh; and that the love and union now commencing between them, were to be indissoluble. He said, "This is now bone of my bone, and flesh of my flesh: she shall be called woman, because she was taken out of man. Therefore shall a man leave his father and his mother, and shall cleave unto his wife; and they shall be one flesh."

Of the bliss of our first parents in their state of innocence, we can form but very imperfect conceptions. We know that even in the present imperfect state, the pleasures arising from domestic affection and intercourse, are the most refined and exquisite of earthly enjoyments: but to suppose such union and intercourse perfectly free from all the present interruptions and imperfections; no obstacles or difficulties in the way of union, where choice and affection were fixed; no differences of views, tastes, and dispositions; no imperfections of temper, to ruffle the harmony, or disturb the enjoyment, of the domestic scene; no scantiness of the means of support and gratification; no sickness, to awaken sympathy; no dread of separation:—but we cannot imagine it; let us be thankful that, even in our very imperfect state, we are capable of receiving and imparting so much happiness; and that our very sufferings, trials, and forebodings, are employed to call into exercise the best feelings and dispositions of our nature, and remotely to prove a source of real enjoyment.

How long our first parents continued in a state of innocency and bliss, Scripture does not inform us; but there is considerable reason to conclude, that that state was not of long duration. Seduced by the wily artifices of Satan, the great enemy of God and man, Adam and Eve transgressed against God by eating of the fruit of a particular tree in the garden, from which they were expressly interdicted, as a test of obedience to their Divine Creator. In this transgression, Eve was first: led away by a vain and rash curiosity, she proceeded to scepticism as to the Divine veracity, and then presumed on disobedience to the Divine command: she hearkened to the father of lies [John 8:44], and, flattering herself that evil was good and good evil, "she took and did eat." Finding that no immediate ill effects ensued, the transgressor became a tempter. She next took of the fruit and gave to her husband, and he did eat. Thus was accomplished the fatal act, that "brought death into our world, and all our woe."

In dealing with the transgressors, the sovereign and righteous Judge had especial regard to the particular modes of transgression. Eve had been first in the offence; and a peculiar punishment was inflicted on her in consequence, which should more or less mar the seasons of the most exquisite domestic felicity. In pain, sorrow, and apprehension she should bring forth her off-spring; and thus, in the consummation of her fondest wishes, be painfully and humblingly reminded of her sin and disgrace. She had abused her influ-ence over her husband, and hence forth she should be brought into subjection unto him. The influence of the gospel has moderated the curse, by equalizing the condition of the sexes, and softening down the ferocious passions of man, which, where they reign in their native violence, render authority oppressive, and subjection galling. The sorrows of child-bearing are also soothed and consecrated by the consideration, that, as they were occasioned by sin, they became also subservient in introducing to mankind salvation from sin; even the "Seed of the woman," who should "bruise the head of the serpent," and raise mankind from the ruins of the fall.

After their expulsion from paradise, Adam and Eve became the parents of a numerous progeny. Only three, viz. Cain, Abel, and Seth, are particularly mentioned, with an intimation of daughters, who became their wives. The remarks of Eve, in giving names to these children manifest a spirit of faith in the Divine promise, and resignation to the Divine dispensations. In the fulness of her joy, on the birth of her first-born, she exclaimed, "*A posses-sion*! I have gotten a man from the Lord;" which, however mistaken in her expectations with respect to that child, indicates that her eye was fixed on the fulfilment of the promise of mercy. Abel she called vanity, perhaps from a growing conviction of the vanity and frailty to which all sublunary enjoy-ments were reduced by sin; and on receiving Seth she devoutly acknowledged the good hand of God upon her, saying, "God hath appointed me another seed instead of Abel, whom Cain slew." After this, we are informed in general, that Adam and Eve had more sons and daughters; but no further particulars are furnished, either of their lives or their death.

Gen. i.–iv.; v. 1–5. 1 Tim. ii. 13–15.

§4 Favell Lee Mortimer
(1802–1878)

Favell Lee Mortimer was born in London, the second daughter of David Bevan, a banker, and Favell Bourke. She was educated at home and loved reading from a young age. Early evangelical influences on her life included a governess and an independent minister. At 25 she experienced a conversion which made her leave her busy social world in London for a life devoted to the poor on her father's Wiltshire estate, where she began a school. Her experience teaching prompted her to write her first book published in 1836, *The Peep of Day or A Series of the Earliest Religious Instruction the Infant Mind is Capable of Receiving.* The book demonstrated her belief that the best way to teach children Christianity was by using simplified Bible stories. This first book became very popular. It was published many times in English in both Britain and North America, and translated into thirty-seven other languages for use in mission education. As a follow-up to *The Peep of Day,* Mortimer wrote other books on the Bible for children, including *Line upon Line* (1841), *Precept upon Precept* (1867), and *The Kings of Israel and Judah* (1872). She also wrote books on geography and on how to teach children to read. In 1841 Favell Bevan married the Rev. Thomas Mortimer, a widower with two daughters. After her husband died in 1850, Mortimer continued to write. She moved to Norfolk in 1862 where she also looked after six orphans. She died in August 1878.[14]

Mortimer's primary audience was young children. Her lessons focused on the ideas of sin and forgiveness which she explained using simple language. She highlighted the contrast between the happy life of Eve and Adam in the garden and their aging and death after the fall. Like Barton, Mortimer did not indicate that there was any difference between the punishment given to Adam and that given to Eve: both were driven from the garden and would eventually die. Their redemption came through God's Son. Mortimer connected the story of the fall and its consequences directly to the New Testament and atonement theology.

Like Barton, Mortimer's teaching was moralistic: they both emphasized the importance of good behaviour. Unlike Barton, who called children to repent, Mortimer assumed her readers' sins were covered and directed them to love God the Father and the Son, who had pity on us. Mortimer took a

[14] Source: Rosemary Mitchell, "Mortimer, Favell Lee," in *The Oxford Dictionary of National Biography* 39:377–78.

different approach in her discussion of the fall and redemption than Barton. Whereas Barton asked her readers to empathize with Eve as they would probably have eaten the fruit as she did, Mortimer emphasized her readers' relationship to Adam and Eve—they were children of Eve, and so would die as she did.

From Favell Lee Mortimer, *The Peep of Day, or A series of the Earliest Religious Instruction the Infant Mind is Capable of Receiving* (London: J. Hatchard & Son, 1833). [Text taken from a later edition (London: The Religious Tract Society, n.d), 76–86.]

Lesson XI
The First Sin: Gen. iii

Adam and Eve were very happy in the garden of Eden. They talked to each other, and walked together, and they never quarrelled, and they praised God for all His kindness to them.

God used to talk with them sometimes. They were pleased to hear His voice, for they were not afraid of Him.

There was one thing that God had told them not to do.

There was a tree in the middle of the garden; it grew by the side of the river. Some beautiful fruit grew upon it; but God said to Adam and Eve, 'You must not eat of the fruit of that tree; for if you eat of it, you shall die.'

Adam and Eve liked to obey God, and they did not wish to eat of this fruit.

You know that the wicked angel, Satan, hates God, and he hated Adam and Eve.[i] He wished to make them naughty, that they might go to hell and be burned in his fire. So he thought he would ask them to eat of that fruit. He went into the garden, and looked like a serpent.[ii] He saw Eve alone near the tree. He said to her, 'Why do you not eat of this nice fruit?'

Eve answered, 'No, I will not; we must not eat of that fruit. If we do, God has said we shall die.' Then the serpent said, 'You shall not die; that fruit will make you wise.'

Eve looked at the fruit, and thought it seemed nice and pretty, and she picked some and ate it; and she gave some to Adam, and he ate it.

It was very wicked of them to eat this fruit. Now they were grown naughty, and did not love God.[iii]

Soon they heard God speaking in the garden; then they were frightened, and then went and hid themselves among the trees. But God saw them, for He can see everywhere.

And God said, 'Adam, where art thou?' So Adam and Eve came from under the trees.

God said to Adam, 'Have you eaten the fruit that I told you not to eat?'

And Adam said, 'It was this woman who asked me to eat some.'

And God said to Eve, 'What is this that thou hast done?'

And Eve said, 'The serpent asked me to eat.'

God was very angry with the serpent, and said he should be punished for ever and ever.[iv]

God said to Adam and Eve, 'You shall die. I made your bodies of dust, and they will turn to dust again.'

God would not let them stay in the sweet garden, but He sent an angel with a sword of fire, and he drove them out.

The angel stood before the gate with his sword, so that they could not come again into the garden.

[Mortimer includes a poem at this point. The final verses follow.]

> O, why did Eve to Satan's lies
> So readily attend?
> Upon the fruit why fix her eyes,
> Then pluck it with her hand?

> No more shall Eve or Adam stay
> Within that garden fair;
> An angel stands to guard the way,
> That none may enter there,

[i] 'Love is of God; and every one that loveth is born of God, and knoweth God.' I John iv.7.

[ii] 'That old serpent, called the devil, and Satan, which deceiveth the whole world.' Rev. xii.9.

[iii] 'By one man's disobedience many were made sinners.' Rom v.19.

[iv] 'It shall bruise thy head.' Gen iii.15.

Lesson XII
The Son of God: Gen iii.14–24

Are you not very sorry to hear that Adam and Eve were turned out of the garden?

It was not so pleasant outside of the garden. A great many weeds and thistles grew outside; but in the garden there were only pretty flowers and sweet fruits.

Adam was forced to dig the ground till he was hot and tired, for he could not always find fruit upon the trees.

Now Adam felt pain in his body sometimes; and his hair became grey, and at last he was quite old.

Eve was very often sick and weak, and tears ran down her cheeks. Poor Adam and Eve! if you had obeyed God, you would have been happy for ever.

Adam and Eve knew that they must die at last. God gave them some little children, and Adam and Eve knew that their children must die too. God had told them that their bodies were made of dust, and that they must turn to dust again.

But there was something more sad still. They were grown wicked. They did not love praising God as they once had done, but they liked doing many naughty things.[i] They were grown like Satan, so Satan hoped that when their bodies were put into the ground, their spirits would be with him; for Satan knew that the wicked could not live with God in heaven.[ii]

And they would have gone to hell, and all their children too, had not God taken pity upon them. God, who is very kind, had found out a way to save them.

God had said to His Son a long, long while before, 'Adam and Eve, and all their children, must go to hell for their wickedness, unless You die instead of them.[iii] My beloved Son, I will send You; You shall have a body; You shall go and live in the world, and You shall obey Me, and You shall die for Adam and his children.'[iv]

The Son said to his Father, 'I will come; I will do all that You desire Me to do. It is My delight to obey You.'[v]

So the Son promised that He would die for Adam and Eve, and for their children.

How kind it was of the Father to spare His dear Son, Whom He loved so very much![vi] How kind it was of the Son to leave His throne of light, His bright angels, and His dear Father, and to take a body and to die![vii]

You know that we are some of Adam's children's children. It was for us Jesus came to die. We are wicked, and we should go to hell if Jesus had not promised to die for us.[viii] We ought to love the Father, and the Son, because They had pity on us.

[i] 'The carnal mind is enmity against God: for it is not subject to the law of God, neither indeed can be.' Rom. viii.7.

[ii] 'And the Lord said, Simon, Simon, behold, Satan hath desired to have you.' Luke xxii.31.

The constant efforts of Satan to tempt men to commit sin, show that he is aware of the destructive nature of sin, as it is undeniable that he desires to destroy man.

[iii] 'Herein is love, not that we loved God, but that He loved us, and sent His Son to be the propitiation for our sins.' I John iv.10. 'Who verily was fore-ordained before the foundation of the world.' I Pet i.20.

[iv] 'I have kept My Father's *commandments*, and abide in His love.' John xv.10.

[v] 'Then said I, Lo, I come: I delight to do Thy will, O my God: yea, Thy law is with my heart.' Ps. xl.8.

^{vi} 'Thou lovedst me before the foundation of the world.' John xvii.24.
^{vii} 'The glory which I had with Thee before the world was.' John xvii.5.
^{viii} 'As in Adam all die, even so in Christ shall all be made alive.' I Cor xv.22.

§5 Sarah Moore Grimké
(1792–1873)

Sarah Grimké was born in Charleston, South Carolina, the sixth of four-teen children born to John Grimké and Mary Smith. Her father, of French Huguenot descent, was a well-known judge, educated in England; her mother, of Irish and Puritan ancestry, came from a prominent Carolina family. Private tutors educated Sarah Grimké in subjects considered appropriate for young ladies. She also learned what she could of Greek, Latin, philosophy and law from her brothers and father. Grimké encountered the Society of Friends on a trip with her father to Philadelphia and New Jersey; afterwards Grimké left the Episcopal church and joined the Society of Friends. She was drawn to Quaker piety and their abhorrence of slavery, though later she would become disenchanted with orthodox Quakerism, and be dismissed from the society. Sarah Grimké and her sister Angelina Weld became well known for their antislavery work. At a time when women did not speak in public they spoke publicly to audiences of both men and women as a part of their abolition work. Opposition to their public speaking led the sisters to involvement in the early feminist movement.

Sarah Grimké wrote *Epistle to the Clergy of the Southern States* (1836) to refute the argument that slavery in biblical times justified slavery in the United States. She wrote *Letters on the Equality of the Sexes, and the Condition of Women* (1838) in defense of the right of women to have a public voice in the abolition movement.[15] She was a major theoretician of the women's rights movement.

Grimké, like Crocker, was an American arguing for the rights of women. Like Crocker, she realized that the interpretation of Genesis 1–3 greatly influ-enced views on women's role in family and society. Grimké read the text in the original Hebrew, and used this knowledge in her interpretation. For example, the Hebrew word 'adam' can be used as a generic term for human-

¹⁵ Source: Betty L. Fladeland, "Grimké, Sarah Moore and Angelina Emily," in *Notable American Women 1607–1950: A Biographical Dictionary*, ed. Edward T. James, Janet Wilson James, and Paul S. Boyer, vol. 2 (Cambridge, Mass.: Harvard University Press, 1971), 97–99.

ity, and Grimké used this to argue for the coregency of women and men over creation. She called the account of the creation of Eve in Genesis 2 a recapitulation of the story of the creation of humans in Genesis 1, and so she subordinated her interpretation of the second chapter of Genesis to the theology she found in the first chapter. Grimké redefined the term 'helpmeet' so that women were not subordinate to men, but companions in every way equal to them. Like Crocker, she compared the temptation of Adam and Eve and concluded that Eve's temptation was more difficult. Unlike Crocker, Grimké argued that while both Adam and Eve fell from innocence, they did not fall from equality. The consequence of the fall for women (you will [not shall] be subject to your husband) was prophetic, not prescriptive. The consequence of the fall was a struggle for dominion between women and men.

From Sarah Grimké, *Letters on the Equality of the Sexes, and the Condition of Woman* (Boston: I. Knapp, 1838).

Letter I: The Original Equality of Woman
Amesbury, 7th Mo. 11th, 1837

My Dear Friend,

In attempting to comply with thy request to give my views on the Province of Woman, I feel that I am venturing on nearly untrodden ground, and that I shall advance arguments in opposition to a corrupt public opinion, and to the perverted interpretation of Holy Writ, which has so universally obtained. But I am in search of truth; and no obstacle shall prevent my prosecuting that search, because I believe the welfare of the world will be materially advanced by every new discovery we make of the designs of Jehovah in the creation of woman. It is impossible that we can answer the purpose of our being, unless we understand that purpose. It is impossible that we should fulfil our duties, unless we comprehend them; or live up to our privileges, unless we know what they are.

In examining this important subject, I shall depend solely on the Bible to designate the sphere of woman, because I believe almost every thing that has been written on this subject, has been the result of a misconception of the simple truths revealed in the Scriptures, in consequence of the false translation of many passages of Holy Writ. My mind is entirely delivered from the superstitious reverence which is attached to the English version of the Bible. King James's translators certainly were not inspired. I therefore claim the original as my standard, believing that to have been inspired, and I also claim to judge for myself what is the meaning of the inspired writers, because I believe it to be the solemn duty of every individual to search the Scriptures for themselves, with the aid of the Holy Spirit, and not be governed by the views of any man, or set of men.

We must first view woman at the period of her creation. "And God said, Let us make man in our own image, after our likeness; and let them have dominion over the fish of the sea, and over the fowl of the air, and over the cattle, and over all the earth, and over every creeping thing that creepeth upon the earth. So God created man in his own image, in the image of God created he him, male and female created he them." In all this sublime description of the creation of man, (which is a generic term including man and woman), there is not one particle of difference intimated as existing between them. They were both made in the image of God; dominion was given to both over every other creature, but not over each other. Created in perfect equality, they were expected to exercise the viceregence intrusted to them by their Maker, in harmony and love.

Let us pass on now to the recapitulation of the creation of man—"The Lord God formed man of the dust of the ground, and breathed into his nostrils the breath of life; and man became a living soul. And the Lord God said, it is not good that man should be alone, I will make him an help meet for him." All creation swarmed with animated beings capable of natural affection, as we know they still are; it was not, therefore, merely to give man a creature susceptible of loving, obeying, and looking up to him, for all that the animals could do and did do. It was to give him a companion, *in all respects* his equal; one who was like himself a *free agent*, gifted with intellect and endowed with immortality; not a partaker merely of his animal gratifications, but able to enter into all his feelings as a moral and responsible being. If this had not been the case, how could she have been an help meet for him? I understand this as applying not only to the parties entering into the marriage contract, but to all men and women, because I believe God designed woman to be an help meet for man in every good and perfect work. She was a part of himself, as if Jehovah designed to make the oneness and identity of man and woman perfect and complete; and when the glorious work of their creation was finished, "the morning stars sang together, and all the sons of God shouted for joy" [Job 38:7].

This blissful condition was not long enjoyed by our first parents. Eve, it would seem from the history, was wandering alone amid the bowers of Paradise, when the serpent met with her. From her reply to Satan, it is evident that the command not to eat "of the tree that is in the midst of the garden," was given to both, although the term man was used when the prohibition was issued by God. "And the woman said unto the serpent, WE may eat of the fruit of the trees of the garden, but of the fruit of the tree which is in the midst of the garden, God hath said, YE shall not eat of it, neither shall YE touch it, lest YE die." Here the woman was exposed to temptation from a being with whom she was unacquainted. She had been accustomed to associate with her beloved partner, and to hold communion with God and with angels; but of satanic intelligence, she was in all probability entirely ignorant. Through the subtlety of the serpent, she was beguiled. And "when she saw that the tree was good for food, and that it was pleasant to the eyes, and a tree to be desired to make one wise, she took of the fruit thereof and did eat."

We next find Adam involved in the same sin, not through the instrumentality of a supernatural agent, but through that of his equal, a being whom he must have known was liable to transgress the divine command, because he must have felt that he was himself a free agent, and that he was restrained from disobedience only by the exercise of faith and love towards his Creator. Had Adam tenderly reproved his wife, and endeavored to lead her to repentance instead of sharing in her guilt, I should be much more ready to accord to man that superiority which he claims; but as the facts stand disclosed by the sacred historian, it appears to me that to say the least, there was as much weakness exhibited by Adam as by Eve. They both fell from innocence, and consequently from happiness, but not from equality.

Let us next examine the conduct of this fallen pair, when Jehovah interrogated them respecting their fault. They both frankly confessed their guilt. "The man said, the woman whom thou gavest to be with me, she gave me of the tree and I did eat. And the woman said, the serpent beguiled me and I did eat." And the Lord God said unto the woman, "Thou wilt be subject unto thy husband, and he will rule over thee." That this did not allude to the subjection of woman to man is manifest, because the same mode of expression is used in speaking to Cain of Abel. The truth is that the curse, as it is termed, which was pronounced by Jehovah upon woman, is a simple prophecy. The Hebrew, like the French language, uses the same word to express shall and will. Our translators having been accustomed to exercise lordship over their wives, and seeing only through the medium of a perverted judgment, very naturally, though I think not very learnedly or very kindly, translated it shall instead of will, and thus converted a prediction to Eve into a command to Adam; for observe, it is addressed to the woman and not to the man. The consequence of the fall was an immediate struggle for dominion, and Jehovah foretold which would gain the ascendency; but as he created them in his image, as that image manifestly was not lost by the fall, because it is urged in Gen. 9:6, as an argument why the life of man should not be taken by his fellow man, there is no reason to suppose that sin produced any distinction between them as moral, intellectual and responsible beings. Man might just as well have endeavored by hard labor to fulfil the prophecy, "thorns and thistles will the earth bring forth to thee," as to pretend to accomplish the other, "he will rule over thee," by asserting dominion over his wife.

> Authority usurped from God, not given.
> He gave him only over beast, flesh, fowl,
> Dominion absolute: that right he holds
> By God's donation: but man o'er woman
> He made not Lord, such title to himself
> Reserving, human left from human free.[16]

Here then I plant myself. God created us equal;—he created us free agents;—he is our Lawgiver, our King and our Judge, and to him alone is woman bound to be in subjection, and to him alone is she accountable for the use of those talents with which her Heavenly Father has entrusted her. One is her Master even Christ.

Thine for the oppressed in the bonds of womanhood,

Sarah M. Grimké

§6 Angelina Emily Grimké Weld
(1805–1879)

Angelina Weld was Sarah Grimké's younger sister and coworker in the abolitionist cause. Weld wrote and lectured on human rights, and was a powerful speaker. After her marriage to Theodore D. Weld, also an abolitionist, her ill health prevented her public work in the anti-slavery cause.[17]

Weld's *Letters to Catherine Beecher* was part of an ongoing discussion between Catharine Beecher (1800–1878) and Weld on the slavery issue.[18] Throughout this work Weld quoted from Beecher's *An Essay on Slavery and Abolitionism addressed to A.E. Grimké.* Letter XII is an argument for universal human rights, independent of gender, in which Weld used Eve's relationship to Adam to argue that women and men were equal. The letter does not begin with scripture, but uses scripture as an authoritative source of evidence for Weld's argument. While Weld's *Letters to Catherine Beecher* were published before Grimké's *Letters on the Equality of the Sexes,* Weld referred to Grimké's

---

[16] Here Grimké cites John Milton's *Paradise Lost*, book 12.

[17] Fladeland, "Grimké," 97–99.

[18] Note that Beecher's first name is misspelled in the printed edition of the letters.

work in this letter, and possibly based her interpretation of Genesis 2 on her sister's work. Like Crocker and Grimké, Weld used the Genesis texts to support her argument for equality between women and men.

From Angelina E. Grimké, *Letters to Catherine Beecher* (Boston: Isaac Knapp, 1838), 114–21.

Letter XII
Human Rights Not Founded on Sex.

East Boylston, Mass. 10th mo. 2d, 1837.
Dear Friend: In my last, I made a sort of running commentary upon thy views of the appropriate sphere of woman, with something like a promise, that in my next, I would give thee my own.

The investigation of the rights of the slave has led me to a better understanding of my own. I have found the Anti-Slavery cause to be the high school of morals in our land—the school in which *human rights* are more fully investigated, and better understood and taught, than in any other. Here a great fundamental principle is uplifted and illuminated, and from this central light, rays innumerable stream all around. Human beings have *rights*, because they are *moral* beings: the rights of *all* men grow out of their moral nature; and as all men have the same moral nature, they have essentially the same rights. These rights may be wrested from the slave, but they cannot be alienated: his title to himself is as perfect now, as is that of Lyman Beecher:[19] it is stamped on his moral being, and is, like it, imperishable. Now if rights are founded in the nature of our moral being, then the *mere circumstance of sex* does not give to man higher rights and responsibilities, than to woman. To suppose that it does, would be to deny the self-evident truth, that the 'physical constitution is the mere instrument of the moral nature.' To suppose that it does, would be to break up utterly the relations, of the two natures, and to reverse their functions, exalting the animal nature into a monarch, and humbling the moral into a slave; making the former a proprietor, and the latter its property. When human beings are regarded as *moral* beings, *sex*, instead of being enthroned upon the summit, administering upon rights and responsibilities, sinks into insignificance and nothingness. My doctrine then is, that whatever it is morally right for man to do, it is morally right for woman to do. Our duties originate, not from difference of sex, but from the diversity of our relations in life, the various gifts and talents committed to our care, and the different eras in which we live.

[19] Lyman Beecher (1775–1863) was Catharine Beecher's father. Lyman Beecher was a prominent Congregational minister, revivalist, and social reformer.

This regulation of duty by the mere circumstance of sex, rather than by the fundamental principle of moral being has led to all that multifarious train of evils flowing out of the anti-christian doctrine of masculine and feminine virtues. By this doctrine, man has been converted into the warrior, and clothed with sternness, and those other kindred qualities, which in common estimation belong to his character as a man; whilst woman has been taught to lean upon an arm of flesh, to sit as a doll arrayed in 'gold, and pearls, and costly array,' [1 Tim. 2:9] to be admired for her personal charms, and caressed and humored like a spoiled child, or converted into a mere drudge to suit the convenience of her lord and master. Thus have all the diversified relations of life been filled with 'confusion and every evil work,' [James 3:16]. This principle has given to man a charter for the exercise of tyranny and selfishness, pride and arrogance, lust and brutal violence. It has robbed woman of essential rights, the right to think and speak and act on all great moral questions, just as men think and speak and act; the right to share their responsibilities, perils and toils; the right to fulfil the great end of her being, as a moral, intellectual and immortal creature, and of glorifying God in her body and her spirit which are His. Hitherto, instead of being a help meet to man, in the highest, noblest sense of the term, as a companion, a co-worker, an equal; she has been a mere appendage of his being an instrument of his convenience and pleasure, the pretty toy with which he wiled away his leisure moments, or the pet animal whom he humored into playfulness and submission. Woman, instead of being regarded as the equal of man, has uniformly been looked down upon as his inferior, a mere gift to fill up the measure of his happiness. In 'the poetry of romantic gallantry,' it is true, she has been called 'the last *best* gift of God to man';[20] but I believe I speak forth the words of truth and soberness when I affirm, that woman never was given to man. She was created, like him, in the image of God, and crowned with glory and honor; created only a little lower than the angels, [Ps. 8:5]—not, as is almost universally assumed, a little lower than man; on her brow, as well as on his, was placed the 'diadem of beauty,' and in her hand the sceptre of universal dominion. Gen. i:27, 28. 'The last *best gift* of God to man!' Where is the scripture warrant for this 'rhetorical flourish, this splendid absurdity?' Let us examine the account of her creation. 'And the rib which the Lord God had taken from man, made he a woman, and brought her unto the man.' Not as a gift—for Adam immediately recognized her *as a part of himself*—('this is now bone of my bone, and flesh of my flesh')—a companion and equal, not one hair's breadth beneath him in the majesty and glory of her moral being; not placed under his authority as a *subject*, but by his side, on the same platform

---

[20] Weld is probably referring to Milton's *Paradise Lost*, book 6, l.19, which reads "Heav'ns last best gift, my ever new delight."

of human rights, under the government of God only. This idea of woman's being 'the last best gift of God to man,' however pretty it may sound to the ears of those who love to discourse upon 'the poetry of romantic gallantry, and the generous promptings of chivalry,' has nevertheless been the means of sinking her from an *end* into a mere *means*—of turning her into an *appendage* to man, instead of recognizing her *as a part of man*—of destroying her individuality, and rights, and responsibilities and merging her moral being in that of man. Instead of *Jehovah* being *her* king, *her* lawgiver, and *her* judge, she has been taken out of the exalted scale of existence in which He placed her, and subjected to the despotic control of man.

I have often been amused at the vain efforts made to define the rights and responsibilities of immortal beings as *men* and *women*. No one has yet found out just *where* the line of separation between them should be drawn, and for this simple reason, that no one knows just how far below man woman is, whether she be a head shorter in her moral responsibilities, or head and shoulders, or the full length of his noble stature, below him, i.e. under his feet. Confusion, uncertainty, and great inconsistencies, must exist on this point, so long as woman is regarded in the least degree inferior to man; but place her where her Maker placed her, on the same high level of human rights with man, side by side with him, and difficulties vanish, the mountains of perplexity flow down at the presence of this grand equalizing principle. Measure her rights and duties by the unerring standard of *moral being*, not by the false weights and measures of a mere circumstance of her human existence, and then the truth will be self-evident, that whatever it is *morally* right for a man to do, it is *morally* right for a woman to do. I recognize no rights but *human* rights—I know nothing of men's rights and women's rights for in Christ Jesus, there is neither male nor female. It is my solemn conviction, that, until this principle of equality is recognised and embodied in practice, the church can do nothing effectual for the permanent reformation of the world. Woman was the first transgressor, and the first victim of power. In all heathen nations, she has been the slave of man, and Christian nations have never acknowledged her rights. Nay more, no Christian denomination or Society has ever acknowledged them on the broad basis of humanity. I know that in some denominations, she is permitted to preach the gospel; not from a conviction of her rights, nor upon the ground of her equality as a *human being*, but of her equality in spiritual gifts—for we find that woman, even in these Societies, is allowed no voice in framing the Discipline by which she is to be *governed*. Now, I believe it is woman's right to have a voice in all the laws and regulations by which she is to be governed, whether in Church or State; and that the present arrangements of society, on these points, are *a violation of human rights, a rank usurpation of power,* a violent seizure and confiscation of what is sacredly and inalienably hers—thus inflicting upon woman outrageous wrongs, working mischief incalculable in the social Circle, and in its influence on the world producing only evil, and that continually. *If* Ecclesiastical and Civil governments are ordained of God, *then* I contend that woman has just as much right to sit in solemn counsel in Conventions, Conferences, Associations and General Assemblies, as man—just as much right to it upon the throne of England, or in the Presidential chair of the United States.

Dost thou ask me, if I would wish to see woman engaged in the contention and strife of sectarian controversy, or in the intrigues of political partizans? I say no! never—never. I rejoice that she does not stand on the same platform which man now occupies in these respects; but I mourn, also, that he should thus prostitute his higher nature, and vilely cast away his birthright. I prize the purity of *his* character as highly as I do that of hers. As a moral being, *whatever it is morally wrong for her to do, it is morally wrong for him to do.* The fallacious doctrine of male and female virtues has well nigh ruined all that is morally great and lovely in his character: he has been quite as deep a sufferer by it as woman, though mostly in different respects and by other processes. As my time is engrossed by the pressing responsibilities of daily public duty, I have no leisure for that minute detail which would be required for the illustration and defence of those principles. Thou wilt find a wide field opened before thee, in the investigation of which, I doubt not, thou wilt be instructed. Enter this field, and explore it: thou wilt find in it a hid treasure [Matt. 13:44], more precious than rubies [Prov. 3:15]—a fund, a mine of principles, as new as they are great and glorious.

Thou sayest, 'an ignorant, a narrow-minded, or a stupid woman, cannot feel nor understand the rationality, the propriety, or the beauty of this relation'—i.e. subordination to man. Now, verily, it does appear to me, that nothing but a narrow-minded view of the subject of human rights and responsibilities can induce any one to believe in this *subordination to a fallible being.* Sure I am, that the signs of the times clearly indicate a vast and rapid change in public sentiment, on this subject. Sure I am that she is not to be, as she has been, *'a mere second-hand agent'* in the regeneration of a fallen world, but the acknowledged equal and co-worker with man in this glorious work. Not that 'she will carry her measures by tormenting when she cannot please, or by petulant complaints or obtrusive interference, in matters which are out of her sphere, and which she cannot comprehend.' But just in proportion as her moral and intellectual capacities become enlarged, she will rise higher and higher in the scale of creation, until she reaches that elevation prepared for her by her Maker, and upon whose summit she was originally stationed, only 'a little lower than the angels' [Ps. 8:5]. Then will it be seen that nothing which concerns the well-being of mankind is either beyond her sphere, or above her comprehension: *Then* will it be seen 'that America will be distinguished above all other nations for well-educated women, and for the influence they will exert on the general interests of society.'

But I must close with recommending to thy perusal, my sister's Letters on the Province of Woman, published in the New England Spectator, and republished by Isaac Knapp of Boston. As she has taken up this subject so fully, I have only glanced at it. That thou and all my country-women may better understand the true dignity of woman, is the sincere desire of

Thy Friend,
A. E. GRIMKÉ.

§7 Catherine Hunt Putnam
(1792–1869)

Catherine Hunt Putnam (née Palmer) was born in Framingham, Mass. Little is known about her education and upbringing. She married Henry Putnam, a lawyer trained at Harvard. Catherine Putnam ran a successful preparatory school, which supported the family through her husband's ill health. She was remembered for her benevolence. The Putnam's son, George Palmer Putnam, worked in publishing, and founded the firm eventually known as G. P. Putnam's Sons. Catherine Putnam died in New York in 1869.[21]

Catherine Putnam's publications, *Scripture Text-Book* (1837), and *The Gospel by Moses in the Book of Genesis; or, The Old Testament Unveiled* (1854) demonstrate that she was a well-educated and thoughtful Christian who confidently entered into the contemporary debate about typology. She supported her own position on typology with the views of the Scottish biblical scholar, Patrick Fairbairn (1805–1874), whose well-known book, *Typology of Scripture* (1845) advocated the continued use of typology, against the views of her American contemporaries, Calvin Stowe (1802–1886) and Moses Stuart (1780–1852). She published her first book anonymously as "a teacher," but she identified herself as the author of her second book.

Putnam's reading is very different than that of Grimké and Weld. Where Grimké found meaning in a fresh literal reading of the text, Putnam looked

---

[21] Sources: Ronald J. Zboray, "George Palmer Putnam," in *American National Biography* 18:6–8. See also "Israel Putnam" published online at http://www.virtualology.com/virtualwarmuseum.com/revolutionarywarhall/ISRAELPUTNAM.ORG/ (accessed November 3, 2004).

for the hidden spiritual meaning of the text through typology. This reading gave her a different understanding of the theological and practical implications of the text. Putnam's work was laid out in two columns, one called "The Letter" and the other "The Spirit." The column entitled "The Letter" contains verses from Genesis and notes on the typological reading of the text. The column entitled "The Spirit" contains the intertexts for her reading: verses from the rest of the Bible, which support her typological reading of Genesis. These texts are not always quoted from the King James Version. We suggest this selection will make the most sense if one first reads the column entitled "The Letter," including Putnam's Note, then the column entitled "The Spirit."

Putnam's reading elevated Adam to a Christ-figure, and Eve to a type of the individual Christian in the church. Putnam's typological approach is important as it shows how typology can force the meaning of a text. Any typological reading of a male figure as God and a female figure as the church necessarily elevates the male figure and lends weight to the traditional understanding of women being subordinate to men. A typological reading of Adam as Jesus and Eve as the church is quite traditional; however, Putnam pushed this reading much further than most interpreters.[22] As a divine type, Adam could do no wrong. Thus, Putnam had to reinterpret Adam's eating of the fruit. Putnam had Adam become the substitute for Eve in taking the fruit and sinning with her; Adam ate the fruit out of love for Eve, and bore her curse in his body, as Christ did for the Church.

Selections from Catherine H. Putnam, *The Gospel by Moses, in the Book of Genesis; or, the Old Testament Unveiled* (New York: Edward H. Fletcher, 1854), 35–37; 39–42.

The Letter	*The Spirit*
21. And the Lord God caused deep sleep to fall upon Adam, and he slept; and he took one of his ribs, and closed up the flesh instead thereof:	ACTS xx. 28. * * Feed the church of God, which he hath purchased with his own blood.
22. And the rib, which the Lord God had taken from man, made he a woman, and brought her unto the man.	PHIL. ii. 6. Who, being in the form of God, thought it not robbery to be equal with God
	7. But made himself of no reputation,

---

[22] Compare Putnam's reading with peers such as Mary Wardle, in *The Law: Moral, Ceremonial and Judicial. [Explanation of Chapters of the Books of Genesis, Exodus and Deuteronomy]* (London: 1879), 5–6. For Origen's reading of Eve as the church, see Gary A. Anderson, *The Genesis of Perfection: Adam and Eve in Jewish and Christian Imagination* (Louisville: Westminster John Knox, 2001), 101–3.

Note

Regarded as nothing more than a literal narrative of common facts, this would seem a remarkable method of procuring a help-meet for Adam. But if we look through the veil of material things to that which is hidden behind, we may see that no other could be adopted. Through this figure was to be shown forth the vital union of Christ and the church: that she is one with him, members of his body; that she was originally and *always with him* and *in him*! How then could this be represented but by taking a part of Adam's self; the bones of his own body!

Again, another idea must be involved, —it was accomplished by means of death, for with nothing less than the blood of Christ could the church be purchased. A "deep sleep" then must fall upon Adam to show that the good shepherd laid down his life for the sheep.

It was the hand of God that laid this deep sleep upon Adam, and that also brought to him the help-meet which he had moulded and fashioned after his own image. So it is the work of the Father to bring to Jesus all that are his, when he has taught them by his Spirit, and conformed them to the image of his Son.

and took upon him the form of a servant, and was made in the likeness of men:

8. And being found in fashion as a man, he humbled himself, and became obedient unto death, even the death of the cross.

Col. i. 20. And, having made peace through the blood of his cross, by him to reconcile all things unto himself; by him, I say, whether they be things in earth, or things in heaven.

21. And you, that were some time alienated and enemies in your mind by wicked works, yet now hath he reconciled.

22. In the body of his flesh through death, to present you holy, and unblamable, and unreprovable, in his sight.

John vi. 44. No man can come to me, except the Father which hath sent me draw him: and I will raise him up at the last day.

1 Pet. ii. 25. For ye were as sheep going astray: but are now returned unto the Shepherd and Bishop of your souls.

Heb. ix. 15. And for this cause he is the mediator of the new testament, that by means of death, for the redemption of the transgressions that were under the first testament, they which are called might receive the promise of eternal inheritance.

16. For where a testament is, there must also of necessity be the death of the testator.

The Letter

23. And Adam said, This is now bone of my bone, and flesh of my flesh she shall be called Woman, because she was taken out of man.

24. Therefore shall a man leave his father and his mother, and shall cleave

The Spirit

Eph. v. 30. For we are members of his body, of his flesh and of his bones.

Col. i. 22. In the body of his flesh through death, to present you holy and unblamable and unreprovable in his sight.

unto his wife: and they shall be one flesh.

25. And they were both naked, the man and his wife, and they were not ashamed.

Note

As a literal fact, Adam would hardly have recognised the rib which had been taken from him in the unconsciousness of deep sleep, in the fair woman, thus *made ready* and presented to him without spot or wrinkle, or any such thing! But the divine Redeemer was fully aware of the whole process, when his body was broken and his blood shed for his people. This people were recorded by name in his body, and worn upon his heart, as in the book of life, and not one shall finally be taken from him. They are of his body, his flesh and his bones, in an everlasting union which death could not dissolve.

Jesus left the bosom of the Father and the glory which he had with him before the world was, that he might seek and save that people which had gone astray, like lost sheep; and when he has again brought them back to the Shepherd and Bishop of their souls, he calls upon them to forsake all for him; and that they henceforward live not to themselves, but to him who died for them, that they might have life.

They were "both naked," for as yet they had no guilt to require the garment of imputed righteousness. Adam was naked, as being exposed to the consequences of becoming bondsman for the woman; but as yet there was no transgression, and therefore no shame or fear.

iii. 10. And have put on the new man, which is renewed in knowledge after the image of him that created him.

i. 24. Who now rejoice in my sufferings for you, and fill up that which is behind of the afflictions of Christ in my flesh for his body's sake, which is the church.

EPH. v. 22. Wives, submit yourselves unto your own husbands, as unto the Lord.

23. For the husband is the head of the wife, even as Christ is the head of the church: and he is the Saviour of the body.

24. Therefore as the church is subject unto Christ, so let the wives be to their own husbands in everything.

REV. xix. 7. Let us be glad and rejoice, and give honour to him: for the marriage of the Lamb is come, and his wife made herself ready.

8. And to her was granted that she should be arrayed in fine linen, clean and white: for the fine linen is the righteousness of saints.

9. And he saith unto me, Write, Blessed are they which are called unto the marriage-supper of the Lamb. And he saith unto me, These are the true sayings of God.

LUKE xiv. 26. If any man come to me, and hate not his father, and mother, and wife, and children, and brethren, and sisters, yea, and his own life also, he cannot be my disciple.

33. So likewise, whosoever he be of you that forsaketh not all that he hath, he cannot be my disciple.

The Letter

6. And when the woman saw that the tree *was* good for food, and that it was pleasant to the eyes, and a tree to

The Spirit

JAMES i. 12. Blessed is the man that endureth temptation; for when he is tried he shall receive the crown of life, which be desired to make *one* wise; she took of the fruit thereof, and did eat, and gave also unto her husband with her, and he did eat.

7. And the eyes of them both were opened, and they knew that they were naked: and they sewed fig-leaves together, and made themselves aprons.

Note

The old leaven of malice and wickedness, infused by the enemy of all righteousness into the entire lump of clay—or body of *flesh*, out of which the Divine Potter would form the vessels for his own use and service-had already begun to work! "When lust hath conceived it bringeth forth sin; and sin when it is finished bringeth forth death!"

Thus had the *enemy* succeeded in sowing "*his tares*" upon the fair field of the Son of man! planting his *lie* where God had breathed the breath of life! and thus subjected the entire *field* to his own dominion, until the "one nearest of kin should appear to redeem his possession."

But it is written, "*Adam was not deceived, but the woman being deceived, was in the transgression.*" If Adam was not deceived—if he was fully aware of the penalty that awaited him if he took the fruit from the woman—why did he eat? There can be but one answer to this question: it was, "*for the great love wherewith he loved her!*" Having himself been entrusted by God with the law of the garden, to keep it from pollution and dishonour, he was bound to take upon himself the vindication of that law by the best possible manner, in showing that he would himself suffer its sentence rather than that it should be violated with impunity. Again: he saw that his wife, the

the Lord hath promised to them that love him.

13. Let no man say when he is tempted, I am tempted of God: for God cannot be tempted with evil, neither tempteth he any man.

14. But every man is tempted, when he is drawn away of his own lust, and enticed.

15. Then, when lust hath conceived, it bringeth forth sin ; and sin, when it is finished, bringeth forth death.

HEB. xii. 2. Looking on Jesus, the author and finisher of faith, who having joy proposed unto him, underwent the cross, despising the shame; and sitteth on the right hand of the throne of God.

3. For think diligently upon him who endureth such opposition from sinners against himself; that you be not wearied, fainting in your minds.

4. For you have not yet resisted unto blood, striving against sin.

ECCL. ix. 14. There was a little city, and few men within it; and there came a great king against it, and besieged it, and built great bulwarks against it:

15. Now there was found in it a poor wise man, and he, by his wisdom delivered the city; yet no man remembered that same poor man.

ROM. v. 6. For when we were yet without strength, in due time Christ died for the ungodly.

7. For scarcely for a righteous man will one die: yet peradventure for a good man some would even dare to die.

8. For God commendeth his love toward us, in that while we were yet sinners, Christ died for us.

woman whom God had given him, and for whom he had been made responsible, was under condemnation, and must suffer the penalty of transgression. Therefore he felt himself bound also to bear her curse in his own body; and the only possible way to do this, was to take upon himself her sins. Satan, her murderer, must also be slain, and *he* only could become the *avenger of blood*. Thus, as far as natural

things can represent spiritual, Adam is, in this act, a "figure of Him that was to come." The first attempt to cover sin, was by the fig-leaf righteousness of the law. But it proved ineffectual, and the sinner still remained exposed until God himself provided a garment.

From 1 Tim. ii. 11-15, it would appear that from this time the woman was put in *subjection* to the man.

The Letter

8. And they heard the voice of the Lord God walking in the garden in the cool of the day: and Adam and his wife hid themselves from the presence of the Lord God amongst the trees of the garden.

9. And the Lord God called unto Adam, and said unto him, Where *art* thou?

Note

The call of God upon Adam, *in the cool of the day*, or, as it might be rendered, the *wind of the day*, shows forth the recognition of Jesus as the propitiation for sin, "through the forbearance of God."

The woman had sinned, and with her whole posterity had come short of the glory of God. But instead of visiting upon her the fierceness of his anger, God calls upon her bondsman, her substitute; on whom he had "*laid help*" by his own special appointment: "*Adam, where art thou?*"

The fig-leaf covering had been tried; the righteousness which is of the law; but it was found "weak through the flesh;" it "could never take away sin." Therefore, "*when he cometh into the world he saith, Sacrifice and offering for sin, thou wouldst*

The Spirit

ROM. iii. 20. Therefore by the deeds of the law, there shall no flesh be justified in his sight, for by the law is the knowledge of sin.

21. But now the righteousness of God without the law is manifested, being witnessed by the law and the prophets.

22. Even the righteousness of God which is by faith of Jesus Christ, &c.

23. For all have sinned, and come short of the glory of God.

24. Being justified freely by his grace through the redemption that is in Christ Jesus.

25. Whom God hath set forth to be a propitiation through faith in his blood, to declare his righteousness for the remission of sins that are past, through the forbearance of God.

ISA. liii. 5. But *he was* wounded for our transgressions, *he was* bruised for our iniquities: the chastisement of our peace *was* upon him; and with his stripes we are healed.

6. All we, like sheep, have gone astray; we have turned every one to his own way; and the Lord hath laid on him the iniquity of us all.

12. * * And he was numbered with the transgressors; and he bore the sin

not; then said I, Lo, I come; in the volume of the book it is written of me; I delight to do thy will, O God."

It may be thought, that if Adam here represented Jesus, coming forth for the salvation of his people, and to answer for their transgressions; why did he *hide* himself? But was not Jesus, the sinner's substitute, the Lamb of God, that taketh away the sins of the world, found hid under a veil of flesh, made like unto his brethren? like unto the trees of the garden? and walking among them?

"They word was made flesh and dwelt among us," &c.

of many and made intercession for the transgressors.

Heb. x. 7. * * Lo, I come to do thy will, O God, &c.

Ps. xl. 8. I delight to do thy will, O my God; yea, thy law is within my heart.

The Letter

10. And he said, I heard thy voice in the garden; and I was afraid, because I *was* naked; and I hid myself.

11. And he said, Who told thee that thou *wast* naked? Hast thou eaten of the tree whereof I commanded thee, that thou shouldest not eat?

12. And the man said, The woman, whom thou gavest *to be* with me, she gave me of the tree, and I did eat.

Note

In view of the fearful responsibility he had assumed, and all that he must endure, in bearing the sins of his people, Jesus said, "Now is my soul exceeding sorrowful, even unto death." And by the mouth of the prophets he set forth the anguish and terror he felt in prospect of the mighty conflict that awaited him, when, in the fulness of time, the sword of Justice would be called upon to *awake* against him, and full satisfaction for transgression be demanded at his hands.

"By the law is the knowledge of sin;"

The Spirit

Ps. lxxxviii. 15. I *am* afflicted and ready to die from *my* youth up: while I suffer thy terrors, I am distracted.

16. Thy fierce wrath goeth over me; thy terrors have cut me off,

17. They came round about me daily like water; they compassed me about together.

lv. 4. My heart is sore pained within me, and the terrors of death are fallen upon me.

5. Fearfulness and trembling are come upon me; horror hath overwhelmed me.

1 Pet. ii. 22. Who did no sin, neither was guile found in his mouth:

23. Who, when he was reviled, reviled not again; when he suffered, he threatened not; but committed *himself* to him that judgeth righteously:

24. Who his own self bare our sins in his own body on the tree, that we, being dead to sins, should live unto righteousness: by whose stripes ye were healed.

therefore, Adam could be conscious of nakedness only by transgression. Neither could Jesus become exposed to the stroke of Justice in any other way than standing in the sinner's place.

It was the woman that the Father had given him; the people chosen in him from the foundation of the world, whom Jesus pledged himself to keep, and that "they should never perish, neither should any pluck them out of his hand;" on whose account and for whose sake he became a sin offering, that "they might be made the righteousness of God in him."

§8 E. C. C. Baillie
(fl. 1853–1873)

E. C. C. Baillie was a well-educated British Christian writer, thinker, poet, and world traveler. In the series of essays she published as *The Protoplast* (1853), Baillie explored a number of religious and philosophical subjects united by the theme of "firsts." This book was followed by seven others: *Snatches of Sacred Song* (1854); *Our Infirmities* (1858), which dealt with such issues as sin and conduct of life; *The Way of the Wilderness, and Other Poems* (1862); a devotional book called *Hours of Rest, or, Sabbath-thoughts for Sabbath-days* (1867); *A Memoir of General Latter* (1870); and a journal of her travels to Turkey, *A Sail to Smyrna: or, An Englishwoman's Journal; Including Impressions of Constantinople, a Visit to a Turkish Harem, and a Railway Journey to Ephesus* (1873). A letter to a Miss Philpot suggests that she lived with her husband in the Wyvenhoe Rectory, Colchester, circa 1879.[23]

Like Putnam, Baillie upheld a very traditional view of women and men. Baillie saw Eve as a type or model for all women, but she did not spiritualize the text to the extent Putnam did. Baillie and Putnam articulated the traditional interpretation of the Genesis texts that Grimké and Weld argued against. Like Copley, Baillie argued that women were not given to men for their amusement; women were to be a helpmeet for men, not a plaything. In contrast to this portrait of the ideal submissive woman, Baillie's self-portrait in her published travel journal presented a woman who was powerful, independent, and self-assured. Further, her vocation as a writer, especially as the author of a volume of weighty theological essays, did not fit with the ideal for women she espoused in the essays.

Baillie argued that Eve's submissive role as Adam's helpmeet was part of the created order, and so permanent. As Eve was to be Adam's helper, the fact

[23] Source: John R. Yamamoto-Wilson, "Victorian Women," http://rarebooksinjapan.com/Victorian/ (accessed November 12, 2004).

that she became his seducer made her sin more heinous. Women's subservient role will only change in the new heaven and the new earth.

From E. C. C. Baillie, *The Protoplast: A Series of Papers* (London: Wertheim & MacIntosh, 1853). [Text from 2nd ed. (London: Wertheim & MacIntosh, 1855), 251–53.]

The First Woman

Adam was lonely in the Paradise of God. Although there was outspread before his admiring gaze the magnificent vegetation of the newborn earth, although there were gathered around him the beautiful forms of the animal creation, a void was in his heart; and there arose within him a consciousness of the fact that for him alone no companion was provided. There was no one to whom he could tell the feelings and the aspirations of his noble nature; no one to understand his greatness; no one to appreciate his glory. The beasts of the field, the fowls of the air, passed in review before him; he gave names to them all; but amongst them there was not found an help-meet for himself.

Yet the Creator of man only suffered him to experience a vague, undefined want of some hitherto ungiven good, and then supplied it according to His eternal purpose. The Lord God had said, "It is not good that the man should be alone."

By the side of the sleeping Adam there stood a beautiful and perfect creature, formed, not from the ground, as he was, but from his bone and flesh, like unto himself, and yet differing from himself; so nearly his equal as to be fit to commune with him; so much his inferior as to be fit to serve and obey him; less majestic, but more graceful; less strong, but more endearing; less noble, but more gentle. Such was the First Woman! From the moment that the man arose from his blessed slumber to welcome her, she was given unto him to be his companion and his friend; to walk hand in hand with him through the Eden of beauty; to share his occupations in the day; to rest with him at the eventide; to converse with him on the highest subjects presented to his intelligence; to bow with him in adoration and worship before the Maker of the universe. Let us notice three particulars respecting her.

First, the *Subserviency of her being*. It is very important that we recognise this fact. St. Paul touches upon it, 1 Cor. xi. 7, 8, 9: "He" (man) "is the image and glory of God; but the woman is the glory of the man. For the man is not of the woman; but the woman of the man. Neither was the man created for the woman, but the woman for the man." Again, 1 Tim. ii. 13: "Adam was first formed, then Eve."

Eve was not created simultaneously with Adam, upon a footing of perfect equality with him, to occupy the same rank in the scale of creaturehood, and to bear before the Lord a similar glory; but, on the contrary, she was bestowed upon him for his use and benefit, to add to his happiness, and to render unto him assistance. The admission of this truth strikes at the root of the false assumption that man and woman are on a level with regard to all rights and privileges: a principle which, in its development and working out, has, to a very great extent, led to the misery and degradation of the weaker sex. We shall see this as we advance in the study of our subject. Even in innocence the superiority of the man to the woman was most distinctly marked; to him pertained authority and government; to her subjection and servitude. Both were the glorious creatures of God, but the one was the head of the other.

Secondly, *the Purpose of her being.*

Doubtless, the ultimate end of her existence was to bring honour unto the Almighty Artificer of all things. Like Adam, she came into the world to show forth her Maker's praise; yet the Spirit calls attention to the intermediate, secondary object in her creation. She was designed as a "*help*" for man.

Eve was not given to Adam that he might rejoice in her beauty, or as a thing to be gazed upon, caressed, and loved alone; she was not given to him that she might minister to his amusement, or as a thing to be trifled with and played with. God intended her to be the partner of his highest pleasures, and the assistant in his noblest avocations; her office was "*to do him good*" in all the future which lay before them; she was to interchange her thoughts for his thoughts, her feelings for his feelings, her views for his views; she was to co-operate with him in all his work for God. Would that this were borne in mind; would that it were duly felt, that whatever may be the influence given to woman over man by the spell of her loveliness; whatever fascination she may exercise in the idle hours of his pastime and relaxation; if she stand not by his side when weighty and serious realities engage his attention; if she take not her share in the *business* of life, her mission remains unfulfilled.

Thirdly, *the Adaptation of her being.* God called her a help *meet* for the man.

Eve was not a creature resembling Adam, only inferior to him. There was a difference between her, and her appointed head, not merely in the *degree*, but in the character of her physical and mental beauty,—she was *perfect after her kind*. Just as the morning stars in God's heavenly constellation, archangels and angels, principalities, powers, and dominions differ, each from each, in glory, so the First Woman, although occupying a lower grade than man, was in her own order exquisite and faultless. This being the case, we see her suitability for her office. Had she been made after the model of man, with just a deficiency of his noblest qualifications, she would have been no *help* for him; she would have only reflected back his thoughts, and echoed back his language. It was her distinctiveness which rendered her worthy of his notice:

again, had she been made equal to him in greatness, she would have been unfitted to bow to his yoke, to wait for his law, and to render unto him a perpetual service. But her woman-nature, so constituted as to differ essentially from man's nobler being, inferior to it, and yet perfect in itself, gave to her a capability of performing the work, which God in His wisdom and in His sovereignty assigned to her.

A time came when she who had been given to man as a "help," became his seducer unto evil. Yet, blessed be God! no sooner were the seeds of mutual wrong and mutual recrimination sown in the hearts of Adam and Eve, than grace healed the breach between them; they were united again by their common faith in the promised Saviour, and became fellow-heirs of the life and immortality to be brought by Him to light.

We must remember that in Eve we find the Protoplast of womanhood: in her relation to Adam she stands to us as the type of all that man's companion is to be to him, in the economy of God's providence, till the dispensation of the present has passed away.

§9 Cecil Frances (Fanny) Alexander
(1818–1895)

Fanny Alexander was born in 1818 in Dublin, Ireland, the second daughter of Major John Humphreys and Elizabeth Frances Reed. In 1833, the family moved to Milltown House in Strabane, County Tyrone, where Major Humphreys served as agent to the Marquess of Abercorn. While living at Milltown House, Alexander wrote some of her best-known poetry and hymns. In 1846, she published *Verses for Holy Seasons*, and in 1848 *Hymns for Little Children* was published, with a preface by John Keble. The purpose of this immensely popular collection was to explain the Apostles' Creed to children using concrete images in hymns. "Where was Jesus born?" was answered by "Once in Royal David's City"; the answer to "Why did he have to die?" was found in "There is a Green Hill Far Away." Alexander's poetry reflected her interest in the teachings of the Anglo-Catholic Oxford Movement; this movement and its leaders continued to influence her throughout her life.

In 1850 Alexander was married to the Reverend William Alexander, a supporter of the Oxford Movement and rector of a parish in County Tyrone, Ireland. She became devoted to parish work. She continued to write and publish poetry when health and other responsibilities allowed. Her early hymn writing was so highly regarded that she was consulted by Sir Henry Baker

(1821–1877), the editor-in-chief of *Hymns Ancient and Modern.* The inclusion of her hymns in that volume helped her own reputation and also helped popularize the collection. In 1867, her husband became bishop of Derry and Raphoe and Alexander moved with her husband and four children to the bishop's palace in Londonderry.[24]

Alexander's poem, "The Temptation," linked Eve's temptation (Gen. 3:6) and Jesus' temptation (Matt. 4:11). Alexander's poetic comparison of the two temptation scenes highlighted similarities and differences between them. She then compared both temptations to our own temptations. By comparing Eve's temptation to Christ's temptation and our own, Alexander elevated Eve. Her poem's positive look at Eve, the "daring spirit," provides a refreshing change from the negative portrayal found in the work of her contemporaries, Putnam and Baillie.

> From Mrs. C. F. Alexander, "The Temptation," in *Poems on Subjects in the Old Testament* (London, 1854). [Text from 3rd ed. (London: J. Masters & Co., 1888), 4–5.]

The Temptation

"She took of the fruit thereof and did eat."—Gen. iii. 6.
"Then the devil leaveth Him."—S. Matt. iv. 11.

IT was in GOD'S own garden-bowers,
　　The sweetest spot earth ever knew,
Eve met the serpent in the flowers—
　　When soft as drops of honied dew,
　　He poured the poisoned words untrue,
That lost this world of ours.

He said the golden fruit was good,
　　He showed it pleasant to the eyes,
He spake of knowledge by that food
　　To make the daring spirit wise:
　　In the full heart of Paradise,
She pluck'd it where she stood.

It was a wild unlovely place
　　That fed no trees with fruitage crowned,
Nor bore upon its barren face

---

[24] Source: Leon Litvack, "Alexander, Cecil Frances," in *The Oxford Dictionary of National Biography* 1:661–62.

Bright blossoms shedding fragrance round,
   Where Satan erst the SAVIOUR found
Who raised our ruined race.

In vain His soul with hunger tried
   He tempted in that lonely hour
To make the bread of Heaven denied;
   In vain he showed earth's pomp and power,
   And prompted from the Temple tower
The deed of daring pride.

Him fleshly lusts might not ensnare,
   Nor gorgeous pomps with pleasure rife
That seem to worldly eyes so fair;
   He heeded not the pride of life,
   But rose triumphant in the strife,
And bruised the serpent there.

LORD, by that threefold promise spoken,
   O'er the baptismal water bright,
And by Thine own dear anguish taken,
   We too are pledged to that stern fight.
   Look on us, help us with Thy might,
Nor let our vows be broken.

In all our paths the tempter strays,
   For each a separate snare he knows,
The Eden of our happy days—
   The desert of our lonely woes—
   Thou that hast fought, and foiled our foes,
Lead us in all our ways!

§10 Sophia Goodrich Ashton
(1819–1872)

Sophia Ashton wrote two books, *Mothers of the Bible* and *Women of Worth*.
The little that is known about her is derived from these books. Her writings show that she was a devout evangelical, probably a Congregationalist

from Boston, well educated, a teacher with a real concern for the spiritual well-being of others. The preface to her book was written by Andrew Leete Stone, the congregational minister of Park Street Church in Boston from 1849–1866. Ashton was probably a parishioner in his church.

Ashton understood the challenges and responsibilities of motherhood. She wrote to instruct and encourage other mothers in their important work. She also explored a theology of motherhood. In her books, she held up the mothers of the Bible and the worthy women of history as examples to be followed by women of nineteenth-century America. In her works, Ashton emphasized the sacred aspect of motherhood and the virtues appropriate to women.

Ashton emphasized the contrast between Eve in Eden, the only woman who experienced "true conjugal bliss," and Eve after the fall, when her life "led often through dark, and wretched, and jarring scenes." Instead of Eve being the temptress, Ashton portrays her as an object of pity, "the victim of Satan's artful wiles." This contrasts with Alexander's reading of Eve as a "daring spirit."

From S. G. Ashton, *Mothers of the Bible* (Boston: J.P. Jewett & Co., 1855), 11–13.

–Eve–

PERHAPS no character of earthly history, if we except only our Lord Jesus Christ, gathers about itself so much of interest, calls forth such deep and varying emotions, or affords such important instruction, as does that of our first mother, certainly in no other do we find such marked contrasts, such strange vicissitudes. Hers was indeed a checkered life. It could hardly be compared, like ours, to an "April day;" the clouds were too black and portentous, the sunshine too brilliant. Not on her path shone "a little sun," nor dropped "a little rain." The effulgence of heaven and the driving tempest were fitter types. To her lips was presented a draught of pure, unalloyed, and perfect happiness. For a few brief days she tasted bliss complete. But the cup from which she drank through lingering centuries contained dregs of bitterest woe. She listened, delighted, to the thrilling tones of nature's harp, touched by Almighty skill, and tuned to nicest harmony; and on her ear grated the harsh and fearful discord, when the curious strings were shattered by her own disobedient hand. To her it was given to look upon life in its perfection, when the earth yielded her luxuriant fruits spontaneously; when flowers of every hue and thornless roses blossomed about her path; when animals of various names, obedient to man, and gentle in disposition, gambolled and frisked at her side, and there was none to molest or make afraid. And she gazed also, in sorrowful amaze, at the bitter contrast, when the ground, cursed for man's sake, brought forth thorns and thistles, and universal war raged among the tribes of the forest. She alone, of all her daughters, enjoyed in its completeness, unmarred and entire, true conjugal bliss. Fairest of them all in person, and most excellent in character, she was most worthy of the love which she received from her husband, such love as no son of Adam has since been able to bestow. But even on this domestic happiness she saw the blighting mildew fall, and her path of life thenceforth, even when trodden by her husband's side, led often through dark, and wretched, and jarring scenes. Our mother Eve! How has her name ever summoned the most conflicting emotions and thoughts,—approval and censure, admiration and contempt, blessing and cursing! Around her poetry has thrown all its enchantments, portraying her beautiful and lovely beyond compare; and on her devoted head have the maledictions of a race been showered, as on the most sinful of God's creation. The stern and truth-telling oracles of God, neither charmed by poetry nor swayed by prejudice, present her to us, in one hour exalted, dignified, and holy, the fit companion of man in his best estate, worthy the society of angels, and even of God himself; in the next, fallen, weak and sinful, the victim of Satan's artful wiles, an object of pity to all holy beings, and the wretched subject of divine displeasure.

§11 Christina Georgina Rossetti
(1830–1894)

Christina Rossetti was born in London, the fourth child of Gabriele Rossetti, an Italian poet in exile, and Frances Polidori Rossetti. The Rossettis encouraged their children to develop their artistic and scholarly talents. Rossetti was educated at home by her mother, and influenced by her evangelical faith. Christina Rossetti became a devout High Anglican under the influence of the Tractarians in the 1840s together with her mother and her sister Maria, who eventually became an Anglican sister. Rossetti is best known for her poetry, but she also published a number of other devotional prose works, including two devotional commentaries on Scripture.

Rossetti featured Eve in both her poetry[25] and prose.[26] Some recent Rossetti scholars regard her use of Eve in these prose works as evidence of "the

[25] See "Rossetti's Eve and the Woman Question," in Diane D'Amico, *Christina Rossetti: Faith Gender and Time* (Baton Rouge: Louisiana State University Press, 1999), 118–46.

[26] See for example, Christina Rossetti, *The Face of the Deep: A Devotional Commentary on the Apocalypse*, 2nd ed. (London: SPCK, 1893), 310–12, 357–58, 400. Also see Christina Rossetti, *Letter and Spirit: Notes on the Commandments* (London: SPCK, 1883), 16–19. Also see her unpub-

unconventional and proto-feminist qualities of Rossetti's devotional prose."[27]
But Rossetti's stance on gender issues was complex. As Diane D'Amico and
David Kent point out, "Her work simultaneously reveals both conservative
and progressive qualities, and there seem to be moments of real uncertainty
or at least profound ambivalence in her views."[28] Rossetti's two poems on Eve,
one published in 1866, and the other in 1888, display some of this tension
in her views on gender.

The first poem, "Eve," portrayed Eve as the grieving mother. The first four
stanzas of this poem were written as the words of Eve after the death of Abel.
Grief and guilt combined in this imagined speech. Eve grieved that Adam had
not resisted her offer of the fruit, reasoning that then he could have stayed in
the garden. After Eve's speech, Rossetti portrayed the rest of creation as grieving with Eve—except the serpent, who grinned.

The second poem, "A Helpmeet for Him," was written in the context of
the woman's suffrage movement, which was prominent in British public life
in the 1880s. This poem is an anti-suffrage work. Diane D'Amico noted that
the poem must be understood in the political context of the time it was written. "In tones both soothing and inspiring, 'A Helpmeet for Him' urges the
women of the 1880s to accept a supporting role in the world's affairs, for such
is God's ordinance regarding the daughters of Eve."[29]

"Eve" from *The Prince's Progress and Other Poems*, 1866.

"While I sit at the door
Sick to gaze within
Mine eye weepeth sore
For sorrow and sin:
As a tree my sin stands
To darken all lands;
Death is the fruit it bore.

"How have Eden bowers grown
Without Adam to bend them!
How have Eden flowers blown
Squandering their sweet breath
Without me to tend them!

---

lished fragmentary notes quoted in Diane D'Amico and David A. Kent, "Christina Rossetti's
Notes on Genesis and Exodus," *Journal of Pre-Raphaelite Studies* 13 (2004): 72, n. 20.

[27] D'Amico and Kent, "Notes," 52.

[28] D'Amico and Kent, "Notes," 53.

[29] Diane D'Amico, "Christina Rossetti's Helpmeet," *Victorian Newsletter* (Spring, 1994), 26.

The Tree of Life was ours,
Tree twelvefold-fruited,
Most lofty tree that flowers,
Most deeply rooted:
I chose the tree of death.

"Hadst thou but said me nay,
Adam, my brother,
I might have pined away;
I, but none other:
God might have let thee stay
Safe in our garden,
By putting me away
Beyond all pardon.

"I, Eve, sad mother
Of all who must live,
I, not another,
Plucked bitterest fruit to give
My friend, husband, lover;—
O wanton eyes, run over;
Who but I should grieve?—
Cain hath slain his brother:
Of all who must die mother,
Miserable Eve!"

Thus she sat weeping,
Thus Eve our mother,
Where one lay sleeping
Slain by his brother.
Greatest and least
Each piteous beast
To hear her voice
Forgot his joys
And set aside his feast.

The mouse paused in his walk
And dropped his wheaten stalk;
Grave cattle wagged their heads
In rumination;
The eagle gave a cry

From his cloud station;
Larks on thyme beds
Forbore to mount or sing;
Bees drooped upon the wing;
The raven perched on high
Forgot his ration;
The conies in their rock,
A feeble nation,
Quaked sympathetical;
The mocking-bird left off to mock;
Huge camels knelt as if
In deprecation;
The kind hart's tears were falling;
Chattered the wistful stork;
Dove-voices with a dying fall
Cooed desolation
Answering grief by grief.

Only the serpent in the dust
Wriggling and crawling,
Grinned an evil grin and thrust
His tongue out with its fork.

From "A Helpmeet for Him" in *Poems*, 1888.

Woman was made for man's delight;
Charm, O woman, be not afraid!
His shadow by day, his moon by night,
Woman was made.

Her strength with weakness is overlaid;
Meek compliances veil her might;
Him she stays, by whom she is stayed.

World-wide champion of truth and right,
Hope in gloom and in danger aid,
Tender and faithful, ruddy and white,
Woman was made.

§12 Charlotte Maria Tucker (A.L.O.E.)
(1821–1893)

Charlotte Maria Tucker was born in Barnet, Hertfordshire, the sixth child of Henry St. George Tucker, and his wife, Jane Boswell. The year after Tucker's birth, the family moved to London. Henry Tucker was the chairman of the East India Company, and the family was wealthy and well connected. Tucker's father disapproved of women working, so Tucker only began to publish her writing after his death in 1851.[30] She did not need to earn a living because of her family's wealth, but wanted to instruct others in the Christian faith. In addition to writing, Tucker energetically engaged in volunteer work in London. After her mother's death in 1869, she moved to India as a self-supporting missionary. She spent the last part of her life working in schools in India, first a normal school, then a boys' high school. Tucker died and was buried in India.[31]

Tucker wrote under the pseudonym A.L.O.E. (A Lady of England). She directed her stories and books to children with the intention of teaching them about the Christian faith. The selection below, "Forbidden Fruit," comes from *House Beautiful; or, The Bible Museum* (1868). Tucker named the book after the House Beautiful in *Pilgrim's Progress*;[32] in the preface to the book, she explained that she was going to write about objects mentioned in scripture, so the book was like a museum. Tucker explained to her readers that they could gain instruction from each of the objects described in this book. From the "Forbidden Fruit" chapter readers learned about Eve's and Adam's fall, and the ways that they could be tempted like Eve.

Like Barton and Mortimer, Tucker's audience was children. Tucker approached the subject of sin and the fall from a different perspective than either Barton or Mortimer. Like Barton, Tucker argued that her audience would have fallen as Eve did; like Mortimer, Tucker presented the consequences of sin. Tucker, however, focused on the words of the serpent, "Thou shalt not surely die," and asked her readers to think about the excuses they

[30] Tucker was a prolific writer. Her works included *The Young Pilgrim: a tale illustrative of "The Pilgrim's Progress"* (1860), *A.L.O.E.'s Sunday Picture Book: illustrating the life of the Lord Christ: in a series of short poems* (1871), and *Pride and his Prisoners* (1876).

[31] Source: Kimberly Reynolds, "Tucker, Charlotte Maria [pseud. A.L.O.E.]," in *The Oxford Dictionary of National Biography* 55:494–95.

[32] See the description of the house in John Bunyan, *The Pilgrim's Progress*, ed. with intro. by Roger Sharrock (London: Penguin Books, 1987), 89–101. While staying at this house, Christian was shown a variety of objects and learned lessons from them.

made for "little sins." She warned them to be on their guard against temptation. Tucker's focus on an object, the fruit Eve ate, rather than on people, meant she did not deal with the issues like gender difference and hierarchy; in fact, Adam was absent from her treatment of Genesis 3. Tucker asked all of her readers, both male and female, to relate to Eve and her temptation.

From A.L.O.E. (A Lady of England). *House Beautiful; or, The Bible Museum* (London: T. Nelson & Sons, 1868), 9–11.

"Forbidden Fruit"

Can this object, so small, so beautiful, be yet through its effects more deadly than any weapon of war ever forged for man's destruction, more deadly than the poison-flask, the dagger, or the thunderbolt! It lies before us fresh and fair as when, nearly six thousand years ago, it hung amongst the green foliage of Paradise, more beautiful than any fragrant peach on which the last ripening sunbeam glows in a now fallen world. On the fruit of Eden, which could so lightly yield to Eve's touch, and be marked by the soft pressure of her fingers, we see not the trail of the serpent; it is goodly to look upon, and what mortal dare say that had he been in the place of our first parents, the fair but fatal fruit would have hung untasted on the bough? In looking on it, how awful a lesson we learn of the poisonous nature of what we dare to call *little sins*! Who amongst us, beholding Eve in her beauty plucking the fruit which tempted her eye, would not have been ready to have echoed the first lie ever breathed on our planet, *thou shalt not surely die*. Bright, guileless, and, until now, sinless being; God will not severely judge thee, He has threatened, but He will not perform.

Is not the same deluding idea at the bottom of all our carelessness, our neglect of duty, our grasping at forbidden pleasure? *Thou shalt not surely die* has been the whisper of the Tempter from Eve's time till now. Let us answer him by pointing to that fruit. Was not the death of myriads enclosed, as it were, in its rind? Could the stain left by its fatal juice be washed out by floods of tears or rivers of blood? Had no sin but that one sin of plucking it been ever committed upon earth, could that sin have been atoned for by anything less than the sacrifice of an Incarnate God?

Sin stands not alone by itself: as the seed is contained in the fruit, so one transgression is the parent of many. Coveting what God had withheld, longing for a luxury forbidden, ambitiously aiming at gaining knowledge which should make her independent as a God, Eve at once received into her heart the *lust of the eye, the lust of the flesh, and the pride of life*. They came as guests—to remain as tyrants. When we feel their influence within ourselves, when covetousness, love of pleasure, or pride of intellect would draw us from our lowly allegiance to God, from our simple obedience to His word, let us look on the forbidden fruit and tremble—let us look on it, and watch and pray.

The fruit of knowledge still,
Plucked by pride, may death distil.

When we make of intellect an idol; when we exalt reason above revelation, and would draw down God's hidden mysteries to the level of our finite comprehension, we are putting forth our hand, like Eve, to pluck and taste the forbidden fruit; forgetful of the warning of the Saviour: *He that receiveth not the kingdom of heaven as a little child shall in no wise enter therein* [Mk. 10:15].

§13 Sarah Town Martyn
(1805–1879)

Sarah Martyn was born in New Hampshire. Her father, Reverend Ethan Smith, a Congregational minister, educated her at home. Martyn volunteered in the temperance and abolition movements for most of her adult life. She edited a number of religious and women's magazines, including the *Ladies' Wreath*, which she founded. The American Tract Society published more than twenty of her books; most were historical fiction set around the time of the Reformation. She was married to Reverend Job H. Martyn, also a Congregational minister. They lived with their four children in New York City and Wausheka, Wisconsin.[33]

Like Ashton's work, Martyn's book, *Women of the Bible* (1868), is marked by its romanticized approach to biblical women. She appealed to the reader's imagination and wondered about Adam's and Eve's imagination. While Martyn clearly recognized the historical distance between the world of the biblical text and her own world, she attempted to minimize this distance by appealing to the similarity of feeling and passion between the women of the Bible and the women of the nineteenth century. Martyn's discussion of Eve and Adam as parents helped her make the connection between her readers and the biblical characters. Martyn was aware that Genesis story could be read as myth. She appreciated the sparse narrative style of the Hebrew text, as well as the poetic and mythic qualities of the story.

---

[33] "Martyn, Sarah Towne (Smith)," *American Authors 1600–1900: A Biographical Dictionary of American Literature*, ed. Stanley J. Kunitz and Howard Haycroft (New York: The H. W. Wilson Co., 1938), 512.

Milton's poetry was an important interpretive tool for Martyn. She frequently quoted him, and used his images throughout her discussion of Eve. Her romantic view of the text did not, however, prevent her from asking difficult interpretive questions. She wondered how evil could possibly enter "the garden of the Lord, hallowed by his frequent presence, and guarded by his omniscient eye." It is easy to miss the theological richness of this document, because Martyn did not use traditional theological language.

Martyn's underlying purpose was to redeem Eve. She acknowledged Eve's sin, but emphasized both Adam and Eve as fallen. She avoided the use of the term "helpmeet" and looked forward to a time when women's lot would be better than Eve's through redemption. She concluded this chapter on a very positive note, calling us to regard Eve with "tenderness and veneration."

From S. T. Martyn, *Women of the Bible* (New York: American Tract Society, 1868), 9–23.

–Eve–
The Mother of Mankind

THE WOMEN of the Bible! Separated from us by scores of centuries, with language, customs, and manners utterly different from our own, and yet as distinct and real to our mental vision as the familiar friends of childhood, who can doubt that the pencil of inspiration sketched portraitures that thus appeal to the universal human heart?

Brief and unadorned as they are, they present a more graphic picture of the life and character of their subjects, and interest us more in their behalf than whole volumes of biography filled with analysis, and eloquent with panegyric.

It is delightful thus to go back into the dim and shadowy recesses of the past, and to ascertain how our sisters of that early age thought and felt and acted, with the certainty that we may rely on the authenticity of the record. We are admitted into the sanctuary of home; we become acquainted with the inmates of that hallowed spot in their everyday joys and sorrows; and finding them subject to the same passions as ourselves, the flood of time is rolled backward, bygone ages come up before us, and we feel that the human heart in all climes and ages knows the same necessities, and finds the same utterance.

Foremost among the women of the Bible, in point of interest as of time, is Eve, daughter of God, and wife of the first man; the majestic mother of the human race. As we look back through the long vista of the ages, and behold her standing in the portal of the world's history, she seems to us like one of the unreal visions of mythology, rather than a living, breathing woman, who actually loved and joyed and sorrowed, as her daughters have done ever since the fall. But the few particulars concerning her given us in the sacred book are so lifelike, so true to nature, that they invest her with a wondrous reality, and bring her at once within the pale of human affection and sympathy.

Adam, the first man, had been placed, immediately after his creation, in the garden of Eden, filled by the divine hand with every thing that could conduce to the gratification of his newly awakened senses. He was formed in the image of his Creator, splendidly endowed with physical and mental gifts, which qualified him to enjoy to the utmost all the advantages which the munificence of the Creator had lavished upon him. But not all the gorgeous splendor of oriental scenes with which he was surrounded; not the song of birds rejoicing in the gladness of their new creation; not the forms of beauty wooing him on every side; not his imperial dignity, though gifted with supremacy over every living thing; not even the companionship of angels, could fill the void in his heart and make him fully blessed. He needed communion with a kindred soul, with one whose wants and joys were like his own, and who should be bone of his bone and flesh of his flesh.

> "The earth was sad, the garden was wild,
> And man the hermit sighed, till woman smiled."[34]

"It is not good for man to be alone," was the word of unerring wisdom, and then, as the crowning work of creation, woman was made and brought to her lord, that last best gift, which doubled the value of every other.

Milton's exquisite picture of our common mother as she appeared to her enraptured companion, though skilfully painted, undoubtedly fails to do full justice to the matchless original:

> "So lovely fair,
> That what seemed fair in all the world, seemed now
> Mean, or in her contained and in her looks."
> "Grace was in all her steps, heaven in her eye,
> In every gesture dignity and love."[35]

With what delight must Adam have gazed on this beautiful being, who was henceforth to be his own, the partner of his joys, the sharer of his earthly destinies and his heavenly inheritance. He says of her to the angel Raphael:

> "What she wills to do or say
> Seems wisest, virtuousest, discreetest, best;
> All higher knowledge in her presence falls
> Degraded; wisdom in discourse with her

[34] The author of this couplet is unknown to us.
[35] *Paradise Lost*, book 8.

> Loses discountenanced, and like folly shows;
> Authority and reason on her wait,
> As one intended first, not after made
> Occasionally; and to consummate all,
> Greatness of mind and nobleness their seat
> Build in her loveliest, and create an awe
> About her, as a guard angelic placed."[36]

The imagination loves to linger about the bowers of Eden after this bridal morn, and endeavor to picture the bliss of the newly formed pair, as hand in hand they explore the wonders of their delightful abode, and talk of the goodness of their heavenly Benefactor; while the shining way from earth to heaven, still open to them, was radiant with celestial forms coming down to gaze with delight and admiration on this latest work of the almighty hand.

Surely one might suppose such happiness was beyond the power of chance or change. Surely nothing evil could find entrance into the garden of the Lord, hallowed by his frequent presence, and guarded by his omniscient eye.

Alas, from the hour in which Lucifer, "son of the morning," fell from his estate among the angels of light [Isa. 14:12], he has been continually roaming through the universe of God, seeking whom he might seduce from their allegiance to the Most High. The garden of Eden with its innocent and happy inhabitants was not likely to escape his observation; and assuming a convenient disguise, he awaited the opportunity of making his grand experiment on the firmness and integrity of our first parents. With that sagacity which for thousands of years has given Satan his "bold, bad eminence" over the fallen angels, he carefully avoided meeting Adam and Eve when in company; but selecting the woman as the one who might be most easily wrought upon, he no sooner found her alone than he ventured to address her.

Stimulated by wonder and curiosity, for before the fall the serpent had none of the repulsive attributes with which he has since been invested, Eve listened eagerly, thus giving the tempter an advantage of which he was not slow to avail himself. Skilfully mingling, delicate flattery with insinuations against the benevolence of the Creator, he endeavored to awaken in her breast vanity and ambition, by informing her of the glorious effects which would result from disobedience to the divine command. Incredible as it may seem, that a being so favored and blessed should for a moment listen to any reflection on the glorious Giver of all her enjoyments, Eve suffered the poison of the serpent to enter her ear, and thus gain access to her heart. Could it be that she and her beloved Adam might at one step become like the glorious spirits who

---

[36] *Paradise Lost*, book 8.

often visited them, simply by eating of the fruit of that wonderful tree which had been so strictly prohibited by God? Why this strange prohibition?

Listening for a moment was Eve's first step in the downward course; daring to question the goodness of God the second; and from these to the third, actual disobedience, the transition was easy and natural.

> "She plucked, she ate;
> Earth felt the wound, and nature from her seat,
> Sighing through all her works, gave signs of woe,
> That all was lost."[37]

With a thrill of fiendish exultation the tempter retired, leaving to his victim the task of rendering the victory complete, by persuading Adam to join in her transgression. Hapless pair! but lately so innocent and joyous, now so lost and miserable. When the glory of the Shechinah announced the presence of the Lord God in the garden, instead of running to welcome the divine Guest, Adam fled, and vainly hoped to hide himself, ashamed to meet his injured Maker. Compelled at length to appear and answer to the question, "Hast thou eaten of the tree whereof I told thee thou shalt not eat of it?" he attempts to shelter himself behind his partner in guilt: "The woman whom thou gavest to be with me, she gave me of the tree, and I did eat."

Oh the infinite malignity of sin, which in so short a time could thus derange the moral nature of Adam, and render him capable of resorting to such a subterfuge! There is in this speech a tacit insinuation that the gift was not a wise one, and thus an attempt to throw a portion of the blame on God himself.

This whole scene in the garden presents the divine character in a light the most sublime and glorious of which we can conceive. Never were the mercy and long-suffering kindness of our God more strikingly manifested, while at the same time his justice asserts its claims in thunder tones.

The offenders had drawn upon themselves the penalty of death, and it must be paid to the full extent of the violated law; but while announcing this awful fact, infinite Wisdom found a remedy by which the claims of justice might be fully satisfied, and yet the ruins of the fall more than repaired by that mysterious Seed of the woman who was to bruise the serpent's head.

The sentence pronounced on Eve was so merciful, so mingled with blessing, that her very heart must have melted with gratitude and contrition as the eye of the Judge rested upon her. Personal suffering and subjugation were to be her lot, but love would sweeten both and render them welcome; while by faith in the coming Conqueror, she might hope to regain all and more than all she had lost.

[37] *Paradise Lost*, book 8.

At the close of this memorable interview, the offending pair, having been clothed by the hand of God, were driven from their delightful home, henceforth to become acquainted with care and sorrow, and to earn their daily bread by daily toil. True woman as she was, Eve undoubtedly felt that while Adam was beside her, no lot could be wholly miserable; but as we contemplate the terrible change in her condition, we forget to censure, in our compassion for her grief. What must have been her emotions as she sends back a last lingering gaze at the flowery lawns, verdant walks, and embowering shades of Eden, and sees the bright cherubim and the flaming sword guarding the gates of the lost paradise she was never more to enter.

But though fallen and chastened, our first parents were not utterly forsaken. The eye of a forgiving God was upon them in their altered condition, and in process of time a ray of hope and joy found its way into their hearts and home. A son was given to them, a pledge of pardon and peace; and in the first blessedness of maternity, that crowning glory of womanhood, the happy mother forgot her past sorrows as she exclaimed, "I have gotten a man," or the Man, "from the Lord."

She perhaps hoped this precious babe might be the promised Seed whose coming was foretold in the garden, and who was to restore to her posterity the blessings of which her sin had deprived them. If such were her thoughts, how fearful was the disappointment which awaited her in the coming future.

We are next informed of the birth of Abel, but there were doubtless many others not mentioned in the sacred record; and in her children Eve renewed her own life, and learned to bow with humble submission to her lot.

But too soon there came a time when the first mother was to witness that death of which she had so often heard, and to see it too under circumstances so dreadful, that her terror and anguish must have been overwhelming.

Abel, the second son of Adam, pleasant and beloved of God and man, was found dead, slain by the hand of his brother, her first-born Cain, who was henceforth to be a wanderer on the face of the earth. It is impossible for us who witness daily the ravages of the king of terrors, even to imagine the feeling of the first pair as they looked on the lifeless body from which the animating soul had departed. Yesterday he was all life, health, and vigor; now pale, cold, and still, he heeds not their sighs and tears—he will never heed them more.

Then for the first time they realized to some extent what they had done in bringing sin, and death through sin, into the world; and if in imagination they looked down through the ages and saw similar deeds of blood and horror multiplied and accumulated to the end of time, how fearful must have been the weight of anguish and remorse pressing on the hearts of the self-convicted authors of all this misery. Nothing but unwavering faith in the power and mercy of Him who bringeth good out of evil, could have saved them at such a moment from utter despair. It is doubtful if the murderer ever again revisited his childhood's home, or looked again on the faces of his parents. He too, as well as Abel, was dead to them, and in a sense far more painful to endure. The one, after a sharp but short agony, had gone to his everlasting rest, and there awaited their arrival, never again to be parted from them; the other, the "living dead," was a branded outcast from all he had hitherto held dear; without God and without hope in this world or the next.

But the mourning parents were not forsaken. God graciously gave them another son, whom in the fulness of her joy Eve named Seth; "for God," she said, "hath given him to me instead of Abel, whom Cain slew." After the birth of this cherished son, we hear no more of the mother of mankind, and can only suppose it probable that, at the close of a long life checkered by joys and sorrows of no ordinary kind, she was the first of her sex to go down to the grave which has since closed over so many generations of her descendants.

She sinned and suffered greatly, but judgment belongeth unto God; and while, in the light of a completed redemption, we see how gloriously "the Seed of the woman" has triumphed over the devil, changing a seeming victory into an overwhelming defeat, and leading captivity captive, it becomes us to regard the mother of the race with tenderness and veneration, leaving her to that mercy which even in the first moment of transgression was so signally manifested in her behalf.

§14 Elizabeth Rundle Charles
(1828–1896)

Elizabeth Rundle Charles was born in Devon, England, the only child of John Rundle, a member of Parliament, and his wife, Barbara Gill. Charles was educated at home and began writing at a young age. She joined a women's essay-writing group where she learned to write about particular historical periods. This equipped her for writing historical fiction later. She was influenced by the Oxford Movement and almost converted from Anglicanism to Roman Catholicism. She did not convert due to the influence of a Swiss protestant minister who upheld the "invisible church of all believers." Charles retained evangelical sympathies throughout her life.

After her marriage to Andrew Paton Charles in 1851, Elizabeth Charles lived in London. Because of her husband's ill health, the couple travelled to warmer countries: Egypt, the Holy Land, Turkey, the Greek islands, and Italy.

This trip resulted in Elizabeth Charles's 1861 book, *Wanderings over Bible Lands and Seas*. Charles published a number of novels, the most famous of which, *The Chronicles of the Schonberg-Cotta Family* (1864), was reprinted numerous times and translated into many languages. Charles regarded her writing as a religious calling, although after her husband's death it became her main source of income. In addition to writing novels, Charles did translation work and wrote a number of devotional books that clearly reflect her High Church thinking.[38]

Sketches of the Women of Christendom addressed the women of India. It attempted to show what Christianity had done for women by telling the life stories of Christian women. Charles began this work by telling the story of Eve. Like Crocker, she then moved directly to the story of the Virgin Mary. The chapter on Eve told the story of the fall; the rest of the book told the story of women who were redeemed, and could still be redeemed, despite the fall.

Charles wrote *Sketches* using very simple language. She tried to make the story understandable for her readers in India. For example, she referred to the climate of India as an aid to understanding what the garden of Eden might have been like. Despite the simplicity of her language, Charles addressed some sophisticated hermeneutical issues. She clearly stated that the literal historical sense of the biblical text was not enough for understanding the story of Eve; all histories must be "read also as parables and poems." She read the text carefully, noting that Adam's first recorded speech does not occur until he saw Eve, "another creature who could understand and respond to his speech."

Like Alexander and Tucker, Charles attempted to understand our temptation by understanding the nature of Eve's temptation. Eve sinned by not trusting God rather than by taking the fruit. Adam fell deeper into sin than Eve when he accused her of offering him the fruit. Charles called the story of Adam and Eve a parable of the temptation of all men and women. Despite Adam's accusation of Eve, only through Eve, the mother of all the living, could "he and the world be delivered."

From Elizabeth Rundle Charles, *Sketches of the Women of Christendom* (New York: Dodd, Mead & Co., 1880), 4–13.

–Eve–

Both parts of our Sacred Scriptures begin with the story of a woman.

The first is the sad story of a fall; how this world of ours went wrong. And the heart that drank in the poison which poisoned our whole race was the heart of a woman.

[38] Source: Elisabeth Jay, "Charles, Elizabeth Rundle," in *The Oxford Dictionary of National Biography* 11:160–61.

The second is the glorious story of the rising again; of redemption and restoration. And here, too, the lowly and loving heart which received the creative word which renews the world was the heart of a woman.

Eve and Mary begin the two histories which make up our Scriptures, the history of the fall, and the history of the redemption and rising again of men.

Throughout the history it is the same.

The worst, and the best, in the long story of our world, in all times and places are continually springing from the influence of bad or good women.

So closely has God bound us together that it is impossible for man to lower woman without lowering himself; as it is impossible for women to be made nobler and wiser without ennobling and raising the men of their race.

Our first story begins in a garden.

Perhaps you will say, Is the story fact, or poem? parable, or history?

It is both: true, with the deepest truth, always renewed in various forms. To get at truth in all histories we must read them also as parables and poems; that is, as a sacred story which does not merely gossip about the external facts, but penetrates to the divine and human meanings enfolded in these.

The garden or paradise was such as you can picture better than I can, for it was flooded with your glowing Southern sunshine, and filled with the fruitful trees and fragrant flowers of your Eastern lands.

The almighty and all-loving God Himself had planted it, and no-one had spoiled it.

Every tree that is pleasant to the eye and good for food was in it, every delicious fruit you can think of; and the shady woodlands and sunny lawns were watered by cool brooks flowing musically to the four rivers which bounded the garden.

And in all this beautiful region at first lived only one solitary man, Adam, whom God had made king and lord of it all.

He was not made to be idle. God loved him too much, and knew him too well, for that. The garden was given him to dress and to keep.

From the beginning God himself has always been working. Every day He is creating, upholding, restoring. And He made man to be like Himself, happy in beneficent work.

But man needs something besides work to make him blessed. He needs companionship, a home, love.

And in all the beautiful paradise Adam, the first man, found no companion. Among all the swift, and strong, and beautiful creatures that coursed through the meadows, or roamed in the forests, or sang their sweet songs on the trees, for Adam was no helpmeet found.

None else of the creatures were alone; all had their associates and mates. But Adam had no one.

He could call every creature by its name, which described what it was; but none of them could answer him in speech like his own.

It seems as if Adam were left by himself just long enough to show how he needed the gift which God meant to give him.

Then in a deep sleep the mighty hand of the Creator was laid on him, and from his very flesh and bones, from his own side, a portion of his own life was taken and made woman.

And God Himself brought her to him.

And then the first man, forefather of us all, spoke the first human words which are recorded.

He said, "This is now bone of my bone, and flesh of my flesh."

For here at last was another creature who could understand and respond to his speech.

And Adam had found the helpmeet he needed, and was no more alone. The husband and the wife, the sacred two, no more two, as Adam said, but one, made a full world for each other, a sacred source of life for the ages.

But then the simple, happy story is broken by a glimpse into an earlier world.

In the garden, before Eve was made, there was a tree called the tree of the knowledge of good and evil.

God had told Adam not to eat of this tree; for if he ate of it he would die.

God knew, and told Adam.

And Adam told Eve.

But in that earlier world, which lay hidden around them, which they could not see, were beings who hated Adam and Eve, and wished to spoil their peace.

One of them especially set himself to this. He had been good and very glorious himself once.

God made all creatures good. But this once good and glorious creature had fallen into self-love and untruth, and now he wanted to make Adam and Eve fall from light and peace into darkness and strife, as he had.

He knew he could not do either of them the least harm except by making them do wrong. He knew he could not make them do wrong as long as they trusted God. He appeared to Eve as a serpent.

He knew all about the tree whose fruit they were not to eat.

He knew quite well that what God had said about it was true.

He knew that God loved the man and the woman He had made as a father loves his own children. He knew he could only bring unhappiness into this beautiful new world by separating the hearts of these beautiful new children of God from their Father.

And he knew he could only so separate them by making them believe a lie about God.

Do you ask me why this Evil One hated the man and woman?

I cannot answer you, except by asking you to look into your own hearts.

He had been happy and beautiful and good himself once. He had fallen, and when he saw these new creatures happy and beautiful and good as he had been, he wanted to make them like himself.

If you have lost, especially through your own fault, any good or beauty you once had, do you never know what it is to be unhappy to see others still enjoy it?

Did you never see those who have done wrong themselves become tempters of others?

We call this Evil One the hater, Satan, the Enemy, the Tempter.

And it was Eve, the woman, he set himself to tempt.

He began his temptation very subtly, with a question, "Yea, has God said you may not eat of every tree of the garden?"

He knew how apt we are, at the fullest table of blessings, just to think the one thing refused us is the thing which we want most.

And Eve said, "We may eat of the fruit of the trees in the garden; but of the fruit of the tree in the midst of the garden, God hath said, Ye may not eat of it, nor may ye touch it, lest ye die."

It seems as if Eve looked round from the abundance she might enjoy, to the tree she might not taste, and at once that one forbidden tree became, "in the midst of the garden," the central point of it all to her.

And then the enemy ventured with a bolder lie, though like all his previous lies, made credible by being hidden in a truth.

"Ye shall not surely die," he said. "For God doth know that in the day ye eat thereof, then your eyes shall be opened, and ye shall be as gods, knowing good and evil."

The poisoned sting found its way into her heart.

She looked at the forbidden tree; it was beautiful, and seemed good.

We are not tempted, man, woman, or child, except with things which seem, and probably are, beautiful and good in themselves, only not just *then*, or not *for us*.

No one does a wicked thing because it is wicked, but because it seems the way to something good.

The tree was pleasant to the eyes and good for food; did not falsely *seem* so, but really *was* so, *at the right time*.

And then the subtle enemy had said it would make her wise!

To be wise in a moment, without trouble of training or learning, seems so pleasant!

Beautiful, happy Eve! see her with her hand stretched out to gather the fruit.

The enemy could not *give* it her. He cannot give us anything, whatever he may try to persuade us.

God only can give us good. And He will always give us the very best, at the best time, if we wait on Him and for Him.

We may snatch real blessings at the wrong time, and so make them curses.

But God only can really give good.

Did Eve fall when she took the fruit into her hand? Was such a very little thing as gathering a forbidden fruit the beginning of so much misery? No; Eve did not fall when she touched the forbidden fruit. She fell first, in her heart, when she believed evil of the good God, who had given them everything and each other; believed that He could withhold anything from them, not for their good and real gain, but for their harm and real loss.

The gathering of a fruit is a very little thing.

But distrusting God is the great evil; the fall from heaven to hell, from light to darkness.

And moreover, the thing Satan really tempted Eve with was not a fruit, but nothing less than deification. "Ye shall be as gods," he said.

The fruit was only to be a magical charm to lift them up to the throne of the universe; to know all, like God, and therefore to be able to rule and possess all.

All the terrible steps followed quite naturally from this first step.

Poor, tempted, fallen Eve's next step was to become herself a tempter, like the serpent.

She gave the fruit to her husband, and he did eat.

And then they found out that part, at least, of what the enemy said was only too true.

They did "know good and evil," as he had said, by having done evil, and so far become evil.

The blessed innocence and freedom were all gone.

And Adam's next step was another, deeper descent into the likeness of the serpent, the accuser of the brethren.

When God called to him, as of old, in the garden, and asked what he had done, Adam, to throw the blame off from himself, accused poor fallen Eve, unhappy enough by this time. He even accused God.

"The woman *Thou gavest* to be with me," he said, "tempted me, and I did eat."

The dreadful lie of the enemy about the good God had indeed taken root, and has been bearing fruit, upward and downward, ever since.

For the histories of our Sacred Scriptures have this remarkable characteristic.

They are not stories of something that *was once*, and *is done with*.

They are unveilings in one picture and parable of *what is happening always*, again and again.

Did God give the man and woman up—let them alone, to reap the fruits of their sin?

No! he was the Father, and loved and pitied them; he pitied that man and woman, and all men and women ever since.

Their sin made him grieved at His heart, but it did not make Him cease to be their Father.

He began at once His unsparing, unfailing discipline of love. He met them at once with merciful punishments and merciful promises.

He drove them from the garden, where the leisure and plenty would no longer have been blessings to them, into the wilderness, to toil and to suffer. Adam to earn his bread in the sweat of his brow; Eve to become the mother of children, and suffer most through her deepest joys.

And, ever since, our race has been in the wilderness, and not in the garden; the fathers toiling, the mothers suffering.

But God never cursed the man and the woman. He cursed the tempter who had betrayed them. He cursed the ground, making it barren with thorns and thistles, for their sakes.

But his disobedient children he *punished*, which is a very different thing from cursing.

He punished them with hard labor, and anguish and pain, to make them good, to drive them back to himself.

And He gave them, wrapped up in the very curse on the serpent, the promise whose fulfilment is the subject of my next story.

God said to the serpent,

"I will put enmity between thee and the woman, and between thy seed and her seed; *it shall bruise thy head*, and thou shalt bruise his heel."

The enemy was not the conqueror, however for the time he might terribly seem to be so.

God was and is the conqueror; for He is mightier than the devil; and He is love.

And God announced, that the victory should be through the seed of the woman—the poor tempted, fallen woman—of whose seed the victorious and holy Saviour should one day be born.

Adam might accuse Eve as he would (no doubt he was sorry for it afterward, and they repented and wept together), but it was only through Eve, his wife, mother of his children, mother of all living, that he and the world could be delivered.

And now, ever since, the best places for any of our race are not the paradises, but the wildernesses; not the easy, luxurious gardens where we can rest, but the hard earth which we must subdue, and where we may serve each other in the sweat of the brow, with fruitful toil and anguish.

§15 Etty Woosnam
(1849–c.1883)

Etty Woosnam was born in India to British parents. Her family returned to England to reside in Somerset when Woosnam was a teenager. Woosnam married John R. Theobalds, in 1882. She died soon after.[39]

Woosnam wrote *Women of the Old Testament* (1881) and *Women of the New Testament* (1885) to edify and instruct young ladies in a Bible class in Weston-super-Mare, Somerset, England. In each chapter Woosnam chose one application for particular emphasis, and drew on a variety of sources to make her point. She was aware of the debates about woman's nature, character, and role and used her studies on biblical women as an opportunity to teach her students what she thought every Victorian young woman should know.

The application Woosnam drew from the story of Eve was that "woman's influence is appallingly great." As Eve influenced Adam to sin, so all women have the ability to influence others, especially men, for evil as well as good. She encouraged her readers to pray that the God would check the evil that their words might do, and diligently use their influence for good.

Woosnam compared Eve before the fall with the situation of women in England in the nineteenth century. Like Martyn, she saw an enormous difference between Eve in the garden and the life of women after the fall. Woosnam, however, did not consider Eve to be innocent in Eden; she argued that "she was innocent only as long as she was untried."

From Etty Woosnam, *The Woman of the Bible: Old Testament* (London: S. W. Partridge, 1881), 7–17. [Text take from the 4th ed, n.d.]

–Eve–
Woman's Influence

IT is a very humbling reflection that woman's first appearance in the world's history is the story of the Fall. The name Eve was given by Adam to his wife

[39] Source: Donna Kerfoot, "Etty Woosnam: A Woman of Wisdom and Conviction" (term paper, Wycliffe College, 2004).

"because she was the mother of all living." She might as appropriately have been called "the mother of death"; for by her, sin entered into the world, and death by sin. Shame, like distress, is more easily borne in company than singly; and this may be one reason why we are not all more humbled by our ancestry.

And yet which one of us women might not any day fall into the very same temptation, or combination of temptations, that led our first mother astray? They were: "the lust of the flesh," (it was good for food-Gen. iii. 6), "the lust of the eyes" (pleasant to the eyes); and "the pride of life" (to make one wise) [1 John 2:16]; and it is evident that we are as prone to yield to these considerations in 1883, as Eve was, and as the early Christian Church was when St. John found it necessary by his first epistle to warn it about the year 90 A.D. Satan even had the presumption to use these very darts against the Holy One of God; and He was tempted by them in some sense which we cannot understand, though sinless under them. Let us know, then, that it is no easy task for any of us to withstand the power of the lust of the flesh, the lust of the eyes, and the pride of life.

Different points and lessons might be drawn from Eve's history by every one reading it through carefully. Many lie on its surface. For many more, deeper digging is needed. To me the most salient is the power of Woman's Influence.

Surrounded with all she could want or wish for—exempt from toil, pain, and even anxiety or thought for the future, Eve uses her perfect liberty to yield to the first suggestions of Satan that she had some grievance, some unfulfilled desire; and the climax of the narrative is—"She took of the fruit and did eat, and gave also unto her husband and he did eat." Verily, it does not say much for either of them! She disregards God, the giver of all her happiness and her powers to please herself; and Adam, as dead as his wife to all the noble sentiments of loyalty and gratitude, unhesitatingly fellows her. Imitation is very natural to men and women. I remember some years ago that a young man stood in the streets of London looking steadily up at the lion on the top of a monument. Some one else, passing, stood and looked, too, and then asked him what he was looking at. He said—"I hear that that lion wags his tail precisely at twelve o'clock every day." "You don't believe that, surely?" said the second watcher. "No, but I am just going to wait a minute till the clock strikes twelve, to see and test it." They waited together! Soon others joined them, *without knowing or hearing why!* and by the time twelve o'clock sounded, quite a small crowd had collected. It is needless to add that the lion never did wag his tail, and the crowd dispersed as quietly as it had gathered. It is not only silly, ignorant people who make crowds, or who walk after each other. By a sort of instinct we follow the lead of others; as when the disciples were standing by the lake of Galilee, Simon Peter said, "I go a fishing," the other six men instinctively said—"We also go with thee," and so they did [John 21:3]. Again, as St. John himself tells us, St. Peter was going to see the sepulchre, so he went too; and they ran together. St. John got there first. But when St. Peter got there, *he went in*; and "then went in also that other disciple" [John 20:3-8]. Nor is it only men who copy each other and lead each other.

Woman's influence is appallingly great. For one thing, it is so often thrown into the same side of the balance as the men's inclinations, and made to weigh against their duty—as in Adam's case—that what wonder if it turns the scale? I once heard the remark made, that the more a woman loves you, the more she will hinder you from right purposes, and strew flowers on the road that leads to hell. I thought it a terrible libel, roughly worded; but ever since then, I have seen it is often too true, though not always so, let us fervently hope and pray.

Very often affectionate sisters and wives encourage their brothers and husbands to lounge and idle instead of letting them go to their work when duty calls. The breadwinner of a family is constantly disturbed in his laborious train of thought to suit the convenience or amusement of less well-occupied women. I hope you never hear young men willingly persuaded to go to enervating and very questionable places of amusement, instead of being helped in their work and sympathized with in the healthy pleasure that comes in duty's path? If you do not, I often do. I hope you never hear young or even older women pressing a young man to take wine or spirits against his will because he is tired or his nervous system jaded, instead of recommending and making it possible for him to use the natural remedy of rest and sleep; for if you do not, I often do. I knew a young man in his first term at Cambridge, working for honours, give up a self-indulgence to please his father. A smile and sneer from a fast young lady made him ashamed of his softness and he resumed the forbidden pleasure.

Shall we ask for Women's Rights? and seek for more power? or make it the object of our existence to use better what we have? It is a powerful weapon that we can make great havoc with, if we do not kneel down humbly and shamefacedly before the Master's Throne, and beseech of Him to teach us the proper use of it, or rather to take it from us than suffer it to make one of His little ones to offend. As for female suffrage, women do virtually give away a great many votes for members of parliament, as you know if you have ever been with those canvassing in agricultural districts before an election. If you ask an uneducated man on which side he is going to vote he parries all your efforts to find out and finally says: "I'll wait till my missis and I have talked about it." The "missis" has private reasons for knowing whether more coal and blankets are to be had out of one party or the other. And it is not only among the labourers and colliers that the "missis" is such a guiding-star in the way of counsel. Wife-power and mother-power are often quite as great forces in the more educated classes up to the very highest—as was shown by the infatuation of Mr. John Stuart Mill [1804–1873] for his wife.[40] And by the graceful tribute paid by the late Lord Beaconsfield [1804–1881] to his when he dedicated one of his books to her as "The severest of Critics and the best of Wives."[41] Influence is a weighty responsibility. How terribly women have abused it we shall see as we read the Bible—as we read history, and as we read human nature. Probably it is not so great now as it might and would be if more women had lived in the fear of God.

What good effect was produced on Herod by the elegant dancing and charming deportment of Herodias' daughter? [Matt. 14:6-8]It is a force—this influence of women—so subtile [sic], that it is strongest where the possessor is unconscious of it. We hardly dare to speak of it aloud, and if a woman boasts of her individual power over any or over many, we may be sure she has very little of it, and that such as it is, it will soon dwindle away from having been brought out into the sun. Let us ask God most earnestly every day, to check and counteract the evil that our unwise and sinful words may do, and help us to use so diligently the influence we have for His glory and for good that He may some day see fit to double our charge as the Lord did to the well-used talents in the parable.

We must see very distinctly from Eve's punishment how irreversible are God's decrees. The carelessness of a moment—the yielding to temptation— what never-ending results they produced! And so every sin is like a seed which springs and bears fruit a hundredfold. It is carefully watered and tended by the evil one, and propagates long after we had forgotten about it and our consciences have closed comfortably over the sting, and inconvenience us no longer. She took of the fruit and did eat; and mankind has reaped the results for the last 6000 years. If she could have foreseen the consequences, would she have done it? If in her unbroken enjoyment she could have seen a picture of the future Eve, in grief and pain, struggling through the waves of a blighted and troublesome life, surely she would not have disobeyed. And if afterwards, when she had her firstborn son in her arms and hushed the innocent babe to her bosom, she had been told he would be a murderer and die a beggar, would not sin have seemed more loathsome, and the serpent's insinuations less beguiling?

[40] In 1851 Mill married Mrs. Harriet Taylor, a long standing friend of his, after her husband died.

[41] Lord Beaconsfield was Benjamin Disraeli; his wife was Mary Anne Lewis, the widow of a political colleague.

We get a fair idea of the results of sin by comparing in our minds the Eve before the Fall, so joyous, beloved, and peaceful, with one other descendants of the present day—a modern poor wicked woman, wandering houseless in the streets of one of our crowded cities, in sickness, suffering, and shame. We are often mortified and surprised when we have said or done things which our better selves revolt against. If any one had told us we were capable of saying that bitter sarcastic word to a weary and burdened fellow-pilgrim—or showing petulance to a poor dependant child or servant, we should have said, as Hazael did: "Is thy servant a dog that he should do this great thing?" [2 Kgs. 8:13]. Dr. Joseph Cook [1838–1901] says in one of his valuable lectures, that a French atheist once confessed when in advanced age, that, "if at eighteen years old he had known what a hard time he was going to have of it, he would have hung himself."— Truly, "the way of transgressors is hard;" and transgressors' children and grandchildren to all generations reap the fruits of our wrong doings.[42]

It is customary to speak of Eve before the disobedience, as in a state of innocence; but this appears to be rather a phrase of commentators than of the Bible. She was innocent only as long as she was untried, and it has been well said,* "the innocence of ignorance is a poor thing."—An old proverb of the Talmud is: "When the thief has no opportunity for stealing, he considers himself an honest man." We speak of children's innocence because they are quite unable to understand or carry out much that is wrong, their liberty is comparatively so very small. But yet they soon show their sinfulness. Before they can speak clearly they try on their little artifices, their petty deceits. "As soon as they be born they go astray" in wilfulness, disobedience, and lying.

And the so-called purity of girlhood, too, amounts pretty much to the fact that, in the present state of civilization, young women of the upper classes are so carefully hedged in by parents and teachers—their very movements and expressions so closely criticised—they are hardly at liberty to do wrong noticeable to human eyes, or to behave unseemly. But they have no reason to flatter themselves as to their simplicity and innocence. We might as well talk of glass as not being brittle because no one had tried to break it. God's Word seems to recognise no such maiden goodness. Christ's righteousness is the only white robe that will bear Divine scrutiny; and the smile of God's approval rests on those who have fought the good fight of faith. The sevenfold blessing is bestowed on "him that over-cometh,"—on her who overcometh her temper, her frivolity, a mean purpose, a jealousy, a rising of pride. Every time that, by God's grace, a passion, a foolish or unkind thought, or a longing for some

---

[42] It is possible that Woosnam is referring to Cook's *Monday Lectures* (London, 1877).

ungranted good, is subdued, a step is gained towards that positive purity, that holiness, without which no man can please God here or see Him hereafter.

In Genesis iii. 6, it is seen that the last, and perhaps prevailing inducement to take the fruit was in the fact of its being "a tree to be desired to make one wise," and in Genesis ii. 17, it is called "the tree of knowledge." The curiosity of our first parents, then, led them to disobedience—the desire for more knowledge than God had put within their reach. To attain all useful knowledge we cannot be too keen, as the Bible (and specially the book of Proverbs) emphatically reiterates. But generally, just in proportion as we are willing to be ignorant of what we ought to know, to be superficial readers of the Bible and of the wonders of God in Nature, we are inquisitive as to what is hidden from us. We hold loosely to that which is precious food, and which is revealed for our learning so plainly that a running man may read, and by which a fool shall if docile and willing be taught and not go astray. And yet we speculate and argue about "the secret things which belong unto God"—(Deut. xxix. 29). What will Heaven be? What will future punishment be?—All such conjectures are vain. "Teach thy tongue to say, I do not know." It is presumptuous to intrude into God's mysteries—"to pick the lock where He has not allowed the key." And it is vain. For if we were to see, we could not understand. We are spiritual owls and have eyes, suited to this world, which could not bear the blaze of heavenly glory. As well might a mole accustomed to burrow under ground be expected to see the glories of a flower-show, or understand the use and mechanism of a telescope, as we to comprehend all God's designs and the wonders of the world to come. Trench says†:—"Our old bottles could not bear the new wine of the Kingdom. It is probable that a clear view of things above would blind us both bodily and mentally. If the light of the sun were sevenfold, as the light of seven days (Isaiah xxx. 26) it would literally blind us, for our eyes are made exactly to match the light we have; and a fuller knowledge of things above than God has placed within our reach would probably unfit us altogether for the necessary business of this life." Trench then gives an extract from Dr. Pierre's travels:—"I remember on my return to France after a long voyage to India, as soon as the sailors had discovered the shores of their native country, they became, in a great measure, incapable of attending to the duties of the ship; some looked at it wistfully, others dressed themselves in their best clothes, some talked, others wept. As we approached, their joy became greater; and still more intense was it when we came into port, and the sailors saw on the quay their parents and children, so that we had to get another set of sailors to bring us into the harbour." Thus might it be with God's children if they saw the full and unclouded glory of eternity before they reach the eternal haven. Christ said, "I have many things to say unto you, but ye cannot bear them now" [John 16:12]. With all reverence let us accept and acknowledge our ignorance of "many things," and be all the more zealous to ask God that the Comforter may bring all things to our remembrance whatsoever Christ has said unto us.

Much as there is to humble us in the Chapter of the Fall, to awe and to solemnize, one most blessed thought is there too to give hope and comfort to fallen humanity. Behind the cloud of sin and misery the Sun of Righteousness shone forth with healing in His wing [Mal. 4:2]; and on the same sacred page that records the entrance of sin, disease and death, there gleams the promise of Him who would bring life and immortality to light; who through death should destroy him that had the power of death, and be the life of every repentant sinner who believes and lives in Him.

* In "Seekers after God," by Canon Farrar.
† In "Things Above," by Frederick Fitzwilliam Trench.

§16 Ray Frank
(1861–1948)

Ray Frank was born in San Francisco, to Leah and Bernard Frank. Ray Frank completed high school and taught school in Nevada for six years. She moved back to Oakland to help her family and supported herself through teaching and writing. She taught Sabbath school classes and became the superintendent of the religious school of the First Hebrew Congregation in Oakland. In 1890, she traveled to Spokane, Washington, and preached to 1,000 Jews of the community at the Opera house several times, encouraging them to drop their religious differences and form a permanent congregation. She continued to work as a journalist and preach and lecture throughout western and northwestern United States. Local newspapers called her a "latter-day Deborah," and even "Lady Rabbi." She studied at Hebrew Union College in Cincinnati in the spring of 1893, but declined to serve as a spiritual leader of a congregation. She delivered the opening prayer at the first Jewish Women's Congress, held in Chicago in conjunction with the World Parliament of Religions in 1893. In 1901 she gave up her career as a journalist and preacher and she married Simon Litman, a professor of economics, first at the University of California and later at the University of Illinois. In Illinois, Frank was involved in Jewish student life and active in the larger Jewish community.

Frank is remembered as the first Jewish women to preach from a pulpit in the United States and the first female Jewish religious leader.[43]

The interpretation of Eve given here is an excerpt from the address Frank gave at the Jewish Women's Congress in 1893, entitled "Women in the Synagogue." It is very different from Christian women's interpretations of Eve. From Eve, Frank argued for women's spiritual superiority and their responsibility to teach and lead others to God. She believed women were able to be rabbis or presidents of congregations, but felt that women's "noblest work" was in the home. She believed that Eve's repentance and the collective faith of all women through the ages redeemed Eve.

From Ray Frank, "Women in the Synagogue" in *Papers of the Jewish Women's Conference* (Philadelphia: The Jewish Publication Society of America, 1894), 52–53.

Duality manifests itself in all things, but in nothing is this two-foldness more plainly seen than in woman's nature.

The weaker sex physically, it is the stronger spiritually, it having been said that religion were impossible without woman. And yet the freedom of the human soul has been apparently effected by man. I say apparently effected, for experience has demonstrated, and history records, that one element possessed by woman has made her the great moral, the great motif force of the world, though she be, as all great forces are, a silent force.

It may be true that sin came into the world because of the disobedience of the first woman, but woman has long since atoned for it by her loving faith, her blind trust in the Unknown. Down through the ages, traditional and historical, she has come to us the symbol of faith and freedom, of loyalty and love.

From the beginning, she sought knowledge; perceive, it does not say wisdom, but knowledge; and this was at the expense of an Eden. She lost Eden, but she gained that wisdom which has made sure of man's immortality.

She walked upon thorns, she bled; but so sincerely repentant was she, so firmly rooted had become her faith in the Almighty, that no amount of suffering, no change of time and circumstance, could destroy it. With repentance something had sprung up, and blossomed in her being, an imperishable flower, beautiful, fragrant, making the world bright and sweet.

This flower twined itself round man, its odors refreshed and strengthened him; its essence healed him when wounded, and nerved him on to gallant and

[43] Source: Ellen M. Umansky, "Frank, Ray," in *American National Biography* 8:366–67.

noble deeds. It is the breath of life in him, and he must needs be careful of its clinging stems, its tender leaves, for they are rooted in a woman's heart.

In mother, wife, sister, sweetheart, lies the most precious part of man. In them he sees perpetual reminders of the death-sin, guarantees of immortality. Think, woman, what your existence means to man; dwell well on your responsibility; and now let us turn to that part of time called the past, more particularly biblical days. The religious life of the early Israelites is so closely interwoven with their domestic and political life, that it cannot be separated and treated alone. Amidst all kind of tribal and national strife, the search for knowledge of Javeh [sic] went on in so even a way, so indifferent to men and things, as no other investigation has done. The soul of mankind could not be quieted concerning this matter, and religion from its very nature evolved itself.

§17 Henriette Greenebaum Frank
(1854–1922)

Henriette Frank was born in Chicago to Michael and Sarah Spiegel Greenebaum. She was educated in Chicago and Frankfurt, Germany. She married Henry L. Frank in 1873. Frank became a member of the Chicago Woman's Club in 1877 and served as its president in 1884–1885. She was also active in the Chicago branch of the Council of Jewish Women.[44]

Like Ray Frank, Henriette Frank gave a paper at the Jewish Women's Congress. The excerpt given below is from her paper, "Jewish Women of Modern Days." Frank read the story of Eve as a wisdom tale. She removed sin from the story. Her reading of the Genesis text presented women very positively.

> From Henriette[45] G. Frank, "Jewish Women of Modern Days," in *Papers of the Jewish Women's Congress* (Philadelphia: The Jewish Publication Society of America, 1894), 43.

The woman of our day, like Eve, the All-Mother, stretches out her hand for the fruit of the tree of knowledge that she may know good from evil; though she lose the paradise of ignorance, she may gain the field of honest

[44] Source: *Obituary in Publications of the American Jewish Historical Society* 29 (1925), 159–60.

[45] In *Papers of the Jewish Woman's Congress*, Franks's name is listed as Henrietta G. Frank. Her biographical material spells it as Henriette.

endeavor. The serpent appears to her not as Satan, the tempter, but rather as the companion of Minerva, the symbol of wisdom and of eternity.[46] If Adam had eaten more freely of the fruit tendered him by Eve, his descendants might have become too wise to deny to women capabilities equal to men's. Would Adam have given Eve of the fruit, had he been the first to taste of it? Adam now permits Eve to enjoy the fruit, while he digs about the roots of the tree, until he lands at the antipodes in his effort to reach final causes.

§18 Julia Wedgwood
(1833–1913)

(Frances) Julia Wedgwood was the daughter of Frances Emma Mackintosh and Hensleigh Wedgwood, a barrister and philologist, and grandson of Josiah Wedgwood, founder of the Etruria Pottery Company. From an early age Wedgwood lived surrounded by intellectuals debating questions of science, history, and religion, but she received almost no formal education. Her strong academic gifts pushed her to resist her parents' idea that marriage was a woman's only vocation. She taught herself Latin, Greek, French, and German, worked as a research assistant, and became a renowned conversationalist and debater, despite her deafness. Her intellectual powers brought her the admiration of men like the poet Robert Browning (1812–1889), her relative the naturalist Charles Darwin (1809–1882), and the theologian and Christian socialist F. D. Maurice (1805–1872). Wedgwood's intense rationalism was wed to deep spirituality and mysticism. She was critical of the low expectations Christians had for intellectual engagement in church. Wedgwood recognized with considerable regret that her life could "have been so much more than it has been," if she had had the advantages of university education and been free from the duties required of her as a woman.[47]

Julia Wedgwood began her writing career as a novelist. Later she wrote numerous articles, including one on the theological significance of the *Origin*

---

[46] Minerva is the goddess of wisdom, crafts and war, the daughter of Jupiter. She is often depicted with a python draped around her neck.

[47] Sources: Jose Harris, "Wedgwood, (Frances) Julia," in *The Oxford Dictionary of National Biography* 57:927–29. L. Robert Stevens, "Intertextual Constructions of Faith: Julia Wedgwood (1833–1913)," in *Women's Theology in Nineteenth-Century Britain: Transfiguring the Faith of their Fathers*, ed. Julie Melnyk (New York: Garland, 1998), 83–93. Richard Curle, ed. *Robert Browning and Julia Wedgwood: A Broken Friendship as Revealed in their Letters* (London: John Murray & Jonathan Cape, 1937).

of Species. Darwin liked her analysis of his work and wrote: "I think that you understand my book perfectly, and that I find a very rare event."[48] Wedgwood also wrote a number of works of non-fiction, including an acclaimed study of the life and historical significance of John Wesley (1870), and a book which popularized the modern critical approach to the study of the Bible. Her severest critics, her family, wrongly judged *The Message of Israel in the Light of Modern Criticism* (1894) to be "tiresome and old-fashioned."

In *The Message of Israel*, Wedgwood used the results of contemporary biblical criticism to elucidate the message of the Bible. She noted her particular indebtedness to Canon S. R. Driver (1846–1914), whose *Introduction to the Literature of the Old Testament* (1891) convinced many in the English-speaking world of the legitimacy of the higher-critical approach to the study of the Scriptures. She discussed the issues of inspiration, criticism, and authorship of the Old Testament. She reconstructed the history of ancient Israel based on the literary sources that source critics such as J. Wellhausen (1844–1918) assumed stood behind the present shape of the biblical text. She wrote about Eve in the context of her discussion of the Priestly Code, which she described as "an anonymous and annotated work" from the post-exilic period. She contrasted the depiction of the creation of woman in the Priestly Code in Genesis 1 with that found in the earlier and more anthropomorphic Genesis 2–3, which she attributed to the Jehovist source.

From Julia Wedgwood, *The Message of Israel in the Light of Modern Criticism* (London: Isbister, 1894), 87, 244, 261–62.

The work of the Hebrew Creator appears as a series of blunders. "It is not good for man to be alone," Jahveh has said when he created a companion for the first man, and to judge from the result it would have been far better for man to be alone than to have had Eve for a companion. "I have gotten a man with the help of Jahveh," is the glad exclamation of Eve at the birth of Cain, and the man is the first murderer. . . .

The general limits of the Priestly Code may be briefly suggested as being identical with the book of Leviticus, together with all that prefaces or recalls it. The work supplies a statistical and chronological commentary on the early history of Israel, made in the interest of the priesthood, and constitutes a ritual directory of worship in all its branches. Wherever, through the Pentateuch and Joshua, these interests come into prominence we recognize the hand of the Priestly narrator, but we do not thus give an exhaustive analysis of his work; he sometimes tells the story of the Jehovist over again, occasionally (as in the first chapter of Genesis) from a more spiritual point of view, and with

[48] Curle, *Robert Browning*, 7.

what might appear the design of correcting the crude anthropomorphism of his forerunners. . . .

We must to a certain extent turn back to the Jehovist to understand his later associate. We may gather up the characteristic differences of the two by saying that the Jehovist starts from Man and ends with Woman, and the Priestly narrator stars with a chaos and ends with a cosmos. With the Jehovist the creation of woman is an afterthought; it seems almost implied that some demand from Adam, some expression of the unsatisfactoriness of non-human companionship, lies at the root of her being. The animals seem, according to this account, to have been created with a view to providing man with that "fit help," which he was only to find in Woman, after they had been tried as companions and failed. She is far more closely related to him; they are made of the dust of the field, she is literally "bone of his bone"; but her creation, as much as theirs, is subordinate to his. Milton's line, "He for God only, she for God in him," is an accurate reflection of the feeling of the Jehovist. It is to a different order of conceptions we are carried by the story of the Priestly writers. Mankind is male and female from its first existence, the sexes are coeval. It would appear, indeed, that this writer recognizes sex as older than humanity. "In the image of God created he him, male and female created he them," seems to suggest that the divine nature embodied this dual element as well as the human. Sex, in some mysterious form, would seem embodied in the divine nature. At any rate it is a primeval fact in human nature. Woman is no afterthought, no postscript, as it were, to the work of creation, but shares with man the first thought of God, and derives her being directly from Him.

The different sense of sex in the two writers would appear with a different feeling with regard to that creation of new life which gives the deepest significance to the fact of sex. "Be fruitful, and multiply and replenish the earth," says Elohim to the newly created pair. "In sorrow shalt thou bring forth children," says Jahveh to Eve. The two speeches are hardly made in circumstances sufficiently comparable to be called inconsistent. The injunction is given to unfallen human beings who are looking forward into a wide world which they are to "replenish and subdue"; the penalty announced to Eve succeeds the Fall; it is not logically impossible to arrange the two speeches in a single narrative. And yet, taken with their context, we may say that their effect is inconsistent. There seems a sympathy with the desire for offspring in the Priestly story which we fail to discover in its predecessor, in this respect marking the later narration with a far more Hebrew tinge of feeling than the earlier one. But we are reminded, in this particular as in all others, that the Jehovist is giving us a picture of a soul's temptation, and the Priestly historian is giving an account of the protoplasts of humanity. The aims of the two writers are not only different, they are totally heterogeneous. The Jehovist need not consider the life of man in any other aspect than that of his relation to God. The Priestly writer is consciously starting a history of the world, and must lay some foundation for whatever is of importance in all subsequent history. If the two accounts are not inconsistent, it is because they are incomparable.

§19 Lillie Devereux Blake
(1833–1913)

Lillie D. Blake was a suffragist, writer, women's rights activist, and president of New York City Woman's Suffrage League. In her novels[49] and published lectures[50] she addressed women's issues.

Blake contributed to *The Woman's Bible* edited by Elizabeth Cady Stanton.[51] For Stanton and her colleagues, the Bible was the authority used to keep women in an oppressed state. This attitude to the Bible sets this work apart from the other works in this chapter. *The Woman's Bible* undermined the authority of the Bible by suggesting that its message was primitive, immoral, and oppressive. Stanton regarded the Bible as a human document, so she and the revising committee felt free to expurgate objectionable texts. "The Bible cannot be accepted or rejected as a whole, its teachings are varied and its lessons differ widely from each other."[52]

The women working on the commentary used the literal Bible translation of their contemporary Julia Evelina Smith (1792–1886).[53] Blake marked her citations from Smith's work by calling it a "literal translation."

---

[49] For example, *Fettered for Life, or Lord and Master* (1874).

[50] *Woman's Place To-Day: Four Lectures, in Reply to the Lenten Lecures on "Woman" by the Rev. Morgan Dix* (1883).

[51] For more information on Stanton, see part 5, "Leah and Rachel—Founders of the House of Israel."

[52] Elizabeth Cady Stanton, *The Woman's Bible* (New York: European Publishing Co., 1895), 13.

[53] Smith began her translation work by producing English versions from the Greek New Testament, the Septuagint, and the Latin Vulgate. She then taught herself Hebrew so that she could translate the Old Testament from the Hebrew original. Smith published one of her translations with her own money in 1876. Professor Young of Harvard College was one of the many men who commented on the literalness of her translation and he was apparently "much astonished that she had translated so correctly without consulting some learned man." Marla J. Selvidge, *Notorious Voices: Feminist Biblical Interpretation, 1500–1920* (New York: Continuum, 1996), 215. For a full treatment of Julia Smith and her family see Susan J. Shaw, *A Religious History of Julia Evelina Smith's 1876 Translation of the Holy Bible: Doing More Than Any Man Has Ever Done* (San Francisco: Mellen, 1993).

Blake's writing on the fall was highly polemical and argued for women's supremacy over men. She thought that Adam was with Eve when the serpent tempted her. Blake, like many other women, argued that Adam was much weaker than Eve in resisting temptation. Blake stated what other women only implied: it was ludicrous that men had used this account to argue for male superiority for so long.

From *The Woman's Bible*, edited by Elizabeth Cady Stanton (New York: European Publishing Co., 1895), 26–27.

Note the significant fact that we always hear of the "fall of man," not the fall of woman, showing that the consensus of human thought has been more unerring than masculine interpretation. Reading this narrative carefully, it is amazing that any set of men ever claimed that the dogma of the inferiority of woman is here set forth. The conduct of Eve from the beginning to the end is so superior to that of Adam. The command not to eat of the fruit of the tree of Knowledge was given to the man alone before woman was formed. Genesis ii, 17. Therefore the injunction was not brought to Eve with the impressive solemnity of a Divine Voice, but whispered to her by her husband and equal. It was a serpent supernaturally endowed, a seraphim as Scott[54] and other commentators have claimed, who talked with Eve, and whose words might reasonably seem superior to the second-hand story of her companion, nor does the woman yield at once. She quotes the command not to eat of the fruit to which the serpent replies "Dying ye shall not die," v. 4 literal translation. In other words telling her that if the mortal body does perish, the immortal part shall live forever, and offering as the reward of her act the attainment of Knowledge.

Then the woman fearless of death if she can gain wisdom takes of the fruit; and all this time Adam standing beside her interposes no word of objection. "Her husband with her" are the words of v. 6. Had he been the representative of the divinely appointed head in married life, he assuredly would have taken upon himself the burden of the discussion with the serpent, but no, he is silent in this crisis of their fate. Having had the command from God himself he interposes no word of warning or remonstrance, but takes the fruit from the hand of his wife without a protest. It takes six verses to describe the "fall" of woman, the fall of man is contemptuously dismissed in a line and a half.

The subsequent conduct of Adam was to the last degree dastardly. When the awful time of reckoning comes, and the Jehovah God appears to demand

---

[54] Probably Thomas Scott (1747–1821), an Anglican priest, whose notes on the Bible were published with the text of the Bible and at times combined with Matthew Henry's commentary. Many editions of Scott's comments exist; they were initially published serially.

why his command has been disobeyed, Adam endeavors to shield himself behind the gentle being he has declared to be so dear. "The woman thou gavest to be with me, she gave me and I did eat," he whines trying to shield himself at his wife's expense! Again we are amazed that upon such a story men have built up a theory of their superiority!

Then follows what has been called the curse. Is it not rather a prediction? First is the future fate of the serpent described, the enmity of the whole human race "it shall lie in wait for thee as to the head" (v. 15, literal translation). Next the subjection of the woman is foretold, thy husband "shall rule over thee," v. 16. Lastly the long struggle of man with the forces of nature is portrayed. "In the sweat of thy face thou shalt eat food until thy turning back to the earth" (v. 19, literal translation). With the evolution of humanity an ever increasing number of men have ceased to toil for their bread with their hands, and with the introduction of improved machinery, and the uplifting of the race there will come a time when there shall be no severities of labor, and when women shall be freed from all oppressions.

"And Adam called his wife's name Life for she was the mother of all living" (v. 20, literal translation).

It is a pity that all versions of the Bible do not give this word instead of the Hebrew Eve. She was Life, the eternal mother, the first representative of the more valuable and important half of the human race.

—L. D. B.

§20 Elizabeth Baxter
(1837–1926)

Elizabeth Baxter was born to Thomas Nelson Foster (1799–1858), a Quaker, and his second wife, Elizabeth Gibbs. She was initially educated at home by a governess, then sent to a boarding school at the age of eleven. Her conversion experience in her late teens exposed her to the wider evangelical world. In 1868, she married Reverend Michael Paget Baxter (1834–1910), an eccentric, end-times lecturer and author of a popular book, *Louis Napoleon, The Destined Monarch of the World* (1863). The Baxters spent the first fifteen years of their married life as itinerant preachers: Michael spoke about the Second Coming and Elizabeth followed his lecture with an evangelistic appeal. Two children were born during this time; the first died in infancy. The Baxters also became involved with the evangelistic work of the celebrated American evangelist Dwight L. Moody (1837–1899) and his associate Ira D. Sankey (1840–

1908) during their British crusades in 1873–1875.[55] Elizabeth was involved in the crusade's ministry to women and read and expounded Scripture to as many as 1,500 women each week.

The Baxters initiated a number of publishing endeavors. Elizabeth did most of the writing and handled the practical details of the business. A breakdown in her health in 1876 took her to Europe where she again got involved in preaching and teaching and evangelistic missions. From 1882 on, she was involved in initiating a variety of ministries, including the Bethshan home for divine healing, a missionary training home, and several foreign missions. In 1894, she was involved in a world mission tour. Although she remained an Anglican all her life, her sense of a prophetic call impelled her to carry out independent preaching and teaching ministries, and to become involved with many evangelical organizations.[56]

During her life, Elizabeth Baxter published some 40 books and a great number of smaller booklets, tracts, and brief appeals, as well as expositions, and weekly Sunday School lessons in her husband's successful paper, *The Christian Herald*. Most of her books are expositions of scripture, which grew out of her extensive teaching ministry. She often focused her studies on characters in scripture, as she does in *The Women in the Word* (1897) and *The School of the Patriarchs* (1903), though she also wrote commentaries on particular books, including *Ezekiel Son of Man: His Life and Ministry* (1902), *Portraits from Proverbs* (1891), and *Job* (1894). She also wrote on diverse topics from divine healing to the Second Coming, as well as a guide to the use of the Anglican *Book of Common Prayer*.[57]

In *The Women in the Word*, Baxter used the idea of "helpmeet'" to judge biblical women. Women were good wives if they helped their husbands and bad wives if they hindered them. Eve failed as Adam's helpmeet when she acted without considering her husband's good in taking the fruit: "Adam's helpmeet had become Satan's instrument of temptation!'"

Like Baillie and Putnam, Baxter upheld a traditional view of women's roles in society and church. Despite Baxter's negative portrayal of Eve in this selection, there is a curious subtext of equality. She holds both Eve and Adam to a high standard of conduct. In spite of Baxter's commitment to a clear

[55] For a summary of Moody and Sankey's evangelistic work in Britain see D. W. Bebbington, *Evangelicalism in Modern Britain: A History from the 1730s to the 1980s* (London: Unwin Hyman, 1989), 162–64.

[56] Source: Nathaniel Wiseman, *Elizabeth Baxter: Saint, Evangelist, Preacher, Teacher and Expositor* (London: The Christian Herald, 1928). See further, Nathaniel Wiseman, *Michael Paget Baxter: Clergyman, Evangelist, Editor and Philanthropist* (London: The Christian Herald, 1923).

[57] Respectively, *Divine Healing* (1900), *His Last Word: Bible Readings on Revelation* (1896), and *Thoughts for Worshippers* (1871).

hierarchy of relationships between God, man, and woman, she is very committed to mutuality in marriage relationships. Baxter's own marriage seemed to follow this model of mutuality rather than hierarchy.[58]

Baxter read Greek and, like Grimké, was sensitive to issues of translation. She used commentaries but moved beyond the interpretations of others to her own interpretation of Eve and her selfishness. She saw Eve's exclamation at the birth of Cain as evidence of Eve's selfishness rather than Eve's faithfulness, as did other women.

From Elizabeth Baxter, *The Women in the Word*, 2nd ed. (London: Christian Herald, 1897),1–8.

–Eve–

The Lord God said, "It is not good that the man should be alone."
—Gen. ii. 18

When the Lord God formed man out of the dust of the ground, and breathed into his nostrils the breath of life, and man became a living soul, He said, "It is not good that the man should be alone" (Gen. ii. 18). Even unfallen human nature was possessed of a selfish principle, which needed the discipline of considering and of caring for others. There are very few unmarried men who are not selfish, and only those unmarried women can be unselfish who have found something definite to live for. It needs the check of another will, the friction of the dispositions in another which are contrary to our own, in order to develop in us the consideration and thoughtfulness for others which are so characteristic in the life of Jesus.

It was God's own thought that man should not be alone; He said: "I will make him an help meet for him" (Gen. ii. 18, or R.V. "answering to him"). God saw the need, and God created the supply. He had already made every beast of the field, and every fowl of the air, and had brought them to Adam that he might give names to them; but in all God's fair creation there was no true companion found for Adam. He alone was made in the image of God and in His likeness; he alone had dominion over the animal creation; there was not an equal to be found for him.

In order that a helpmeet should be created who should respond to the necessities of man, who should be the complement of himself and his

---

[58] Baxter's biographer, Nathaniel Wiseman, noted that "there was in Mrs. Baxter an individuality saturated with the ideas that governed her husband, but one that claimed complete independence of both thought and freedom. In this difference and freedom Mr. Baxter gleefully reveled and by it he was forcefully and persistently moulded and shaped, perhaps unconsciously, to what he became" (Wiseman, *Elizabeth Baxter*, 10).

representative, Adam must suffer loss. "The Lord God caused a deep sleep to fall upon Adam, and he slept: and He took one of his ribs, and closed up the flesh instead thereof; and the rib, which the Lord God had taken from man, made He a woman, and brought her unto the man" (Gen. ii. 21, 22). It was a type of death and resurrection. Adam suffered loss in order to gain what was better. It was a true picture of the death of Christ, in order that the Church, His Bride, might be taken from His pierced side, blood-bought, living out of His death. Just as man proceeded from God, and was made alive with His very breath, so woman proceeded from man, and we understand the depth of that word of Paul's, "He that loveth his wife loveth himself" (Eph. v. 28).

After man had sinned, he no longer trusted God to prepare a help meet for him. "And it came to pass, when men began to multiply on the face of the earth, and daughters were born unto them, that the sons of God saw the daughters of men that they were fair; and they took them wives of ALL WHOM THEY CHOSE" (Gen. vi. 1, 2). Their object was a selfish one. They sought in their wives what should please them, and, doubtless, the wives sought in their husbands what should please them. Every marriage entered into with a selfish object produces bitter fruit; it is wrong at the very root.

Eve was created for Adam's sake, and Adam said of her: "This is now bone of my bones, and flesh of my flesh: she shall be called Woman, because she was taken out of Man. Therefore shall a man leave his father and his mother, and shall cleave unto his wife: and they shall be one flesh" (Gen. ii. 23, 24). There must be sacrifice on both sides.

One of the happiest marriages we know was entered into by a dear Christian woman on the continent with a blind minister for the very purpose of caring for him. Being eyes to him, she enables him to carry out his ministerial work. Why is it so happy? Because it is unselfish; she is a helpmeet for her husband, and she has found in him a patience and a self-denial which, with her naturally impetuous and impulsive disposition, makes the gain as much hers as his.

When a wife seeks in her husband the affection which shall satisfy her, or the attention which shall gratify *her* self-love, she is not acting as a helpmeet; she is making her husband minister to her, instead of taking her place as minister to him. And when a husband is exacting with his wife, claiming all her time, all her attention, all her thoughts to revolve around *him*, he will never be fully satisfied with her. Selfishness is a plant that produces sour fruit, and sows discord wherever it grows.

There was no jar in the union of Adam and Eve until the serpent made his appearance. He approached the weaker vessel, saying to the woman,

"Yea, hath God said, Ye shall not eat of every tree of the garden?" (Gen iii. 1).

How should Eve act? Created to be Adam's helpmeet, her duty was to sustain her position and dominion over the lower creation. How could she consistently listen to a serpent, and how could she, who shared Adam's dominion over all but God, endure that her God should be called in question? The very listening to the reptile was a departure from God and a treachery against her husband.

Her answer was a true one, but she ought never to have answered at all. It gave ground to the serpent to continue his temptation. The serpent had already found out that it was more easy to draw the woman into conversation than the man; and her first answer gave him ground to speak again:

"Ye shall not surely die: For God doth know that in the day that ye eat thereof, then your eyes shall be opened, and ye shall be as gods, knowing good and evil" (Vers. 4, 5).

The enemy of souls was wise in his tactics. He knew that in these early days, when man was fresh from the hand of his Creator, he had not yet become flesh (Gen. vi. 3). The spirit, which responded to God, had still the upper hand, and he addressed his chief temptation to the higher and not the lower part of man's nature: "Ye shall be as gods, knowing good and evil."

Eve's ambition was stirred. Could there be anything wrong in desiring to be like God? But Eve, in entertaining such thoughts without reference to her God, failed in her position of helpmeet to Adam. She acted without respect to him, and without considering either God's authority or her husband's good. It was THE FIRST MANIFESTATION OF SELF in God's creation. It is, however, this very object of being like God that He sets before His people now, "Whom He did foreknow, He also did predestinate to be conformed to the image of His Son" (Rom. viii. 29). It is only through Christ that we find the way to be conformed to Him. Disobedience towards God can never lead to God, and Satan's short cut was a fatal one. No sooner had the enemy laid hold of Eve on this point than he could appeal to her on lower ground.

"The woman saw that the fruit of the tree was good for food," and "the lust of the flesh" began to work within her; "and that it was pleasant to the eyes;" "the lust of the eyes" was awakened too; "and a tree to be desired to make one wise," "the pride of life" (I John ii. 16) was working, and acting upon her own judgment, —a judgment biased by the serpent—"she took of the fruit thereof and did eat." With this fatal act, every unselfish instinct seemed to die within her; "she gave also unto her husband with her, and he did eat" (Ver. 6). Adam's helpmeet had become Satan's instrument of temptation! The knowledge of evil awoke within them, and the man and his wife began to be afraid of God.

It was a new experience to them to find evil where they had not formerly suspected it, and to feel the need to hide themselves away from God. It was

an awful moment when the man and the woman made in God's image found
within them an impulse to flee from Him, as though their Father and their
Creator were their enemy. The sin of the first woman brought about this
grievous, this disastrous change. But neither the fig-leaves nor their hiding-
place among the trees of the garden answered their purpose. God found them
out, and He said unto Adam:

"Where art thou?"

The man's answer condemned him: "I heard Thy voice in the garden,
and I was afraid, because I was naked; and I hid myself." UNTRUTH WAS
DEVELOPED ALREADY.

"Who told thee that thou wast naked ? Hast thou eaten of the tree whereof
I commanded thee that thou shouldst not eat?"

Adam lost his manliness and said: "The woman whom Thou gavest to be
with me, she gave me of the tree, and I did eat."

Eve had become, not a helpmeet, but a hindrance to her husband. Adam
had become, not a protector, but an accuser to his wife; sin and selfishness
came in together, and the seeds of disunion were sown which were to bring
forth the harvest of earth's sorrow. And when God questioned the woman:

"What is this that thou hast done?" she said: "The serpent beguiled me,
and I did eat."

It is a sorry history; but oh, what a picture of many a household where
self is ruling! How often, when a loss occurs in business, and the husband is
deeply mortified, the wife will speak bitter words of reproach: "If you had
only done as I advised you, you would not have ruined us all." Or the husband will bitterly retort: "If only you had not been so extravagant, things
would never have come to this pass; you have yourself to thank for it." How
often when a son or a daughter brings shame and grief upon their parents,
bitter words of recrimination and retaliation are spoken! The wife, given to
be a helpmeet, a blessing to her husband, to win him back when he has
wandered, only galls the open wound; and the history of fallen Adam and
Eve is constantly repeated even in the houses of God's children! If only the
wife could recognise her high calling to suffer for Christ and with Christ in
relation to her husband; the Bible tells us that the husband, even without the
Word, may be won by the conversation, or manner of life, of the wife, which
they behold with fear (I Pet. iii. 1, 2).

But Adam and Eve were still in Eden, and before the Lord cast them out,
He gave them the promise, spoken, neither to the fallen man nor yet to the
fallen woman, but to the serpent—that her Seed should bruise the serpent's
head, and a way of salvation should be made.

There is just one other instance of self-life recorded of Eve. Sent out from
the garden into the world which had become full of thorns and briars, Eve

became a mother, and named her first son Cain, saying, "I HAVE GOTTEN a man from the Lord." The selfish wife becomes a selfish mother. "I have gotten" expresses her thoughts regarding her boy. If the first idea in the possession of a child is the selfish one, what we have got, and what the child is to be to us—how can we be fit to train him for heaven? It is only as we count our children to be the Lord's possession that we can bring them up in His nurture and admonition.

Eve became a mother a second time, and had the bitterness of seeing her child's blood shed by the very son whom her selfish heart had named Cain; and, perhaps, it was only when she learnt the lesson of sacrifice from Abel's altar that God could trust her with her son Seth, who was "appointed" or "put" by the hand of God in the place of his slain brother. Seth was, so to speak, a resurrection child, and through him the family of the faithful descended.

Conclusion

Nineteenth-century women recognized Eve's importance. Ashton wrote, "Perhaps no character of earthly history, if we except only our Lord Jesus Christ, gathers about itself so much of interest, calls forth such deep and varying emotions, or affords such important instruction, as does that of our first mother."[59] Women looked to Eve, their mother, for self-understanding, self-knowledge, guidance, and direction as they came to terms with key issues of the century. The nineteenth century was a time of tremendous change in the status of women. Discussion of the woman's place in home and society invoked the Bible as an authoritative text and discussed Eve as a foundational ancestress. Even women who seemed to follow traditional understandings of Eve challenged these understandings in subtle and surprising ways.

The authors represented in this chapter tried to redeem Eve from a long theological tradition that blamed her for sin, characterizing Eve, and thus every other "daughter of Eve," as a temptress.[60] Yet, as we have seen, many

---

[59] Ashton, *Mothers of the Bible*, 11.

[60] The tradition of blaming Eve for the sin of both men and women is ancient, and can be seen in the following tenth century penitential prayer to the Virgin Mary.

"Hail, Holy Queen, Mother of mercy!
Hail, our life, our sweetness and our hope!
To Thee do we cry, poor banished children of Eve.
To Thee do we send up our sighs,
mourning and weeping in this valley of tears.
Turn then, most gracious Advocate

women found positive characteristics in Eve and negative characteristics in Adam. When the temptations of Eve and Adam were compared, Adam's sin was often argued to be greater. Some authors redeemed Eve by looking to Mary; they minimized Eve's guilt by saying her fall led to redemption. They questioned the punishment, or at least the traditional weight given to the punishment of Eve, and the depiction of her as the evil seductress.

Nineteenth-century women held a variety of positions on the Woman Question. Their voices resonate with the multiplicity of perspectives that exist today. We have heard traditional voices such as Esther Copely[61] reminding her audience to maintain tradition: "She was designed to be a help meet for man—that is, 1. a suitable companion, capable of holding rational and spiritual communion with him; and, 2. a willing and active assistant to him in all his cares and enterprises; the sweetener of his toil, and (since sorrow, through sin, has become man's sad inheritance) the soother of his sorrows." We have heard voices such as Hannah Crocker[62] pushing tradition forward: "For she is bone of my bone, and flesh of my flesh, and therefore she shall be my equal. She shall have equal right to think, reason and act for herself, with my advice corroborating." And we have heard other voices such as H. G. Frank arguing for a different understanding of women and men: "If Adam had eaten more freely of the fruit tendered him by Eve, his descendants might have become too wise to deny to women capabilities equal to men's."[63]

Nineteenth-century women recreated Eve in their own image. The retellings of Eve's story tell us as much, or more, about the life of nineteenth-century women as they do about the biblical text. We learn the questions these women asked, the books they read, and the battles they fought. We hear their own voices of protest and of self-understanding as they enter the forbidden realms of theological and political discourse. We hear them preach with their pens. We see them teach the content and moral lessons of the Bible. We see how the biblical text functioned in their lives.

Thine eyes of mercy towards us
and after this, our exile,
show unto us the blessed fruit of Thy womb, Jesus,
O clement, O loving, O sweet Virgin Mary!"

[61] Copely, *Scripture History for Youth*, 18.

[62] Crocker, *Observations*, 11.

[63] Frank, "Jewish Women of Modern Days," 43.

Part 2

Sarah—The First Mother of Israel

Introduction

The first matriarch of Israel, originally named Sarai, entered the story of salvation history as the wife of Abram; Genesis 11:27–23:20 contains her story. Ambiguity surrounds Sarai's ancestry but not her fertility. Genesis 11:30 reads, "But Sarai was barren; she had no child." When God commanded Abram to leave his homeland and go to the land of promise, Sarai traveled with her husband and his nephew, Lot, to Canaan. A grievous famine prompted them to take refuge in Egypt, where Abram, fearing that the Egyptians would kill him because of Sarai's beauty, instructed her to say she was his sister. Pharaoh's officials took Sarai into the palace; disease afflicted Pharaoh and his household until Sarai was returned to Abram. God promised Abram many descendents, but Sarai was barren. Sarai decided to solve the problem of her barrenness by giving Abram her Egyptian maid, Hagar, as a second wife (Gen. 16). The pregnancy of Hagar precipitated a conflict that led to Sarai's harsh treatment of her and her subsequent flight into the desert. Hagar returned to Sarai's household and gave birth to Abram's son Ishmael. In Genesis 17:15, God changed Sarai's name to Sarah and promised that she would bear the child of promise. On different occasions, both Abraham and Sarah laughed when they heard this promise (Gen. 17:15-19, Gen. 18:9-15).

When Abraham and Sarah moved to Gerar (Gen. 20), Abraham again claimed that Sarah was his sister. Abimelech, the king of Gerar, took Sarah into his household, but returned her to Abraham after God visited him in a dream. Abimelech gave Abraham and Sarah gifts, and Abraham prayed for the healing of the king and his household, as God had made every female in the household barren "because of Sarah, Abraham's wife."

As God had promised, Sarah gave birth to Isaac (Gen. 21). At the feast of his weaning, the teenaged Ishmael "mocked" his young brother. Sarah told

Abraham to send Hagar and Ishmael away, a decision God confirmed. When Sarah died at the age of 127, Abraham bought a cave in a field in which to bury his wife (Gen. 23).

Old Testament scriptures present Sarah primarily as the wife of Abraham and matriarch of Israel (Isa. 51:2). Tradition also identified her strongly with her burial place, the cave of Machpelah (Gen. 23:19-20; 49:31), and as the mother of Isaac, Abraham's heir (Gen. 24:36). Sarah's tent became the bridal suite for Rebekah and Isaac and the place where Isaac found comfort after Sarah's death (Gen. 24:67). The New Testament held Sarah up as an example of faith (Heb. 11:11) and of submission to her husband (1 Peter 3:6). In Galatians 4:21-31, Paul did not name Sarah, but called her the free woman who bore a son to Abraham, thus establishing her as a type or symbol of Gentile Christians.

Nineteenth-century British and American women lived in a very different world than Sarah, so her story presented them with a variety of interpretive issues. These issues included the ages of characters, the timing and chronology of events in the story, marriage customs, ethics, and morality.

Nineteenth-century women also saw similarities between Sarah's story and their own lives. They related to her as a woman, wife, and mother. The association of Sarah and submission was well known to Christian interpreters as 1 Peter 3:6 was embedded into most marriage ceremonies. Most writers used this text as an interpretive lens for Sarah's story and emphasized the theme of wifely submission, a quality enshrined in the cult of domesticity. Some authors carefully nuanced the meaning of submission. Harriet Beecher Stowe, for example, noted that if Sarah was an example of the proper behaviour of a wife, then "no very alarming amount of subjection or submission is implied."

British and American women understood Sarah in different ways based on their cultural context. Jewish authors living in both Great Britain and the United States presented a very positive portrait of their first mother and matriarch. She was called a "queen," a title which invites comparison with the Virgin Mary, Queen of Heaven. Many British women read Sarah's story in light of their own experiences as women of wealth, power, and position. Their own experiences with household servants became a lens for understanding Sarah's relationship with Hagar. Frances King was troubled by Sarah's preparation of a meal for strangers—in her experience ladies did not work in the kitchen. American women were less troubled by Sarah's presence in the kitchen, a place where they exercised considerable influence. They read Sarah's story in the light of the American institution of slavery. Many identified Sarah as the rich, white mistress and Hagar as the oppressed black slave. Women's first-hand experiences of power in the domestic sphere, classism, racism, and patriarchy enabled them to read Sarah's story with considerable insight and empathy.

In conjunction with their experiences as women, the authors used a variety of other resources to help them understand the story of Sarah. They interpreted her story by viewing it within the larger canon of scripture. In addition to the texts listed above, which specifically refer to Sarah, they used Proverbs 31:10-31, a passage that described a virtuous woman. Some compared Sarah with other biblical women such as Eve and the Virgin Mary. They found background information in Josephus and other historical resources, Christian and Jewish biblical commentaries, and Middle East travel accounts. They used the language of evolutionary development to explain "questionable" and "primitive" moral behaviour on the part of the characters. Many used their imaginations to fill in details missing from scripture about the internal and external world of Sarah. They recognized the absence of Sarah's perspective in the wife-sister stories and they accounted for her non-appearance in the story of the sacrifice of her only son.[1] Nineteenth-century women used available scholarly tools, as well as their own beliefs, assumptions, and perspectives, to interpret and apply the story of Sarah to their various audiences.

§21 Sarah Trimmer
(1741–1810)

Sarah Trimmer (née Kirby) was born in Ipswich and lived there until her family moved to London. She was educated in the Christian faith by her father and studied English and French in a small school for young women in Ipswich. The family moved to London so her father, Joshua Kirby, an artist and architect, could take up a post teaching drawing to the future George III. Kirby was later appointed clerk of the works of the palace at Kew. The only lay member of a clerical club, Joshua Kirby immersed himself in theology. He passed on his appreciation of the established Church of England and knowledge of divinity to his daughter.

---

[1] Modern feminists also fill in gaps and rewrite Sarah's story. Though the tools modern readers bring to the task of interpretation may be much more sophisticated and the convictions and experiences more varied, they share much in terms of approach with their nineteenth-century foremothers. Compare Grace Aguilar to Phyllis Trible, "Genesis 22: The Sacrifice of Sarah," in *Not in Heaven: Coherence and Complexity in Biblical Narrative*, ed. Jason Rosenblatt and Joseph Sitterson, Indiana Studies in Biblical Literature (Bloomington: Indiana University Press, 1991), 170–91.

Sarah Kirby married James Trimmer in 1762, living with her husband and twelve children in Brentford, England, a town just outside London. Trimmer educated all of her children at home and sent her sons out to learn classics from a local clergyman. After seeing Anna Barbauld's book, *Easy Lessons for Children*, Trimmer's friends persuaded her to write about her experiences of teaching her own children. Trimmer's career as a writer was thus born. She was involved in the Sunday School and charity school movements and wrote extensively on many aspects of education.[2] She published twenty-five titles, including *An Easy Introduction to the Knowledge of Nature* (1780), *Sacred History Selected from the Scriptures, with Annotations and Reflections* (1782–1784), *The Economy of Charity* (1786), and *An Essay on Christian Education* (1812).[3]

It will come as a surprise to many twenty-first century readers that Trimmer wrote a commentary on the entire Bible, including the Apocrypha.[4] She was one of the few women in history to write a work like this. She wrote to assist people in reading and studying the Bible. By following the standard commentary format, she was able to comment on exegetical and interpretive issues that she felt needed clarification. Most often she avoided engaging moral or ethical problems raised in the biblical texts. She did not highlight the significance of particular texts for women because she sought to educate both men and women. Unlike most other women writers, she did not focus on the character and emotions. However, by noting the Hebrew word translated as 'laugh,' could also be translated as 'rejoice,' she subtly redeemed Sarah from the judgment of the divine visitors when she "laughed" at the notion that she would become pregnant. Further, Trimmer noted the fulfillment of God's promises to Sarah as well as Abraham.

In addition, Trimmer's treatment of the encounter of Sarah and Abraham with Abimelech demonstrated her ability to raise difficult textual issues on the one hand, and, on the other, her unwillingness to encourage readers to wrestle with moral questions that might raise theological questions or doubts.[5]

---

[2] Source: *Some Account of the Life and Writings of Mrs. Trimmer* (London: F. C. & J. Rivington, 1814). Trimmer's son Henry may have authored this unsigned memoir of his mother's life.

[3] The dates given are for the first edition, except *An Essay on Christian Education* which was initially published as part of a periodical edited by Trimmer, *The Guardian of Education* (1802–1806).

[4] Mrs. Sarah Trimmer, *A Help to the Unlearned in the Study of the Holy Scriptures: Being an attempt to explain the Bible in a familiar way* (London: F.C. & J. Rivington, 1805).

[5] In her tendency to avoid introducing readers to theological controversy, Trimmer was typical of many late eighteenth-century figures writing for women, although Trimmer's intended audience was not exclusively female. See Julie Straight, "Religious Controversy in Hester Chapone's *Letters on the Improvement of the Mind*," *Nineteenth-Century Contexts* 27.4 (2005): 315–34.

For example, she raised the issue of the story's chronology and noted that this episode may have occurred earlier in Sarah and Abraham's life. Trimmer no doubt recognized moral problems in the behaviour of Abraham and Sarah in Genesis 20 but ignored them, advising her readers that the chapter did not "require particular meditation." Trimmer wanted to encourage faith in her readers and tried to avoid burdening her readers with problematic moral and ethical issues rooted in social, religious, and cultural differences between the world of the text and the world of the reader.

From Mrs. Sarah Trimmer, *A Help to the Unlearned in the Study of the Holy Scriptures: Being an attempt to explain the Bible in a familiar way* (London: F.C. & J. Rivington, 1805), 20–21, 24–25.

Chapter XVII

Ver. 1. Observe, that the Divine Being who appeared to Abram, called himself the ALMIGHTY GOD, and that he renewed his covenant with Abram, and appointed circumcision as a sign, or token, to distinguish the posterity and family of Abram from the idolatrous nations. The word ABRAM, in the Hebrew language, signifies *high father*. ABRAHAM, signifies *a father of many nations*. SARAI, signified a *lady*. SARAH, a *princess*.[6] Observe, that though it seemed scarcely possible to Abraham that he should have a son, he believed the promises of GOD, and testified his faith in the way which GOD had commanded.

Chapter XX

This chapter affords another proof that the best men are not perfect. It also shows that the knowledge of the true God was not quite lost in the country of which Abimelech was King. What is related here most probably happened at an earlier period of Abraham and Sarah's life. However it was, this chapter is one of those which do not require particular meditation. But we learn from it that Abraham was a prophet, that is, one to whom the LORD made known things that were to come to pass at a distant period, that through him they might be made known to the world.

Chapter XXI

Ver. 1 to 9. We have here an account of the fulfilment of the promises which God had made to Abraham and Sarah, that he would give them a son in their old age; and we find that Abraham's faith had in this instance its reward, though it pleased GOD to keep him for a number of years in expectation

[6] Scholars today regard Sarai as an older form of the name Sarah, meaning "princess."

of it; from which we should learn to trust in the promises of God written in scripture. It was certainly a wonderful thing when the lives of mankind were so much shortened, that such aged people as Abraham and Sarah should have a child, and it was matter of great joy to them. The word laugh, ver. 6, signifies to rejoice.[7]

§22 Frances Elizabeth King
(1757–1821)

Frances Elizabeth King was born in Lincoln, England, the eighth child of Sir Francis Bernard, baronet, provincial lawyer and governor of New Jersey, and his wife, Amelia.[8] King was educated at home by her older sister, Jane, and her guardian while the rest of the family lived in America. In 1782, against her family's wishes, she married Rev. Richard King. The Kings had four children, of whom two died young.

King's writing career began when she authored papers for her brother's reports for the Society for Bettering the Condition and Improving the Comforts of the Poor (SBCP), an organization which she helped to establish. In 1811, King published her popular book *Female Scripture Characters* to correct the late Rev. Thomas Robinson's omission of women in his book on Scripture characters.[9] King likened her interpretive work to that of the apostle Paul.[10] Her writing on women brought her into the ongoing discussions featured in popular conduct books of the period written by women and men

---

[7] Here Trimmer may have been using one of the multiple editions of Bishop Symon Patrick's *A Commentary upon the First Book of Moses, called Genesis* (London: Printed for R. Chiswell, 1695). The etymological suggestion Trimmer included has not been accepted by scholars.

[8] Source: an unsigned memoir in the ninth edition of her book, *Female Scripture Characters; Exemplifying Female Virtues* (London: F.C. & J. Rivington, 1813, 1822).

[9] Thomas Robinson, *Scripture Characters, or a practical improvement of the principal histories in the Old and New Testament*, 3rd ed. (London, 1793).

[10] King wrote of the "dread" that writing the book "excites in her mind," and worried that after she preached to others, she might be herself a cast-away (1 Cor. 9:27). King asked her readers to join with her in prayer that "the opportunities they have both enjoyed of gaining divine instruction, may never hereafter rise in condemnation against them" (xii). King's citation of the concluding verse of Paul's defense of his apostolic authority (1 Cor. 9:1-27), raises the issue of King's authority for preaching with the pen (*Female Scripture Characters; Exemplifying Female Virtues*, 9th ed. [London: F.C. & J. Rivington, 1822], xii). King's book was put out initially in periodical form. It went through at least twelve editions and became a school textbook.

about the capabilities, religion, virtues, intelligence, work, and character of women.[11]

King used the New Testament depiction of Sarah as a lens for reading the Genesis narrative, taking her cue from 1 Peter 3:6 to look for Sarah's domestic and wifely virtues. She also compared Sarah to the Virgin Mary. She highlighted values associated with her nineteenth-century British context (for example, obedience, polite speech to husbands, truth telling, piety, remaining in one's proper sphere, selflessness, domestic accomplishments, and beauty without vanity). Sarah, like the ideal wife in Proverbs 31, was an example to all wives and mothers.

King's gender and social location as a woman of rank from a titled family informed her interpretation of Sarah. She portrayed Sarah, the mistress of Abraham's household, as a woman of rank and wealth. An inheritance was an important part of King's world, and she saw Ishmael's loss of status as Abraham's heir as the reason he 'mocked' Isaac. She even wrestled with the idea of Sarah as a lady of rank baking cakes for visitors.

As an informed and careful reader of the Bible, King used sophisticated resources such as Josephus and several biblical commentaries undoubtedly borrowed from her husband's theological library. She was sensitive to issues of language and translation. Unlike Trimmer, King did not avoid the moral issues raised by the story but rather faced them, drawing lessons from them based on her nineteenth-century understanding of morality and ethics. Consequently, readers have no difficulty observing King's strong sense of her own agency as a female interpreter, theologian, and preacher.

From Frances Elizabeth King, *Female Scripture Characters; Exemplifying Female Virtues* (London, 1813). (This text from the 9th ed. [London: F.C. & J. Rivington, 1822], 21–33.)

–Second Character, Sarah–

The book of Genesis presents to us many interesting pieces of family history, which come so home to our own domestic circle, that they seem almost divested of the remote antiquity with which they are stamped: they charm us by their resemblance to ourselves, and the family scenes with which we are surrounded; the same workings of the human mind, the same trials and temptations, and the same conquests over evil.

The history of Sarah is one of this description; and presents an example of that mixture of character we daily see around us. She appears to have

---

[11] For example, Hester Chapone, *Letters on the Improvement of the Mind, Addressed to a Young Lady* (London: H. Hughes, 1773). See Julie Straight, "Religious Controversy."

possessed many of those domestic virtues, so appropriate in a woman: she is recorded as a good and obedient wife; and is recommended as an example to wives, by St. Peter, in his first Epistle, 3d chapter, and 6th verse, "Even as Sarah obeyed Abraham, calling him lord; whose daughters ye are, as long as ye do well, and are not afraid with any amazement."

The example proposed in this verse is well worth our study: for married women will find, on reflection, that familiarity and freedom of speech to their husbands, is subversive of that respect and deference which every wife owes to him. "The husband is the head of the wife;" [Eph. 5:23] he is in every respect her lord; and ordained by God to be her master and ruler; and it is essentially necessary towards her obedient and gentle submission to him, that she should cultivate in her heart, and evince by her conduct, respect for his person, and deference for his opinion: and that she should studiously preserve every outward form of politeness and attention to him. If she does well, and performs her duty, she need not "be afraid with any amazement:" [1 Pet. 3:6] she may preserve in her mind due respect for him, perfectly free from any fear or apprehension which is consistent with the most tender affection, and the most perfect confidence.

Sarah is recorded by Josephus,[12] as well as by the sacred historian, to have been a woman of extraordinary beauty and attraction; and this circumstance seems to have offered a temptation to err, in the first action of her life that is mentioned.

The dread of Pharaoh's licentious attachment induced her, in conformity to her husband's wishes, to profess herself his sister, instead of his wife. But this conduct has been censured by most writers on the subject; and, in every respect, it is very reprehensible, as a departure from that integrity of speech, which the laws of God enjoin, and the well-being of society requires.

The object of speech is to convey truth, and, if it is ever used to deceive, it is a wicked abuse of one of the best blessings, and most distinguishing faculties allotted to man. It is a crime which does not merely consist in a wilful falsehood; it extends to all those little prevarications and mental reservations which mislead the judgment of others.

Sarah's profession was not a positive falsehood; for she was, according to the degrees of Jewish consanguinity, actually the sister of Abraham; but she nevertheless meant to deceive; for she concealed the whole truth, in not also professing herself his wife. She had herself a fearful lesson on the sin of this deceit: for it was the very means of nearly plunging her into the misfortune from which she intended to save herself.

---

[12] Josephus, *Antiquities of the Jews,* 1.8.

The history certainly represents Abraham as most culpable in this transaction: Sarah was merely acting in obedience to his commands. But here I would remark, that compliance with the wishes of a husband, or any human being, is not to extend to any act that is a breach of the laws of God.

Let us, from the example now before us, strictly and impartially examine our own hearts: are we not all given, even on a slighter temptation than this, to prevaricate and misrepresent, where our own feelings and interest are concerned? and, though we might shrink from a falsehood deliberately fabricated, are we always careful to represent facts exactly as they are, at all risks of our own character and advantage? Alas! I fear we shall none of us stand the scrutiny. A deceitful word or look, a concealment of the truth, is equally lying in its injury to society, is an equal crime in His sight, to whom "lying lips are an abomination" [Prov. 12:22]. Let us then humbly beseech the Almighty, that "He will set a watch upon our mouths, and keep the door of our lips, and that our hearts may not be inclined to any evil thing" [Ps. 141:3-4]. Let us restrain in ourselves even deceitful thoughts, and let us weigh well our words, and "speak every one truth to his neighbour" [Eph. 4:25]; resting assured, that if we act with integrity and uprightness, the Almighty will "cause all things to work together for good to those who love and fear him" [Rom. 8:28].

We next see Sarah under the influence of very blameable discontent and distrust of the Almighty, because she had no children; and, instead of confiding in the promises given, resorting to human means to effect what was in the hands of God. Impatient to raise an heir to her husband's great possessions, she gave him her hand-maid, Hagar, as a second wife.

Though the commandment against adultery was not then promulgated, and no positive law against polygamy existed, yet the express words of God himself, in his institution of marriage, plainly imply, that a man shall cleave to one wife only [Gen. 2:23-24]. But, in this instance, it appears to have been over-ruled by the Almighty, in order that Abraham might become the father of two nations, the Jewish and the Gentile race. Yet we see in the miserable family dissentions that ensued, a lesson against its practice:—Hagar, finding herself in a situation that would give her consequence in her master's family, was inflated with pride, and behaved impertinently to her mistress; and Sarah, in resentment and anger against her, "dealt hardly by her." In this instance, both were to blame, as in all family dissentions is the case. Hagar was wrong in forgetting her subjection and obligations to her mistress; and Sarah, for not allowing for the force of those temptations to which she had subjected her, by raising her out of her proper sphere; but how exactly do we see in this, the mistress and servant of the present day; and how useful a lesson it presents to each. Hagar in dismay and anger, fled from her mistress; but was arrested in her flight, by an angel sent from God to counsel her to return and submit herself to her mistress;—he also foretold to her what would be the character and habits of life of the child she would bear; that he would be the father of a great nation, but a wild, irreligious, and lawless people; a prophecy, which to this day, is fulfilled in his descendants, who are the wandering, wild, and plundering Arabians. After the birth of Ishmael, Sarah is recorded by Josephus,[13] as being extremely attached to him, treating and distinguishing him as her husband's heir: a good example to wives, in receiving with affection, their husband's offspring, though unconnected with themselves; but we shall, afterwards, see her falling off from this praiseworthy conduct, under the influence of ardent attachment to her own son. We are all like Sarah in this respect, too selfishly fond of what belongs to ourselves, to pay proper attention and regard to others.

When Sarah was well stricken in years, and all hope was relinquished of her having a child, the Almighty vouchsafed her a renewal of his promise, through the mouth of a divine messenger, expressly sent, who condescended to become their guest. Instead of receiving the promise with faith and gratitude, like the Virgin Mary, to whom a more improbable event was prophesied, Sarah laughed in contempt and disbelief, and added to her sin a flat denial of this act of folly.

Here too, our reflections are arrested by the important question to ourselves, whether our faith is always humbly and implicitly given to every promise vouchsafed us by the Almighty, through his Divine Messenger in the Holy Scriptures? Are we not apt to doubt, and even treat with contempt, what, to our narrow and dark understandings, appears incomprehensible? not considering that faith is, in its nature, an implicit belief of what we cannot understand, humbly relying that what God hath said, he will most assuredly do.

We are here also offered another lesson, on that pride of heart and fear of worldly censure, which betrays us into the sin of self-justification, by denying or palliating our faults and errors, though the humble acknowledgment of them, both to God and man, is the only means, on our parts, that can ever render our repentance acceptable.

In due time this extraordinary promise was fulfilled; Sarah, in her ninetieth year, gave birth to her son Isaac; great were the rejoicings and gratitude of the happy parents on this event: Sarah performed the duty of a tender mother and nurse to her child; "and Abraham made a great feast the same day that Isaac was weaned." But Sarah's trial was now to commence, in the confusion of families she had been the means of introducing into her husband's house, through her impatience and want of confidence in God's promises. As defective human beings, they made little effort to subdue those feelings of envy

---

[13] Josephus, *Antiquities of the Jews,* 1.12.

and ill-will, which the jarring of interests give rise to—"Sarah saw the son of Hagar the Egyptian, which she had borne unto Abraham, mocking." Ishmael probably felt that too natural sensation of the human heart, bitter regret for the loss of his expected large property, and envious ill-will against the child that had superseded him in it. Whatever meaning is conveyed to us, under the term of Ishmael *mocking*, it gave grievous offence to Sarah; and instead of trying to conciliate the disappointed youth, and his blameless mother, and submitting herself to the feelings and wishes of their father, to whom, as his own children, they were both dear, she positively demanded the dismission of the child and his mother from their father's family; urging, that they were not worthy to share the same house, and partake the same inheritance with her and her son.

Here is a lesson to step-mothers, to resist that pride, arrogance, and self-ishness, which lead them to over-rate the claims of their own offspring, and to shut out others from a participation of those family blessings and comforts to which the children of the same father are entitled.

Abraham bitterly lamented, and at first resisted this act of violence and resentment in Sarah; but with the piety and confidence in God, which uniformly marked his conduct, he addressed himself, in this strait, to the Almighty, who graciously announced to him his will, that Ishmael should be separated from Isaac; for though he means to make a great nation of each, they were to be so distantly situated, that the family of Ishmael should never interfere with that of Isaac, who was the child of promise, and in "whose seed all the families of the earth were to be blessed."

The Almighty saw fit to over-rule the misconduct of Sarah, to his own wise purposes; but it, nevertheless, was misconduct; and, viewed without reference to the end which was to be accomplished, we must know that every act of injustice and ill-will is offensive to God.

Ishmael settled in Arabia, which country he peopled with those whose descendants are the present race of wild and lawless Arabs; and Isaac continued with his father in the land of Canaan.

Nothing is recorded of Sarah, after these events, but that she lived to a good old age, and died greatly lamented by her husband and son: from whence, we may justly conclude, her general character was that of a good wife and affectionate mother. The little that is said of Sarah, uniformly represents her in a retired and domestic situation; performing the appropriate duties of her sex; and presenting an example to women of rank and fortune, in attention to family cares; for though she was the most distinguished female of her time, from the wealth and splendid situation of her husband, she is represented as making the cakes with which she entertained the two angels. Doubtless, the ladies of rank and fortune of the present day, will shrink from the example here offered, and consider it as useless and singular; but the example is not singular; for in primitive times, all women considered their household business as their principal employment; and the daughters of monarchs thought it not beneath them to perform the menial offices of domestic life. In Homer's Iliad, Nausicaa, the daughter of Alcinous, king of Phaeacia, is represented as washing the robes of the state, while

> The queen, her hours bestow'd,
> In curious works; the whirling spindle glow'd
> With crimson threads; while busy damsels call
> The snowy fleece, or twist the purpled wool.[14]

Such were the manners of those times, and such have been the manners of later periods; for we have many memorials of the industry of our own queens, within a century or two back; and even the memories of many elderly persons, will recal [sic] far better housewives in culinary and family concerns, than exist in the present day.

Such may be the effects of modern refinement; but it seems doubtful, whether it is any improvement in the female character. It does not appear necessary, that a woman of rank and fortune should be a domestic drudge, or that she should perform any menial offices in her family; but she should certainly be sufficiently mistress of all household concerns, to know that they are rightly performed, and to save herself and her servants from that useless waste, idleness, and extravagance, which ruin the morals of domestics, and dissipate the largest properties.

In another instance, Sarah's character offers a useful example to her sex; for it appears that she possessed eminent beauty, without vanity; and winning attractions, without the desire of admiration.

It is not by the voice of fame, or the applause of the world, that a woman's virtues are to be estimated: from such testimonies, a female of a modest and gentle character shrinks with alarm.

A Woman's Noblest Station is Retreat

Pope[15]

---

[14] Homer, *Iliad*, book 6.

[15] King may be thinking of the poem "Epistle 11: To a Lady (Of the Characters of Women)" by Alexander Pope (1688–1744). But this line is found in George Lyttelton's poem (1733) "Advice to a Lady." Compare lines 60–64:

> Seek to be good, but aim not to be great:
> A woman's noblest station is retreat;
> Her fairest virtues fly from public sight,
> Domestic worth, that shuns too strong a light.

Her virtues can only be known by the near and dear relatives that form the domestic circle. "If she openeth her mouth with wisdom, and in her tongue is the law of kindness. If she looketh well to the ways of her household, and eateth not the bread of idleness. If her children rise up and call her blessed; her husband also, and he praiseth her" [Prov. 31:26-28]. If to all these she add the "fear of God" [Prov 31:30], such a "woman's price will be far above rubies; she will be above the deceitfulness of worldly favour; above the vanity excited by beauty. The heart of her husband will safely trust in her" [Prov. 31:10-11]; and she will, like Sarah, live beloved and die lamented.

§23 Sarah Ewing Hall
(1761–1830)

Sarah Ewing Hall, born and raised in Philadelphia, had little formal education, but her father, the Reverend John Ewing, was a scholar. He was Provost of the University of Pennsylvania and pastor of First Presbyterian Church in Philadelphia. Sarah Hall thus had access to the academic world through her father and the guests who frequented the Ewing home. Hall read broadly and developed a taste for literature and history as well as astronomy. By listening to her brothers' Greek and Latin lessons, as well, she became familiar with the subject matter of classical works and frequently stayed up late at night to read and study.

After her marriage to John Hall, the son of a Maryland planter, Sarah Hall moved to Maryland. Later she returned to Philadelphia where she became acquainted with the city's literary figures. Hall contributed letters to the editor and poetry to *Port Folio*, a literary journal founded in 1800. *Conversations on the Bible* was her only major work. It paraphrases and comments on the Old Testament using the form of a conversation between a mother and her three children (Catherine, Fanny, and Charles). Hall's book went through three American and one British edition.[16]

The following excerpt from Hall's *Conversations* examines the second wife-sister story in Genesis 20. Unlike Trimmer, who did not recommend meditation on this passage, Hall gave the details without justifying Abraham's behaviour. Hall's "Mother" astutely said: "It is not for me to soften or disguise the characters I present to you. The scriptures have not done it." Like King,

---

[16] The first edition was published in 1818, and a second enlarged edition in 1821. The third edition was published in England without Hall's knowledge. The fourth edition was updated in style and content.

Hall emphasized the importance of truth telling. Both women countered the views of those who thought women should avoid religious and theological controversy and, instead encouraged women (and children in Hall's case) to wrestle with difficult issues, to study and to understand the scriptures.[17]

> From Sarah Hall, *Conversations on the Bible* (Philadelphia: Harrison Hall, 1818), 33–34. [Text from 4th ed., 1827].

MOTHER. Journeying still farther south, Abraham came into Philistia on the border of the Mediterranean, and halted near Gerar, the residence of the king. Again he was tempted to represent the fair Sarah as his sister, and a second time she was taken to the palace; but Abimilech, yet unconscious of the wrong he had done, was warned in a dream—"Thou art but a dead man for the woman whom thou hast taken—for she is a man's wife," was the appalling sentence. With unfeigned horror the terrified prince received it, and appealed to Omniscience—"In the innocency of my heart I have done this. Said he not unto me, she is my sister? And she—even she herself said, he is my brother. Lord, wilt thou also slay a righteous nation?" "Restore the man his wife," said his just Judge, "for he is a prophet and shall pray for thee, and thou shalt live. But if thou restore her not, thou shalt die, thou and all thy house." In the morning early, therefore, Abimilech collected his servants and related his dream, and sent for the strangers and reprehended them both; inquiring wherein he had offended, that they should lead him into such imminent danger; or what evil disposition they had seen in him to justify their suspicion of his integrity? "Because I thought," replied the timid husband, "surely, the fear of God is not in this place, and they will slay me for my wife's sake, and yet indeed she is my sister, the daughter of my father, but not the daughter of my mother."

CATHERINE. I hope Abraham was not really married to his sister!

MOTHER. Not his sister as we understand that appellation, but as it is commonly used in scripture, where relatives of the same stock are called brethren, or sisters, though not children of the same father and mother. Taking advantage of this custom, Abraham imagined he might with impunity defend himself by a mental reservation.

CATHERINE. But in his case it was a duty to tell the whole truth, because his concealment of a part not only exposed him to the danger of losing his wife, but entangled the king, who it appears was an upright man.

MOTHER. The vicious state of public morals had not permitted Abraham to hope that he should again find such disinterested virtue, united with power,

---

[17] For examples of those advocating avoiding controversy, see Straight, "Religious Controversy."

as he had seen in Pharaoh. But the king of Gerar was equally just, and yet more liberal: for together with Sarah, he sent large presents to Abraham, of cattle and servants and silver; and nobly offered him the choice of his whole domain to settle wheresoever he pleased. Thus by his piety and munificence he obtained the prayers of Abraham, and the blessing of heaven.

You may perhaps think, my children, that I speak with lenity of the errors of this distinguished patriarch in the two instances I have related. It is not for me to soften or disguise the characters I present to you. The scriptures have not done it. They show us that the best of men were fallible. I have told you the facts, and the reasoning by which Abraham excused himself—but he was not innocent. No deviation from the truth can be justified. The little artifices by which we think to advance our own interests, often recoil upon ourselves. What must have been the remorse of Abraham when he found himself surpassed in uprightness by two heathen kings!

The following year the promise of a son to Abraham and Sarah, was verified in the birth of Isaac; the father was in the hundredth year of his age, and his wife in her ninetieth, at this period.

§24 Grace Aguilar
(1816–1847)

Grace Aguilar, born in Hackney, Middlesex, a suburb of London, England, was the eldest of the three children of Emanuel and Sarah Aguilar. Emanuel Aguilar was the leader of a Spanish and Portuguese Jewish congregation in London. Grace Aguilar's gifts as a writer showed themselves at an early age in the family home where she received her education.

In 1828, due to Emanuel Aguilar's poor health, the family moved to Devon. There Grace Aguilar associated with Christians and attended services at the Methodist church. She wrote that worshipping with those of another faith broadened her. When her family returned to London, she ran a school for Jewish boys with her mother and continued her writing career. She died at the age of thirty-one in Germany. The Jewish communities in Britain and America deeply mourned the loss of this creative and brilliant female writer, theologian, and apologist. Aguilar's mother published many of her writings after her death.

Many of Aguilar's published works were written in support of Judaism and religious tolerance at a time when British Jews were under great pressure to convert to Christianity. In 1845, Aguilar published *The Women of Israel,* a book of essays on Old Testament heroines. She intended her book to refute the writings of women such as Sarah Ellis who argued in her book *The Women of England*,[18] that "to Christianity alone they [women] owe their present station in the world: their influence, their equality with man, their spiritual provision in this life, and hopes of immortality in the next."[19] Aguilar wrote *The Women of Israel* to encourage young Jewish women to be proud of their heritage and see the benefits of their own religion for women. Aguilar also intended her book to be "as instructive as interesting, as full of warning as example, and tending to lead our female youth to the sacred volume, not only as their guide to duty, their support in toil, their comfort in affliction, but as a true and perfect mirror of themselves."[20] Aguilar's *The Women of Israel* joined the many books of the mid-nineteenth century that addressed issues related to "woman's capabilities, influences and mission," but her experiences as a devout Jewish woman familiar with Christian worship and tradition, together with her gifts as a writer, set her book apart from many others. *The Women of Israel* became a popular gift book for Jews and Christians alike.

Aguilar's aim of making young Jewish women proud of their foremothers pushed her to portray the mothers of Israel positively. In her assessment of Sarah's behaviour toward Hagar after Hagar became pregnant, Aguilar noted that it was easy on a superficial reading of the text to blame Sarah for being unduly harsh. She herself admitted that "until lately we too thought Sarai harsh and unjust, and rather turned from than admired her character: but we have seen the injustice of this decision, and, therefore, without the smallest remaining prejudice, retract it all together." Without this change of mind, Aguilar could not have written as positively about Sarah as she did.

Aguilar's project made her very aware of the gaps and silences in the stories about women of Israel. She reasoned that "the record of Moses is too important to descend to the thoughts and feelings of woman," and so she freely imagined what Sarah's feelings were in many situations. Aguilar's assumptions about women's duties, influence, and nature shaped her midrashic embellishments of the story. Like King, Aguilar commended Sarah for her domestic accomplishments.

Aguilar was a careful and competent reader of Scripture. She noticed and raised questions about many details in the text. Sometimes Aguilar answered these questions in the embellishments she added to the text. For example, she noted Abimelech's gift of a veil in Genesis 20 and suggested that Sarah's beauty had been supernaturally restored. Aguilar's portrait of Sarah in *The*

[18] Sarah Stickney (Ellis), *The Women of England, Their Social Duties, and Domestic Habits*, 2nd ed. (London, 1839).

[19] Grace Aguilar, *The Women of Israel*, new ed. (New York: Appleton, 1901), 2.

[20] Aguilar, *The Women of Israel*, 1.

Women of Israel consists of thirty-one pages of dense prose. The edited version below excludes the passages which do not feature Sarah.

From Grace Aguilar, *The Women of Israel New Ed.* (New York: Appleton, 1901), 35–66. (Orig. publ. London, 1845).

–Sarah–

[Aguilar introduces her readers to Sarah as "the beloved partner of Abraham," who "ought to be a subject of reverence and love to her female descendants." She raises the issue of Sarah's relationship to Abraham—was she his niece or half-sister as well as his wife? Aguilar argues that she was his half sister, but leaves the final decision to "more curious speculators."]

The first notice we have of Sarai is her accompanying her husband and Lot from the home of her kindred to a strange country, among all strange people, in simple obedience to the word of God. . . .

To Sarai the trial [of leaving home] must have been more severe than to her husband. She was to go forth with him indeed; but it is woman's peculiar nature to cling to home, home ties, and home affections—to shrink from encountering a strange world, teeming with unknown trials and dangers. . . .

One cause for the love of home ties and associations, in the heart of a right-feeling woman, originates in the belief that there she can do so much more good than elsewhere—that, unfitted by the weakness and infirmities of her frame from active toil, and the pursuit of goodly service, as falls to the lot of man, she can yet benefit her friends, children, and domestics, in the hallowed circle of home; and better manifest the blessings of the Lord and the love she bears Him, there than among strangers. And this was especially the case with Sarai. . . . All was mental darkness in the world around her, except her husband and those few whom he had been enabled to teach a partial knowledge of his God. They stood alone in their peculiar faith; and how often, in such a case, do doubts and fears enter the breast of woman! Yet it was enough that her husband prepared without question or hesitation to obey his God—to leave his aged father, his kindred, and his friends; and, with simple and loving faith, she went with him where the Lord should lead. Well is it for us when we can do so likewise; when, in some of those bitterest trials that woman's heart can know, the change of home or land, be it with our parents, or husband, or more fearful still, alone, we can yet so stay upon our God that we can realize His presence, His loving mercy directing our weary way, and resting with us still. His direct communing by voice or sign, or through angelic messengers, is indeed no longer ours; but those that seek to love and serve Him may yet hear His still small voice breathing in the solemn whisper of their own hearts, and through the individual promises of His Word.

Accompanied by Lot and their household—expressed in the term "the souls they had gotten in Charran," who were probably those whom they had instructed in the true faith—and carrying with them the substance they possessed, Abram and Sarai "went forth into the land of Canaan," which was inhabited by a fierce people, and gave little hope of ever being possessed by the patriarch and his family, for by their constant journeyings it would seem as if they could not even obtain sufficient land to fix their home. Yet, there again the Lord appeared to the patriarch and renewed His promise—thus proving His tender compassion for the human weakness of His creatures, and encouraging their faith, when, without such encouragement, He knew it must have failed. To add to their numerous human discomforts and trials, a famine broke out in the land, so severe and grievous that Abram sought the land of Egypt; and there, rendered fearful by the exceeding beauty of his wife, and the supposed barbarity of the land, he bade Sarai call herself his sister, not his wife. . . .

This part of Sarai's history gives us information generally very interesting to young female readers—that she was very beautiful. We are wont to imagine that the charms of sixty-five could not be very remarkable; but reckoning according to the age to which mortals then lived, she was not older than a woman of thirty or five-and-thirty would be now, consequently in her prime; endowed, as her history gives us authority to suppose, with a quiet, retiring dignity, which greatly enhanced her beauty, and rendered it yet more interesting than that of girlhood.

Protected from this danger, his substance greatly increased by Pharaoh's gifts, Abram, his wife, and household, retraced their steps to where "his tent had been at first, between Bethel and Hai."[21] The altar which he had originally erected was still there, and again he and his family "called on the name of the Lord." The command of Pharaoh—"Go thy way"—was most probably regarded and acted on by the patriarch as a warning, that his safest and most hallowed home was in the land to which the Lord had originally guided him.

In the events which follow—the separation of Abram and Lot—the battle of the kings—the imprisonment and rescue of Lot—the blessing of Melchisedek—Holy Writ makes no mention of Sarai. She was performing those duties of an affectionate wife and gentle mistress of her husband's immense establishment, which are nothing to write about, but which make up the sum of woman's life, create her dearest and purest sources of happiness, and bring her acceptably before God. . . .

---

[21] "Ai" is the normal spelling of this place name.

The beautiful confidence and true affection subsisting between Abram and Sarai, marks unanswerably their *equality*; that his wife was to Abram friend as well as partner; and yet, that Sarai knew perfectly her own station, and never attempted to push herself forward in unseemly counsel, or use the influence which she so largely possessed for any weak or sinful purpose. Some, however, would have found it difficult to preserve their humility and meekness, situated as was Sarai. A coarser and narrower mind would have prided herself on the promises made her husband, imagining there must be some superlative merit, either in herself or Abram, to be so singled out by the Eternal. There is no pride so dangerous and subtle as spiritual pride, no sin more likely to gain dominion in the early stages of religion—none so disguised, and so difficult to be discovered and rooted out. But in Sarai there was none of this; not a particle of pride, even at a time when, of all others, she might have been *almost* justified in feeling it. She was, indeed, blessed in a husband whose exalted, yet domestic and affectionate character must ever have strengthened, guided, and cherished hers; but it is not always the most blessed and distinguished woman who attends the most faithfully to her domestic duties, and preserves unharmed and untainted that meekness and integrity which is her greatest charm.

Abram's warlike expedition was the only one in which his wife did not accompany him. With what joy she must have welcomed her warrior lord! How gratefully must her loving heart have delighted to ponder on his magnanimity, in going instantly to the rescue of his weak and little grateful nephew—on his courage—his success; and yet more on his noble refusal of all gifts from the king of Sodom, lest the glory should be taken from the Lord, and any mortal should say, "I have made Abram rich.". . . It was indeed enough for a woman to glory in; and, though nothing is said, for the record of Moses is too important to descend to the thoughts and feelings of woman, we may well imagine the grateful and rejoicing feelings of Sarai, as she welcomed her husband home—forgetting all the pangs of parting and loneliness of separation, in the triumph and delight of such a meeting. . . .

Great must have been Sarai's joy when this gracious promise was made known to her. If to Abram being childless was a source of deep regret, it must have been still more so to her. Loving and domestic, as her whole history proves she was, how often may she have yearned to list the welcome cry of infancy; to feel one being look up to her for protection and love, and call her by that sweet name—Mother. But this joyful anticipation could only have been of short duration. Sarai, as is woman's nature, in all probability imagined the *fulfilment* would immediately follow the *promise*. The most difficult of all our spiritual attainments is to *wait* for the Lord: to believe still, through long months, perhaps years, of anticipation and disappointment, that as He has said it, so it *will be*, so it *must be*, though our finite wisdom cannot pronounce the *when*. Did the Eternal fulfil His gracious promises on the instant, where would be the trial of our faith, and of our confidence and constancy in prayer?

Finding still there was no appearance of her becoming a mother, we are led to suppose, by the events which follow, that all Sarai's joyous anticipations turned into gloomy fears, not merely from the belief that she herself would not be blessed with a child, but that Abram might, as was and is the custom of Eastern nations, take another wife; an idea excited, perhaps, by the recollection that *her* name had not been mentioned as the destined mother of the promised seed, but precisely the most painful which could find entrance in a heart affectionate and faithful as her own. To prevent this misfortune, and yet to further (as she supposed) the will of the Eternal, Sarai had recourse to human means.

All women in her position, and influenced as she was by the manners and customs of the East, would have both felt and acted as she did, but few, we think would have waited so long. It was ten years after Abram had left Egypt to fix his residence in Canaan, before Hagar became his wife. . . .

The first human evidence that Sarai's scheme would be productive of vexation and sorrow, as well as of joy, was her disappointment with regard to Hagar's continued humility and submission. Forgetful that it was to her mistress, humanly speaking, she owed the privileges now hers, the Egyptian so far forgot herself, as to feel and make manifest that Sarai "was despised in her eyes." Alas, how mournfully does that brief sentence breathe of woman's fallen nature! How apt are we to exalt ourselves for imaginary superiority—to look down on those who have served us, when God has bestowed on us privileges of which they are deprived. We forget, often through thoughtlessness, that those very things of which we are so proud, come not from ourselves, but from Him who might equally have vouchsafed them to others. We may not indeed have the same incitement to pride and presumption as Hagar, but have we *never* despised others for the want of those accomplishments, those advantages, that beauty, and other gifts from God, which we ourselves may possess? . . .

And this was the case with Hagar. A superficial reading of the Bible often causes Sarai to be most unjustly blamed for undue harshness. We think only of Hagar's wanderings in the wilderness, and pity her as cruelly treated, and suppose, that as the Most High relieved her through His angel, she had never been in any way to blame. Now, though to sympathize with the sorrowing and afflicted be one of our purest and best feelings, it must not so blind us as to prevent our doing justice to the inflictor of that affliction. We candidly avow, that until lately we too thought Sarai harsh and unjust, and rather turned from than admired her character: but we have seen the injustice of this decision, and, therefore, without the smallest remaining prejudice, retract it altogether: retract it, simply because the words of the angel are quite sufficient proof that Hagar had been *wrong*, and Sarai's chastisement just, or he would not have commanded her, as Sarai's *bondwoman*, to return and submit herself to her mistress's power, without any reservation whatever.

It must indeed have been a bitterly painful disappointment to Sarai, that instead of receiving increased gratitude and affection from one whom she had so raised and cherished, she was despised with an insolence that, unless checked, might bring discord and misery in a household which had before been so blessed with peace and love. Sarai's was not a character to submit tamely to ingratitude. There was neither coldness nor indifference about her. In no part of the Bible, either in character or precept, do we perceive the necessity or the merit of that species of cold indifference, which is by some well-meaning religious persons supposed to be the self-control and pious forgiveness of injuries most acceptable to God. The Patriarchal and Jewish history alike prove, that natural feelings were not to be trampled upon. The Hebrew code was formed by a God of love for the nature of man, not angels—formed so as to be *obeyed*, not to be laid aside as impracticable. The passions and feelings of the East were very different to those of the calmer and colder North; and nowhere in Holy Writ are we told that those feelings and emotions must be annihilated. *Subdued* and *guided* indeed, as must be the consequence of a true and strict adherence to the law of God, and impartial study of His Word; but in the sight of a God of love, indifference can never be, and never was, religion.

Yet even this, an affair of feeling entirely between herself and Hagar, could not urge Sarai to any line of conduct unauthorized by her husband. Naturally indignant, she complained to him, perhaps, too, with some secret fear that Hagar, favored so much above herself by the hope of her giving him a son, might be unduly justified and protected. But it was not so. Abram's answer at once convinced her that Hagar had not taken her place; nay, that though Abram could not do otherwise than feel tenderness and kindness toward her, he at once recognized Sarai's supremacy, both as his wife and Hagar's mistress, and bade her "do with her what seemeth good to thee." We have so many proofs of Abram's just, affectionate, and forgiving character, that we may fully believe he would never have said this, if he had not been convinced that it was no unjust accusation on the part of Sarai. He knew, too, that she was not likely to inflict more punishment than was deserved, particularly on a favorite slave; and, therefore, it was with his full consent "Sarai afflicted her, and she fled from her presence."

Whatever the nature of this affliction, it could not have been very severe—neither pain nor restraint—for Hagar had the power to fly. Reproof to an irritable and disdainful mind is often felt as intolerable, and given too, as it no doubt was, with severity, and at a time when Hagar felt exalted and superior to all around her, even to her mistress, her proud spirit urged flight instead of submission, and not till addressed by the voice of the angel did those rebellious feelings subside.

There was no mistaking the angelic voice, and his first words destroyed the proud dreams which she had indulged. "Hagar, Sarai's bondwoman!" he said, and the term told her in the sight of God she was still the same, "whence camest thou, and whither art thou going?" It was not because he knew not that he thus spoke. The messengers of the Lord need no enlightenment on the affairs of men, but their questions are adapted to the nature of men, to awaken them to consciousness, to still the tumult of human passion, and by clear and simple questioning compel a clear and true reply. Had his command to return been given without preparation, Hagar's obedience would have been the effect of fear, not conviction. . . . thus meekly acknowledging that Sarai was still her mistress, and that her derision had indeed been wrong. Reproof, therefore, followed not; but the angel bade her, "Return to thy mistress, and submit thyself to her power." And, perceiving that her repentance was sincere, and would lead to obedience, he continued graciously to promise that her seed should be multiplied, so that it should not be numbered for multitude; that her son should bear a name which would ever remind her that God had heard her affliction, with other promises concerning that son, *yet none* which might lead her to the deceitful belief that he would be Abram's promised seed. . . .

In due course of time the promise was fulfilled, and Hagar, to the great joy of Abram, had a son, whom Abram called Ishmael, thus proving that Hagar must have imparted the visit of the angel, and his command as to the name of her son. . . .

It may be that Sarai's correction of Hagar was unduly harsh, although we have no warrant in Scripture for so believing; but it is evident, as there is no further mention of contention and disagreement between them, that she received her submission with gentleness, and restored her to favor. . . .

For thirteen years Abram and Sarai must have looked upon Ishmael as the promised seed; for, though not actually so said, there was neither spiritual sign nor human hope of the patriarch having any other child. At the end of that period, however, the Most High again appeared unto Abram, proclaiming Himself as the ALMIGHTY—a fit introduction to the event He was about to foretell; and bidding His favored servant, "Walk before Me, and be thou perfect," perfect in trust, in faith, without any regard to human probabilities, for, as Almighty God, all things were possible with Him. The name of the patriarch was then changed, as a sign of the many nations over whom he was appointed father—the land again promised him—and the covenant appointed which was to mark his descendants as the chosen of the Lord, the everlasting inheritors of Canaan; and bear witness, to untold-of ages, of the truth of the Lord's word, and the election of His people. This proclaimed and commanded the Eternal commenced His information of the miracle He was about to perform, by desiring Abraham to call his wife no longer Sarai שָׂרָי but Sarah שָׂרָה a change which our ancient fathers suppose to mean the same as from Abram to Abraham. "Sarai, signifying a lady or princess in a restricted sense, imported that she was a lady, or princess, to Abram only; whereas the latter name signifies princess or lady absolutely, indicating that she would thus be acknowledged by many, even as Abraham was to become the father of many nations."* A meaning perfectly reconcilable with the verse which follows: "And I will bless her, and give thee a son also of her: yea, I will bless her, so that she shall be a *mother of nations; kings of people* shall be of her." She was, therefore, no longer a princess over Abraham's household, but a princess in royal rank, from whom *kings* should descend. Joy must have been the first emotion of Abraham's heart at this miraculous announcement, mingled with a feeling of wonder and astonishment how such a thing could be; but then in his peculiarly affectionate heart, came the thought of his first-born Ishmael, and with earnestness he prayed, "Oh! that Ishmael might live before thee!" And though the Eternal could not grant this prayer, for the seed of Abraham, from whom His chosen people would spring, must be of pure and unmixed birth, He yet, with compassionating tenderness, soothed the father's anxious love, by the gracious promise that, though Sarah's child must be the seed with whom His covenant should be established, yet Ishmael also should be blessed and multiplied exceedingly, and become, even as Isaac, the father of a great nation. "And for Ishmael I have also heard thee." . . .

The acceptance of the covenant throughout Abraham's household, and the change in her own name, must, of course, have been imparted by Abraham to his wife, with the addition of the startling promise, that she too, even at her advanced age, should bear a son. Yet by her behavior, when the promise was repeated in the following chapter, it would appear that, though informed of it, she had dismissed it from her mind as being a thing impossible. Accustomed to regard Ishmael as the only seed of Abraham—to suppose her scheme had been blessed, more particularly as she had never been named before as the mother of the chosen seed—the hope of being so had long since entirely faded; and, not having attained the simple questionless faith of her husband, she, in all probability, dismissed the thought, as recalling too painfully those ardent hopes and wishes, which she had with such difficulty previously subdued. Engaged, as was her wont, in her domestic duties, she was one day interrupted by the hasty entrance of her husband, requiring her "quickly to prepare three measures of fine meal, knead it, and make it into cakes." Patriarchal hospitality was never satisfied by committing to hirelings only the fit preparations for a hearty welcome. We see either Sarah herself making the desired cakes, or closely superintending her domestics in doing so; and the patriarch hastening, in the warmth of his hospitality, himself to fetch a calf from the herd, to give it to a young man to dress it, though he had abundance of servants around him to save him the exertion. Yet both Abraham and Sarah were of the nobility of the Eternal's creating. He had raised them above their fellows, and bestowed on them the patent of an aristocracy, with which not one of the nations could vie, for it came from God Himself. He had changed their names to signify their royal claims—to make them regarded in future ages as noble ancestors of a long line of prophets, kings, princes, and nobles; and there was a refinement, a nobleness, a magnanimity of character in both the patriarch and his wife, which, breathing through their very simplicity, betrayed their native aristocracy, and marked them of that princely race which has its origin in the favor and election of the King of kings. The primitive simplicity of our first fathers generally impresses the mind with the mistaken idea of their being simply farmers or agriculturists, both of which they certainly were, but not these alone, as supposed in the present acceptation of the term. They were princes and nobles, not only in their mental superiority but in their immense possessions—in their large and well-ordered households, in the power they possessed both in their own establishments and in the adjoining lands, and in the respect and submission ever paid them by the nations with whom they might have held intercourse. Abraham was never addressed save as "My Lord," either by his own domestics or other nations; thus acknowledged as superior, and of noble if not royal rank, by those who could scarcely be supposed to understand why he was so, save by the outward signs of landed possession and large establishment. Those who think so much of noble descent and princely connection, would do well to remember this—that impoverished, scattered, chastised, for a "little moment," as we are—yet, that if we are children and descendants of Abraham—ISRAELITES not only in seeming but in heart—we are descended from the aristocracy of the Lord—from a higher and nobler race than even Gentile kings may boast; a privilege and glory of which no circumstance, no affliction, no persecution can deprive us—ours, through all and every event of life, unless we cast it from us by the dark deed of forsaking, for ambition, or gold, or power, the banner of our blessed faith—the religion of our God. . . .

Sarah joined not her husband or his guests. The modest and dignified customs of the East prevented all intrusion, or even the wish to intrude. Unless particularly asked for, the place of the Eastern and Jewish wife was in the retirement of home; not from any inferiority of rank, or servitude of station, but simply because their inclination so prompted. The strangers might have business with Abraham, which, if needed, he would impart to her; there was no occasion for her to come forward. But, while seated in the inner tent, engaged in her usual avocations, she heard her own name, "Where is Sarah, thy wife?" and her husband's reply, "She is in the tent," followed by words that must indeed have sounded strange and improbable, "Sarah, thy wife, shall bear a son"; yet, improbable as they might have seemed, there is no excuse for the laugh of incredulity with which they were received. Already prepared by the previous promise of the Lord, the words should at once have revealed the heavenly nature of those who spake, and been heard with faith and thankfulness; but Sarah thought only of the human impossibility. Strange as it is, that such unbelief should be found in the beloved partner of Abraham, yet her laugh proves that even she was not exempt from the natural feelings of mortality— the looking to human means and human possibilities alone; forgetting that with God all things are possible [Matt. 19:26]. Yet, to us, the whole of this incident is consoling. It proves that even Sarah was not utterly free from human infirmities; and yet that the Eternal, through His angel, deigned graciously to reprove, not to chastise. It proves that God has compassion on the nature of His erring children; for He knows their weakness. Man would have been wroth with the laugh of scorn, and withdrawn his intended favor; but "the LORD said unto Abraham, Wherefore did Sarah laugh, saying, Shall I, who am old, indeed bear a child? Is anything too mighty for the Lord? At the time appointed I will return unto thee, and Sarah shall indeed have a son." The gracious mildness of the rebuke—the blessed repetition of the promise—must, to one so affectionate as Sarah, have caused the bitterest reproach; but, weakly listening to fear instead of repentance, she denied her fault, seeking thus mistakenly to extenuate it. But He said, "Nay, but thou didst laugh," proving that her innermost thoughts were known; and, silenced at once, left to the solitude of her own tent, for Abraham accompanied his guests on the road to Sodom, we know quite enough of Sarah's character to rest satisfied that repentance and self-abasement for unbelief, mingled with, and hallowed the burst of rejoicing thankfulness with which she must have looked forward to an event so full of bliss to her individually, and so blessed a revelation of the Lord's deep love for Abraham and herself. Nearly twenty years had passed since the first promise of an heir in his own child had been given.

    . . . Sarah had imagined she was too old to enjoy the felicity of becoming a mother—too old in any way to excite admiration, save to the beloved husband of her youth; and, ignorant that her beauty had been supernaturally renewed, neglected to assume the veil, which was worn by all Eastern women dwelling in towns. This explains Abimelech's present of a "covering for the eyes," and the words, "thus she was reproved," or warned, that her beauty subjected her to as much danger as had been the case in her youth.

Miraculously protected by the Eternal, and publicly vindicated from all dishonor by the King of Gerar, Sarah and her husband continued to dwell in Abimelech's dominions, some few miles to the south of Gerar; a place afterward called Beer-Sheba, or Well of the Oath, from the covenant of peace there made between the patriarch and the king. Here it was that at the appointed time "God visited Sarah as He had said"; and the promised seed—the child of rejoicing—Isaac was born. What must have been the emotions of Sarah on beholding him? Not alone the bliss of a mother; but that in him the infant claimer of a love and joy which she had never so felt before, she beheld a visible and palpable manifestation of the wonderful power and unchanging love of the Most High God. Devoted, as Sarah had been to the service and love of the Lord, how inexpressibly must those emotions have been heightened as she gazed upon her babe, and held him to her bosom as her own, her granted child! To those who really love the Lord, joy is as dear, as bright, as close a link between the heart and its God, as grief is to more fallen natures. We find the hymn of rejoicing, the song of thanksgiving, always the vehicle in which the favored servants of the Lord poured forth their grateful adoration, thus proving that the thought of the beneficent Giver ever hallowed and sanctified the gift; and therefore we believe with our ancient fathers, that though *not translated metrically*, Sarah expressed her joy in a short hymn of thanksgiving. The peculiar idiom of the Hebrew text confirms this supposition,† and we adopt it as most natural to the occasion. Her age had had no power, even before she became a mother, to dull her feelings, and her song of thanksgiving well expresses every emotion natural, not alone to the occasion, but to her peculiar situation. As a young mother, full of life, of sentiment, of affection, she felt toward her babe—giving him his natural food from her own bosom—tending his infant years—guiding him from boyhood to youth—from youth to manhood, and lavishing on him the full tide of love which had been pent up so long. The very character of Isaac, as is afterward displayed—meek, yielding, affectionate almost as a woman's—disinclined to enterprise—satisfied with his heritage—all prove the influence which his mother had possessed, and that his disposition was more the work of her hand than of his father's.

"The child grew and was weaned," Holy Writ proceeds to inform us; "and Abraham made a great feast the day Isaac was weaned"—a feast of rejoicing that the Eternal had mercifully preserved him through the first epoch of his young existence. He was now three years old, if not more—for the women of the East, even now, do not wean their children till that age. The feast, however, which commenced in joy, was, for the patriarch, dashed with sorrow ere it closed. Educated with the full idea that he was his father's heir—though the words of the angel before his birth gave no warrant for the supposition—to Ishmael and his mother, the birth of Isaac must have been a grievous disappointment. And we find the son committing the same fault as his mother previously had done—deriding, speaking disrespectfully of Sarah and her child. The youth of Ishmael, and Sarah's request that the bondwoman might also be expelled, would lead to the supposition that it was Hagar who had instigated the affront. The age of Sarah and the decidedly superhuman birth of Isaac, must, to all but the patriarch's own household, have naturally given rise to many strange and perhaps calumniating reports. In the common events of life all that is incomprehensible is either ridiculed, disbelieved, or made matter of scandal; and, therefore, in a case so uncommon as this, it is more than probable reports very discreditable both to Sarah and Abraham were promulgated all around them. Hagar, indeed, and Ishmael must have known differently—that it was the hand of God which worked, and therefore all things were possible; but it was to Ishmael's interest to dispute or deny the legitimacy of Isaac; and therefore it was not in human nature to neglect the opportunity. No other offence would have so worked on Sarah. We are apt to think more poetically than justly on this part of the Bible. Hagar and her young son, expelled from their luxurious and happy home, almost perishing in the desert from thirst, are infinitely more interesting objects of consideration and sympathy, than the harsh and jealous Sarah, who, for seemingly such trifling offence, demanded and obtained such severe retribution.

We generally rest satisfied with one or two verses; whereas, did we look further and think deeper, our judgment would be different. In a mere superficial reading we acknowledge Sarah does appear in rather an unfavorable light; as if her love for Isaac had suddenly narrowed and stagnated every other feeling; and, jealous of Ishmael's influence over his father, she had determined on seizing the first opportunity for his expulsion. That this, however, is a wrong judgment is proved by the fact, that the Eternal Himself desires Abraham to hearken to the voice of Sarah in all that she shall say; for in Isaac was to be the promised seed, though of Ishmael also would He make a nation, because he was Abraham's son. That Sarah's advice was not to be displeasing to him, because of the lad and his mother.

Now, had Sarah's advice proceeded from an undue harshness, a mean and jealous motive, the Most High would in His divine justice, have taken other means for the fulfilment of His decrees. He would not have desired His good and faithful servant to be so guided by an evil and suspicious tongue. There are times when we feel urged and impelled to speak that which we are yet conscious will be productive of pain and suffering to ourselves. All such impulses are of God; and it must have been some such feeling which actuated Sarah, and compelled her to continue her solicitation for the expulsion of Hagar and Ishmael, even after the moment of anger was passed. We know that Hagar had ever been her favorite slave; it was impossible for one affectionate as was Sarah, to have regarded Ishmael as her son for thirteen or fourteen years and yet not have loved him, though of course with less intensity than his father. The birth of Isaac naturally revealed yet stronger emotions; still Ishmael could not have been so excluded from her affections as to render her separation from him void of pain. And still she spoke, still urged the necessity, conscious all the time she was inflicting pain not only on her husband but on herself. This appears like contradiction; but each one who has attentively studied the workings of his own heart, will not only feel but pronounce it *truth*. Anger caused the demand: "Expel this bondwoman and her son; for the son of this bondwoman shall not inherit with my son, even with Isaac"; and calmer reflection continued to see the necessity. Abraham's possessions were sufficient for the heritage of both his sons; but as the course of nature was changed, and the younger, not the elder, was to be the heir of promise, confusion and discord would have ensued, and the brothers continually have been at war. Sarah's penetration appears to have discovered this; and as it was necessary for Ishmael to form a separate establishment, it was an act of kindness, not of harshness, to let him depart with Hagar, instead of going forth alone. From her own feelings she now knew the whole extent of a mother's love; and therefore, though Ishmael had been the sole offender and the only one whose claims were likely to clash with Isaac's, she would not separate the mother from the son, and so urged Abraham to separate from both. . . .

Few other events mark the life of Sarah. The Most High had brought her forth from the trials, anxieties, and doubts of previous years. He had, in His infinite mercy, fulfilled His word, and bestowed on her the blessed gift for which, in the midst of happiness, she had pined. Continuing His lovingkindness, He lengthened her days much beyond the usual sum of mortality, that she might rear her child to manhood, and receive all the blessed fruit of her maternal care in Isaac's deep love and reverence for herself. In a mere superficial perusal of the life of Sarah as read in our Sabbath portions, we are likely to overlook much of the consoling proofs of the Eternal's compassionating love for His female children, which it so powerfully reveals. Sarah was ninety years of age when Isaac was born. In the course of nature, ten or twelve years more would either have closed her mortal career, or rendered it, from the infirmities of so great an age, a burden to herself and all around her. There was no need of her preservation to forward the decrees of the Lord. In giving birth to the child of promise, her part was fulfilled, and at the age of ten or twelve the boy might have done without her. But God is LOVE and the affections of His children are, in their strength and purity, peculiarly acceptable to Him. He never bestoweth happiness to withdraw it; and there-fore, to perfect the felicity of Sarah and her child, His tenderness preserved her in life and vigor seven and thirty years after she had given him birth.[22] In this simple fact we trace the beneficent and tender Father, sympathizing not alone in every grief and pang, but in every joy and affection of His creatures. We feel to our heart's core the truth of the words of Moses, "Who hath God so near to Him" [Deut. 4:7] as Israel? What nation can so trace, so claim the love of the Eternal?

Nor was the preservation of Sarah the *only* proof of our Father's loving tenderness toward her, and of His condescending sympathy with the love she bore her child. The trial of faith in the sacrifice of his son was given to the *father*; but the *mother* was spared the consuming agony which must have been her portion, even had her faith continued strong. God had compassion on the feebler, weaker nature of His female servant. He demanded not from her that which He knew the mother could not bear. He spared her, in His immeasurable love, the suffering which it pleased Him to inflict upon the father—suffering and temptation *not* to satisfy the Lord, for His omniscience knew that His faithful servant would not fail; but to prove to future ages the mighty power of spiritual faith and love, even while in the mortal clay.[23] . . .

It is His [God's] loving-kindness manifested toward Sarah that we, her female descendants, must take to our hearts, thence to derive alike strength and consolation. The conviction of the Eternal's love for us *individually* is necessary for woman's happiness, and peculiarly adapted to its bestowal.

It is woman's *nature* to yearn and droop for love—to shrink in agony from a lonely path—to long for some supporting arm on which to rest her weakness; and it is woman's *doom* too often to find *on earth* no loving rest, and therefore is her lot so sad. But when she can once realize that she is the subject of a love as immeasurably superior in consolation, strength, and changeless sympathy, to that of man, as the heaven is above the earth: when she can once feel she has a friend who will never "leave her nor forsake" [1 Kgs. 8:57]—in whose pitying ear she may pour forth trials and griefs, either petty or great, which she would not even if she might confide to man, secure not only of pity but of *healing*—when she is conscious that she is never lonely—never left to her own weakness, but in her every need will have strength *infused*—then, then is she so blessed that she is no more lonely, no more sad! And the Word of God will give us this thrice-blessed consolation, not in His gracious prom-ises alone, though they in themselves would be sufficient, but in His dealings with His creatures.

---

[22] Ashton quotes from this paragraph in her essay later in this chapter.
[23] Compare Phyllis Trible, "Genesis 22: The Sacrifice of Sarah."

As the ancestor of His beloved, we find Sarah's death and age particularly recorded; being the first woman of the Bible whose death and burial are mentioned. The deep grief of her husband and son are simply but touchingly betrayed in the brief words, "And Abraham came to mourn for Sarah, and to weep for her"; and, at a later period, not till his marriage with Rebekah, "and Isaac was comforted after his mother's death." Words that portray the beauty and affection of Sarah's domestic character, and confirm our belief that, although perhaps possessing many of the failings of her sex, she was yet a helpmeet for Abraham—a tender and judicious parent to her son—and a kind, indulgent friend to the large household of which she was the mistress. Her noble or rather princely rank, received as it had been direct from the Lord, is still more strongly proved by the intercourse between Abraham and the sons of Heth, when seeking from them a place to bury his dead: "Hear us, my lord," is their reply, "thou art a *mighty prince of God* among us; in the choicest of our sepulchres bury thy dead"; and it was with difficulty Abraham could elude the offered gift, and procure the cave as a purchase. His princely rank, however, and in consequence that of his wife, we see at once acknowledged, even by strangers, and the promise of the Lord, expressed in changing the name of Sarai into Sarah, clearly fulfilled.

The grief of Isaac appears to have lasted yet longer than that of his father, and beautifully illustrates the love between the mother and son. . . . Except the three days' journey to Mount Moriah with his father, Isaac does not appear to have been separated a single day from his mother; and her care, her guiding and fostering love, had so entwined her round his heart, that for three years after her death her son could find no comfort. How exalted and lovely must have been that mother's character to demand such a term of mourning from her son; whose youth and sex would, in some, have speedily roused him from sorrow, or urged its forgetfulness in scenes of pleasure!

We have little more to add on the spiritual lesson and divine consolation which Sarah's life presents to her female descendants, than those hints already given. Differently situated as we are, with regard to station, land, and customs, we may yet imitate her faithfulness in all her household duties—her love and reverence to her husband—her tenderness to her child—her quiet, unpretending, domestic, yet dignified fulfilment of all which she was called upon to do. We may learn from her to set no value on personal charms, save as they may enhance the gratification of those who love us best; or of rank and station, save as they demand from us yet deeper gratitude toward God, and more extended usefulness toward man. We may learn too from her history that it is better to wait for the Lord—to leave in His hands the fulfilment of our ardent wishes —than to seek to compass them by human means. We may trace and feel that nothing, in truth, is too wonderful for the Lord; that He will do what pleaseth Him, however we may deem it hopeless and in vain. Direct revelations, as vouchsafed to Sarah, indeed we have not, but God has, in His deep mercy, granted us His Word—the record of all HE HAS DONE—that we may feel He is still OUR God; and though He worketh now in secret—for our sins have hid from us His ways—yet He worketh for us still, and hath compassion and mercy and love for each of us individually, even as He had for Sarah, and her bondwoman Hagar. All these to us, as women, her history reveals: as women of Israel, oh! yet more. It is of no stranger in race, and clime, and faith we read. It is of OUR OWN—of one from whom Israel hath descended in a direct, unshadowed line—of one—the beloved and cherished partner of that chosen servant and beloved friend of the Eternal, for whose sake revelation was given to mankind—Israel made not alone the nation, but the FIRST-BORN of the Lord; and that law bestowed, which revealed a God of "love, long-suffering and gracious, plenteous in mercy and truth" [Ps. 86:15]—instructed us how to tread our earthly path, so as to give happiness to ourselves and fellow-creatures—to be acceptable to Him—and pointed with an angel-finger to that immortal goal, where man shall live forever!

Is it nothing to be the lineal descendants of one so favored—nothing to hold in our hands and shrine in our hearts, the record of her life from whom the race of promise sprang? Nothing, to peruse the wonderful manifestations of the Lord's love to her—to feel that from Him direct was Sarah's patent of nobility, and yet possess the privilege of being her descendant? Will the women of Israel feel this as nothing? Will they disdain their princely birth, their heavenly heritage? Will they scorn to look back on Sarah as their ancestor, and yet long for earthly distinctions, earthly rank? No! oh, no! Let us but think of these things, of those from whom we have descended, and our minds will become ennobled, our hearts enlarged. We shall scorn the false shame which would descend to petty meannesses to hide our faith, and so exalt us in the sight of a Gentile world. Humbled, cast off for a little moment as we are—liable to persecution, scorn, contumely—to be "despised and rejected" [Is 53.3] of men—to bear the burden of affliction from all who choose to afflict—still, still we cannot lose our blessed heritage unless we cast it off; we cannot be deprived of our birthright unless, like Esau, we exchange it for mere worldly pelf,[24] and momentary (because *earthly*) gratification. We are still Israelites—still the chosen, the beloved, the ARISTOCRACY of the Lord.

* See note to Gen. xvii. 15, in the Rev. D. A. De Sola's translation of the Bible. [D. A. de Sola, I. L. Lindenthal, and the Rev. Morris, *The Sacred Scriptures in Hebrew and English: A New Translation with Notes Critical and Explanatory* (J. Raphall. London: Samuel Bagster & Son, 1844).]

† See the Rev. D. A. De Sola's translation, and note thereon.

[24] Booty or spoil.

§25 Rebekah Hyneman
(1812–1875)

Rebekah Hyneman (née Gumpert) was born in Philadelphia, the daughter of a Jewish-German storekeeper and a Christian mother. She had no formal education but acquired her literary education and a mastery of French, German, and later Hebrew through self-study. She married Benjamin Hyneman, a Jewish jewelry salesman in 1835, but when she was pregnant with their second son, he disappeared on a trip and was presumed murdered. She never remarried. Hyneman wrote short stories, novellas, including *Woman's Strength,* and serial novels published in a newspaper edited by her brother-in-law, Leon Hyneman. Her poetry was published in the Jewish journal, *The Occident,* and later as a collection, *The Leper and Other Poems* (1853). Her poetry intimated that her Jewish faith sustained her through loneliness and tragedy.[25]

Like Aguilar, Hyneman exalted Sarah. She developed the significance of the meaning of Sarah's name as "princess," naming her "queen of a high and noble race; proud mother of a princely line." Her use of jewelry images recalls her murdered husband's profession. In a surprising interpretive move, Hyneman put a positive spin on the wife-sister stories in Genesis 12 and 20. She imagined Sarah protected by Abraham's arms when she was taken into the households of Pharaoh and Abimelech, who "bent in homage to her charms." Hyneman's identification of Sarah as queen and her association of Sarah with heaven may provide a Jewish counterpart to the Roman Catholic designation of Mary as Queen of Heaven.

From Rebekah Hyneman, "Sarah," *The Occident and American Jewish Advocate* 4.4 (June 1846).

–Sarah–

Room! for that queenly one;
Room! for the peerless gem;
Place on her form the regal robe,

[25] There is some debate about Hyneman's date of birth and about whether she was a Jew all her life or converted to Judaism after her husband died. See Abraham J. Karp, *From the Ends of the Earth: Judaic Treasures of the Library of Congress* (Washington D.C.: Library of Congress, 1991). Excerpts located online at Jewish Virtual Library. http://www.jewishvirtuallibrary.org/jsource/biography/Hyneman.html; also see Jewish-American History on the Web, "Biography of Rebekah Hyneman" http://www.jewish-history.com/Hyneman/hynemanbio.html.

On her brow the diadem.
And hail her as the queen
Of a high and noble race;
Proud mother of a princely line,
Radiant in every grace.
She comes, a husband's pride,
Protected by his arms;
And haughty kings and princes bend
In homage to her charms.
From her our race hath sprung—
She has given us a dower
More dear than gems or robes of price,
Or the pomp of earthly power.
Then blest, forever blest!
Be she, who thus hath given
Unto her weary, earth-born sons,
A heritage in heaven.

§26 Elizabeth Fries Ellet
(c.1810–1877)

Elizabeth Fries Ellet was one of six children born to Dr. William A. Lummis and his second wife, Sarah Maxwell. She was educated at the Friends' Female Seminary in Aurora, New York. In 1835, she married Dr. William H. Ellet, a professor of chemistry at Columbia College in New York City. Soon after their marriage, the Ellets moved to Columbia, South Carolina, where Dr. Ellet took a position as chemistry professor. They returned to New York City in 1849.

Ellet published eighteen books between 1835 and 1870. She was interested in women's history, as seen in one of her best-known works, *Women of the American Revolution* (1848). In this work Ellet used previously ignored sources to trace the lives and contributions of women to the American revolutionary war.

Another of Ellet's books, *Family Pictures from the Bible*, focused on lessons for families found in scripture. She considered the Bible a sourcebook of principles for family life. For example, Genesis 18:19 implied Abraham offered leadership in teaching his household and so taught that fathers should lead their households. Unlike Aguilar and Hyneman, who idealized Sarah,

Ellet recognized Sarah's complexity as a character and did not see a problem in describing Sarah as both "imperious and haughty" and yet also as "subject to Abraham." Her emphasis on subjection follows the interpretive guide of 1 Peter 3:6, which King also used.

Ellet was a historian. Like her contemporaries, she recognized the importance of reading the stories in light of their ancient setting. She highlighted historical and cultural differences in her choice of language. For example, she used the phrase "the pastoral simplicity of the world's infancy" to describe the scene in Genesis 18. She also called polygamy a practice of primitive times. But, unlike Moses Stuart (1780–1852), Calvin Stowe (1802–1886), and other early American biblical scholars,[26] Ellet did not examine the Bible as she would any other historical or literary text. She wrote to teach and encourage Christian readers. She resolved not to embellish the story very much, sensing that the "beauty of simple truth in Holy Writ would be marred, rather than improved or set forth by embellishment."[27] Despite this, she did suggest the use of imagination in picturing the scenes from the Bible; she did not adorn the text as much as Aguilar and other writers, and she did inform the reader when something was added.

> From Mrs. Ellet, *Family Pictures from the Bible* (New York: G. P. Putnam, 1849), 16–23.

But little is said in the Scriptures, by which we may learn the character of Sarai. She appears to have been wanting in the faith so eminent in her husband, and which "was counted unto him for righteousness" [Gen. 15:6]. Despairing of the fulfilment of the promise so often and so solemnly repeated, she ventures to propose means for bringing about the desired accomplishment. Perhaps the annoyances she afterwards suffered from the insolent behavior of her maid, the natural consequence of her folly, were intended as a reproof for her want of trust, and irreverent impatience. She seems to have been of a haughty and imperious temper, and felt bitterly the arrogant insults of the servant whom she had elevated to the dignity of a wife. She complains to her husband of the humiliating treatment she has received, and lays to his charge the responsibility. "The Lord judge," she says, "between me and thee." The appeal was answered by Abram with permission to his wife to do with her maid as she pleased. He exhibits none of the feeling shown on a subsequent occasion, when the dissensions in his family rendered it necessary for him to

---

[26] John H. Giltner, *Moses Stuart: The Father of Biblical Science in America* (Atlanta: Scholars Press, 1988).

[27] Mrs. Ellet, *Family Pictures from the Bible* (New York: G. P. Putnam, 1849), 4.

part with his son Ishmael; for it is evident he had not wronged Sarai by any transfer of his affections.

The jealous pride of the mistress, roused by the presumptuous conduct of Hagar, prompts her to treatment so harsh that the slave flies from the oppression, and wanders in the wilderness.[28] Careless of her own fate, or that of her unborn child, she desires only to escape from present evil; she can give no answer to the angel who asks whither she would go, but confesses that she has fled from the face of her mistress. It is a touching trait in the character of Hagar, that she makes no attempt to justify herself by complaint of the unkind usage she has received; indeed the consciousness of the presence and omniscience of God, which she expresses in the name given to Him who spake to her—seems to imply that her thoughts dwelt on her own faults. The angel comforts her by an assurance that her affliction has been regarded, and a promise of numerous descendants; and bids her return and submit herself to lawful authority.

The race of which the Messiah was to be born must be "beyond every possible impeachment of its legitimacy;" and after the lapse of fourteen years another revelation renews the covenant; and the names of Abram and Sarai are changed by the Divine command, in token of their parentage of many nations. At the announcement that the covenant is to be established with the son whom Sarah was to bear, the father's love for his first-born is touchingly exhibited. His whole heart is poured out in the prayer for Ishmael. The blessing is to be inherited by one unborn. What should become of the boy whose birth had first brought joy to his tent—in whom his soul was bound up! The strength of the parental feeling in Abraham's bosom is thus shown in his tender solicitude for the child who had first awakened it. His prayer is answered by the promise of the blessing, though a subordinate one, to Ishmael.

The pastoral simplicity of the world's infancy comes before us, as we contemplate the picture presented in the eighteenth chapter of Genesis—of the aged patriarch sitting in his tent-door in the heat of the day, the approach of the three strangers, and his reception of them with oriental hospitality. . . . The quick preparations for their entertainment, in which the master and mistress are active as well as their servants, and the particulars related, strongly mark the simple and generous character of that ancient hospitality. The meal was partaken of under the spreading tree which shaded the tent; and then the chief of the three strangers renewed the promise of a son before given, and fixed the time of his birth. The laughter of Sarah, who heard this promise in the tent-door behind, indicated the unbelief of her heart, and was reproved, though mildly, by the Almighty visitant.

[28] Contrast Aguilar who infers a restrained action from the same text.

It is remarkable, that by a few words in the verses succeeding, light is thrown upon the character of both Abraham and Sarah in their domestic relations. The patriarch's habitual exercise of due authority over his household, and pious zeal in instructing them, is attested by the Lord in the disclosure of his gracious purpose towards him. "I know him, that he will command his children and his household after him," is not said as a reason for the bestowal of the blessing at first promised—for the very fitness to receive it was a gift from above—but it was part of the plan of benevolence. The father of the faithful had once listened to the persuasions of his wife, and obeyed them in espousing Hagar; instances of misconduct and criminal distrust of God's protection through scenes of peril, are also recorded of him; but his heart, by the Divine aid, was set to do that which was right, and the same grace would be granted to keep him faithful to the end, and to cause his descendants to "keep the way of the Lord" [Jud. 2:21-22]. It appears from several particulars mentioned, that the patriarch was naturally disposed to exercise his own judgment in shaping his course. His disingenuous equivocation concerning his relations to Sarah, in Egypt and in Gerar, strongly evinces this tendency; but under the appointed discipline, these corrupt inclinations were gradually overcome. The last severe ordeal through which he was called to pass —in the sacrifice required of his only son—was met in a manner that showed him then advanced in the life of faith beyond the weakness which had marked its early growth; and thenceforward we hear of no more doubts or shortcomings.

The expression of Sarah in the eighteenth chapter, calling Abraham "my lord," seems to be referred to by St. Peter in his commendation of her obedience to him. The life of this couple—growing old in faithful affection, and in expectation of the blessing mysteriously promised—is simply and beautifully delineated. Sarah was subject to Abraham as her head, superior, and guide. Abraham, "the friend of God," leaned on the Divine counsel and support. The son born to them—the child of promise—the heir of unknown blessing—the channel of mercy fore-ordained for the whole race of mankind, was a gift received from the hand of the Creator, and unspeakably precious. The circle of the family life was thus complete. The bondwoman and her son had no proper part therein and they were to be removed from the association. The custom of men in that primitive age allowing a plurality of wives, it was not expressly censured; but that the practice was a violation of the principle on which the marriage relation was founded, and tended to the subversion of domestic comfort and peace, is plain from the examples in the case of the patriarchs. Abraham was doomed to suffer the consequences of his own fault, by the necessity of parting with the son borne to him by Hagar. The haughty spirit of Sarah could ill brook the boyish insolence of Ishmael; and remembering Abraham's former yielding to her complaints, she demanded peremptorily the expulsion of the boy and his mother. It was hard for the father to send from him the child he had first loved, and in whose opening faculties, wild as his nature was, he felt a parent's pride. "The thing was very grievous in his sight;" and in his anguish he doubtless sought the direction of that great Being by whom hitherto his steps had been guided. The answer, couched in gracious and comforting terms, commands him to comply with the apparently unreasonable demand, and to yield to his wife the unlimited control over her servant assigned her by the usage of pastoral tribes. An intimation is added of blessing destined Ishmael for Abraham's sake; and Abraham, obedient to the Divine vision, rose up early to make preparations for the departure of the two. There is something unspeakably touching in the very simplicity of the account, which leaves room for imagination to dwell upon the melancholy scene. The aged and affectionate father, placing in Hagar's hands the provisions which could sustain them only a brief way on their lonely journey, and sorrowing that he should see the face of his child no more—the Egyptian mother, bowed down in humiliation for this abrupt dismission from the home that had been hers so long; perhaps reproaching herself for the unseemly pride and arrogance which so provoked her mistress—and the spirited lad, who would naturally feel the separation less keenly, in his youthful love of adventure, to be indulged without restraint in the wild and uninhabited districts where they were to seek their fortune. What a scene, with its deep pathos, for the embellishment of poetry! We may well believe that tears in abundance were shed as the patriarch bade farewell to Hagar, and strained his son for the last time to his bosom in agonized embrace. The heart of Sarah must have melted at the sight of his grief, and her anger have given way to a willingness for reconciliation. She could not see the suffering of him she loved; she could not see the handmaid who had served her so long, the boy who had grown from infancy by her side, go forth from her door, driven thence by her severity, to wander through the world, without a revulsion of feeling. But a higher purpose than hers was to be accomplished; and the words she had uttered in anger were exponents of the decree fulfilled in after ages. Abraham obeyed, not the imperious demand of his wife, but the Divine direction; and the consciousness of this, and that he was committing Ishmael, not to the uncertainties of a dreary future, but to the care of One who had promised to protect him, took away from the bitterness of parting. The fervent prayer with which he commended the boy to the keeping of his Heavenly Father, ascended upwards from his pious heart on the wings of faith, and was heard. Then the Egyptian and her son went forth from the patriarch's dwelling.

The wandering of the outcast Hagar and Ishmael in the wilderness—their sufferings from the failure of the supply of water, and the anguish of the mother, who lays down her child to die, and retires to weep, that she may not behold his last agonies—are recounted in a description which has never been surpassed in simple pathos. Here again is a scene for the artist, whose fancy could add no coloring more striking than is presented. The familiar story, with its typical meaning, need not be dwelt upon here, as the Egyptian and her son were no longer a portion of the family of Abraham.

When the command came—the keenest trial to the parental feeling as well as to the faith of Abraham—to offer up Isaac in sacrifice, we read of no struggle nor hesitation, as in the case of Ishmael. He utters no murmur, though bidden to cut short, with his own hand, the life on which his expectation depended of a numerous posterity, and the blessing which, through him, was to pervade the whole earth. As before, after the vision, he "rose up early in the morning," and prepared for his journey, having prepared wood for the burnt-offering. Those who were with him knew not of his intention; and it is not likely that he confided the matter to Sarah, whose feebler faith and maternal anxiety might have interposed obstacles. . . .

The expression so often used in Scripture, "gathered to his fathers," [e.g. Job 27:19] appears to have a meaning which throws light upon the customs of primitive ages. We learn that each tribe or family had its own place of burial—sometimes a spacious sepulchre, hewn from the rock, and divided into several chambers, where the dust of many branches of the clan might be deposited.[29] The chief had here his appointed place, and round him were assembled the children who came one by one to moulder at his side. Thus the family union was preserved even in the grave. No stranger dust was permitted to mingle with the kindred remains; and from generation to generation the descendants of the same progenitor occupied their last resting-place together. Thus Abraham, when Sarah died, applied to the chiefs of the clan of Heth to purchase a cemetery; for as yet he had been a stranger and a sojourner, and in his wandering life had possessed no place to bury his dead. His home was fixed now in the land of Canaan; and there was to be the sacred deposit, which he would guard with jealous care from foreign intrusion. He declines the complimentary offer of the chief, of permission to bury his dead in the choicest of their own national sepulchres; he refuses to accept as a gift from Ephron the cave and field he had selected as suitable for the purpose, though it was proffered publicly, as a mark of high respect. He will have this sacred possession isolated from all others, and take it only on condition of being permitted to pay the price to its owner. The bargain is ratified, and the field

---

[29] Ellet's observation has been confirmed by numerous excavations of Iron Age bench tombs. An added feature in keeping with the spirit of her observation is that underneath the bench was a repository of the bones of the ancestors. Thanks to Glen Taylor for this note.

secured to him, with its rock and the trees that were to shade the graves of his household. . . .

The line of the Messiah being thus cared for [in the marriage of Isaac], and Isaac constituted the sole heir to all the wealth of Abraham, the patriarch married again. But his other children, having received gifts from him, were sent away into the east country; nor were their descendants, though noticed in the Hebrew annals, considered as belonging to the same stock with the Jews. Ishmael, indeed, joined with Isaac in the last duties to their father, interring his remains in the cave of Machpelah, where the dust of Sarah reposed.

§27 Catherine Hunt Putnam
(1792–1869)

Catherine Hunt Putnam[30] was an American writer whose son, George Putnam, owned the firm that published Mrs. Ellet's *Family Pictures from the Bible*. In writing *The Gospel by Moses in the Book of Genesis; or, The Old Testament Unveiled* (1854), Putnam aimed to recover a spiritual sense of Genesis through typology. In her preface to the volume, Putnam claimed that she did not read this spiritual sense into the text, but discovered it within the text. She used three categories to discuss Genesis. "The Letter" gave the verses to be considered; under "Note," she gave an explanation of the spiritual sense of the Genesis passage. "The Spirit" listed other scripture verses that complemented her spiritual reading of Genesis.

Putnam knew that readers might find her interpretation troublesome. She asked them "to lay aside preconceived notions, and look into these things in the spirit of candid inquiry," and so discover "that many a scripture whose *dead letter* yielded nothing to their perception but barren historic detail, is really a 'well of salvation,' out of which they may draw '*living water*'"[John 4:11-13].[31] Putnam's book was the result of thirty years of study, so she asked readers not to be too hasty in their judgment, as she had not been hasty in drawing her conclusions.

Putnam interpreted Abraham as a type of Christ and Sarah as a type of the church. This interpretation allowed her to read the wife-sister story in Genesis 12 in an entirely different way. She disregarded the historical sense

---

[30] For a more complete biography of Putnam, see part 1, "Eve—The Mother of Us All."

[31] Catherine Putnam, *The Gospel by Moses in the Book of Genesis; or, the Old Testament Unveiled* (New York: Edward H. Fletcher, 1854), xi.

and avoided all the moral questions that all the other women interpreters asked: whether Abraham and Sarah were lying, whether they should have gone to Egypt, and whether they were displaying faith in this episode of their life. Instead, Putnam saw this episode as illustrating the true relationship between Christ and the Church, which is never understood by the world (Egypt). She also saw the true glory of the Church revealed in the discussion of Sarah's beauty: the world may admire the beauty of the Church, but cannot recognize her spiritual character or hidden nature. On the other hand, Christ, the Church's husband, guards her "with watchful jealousy."

Like Ellet, Putnam regarded Abraham highly; however, Putnam went rurther and exalted Abraham. He could do no wrong because he represented Christ. Putnam's reading of Abraham and Sarah was similar to her reading of Adam and Eve (found in the previous chapter on Eve). Both readings are christological, as the title of the work, *The Gospel by Moses*, implies.

From Catherine Putnam, *The Gospel by Moses in the Book of Genesis; or, the Old Testament Unveiled* (New York: Edward H. Fletcher, 1854), 114–16.

[Genesis chapter 12, labeled in Putnam chapter 11.]

The Letter

7. And the Lord appeared unto Abram, and said, Unto thy seed will I give this land: and there builded he an altar unto the Lord, who appeared unto him.

8. And he removed from thence unto a mountain on the east of Beth-el, and pitched his tent, *having* Beth-el on the west, and Hai on the east: and there he builded an altar unto the Lord, and called upon the name of the Lord.

9. And Abram journeyed, going on still toward the south.

10. And there was a famine in the land: and Abram went down into Egypt to sojourn there; for the famine *was* grievous in the land.

11. And it came to pass, when he was come near to enter into Egypt, that he said unto Sarai his wife, Behold now, I

The Spirit

DEUT. xxxiii. 7. Remember the days of old, consider the years of many generations: ask thy father, and he will show thee; thy elders, and they will tell thee.

8. When the Most High divided to the nations their inheritance, when he separated the sons of Adam, he set the bounds of the people according to the number of the children of Israel:

9. For the Lord's portion *is* his people; Jacob *is* the lot of his inheritance.

2 SAM. vii. 10. Moreover I will appoint a place for my people Israel, and will plant them, that they may dwell in a place of their own, and move no more; neither shall the children of wickedness afflict them any more, as beforetime.

11. And as since the time that I commanded judges *to be* over my people Israel, and have caused thee to rest from

know that thou *art* a fair woman to look upon:

12. Therefore it shall come to pass, when the Egyptians shall see thee, that they shall say, This *is* his wife: and they will kill me, but they will save thee alive.

13. Say, I pray thee, thou *art* my sister: that it may be well with me for thy sake; and my soul shall live because of thee.

Note

The promise increases in its fulness and clearness. At first it was an indefinite blessing; now it assumes a more distinct form. "*Unto thy seed will I give this land.*" Paul in Gal. says, this *seed* is *Christ*. If so, then the *land* given is not *literal Canaan*, but that which Canaan represents, the "inheritance incorruptible, undefiled, and that fadeth not away, which is reserved in heaven" for Christ and his people.

Upon receiving this promise Abram sets up an altar, or memorial of it on the east of Bethel, because *there*, in that *very spot*, would this promise be hereafter more fully developed.

Abram then proceeds to Egypt, a place which is often mentioned in this typical history. Egypt appears to represent the *world* in distinction from the *church*, or the earth in distinction from the heavens, in their mystical sense.

The true relationship between Christ and the church is never understood by the *world*; it is to them a *hidden mystery*. For Jesus manifests himself to her as he does not to the world ; and in their view treats her more as a *sister* than a *spouse*.

This act of Abram may also intimate that which in the "fulness of time" would actually take place in the spiritual Egypt, where Jesus would redeem the church with his blood.

all thine enemies. Also the Lord telleth thee, that he will make thee a house.

12. And when thy days be fulfilled, and thou shalt sleep with thy fathers, I will set up thy seed after thee, which shall proceed out of thy bowels, and I will establish his kingdom.

13. He shall build a house for my name; and I will stablish the throne of his kingdom for ever.

14. I will be his father, and he shall be my son. If he commit iniquity, I will chasten him, with the rod of men, and with the stripes of the children of men.

ACTS iii. 30. Therefore being a prophet, and knowing that God had sworn with an oath to him, that of the fruit of his loins, according to the flesh, he would raise up Christ to sit on his throne.

SOL. SONG iv. 12. A garden enclosed is my sister, my spouse; a spring shut up, a fountain sealed.

EPH. v. 29. For no man ever yet hated his own flesh ; but nourisheth and cherisheth it, even as the Lord the church.

30. For we are members of his body, of his flesh, and of his bones.

31. For this cause shall a man leave his father and mother, and shall be joined unto his wife, and they too shall be one flesh.

32. This is a great mystery; but I speak concerning Christ and the church.

The Letter

14. And it came to pass, that when Abram was come into Egypt, the Egyptians beheld the woman that she was very fair.

15. The princes also of Pharaoh saw her, and commended her before Pharaoh: and the woman was taken into Pharaoh's house.

16. And he entreated Abram well for her sake: and he had sheep, and oxen and he-asses, and men-servants, and maid-servants, and she-asses, and camels.

17. And the Lord plagued Pharaoh and his house with great plagues because of Sarai, Abram's wife.

18. And Pharaoh called Abram, and said, What *is* this *that* thou hast done unto me? why didst thou not tell me that she *was* thy wife ?

19. Why saidst thou, She *is* my sister? so I might have taken her to me to wife: now therefore behold thy wife, take *her,* and go thy way.

20. And Pharaoh commanded *his* men concerning him: and they sent him away, and his wife, and all that he had.

Note

The external glory of the church under the first testament, made her an object of admiration and wonder to the world. Not discerning her spiritual nature or hidden character, and mistaking her outward ceremonies and adornments for a token of oneness and similitude with themselves, they claim a right to her blessings and privileges as their own. But though her Lord and Husband does not openly recognise his own exclusive title and relationship to Zion, yet he guards with watchful jealousy against the claims and encroachments of "other lords."

The Spirit

1 JOHN iii. 1. Behold what manner of love the Father hath bestowed upon us, that we should be called the sons of God! therefore the world knoweth us not, because it knew him not.

2. Beloved, now are we the sons of God; and it doth not yet appear what we shall be: but we know that, when he shall appear, we shall be like him; for we shall see him as he is.

Ps. xlviii. 2. Beautiful for situation, the joy of the whole earth, *is* mount Zion, *on* the sides of the north, the city of the great King.

3. God is known in her palaces for a refuge.

4. For lo, the kings were assembled, they passed by together.

5. They saw *it, and* so they marvelled they were troubled, *and* hasted away.

6. Fear took hold upon them there, *and* pain, as of a woman in travail.

7. Thou breakest the ships of Tarshish with an east wind.

8. As we have heard, so have we seen in the city of the Lord of hosts, in the city of our God: God will establish it for ever. Selah.

9. We have thought of thy loving kindness, O God, in the midst of thy temple.

10. According to thy name, O God, so is thy praise unto the ends of the earth; thy right hand is full of righteousness.

11. Let mount Zion rejoice, let the daughters of Judah be glad, because of thy judgments.

12. Walk about Zion, and go round about her: tell the towers thereof.

JOB xxi. 14. Therefore they say unto God, Depart from us; for we desire not the knowledge of thy ways.

If the ungodly put unholy hands upon his chosen, they are given to understand that she is not to be defiled, polluted, or held in bondage with impunity; that "he who touches her touches the apple of his eye." [Ps. 122:6; Zech. 2:8] They may boast of their power over her, and what they might do, either to favor or destroy her; but the language of her sovereign Lord is, "Touch not mine anointed, and do my prophets no harm" [1 Chron. 16:22].

15. What *is* the Almighty, that we should serve him? and what profit should we have, if we pray unto him?

16. Lo, their good *is* not in their hand: the counsel of the wicked is far from me.

§28 Sophia Goodrich Ashton
(1819–1872)

Sophia Ashton,[32] American author of *The Mothers of the Bible*, wrote to encourage women in their vocations as mothers. Ashton emphasized the sacred aspect of motherhood and female virtues. In the chapter of *The Mothers of the Bible* entitled "Sarah and Hagar," Ashton retold the intertwined stories of Sarah and Hagar, the mothers of Abraham's sons, Isaac and Ishmael.[33] She interpreted all of Sarah's life in light of her calling as mother. She imagined Sarah as a mother even before the birth of Isaac and portrayed her as the mother and catechizer of the large household of Abraham. Like Hyneman, she designated Sarah as "queen."

Like Aguilar, Ashton filled in the many gaps in the biblical portrait of Sarah, calling on her readers to imagine the scenes she described. She wanted to know more about Sarah as mother and wife, and, to that end, used passages from Hebrews 11 and 1 Peter 3 to infer more about Sarah than the Genesis account allows. She also drew on the expertise of others. She used the six-volume reference work on the Bible written by the British Methodist, Dr. Adam Clarke (1760?–1832).[34] Ashton plagiarized Aguilar's *The Women*

---

[32] For a more complete biography of Ashton see part 1, "Eve—The Mother of Us All."

[33] The sections which focus primarily on Hagar have been edited out for the purposes of this chapter.

[34] Adam Clarke, *The Holy Bible, Containing the Old and New Testaments, according to the Authorized Translation; with all the parallel texts and marginal readings: to which are added, notes, and practical observations, designed as a help to a correct understanding to the sacred writings* (Liverpool, 1813). This work was republished numerous times.

of Israel without using quotation marks or acknowledging her source. This dependence demonstrates the transatlantic crosspollination of ideas. Women read one another and used each other's work in addition to reading the works of male scholars and theologians.

Ashton wrote for women retelling the story through a distinctively feminine lens: "Sarah nourished her infant at her own breast; and only a mother can imagine her heartfelt happiness and gratitude during that delightful time." Ashton ended this chapter with a reflection on God as mother, based on Isaiah 49:15. This feminine image of God provided a striking conclusion to Ashton's reflections on Sarah as mother.

From S. G. Ashton, *The Mothers of the Bible* (New York: The World Publishing House, 1855), 31–59.

–Sarah and Hagar–

IN pursuance of the plan which he had devised for the redemption of the race of man, God appeared to Abraham, the son of Terah, in a city called Ur, in Chaldea, and directed him to leave his country, and dwell in the land of Canaan. Among the nations, perhaps the Chaldeans had departed less from the simplicity of a true faith and worship than many others; but they were still idolaters, and Ur, as appears from recent discoveries, was their sacred city. It is not necessary that we should dwell upon the familiar details of Abraham's separation from his country and kindred. Suffice it, that the object of his being thus separated by God was, that through his faith and obedience, through his instructions to his family, and through the seed afterward promised, the knowledge and worship of the only true God should be gradually disseminated.

Abraham obeyed the command of Jehovah, and was accompanied in his wanderings by the wife of his youth; henceforth the partner of his exile, and a helpmeet in his cares. They had spent hardly a year in Canaan, when a famine compelled them to repair to Egypt, where they remained three months. Sarah was a very beautiful woman, and Abraham knew that she would be peculiarly attractive to the Egyptians, because so much more fair than their swarthy countrywomen; and the account of his deception in calling her his sister, with the consequent trouble, stands on the sacred page, a beacon against the folly of distrusting God, and resorting to prevarication. The beauty of the fair Chaldean was soon in every mouth, and Sarah was taken from her supposed brother to the king's household, to go through the preliminary ceremonies and purifications which were requisite to her becoming his wife, and which usually occupied about a month. What Abraham suffered during this interval, and what were her own trials, we can only imagine. Nothing is said of the prayers which the patriarch must have offered to God; nothing recorded of the anguish and tears of the wife, who had taken, as she believed, a final leave of her husband, and was destined to the honor of being a favorite of Egypt's monarch. The trial was severe. God, however, interposed to save them from their fears. His judgments caused Pharaoh to inquire into the truth, and to restore Sarah before the month of preparation was ended. He dismissed them from his dominions without injury, but not without severe rebuke, and they returned to Canaan.

Ten years passed away, during which time Sarah's name is not mentioned. They had no children, but it must not be inferred that, because she had not a mother's cares, she was therefore unoccupied. It is recorded that at one time Abraham went out to fight against the Assyrian king with more than three hundred trained servants. These were all born in his house, the sacred writer informs us, and were capable of bearing arms. If we add to these those who must have remained in charge of the flocks and herds, and the women and children, we may, perhaps, form some idea of the family over which Sarah presided as mistress. The phrase "trained servants" signifies catechised, or instructed. We know that wherever Abraham pitched his tent, as he removed from place to place, he erected an altar, and in the midst of his assembled family offered sacrifices to God. "I know him," said the Lord, "that he will command his children and his household after him, and they shall keep the way of the Lord." That Sarah was a faithful wife, a prudent and discreet housekeeper, and willing to aid her husband in this important work of training his household to serve God, we have no reason to doubt. That she "labored, working with her own hands," or strictly superintended the labor of her servants, we infer from the fact that when strangers were to be entertained, Abraham calls upon her to prepare the needed food. We think of her as the energetic, active head of a large and well-ordered family, and God doubtless aided and qualified her for the station she occupied.

Soon after their return from Egypt, God had appeared again to Abraham, and renewed his covenant with him, assuring him that the land should be given to his posterity, who should be as the sands of the sea-shore, innumerable. But the years rolled by, and there was no sign of the fulfillment of this promise. Sarah, who seems not to have possessed the unshaken faith which characterized her husband, despairing of herself becoming a mother, resorted at length to an expedient which is revolting to us, and which proved disastrous to the peace of all concerned in it. The laws and customs of the land countenanced polygamy, and Abraham, in compliance with Sarah's wishes, took Hagar, her bond-woman, for a secondary wife, in hope of gaining the long-desired blessing. Hagar was an Egyptian, and had probably become one of their family during their sojourn in her native land. She seems to have been a favorite servant, and was certainly honored in being selected as the object of her master's regards. The desired end was obtained. Hagar soon had the prospect of becoming a mother. But the happiness which Sarah anticipated did not follow. As might have been foreseen, her own jealous feelings were roused, and Hagar soon manifested the vanity and insolence which her situation, now so superior to that of her mistress, naturally called forth. She manifested her contempt in a manner so marked that Sarah's indignation could not be controlled; but, instead of blaming only herself, she reproached her husband. She insinuated that Hagar stood too high in his estimation, and called upon God to witness that she was wronged. The most serious unhappiness now reigned in this hitherto quiet family. Abraham might have remonstrated with Sarah, or reproached her in turn, he might have claimed the right to protect Hagar as his wife; but the dignity and excellence of his character appear in his answer: "Thy maid is in thine hand; do to her as it pleaseth thee." "Sarah afflicted her." Whether it is intended that she inflicted personal chastisement upon her, as some commentators affirm, or whether the affliction consisted of bitter words, which to a sensitive spirit are worse than blows, we cannot decide. Whatever was done was sufficient to drive Hagar, in desperation, from her presence. She fled hastily to go to Egypt, her native land, but sank exhausted, friendless, and ready to perish, by a fountain in the wilderness of Shur. Most beautiful is the description which follows the account of her flight, and wonderfully does it show the tender mercy of God toward those who are in trouble. An angel of the Lord seeks her in her woe. He, without whose notice the sparrow cannot fall, is not unmindful of helpless, suffering woman [Matt. 10:29, 30]. "And he said, Hagar, Sarah's maid, whence camest thou? and whither wilt thou go?" He does not call her *Abraham's wife*. It is not his part to increase her pride, and aggravate her discontent. He reminds her of her true condition, and calls up entirely different thoughts from those which she has been indulging. Those simple questions startle her from the tumultuous emotions of rebellion and presumption. Whence had she come? From a happy, loving home, where she had been the favorite of an indulgent and gentle mistress; a home which would speedily be yet dearer to her as the birth-place of her child,—that child who was to be the supposed heir to her master and all his sainted privileges; from friends, from companions, all whom she loved; and she had left them! and whither was she going? How might she answer, when she knew not? How idle and impotent now seemed her previous feelings! Those questions had flashed light on her darkened heart, and humbled her at once; and simply and truthfully she answered, "I flee from the presence of my mistress Sarai."[35] . . .

---

[35] Ashton is quoting Aguilar here. See Aguilar's essay on Sarah earlier in this chapter.

Nearly thirteen years passed quietly on, bringing with them no events of sufficient importance to be noticed by the inspired penman. No further revelation from God disturbed the delusion under which Abram and Sarah labored, that Ishmael was the promised seed, the heir of the covenant; and he was doubtless trained up in his father's house in a manner suitable to his future expectations. The time, however, at length came when Jehovah would more fully unfold his plans. Abram had nearly reached the age of a hundred years, and Sarah was almost ninety, when he once more appeared, and said, "I am God all-sufficient; walk before me, and be thou perfect." This language seems to convey a reproof for their want of faith in his promises, and resorting to expedients of their own devising, and bids them henceforth act with more simplicity, and leave God to bring about his designs in his own way. He then entered into a solemn covenant with Abram, in which he included all his posterity to the latest generation. He also changed their names. Abram, which signifies "an eminent father," he called Abraham, "an eminent father of a multitude;" and Sarai, "my princess," or, as we more familiarly say, queen of her own household, he called Sarah, "princess of a multitude;" and then for the first time announced that the promised seed should descend from her: "I will give thee a son also of her;" "she shall be a mother of nations."

Not long after this, the Lord again reiterates his promise, in an interview which is beautifully described in the sacred volume.

In the delightful oak-grove of Mamre, in the midst of a sultry summer day, the patriarch sat at the door of his tent, enjoying the slight breeze, and resting from toil, which the intense heat of the Eastern climate forbids during certain hours. All around, at short distances, were the tents of his numerous dependants, their occupants reposing like himself, or scattered abroad with the flocks and herds. All was quiet and peaceful, until the sound of coming footsteps disturbed his meditations, and warned him of the approach of strangers. Abraham, obeying the quick impulse of hospitality, hastened to greet them, and invite them to repose under the grateful shade, and offer them the refreshments they needed. He provided water for their feet, and, entering the tent, directed Sarah to prepare food and set it before them; which being done, he served them himself, according to the custom of his time. While they sat eating, the chief of them suddenly asked him, "Where is Sarah, thy wife?" It was an extraordinary question. The women of the East live in the closest seclusion, having no intercourse with strangers, nor with any of the opposite sex, save their husbands, and with them they are never permitted to sit at the same table. A traveller remarks that one who should ask another of the health of his wife and family would be considered as offering him a downright insult. The question must, therefore, have greatly surprised Abraham. He answered, briefly, that Sarah was in the tent. "I will certainly return unto thee," continued his mysterious, though now no longer unknown visitor, "and, lo, Sarah thy wife shall have a son." Their table was spread at no great distance from the tent door, and Sarah, in her private apartment, was an astonished listener to this strange conversation. We have before said that she did not partake of her husband's implicit faith. When she heard the announcement that she should bear a son, it was to her only ridiculous. The infinite power of him who promised she wholly overlooked, and remembered only that she had long passed the age when maternity was possible, in the ordinary course of events. She laughed incredulously at what she heard. Omniscience pierces any barrier. "Wherefore did Sarah laugh?" said he. "Is anything too hard for the Lord?" Terrified at being detected, Sarah now came forth from the tent, and, in her fear and confusion, "denied, saying, I laughed not." One penetrating look, and the quiet, firm reply, "Nay, but thou didst laugh," were sufficient to send her back to her retirement in penitence, a wiser and a better woman. From this time her character seems to have undergone a change. Her distrust of God was gone, and Paul, in days long after, numbers her among those who were illustrious for their faith, attributing the birth of Isaac to her implicit reliance on the word of the Almighty: "She judged him faithful who had promised, and received strength" [Heb. 11:11].

Not long after this, Abraham removed from Mamre, where he had long resided, and went to dwell in Gerar, the capital of the Philistines. Here was reenacted the same folly which had formerly cost them so much in Egypt, and which it is most marvellous to us should have ever been forgotten. Sarah was again taken by a heathen king, and only restored to her husband by the intervention of Jehovah. She was at this time ninety years of age, yet so remarkable was her beauty that she was as much an object of attraction as in her youthful days, and Abimelech, after reproving Abraham for his deception, hinted to her, that it would be becoming in her to wear, when among strangers, a closely-covering veil, such as was universally customary among females resident in towns, in order to avoid the dangers to which her beauty exposed her. So far as we can gather from the sacred volume, Sarah was at this very time pregnant, by the miraculous power of Jehovah, which renders the whole scene still more remarkable.

Whether they remained long in Gerar, we are not informed, nor where Isaac was born. But the joyful day came at length. "After a childless union of more than sixty years," Abraham and Sarah welcomed with delight the heir of the promises, the covenanted gift of Jehovah. They called him Isaac. "There shall be laughter;" "All that hear will laugh with me," said Sarah; and, indeed, few events, if any, recorded on the sacred page, were welcomed with so much rejoicing. Nearly three years, according to the custom of her nation, Sarah nourished her infant at her own breast; and only a mother can imagine her heartfelt happiness and gratitude during that delightful time. "And the child grew and was weaned, and Abraham made a great feast the same day that Isaac was weaned." It was a bright, joyous day; friends were congregated, tables of abundance were spread, congratulations were poured forth; while the unconscious object of all, the pride and joy of fond parents, the hope of generations to come, pursued his childish sports and expressed his childish wonder at the scene. But, like many sunny mornings of earth, it was to be overhung with clouds, its joy to be dampened by deep sorrow.

Two hearts were there which no gladness visited, and in which no good feelings were cherished. Ishmael and his mother were envious and discontented witnesses of all that occurred. The happiness of others was their sorrow, the fulfilment of hope to Abraham and Sarah was their bitter disappointment; and they manifested their dissatisfaction; Hagar, probably, by pouring out her thoughts to her son, and he by ridiculing and speaking contemptuously of Isaac. Sarah saw and heard, and all that was to come in the future—the discord and wrangling, the endless disputes and heart-burnings, the evil and perhaps malicious influence over her precious child— flashed instantly upon her mind, and, urged by an impulse too strong to be resisted, she sought her husband, and demanded that Hagar should be divorced, and Ishmael disinherited. It was a grievous request to Abraham. Ishmael was his own son, his first-born and first-beloved; and toward Hagar he felt the tenderness of a father for the mother of his child. He appears to have appealed to God, who bade him do as Sarah had said, for Isaac was to be his only heir; but, at the same time, soothed his grief, and allayed his anxieties, by promising that Ishmael, for his sake, should be abundantly prospered and blessed.

Early on the morning which followed the weaning feast, Abraham arose to execute his sorrowful task. Calling Hagar, he gave her the necessary directions for her future course, placed on her shoulder a leathern bottle of water, and bread sufficient for their present wants, and then, putting Ishmael's hand in hers, he bade them a final farewell, and sent them on their way. Wonderful, indeed, was the faith and obedience of Abraham! . . .

After the departure of Hagar and Ishmael little is recorded concerning the family of Abraham. They dwelt at Beersheba, and, so far as we know, their life passed quietly. Of Sarah's character as a mother we earnestly wish to know more than we are told. Not a word is said of her instructions to her cherished son, and we can only gather the proof of her faithfulness from the excellent character of Isaac. We know that daily lessons of obedience to his parents were instilled into his young mind, for he hesitated not to follow his father, unquestioned, to the Mount of Moriah, and to do his bidding to the utmost. . . .

The strongest earthly ties are frail when death appears. Sarah's death and the circumstances of her burial are touchingly described in the sacred volume, and it is worthy of notice, that she is the only woman to whom such honor is given. Abraham was a stranger and sojourner in the land of Canaan, and had hitherto owned not a foot of the land promised to his descendants, nor had he needed such possession. Cared for by God, and surrounded by those he loved, every place was home. But now, death had removed the light of his eyes, the fond companion of his days. Nearly a century had she shared his every joy and sorrow, and cheered his pilgrim lot. But now she would no longer gladden his tent, nor accompany him in his wanderings. She had daily bowed with him, through those long years, in sincere and humble worship of the living God, and their united faith had drawn from him wonderful, even miraculous blessings. But now her familiar form would appear no more at the sacred altar, nor her confidence in the Almighty strengthen his own. He had loved her in their early days, when she was the pride and joy of his Chaldean home, but she was far dearer to him when he looked upon her, after nearly a century had passed over her head, with beauty unimpaired, her youth renewed by the kindness of God, folding to her mother's breast the long-desired and most precious son of promise. "A babe in a house is not merely a well-spring of pleasure," and "a messenger of peace and love," but infancy and childhood ever bring with them freshening and revivifying influences. Abraham had felt their influences himself, and seen their effect on Sarah, and we can well believe that their evening-time had been brighter than the morning.

But she was gone, and the question came, "where should he lay, for their last repose, the remains of his beloved and faithful wife?" Not in the burying-places of the idolaters! He could not endure the thought. He purchased the cave of Machpelah, and, with weeping and mourning, buried his dead out of his sight.

Around that grave of Sarah how many sacred associations linger. There, when years had passed, Isaac and Ishmael met, for the first time, perhaps, since the weaning feast, to lay their honored father by her side. "There they buried Isaac and Rebecca his wife; there Jacob buried Leah," and thither went up from Egypt the "chariots and horsemen, a very great company," who, with Joseph, bore the body of Jacob also to the same quiet resting-place [Gen. 49:31; 50:9]. Upon the hills of that beautiful region the mighty Anakims dwelt [Gen. 6:4], and from thence, more than four hundred years after, when the descendants of Abraham were returning from bondage, the spies sent by Moses brought back the evil report which resulted in the many wanderings of the wilderness [Num. 13:25–14:25]. On that spot stood one of the most ancient cities of the world—the possession of Caleb, the son of Jephunneh, where the tribes received their inheritance, and later, a city of refuge, and assigned to the Levites [Josh. 14:12-15, 15:14; 20:1-7]. There David held his court seven years [2 Sam. 5:5], and there Absalom raised the standard of revolt [2 Sam. 15:7]. And when centuries had rolled away, when the long-expected Messiah was at hand, to that sacred "city in the hill-country of Judah, went, in haste," the most highly favored among women, the virgin mother of Jesus, to exchange congratulations with her only less favored cousin, and to pour forth her song of exultation and triumph [Luke 1:39-55]. The spot on which Abraham and Sarah dwelt so long and where their bones reposed, where the Almighty had reiterated his solemn promises, thousands of years after, witnessed Mary's joy, and echoed her song of gratitude to him whose word abideth forever, for the fulfilment of those very assurances. "My soul doth magnify the Lord; he hath holpen his servant Israel in remembrance of his mercy; as he spake to our fathers, to Abraham and his seed forever" [Luke 1:46, 54-55].

A multitude of reflections crowd upon us as we draw to a close our account of Sarah and Hagar, to which we can do no justice. Indeed, we feel that we have given a meagre transcript of our own thoughts while studying this deeply interesting history. We earnestly request those who have read these pages, not to rest for a moment satisfied, but to take the sacred book, and, asking light from above, give themselves to the work of gaining all the instruction it affords upon this theme. We assure them that encouragement, strength, and blessing will be their reward. Especially, they shall gain delightful views of the character of Jehovah, and be able to sing as never before, "Exalt the Lord our God" [Ps. 99:5]. "Praise ye the Lord, for his mercy endureth forever" [Ps. 106:1].

Sarah, notwithstanding her dignified station, her wonderful beauty and noble character, was still an imperfect woman; yet how kindly was she dealt with; what honor has God put upon her. She consented to prevarication and deceit with her husband, but the evil consequences which they deserved were once and again prevented by divine interposition. She laughed incredulously at his gracious words of promise, and then denied her fault. Yet, in consideration of her "fear and amazement," she was not severely reproved, the blessing was not withheld, nor was her fault noticed to the exclusion of what was otherwise good in her conduct, for, by the mouth of Peter, God afterward commends her reverence for her husband, manifested at that very time. She was faithless, and jealous, and angry in her dealings with Hagar, yet the Almighty did not take his favor from her, while he suffered her to reap the bitter fruit of her folly. As a mother, how remarkable is his kindness to her. "She was ninety years of age when Isaac was born. In the course of nature ten or twelve years would have closed her mortal career, or rendered it, from the infirmities of age, a burden to herself and all around her. There was apparently no need of her preservation to forward the decrees of the Lord. In giving birth to the child of promise, her part was fulfilled, and at the age of ten or twelve the boy might have done without her. But God is LOVE, and the affections of his children are, in their strength and purity, peculiarly acceptable to him. He never bestoweth happiness to withdraw it; and therefore, to perfect the felicity of Sarah and her child, his tenderness preserved her in life and vigor seven and thirty years after she had given him birth. The trial of faith, also, in the sacrifice of his son, was given to the father. He demanded not from her what he knew the mother could not bear."[36] . . .

Would that, amid our many cares, anxieties, and sorrows, we could ever bear in mind the love of him who wove the ties by which our hearts are bound to our children, whose tenderness and sympathy are never-failing, who says to every one of his redeemed children, "Can a mother forget her child? Yea, they may, yet will I not forget thee" [Isa. 49:15].

§29 Harriet Beecher Stowe
(1811–1896)

Harriet Beecher Stowe was the seventh of thirteen children of Lyman Beecher (1775–1863), a famous Congregational minister and seminary president. She received a fine education at home and at Hartford Female Seminary, a school established by her older sister, Catharine. She obtained a remarkable theological education from her father. As Mary Kelley suggested, "Had Stowe been a male she undoubtedly would have followed her father's example and embarked upon a ministerial career."[37] After her marriage to the distinguished biblical scholar Calvin Ellis Stowe in 1836, she wrote for local religious periodicals and newspapers to supplement her husband's inadequate salary. She is best remembered for her novel *Uncle Tom's Cabin*, originally published as a serial (1851–1852). Her later prose writings on the Bible, *Woman in Sacred History* (1873) and *Footsteps of the Master* (1878), are particularly fine examples of the interpretive work of a woman who effectively blended the resources of the male academy and the church with insights and questions honed in a woman's world. Stowe constantly relied on her husband's literary and scholarly judgment and used him as a resource for her own writings.[38]

---

[36] Here Ashton quotes Aguilar without noting her source.

[37] Mary Kelley, *Private Woman, Public Stage: Literary Domesticity in Nineteenth-Century America* (New York: Oxford University Press, 1984), 82.

[38] Marie Caskey wrote: "Calvin read and criticized her drafts, suggested lines of investigation and brought many sources, including apocryphal and traditionary ones, to her attention" (*Chariot of Fire: Religion and the Beecher Family* [New Haven: Yale University Press, 1978], 183).

With the assistance of her own "Rabbi," as she affectionately called her husband, Stowe added a critical and scholarly dimension to the exegetical and practical homiletical skills she had learned from her father. Her experiences as a daughter, wife, and mother (the Stowes had seven children) added a distinctively feminine hue to the exegesis, exposition, and preaching that she wove into her writing.

Stowe began *Woman in Sacred History* with the story of Sarah, not of Eve. Stowe's purpose in the book was to trace the story of salvation history, and so she began with Sarah as the wife of Abraham and mother of the chosen line.

Stowe recognized a disparity between the "despotic" wife portrayed in Genesis, and the New Testament and other traditional portraits of Sarah as an exemplary submissive wife. Taking her cue from the meaning of the Hebrew name, Sarah, "princess," Stowe argued that "crowned with the power of eminent beauty, and fully understanding the sovereignty it gave her over man Sarah was virtually empress and mistress of the man she called 'lord.'" Like Hyneman and Ashton, Stowe elevated Sarah from princess to queen; Sarah was a beautiful, queenly, and despotic woman. "Over the heart of such a man," Abraham's strong, domineering wife exerted powerful control, expecting him "to use his authority in the line of her wishes." Stowe did not find such a model of submission objectionable. Doubtless, Sarah's submission mirrored the experience of many nineteenth-century women who ruled the home and expected their husbands to use their "authority" in accordance with their wives' wishes. Ellet's discussion of authority of the father in the home lacked the subtlety and candor of Stowe's discussion. Wagenknecht suggested that Stowe "knew that on the domestic front women are more than a match for men and always have been, that if a man loves a woman she has a hold over him which no legal privilege that he may hold can possible counter-balance, and that if he does not wish to kill her or discard her, he *must* please her."[39]

Stowe liked Sarah. However, unlike Aguilar and Hyneman, she stressed that Sarah was "real flesh and blood as any woman in the pages of Shakespeare,— not a saint, but an average mortal, with all the foibles, weaknesses, and variabilities that pertain to womanhood, and to womanhood in an early age of imperfectly developed morals." Like Ellet, on the other hand, Stowe used developmental language to portray the biblical era as "naïve" and undeveloped. She recognized the importance of being sensitive to literary genre and historical context.

[39] Edward Wagenknecht, *Harriet Beecher Stowe: The Known and the Unknown* (New York: Oxford University Press, 1965), 56.

From Harriet Beecher Stowe, *Women in Sacred History* (New York: Fords, Howard, & Hulbert, 1873), 25–31.

–Sarah the Princess–

ONE woman in the Christian dispensation has received a special crown of honor. Sarah, the wife of Abraham, mother of the Jewish nation, is to this day an object of traditional respect and homage in the Christian Church. Her name occurs in the marriage service as an example for the Christian wife, who is exhorted to meekness and obedience by St. Peter, "Even as Sarah obeyed Abraham, calling him lord; whose daughters ye are, so long as ye do well,and are not subject to a slavish fear" [1 Pe. 3:6].

In turning to the narrative of the Old Testament, however, we are led to feel that in setting Sarah before wives as a model of conjugal behavior, no very alarming amount of subjection or submission is implied.

The name Sarah means "princess"; and from the Bible story we infer that, crowned with the power of eminent beauty, and fully understanding the sovereignty it gave her over man, Sarah was virtually empress and mistress of the man she called "lord." She was a woman who understood herself and him, and was too wise to dispute the title when she possessed the reality of sway; and while she called Abraham "lord," it is quite apparent from certain little dramatic incidents that she expected him to use his authority in the line of her wishes.

In going back to these Old Testament stories, one feels a ceaseless admiration of the artless simplicity of the primitive period of which they are the only memorial. The dew of earth's early morning lies on it, sparkling and undried; and the men and women speak out their hearts with the simplicity of little children.

In Abraham we see the man whom God designed to be the father of a great sacerdotal nation; through whom, in the fullness of time, should come the most perfect revelation of himself to man, by Jesus Christ. In choosing the man to found such a nation, the Divine Being rejected the stormy and forcible characters which command the admiration of rude men in early ages, and chose one of gentler elements. Abraham was distinguished for a loving heart, a tender domestic nature, great reverence, patience, and fidelity, a childlike simplicity of faith, and a dignified self-possession. Yet he was not deficient in energy or courage when the event called for them. When the warring tribes of the neighborhood had swept his kinsman, Lot, into captivity, Abraham came promptly to the rescue, and, with his three hundred trained servants, pursued, vanquished, and rescued. Though he loved not battle, when roused for a good cause he fought to some purpose.

Over the heart of such a man, a beautiful, queenly woman held despotic sway. Traveling with her into the dominions of foreign princes, he is possessed by one harassing fear. The beauty of this woman,—will it not draw the admiration of marauding powers? And shall I not be murdered, or have her torn from me? And so, twice, Abraham resorts to the stratagem of concealing their real relation, and speaking of her as his sister. The Rabbinic traditions elaborate this story with much splendor of imagery.[40] According to them, Abraham being obliged by famine to sojourn in Egypt, rested some days by the river Nile; and as he and Sarah walked by the banks of the river, and he beheld her wonderful beauty reflected in the water, he was overwhelmed with fear lest she should be taken from him, or that he should be slain for her sake. So he persuaded her to pass as his sister; for, as he says, "she was the daughter of my father, but not of my mother." The legend goes on to say, that, as a further precaution, he had her placed in a chest to cross the frontier; and when the custom-house officers met them, he offered to pay for the box whatever they might ask, to pass it free.

"Does it contain silks?" asked the officers.
"I will pay the tenth as of silk," he replied.
"Does it contain silver?" they inquired.
"I will pay for it as silver," answered Abraham.
"Nay, then, it must contain gold."
"I will pay for it as gold."
"May be it contains most costly gems."
"I will pay for it as gems," he persisted.

In the struggle the box was broken open, and in it was seated a beautiful woman whose countenance illumined all Egypt. The news reached the ears of Pharaoh, and he sent and took her.

In comparing these Rabbinic traditions with the Bible, one is immediately struck with the difference in quality,—the dignified simplicity of the sacred narrative contrasts forcibly with the fantastic elaborations of tradition.[41]

The Rabbinic and Alcoranic[42] stories are valuable, however, as showing how profound an impression the personality of these characters had left on

[40] Louis Ginzberg, *The Legends of the Jews*, vol. 1 (Philadelphia: The Jewish Publication Society of America, 1909), ch. 5: Abraham: His Sojourn in Egypt.

[41] The influence of Calvin Stowe is clear here. He used the comparative method in his discussion of the criteria for inclusion of books in the New Testament canon. See his *Origin and History of the Books of the Bible, Both the Canonical and the Apocryphal,* designed to show what the Bible is not, what it is, and how to use it. (Hartford: Hartford Connecticut Publishing, 1867).

[42] Calvin Stowe introduced his wife to the stories about Sarah and Abraham in the rabbinic sources and in the Koran.

mankind. The great characters of the Biblical story, though in themselves simple, seemed, like the sun, to raise around them many-colored and vaporous clouds of myth and story. The warmth of their humanity kept them enwreathed in a changing mist of human sympathies.

The falsehoods which Abraham tells are to be estimated not by the modern, but by the ancient standard. In the earlier days of the world, when physical force ruled, when the earth was covered with warring tribes, skill in deception was counted as one of the forms of wisdom. "The crafty Ulysses" is spoken of with honor through the "Odyssey" for his skill in dissembling; and the Lacedaemonian youth were punished, not for stealing or lying, but for performing these necessary operations in a bungling, unskillful manner.[43]

In a day when it was rather a matter of course for a prince to help himself to a handsome woman wherever he could find her, and kill her husband if he made any objections, a weaker party entering the dominions of a powerful prince was under the laws of war.

In our nineteenth century we have not yet grown to such maturity as not to consider false statements and stratagem as legitimate war policy in dealing with an enemy. Abraham's ruse is not, therefore, so very far behind even the practice of modern Christians. That he should have employed the same fruitless stratagem twice, seems to show that species of infatuation on the one subject of a beloved woman, which has been the "last infirmity" of some otherwise strong and noble men,—wise everywhere else, but weak there.

The Rabbinic legends represent Sarah as being an object of ardent admiration to Pharaoh, who pressed his suit with such vehemence that she cried to God for deliverance, and told the king that she was a married woman. Then—according to this representation—he sent her away with gifts, and even extended his complacency so far as to present her with his daughter Hagar as a handmaid,—a legend savoring more of national pride than of probability.

In the few incidents related of Sarah she does not impress us as anything more than the beautiful princess of a nomadic tribe, with many virtues and the failings that usually attend beauty and power.

With all her advantages of person and station, Sarah still wanted what every woman of antiquity considered the crowning glory of womanhood. She was childless. By an expedient common in those early days, she gives her slave as second wife to her husband, whose child shall be her own. The Rabbinic tradition says that up to this time Hagar had been tenderly beloved by Sarah. The prospect, however, of being mother to the heir of the family seems to have turned the head of the handmaid, and broken the bonds of friendship between them.

---

[43] Homer's Greek epic poem, the *Odyssey*, was a tale of Ulysses's wanderings.

In its usual naïve way, the Bible narrative represents Sarah as scolding her patient husband for the results which came from following her own advice. Thus she complains, in view of Hagar's insolence: "My wrong be upon thee. I have given my maid unto thy bosom, and when she saw that she had conceived, I was despised in her eyes. The Lord judge between thee and me."

We see here the eager, impulsive, hot-hearted woman, accustomed to indulgence, impatient of trouble, and perfectly certain that she is in the right, and that the Lord himself must think so. Abraham, as a well-bred husband, answers pacifically: "Behold, thy maid is in thy hand, to do as pleaseth thee." And so it pleased Sarah to deal so hardly with her maid that she fled to the wilderness.

Finally, the domestic broil adjusts itself. The Divine Father, who watches alike over all his creatures, sends back the impetuous slave from the wilderness, exhorted to patience, and comforted with a promise of a future for her son.

Then comes the beautiful idyl of the three angels, who announce the future birth of the long-desired heir. We could wish all our readers, who may have fallen out of the way of reading the Old Testament, to turn again to the eighteenth chapter of Genesis, and see the simple picture of those olden days. Notice the beautiful hospitality of reception. The Emir rushes himself to his herd to choose the fatted calf, and commands the princess to make ready the meal, and knead the cakes. Then comes the repast. The announcement of the promised blessing, at which Sarah laughs in incredulous surprise; the grave rebuke of the angels, and Sarah's white lie, with the angel's steady answer, — are all so many characteristic points of the story. Sarah, in all these incidents, is, with a few touches, made as real flesh and blood as any woman in the pages of Shakespeare, — not a saint, but an average mortal, with all the foibles, weaknesses, and variabilities that pertain to womanhood, and to womanhood in an early age of imperfectly developed morals.

We infer from the general drift of the story, that Sarah, like most warm-hearted and passionate women, was, in the main, a kindly, motherly creature, and that, when her maid returned and submitted, she was reconciled to her. At all events, we find that the son of the bondwoman was born and nurtured under her roof, along with her own son Isaac. It is in keeping with our conception of Sarah, that she should at times have overwhelmed Hagar with kindness, and helped her through the trials of motherhood, and petted the little Ishmael till he grew too saucy to be endured.

The Jewish mother nursed her child three years. The weaning was made a great fête, and Sarah's maternal exultation at this crisis of her life, displayed itself in festal preparations. We hear her saying: "God hath made me to laugh, so that all that hear will laugh with me. Who would have said unto Abraham that Sarah should have given children suck? for I have borne him a son in his old age."

In the height of this triumph, she saw the son of the Egyptian woman mocking, and all the hot blood of the woman, mother, and princess flushed up, and she said to her husband: "Cast out this bondwoman and her son; for the son of this bondwoman shall not be heir with my son, even with Isaac."

We are told "the thing was very grievous in Abraham's sight because of his son." But a higher power confirms the hasty, instinctive impulse of the mother. The God of nations saw in each of these infant boys the seed-forms of a race with a history and destiny apart from each other, and Abraham is comforted with the thought that a fatherly watch will be kept over both.

Last of all we come to the simple and touching announcement of the death of this woman, so truly loved to the last. "And Sarah was a hundred and seven and twenty years old: these were the years of the life of Sarah. And Sarah died in Kirjath-arba; the same is Hebron in the land of Canaan; and Abraham came to mourn for Sarah, and to weep for her." It is a significant token of the magnificent physical vigor with which that early age was endowed, that now, for the first time, the stroke of death has fallen on the family of Abraham, and he is forced to seek a burial-place. Sarah, the beautiful princess, the crowned mother of a great nation, the beloved wife, is dead; and Abraham, constant lover in age as youth, lays her away with tears. To him she is ever young; for love confers on its object eternal youth.

A beautiful and peculiar passage in the history describes the particulars of the purchase of this burial-place. All that love can give to the fairest, most beautiful, and dearest is a tomb; and Abraham refuses to take as a gift from the nobles of the land so sacred a spot. It must be wholly his own, bought with his own money. The sepulchre of Machpelah, from the hour it was consecrated by the last sleep of the mother of the tribe, became the calm and sacred resting-place to which the eyes of children's children turned. So Jacob, her grandson, in his dying hour, remembered it:—

> "Bury me with my fathers in the cave that is in the field of Ephron the Hittite. There they buried Abraham and Sarah his wife; there they buried Isaac and Rebekah his wife, and there I buried Leah." [Gen. 49:29]

Two powerful and peculiar nations still regard this sepulcher with veneration, and cherish with reverence the memory of Sarah the Princess.

§30 Etty Woosnam
(1849–c.1883)

Etty Woosnam[44] was born in India to British parents and as a teenager returned to England to reside in Somerset. Her essays on women in the Bible for young ladies' Bible classes read like powerful sermons. Her elaborate depictions of women's lives reveal much about the lives and values of privileged women in nineteenth-century Britain.

Woosnam, like Stowe, recognized the complexities of Sarah. She praised her qualities that matched the ideals of the cult of domesticity but also acknowledged her weaknesses. She connected Sarah's strengths and weaknesses to the lives of women of her day. Sometimes Woosnam attributed great power and influence to women, though that power was exercised within circumscribed roles and spheres. Other times, she calls women weak and inferior to men. Woosnam's personal ambivalence over the Woman Question reflects the tension found in the writings of many women throughout the nineteenth century.[45]

Woosnam used a wide variety of resources to support her various arguments, including academic resources, literary sources, and devotional writings. Woosnam, a strong supporter of the cult of domesticity, developed a theology of work for women. She argued that women should see their household duties as a part of the pious life. Woosnam's discussion of women's work is part of a larger debate over how far the boundaries of the domestic sphere should extend. In an address to a class of "lady students" at Oxford in 1897, Elizabeth Wordsworth, Principal of Lady Margaret Hall, Oxford, argued for very wide boundaries when she encouraged women to enlarge their sphere of sympathy, and "yearn for the ignorant, the untaught, the unevangelized, of every race and of every clime. She must be always lengthening her cords and strengthening her stakes (Isa liv. 2) . . . She, too, must use those handmaidens—all art, all knowledge, all study, all skill—to bear her company in the service of the King."[46]

---

[44] For a more complete discussion of Woosnam, see part 1, "Eve—The Mother of Us All."

[45] See the discussion of the Woman Question in the introduction.

[46] Elizabeth Wordsworth, *Psalms for the Christian Festivals* (London: Longmans, Green, 1906), 18.

From Etty Woosnam, *The Woman of the Bible: Old Testament* (London: S. W. Partridge & Co., 1881), 18–30. [Text taken from the 4th ed., n.d.]

–Sarah–
Women's Temptations

THE thought of Sarah, Abraham's wife, comes like a breath of home air. Around her name cluster the associations of those wifely domestic virtues which shone in the holy women of old who trusted in God, who had the ornament of a meek and quiet spirit, and were in subjection unto their own husbands. Not of those who through petulance and haughtiness mar the peace of the family circle, or rule over their husbands and friends, and excuse themselves by saying how much they love them. Sarah had no greater pride than to "obey" Abraham, calling him lord. "A meek and quiet spirit" [1 Pet. 3:4] is of great price in God's sight, and of great power over the hearts and minds of men and women. And the women so adorned are the best. As an eminent saint of two hundred years ago expressed it—"It is their very gentleness that makes them powerful. Do you know that pliable steel is far stronger than rough iron?"

Sarah is quoted in the New Testament as an ensample of the practice of little domestic virtues. Have you ever noticed that where St. Paul in his Epistle to the Colossians (chapter iii), or to the Ephesians (chapter v), or St. Peter in his 1st Epistle, instructs as to the duties of the different relations of life, the conduct of the *wife* is always put first, as of the greatest importance? It has been said—"Women control and form the manners of the age in which they live." They are the arbiters of the social customs which prevail. The first name that woman ever received was the beautiful one which God gave to her when as yet man only existed, "an help-meet for him;" and the first object of every wife should be to help her husband to love and serve God better. Milton's line "He for God only—she for God in him,"[47] sounds like a lovely song whose echoes never die away. God does not in His holy Word anywhere encourage women to seek distinction or eminence for themselves, but shows how good women make it easier for men to rise. "A virtuous woman is a crown to her husband" [Prov. 12:4]. The reward held out to a faithful wife is his success. "Her husband is known in the gates when he sitteth among the elders of the land" [Prov. 31:23]. And what greater honour need any woman look for, than

[47] *Paradise Lost* (1667), book 4, l. 296–98. In these lines, Milton writes of the difference between Adam and Eve, and, by extension, between all men and women:

For contemplation he and valor formed,

For softness she and sweet attractive grace;

He for God only, she for God in him.

that "the heart of her husband (or her brother, father, son, friend) doth safely trust in her" [Prov. 31:11]?

Though Sarah's beauty was striking, and her position high, she performed the homeliest duties. Abram said to her: "Make ready quickly three measures of fine meal, knead it, and make cake upon the earth;" and so she at once engaged in

> "the tender ministries
> Of female hands and hospitality."[48]

She was "in the tent" when the angels came to her with the happy news. It has always been in the ordinary routine of duty that the angels of God have found His servants. The shepherds were keeping watch over their flocks by night when the heavenly minstrels sang to them of the birth of infant Jesus [Luke 2:8-15]. Matthew Henry quaintly says—"there is nothing to be got by gadding;"[49] and (in Titus ii. 5), St. Paul says young women are to be "Keepers at home," as well as good and obedient to their own husbands. How many verses in the description of the perfect woman of Solomon allude to her doing household work! [Prov. 31:10-31] though she is the most refined and highly cultured of her sex. What a mistake it is to suppose that piety consists in attending services, addressing classes, hymn singing and prayer merely. And what a very great pity it is that when inquiring as to the best work-man or work-woman, you are often told the one is the better person—the sober, respectable, religious man or woman—but *the other will do your work best*. The power of true godliness would be much greater in the world if all Christians tried earnestly to do things as well as they can possibly be done; if, with their Church-going, they combined great diligence in the exercise of their callings. Saintliness is not only to meditate much and have a solemn manner. A good Christian is not a man shut up in a cave or in a hermitage, nor is he an unpractical dreamer. He is "a workman approved unto God, that needeth not to be ashamed" [2 Tim. 2:15], either before the eye of God, or the criticism of men. What better type of woman can we imagine than the one who is diligent in the discharge of her home duties: the one who makes a house look bright, and the people in it feel happy and comfortable; who is sunshiny and even in temper; and who does all she does as well as possible? The most trifling things must be thought of and carefully measured to get

---

[48] Lord Alfred Tennyson, "The Princess," VI.

[49] Woosnam cites Matthew Henry's *Commentary* on Genesis, ch.18: "Where is Sarah thy wife? was asked. Note the answer, In the tent. Just at hand, in her proper place, occupied in her household concerns. There is nothing got by gadding. Those are most likely to receive comfort from God and his promises, who are in their proper place, and in the way of their duty."

the right result, whether in needlework, painting, music, literary composition, sculpture, gardening, nursing, or cooking. The most successful workers in every department have been those who were most careful in the minute details. Michael Angelo said well:—"Trifles make perfection, and perfection is no trifle." It does not reflect much lustre on our religion if we do our work worse than the sin-loving worldlings; and we are told that all actions—"whatsoever we do"—must be done to the Glory of God [1 Cor. 10:31]. Can you imagine that St. Paul and Aquila had the reputation of being the worst tent makers in Corinth, though the best expounders of the Gospel [Acts 18:1-22]? . . .

If the brief outline of Sarah's life and character suggests the thought of the domestic duties of woman, it reminds us as forcibly of her special temptations. Sarah must have been a prey to several.

(i.) She was beautiful. It was not only in the imagination of a partial husband, but in the land of Egypt, "the Egyptians beheld the woman that she was very fair." Personal appearance is a great temptation to women. If a young woman has beauty, she gains so easily the goodwill and admiration of strangers, and receives so much flattery from friends, that she is prone to concern herself very little about real self denying efforts to do good—to see no great reason to struggle after that inward sanctification which alone can please God. She is likely to become overbearing and proud, expecting from all, the homage she has obtained from the shallow. She is likely to find this world so pleasant that heaven is forgotten and the object of life missed. She receives exaggerated praise and believes it to be her due; and when her beauty passes away and she is treated with indifference, she is tempted to become bitter and harsh in her thoughts of others, to find her friends are vain, and yet not seek a friend in God.

To have an unattractive exterior is also a great temptation to women. I believe Satan leads many a girl through her plain face or clumsy figure. She is self-conscious; tries to deceive herself that she is better inside than outside; is tempted to repine at God's having withheld from her not only the pleasing looks but all the love and approbation which seem to be their result. The only cure for both these searching trials is to humble the soul before God, and beseech Him to sanctify and adorn it with all the graces of the Holy Spirit. "You who are beautiful, be beautiful to the Lord and give God thanks; and you who are not beautiful, rest assured you will be fair enough yonder and give God thanks." If we desired holiness above all things and allowed God's Spirit to work out His graces in our life, we would be lovely enough in the eyes of our fellow-creatures to win much love, and have much power to help others and lead them nearer to God.

(ii.) Sarah had position. In Genesis xvii.15, the margin shows her name meant "Princess," and it was appropriate to her dignity—wife of the first patriarch of the chosen people of Jehovah—of the father (spiritually) of all the faithful, and the "Friend of God" [James 2:23]. If in the course of her history we find some petulance or arrogance towards her handmaid Hagar, she was in special danger to the temptation of pride. Satan loves to see souls perched on pinnacles of the temple, for he knows they are slippery places; and for easy slippery roads we need to be very carefully rough-shod with nails, "the preparation of the Gospel of peace" [Eph. 6:15]. Prosperity tries the disposition even more than adversity, and has in it the element of making the soul imagine it is less absolutely dependent on God for safety. If we are "well-born" (as custom ridiculously expresses it) or "well-connected," or situated in comfortable circumstances, then we have particular need to guard against temptations to indolence, pride, apathy, self-indulgence, and self-sufficiency. It takes more effort on the part of rich people to resist and keep under the fleshly lusts which war against the soul, and to discipline themselves, than on that of those who are subdued by want and the poverty of God's appointment.

> "Others beside the violet
> Are safest in the shade."

Those in a slightly higher social standing than their neighbours have a tendency to be dogmatical and authoritative. They are listened to with servility by their humbler neighbours, and often take flattery and the most unwarrantable praise as if it were true. The fact of being a mistress over several household servants, or a governess instructing young children, gives many women the consequential oracular manner which spoils their womanliness, and diminishes their influence in general society. Let us beware of the traps and gins[50] spread by Satan in front of respectable positions.

(iii.) Sarah's wifely and domestic affections were very keen. Women's love is often a stronger temptation than beauty or high place. The love of approbation, or the still more general love of love, is one of the severest of masters. It is extremely difficult for women to resist doing *anything* to please those whom they love. Husbands and children take such a hold of life and heart that little is left for communion with God; and where women have not such strong claims as these, fathers, mothers, sisters, brothers, cousins, and friends, often exercise too powerful a sway over all the views and actions. Afraid to thwart others in wrong or foolish purposes—yielding easily to stronger wills—sacrificing principle and good resolutions to the irrepressible desire to please—is not this the character of the majority of our sex?—of even the better majority.

---

[50] A snare or trap for game.

"O Earth! thou art too beautiful,
    And thou, dear Home, thou art too sweet,
The winning ways of flesh and blood
    Too smooth for sinners' pilgrim feet."

Faber[51]

If we put things in their right place, we should know that "In His favour is life"; and that living solely for the favour of any other, or others, however good or noble, is death. If we desired to please Him before all others, the Holy Spirit, promised to those who earnestly ask, would enable us to do so; and I believe that we should gain besides the favour of God a fair share of the favour of man too. At any rate, let Madame Guyon's rule be ours:—"God first, and what God sees fit to give us afterwards."[52]

(iv.) Sarah was weakminded and fearful. To ensure her husband's safety she thought it necessary to tell a lie. It was lying, because it conveyed a wrong impression, though some men might have said it was a justifiable prevarication to call herself Abraham's sister as she was in reality his half-sister (Gen. xx. 12). The cowardice of woman's nature leads to much shuffling. Instead of doing right, come what may, and leaving the results to God, our wise and loving Father, we are given to calling out directly a storm is going to rise, "Lord, we perish!" [Matt. 8:25]. But He who sends the storm will steer the vessel. We may trust to the Strong Arm at the rudder.

"One who has known in storms to sail
I have on board.
Above the roaring of the gale
I hear my Lord.
He holds me when the billows smite,
I shall not fall.
If sharp, 'tis short; if long, 'tis light,
He tempers all."

Out of our very timidity our faith should rise strong. Our very helplessness and ignorance should perfect our trust, as many precious blessings are the outgrowth of disease and weakness. "I have been told," says Dr. DeWitt

---

[51] Frederick W. Faber (1814–1863) was a theologian and hymn writer involved in the Oxford movement. He converted from Anglicanism to Roman Catholicism and worked as a priest at the Brompton Oratory in London.

[52] Jeanne Marie Bouvier de la Mothe (1647–1717), better remembered as Madame Guyon, was a Roman Catholic mystic. Her book on prayer is a classic in spirituality. She wrote biblical commentaries, letters, an autobiography, poems, and canticles.

Talmage,[53] "that the pearl in an oyster is merely the result of a wound or a sickness upon it, and I do not know but that the brightest gems of Heaven will be found to have been the wounds of earth kindled into the jewelled brightness of eternal glory." That women are weaker in will and moral force than men is evident from the greater incapacity they show for correcting themselves of bad habits. Owing to a more defective education, they have less self-control than men of the same class—less power to subdue the flesh under the spirit; and therefore they need more grace, to lean more implicitly on the strength of Jesus who came to save His people from their sins. I once asked Mr. Mark Knowles if it were true that though drinking men are frequently known to become total abstainers and keep their pledge, it is impossible to reclaim female drunkards. He said that throughout the whole course of his experience he had known but one woman who had been able for any length of time to adhere to her resolution, and this woman could never yet trust herself to walk home alone, for going past a gin-shop gave her the irresistible craving, and she waited at a factory or wherever her work was till her daughter came with a sturdy arm and unflinching will to drag her safely past. Sometimes when she was hot and tired, and the fumes of the spirits were hot and very perceptible, she had to run with all her might, holding her hand over her nose to escape the danger. This was the only woman who had, in Mr. Mark Knowles' knowledge, ever overcome the habit of drinking, and the love of it seemed as strong as ever! Miss Emily Weston, who has worked for years in the Temperance cause, answered my question: "No, I never have. They keep steady for a little while, but women all relapse into drunkenness." And the Evil One has other chains as strong as this of strong drink. How often is it noticed that when a young man is aroused to thoughts of his immortal soul, and makes up his mind by God's grace to try and do his duty, he turns over a new leaf boldly. He puts a good distance between himself and his old courses. He gives a good-natured nod to his former frivolous companions, as much as to say: "I'm not going along with you; and so, unless you are going to turn round and come with me, we must part company, old friend." But girls are changed in a very different way, and one which does not glorify God in the eyes of the world half so much. They are affected over and over again by sermons, or touched by special dispensations, or softened by sorrows, before the worldliness is knocked out of them; and there is often much hankering after sentimental and unsatisfying pleasures, after they have begun to sip at the fountain of living water. Like Israel in the Wilderness, women are particularly apt to grumble for the fruits and flesh pots of Egypt when living by faith on the heavenly manna [Exod. 16:3].

[53] Thomas DeWitt Talmage (1832–1895) was a well-known preacher at Central Presbyterian Church, Brooklyn; his sermons were widely read.

(v.) Sarah was in a very trying and singular manner tempted to a sin, which is about the commonest in the world—commonest in the Church—which clings leech-like to all Christians, and like the hydra develops a new head and a fresh life for every one that is destroyed—a sin which has caused as much disorder, malice, misery, and sin in others, as strong drink, and probably more; and has done as much as anything else to extinguish the light of truth and to mar the work of God's servants. Sarah was jealous. If any one ever had an excuse for envy, she had. More than all other women, the Hebrews desired children, in the hope of being the honoured mother of the Messiah. To Abraham the glorious promise had been made, and Hagar the handmaid had a son. Hagar had been, no doubt, impertinent and taunting in her manner, as Sarah appeals to Abraham to redress her wrongs, and says she is despised in Hagar's eyes (Gen. xvi. 5). Perhaps any one would have thought and said in her place, that it was more than flesh and blood could stand. Every woman on the face of the earth is subject to repeated assaults of the adversary through this door of envy, and who is sufficient for these things? My dear sisters, you and I are not, and God has not promised to remove the thorn that pricks and galls, from our flesh, but He says: "My grace is sufficient for thee" [2 Cor. 12:9]. Christ will beat down Satan, hydra-headed though he be, shortly. We are more than conquerors through Him that loved us [Rom. 8:37].

Our life, then, is one of temptation. There are dangers to the right of us, dangers to the left of us, dangers behind us; and our only safety is in pressing forward, looking unto Jesus [Heb. 12:2]. He will hear and answer our daily prayer: "Lead us not into temptation" [Matt. 6:13]. "God is faithful who will not suffer you to be tempted above that ye are able; but will with the temptation also make a way to escape, that ye may be able to bear it" [1 Cor. 10:13]. Temptation is not sin. To be tempted and to overcome is Christ-like—is glorious.

"Talk of our sins being strong and our fear lest, if they do not now, they will at some time overcome us; why, it is the Lord of heaven and earth who invites us to confide in Him. His strength, which supports the universe, is surely sufficient for us. It is He who overcame all hell in banded opposition when He redeemed the world. Surely we need not fear that He will be powerful enough to save us. Besides that is His very object. He invites us to rest in Him and lay our self-hood aside, that He may redeem us from all our iniquities, and impart to us perfect peace. And what He says, He will undoubtedly perform. Rest then in the Lord."*

* Dr. Bayley [(1810–1886) was a public speaker and authored several books including *Religion: its influence on the working man, as a lover, husband, and father: a lecture delivered in the Concert Hall, Liverpool, on Sunday, September 19th, 1852; Observations made during a tour through Norway, Sweden, Finland, and Russia in the summer of 1866*, and *The Magnificent Scenes in the Book of Revelation* (1878)].

§31 Julia Wedgwood
(1833–1913)

Julia Wedgwood[54] was born into a privileged British family and spent her life surrounded by intellectuals. She wrote novels, articles, and a number of works of non-fiction, including *The Message of Israel in the Light of Modern Criticism* (1894), in which she used the results of contemporary Biblical criticism to elucidate the message of the Bible.

In this brief excerpt, Wedgwood described Abraham's timidity when faced with external challenges. Sarah, as Stowe intimated, controlled Abraham and he did not protect her from Pharaoh, as Hyneman imagined.

From Julia Wedgwood, *The Message of Israel in the Light of Modern Criticism* (London: Isbister, 1894), 157.

Towards his human kindred he [Abraham] is cowardly even when he is loving. He lacks the physical courage to protect Sarah against Pharaoh, and the moral courage to protect Hagar against Sarah. He surrenders the beloved child and the mother to the most miserable death rather than encounter the anger of a woman; he is willing to surrender this woman to what he should have dreaded more than any death, in order to avert an imaginary danger to himself.

§32 Clara Bewick Colby
(1846–1916)

Clara Bewick Colby was born in England and moved to the United States as a child. She graduated from the University of Wisconsin in 1869. She married former Civil War general, later assistant U.S. Attorney General, Leonard Wright Colby. They were divorced in 1906. Colby was active in the Woman's Suffrage movement, helping to bring the movement to Nebraska in 1881. She published the *Woman's Tribune*, the official publication of the

---

[54] For a more complete biography of Julia Wedgwood, see part 1, "Eve—The Mother of Us All."

Woman's Suffrage movement. Later in her life, Colby was interested in esoteric spirituality.

Colby contributed to Stanton's *Woman's Bible* project. In this excerpt, she
commented on the deeper meaning of Sarah's story using 1 Peter 3:6 and
Galatians 4 as a starting point. Colby argued for the freedom of women.
Her nineteenth-century esoteric reading argued for political and economic
freedom and equality for women, not just spiritual freedom. Unlike Putnam,
whose typological reading ignored the literal sense of the text, Colby incorporated the literal sense into her argument, then pushed beyond that and
beyond Putnam's spiritual sense of the text for an entirely new reading of
Sarah in light of the woman's movement.

> From Clara Bewick Colby, *The Woman's Bible,* ed. Elizabeth Cady
> Stanton (New York: The European Publishing Co., 1895), 43–44.

Western thinkers are so matter-of-fact in their speech and thought that it
might not have occurred to them that the true value of this story of Sarah and
Hagar, like that of all else, not only in our own Bible but in the scriptures of
other faiths, lies in the esoteric meaning, had it not been for Paul, that prince
of occult philosophers, who distinctly says, according to the old version, that
it is an allegory; according to the revised, that it contains an allegory: "for
these women are two covenants," one bearing, children unto bondage, the
other unto freedom [Gal. 4:21-31]. It is our privilege, Paul goes on to teach,
to be children of the free woman, but although we are this by birthright, yet
there has to be a personal appreciation of that fact, and an effort to maintain
our liberty. The mystical significance of this allegory has never been eluci-
dated in reference to the position of woman, but it may well be considered as
establishing her claim, not only for personal freedom, but for the integrity of
the home. Acting according to the customs of the day, Sarah connived at her
own degradation. Later, when her womanly dignity was developed by reason
of her motherhood, she saw what should be her true position in her home,
and she made her rightful demand for unrivalled supremacy in that home and
in her husband's affections. She was blessed of God in taking that attitude,
and was held up to the elect descendants of Abraham nearly 1660 years later
by the Apostle Peter as an example to be imitated. And these later women are
to be Sarah's daughters, we are told, if like her, they "are not afraid with any
amazement," or as the new version hath it, if they "are not put in fear by any
terror" [1 Pet. 3:6].

Even as mere history the life and character of Sarah certainly do not intimate that it was the Divine plan that woman was to be a subordinate, either
in person or in her home. Taken esoterically, as all ancient Oriental writings

must be to get their full significance, it is an inspiration to woman to-day to stand for her liberty. The bondwoman must be cast out. All that makes for industrial bondage, for sex slavery and humiliation, for the dwarfing of individuality, and for the thralldom of the soul, must be cast out from our home, from society, and from our lives. The woman who does not claim her birthright of freedom will remain in the wilderness with the children that she has borne in degradation, heart starvation, and anguish of spirit, only to find that they are Ishmaels, with their hand against every man. They will be the subjects of Divine care and protection until their destiny is worked out. But she who is to be the mother of kings must herself be free, and have surroundings conducive to maintaining her own purity and dignity. After long ages of freedom shall have eradicated from woman's mind and heart the thought habits of the slave, then will she be a true daughter of Sarah, the Princess.

C. B. C.

§33 Elizabeth Baxter
(1837–1926)

Elizabeth Baxter,[55] an evangelical Anglican active in many para-church ministries, was a preacher, teacher, evangelist, and prolific writer of some forty books and numerous booklets, tracts, and weekly Sunday School lessons. Her husband, Michael Baxter, a famous end-times lecturer and author, owned *The Christian Herald* paper and publishing house.

Like Stowe, Baxter wrestled with the difference between Sarah as presented in the New Testament and Sarah as presented in Genesis. Baxter used Hebrews 11 as a lens through which to read Genesis. She began and ended the first part of her treatment of Sarah's story with Sarah's faithfulness as recorded in Hebrews 11. Baxter encouraged her readers using the example of Sarah, who acted without faith but was in the end accounted faithful. Baxter assumed spiritual growth in Sarah that is not recorded in the Genesis account.

Unlike Colby, who wanted women to be free from any notion of subordinate roles, Baxter had a high view of help-meets. She thought Sarah failed as a help-meet in many ways. Unlike most interpreters, Baxter emphasized Sarah's culpability in the wife-sister stories. She saw these stories as the reverse of Eden; in these stories, it was the husband, Abraham, who tempted his wife

---

[55] For a more complete biography of Elizabeth Baxter, see part 1, "Eve—The Mother of Us All."

to sin. In Sarah's lack of faith in the promise and in her affliction of Hagar, Baxter considered Sarah unsuccessful as a help-meet.

In part two of Baxter's discussion of Sarah, she asked if the fate of Lot's wife possibly changed Sarah's mind about God's ability to perform his promise of a son to her. Further, Baxter raised the question of the difficulty of the there being two wife-sister stories.

From Elizabeth Baxter, *The Women in the Word*, 2nd ed. (London: Christian Herald, 1897), 9–20.

–Sarah–

"By faith even Sarah herself received power to conceive seed when she was past age, since she counted Him faithful who had promised."—Heb. xi. 11, R.V.

SARAH is the first woman mentioned in Heb. xi. among those who "obtained a good report through faith," and in this picture gallery of His faithful witnesses, the Lord mentions nothing else about Sarah but her faith. All the great imperfections of her life had been forgiven and blotted out, and nothing was remembered against her. But that faith which she exercised in becoming the mother of the child of promise was counted worthy of record side by side with the faith of an Enoch, an Abraham, a Moses, etc.

We have seen in the history of Eve that the vocation of woman, as she came from the hand of her Creator was to be a helpmeet to her husband, and in this vocation Sarah very frequently and very signally failed; yet the germ of faith, which in time brings forth faithfulness, was discernible in her from the first. She accompanied her husband when God called him out of Ur of the Chaldees, leaving behind her country, her kindred, her father's house, and all the familiar friends and the familiar scenes of her childhood. She was one with her husband in his trusting the God who gave him, for all he had lost, only promises of temporal blessing, with, however, a glorious share of spiritual blessing, a reality of communion with God INFINITELY MORE BLESSED than all the benefits he had left in his old home.

Having reached the land of Canaan, Sarah's husband set up memorials to the Lord at every halting-place on his journey, and called upon the name of his God, without fear of the heathen who carried on their worship around. (Gen. xii. 7, 8) But an unexpected trouble came upon them; there was a famine in the land. What should people do in the time of famine? Most men would say: "Do the best you can for yourselves." God says: "Trust in the Lord, and do good; dwell in the land, and verily thou shalt be fed." (Psa. xxxvii. 3) Abraham, accustomed as he was to take counsel with his God, failed in the point of temporal need. He followed after the way of most men, looked round him for ways of escape, and went down into Egypt to sojourn there (ver. 10), without waiting for God's direction. How could it be that he, a man whose faith in God had been such that he could leave all behind him in his own land, for the apparent uncertainty of the promises that God made him, should, in a time of famine, place no reliance on the forethought and care of a God whom he had trusted thus far? . . .

Sarah was at this juncture no real help to her husband. She failed in being a helpmeet. If she had had the confidence to remain in the land of Canaan, and had said, "Our God, who has led us thus far, will never fail us in a time of famine," Abraham might have been spared the failure and the disgrace with which he a witness for God, afterwards returned from the land of Egypt.

Lack of Faith, Lack of Faithfulness

When they were about to enter Egypt, Abraham proposed to Sarah that their relationship should be kept a secret, that they should say she was his sister. Here is the husband tempting the wife to sin. With Eve it was the wife who tempted the husband. Here again, if Sarah had stood on the side of God, and said: "A God who has led us so far cannot fail to take care of me. God has promised to make thee a great nation, to bless thee, to make thy name great, and to make thee a blessing, to bless them that bless thee, and curse them that curse thee. How can He then let harm come to me?"—how she might have encouraged her husband's faith! But instead of looking at things with the eye of faith, Sarah comes down to earthly combinations, and falls into Abraham's plans to deceive Pharaoh. The consequence is that no altar, no memorial for their God was set up in Egypt, and they were made no blessing there. They had to depart from that land, truly with increased riches, but with no increase of honour, and without leaving behind them one saved soul, one altar reared, one vestige of witness for the God for whose sake they had left all at His call in their old Chaldean home. (Gen. xii. 17–20; xiii. 1–3)

We come now to another page of Sarah's history; God had promised Abraham on two separate occasions that his seed should be numerous: "I will make thy seed as the dust of the earth: so that if a man can number the dust of the earth, then shall thy seed also be numbered" (Gen. xiii. 16), and again: "Look now toward heaven, and tell the stars, if thou be able to number them: and He said unto him, So shall thy seed be. And he believed in the Lord; and He counted it to him for righteousness." (Gen. xv. 5, 6) An earthly seed and a heavenly seed; and both innumerable! But year after year went by, and no sign of the promised seed appeared. Sarah began to be impatient, and FAITH IS NOT IMPATIENT. Faith for the promised seed failed her.

Unbelief is full of plans and human propositions; and so was Sarah, when she came to Abraham and said to him:

"Behold, now, the Lord hath restrained me from bearing: I pray thee, go in unto my maid; it may be that I may obtain children by her." (Gen. xvi. 2) Sarah was no helpmeet to her husband in this proposition; it was not of Divine origin. It came from the restlessness of unbelief. But Abraham hearkened to the voice of Sarah, and took Hagar to wife, contrary to the first order of God, that a man should cleave unto his wife; polygamy was never God's order.

When Hagar saw that she was likely to be the mother of a child, she despised her mistress. This was more than Sarah could bear. Anger and indignation took possession of her, and forgetting altogether that it was she who had brought this thing about, she looked at things only from her own point of view. She felt wronged, and reproached her husband:

"My wrong be upon thee: I gave my handmaid into thy bosom: and when she saw that she had conceived, I was despised in her eyes: the Lord judge between me and thee" (ver. 5).

A family quarrel might have ensued. But if Sarah had not her eye upon God, Abraham was looking to the Lord, and he spoke to Sarah as a man who knew how to trust. He could trust his wife, the circumstances, and Hagar too, into the hands of his faithful God:

"Behold, Thy maid is in Thy hand; do to her that which is good in Thine eyes."

Personal feelings were set aside. The question as between man and man had no weight when Abraham looked at things from above. Sarah dealt hardly with her servant, and Hagar fled from her face. Here again Sarah was no helpmeet to her husband. She acted selfishly and cruelly, because she considered herself rather than her God.

How wonderful that such a woman should at last have come to be numbered among the heroes of faith! Let us take courage; let us trust our God to show us our failure, shortcoming, and sin, in many of our household and family relations; let us trust Him to show us where we are wrong, to purify us, and work in us that life of faith which shall be to His glory, that sin may cease and the life of Christ be formed in us.

–Sarah–
Part II

"She judged Him faithful Who had promised" —Heb. xi. 11.

WHEN Abram was ninety-nine years old (Gen. xvii. 1), God appeared to him after thirteen years of silence, the result apparently of his unbelieving step in taking Hagar to wife. But now He speaks of a Covenant, and gives to Abram circumcision as a sign between God and his seed. Then God changes his name, and calls him Abraham, "the father of a multitude of nations." (Gen. xvii. 5. R.V.) And God said unto Abraham:

"As for Sarai thy wife, thou shalt not call her name Sarai, but Sarah (princess) shall her name be. And I will bless her, and moreover I will give thee a son of her: yea, I will bless her, and she shall be a mother of nations; kings of peoples shall be of her." (R.V.)

Thirty long years had elapsed since God's first promise to Abraham. Physical impossibility stood in the way of the fulfilment of that promise, and, at first, Abraham fell upon his face, and laughed, and said in his heart,

"Shall a child be born unto him that is an hundred years old? and shall Sarah, that is ninety years old, bear? O that Ishmael might live before Thee!" (vers. 17, 18)

God could not choose one that was born after the flesh (Gal. iv. 23), and He reiterated His Word that Sarah should bear a son, that through him Abraham's seed should be established, and God's covenant with Abraham.

After this, the long silence which had existed between God and Abraham because of his unbelief was broken, "and the Lord appeared to him by the oaks of Mamre" (xviii. 1, R.V.). It was in the form of three men. And Abraham hastened to his wife into the tent, and called upon her to make cakes for the men who were come to him. Also Abraham himself helped in the preparation of the repast which he would spread before them. And while the men did eat, they said to him,

"Where is Sarah thy wife?"

"Behold, in the tent."

"I will certainly return unto thee when the season cometh round; and, lo, Sarah thy wife shall have a son," was the message the three men brought to him.

"And Sarah heard in the tent door." (R.V.) Her first thought was to consider herself. How could such a thing be possible? All experience of human nature was against such a possibility: and "Sarah laughed within herself." Was this the woman of whom it should be said wheresoever the Word of God should go: "She judged Him faithful Who had promised?" Yes, it was even so.

But a deep work had to be done upon Sarah's heart before she could be recognised as a woman of faith. There was duplicity as well as unbelief within her, and we may well conceive that at this time she was not the helpmeet to her husband she might have been. The Lord said unto Abraham,

"Wherefore did Sarah laugh, saying, Shall I of a surety bear a child, which am old?"

"Is Anything Too Hard for the Lord?"

And God repeats His Word. "At the set time, I will return unto thee when the season cometh round, and Sarah shall have a son. Then Sarah denied, saying, I laughed not." She even told a lie to God!

And yet, in the New Testament neither her unbelief nor her lie are mentioned against her. Before He could place her among the worthies of faith, God had forgiven her, and cast her iniquities into the depths of the sea. (Mic. vii. 19)

But God was not deceived; He could not ignore sin; it must be brought to book; therefore He said, "Nay, but thou didst laugh."

Perhaps the destruction of Sodom, and the fearful judgment upon Lot's wife which intervened between the promise of God to Sarah and its accomplishment, may have done much to deepen Sarah's respect for God, and her faith in His spoken Word.

When, after the destruction of the cities of the Plain, Abraham journeyed into the land of the south, and came to Gerar (xx.1), it seemed almost inconceivable that he should have again repeated his duplicity with regard to Sarah, saying of her, "She is my sister." Perhaps the rebuke of Abimelech in giving Abraham money compensation may have gone far to humble Sarah. "Thus she was reproved." (xx. 16) The judgment upon Sodom, speaking to her of the mighty power of God and His hatred of sin, and then her fall, and her husband's, into untruth, may have shown both of them how their own hearts were not to be relied upon, and Sarah may have been a more serious as well as a more humble woman before the Lord made her the mother of His promised seed.

But the Lord is true. He visited Sarah, as He had said, and a son was born to Abraham in his old age, and he called him, as God had foretold, Isaac (laughter). It may, perhaps, have been in remembrance of his laugh when God declared to him that Sarah should bear a son, that the remembrance of his unbelief might be ever before him, and warn him lest he should fall again into the same sin.

Sarah's joy was, of course, very great. God's promise could never have been fulfilled if her unbelief had not been overcome. BY FAITH SARAH "RECEIVED STRENGTH to conceive seed." And now, at last, she had learnt to look at God rather than herself, at God rather than circumstances. She said:

"God hath made me to laugh, so that all that hear will laugh with me. Who would have said unto Abraham, that Sarah should have given children suck? for I have borne him a son in his old age." (xxi. 6, 7)

Time went on, and the babe grew. But there was in the house one thing, as the fruit of Abraham's and Sarah's unbelief, which must be set in order. There was always the Egyptian Hagar in the house, and the lad Ishmael; and on the day when Isaac was weaned, Sarah saw Ishmael mocking. The old, irritable spirit got the better of her; and yet there was something of the prophetess about her when she said,

"Cast out this bondwoman and her son; for the son of this bondwoman shall not be heir with my son, even with Isaac. (ver. 10.) She saw, at any rate, in a measure, from God's side; Isaac's birth was the fulfilment of God's promise; Ishmael's was not; he was born after the flesh; Isaac was by promise. (Gal. iv. 23) When Abraham took his family affairs and laid them before his God, God justified Sarah, and said,

"In all that Sarah hath said unto thee, hearken unto her voice; for in Isaac shall thy seed be called."

Sarah had fulfilled her vocation; she was God's witness. He was faithful Who promised, and she had responded to Him; faith had taken the place of unbelief within her, so that all the Canaanites around would have the testimony of how great was the God of Abraham. All her former life, all her mistakes and failures to help her husband, were blotted out, and this one fact remains behind, that, as Abraham "considered not his own body" (Rom. iv. 19), but "was fully persuaded that what God had promised He was able also to perform," so Sarah, contrary to experience, and contrary to human reasonings, "judged Him faithful that promised."

Oh, what a lesson it is to us, in all the details of our family and social life, to see things with the eye of God, to take counsel with Him about everything, to justify Him in all His ways and all His providences! So only can a Christian wife be a true helpmeet to her husband.

Only one more thing is told us of Sarah. It is of her burial. Sarah's name means "princess;" and as a princess Abraham buried her. The only land he possessed in all the world was Sarah's grave, which he bought of Ephron the Hittite. But beyond the grave, amidst those who shall sit down with Abraham and Isaac, and Jacob, in the kingdom of heaven, Sarah shall have her place, because "she judged Him faithful that promised."

Conclusion

Sarah, the first mother and matriarch of Israel, commanded the attention of nineteenth-century Christian and Jewish women. Women writers used Sarah's story, which centered on the home and the family, as a springboard for discussing issues that related to them as women. Christian interpreters eulogized her as a model of submission. However, not all interpreted Sarah's submission in the same way: some women used the story of Sarah to preach the message of wifely submission, some nuanced the meaning of submission, and still others redefined it or even ignored it. The meaning of submission in marriage was clearly an issue of considerable debate in the nineteenth century. Even the aristocratic Frances King was careful to include a strategy of "considered" submission which encouraged women to refuse to follow immoral directives. Harriet Beecher Stowe's close narrative reading of the Genesis story took some of the sting from wifely submission. Hers is a revisionist approach to submission.

Christian women who used the New Testament as an interpretive lens also eulogized Sarah as a model of faith, basing their approach on Hebrews 11. Since the Genesis story presented Sarah as anything but faithful, interpreters had to struggle with the issues of polygamy, Sarah's lying, her hard treatment of Hagar, and her disappearance from the story. They invoked various strategies to deal with these and other interpretive issues. Some used the notion of evolutionary development, judging customs and behaviour as "primitive." Others stressed differences in culture and customs. Many faced the moral difficulties of Sarah and accepted her humanity. They reasoned if God accepted Sarah, God could accept them: they shared with Sarah a common humanity. In spite of all the issues that distanced readers from Sarah and her world, many women elevated her.

Jewish women faced similar interpretive challenges. Like Christians, Jews inherited a tradition that elevated Sarah as their matriarch. Aguilar and Hyneman both wanted to continue to exalt Sarah and present her as an example for contemporary Jewish readers. To do this, they recast or omitted negative scenes involving Sarah.

Nineteenth-century women often fashioned Sarah in their own image. The experiences of women of station and wealth, like King, provided a distinctive lens for reading Sarah's story. King's personal wealth made her sensitive to

issues of inheritance; she used that issue as a guide to understanding the feelings of Ishmael and Hagar. Women authors brought their own experiences
of motherhood to their writing. Understanding the importance of mothers
in shaping a child's character, and in educating children and servants, shaped
their own portrayal of Sarah. As a result, they sometimes read Sarah in light
of their own experiences of living in a patriarchal society. Such experiences
helped them fill in the missing details of the story.

The Woman Question looms in many women's disquisitions and sermons on Sarah. Sarah modeled a woman of strength, wealth, and power, a
mother of influence and honour. Though her barrenness initially threatened
the promise, she bore the child of promise, and her burial site marked the
first property acquired in the Promised Land. Many women who elevated
Sarah seemed to need a strong matriarch to emulate. Aguilar calls readers to
"be proud of Sarah." Though Sarah might have been strong, her marriage
to her husband/lord Abraham, and her obedience to his commands, raised
the issues not only of patriarchy, but also of women's roles in marriage and
society. Thus some interpreters who wrestled with the issue of submission
were actually battling larger issues of patriarchy. By redefining and qualifying
submission, some pushed traditional boundaries and moved towards a more
egalitarian view of marriage. Their positions on women's issues varied considerably, however. For example, Baxter promoted the helpmate ideology as
the lens for judging women's success in life, while Colby would want to free
Baxter from what she viewed as an oppressive ideology.

Many women also used the Sarah story to address the issue of ideal womanhood or female character. They taught lessons about female conduct, character, and motherhood; they emphasized such valued virtues as piety, purity,
retreat, modesty, submission, and beauty. At the same time, by taking up
their pens to preach, teach, and entertain, women placed themselves at the
center of the debate over women's education and women's work. As writers,
they also assumed and promoted a woman's status and power as angel of the
home, responsible for the spiritual well-being of her family and, by extension, her community. In their interpretive work, women authors showed the
value of an education. They did not avoid religious and theological controversy, thereby arguing that women should wrestle with difficult issues. They
presented themselves as powerful agents, interpreters, preachers, competent
exegetes, commentators, and writers. They showed the importance of passing
on the faith to the next generation.

Finally, the selections on Sarah show that women's interpretive work
belonged to the category of popular exposition. Though most women were

not on center stage during the great intellectual debates over the Bible during the nineteenth century, their interpretive work shows that they absorbed many of the new ideas and methods that were in the air: the importance of reading texts within their historical and cultural contexts, the notion of evolutionary development, and, during the final decade of the century, the re-evaluation of the nature of Scripture and the use of higher-critical tools. In contrast to the other female interpreters, Wedgwood and Colby stand out as thoroughly modern promoters of German criticism; they were Wellhausen's helpmates.

Part 3

HAGAR—THE WANDERER

Introduction

The story of Hagar is inextricably linked to the story of Sarah and Abraham. In the last chapter, the selections focused on Sarah. In this chapter, the selections we have chosen focus primarily on Hagar.

Hagar's story is found in Genesis 16:1-16, and in 21:8-21. Interpreters have generally assumed that Pharaoh gave Hagar to Sarah in Egypt (see Genesis 12:16). Sarah's solution to the problem of her barrenness was to give Hagar to Abraham as a second wife. After Hagar became pregnant with Abraham's child, her attitude toward Sarah changed. Sarah asked Abraham to do something about the presumptuous slave, and Abraham told her to take care of it. Sarah dealt harshly with Hagar who then ran away.

Hagar encountered the angel of the Lord in the wilderness, who instructed her to return and submit to Sarah. The angel spoke to Hagar twice, promising that her offspring would be greatly multiplied, and that her son would be named Ishmael. Hagar named God, "The God who sees me." She returned to Abraham's household and bore a son, whom Abraham named Ishmael.

After fourteen years, a son, Isaac, was born to Sarah and Abraham. At the feast to celebrate Isaac's weaning, Sarah saw something objectionable in Ishmael's behaviour and asked that Abraham "cast out" Hagar and Ishmael. Abraham was unwilling to do this because Ishmael was also his son. God told Abraham to do as Sarah asked and send Hagar and Ishmael away, which he did. God again spoke to Hagar in the wilderness, showing her a well of water when the supply they carried with them ran out. Ishmael and Hagar made their home in the wilderness, and Ishmael's descendants became a large nation as God had promised.

Like many Hebrew narratives, the two episodes from Hagar's life are told very succinctly. Neither Hagar nor Ishmael are fully developed characters. There are many gaps in the stories, prompting readers throughout history to embellish the story with missing details, or to go behind the text to find reasons for the gaps.

The story of Hagar elicited two main responses from women interpreters. The first was simply confusion, as shown by Susan Warner in the statement of a child, Tiny, who said: "I do not understand that story, uncle Sam." Women writers attempted to explain the difficulties in the story to nineteenth-century readers of various ages in Britain and the United States.

An understanding of ancient Near Eastern culture helped to answer some basic interpretive questions. Scholarly and popular resources provided an understanding of polygamy and the mechanics of ancient households, the importance of male heirs, and the shame of barrenness. Other questions related to the issues of duty, authority, and submission still remained.

The cultural context of both nineteenth-century Britain and America was closer to the ancient patriarchal society than we are today. British women interpreters understood ordered societies. They were comfortable with the idea that Hagar should return to Sarah because it was wrong to abandon one's station in life. American women read the story of Hagar in light of the institution of American slavery. They imagined Hagar as a black slave woman, and Sarah and Abraham as white slave owners. Their understanding of the story was affected by their own experiences and understandings of slavery. Further, the whole concept of duty had a much more positive connotation in the nineteenth century than it does to many people now. Responsibilities or duties were difficult, but they were not to be avoided.

The authors' theological understandings also helped them resolve difficulties they found in the text. Many of the women writers accepted the divine authority of the Bible and did not overtly challenge the message of the text. Many Christian interpreters, including some of these nineteenth-century women, read Hagar's story through the lens of the New Testament, in which both Sarah and Abraham are held up as examples of faith (Hebrews 11). Galatians 4:21–5:1 gives a typological reading of Hagar and her descendants, and for some women this passage was an important lens for understanding Hagar. The authors' understanding of the fulfillment of prophecy and the providence of God contributed to their interpretation of this story.

The second response Hagar's story evoked in these authors was the repeated description of the story as "touching and beautiful." Etty Woosnam began by asking, "Why is it that from our childhood upwards we are so touched by the

pitiful tale of the poor dishonoured, outcast slave?" This story had an enormous appeal to women writers. They had heard the story from the time they
were children, and as adults they empathized with Hagar as a mother and an
oppressed woman.

The appeal of this story for these authors began in childhood. Sarah
Turnock recalled learning the text, "Thou God seest me," as a young girl. A
Bible Alphabet, which had a scripture text for every letter, used this text for
the letter "T."[1] The familiarity of the authors with the story shaped the way
they interpreted it.

The women writers empathized with Hagar's plight as a mother who could
not bear to watch her son suffer and who could not provide for her son's
physical needs. The death of a child was a very real possibility for mothers in
the nineteenth century. The provision of water through the intervention of
the angel of the Lord brought a satisfying conclusion to this touching tale.
Further, the authors brought to their reading of the text assumptions about
women's responsibility for the spiritual formation of those in their household.
They assumed that since nineteenth-century mothers influenced their children, Hagar must also have influenced Ishmael. Whether Hagar's influence
was positive or negative depended on the particular author's interpretation of
this narrative.

The nineteenth-century authors treated Hagar with much more compassion than they did Sarah. Hagar was an oppressed woman, a runaway
slave who had been abused by her mistress. While Sarah was the example
or standard held up for these women, most seemed to delight in discussing her imperfections. Hagar, by contrast was weak, despised and vulnerable,
embodying what many nineteenth-century women experienced. The writers
felt compassion for Hagar because they saw in her a reflection of themselves
or their readers.

Hagar and Ishmael were wanderers: Hagar left Abraham and Sarah's
home twice to wander in the desert. Ishmael eventually lived in the desert
as a wanderer. Some nineteenth-century Christian women associated Hagar
with the wandering lost sheep found by the Good Shepherd (Luke 15, John
10). Jewish women identified with Hagar as a wanderer from their historical
experience of wandering as a part of the Jewish diaspora. Nineteenth-century
women empathized with Hagar the wanderer; they found her story compel-
ling, though difficult to understand.

---

[1] See an example of a Bible Alphabet at The Christian Connection, "Small Bible Alphabet,"
http://www.alphacares.com/christian/Alphabet.html. (Last accessed March 29, 2005.)

§34 Sarah Trimmer
(1741–1810)

Sarah Trimmer was an Anglican author and educator.[2] Trimmer was a middle-class wife and mother, married to the owner of a brick works, and the daughter of a member of the royal court at Kew. She lived within walking distance of the palace at Kew, and some of her books are dedicated to members of the royal family[3] or other members of the upper class. She had a very conservative view of society and class. This is seen especially in her *Essay on Christian Education* in a section regarding dress. She clearly states that attention must be paid to the way one dresses to maintain the distinction between classes. She claimed that St. Paul's injunction to women not to have braided hair or dress excessively (1 Tim. 2:9) was not made to upper-class women. Trimmer's views on class are a part of the social lens through which she read scripture and influenced the applications she drew from the story of Hagar.

The following excerpt on Hagar is from Trimmer's one-volume commentary on the Bible, *A Help to the Unlearned* (1805), which was written as an aid to Bible reading for those who could not afford more expensive study aids. Trimmer assumed the book would be used next to the scriptures. In her introduction, she told her readers how to use the book: first, they should check in the commentary to see how many verses are explained in one paragraph, next read the verses from the Bible, then read her explanation.

In her comments on Genesis 16 and 21, Trimmer anticipated and answered the questions readers of her day might have asked when reading the Bible. Many of these questions are similar to those twenty-first century readers ask, but Trimmer did not always answer them in the way that we might expect. She carefully pointed her readers to lessons for Christian living from the account of Hagar.

From Sarah Trimmer, *A Help to the Unlearned in the Study of the Holy Scriptures: Being an attempt to explain the Bible in a familiar way* (London: F. C. & J. Rivington, 1805), 20–21, 24–25.

Chapter XVI

We may suppose that Abram, Sarai, and Hagar, having all lived in an idolatrous country, and having no holy scriptures to guide them, acted contrary

---

[2] See part 2: "Sarah—The First Mother of Israel" for more information on Sarah Trimmer.
[3] For example, *The Economy of Charity* is dedicated to Queen Charlotte.

to the marriage law *through ignorance*. Observe that, though Sarai treated her maid *hardly*, the angel of the LORD directed Hagar to return and submit herself to her mistress. Take particular notice of the divine promise made to Hagar in verses 10, 11, concerning the son she was to have. Observe, ver.12, what kind of a man Ishmael was to be; and that a great nation was to proceed from him. Hagar's words, ver. 13, show that the Divine Being, called *the Angel of the LORD*, was GOD. Abram testified his faith in GOD'S promise to Hagar, by naming the child Ishmael.

Chapter XXI

Ver. 9 to 22. Isaac and Ishmael could not both have been heads of nations if they had continued together, and it was ordained of GOD, before either of them were born, that Isaac should be heir to the promises which GOD had made to Abraham, respecting the land of Canaan, and *the seed of the woman who was to bruise the serpent's head* [Gen. 3:15], and that Ishmael should be the head of another great nation; for this reason GOD commanded Abraham to hearken to the voice of his wife. When Abraham sent Ishmael and his mother away with only some bread and a bottle of water, he gave a proof of his faith in GOD's promises, by leaving those he loved to be provided for by Providence. If Abraham had not had such promises this would have been a very unnatural and barbarous action. Observe that Hagar's faith failed when she saw her child ready to perish. She had forgotten the promise which GOD had given her concerning Ishmael before he was born, chap. xvi. and those which had been made to Abraham, chap. xvii. which, in this chapter, no doubt, he told her of. But the Lord showed that he had not forsaken Ishmael though he had sent him away from his father's house: let us from this learn never to despair. Young people, in particular, who are obliged to leave their parents in order to get a livelihood, may take comfort from this part of Ishmael's history, as it proves that they may be under the protection and care of their heavenly Father in every place, and that GOD is ever ready to hear the prayer of those who call upon him in the time of their distress, and to help their necessities. Observe, that Ishmael did not live amongst other men in cities, or towns, following any of the usual occupations of life, but in a wilderness, where he maintained and defended himself by means of his bow and arrows; so that he was properly a *wild man*, as was foretold of him; chap. xvi. ver. 12, and he married a woman of the same country as his mother was of.

§35 Sarah Hall
(1761–1830)

Sarah Ewing Hall was a well-educated Presbyterian woman from Philadelphia.[4] *Conversations on the Bible* (1818), her only major work, is a paraphrase of and a commentary on the Old Testament in the form of a conversation between a mother and her three children (Catherine, Fanny, and Charles).

In this short excerpt, we have one question from Catherine asked in the middle of a conversation on the sacrifice of Isaac (Gen. 22). This question prompted the retelling of the story of Hagar and Ishmael, which had been passed over in Hall's earlier discussions of Abraham's family. The question Hall put in Catherine's mouth was not a new question; it was one rabbinic interpreters also asked.

Like Trimmer, Hall invoked the doctrine of the Providence of God in discussing God's protection of Ishmael and Hagar. Unlike Trimmer, who drew a striking application from Ishmael's life for young people who had to leave home, Hall did not explicitly draw lessons for life from the story of Hagar and Ishmael.

> From Sarah Hall, *Conversations on the Bible* (Philadelphia: Harrison Hall, 1818), 37–38. [Text from 4th ed., 1927.]

CATHERINE. Why is Isaac denominated the *only* son of Abraham, when Ishmael was also his son?

MOTHER. Because the *spiritual* promise bestowed upon Abraham was to be transmitted through Isaac to his posterity, and finally from them to all mankind. Ishmael, was the son of Hagar, a wife less honourable than Sarah, who being the first, was considered the superior.

In those days, it was the practice even of good men, to have several wives. Sarah, seems at first, to have adopted Ishmael, supposing him to be the promised heir of Abraham. But when Isaac was afterwards given to her, she instigates her husband (not however without provocation from the unbecoming conduct of both mother and son,) to banish both from his house, declaring that he should not inherit with her son. This unreasonable desire was very grievous to the venerable patriarch, but his unerring Counsellor, commanded him to listen to his wife and comforted him with an assurance, that of Ishmael also, "he would make a great nation." Thus encouraged, he sent

---

[4] For more information on Sarah Hall, see part 2, "Sarah—The First Mother of Israel."

away the unhappy Hagar and her son, furnishing them, however, with such provisions as she could carry. When these were spent, as they wandered in the wilderness of Beer-sheba, despairing of any further supply, she laid her son down under some bushes, and that she might not see him die (B.C. 1892)[5] she sat down to weep at a distance! From this overwhelming anguish she was aroused by a voice of consolation, directing her to "take up the lad, and give him a drink from a well," which she now perceived to be at hand; for "he should live and become a great nation."

Before his birth, when Hagar had fled into the same wilderness from the unkind treatment of her mistress, "The Angel of the Lord" had appeared unto her, and told her, "that her prosperity should not be numbered for multitude, that her son should be a wild man, that his hand should be against every man and every man's hand against him, yet he should dwell in the presence of his brethren." And now that the prophecy might be fulfilled, the hand of providence conducted him to the desert, where he grew up and "became an archer" or a *wild man. . . .*

§36 Grace Aguilar
(1816–1847)

Grace Aguilar, a Victorian Jewish writer, used many different literary genres, including poetry, to explore religious themes relevant to her Jewish audience.[6] Aguilar wrote her poem, "The Wanderers," as a young, single, Jewish woman whose collective memory allowed her to identify very closely with Hagar. In this poem, she explored some of the emotional issues surrounding Hagar's story.

In an article on this poem Daniel Harris suggests that Aguilar found Hagar emblematic of the Jewish diaspora. Hagar is doubly banished, first from her Egyptian homeland, then from Abraham's household. Similarly, the Jewish people were banished from their homeland, then many were also banished from the European countries of their exile. Aguilar's family found refuge in England after banishment from Spain. Harris writes, "The poem presents Hagar's psychic and dramatic displacement as the poetic trope of

---

[5] Hall used the dates of Bishop James Ussher (1581–1656). These dates were commonly used in biblical commentaries in the early nineteenth century and were often printed in the margins of Bibles.

[6] For more information on Aguilar, see part 2, "Sarah—The First Mother of Israel."

Jewish geographical and politico-religious diaspora."[7] In Aguilar's later work, *The Women of Israel* (1845), she emphasized Sarah rather than Hagar, and presented Sarah in a more positive light.

Aguilar, like Hall and Trimmer, highlighted Abraham's faith in the providence and goodness of God as he sent out Ishmael and Hagar. In Aguilar's portrayal, Ishmael seems younger than sixteen. Aguilar clearly depicted Hagar as God's child (God is her Maker), and as a pious mother. In the poem, Hagar instructed her son to kneel, a very Anglican posture for prayer, and "to bless the Hand that saved him."

From Grace Aguilar, "The Wanderers (1838)," as printed in *The Occident and American Jewish Advocate* 3.7 (October 1845).

The Wanderers (1838)
Genesis, 21:14-20

With sadden'd heart and tearful eye the mother went her way,
The Patriarch's mandate had gone forth, and Hagar must not stay.
Oh! who can tell the emotions deep that pressed on Abra'am's heart—
As thus, obedient to his God, from Ismael called to part!

But God had spoken, and he knew His word was changeless truth,
He could not doubt His blessing would protect the friendless youth;
He bade him go, nor would he heed the anguish of his soul;
He turned aside,—a father's wo in silence to control.

Now hand in hand they wend their way, o'er hills and vale and wild;
The mother's heart was full of grief, but smiled in glee her child:
Fearless and free, he felt restraint would never gall him now—
And hail'd with joy the fresh'ning breeze that fann'd his fair young brow.

His mother's heart was desolate, and tears swell'd in her eye;
Scarce to his artless words of love her quiv'ring lips reply.
She only saw the future as a lone and dreary wild:
The present stood before the lad in joyance undefil'd.

She knew, alas! his boyish strength too soon would droop and fade;
And who was, in that lonely scene, to give them food and aid?

---

[7] Daniel A. Harris, "Hagar in Christian Britain: Grace Aguilar's 'The Wanderers,'" *Victorian Literature and Culture* 27, no. 1 (1999): 143–69, 144.

With trembling gaze she oft would mark the flushing of his cheek,
And list in terror, lest he should 'gin falteringly to speak!

Fatigue she felt not for herself, nor heeded cure nor pain—
But nearer, nearer to her breast her boy at times she'd strain;
Beersheba's wilderness they see before them dark and wide;
Oh, who across its scorching sands their wandering steps will guide?

The flush departed from the cheek which she so oft has kiss'd;
To his glad tones of childish glee no longer may she list;
A pallor as of death is spread o'er those sweet features now—
She sees him droop before the blast that fann'd his aching brow.

"Oh, mother, lay me down," he cried, "I know not what I feel,
But something cold and rushing seems thro' all my limbs to steal—
Oh kiss me, mother dear, and then ah, lay me down to sleep—
Nay, do not look upon me thus—kiss me and do not weep!"

Scarce could her feeble arms support her child, and lay him where
Some clustering shrubs might shield him from the heavy scorching air;
His drooping eyelids closed; his breath came painfully and slow—
She bent her head on his a while in wild yet speechless wo.

Then from his side she hurried, as impelled she knew not why,
Save that she could not linger there—she could not see him die—
She lifted up her voice and wept—and o'er the lonely wild
"Let me not see his death!" was borne, "my Ismael, my child!"

And silence came upon her then, her stricken soul to calm;
And suddenly and strange there fell a soft and soothing balm—
And then a voice came stealing, on the still and fragrant air—
A still small voice that would be heard, tho' solitude was there.

"What aileth thee, oh Hagar?" thus it spoke: "fear not, for God hath heard
The lad's voice where he is,—and thou, trust in thy Maker's word!
Awake! arise! lift up the lad and hold him in thine hand—
I will of him a nation make, before Me, he shall stand."

It ceased, that voice; and silence now, as strangely soft and still,
The boundless desert once again with eloquence would fill—

And strength returned to Hagar's frame, for God hath oped her eyes—
And lo! amid the arid sands a well of water lies!

Quick to her boy, with beating heart, the anxious mother flies,
And to his lips, and hands, and brow, the cooling draught applies—
He wakes! he breathes! the flush of life is mantling on his cheek—
He smiles! he speaks ! oh those quick tears his mother's joy shall speak!

She held him to her throbbing breast, she gazed upon his face—
The beaming features, one by one, in silent love to trace.
She bade him kneel to bless the Hand that saved him in the wild—
But oh! few words her lips could speak, save these—"My child, my child!"

§37 Penina Moise
(1797–1880)

Penina Moise lived in Charleston, South Carolina, all her life. Her parents
were Sephardic Jews who emigrated from Alsace to Santo Domingo in the
West Indies, then to Charleston. Moise's father died when she was twelve,
leaving her with the primary responsibility for her family's care, as her mother
was ill. Moise published several collections of poetry, including *Fancy's Sketch
Book* (1833) and a hymnal (1842), which contained a poem on Hagar. She
was actively involved in religious education and was very prominent in the
Jewish community in Charleston. She never married, living first with her
mother, then later with her sister and niece. Moise's health was never good;
her eyesight grew worse with age until she went blind, and for the final fifteen
years of her life, she was confined to her house an invalid.

Like Aguilar's poem, "The Wanderer," Moise's hymn on Hagar focused on
her expulsion from Abraham's family. Unlike Aguilar, she named Sarah and
described her role in the banishment of Ishmael and Hagar. Moise portrayed
Ishmael as an "infant" and had Hagar praying to God that the child would
die, a prayer not recorded in the text. The wilderness became Hagar's new
home, no longer a place of death but a place of freedom.

Moise concluded her poem with a liturgical prayer for God's provision for
those who still wander in "life's waste." Here, she shifted from the past to the

present; the reader was situated in a community of "us" who wander through life's wastes. Moise's prayer thus made the identification of the Jewish community with Hagar more explicit than it was in Aguilar's work.

From Penina Moise, "Genesis, Chap. XXI," as printed in *The Secular and Religious Works of Penina Moise* (Charleston: Nicholas G. Duff, 1911), 15–16. [Originally published in 1842 in a hymnal.]

Genesis, Chap. XXI
(Hymn No. 14 in this collection)

Weeping, and loth from all she loved to part,
    Stood Hagar, trembling at her Lord's decree;
And, oh! how like a desert was her heart,
    When from His gentle presence urged to flee.

But Sarah's looks, full of indignant scorn,
    The truth to her foreboding soul revealed;
Forth with her infant son she fled forlorn,
    And to his Sire above for aid appealed.

Her scanty bread and beverage are spent,
    Yet Ishmael sleeps unconscious of her pain;
A cry of agony to God is sent
    "Would that the child would never wake again!"

The earth grows brighter where the mother stands,
    A hand divine arrests her falling tears;
A cloud of glory gilds the burning sands,
    And a celestial voice the mourner cheers.

"Arise and drink of yonder balmy well!
    Nor from the wilderness henceforward roam;
Father of nations here the lad shall dwell
    With freedom blest for ages yet to come."

Oh, ever Bountiful! forsake us not,
    When driven forth to wander through life's waste:
But cheer with beams of love each barren spot,
    And let us of the spring of mercy taste.

§38 Susan Warner
(1819–1885)

Susan Warner lived most of her life on Constitution Island near West Point. She received an elite education in New York City, where she was a member of a Presbyterian church. She and her sister, Anna Bartlett Warner, wrote to support themselves after their father's financial failure. Susan Warner wrote many devotional guides, children's books and songs,[8] and novels, including the best selling *The Wide, Wide World* (1850). Warner was active in the American Tract Society, and in her later years taught Bible classes to West Point cadets.[9]

Warner used all the tools of the male academy in her interpretation of the Bible. She made numerous allusions to a variety of Old and New Testament passages. She used linguistic tools to find the literal sense of the text. She studied the historical and geographical context of a passage to assist her understanding of it. These tools enabled her to delve into deeper theological meanings of scripture. Warner raised many theological issues from the text: the nature of God and God's promises, the doctrine of perfection, a reformed view of baptism, and eschatology.

Warner wrote *Walks from Eden* as a family conversation about the book of Genesis. Four children, their grandmother, and uncle stayed in the country one September in "a great tract of unbroken mountain and woodland." The narrator, Tiny, her sister Priscilla, and their brothers, Eliphalet (Liph) and Daniel, discussed Genesis with their uncle, Sam, and their grandmother. In the part of the conversation reproduced here, Hagar was the key character under discussion.

Just as Aguilar and Moise read the story of Hagar through the lens of their own social and cultural position, so Warner wrote as an American woman before the Civil War. She read Hagar with the model of American slavery in her mind. Warner went so far as to describe Hagar as having a "pretty black head." Warner's racism was not limited to black slaves; she also portrayed Arabs in a negative light.

This book was written with an educational purpose. Warner focused on geographical and historical details, and expanded those where possible. She

---

[8] The Warner sisters included original song lyrics in their stories for children; other people then set these lyrics to music and they became quite popular. Anna Warner wrote the words to "Jesus Loves Me." Susan Warner wrote the words to "Jesus Bids us Shine."

[9] Patricia Crane, "Warner, Susan," in *The Cambridge Guide to Women's Writing in English*, ed. Lorna Sage (Cambridge: Cambridge University Press, 1999), 652.

emphasized the cultural differences between contemporary European culture and patriarchal culture (identified with contemporary Bedouin culture). Neither Sarah nor Hagar was portrayed positively; Abraham was the exemplary character. Warner's focus, however, was not primarily on the characters, but on God's intervention in their lives.

From Susan Warner, *Walks from Eden* (New York: Hurst & Co. 1866), 266–85.

Sep. 15. The Wilderness of Paran

The fifteenth of September was exceedingly sultry; and in the afternoon, as we could go to church but once in the day, we agreed to take our Bibles and repair to our beloved rock-top; perhaps there would be a breath of air stirring. Not much could be felt, after all; but it was pleasanter at any time under the trees than it was in the house. The forest was very still on Sunday. Insect life indeed was busy, and bird life; yet that did not really break the silence; and no other sound was there to break it. Other days a wood-chopper's axe might now and then be heard; or the voice of the teamster in the distance; little else in truth; but Sundays, the rest of nature was absolute and profound.

"We are in a wilderness," said uncle Sam. "I have always been of opinion that a wilderness is a pleasant place."

"Is *this* a wilderness?" said Priscilla.

"Yes. What is meant by a wilderness, in Bible language at least, is simply 'land not sown' [Jer. 2:2] as one of the prophets speaks it. Land not cultivated, but left to nature."

"And with nobody living in it," said Priscilla.

"That is not a condition. There can be no settled inhabitants of a wilderness; because if settled they would more or less cultivate the ground; but roving inhabitants there may be, and there are. In the wilderness south of Palestine, for instance, the wilderness between it and Egypt, and stretching down into the peninsula of Sinai—there are thousands of Bedouin rovers, feeding their flocks and their camels by the way; but no cultivation that really changes the face of the land. They do sow and reap thin patches of corn here and there as they can. Eight thousand Bedouins are estimated in that region now; when the powerful Amalekite nation dwelt there, the population must have been much greater; and doubtless they cultivated the soil to some greater extent, and so had more grass and trees."

"But I thought a desert was all sand and nothing else."

"That is what we generally mean by a desert, when we think of Africa and Asia. But a wilderness is a different thing; or a desert, as the Bible often mentions the word. In that wilderness of Paran[10] there is but a proportion of sand;

a great deal of it is rock; and every here and there one comes to a green spot, where a small supply of water nourishes a strip of grass or a tuft of palm trees. All the land wants is water; and if the winter rains and torrents were carefully made use of for purposes of irrigation, the desert might even now literally rejoice and blossom as the rose [Isa. 35:1]. The first we hear of the wilderness, in the Bible, is in the story of Hagar."

"I do not understand that story, uncle Sam," said I.

"It is so unlike our European customs, I do not wonder, Tiny. Yet it is all perfectly natural, and right too, according to the customs of the patriarchal days; or even those of the Bedouin Arabs now, though not quite so much. It was not thought wrong for a man to have more wives than one; and is not among them; but one is always the head wife, the mistress of the family, the chief of the household; and the others are under her. And also to have children was considered a very great blessing, and to be without them, a great misfortune. So it was only doing as other people did, when Sarah, seeing that she had no children, proposed to Abraham to take another wife in one of her slaves; for if her slave had children, according to usage they would be reckoned as Sarah's own. 'And Abraham hearkened to the voice of Sarah'—very likely he thought it was the Lord's will he should; and she gave him Hagar, an Egyptian slave of hers, to be his wife."

"But was Hagar *Sarah's* slave, not Abraham's?" Liph asked.

"Sarah's entirely, until she gave her to Abraham. The bondwomen of the wife belonged solely to her and were at her disposal, whether they were hers by gift or by purchase or by dower. This Egyptian slave was probably the gift of Pharaoh to Sarah, at the time when he was loading Abraham with his marks of favour. Now Sarah gave her to her husband to be his wife."

"And made trouble for herself," said my grandmother.

"Ay, and for Abraham too; who hated confusion in the household, I judge, if ever a man did. However, the Lord gave Hagar the blessing of being a mother; and when she had the premise of it, very naturally she assumed a position which was not her right. She despised her former mistress, and would not take orders from her meekly, but carried her pretty black head high. Then Sarah was both jealous and provoked; and appealed to her husband to know if he was going to allow her to be insulted. Sarah was a good deal of a princess, I fancy, in her temper as well as her name."

"But I think Abraham ought not to have let her have her way," said Priscilla. "It was cruel to Hagar, I think."

[10] First mentioned in Genesis 21:21, as indicated in this discussion. Also mentioned in Numbers 10:12, 16; 13:26; Deuteronomy 1:1; 33:2; 1 Samuel 25:1.

"My dear, Abraham could know nothing about the matter, except what his wife told him; the women did not quarrel in his presence; and you cannot wonder that he cared more for Sarah's comfort, whom he loved and had lived with all his life, than for the Egyptian woman. It *was* a little cruel to Hagar; but then Abraham did not know that Sarah would use her power so harshly. At any rate, he gave it all back to her; 'do as it pleaseth thee,' he said; 'thy maid is in thy hand.' After saying that, he could not interfere, even if he had known interference was needed. Sarah 'afflicted her,' the Hebrew has it;[11] punished her well for her impertinence and presumption, I suppose; and Hagar, after her brief taste of liberty and pride, could not bear it. She ran away."

"And so would I," said Priscilla.

"It is a poor way to get rid of trouble, too," said my uncle; "when one runs away from duty. Hagar's way led her into the wilderness—that wilderness I was speaking of. She had set out with the idea of getting home to her own country, no doubt; and that rocky barren desert must have been a weary place for a delicate woman's feet to travel. Poor thing! she was found by a fountain of water in the wilderness—by a fountain in the way to Shur—where her strength and spirits had very likely failed her. I can see the young creature in that desolate solitude, down on the ground by the well's mouth, with maybe the shade of some scrubby palm trees over her head; and no other shelter in earth or heaven, that she knew of."

"Where is Shur?"

"Not known certainly. It was a place just without the eastern border of Egypt—the last Arabian town on the limit of the desert, probably; but Hagar had not got so far. She was only in the great highway of travel between Palestine and that point; on the way."

"And who was it found her, uncle Sam?"

"Who was it?" repeated my uncle. "Who is it, whose eyes are in every place—'whose eyes are upon the ways of man, and he seeth all his goings' [Job 34:21]—and who 'hath not despised nor abhorred the emotion of the afflicted, neither hath be hid his face from him' [Ps. 22:24]?"

"But sir," said Dan, "it says, 'the angel of the Lord found her.'"

"See how that angel spoke to her, a little farther on. It was the same angel that called to Abraham when he was going to sacrifice Isaac and said, 'thou hast not withheld thy son, thine only son, from ME' [Gen. 22:12]. The same that spoke to Jacob and said, 'I have seen all that Laban doeth unto thee' [Gen. 31:12]. The same angel of the Lord who appeared to Moses in a flame

---

[11] Warner is either reading Hebrew, or is reading a commentary that gives this translation of the Hebrew word. This alternate translation "afflicted" sets up a dialogue of this text with texts in Exodus where the descendants of Sarah were "afflicted" by their Egyptian taskmasters.

of fire out of the midst of a bush and said, 'I am the God of thy father, the God of Abraham, the God of Isaac, and the God of Jacob' [Exod. 3:6]. Angel means messenger; and this was that precious messenger who has declared to us all the will of God; who is elsewhere called the 'Word' [John 1:1]."

"Was it Jesus, uncle Sam?"

"Tiny, the Bible says that the Father no man hath seen or can see; 'the only-begotten Son, which is in the bosom of the Father, he hath declared him' [John 1:18]. This was he of whom Jacob said, 'God, before whom my fathers Abraham and Isaac did walk, the God which led me all my life long unto this day, the *Angel which redeemed me from all evil*" [Gen. 48:15-16].

"Was it Jesus?" I said again. "Did He stand there by Hagar at the fountain, and did she see him?"

"Was it unlike him, Tiny? It was the same One who, some two thousand years later, let the blind and the lame come to him, touched the lepers and healed the sick; 'the same yesterday, to-day, and for ever!' [Heb. 13:8] Was it unlike him to stand beside the poor runaway slave in the wilderness, and hear her cry?"

"But—he doesn't do so now," I said.

"Yes, he does! the only difference is, that we cannot see him. He stands by his people when they are in trouble; he brings them comfort, and gives them deliverance, and speaks to them in their hearts. It is the 'angel of his presence' that saves them now, and in all their affliction he is afflicted [Isa. 63:9]. Nothing is true of him then, that is not true of him now; nor true of him now that was not true of him then."

"Sir," said Liph, "do you think Hagar was one of his people?"

"She was the wife of Abraham, and she was to be the mother of his first child; and God took care of everything that belonged to Abraham. But he passes by nothing; he forgets nobody, and nobody's trouble; he died to put sin and sorrow away; and men's perverseness is the only reason why it is not put away. The 'Messenger of the covenant' [Mal. 3:1]—he comes to every heart that will let him in; and the 'Messenger of the covenant' is the same angel who spoke to Moses in Mount Sinai, and the same angel who 'found Hagar by a fountain of water in the wilderness.'"

"'And he said, Hagar, Sarai's maid, whence comest thou? and whither wilt thou go?'"

"That sounds like Jesus,"—I said.

"She, weary and wondering, said, 'I flee from the face of my mistress Sarai.' And then she was told to go back and be patient; 'and the angel of the Lord said unto her, I will multiply thy seed exceedingly, that it shall not be numbered for multitude.' You see what voice speaks there."

"But her children were not to be the Jews?" said Liph.

"No. The people descended from Ishmael, her son, are the great Arabian nation, a people almost as wonderful as their cousins the Jews. Their character was foretold to Hagar. 'Thou shalt bear a son, and shalt call his name Ishmael; because the Lord hath heard thy affliction. And he will be a wild man; his hand will be against every man, and every man's hand against him; and he shall dwell in the presence of all his brethren.' It is the character they have borne, without change, through all the generations of the three thousand seven hundred years since then. They are like no other nation in that. They are a great multitude of many various tribes, spread over the country from Egypt and the Mediterranean coast to the river Tigris and beyond, and westward through Egypt to the northern regions of Africa. And everywhere they are wild men; their hand against every man, and every man's hand against them; but no hand able to put them down or put them out of their possessions. Still they dwell in the presence of all their brethren; their language and manners and habits and abodes remaining the same as they were three thousand years ago, in all essentials." . . .

"How many tribes are there of them?" my grandmother asked. "It was promised that Ishmael should be 'multiplied exceedingly.'"

"It is supposed his descendants are more at the present day than the descendants of Isaac. I do not know at how many millions they are reckoned; but I know there are one hundred and twenty millions of people who speak the Arabic language. As for the tribes, the original twelve have been divided and subdivided until now there are near sixty. Some Arabs, you must remember, in the south of Arabia, are not Ishmaelites, but the descendants of Joktau; others are the children of Keturah; but they have intermarried, doubtless; and the children of Ishmael are said to form now the great mass of the Arabian people."

"I should not think it would have been much pleasure to Hagar to hear all that," said Prissy.

"It was not said for her pleasure, but for our learning [Rom. 15:4]. However, the promise that her son should be the father of a great nation could not be anything but pleasant to her; for children were esteemed a special boon in the East. One thing she ought not to have forgotten—the name her child should bear. Ishmael means, 'God shall hear.' That name might for ever remind her of those sweet words that were spoken to her in her forlornness there—'the Lord hath heard thy affliction.' Amid the weary rocks of that wilderness, the poor slave did not think her tears had been seen; but they were; and Jesus came to speak peace to them."

"But every poor slave's cry is not heard, I suppose," said Liph.

"Yes it is! and registered; and answered when the time comes. For the day and the hour, my boy, we must trust God's wisdom, as being better than ours

[Matt. 24:36]. As it is, God has given his children a message of comfort to carry to every suffering creature. That it is not carried, is the fault of those to whom the message has been committed."[12]

We were all silent a little while upon this. Then Daniel asked where the place was, of that fountain of water where Hagar was found?

"Not certainly known," my uncle said. "Only that it was in what is called 'the south country' [Gen. 20:1; 24:62]—a wide tract of pasture ground between the hills of Judah on the one hand and the desert on the other. It is a dry land without springs; and therefore from the oldest times men dug wells there, which remain to this day. *Beer* means a well; and *Ain,* or *En,* a living spring of water; you can remember that. Hagar's well was called from that time, Beer-lahai-roi; 'the well of him that liveth and seeth.' And *Ishmael* means, 'God hears;' so if people had not the Bible in those times, you see they carried the truth about with them in the names of every day things. We do the other way, I am afraid. It would be good for us if we knew our own well always as 'Beer-lahai-roi.'"

"But that Angel does not come to speak to us there, uncle Sam."

"Doesn't he?" said my uncle. "Ah, little Tiny, you are mistaken. He comes wherever there is a heart that wants to hear him and will be obedient to him—in the forest, or by the spring, or wherever it may be, there comes Jesus."

"But that well is said to have been between Kadesh and Bered," said Liph. "I should think it might have been known."

"It was known when Moses wrote. But Kadesh and Bered are names now and nothing more; we cannot be sure of the exact site of either of them. It doesn't matter. Hagar went home again, and in course of time Ishmael was born. Abraham very likely thought that this son was to be the promised heir of the promises and of the land of Canaan. But it was not so.

"Thirteen more years had passed quietly away, and Abraham was almost a hundred years old; when the Angel that had come to Hagar came again to him. 'The Lord appeared to Abram,' and told him more particularly about the promise than Abraham had ever known before. Now let us look at it. But first, look at the command; for the Lord's promises are always with a condition. '*Walk before me and be thou perfect*' [Gen. 17:1]."

"But it isn't always *that* condition, uncle Sam," said Priscilla.

"Isn't it? Nobody that does not walk before God—as a servant before his

---

[12] Here Warner criticizes the Christian culture of the United States, which has failed to bring a message of comfort to "every suffering creature." Warner seems to clearly indicate that all American slaves should hear a message of comfort from God. She gives the reader a chance to reflect on this cultural critique as the characters pause to think about it.

master—as a child before his father—has anything to do with the Lord's good promises."

"But nobody is perfect, uncle Sam."

"Nobody is without sin, Prissy. But the Bible must mean something, when it says, 'Thou shalt be perfect with the Lord thy God' [Deut. 18:13]; and certainly nobody is perfect who has the least allowance of sin or makes the least compromise with it, anywhere or in anything; whose heart is *not all the Lord's*. That is required, of everybody; and the heart that is all the Lord's, the Lord will keep [Deut. 6:5; 7:13]. Abraham's was such a heart; and with him God made his covenant. The covenant had been given before; now the Lord added two seals to it. The first was Abraham's change of name. He had been Abram; now he was to he called Abraham, which means, 'father of a multitude,' and his wife was to be Sarah, which is, 'princess.' And whenever afterwards the Lord took any one into particular favour, you may notice that it was apt to be marked by a change of name. 'Thou shalt be called by a new name' [Isa. 62:2], was a promise to the church of old; and Jesus says, 'To him that overcometh will I give a white stone, and in the stone a new name written, which no man knoweth saving he that receiveth it' [Rev. 2:17].

"Uncle Sam, I don't think I know exactly what that means."

"We shall not know exactly, till we get it, Tiny. The other seal to the covenant was one which Abraham was to set, and his children after him; it was the sign of circumcision. It was only a sign; but it was like baptism now, the believer's sign of faith in the Lord and pledge of belonging to him. Anybody who did not choose to give it, was cut off from the covenant and had no right to the promises. And then the Lord told Abraham, that his promised child, through whom the blessing was to come, was not Ishmael; but that Sarah should have a son of her own, and with him and his children the covenant should stand."

"'Then Abraham fell upon his face and laughed'"—said Priscilla.

"Fell upon his face in adoring wonder, and laughed for joy. This was not the laughter of one who doubted the Lord's word. 'He staggered not at the promise of God through unbelief; but was strong in faith, giving glory to God; and being fully persuaded that what he had promised he was able also to perform' [Rom. 4:20]. So the Lord told him that this promised son should be called 'Laughter;' he should be joy and a sign of joy. Nevertheless Abraham's heart held very closely his first child, his thirteen year old boy; and he prayed for a blessing upon Ishmael. And the Lord granted it; indeed the blessing given to Ishmael was as great as that given to Isaac, as far as the mere things of this world are concerned. But the covenant belonged to Isaac alone. Only in Isaac, and in that promised One who should come in Isaac's line, was the word to be true to Abraham, 'I will be a God unto thee, and to thy seed after thee.' Only Isaac's children should inherit the land of Canaan 'for an everlasting possession;' even as only those who are Christ's can receive 'the promise of eternal inheritance' [Heb. 9:15]; of which the land of Canaan was a figure."

"But the Jews have not got the land of Canaan now," said Liph.

"Nor we haven't got heaven," said my uncle. "But both will. 'Thus saith the Lord, which giveth the sun for a light by day, and the ordinances of the moon and of the stars for a light by night—If those ordinances depart from before me, saith the Lord, then the seed of Israel also shall cease from being a nation before me for ever' [Jer. 31:35-36]. 'Yea, I will rejoice over them to do them good, and I will plant them in this land assuredly with my whole heart and with my whole soul'" [Jer. 32:4].

"The Arab nations observe circumcision too," said my grandmother.

"Yes, and claim the right of the eldest son of Abraham—a right to the possession of earthly territory. With the faith of Abraham they have nothing to do. And you know, children, that whether it be circumcision or baptism, the real thing is the Lord's inward seal set on the heart. If that is not washed from sin, and wholly given and marked as the Lord's the outward sign is good for nothing. So unless a man had the inward seal as well as the outward sign, he was not one of the true Israel. 'If ye be Christ's'—not otherwise—'then are ye Abraham's seed, and heirs according to the promise'" [Gal. 3:29].

§39 Charlotte Maria Tucker (A.L.O.E.)
(1821–1893)

Charlotte Maria Tucker, a very prolific children's author, wrote under the pseudonym A.L.O.E. (A Lady of England). She lived in London for most of her adult life, then moved to India as a missionary.[13] The following selection, "Hagar's Bottle," is taken from Tucker's book, *House Beautiful; or, The Bible Museum* (1868). This book was like a museum because in it Tucker discussed objects mentioned in scripture. The object discussed in this essay is Hagar's Bottle.

Tucker only discussed the second episode of Hagar's story. Beginning with the empty water bottle and a traveller's account of travel in the desert, Tucker emphasized Hagar and Ishmael's desperate situation. Ishmael's prayer and God's answer rescued the mother and son from certain death. Tucker compared troubles in her readers' lives with the crisis Ishmael and Hagar

---

[13] For more information on Tucker, see part 1, "Eve—The Mother of Us All."

encountered in the desert. Like Trimmer and Hall, Tucker taught that those who turned to God for help would find fresh resources to assist them in their trouble. While Tucker ostensibly wrote for children, in her application of Hagar and Ishmael's story she seemed to preach to adults.

From A.L.O.E. [A Lady of England], *House Beautiful; or, The Bible Museum* (London: T. Nelson & Sons, 1868), 28–32.

"Hagar's Bottle"

An empty skin-bottle is before us, such as is used by Orientals to the present day to carry what they emphatically term "the gift of God;" a title to which our Saviour appears to have alluded when He said to the woman of whom He had asked water, *If thou knewest the gift of God* [John 4:10], seeking to raise her thoughts from the earthly well to the heavenly Fountain.

Of the value of water in the wilderness, we, in our moist climate, can scarcely form an adequate conception. Let me briefly quote from a description of traveling in an Arabian desert, given by a graphic author:* "On either hand extended one weary plain in a black monotony of lifelessness. . . . A dreary land of death, in which even the face of an enemy were almost a relief amid such utter solitude. . . . Day after day found us urging our camels to their utmost pace, for fifteen or sixteen hours together out of the twenty-four, under a well-nigh vertical sun. . . . Then an insufficient halt for rest or sleep, at most of two or three hours, soon interrupted by the often repeated admonition, 'If we linger here we all die of thirst.'"

But the scene which rises before us, the wilderness of Beersheba, is not peopled with pilgrims and travellers urging on their weary camels; there are but two figures in it—an exhausted, grief-stricken woman, and the fainting lad at her side. That skin-bottle in her hands—empty. She has watched it shrinking as the precious fluid within was gradually used, or wasted by evaporation; dry and parched as is her own tongue, she has feared to relieve her burning thirst lest she should too soon exhaust the priceless treasure. With a sickening feeling of fear Hagar has given the last draught to her Ishmael; and then, with faint hope, squeezed the skin hard with her feverish hands, trying to press out one more drop—but in vain. She looks anxiously around her, but can see no means of refilling that empty bottle. Then, in anguish, Hagar turns from the parched shrub under which she has cast her son; she wanders away—but let the account be given in the touching words of Scripture: *She went and sat her down over against him a good way off, as it was a bowshot: for she said, Let me not see the death of the child. And she sat over against him, and lift up her voice and wept.*

While Hagar was weeping her son appears to have been praying; for it is written, *God heard the voice of the lad.* Ishmael's cry was unanswered: *The angel of God called to Hagar out of heaven, and said to her, What aileth thee, Hagar? fear not; for God hath heard the voice of the lad where he is. And God opened her eyes, and she saw a well of water; and she went, and filled the bottle with water, and gave the lad drink.* When the cool bubbling liquid filled out the swelling skin-bottle in the hand of the rejoicing, thankful mother, as she bent eagerly over the well, far more emphatically than the first supply was it to her—the gift of God.

There are times when life appears to us as the wilderness of Beersheba did to Hagar and Ishmael. Our troubles may have been of our own making; like the proud youth who had mocked at his brother, we may, perhaps, be able to trace our sorrows to their source in our sin; but whether it be so or not, we stand in a dry, thirsty land, where no water is; we seem to have drained our last drop of earthly enjoyment—our lips are parched—our bottle is empty—we feel that we can but lie down and die! Few pass the meridian of life, perhaps few reach it, without knowing something of this desolation of heart, this emptiness of all joy. Blessed to Ishmael was the trouble which made him cry to the Lord; blessed to us these disappointments which dry up our cherished supplies, if in our baffled thirst for happiness we turn to our Saviour in prayer. The same God who gave to Hagar a well in the desert has also a message of mercy for us: *Ho, every one that thirsteth, come ye to the waters, and he that hath no money; come ye, buy, and eat; yea, come, buy wine and milk without money and without price* [Isa. 55:1]. Would we seek more specific direction to the Fountain that bursts forth in the desert, to change that desert to an Eden, and supply our deep thirst for peace and joy? The Saviour Himself repeats the invitation: *If any man thirst, let him come unto Me and drink* [John 7:37].

What do we need, dear brethren in affliction, to make us come unto Him in whom the weary find refreshment, and the broken-hearted peace? We need that by the Spirit *our eyes should be opened.* The Fountain is near us, but we see it not until then. We view the bare waste around us, the withered hopes that strew it; we vainly try to press out one more drop of pleasure from the earthly vessel which once held it, and find the bottle utterly empty and dry. In such moments of dreariness, O Thou who art the Comforter indeed, Thou who canst fill up the empty void, and satisfy the aching soul with abundance, come to us, speak to us, open our eyes to behold the depths of Thy loving-kindness; lead us beside the still waters, and let the promise of our Redeemer be graciously fulfilled unto us: *He that cometh unto Me shall never hunger, and he that believeth on Me shall never thirst* [John 6:35].

* Palgrave [W. Gifford Palgrave (1826–1888)]. Here Tucker is probably referring to Palgrave's work *Narrative of a Year's Journey through Central and Eastern Arabia* (1862–1863) (London: Macmillan, 1865).

§40 Sarah Town Martyn
(1805–1879)

Sarah Martyn, an American Congregationalist, was a social activist and writer. She edited a number of religious and women's magazines, and published more than twenty books.[14] Martyn lived and wrote at the same time as Warner, but wrote for an older and primarily female audience, and addressed theological issues much more subtly than Warner. Martyn's book, *Women of the Bible*, was an illustrated gift book that retold biblical stories in a gentle romanticized way. She filled out the characters in the text and emphasized the emotions she imagined they must have experienced. Building on her experience as a writer of historical fiction, she fleshed out the story through creative extrapolation. Martyn saw Hagar as typical of everyone. Like Warner, Martyn was an abolitionist. However, unlike Warner, she did not interpret the Hagar story in light of the American slavery issue.

From S. T. Martyn, *Women of the Bible* (New York: American Tract Society, 1868), 32–36, 45–49.

–Sarah and Hagar–

ON his entrance into the promised land, Abram passed on to Bethel; and from that place turned southward as far as Mamre, or Hebron, twenty miles south of Jerusalem, where he fixed his abode. Lot, his nephew, being obliged to leave his relative because of the constant bickerings between the herdsmen of the two patriarchs, chose the rich vale of Sodom as his place of residence, moved to the step more by the love of mammon than a regard to the glory of God. This unwise choice resulted most disastrously for Lot and his family, none of whom escaped the moral contamination of the guilty and devoted city [Gen. 19, Josh. 6:17].[15]

Soon after Lot's departure, Sarah, who had brought with her from Egypt a young maiden named Hagar as a personal attendant, and who still continued childless, offered Hagar, according to the custom of those times, to Abram as his concubine, hoping by means of children thus obtained, to escape the

---

[14] For more information on Martyn, see part 1, "Eve—The Mother of Us All."

[15] Martyn called Sodom a "devoted city," though it is not called that in Genesis. A "devoted city" was to be completely destroyed so that Israelites would not be contaminated by it. See Leviticus 27 for regulations around devoted things.

reproach of being childless, so much dreaded by an oriental woman.[16] Hagar assuming that, as the mother of Abram's heir she must become the favored and honored wife, very naturally took upon herself the airs of a favorite, even in the presence of her mistress.

Forgetting the fact that the arrangement was one of her own making, the indignant wife complained bitterly to Abram of Hagar's insolence; evidently looking on herself as the innocent and injured party in the whole transaction. With the dignity and wisdom which marked his character, Abram avoided entering into the merits of the case, simply assuring Sarah that Hagar was in her power and subject to her will. We are sorry to find that this appeal to her better feelings was in vain, for her treatment of the poor bondwoman was such that Hagar resolved to fly to the desert rather than endure it longer.

Having wandered for many hours, she seated herself, weary and desponding, beside a fountain, round which a few palms were growing, and gave herself up to bitter meditation. Suddenly her attention was arrested by a voice which inquired, "Hagar, Sarah's maid, whence camest thou, and whither dost thou go?" Filled with wonder and awe at the heavenly visitation, Hagar did not attempt to exonerate herself or censure her mistress, but simply replied, "I fled from the face of Sarah my mistress."

In tones of thrilling sweetness, the heavenly voice directed her to return to her mistress and humble herself before her, at the same time assuring her that her posterity should be multiplied exceedingly, so that it could not be counted for multitude.

The son she was to bear to Abram, and whose name was to be Ishmael, the voice described as a wild man, whose hand should be against every man, and every man's hand against him; still he would dwell in the presence of his brethren.

The heart of the young Egyptian was softened and penetrated by the words of her divine visitant, and in the fulness of her emotion she exclaimed,

"Have I also here looked after him who seeth me?" at the same time naming the heavenly stranger, "Thou God seest me."

How many a poor wanderer ever since that time, fainting in life's wilderness beneath a load of care and sorrow, when some unexpected voice from heaven has cheered and comforted the fainting soul, has had occasion to exclaim with Hagar, "Have I also here looked after him who seeth me?"

Ishmael was born soon after Hagar's return to Hebron, and the boy was regarded generally as the presumptive heir to his father's rich inheritance. But when he was thirteen years old, God appeared again to Abram, renewing the magnificent promises to him and his posterity made before; and assuring him

---

[16] That is, an eastern woman.

that Sarah his wife should bear a son, that God would bless her and make her mother of nations, and that kings of people should be born of her.

Overcome with surprise and joy, Abraham, as he was now by divine direction to be called, fell on his face, and said in his heart, "Shall a child be born to him who is a hundred years old; and shall Sarah, who is ninety years old, become a mother?" Unable to believe that such a miracle could be wrought in his behalf, he proffers a prayer for his wayward but beloved Ishmael, evidently supposing, the promises were to be fulfilled in him. But the Almighty reaffirmed the assurance that a son should be born to him of Sarah, with whom an everlasting covenant should be established, and with his seed after him. At the same time he graciously assured him that Ishmael should be remembered, and made a great nation; but with Isaac, Sarah's son, his covenant should be established, never to be broken. . . .

There is joy and rejoicing in the tent at Mamre, such as never before lighted up its walls; for a new life has there commenced its course, destined to flow on while eternity itself endures. The promise of God is fulfilled; a son has been given to Abraham, and Sarah, as she sheds happy tears on the soft cheek of her first-born, can hardly believe that all this bliss is a reality, that this precious gift of God is indeed her own, a part of herself, from which henceforth nothing can ever separate her affection. The babe is well named Isaac, or *laughter*, for his coming has opened a perpetual fountain of gladness in the hearts of his parents. They see in him not only the child of their old age, the stay and staff of their declining years, but the heir of promise, and the inheritor of a legacy of blessings such as only God could bestow.

But amidst the general rejoicing at the birth of Isaac, one heart feels nothing but mortification and disappointment. Ishmael, who has hitherto looked upon himself as the heir to the vast possessions of his father, regards the advent of this new claimant as a personal injury, and nurses his indignation until he almost hates the beautiful child who, he thinks, has usurped his place in the heart and home of his father.

Such was his state of feeling, though probably the influence of Hagar restrained him from any violent outbreak, until the time came for the weaning of Isaac, when, according to custom, a great feast was made by Abraham in honor of the infant heir. Ishmael could no longer conceal the envy and bitterness with which his heart was overflowing, and some most offensive manifestation of it was made on that occasion. Justly indignant at his presumption, Sarah demanded of her husband the immediate dismissal of Hagar and her son, lest in process of time contentions should arise, which might endanger the safety of her beloved Isaac.

Though the patriarch listened with his wonted serenity to the complaint of Sarah, his heart was deeply troubled. He loved his eldest born, and felt that

Hagar, as his son's mother, was entitled to his kindness and protection while she lived. In this state of mind, God came to his servant, and commanded him to obey the voice of Sarah, in sending away the Egyptian and her son; for in Isaac should his posterity be established, though, as his son, Ishmael should inherit a blessing, and his posterity become a great and mighty nation.

Thus directed, Abraham hesitated no longer; but rising early in the morning, that his parting with Ishmael might be without witnesses, he gave to Hagar bread and water to sustain her until she should reach some spot in which they might abide.

Thus driven from the home in which she had spent so many years, the poor mother wandered into one of those vast arid deserts which lie between Southern Judea and Egypt. The water in her leathern bottle was soon exhausted, and Ishmael, parched and fainting with thirst, entreated for a drink which it was not in her power to give him.

All around her on every side lay the stony desert, on which the rays of the sun were shining with a fierce brightness that seemed to mock her misery. Leaving Ishmael half dead, under a small shrub, Hagar seated herself at a little distance, waiting till death should come to end their misery. Hopeless and despairing, she could not look on her child, but sat lamenting her miserable condition, when a well-remembered voice once more called to her.

"Hagar, what aileth thee? Fear not; for God hath heard the cry of the lad where he lieth. Arise, lift up the child, and hold him in thy hand; for I will make him a great nation."

While the angel yet spoke, she looked around and saw near her a well of water sparkling in the sunbeams, and with joyful heart hastened to fill her bottle, and give Ishmael drink. After this she took up her abode in the wilderness of Paran, where Ishmael grew to maturity, a celebrated hunter and archer, taking a wife from Egypt, his mother's native land. From this son of Abraham, the various tribes of wandering Arabs are lineally descended, thus verifying the prophecy of the wildness and isolation of his posterity.

§41 Harriet Beecher Stowe
(1811–1896)

Harriet Beecher Stowe was a renowned American author who preached the gospel of womanhood and of Christ to a wide audience.[17] Stowe was a con-

---

[17] For more information about Stowe, see part 2, "Sarah—The First Mother of Israel."

temporary of Warner and Martyn. Like Martyn, she had a clergyman father and was involved in the abolition movement, and she published an illustrated gift book on women in the Bible that included a section on Hagar. Both Martyn and Stowe identified with the common humanity of Hagar and made a universal application of her story: Hagar is each of us. Both writers also used their skills as fiction writers to embellish the story. They interpreted Hagar's story, however, in different ways. Stowe's level of engagement with the text in *Women in Sacred History* was much more profound than Martyn's. Stowe used the tools and language of theology and science, including the idea of evolutionary development. Unlike Martyn, Stowe read Hagar's story through the lens of American slavery.

The second excerpt on Hagar by Stowe comes from her book *Footsteps of the Master,* which she wrote to counter the influence of modern skepticism and biblical criticism.[18] She divided the book's chapters liturgically, from Advent to Ascension Day. In the chapter for Advent, called "Christ in the Old Testament," she compared Jacob and Hagar's encounters with God. Stowe read Hagar as the typical Gentile (see Gal. 4:21–5:1), in contrast to Jacob (rather than Sarah), the father of the nation of Israel.

In both books Stowe used language that a twenty-first century reader will find offensive. While she was against American slavery and attempted to differentiate between slavery in the Bible and slavery in the United States, she was unable to completely separate her reading and interpretation of the text from her social setting.

From Harriet Beecher Stowe, *Women in Sacred History* (New York: Fords, Howard, & Hulbert, 1873), 32–42.

–Hagar the Slave–

A STRIKING pendant to the picture of Sarah the Princess is that of Hagar the Slave.

In the Bible narrative she is called simply Hagar the Egyptian; and as Abraham sojourned some time in the land of Egypt, we are to suppose that

---

[18] Stowe was very critical of a strictly academic approach to the Bible that neglected personal piety. She wrote a letter to her scholar husband, Calvin Stowe, saying: "If you studied Christ with half the energy that you have studied Luther . . . If you were drawn toward him & loved him as much as you loved your study & your books then would he be formed in you, the hope of glory . . . But you fancy that you . . . must write courses of lectures . . . and read new German books—all these things you <u>must</u> do & then if there is any time, any . . . strength & mental capability left, why they are to be given occasionally to . . . keeping a kind of a Christian character" (Letter to Calvin E. Stowe, circa May 21, 1844, cited in Gail Smith, "Reading the Word: Harriet Beecher Stowe and Interpretation" [Ph.D. Diss., University of Virginia, 1993], 58).

this acquisition to the family was then made. Slavery, in the early patriarchal period, had few of the horrors which beset it in more modern days. The condition of a slave more nearly resembled that of the child of the house than that of a modern servant. The slave was looked upon, in default of children, as his master's heir, as was the case with Eliezer of Damascus, the confidential servant of Abraham; the latter, when speaking to God of his childless condition says: "Lo! one born in my house is mine heir." In like manner there is a strong probability in the legend which represents Hagar as having been the confidential handmaid of Sarah, and treated by her with peculiar tenderness.

When the fear of being childless seized upon her, Sarah was willing to exalt one, who was as a second self to her, to the rank of an inferior wife, according to the customs of those early days; intending to adopt and treat as her own the child of her handmaid. But when the bondwoman found herself thus exalted, and when the crowning honor of prospective motherhood was conferred upon her, her ardent tropical blood boiled over in unseemly exultation,—"her mistress was despised in her eyes."

Probably under the flapping curtains of the pastoral tent, as under the silken hangings of palaces, there were to be found flatterers and mischief-makers ready to fill the weak, credulous ear with their suggestions. Hagar was about to become mother of the prince and heir of the tribe; her son one day should be their chief and ruler, while Sarah, childless and uncrowned, should sink to a secondary rank. Why should she obey the commands of Sarah?

Our idea of Sarah is that of a warm-hearted, generous, bountiful woman, with an intense sense of personal dignity and personal rights, just the woman to feel herself beyond measure outraged by this unexpected result of what she must have looked upon as unexampled favor. In place of a grateful, devoted creature, identified with her interests, whose child should be to her as her own child, she finds herself confronted with an imperious rival, who lays claim to her place and position.

The struggle was one that has been witnessed many a time since in families so constituted, and with such false elements. Abraham, peace-loving and quiet, stands neutral; confident, as many men are, of the general ability of the female sex, by inscrutable ways and methods of their own, to find their way out of the troubles they bring themselves into. Probably he saw wrong on both sides; yet Hagar, as the dependent, who owed all the elevation on which she prided herself to the good-will of her mistress, was certainly the more in fault of the two; and so he dismisses the subject with: "Thy maid is in thy hand; do with her as pleaseth thee."

The next we hear of the proud, hot-hearted, ungoverned slave girl, is her flight to the wilderness in a tumult of indignation and grief, doubtless after bitter words and hard usage from the once indulgent mistress. But now comes into the history the presence of the Father God, in whose eye all human beings are equal, and who looks down on the boiling strifes and hot passions of us all below, as a mother on the quarrels of little children in the nursery. For this was the world's infancy, and each character in the drama represented a future nation for whom the All-Father was caring.

So when the violent, desolate creature had sobbed herself weary in the lonesome desert, the story says: "And the angel of the Lord found her by a fountain of water, in the way to Shur. And he said, Hagar, Sarah's maid, whence comest thou? and whither wilt thou go? And she said, I flee from the face of my mistress, Sarah."

In this calm question there is a reminder of duty violated, and in the submissive answer is an acknowledgment of that duty. The angel calls her "Sarah's maid," and she replies, "my mistress, Sarah."

"And the angel of the Lord said unto her, "Return to thy mistress, and submit thyself under her hands." Then, as with awe and submission she rises to go, she is comforted with promises of gracious tenderness. The All-Father does not take part with her in her rebellious pride, nor in her haughty desire to usurp the station and honors of her mistress, and yet he has sympathy for that strong, awakening feeling of motherhood which makes the wild girl of the desert begin at once to crave station and place on earth for the son she is to bring into it. So the story goes on: "And the angel of the Lord said unto her, I will multiply thy seed exceedingly, that it shall not be numbered for multitude. And the angel of the Lord said unto her, Behold, thou art with child, and shalt bear a son, and shalt call his name Ishmael, because the Lord hath heard thy affliction. And he will be a wild man; his hand will be against every man, and every man's hand against him; and he shall dwell in the presence of all his brethren. And she called the name of the Lord that spake unto her, Thou God seest me: for she said, Have I also here looked after him that seeth me?"

This little story is so universally and beautifully significant of our every-day human experience, that it has almost the force of an allegory.

Who of us has not yielded to despairing grief, while flowing by us were unnoticed sources of consolation? The angel did not *create* the spring in the desert: it was there all the while, but Hagar was blinded by her tears. She was not seeking God, but he was seeking her. How often may we, all of us, in the upliftings and deliverances of our life, say as she did, "Have I here looked after him that seeth me?"

The narrative adds, "Wherefore the spring was called *The Well of Him that Liveth and Seeth Me*."

That spring is still flowing by our daily path.

So, quieted and subdued and comforted, Hagar returns to her mistress and her home, and we infer from the story, that, with submission on her part, kindness and bounty returned on the part of her mistress. She again becomes a member of the family. Her son is born, and grows up for twelve years under the shadow of Abraham's tent, and evidently, from the narrative, is fondly beloved by his father, and indulgently treated by his foster-mother.

In an hour of confidential nearness the Divine Father announces to Abraham that a son shall be given him by the wife of his heart.

"As for Sarah, thy wife, I will bless her, and give thee a son of her, and she shall be a mother of nations; kings of people shall be of her. Then Abraham fell upon his face and laughed, and said in his heart: Shall a child be born to him that is an hundred years old, and shall Sarah, that is ninety years old, bear?" Yet, in this moment of triumphant joy, his heart yearns after Ishmael; And Abraham said unto God: "that Ishmael might live before thee!" And the Divine answer is: "As for Ishmael, I have heard thee. Behold, I have blessed him, and will make him fruitful, and will multiply him exceedingly; twelve princes shall he beget, and I will make him a great nation."

But now comes the hour long waited for, of Sarah's triumph, the fulfillment of the desires of her life. A generous heart would have sympathized in her triumph. A mother who had known the blessedness of motherhood would have rejoiced when the mistress who had done so much for her was made so joyful. If her own son be not the heir in succession, yet an assured future is promised to him. But the dark woman and her wild son are of untamable elements. They can no more become one in spirit with the patriarchal family, than oil can mix with water. When the weaning feast is made, and all surround the little Isaac, when the mother's heart overflows with joy, she sees the graceless Ishmael mocking; and instantly, with a woman's lightning prescience, she perceives the dangers, the impossibilities of longer keeping these aliens under the same roof, the feuds, the jealousies, the fierce quarrels of the future.

"Cast out this bondwoman and her son," she says, with the air of one accustomed to command and decide; "for the son of this bondwoman shall not be heir with my son, even with Isaac." It appears that Abraham had set his heart on the boy, and had hoped to be able to keep both in one family, and divide his inheritance between them; but it was otherwise decreed. "And God said to Abraham, Let it not be grievous in thy sight, because of the lad and because of thy bondwoman: in all that Sarah hath said unto thee, hearken unto her voice; for in Isaac shall thy seed be called. And also of the son of the bondwoman will I make a nation, because he is thy seed. And Abraham arose up early, and took bread and a bottle of water and gave it to Hagar, putting it on her shoulder, and sent her away with the child; and she departed and wandered in the wilderness of Beersheba." Probably she was on the road towards Egypt. "And the water was all spent in the bottle, and she cast the child under one of the shrubs; and she went away and sat her down over against him a good way off, as it were a bow-shot, for she said, Let me not see the death of the child; and she lifted up her voice and wept."

Poor, fiery, impatient creature!—moaning like a wounded leopardess,—apparently with no heart to remember the kindly Power that once before helped her in her sorrows; but the story goes on: "And God heard the voice of the lad; and the angel of the Lord called to Hagar out of heaven, and said unto her, What aileth thee, Hagar? Fear not, for God hath heard the voice of the lad where he is. Arise, lift up the lad, and hold him in thy hand; for I will make of him a great nation. And God opened her eyes, and she saw a well of water; and she went and filled the bottle with water and gave the lad drink. And God was with the lad, and he grew, and dwelt in the wilderness and became an archer. And he dwelt in the wilderness of Paran; and his mother took him a wife out of the land of Egypt."

In all this story, nothing impresses us so much as the absence of all modern technical or theological ideas respecting the God who is represented here as sowing the seed of nations with a wise foresight of the future. As a skillful husbandman, bent on perfecting a certain seed, separates it from all others, and grows it by itself, so the Bible tells us that God selected a certain stock to be trained and cultivated into the sacerdotal race, through which should come his choicest revelations to man. Of this race in its final outcome and perfected flowering was to spring forth Jesus, spoken of as the BRANCH of this sacred tree. For the formation of this race, we see a constant choice of the gentler and quieter elements of blood and character, and the persistent rejection of that which is wild, fierce, and ungovernable. Yet it is with no fond partiality for the one, or antipathy to the other, that the Father of both thus decides. The thoughtful, patient, meditative Isaac is chosen; the wild, hot-blooded, impetuous Ishmael is rejected,—not as in themselves better or worse, but as in relation to their adaptation to a great purpose of future good to mankind. The ear of the All-Father is as near to the cry of the passionate, hot-tempered slave, and the moans of the wild, untamable boy, as to those of the patriarch. We are told that God was with Ishmael in his wild growth as a hunter in the desert,—his protector from harm, the guardian of his growing family, according to the promise made to Abraham.

When the aged patriarch is gathered to his fathers at the age of a hundred and seventy-five years, it is recorded: "And Abraham gave up the ghost in a good old age, an old man and full of years; and his sons, Isaac and Ishmael, buried him in the cave of Machpelah, in the field that Abraham purchased of the sons of Heth; there was Abraham buried, and Sarah his wife."

The subsequent history of the nation which Ishmael founded, shows that the promises of God were faithfully kept.

The Arab race has ever been a strongly marked people. They have been worshipers of the one God, and, at one time, under the califs, rose to a superiority in art, science, and literature beyond that of so-called Christian nations.

The race of Ishmael is yet as vigorous and as peculiar, and as likely to perpetuate itself, as the race of Isaac and Jacob; and as God was near to the cries and needs of the wild mother of the race and her wild offspring, so, doubtless, he has heard the prayer that has gone up from many an Arab tent in the desert.

The besetting sin of a select people is the growth of a spirit of haughty self-sufficiency among them. In time the Jews came to look upon themselves as God's only favorites, and upon all other nations as outcasts. It is this spirit that is rebuked by the prophet Amos (ix.) when, denouncing the recreant children of Israel, he says, in the name of the Lord: "Are ye not as children of the Ethiopians unto me, O children of Israel? saith the Lord. Have not I brought up Israel out of the land of Egypt? and the Philistines from Caphtor, and the Syrians from Kir?" [Amos 9:7].

There is a deep comfort in this record of God's goodness to a poor, blinded, darkened, passionate slave-woman, nowise a model for imitation, yet tenderly watched over and succored and cared for in her needs. The Father unsought is ever seeking. He who said, "What aileth thee, Hagar?" is he who, in later times, said that he came to seek and to save the lost. Not to the saintly and the righteous only, or mostly, but to the wayward, the sinful, the desperate, the despairing, to those whose troubles come of their own folly and their own sin, is the angel sent to console, to promise, to open the blind eyes upon the fountain which is ever near us in life's desert, though we cannot perceive it.

From Harriet Beecher Stowe, *Footsteps of the Master* (New York: J. B. Ford & Co., 1877), 27–28.

But it was not merely to the chosen father of the chosen nation that this pitying Friend and Saviour appeared. When the poor, passionate, desperate slave girl Hagar was wandering in the wilderness, struggling with the pride and passion of her unsubdued nature, He who follows the one wandering sheep appeared [Luke 15:4] and spoke to her (Genesis xvi). He reproved her passionate impatience; he counseled submission; he promised his protection and care to the son that should be born of her and the race that should spring from her. Wild and turbulent that race of men should be; and yet there was to be a Saviour, a Care-taker, a Shepherd for them. "And she called the name of the Lord that spake unto her, Thou God seest me; for she said, Have I also here looked after him that seeth me?"

Afterwards, when the fiery, indomitable passions of the slave-woman again break forth and threaten the peace of the home, and she is sent forth into the wilderness, the Good Shepherd [John 10:14] again appears to her. Thus is the story told (Genesis xxi):

"And the water was spent in the bottle, and she cast the child under one of the shrubs, and she went and sat down a good way off, for she said, Let me not see the death of the child. And God heard the voice of the lad, and the angel of the Lord called to Hagar out of Heaven, saying, What aileth thee, Hagar? fear not. God hath heard the voice of the lad where he is. Arise, lift up the lad, hold him in thy hand, for I will make of him a great nation. And God opened her eyes, and she saw a well of water."

Thus did he declare himself the Care-taker and Saviour not of the Jews merely, but of the Gentiles. It was he who afterwards declared that he was the living bread which came down from Heaven, which he gave for the life of the WHOLE WORLD [John 6:33, 51].

§42 Etty Woosnam
(1849–c.1883)

Etty Woosnam was a member of a British family with ties to India.[19] Her involvement in a Bible class for young women resulted in the publication of two books on women in the Bible, *The Women of the Bible: Old Testament* (1881) and *The Women of the Bible: New Testament* (1885). Woosnam used her studies of women in the Bible to teach the Christian faith as well as the values of the dominant culture.

Woosnam lived her life in the context of Imperial Britain, as a member of the established Church of England, in an ordered society with clear class divisions. Her social context was very different from that of her American counterparts Stowe, Martyn, and Warner. Woosnam recognized that woman's duty was to submit to authority, just as Hagar was told to return and submit to Sarah. Woosnam acknowledged the difficulties submission created for women but encouraged them to consider submission a cross to bear for the Lord's sake (Matt. 16:24, Mark 8:34, Luke 9:23 and 14:27). Gerda Lerner

[19] For more information on Woosnam see part 1, "Eve—The Mother of Us All."

would suggest that Woosnam's awareness of oppression is a first step in developing a feminist consciousness.[20]

Woosnam's didactic purpose directed her to draw lessons on God's nature and the Christian life from Hagar's story. She used Galatians 4 as a guide for reading the Genesis story. In the end, Hagar was left behind as Woosnam discussed Christian liberty using Isaac and Ishmael as types.

From Etty Woosnam, *The Women of the Bible: Old Testament* (London: S. W. Partridge, 1881), 31–41.

–Hagar–
Bondage and Liberty

Why is it that from our childhood upwards we are so touched by the pitiful tale of the poor dishonoured, outcast slave? That there is an element of good still left in human nature in spite of all its corruptions, is demonstrated by the fact that the sight of sorrow and desolation does still avail to draw from almost every heart the feeling of kindly compassion, which is akin to love. But we sin-burdened and selfish creatures know little of the yearning tenderness, the infinite compassion, the unselfish pure love that ran through every vein of our Saviour, who, with a divine hatred for sin, could hold out a warm, sympathetic, human hand to the sinner, despised of men.

Hagar, a slave in Abraham's house, had become his wife; at Sarah's suggestion, it appears. And when it seemed likely that she was to be the mother of him in whom God's promise to Abraham was to be fulfilled Sarah's envy was stirred. This jealousy, though most natural, was not the less for that, sinful. She "dealt hardly" with her; and Hagar was treated so unkindly, that she chose rather to face the perils of loneliness and destitution in the wilderness, than to remain in her home. Friendless, afflicted, cast out—Hagar is a type of the penitent sinner. It was when she was in this condition that the angel of the Lord came to her and told her to return to her mistress, and submit herself under her hands. It is usually when a heart is in heaviness that it raises entreating eyes to Heaven. Oh, it is well for a soul when it finds the world cold and unkind, when friends seem hollow and selfish, if in its loneliness and desertedness it looks up. In the lifetime of our Heavenly Master on earth, it was the poor, struggling diseased ones that needed Him and were sought by Him, for His mission was to seek the lost [Luke 19:10]. How we notice this in every page of the Gospels! As for instance in St. John ix. i.—"As Jesus passed by he saw a man which was blind from his birth." As He passed, He

[20] Gerda Lerner, *The Creation of Feminist Consciousness* (Oxford: Oxford University Press, 1993), 274.

probably saw a great number of people besides. But this was a blind man, and Jesus "saw" him in a different sense altogether. Then after He had cured him, they seemed to have parted company for a while, until (as told in verse 35) the poor fellow was in disgrace, and experienced that to be in trouble again means to be sought by Jesus again. It is a happy thing to be cast off by friends, if it leads to being found by the Good Shepherd, and led into the fold [John 10:14-16]. It is a good thing for a flower to be thrown out of a man's garden if it fall over the wall into the King's palace grounds, there to be nourished and "watered every moment," and kept and cultivated by degrees into perfection [Isa. 58:11].

We do not read of Hagar's receiving an angel's visit again till she was in that woeful state in the wilderness of Beersheba, when she had moved a bow-shot away from her boy to avoid the agony of seeing him die; and when "she lifted up her voice and wept." Then once more the angel of God called to her out of heaven. In the first scene of her loneliness she was forcibly impressed with the reality of God's All-seeing Eye, and "Thou God, seest me" became the memorial name of the place. In the second, she was graciously made aware of His hearing ear. "What aileth thee, Hagar? fear not; for God hath heard the voice of the lad where he is." The cry of sorrow from the thirsty soul of a slave boy God hears; from "under the shrubs" in the desert God hears; from the lowest depth of misery, from the utmost ends of the earth, God hears. The presence of God is a reality which tries all our consciences, and proves of what sort they are. He is the Unapproachable Light from which the unrenewed shrink and hide, and at which only the humble, penitent, believing ones can gaze. The fool says "Let there be no God" [Ps. 14:1]. . . . In our worship in church; in our Bible reading alone; in our private prayer; let all be begun, continued, and ended with a clear sense that God is now here. In social visiting, at meal times, in general conversation, let us watchfully remind ourselves that God is here. I remember when I was at school, I often found myself talking fast and loud, and wasting much time and many words. But the instant I heard the footsteps of the schoolmistress whom I both loved and feared, I controlled myself and finished my sentence quite differently, or left it unfinished. How many discussions would we avoid, and how many unprofitable things leave unsaid, if we remembered that we cannot talk behind God's back!

Let us note by the way what the angel told Hagar to do when in the first instance she had fled from Sarah. He said:—"Return to thy mistress and submit thyself under her hands." We may take a practical lesson of duty for ourselves. In most cases our sorrows are the plain result of our offences. We have not done what we ought. We have been insubordinate to the authority over us and the circumstances ordained for us. We struggled and found the yoke galling, and we called it enduring affliction. Now when God's help comes in answer to prayer, and we are led to lay hold on the hope set before us, we are generally put back into the path of duty. "Go back and do better" Christ seems to say. "Return to thine own house and show (by a sweetened character, a consistent behaviour, a changed life, rather than by wordy profession) how great things God hath done unto thee" [Luke 8:39]. And if we should have to deal with others who, turning from evil ways desire to follow Christ, we can scarcely advise them better than by some such counsel as the angel gave:—Return to thy home—thy parents, thy work, thy master or mistress—or whoever is in authority over thee, and unto whatever constitutes thy cross, and submit thyself unto it for the Lord's sake [1 Pet. 2:13–3:6].

If Hagar's life teaches us first how tenderly God has compassion on them that are ignorant and out of the way, it has also that other deep lesson involved, which St. Paul educes from it. In Galatians iv. 21, and following verses, he says that Abraham's two sons—the one by a bondmaid, the other by a free woman—are an allegory of the two covenants. The first covenant made on Mount Sinai signified this:—"Thou shalt keep all the commandments of the Lord thy God, and He, on His part, shall bless thee" [Deut. 30:16]. The second made on Mount Calvary signified this:—"Christ hath redeemed us from the curse of the law being made a curse for us" [Gal. 3:13]; and "whosoever believeth in Him, though he were dead, yet shall he live" [John 11:25]. The first covenant meant bondage, for man could not keep it, and was under the curse of a broken law. An Israelite under the law of Moses was bound to obey God. The better covenant means Freedom. "If the Son shall make you free ye shall be free indeed" [John 8:36]. Free, not from the service of God, but from the slavery of Satan. Free, not to disobey the commands of God, but freed by a strong and lively faith from the bands of those sins that tyrannized over us. Free, not to please ourselves, but to serve mankind with a joyful and loving heart for Christ's sake [Gal. 5:13]. When Christ saves from the curse of sin and from the punishment of sin, He saves also from the power and dominion of sin. And then a man is free indeed! If we think that the atonement releases us from duty to God and men, we do not know Jesus aright. The cross was the very embodiment of unselfishness; and if we take Christ's yoke [Matt. 11:29-30] upon us and learn of Him, we must be unselfish too. He did not save us from the bondage of the law by breaking the law, but by perfectly keeping the law. The first covenant meant obligation; the second means love. The first held out death as the penalty of a broken law. The second holds out a lawfully kept and perfect freedom to every one who trusts in Christ's complete fulfilment of it. "Stand fast therefore in the liberty wherewith Christ hath made us free!" [Gal. 5:1].

Who loves chains, and prison bars, and hard rules, and binding engagements, and never-ending toil? Satan gives these.

It is not so much what we do, as the spirit in which we do it, that makes all the difference as to whether we are hardly used or blissfully content. We may do our life-work day by day thoroughly, write letters, pay visits, work hard for charitable objects besides, and be doing it all with a selfish aim and be the devil's drudge all the while, sowing to the flesh to reap death. Or we may do the very same life-work day by day, and write letters and pay visits and work for good objects; and do it like the children of the King—free, gracious, joyful, and blest. There is *everything in the spirit of the thing.* . . .

It is very interesting to observe how the history of nations is foreshown by the lives of individuals. Ishmael, typifying the spirit of servile fear, had had for many years the appearance of being the chosen seed; as for many centuries the Hebrews were the people on whom God set His love. But when they proved faithless to their part of the covenant, and finally rejected the Messiah who "came unto His own" [John 1:11], and who preached first to the lost sheep of the house of Israel [Matt. 15:24], they were cast out like the son of the bondwoman—cast out as Ishmael was the day that Isaac was weaned, when Abraham made a great feast in his house.

And so the wonder came to pass that Ishmael was a figure of Isaac's seed, the people of Israel. And Isaac, the son, the heir of the promises, was a figure of the true and spiritual Israel, of the Gentile believers who should receive the glad tidings of the grace of God and preach the Gospel to all the world. And thus the prophecy has been accomplished: "The elder shall serve the younger" [Gen. 25:23], and God has made known the riches of His Glory to us Gentiles [Col. 1:27] who enter by faith into the new and better covenant, who are God's "peculiar people, that we should show forth the praises of Him who hath called us out of darkness into His marvellous light,"—which in times past were *not a people* (not a united nation at all), but are *now the people of God,* which had not obtained mercy, but now have obtained mercy" [1 Pet. 2:9-10].

The Jerusalem above is free, which is the mother of us all. "Stand fast therefore in the liberty wherewith Christ hath made us free and be not entangled again with the yoke of bondage" [Gal. 5:1].

§43 Mary Elizabeth Beck
(fl. 1872–1908)

Mary Elizabeth Beck was a member of the Society of Friends in England. She was a prolific writer, publishing books on the Bible and on Quaker principles.

She traveled to the Holy Land, but little is know about her life outside of what is mentioned in her published books.

Beck presented Hagar as an example for her contemporaries. She was aware that her contemporaries might connect American slavery with the story of Hagar, and in the first paragraph of this selection clearly stated that not all stories in the Bible contain examples to be followed today. She empathized with Hagar's struggles and circumstances: Hagar was an example of a sorrowful mother, a woman who carried heavy burdens in life. Beck respected Hagar's strength and ability to carry the heavy burdens she was given. The lesson drawn for Beck's readers was that God's love and presence could sweeten the bitter cup of a woman's life; as God heard Hagar's "cry of suffering" and cared for her, so he will hear our prayers and comfort us. Even when Hagar forgot God, God did not forget her; similarly, we may forget God, but he will not forget us no matter what our circumstances. In this application of Hagar's story to her readers, Beck recognized the problems encountered by nineteenth-century women. Beck offered spiritual solace for these difficulties; other women, like Grimké, Weld, Morgan, Balfour, and Stanton worked against the systemic flaws in society in order to end women's oppression.

From Mary E. Beck, *Bible Readings on Bible Women: Illustrated by incidents in daily life* (London: S.W. Partridge & Co., 1892), 17–20.

The Story of Hagar
God's Pity for the Desolate

Water flowing fresh and free,
Fainting soul, it flows for thee.

Read aloud, Genesis xvi. 3-16, and Genesis xxi. 9-21.

WE read last time some stories of slaves in America—here is one of an Egyptian slave woman. It is very familiar to us, but we can always get something that comes home to us in a Bible story if we seek for it. Many things that were done in Old Testament times would not be right for us to do now, and we must always remember that "Life and immortality are brought to light by the Gospel." Still, all through the Bible, from beginning to end, there are wonderful proofs of the love of our Father in Heaven to individual souls. Just as a good earthly father loves each of his children separately, so each one of us, however sad and lonely we may feel, is the object of His pitying care.

Poor Hagar had been very hardly treated by her mistress, and she ran away, not knowing where to go. I suppose she thought no one cared for her, and it did not matter what became of her. But God cared, and sent His angel, "The Angel of the Covenant," to talk to her, and to tell her that the Lord "had heard her affliction." But he also showed her she ought not to flee from her circumstances—she was to return and submit herself to her mistress. And so she did; but her burden was lightened, for she had learned that God could never forget her.

In her joy of heart "she called the name of the Lord that spake unto her, Thou God seest me," and she named the well by which she had been sitting, Beer-lahai-roi, that is, "The well of Him that liveth and seeth me." Our circumstances may be very painful, and we may sometimes be tempted to run away from them, but it is far better to take up the burden of life and carry it patiently, knowing that if we have not brought it on ourselves, it must be the Lord's choice for us, and that even if we have, He is still at our side as we cry to Him, and He can sweeten our bitter cup with His love and presence.

Once more we hear of Hagar, and this time it does not appear that she ran away from her mistress, but Sarah entreated Abraham to cast her out. She had a little son, on whose account she must have suffered far more than on her own. Mothers know that if they have trouble at home, if they have no money and the cupboard is empty, they can bear it for themselves, but they grieve over their poor sick and hungry little ones; they cannot bear to see them pale and thin and only half fed. Poor Hagar! She felt the same when her boy became faint and ill with wandering through that dreary wilderness; and when the water was all gone which Abraham had given her, she was almost in despair. I wonder, when she laid her child under the shade of a shrub, and sat a good way off that she might not see him die, and then wept aloud, whether she remembered that day, long past, when she had thought she was alone in the wilderness, and the angel of the Lord had comforted her. I am afraid in her present trouble she had forgotten this; for how often we forget, when sorrows press upon us, the deliverance of the Lord in times gone by! Yet God was faithful, and the sad mother, far away from the sound of every earthly voice, heard the tender question from Heavenly lips, "What aileth thee, Hagar? Fear not, for God hath heard the voice of the lad where he is." It might have been only the cry of suffering, but He "who giveth to the young ravens their food" [Psalm 147:9] has always a storehouse for His children. God showed her the well of water, which she had not seen before, and her fainting boy lived to be the father of twelve princes. Take courage, sorrowing mother; thy well of comfort may be close at hand, though thy eyes are not yet opened to see it. Look up to the God of Hagar, and He who showed the springs of water to the poor outcast, and restored her boy, can yet make the desert of thy life blossom as the rose [Isa. 35:1].

"Alone! there is no loneliness with God;
    No darkness which He cannot turn to light;[21]
No flinty rock from whence His gracious word
    Cannot pour forth pure water, clear and bright.[22]

There is no wilderness whose desert caves
    Are hid from His all-penetrating eye;[23]
Nor rolls an ocean whose tumultuous waves
    Cannot be silenced when the Lord is nigh.[24]

There is no bark upon the troubled main,
    No pilgrim lone whose path He cannot see.[25]
Peace then, poor mourner, trim thy lamp again;[26]
    The eye that knows no slumber watches thee."[27]

Let us repeat together Hebrews 13, part of verses 5, 6: "Be content with such things as ye have: for He hath said, I will never leave thee, nor forsake thee. So that we may boldly say, The Lord is my Helper."

§44 Harriet Morton
(fl. 1870–1898)

Little is known about the life of Harriet Morton (née Cave) who published as Mrs. G. E. Morton after her marriage. Her publications suggest that she was actively involved in several different Christian ministries in England. Most of her writings were for children and included fiction, for example *A Trio of Cousins: A Tale of 1791* (1891), and educational books on the Bible like *Stories of Christ the Lord in simple verse for little children* (1870) and *From Egypt to Canaan: For little children* (1882). Morton also wrote *Jubilee Echoes: A poem in celebration of the fifty years reign of Queen Victoria* (1837–1887), and several

---

[21] Ps. 139:11-12.
[22] See Exod. 17:6 and Num. 20:8.
[23] See Heb. 11:35.
[24] See Ps. 107:29; Matt. 8:26.
[25] See Ps. 139:3; Ps. 142:3.
[26] Matt. 25:6.
[27] See Ps. 121:3.

books which suggest her interest in encouraging devotional life in the family setting, for example *Short chapters on Genesis: Adapted for use at family prayer* (1898) and *Plain teaching; or, Homely lessons from God's word* (1884). Morton was also involved in the leadership of mothers' meetings, and co-authored *Addresses and stories for mothers' meetings with Anne Hankey* (1883).

Like Warner, Morton emphasized and expanded details when she wrote for children. Morton explained the idea of slavery so children could better understand the story. In her introduction, she emphasized the necessity of using the language of the text as much as possible without sacrificing understanding for children. Despite her stated intention of closely following the scriptural text, she added moralizing details to the story.

Morton drew a moral lesson from the negative example of Hagar and Ishmael, who brought trouble upon themselves and so deserved their expulsion. By contrast, she reflected positively on God's character with her conclusion that God cared for Hagar and Ishmael because God never forgets his promises.

From Mrs. G. E. Morton, *From the Beginning or Stories from Genesis* (London, Edinburgh & New York: Thomas Nelson & Sons, 1893), 72–75, 91–96.

Eight years had passed since God had called Abram away from his own people, and had made him all those gracious promises. You remember what those promises were? God said that he would make of him a great nation, and that he would give all the land of Canaan to him and to his children [Gen. 12:2; 13:14-15].

But now Abram was living in tents in the plains of Mamre, and he could not call one yard of the country his own; and more than that, both he and Sarah his wife were getting very old, and they had not even one little child.

I daresay Abram often wondered when it would please God to give him all the blessings he had promised. But God had not forgotten him; and one night he came and spoke to him in a vision. I do not know what it was that Abram saw; perhaps it was only a bright and shining light—just the visible sign of God's presence and glory. I think he must have felt afraid when he saw it, for God said, "Fear not, Abram; I will take care of you, and will give you great things."

And Abram answered, "Lord God, what wilt thou give me? for I have no child, and when I am dead all my riches will go to one of my servants."

Then the Lord spoke again to Abram, and said, "It is not to a servant, but to a son that you will leave your riches" [Gen. 15:4].

And God made Abram get up and go out of his tent. It was dark, and thousands and thousands of stars—more than could be counted—were shining in the midnight sky. Then God said, "Look now toward heaven, and see if you can tell the number of the stars! so also your grandchildren, and their children's children, shall be more than can be counted."

And Abram believed God. He was sure that God was true, and that he would do everything he had promised in his own good time. And because he believed, he waited patiently.

But Sarah was not patient. She had waited a long time for God to fulfil his promise, and now ten years had passed away since they had come down into Canaan, and she was beginning to be in despair, for she thought that she was getting too old ever to have a baby of her own. So I will tell you what she did.

Sarah had a servant whose name was Hagar, and she was a slave. Those who are slaves belong altogether to their master or mistress; they may never go away from them, even if they are cruelly treated and are very unhappy. And not only that, but everything that the slaves have belongs to the master or mistress—even their children. So Sarah thought that if she were to give her slave to Abram to be his wife, then, if Hagar should have any children, they would belong to *her*.

She spoke to her husband about it, and told him her plan; and Abram agreed to do as she wished, and to take Hagar to be his wife.

In those days it was a common thing for a man to have more than one wife; but in the beginning it was not so. God only created one woman for Adam—he only intended each man to have one wife, and it was the family of wicked Cain who first began to transgress God's laws [see Gen. 2:24; 4:19].

Abram was the first *good* man of whom we read in the Bible who had two wives. Before he took Hagar to be his wife, he ought to have asked God what was his will in the matter; but he and Sarah went their own way about it, and it brought them into a great deal of trouble and difficulty.

When Hagar knew that she would have a baby of her own, she began to be proud, and to behave badly to her mistress, and to be rude to her. Then Sarah complained about it to Abram; and he said, "Behold, your servant is in your own power; do to her as you think right."

So Sarah punished Hagar for her rudeness; but Hagar was too proud to bear it patiently, and she ran away. Was it wrong of her to go away like this? Yes, it was very wrong. She was Abram's wife, and she had no right to leave him; she was Sarah's slave, and her place was by her mistress.

She had gone a long way from home, and was sitting down to rest in a lonely wilderness, near to a well of water. She must have been feeling very sad and miserable, sitting there all by herself, and perhaps she was thinking how foolish she was to have left a comfortable home because she had been punished for a fault. All at once she heard her name called. An angel appeared to her—not a created angel, but the Angel of the Covenant, even the Lord Jesus Christ himself.

He said, "Hagar, Sarah's maid, where do you come from? and where are you going?"

She answered, "I flee from the face of my mistress Sarah."

And the Lord said unto her, "Return to your mistress, and be humble and submissive."

Then the Lord spoke very kindly to her. He said, "When your baby is born, you shall call his name Ishmael" (that means, "God will hear"); "because the Lord has heard your sorrow."

There must have been great comfort to poor Hagar in the name by which God had told her to call her baby-boy. The word Ishmael—"God will hear"— was a promise that God would hear, as he had already heard, in every time of need. And Hagar called the name of the Lord who spoke with her, "Thou God seest me;" and she called the well by which she was sitting, "The well of him who liveth, and who seeth me."

So Hagar got up and returned, and went back to Sarah's tent, and behaved herself humbly to her mistress, as God had told her to do. She must have told her wonderful story about the Lord having appeared to her, and what he said to her; for when her little son was born, Abram called his name Ishmael.

I daresay both he and Sarah rejoiced very much at this baby's birth, and thought that this was the beginning of God's promise to them. But they were mistaken. This was not the child he had promised. Abram's faith and patience were to be tried for a great many years yet.

At last the longed-for time had come when God gave to Abraham and Sarah the little child he had promised to them. Just at the exact time he had said, and when Abraham was a hundred years old, the little baby-boy was born; and the happy parents called his name Isaac, as they had been commanded. It was a time of great rejoicing to them both; and Sarah said, "God has made me to laugh; and all who hear of it will laugh too. For who would have thought of saying to Abraham that Sarah should have a son?"

The child was rightly named Isaac, or "Laughter:" for Abraham laughed with joy when God told him he should be born, and Sarah laughed when she heard the promise given (and I am sure she must always have remembered that with shame and sorrow), because she did not believe; but now again she laughed, with thankfulness and delight; because the promise had come true.

When Isaac was three or four years old, Abraham made a great feast, to which he invited all his friends and neighbours. He wanted them to see his little son, who was now no longer a baby; and he showed Isaac to them, and told them that it was to him, and not to Ishmael, that he would leave all his riches. So they knew that Isaac was his father's heir, as God had said he should be.

It is supposed that at this time Abraham gave his little son a striped robe, or tunic, of different colours, as a token (or sign) of his being the heir.[28] He would have explained to Ishmael that it was God's will that it should be so; and that though he was the eldest son, yet it was Isaac who was to have the special blessing.

But Ishmael was not content with God's will. He felt jealous of his little brother, and angry with him; and Sarah saw him treating her little son unkindly one day, and mocking him. This made her afraid that Ishmael might do him some harm, and so she said to Abraham,—

"Send away this servant and her son; for the son of this slave shall not be heir with my son, even with Isaac."

But Abraham did not wish to send them away. He loved Ishmael, who was now a big lad of about sixteen years of age; and the thought of doing what Sarah had begged him to do filled him with pain. I do not know if he asked God what he should do about it, but I think he must have done so; for those who love God and trust in him, and walk in his ways, always tell him all that is in their hearts, and ask him for help in all their difficulties and sorrows.

God knew how very sad it made Abraham to think of parting with his son, and so he said, "Do not let it be grievous to you because of the lad, and because of his mother: in all that Sarah has said to you, hearken unto her voice; for all the great blessings I have promised you will come to you through Isaac and his children. And Ishmael also will I bless, because he is your son."

As soon as Abraham knew that it was God's will that Hagar and her boy should be sent away, he did not hesitate a moment longer. He rose up early in the morning, and took some bread and a bottle of water, and gave it to Hagar, putting it on her shoulder; then he sent her away, and Ishmael also.

It was a sorrowful parting. Hagar was now turned out of a home where she had lived for a great many years; and her boy, who she hoped would one day be his father's heir, was turned out too. If they had behaved well, this would never have happened; but both Hagar and her boy had proud and passionate tempers, and this was the cause of all the trouble that came upon them.

Abraham, though he was so obedient to God's word, must have had many sad thoughts that early morning as he watched them turning away from his

---

[28] Some commentators suggest this idea that a coat marked the heir, for example, Robert Jamieson, A. R. Fausset, and David Brown, *Commentary Critical and Explanatory on the Whole Bible* (Grand Rapids: Zondervan, n.d.), 28. Jamieson, Fausset, and Brown cite Rosenmüller as their source for this comment. [E. F. K. Rosenmüller, *Scholia in Vetus Testamentum Leipzig*, 1820–1834].

tent door. He would grieve that his son's misconduct had brought this distress upon him and his mother; yet he would feel comfort in remembering God's promise that he would bless the lad for his sake.

Hagar was intending to return to Egypt, which was her home before she became Sarah's servant. But she lost her way, and wandered about in the wilderness, not knowing in which direction to go. It was very hot, and the water in the bottle was soon gone. They looked about for some well or running stream, but they could not find any; and at last Ishmael became so weary and tired, and faint from thirst, that his mother feared he was at the point of death.

She took him up in her arms, and carried him to a shrub or small tree that was growing near, and laid him gently down in the shade. Then she went away from him a little distance, for she could not bear to see him die. She said, "Let me not see the death of the child." And she sat down, and lifted up her voice and wept.

She was so miserable and unhappy; but she did not pray to God to help her, and she seemed quite to forget how he had spoken to her and comforted her many years before, in another wilderness, when she was lonely and sad. She seemed quite to forget, also, the meaning of her boy's name, and the promise there was in it, "God will hear."

But Ishmael cried to God, and God heard him. Abraham had taught his son to worship God and to pray to him, and now in his great need he remembered his father's teaching.

And the Angel of the Covenant, Jesus, who had spoken to Hagar before, called to her again out of heaven and said unto her, "What is the matter with you, Hagar? Fear not; for God has heard the voice of the lad where he is. Arise, lift up the lad, and hold him in your arms; for I will make him a great nation."

Then God opened her eyes, and she saw a well of water. This was a most joyful sight. She ran to the well and filled her bottle with cool, delicious water, and gave it to her boy; and he drank and felt refreshed and strong again.

Did Hagar thank God? Did she love him for all his tender care of herself and Ishmael? I do not know. The Bible tells us nothing more about her, except that some years afterwards she took a wife for her son out of the land of Egypt.

And God was with Ishmael. He never forgets his promises, and so he never forgot that he had told Abraham he would bless the lad for his father's sake. And Ishmael grew, and dwelt in the wilderness of Paran, and became an archer. An archer is one who is skilful, or clever, in the use of a bow and arrows. He was a wild man. His hand was against every man, and every man's hand was against him; which means, that he did not live peaceably with his neighbours. But God prospered him, and gave him twelve sons, who were all princes and great men; and in after years the family of Ishmael became a great and powerful nation, as God had promised.

§45 M. G.
(fl. 1893)

M. G. chose to publish anonymously. The only details of her life that can be recovered are found in the introduction and chapters of her only known publication *Women Like Ourselves: Short Addresses for Mothers' Meetings, Bible Classes, etc.* (1893). M. G. delivered the addresses printed in this book to classes of women, probably in an Anglo-Catholic parish, and later wrote them down from memory. M. G. was an experienced teacher of mothers' meetings (classes held for mothers in a parish) and Bible classes. She published her addresses as an expert, for the benefit of inexperienced teachers. M. G. aimed to present the women of the Bible as real people who were tempted as her contemporaries were and who acted "exactly as we ourselves would be likely to act under the same circumstances."[29] The oral qualities of the addresses, complete with rhetorical questions, sets M. G.'s writing apart from the work of other women.

M. G. read the Bible intertextually and poetically.[30] She moves from Hagar's wandering in the desert to the Luke 15 image of lost sheep wandering off. The image of the lost sheep then set up a connection with John 10's image of Jesus as the Good Shepherd, who knows his sheep by name. The Angel of the Lord who called Hagar by name was thus identified with Jesus the Good Shepherd. Another wanderer associated with Hagar is the bride in Song of Songs. In the verse M. G. referred to, the bride is abused by the watchmen (Song of Songs 5:7); M. G. spiritualized this verse and gave it a positive reading that reinforced the connection with Hagar. This juxtaposition of texts is unusual but consistent throughout this address.

M. G. taught with a heavy hand. She emphasized God's retributive justice rather than God's mercy and grace. She spoke severely to mothers, reminding them of their power over their children and warning them to be careful to teach their children properly. With a mother's great influence comes great responsibility.

[29] M. G., *Women Like Ourselves: Short Addresses for Mothers' Meetings, Bible Classes, etc.* (London: SPCK, 1893), iv.

[30] This kind of reading is also done by Christina Rossetti in *The Face of the Deep*.

From M. G., *Women like Ourselves: Short Addresses for Mothers' Meetings, Bible Classes, etc.* (London: SPCK, 1893), 18–24.

–Hagar–

DID you ever notice how often the wells are mentioned in the Bible? They were of great importance, because water is terribly scarce in Eastern countries, so scarce that it is often called "the gift of God," and therefore the wells were, and are, very valuable. One day a young woman was sitting upon one of these wells, very weary and very desolate, for she had come a long way by a rough and lonely road. She was sad and anxious too, for she felt she could never reach the country she wanted to go to, since it was two hundred miles away, and the road led over rough mountains, where there were few wells and fewer houses, and she was tired out already, and had scarcely been able to drag herself to that well on which she was resting. This lonely woman was Hagar, Sarah's maid, and she was running away from her mistress.

As we heard last week, when Hagar found that she was going to become a mother, she not only "despised her mistress in her heart" for not having been able to bring Abraham the desired son herself, but she became very proud and insolent in her behaviour towards her (Gen. xvi.). We know that Sarah (or "Sarai," as she was called at that time) was very unkind to her and "dealt hardly" with her (see ver. 6); but you see that was no excuse in God's eyes for her rudeness to Sarai, still less for her running away. We are so apt to think that we should be so much better in other surroundings, to throw all the blame of our tempers, or our other faults, upon those we live with, and to try to make out that no one could be good with such trials. Hagar thought Sarai's unkindness was quite reason enough why she should do wrong too; so, instead of bearing it patiently, she ran away, meaning to try and find her way back to her own country, Egypt.

Maybe, while she sat there upon the well, wondering what would become of her, she lifted her heart to the God of Abraham. What a pity that she and Abraham and Sarah had not before asked counsel of God, instead of trying to bring about the birth of the promised son in their own way! But though they had all been wilful, and though Hagar was acting wrongly still, God had never forgotten her. He had watched every step of her hasty flight, and now that her passion had exhausted itself, and she was calm enough to listen, He sent an angel to reason with her and show her that she was in fault. An Angel, did I say? nay, rather, "*the* Angel of the Lord." There is reason to think that by this expression, used here and there in the book of Genesis, is meant our Lord JESUS CHRIST Himself, come down to earth in human form. Here was a poor lost sheep, wandering literally in the wilderness [Luke 15:4], where her sins had driven her, but the Good Shepherd [John 10:11] would not leave her there to perish. See how tenderly He called to her (ver. 8). The Good Shepherd knoweth His sheep by name [John 10:14]. "Hagar, Sarai's maid, whence comest thou?" He knew her name, and who she was; what need then to ask the question? It was asked purposely, to lead her to repentance. God sends His messengers to us still, in the ministers of His Church, to show us our faults; and it is well that we should lay our hearts open to them, and tell them bravely of our wrong-doing, that we may receive from their mouth God's message of pardon for the past and counsel for the future. In the mystical Song of Solomon the Bride describes how she wandered hopelessly about the city, till she was found by the watchmen, the Priests who "watch for souls, as they that must give account" [Heb. 13:17]. "They wounded her" (Cant. v. 7), for "faithful are the wounds of a friend" [Prov. 27:6]; and they took away her veil, that she might not dissemble nor cloke [sic] her sins, nor make excuses for them; the exposure was painful at the time, but it was the means by which she found Him again Whom her soul loved (Cant. iii. 4). But whether we confess our sins to God in the presence of one of His Priests, or whether we confess them in secret to God alone, it is absolutely necessary that they should be fully confessed, not merely in a half-hearted sort of general way that "we are all miserable sinners," but with a definite acknowledgment of each separate sin. "I flee from the face of my mistress Sarai," was the simple, truthful confession of Hagar. God knows all about you and me, just as He knew all about her; but our repentance is not complete till of our own accord we have added confession to our sorrow for sin; and this again would be worthless without amendment of life.

The Angel gave Hagar two commands—"Return unto thy mistress." "Submit thyself at her hands." Neither of these would be easy for her to do. There are few things harder than openly to acknowledge ourselves in the wrong. We often long to go back, as it were; we would give worlds to undo what we said or did yesterday, but it is very difficult to bring ourselves to say to mistress, or parent, or neighbour, "I am sorry I lost my temper." "I did wrong to act as I did." Yet, hard though it is, we cannot hope for God's blessing till we have done this. Even if we have not been the first or the most to blame, if we have put ourselves in the wrong, we must be ready to "return" and make amends. And then she was to "submit to her mistress." However hard and cruel Sarai might be, Hagar must bear it meekly and respectfully, and obey all her orders. You see, though God had watched over her so lovingly, and sent an angel to help her, she was not to escape suffering and punishment. It would be ten times harder for one of Hagar's spirit to go back to Sarai after she had once run away, than if she had remained quietly bearing her unkindness. She would have to face a good deal of reproach, perhaps she would be punished for her desertion; her fellow-servants would laugh at her.

At the same time the angel spoke kind and encouraging words to her, to help her to do what was right.

In after years, too, there came a very great trouble upon Hagar, which was probably permitted by God as a punishment for this running away, to bring her early sins back to her mind and deepen her repentance for them. Fifteen years after her return to Abraham, her son Ishmael was guilty of the same fault for which Sarai had punished Hagar before; he was caught mocking contemptuously at Isaac and Sarah (chap. xxi. 9). We do not read that Hagar was this time to blame, but I suppose Ishmael had inherited that mocking, disrespectful spirit from his mother. Oh, mothers, you know how much your minds and characters tell upon your unborn children; watch and pray, then, that they may not inherit your faults, and develop them in after years, when *you* have conquered them and almost forgotten them.

The punishment came to Hagar in the shape of one of her own former sins. She had run away from Sarai in wilfulness in the old days; now, to her great grief, she and her boy are sent away for ever. Have you never observed how often God sends troubles to us in after life that vividly remind us of our past transgressions? An old man, who could no longer support himself, was taken by his unfilial son to the poor-house. On the way they sat down by a milestone to rest, and as they did so, the old man burst into a sudden burst of tears. When asked the reason, he confessed that many years before he had carried his own old father to the same poorhouse, and that as they then rested at the very same milestone, his father had warned him that God would visit his undutiful conduct upon himself; and now, too late, he felt the words had come true.

I knew a woman once, whom we will call Jane. This woman pretended for many months to be very ill and in pain; because she liked better to be waited upon and fed on dainties, than to be doing ordinary work. After a time she had to go away from all her kind friends, and then she took to work as well as anybody. Very many years after, Jane got a complaint which really caused her a very great deal of pain; and then the retribution came for her former deceit. The people with whom she was then living took up notice of her sufferings, but treated her unkindly, and told her she was only shamming. Such things are hard to bear, and Jane shed many bitter tears over the unjust and cruel remarks; but at length it came home to her that this was her punishment for the sham illness she had acted before.

Many more instances could be given you, for God sees and remembers even what we ourselves forget, and in mercy He brings it forcibly to our remembrance in this life, that repenting here, we may be saved the public exposure of it at the last day. People sometimes think, when troubles come upon them, that God has forgotten them. It is not so, dear friends, the troubles are sent in love, lest we should forget God. In her days of pride and conceit, Hagar thought little of Him. It was not till she was alone in the wilderness, face to face with the Angel, that, conscience-stricken, she exclaimed, "Have I also looked after Him that seeth me?" God's all-seeing Eye is ever upon us, but how seldom we look towards Him with the eye of faith. He has promised (Ps. xxxii. 8), "I will guide thee with Mine Eye;" but if He does this, we must keep our eye fixed on Him, must we not? And what a comfort it is to feel that all through our lives, in our mistakes, and our sins, and our troubles, whatever befalls us, God's Eye is never tired of watching us, God's Ear is always open to hear. The very name the angel told Hagar to give her son—"Ishmael"—means "God hears"; and she proved the truth of the name when Ishmael lay dying of thirst in the wilderness; "God heard the voice of the lad" (Gen. xxi. 17), and again sent His Angel to Hagar to show her the well.

If we could only remember these two great truths, "God seeth me," and "God hears," in our daily life, we should be spared much sin and much sorrow. We should keep from sin, because we should not dare to give way to pride, or disrespect, or wilfulness, or tempers, if we remembered that God sees us always; and we should be saved much sorrow, because, if we could thoroughly believe that His loving Eye was watching us, and His Ear always listening for our feeblest prayers, we should not fret so much over our difficulties and anxieties, but should be content to leave all to His fatherly care, who can make "the parched ground become a pool" [Isa. 35:7], and "waters to break out in the desert" [Isa. 35:6].

§46 Josephine Elizabeth Butler
(1828–1906)

Josephine Butler was the daughter of John Grey and Hannah Annett Grey. The Greys were passionate abolitionists and were also involved in other contemporary social and economic debates; they passed their concern for these types of issues on to their daughter. Butler was raised in the Anglican church, though she had a Methodist governess and attended Wesleyan services. In her teens she experienced a religious crisis; as an adult she practiced the spiritual disciplines of daily prayer and Bible study. She also kept a diary describing her spiritual experiences, which included mystical experiences and direct encounters with Christ.

Butler married George Butler in 1852, and a year later George was ordained an Anglican priest. After the tragic death of her five-year old daughter, Butler began a ministry to women in workhouses, seeing their pain as greater than her own. She was active in working for higher education of women and in the campaign to repeal the Contagious Diseases Acts of 1864, 1866, and 1869. These acts empowered police to detain any woman suspected of prostitution and to insist they undergo a medical examination for venereal disease. Butler protested that these acts applied only to women. She believed they were forced into prostitution because they had no other source of income. Butler's work and writings contributed to the growing feminist movement; she was regarded as a feminist foremother by Edwardian suffragists.[31]

Butler was a prolific author, producing numerous works on a variety of subjects and in a variety of genres; she wrote pamphlets, essays, and books on subjects such as women's education and work. *The Lady of Shunem* (1894), a series of essays on biblical characters, shows that Butler's Christian faith inspired her work for women's rights. Like many women, Butler understood Hagar as typical of all oppressed women; Butler, however, identified this oppression as sexual. Hagar was like the prostitutes she worked with. Butler treated Hagar's relationships with Abraham and Sarah first, denouncing their treatment of Hagar. In the second part of the essay, Butler contrasted God's treatment of Hagar with the actions of Abraham and Sarah; as God cared for Hagar, so contemporary Sarahs should learn to care for contemporary Hagars. Like many women, Butler wrote from her experience as a woman and mother; however, Butler specifically identified her hermeneutical stance, saying, "my reading of it may only be a motherly, a womanly reading of it."

From Josephine E. Butler, *The Lady of Shunem* (London: H. Marshall, 1894), 70–92.

The Bad Sinister

I SAID I would return to Hagar.

The Apostle Paul, in his letter to the Galatians, as you know, makes use of the story of Sarah and Hagar, and their sons, as an allegory to represent "the two Covenants" [Galatians 4:21-31], the two Dispensations, the Jewish

[31] For more biographical information on Butler see Helen Mathers, "Butler, Josephine Elizabeth," in *Biographical Dictionary of Evangelicals*, ed. Timothy Larsen, David Bebbington, and Mark A. Noll (Downers Grove, Ill.: InterVarsity, 2003). For a discussion of Butler's theology see Lucretia A. Flamming, "'And Your Sons and Daughters will Prophesy': The Voice and Vision of Josephine Butler," in *Women's Theology in Nineteenth-Century Britain: Transfiguring the Faith of their Fathers*, ed. Julie Melnyk (New York: Garland Publishing, 1998), 151–64.

and the Christian, the Law and the Gospel. It is a very striking allegory for that purpose. That unworthy page in Abraham's history was typical of the discord between the two principles—that of the old and that of the new Dispensation. The earlier, the imperfect, must needs be expelled before the later born and perfect could have full and free scope.

But in quite another sense I regard the story as typical. It is the earliest recorded embodiment in practice of a humanly decreed injustice which has prevailed ever since in society, more or less, in different times and in different lands, poisoning the sources of human life, and bearing disastrous fruits for the world.

Here are two women—one the lawful, respected, and respectable wife; the other, of inferior rank, no wife at all, not the chosen of man through any high motive of love or soul's election, but simply made use of for a time and purpose—a supplement to what God had already bestowed on man, and claimed by him to serve his own lower interests. Hagar is THE TYPICAL OUTCAST. Sarai, after having herself advised her husband to take Hagar as his concubine, acts the heartless part which respectable womanhood (with noble exceptions) has too frequently acted ever since. "Cast out the bondwoman and her son." This has been the verdict of countless generations. "Cast her out, with her unlawful offspring. Get rid of her, keep her out of sight. Set up a barrier between these and those. Mark, strong and dark, the Bar Sinister[32] athwart her destiny, so that the legitimate wife may never hear or dare to speak of the existence of the outcast, who shall be for ever accursed."

It was long before Ishmael was born that this unworthy drama opened. Hagar was about to become a mother; Sarai remained childless; discord and jealousy arose. Sarai reproached Abraham, who had but acted on her advice; "The Lord judge between me and thee!" she taunted him, and he turned upon her, saying, "Behold, thy maid is in thy hands; do to her as it pleaseth thee." And "when Sarai dealt hardly with her, she fled from her face." What an unlovely story this of the Hebrew matron beating her wretched slave till she was forced to save herself by flight, the husband acquiescing! And because the apostle made use of this incident in his passionate desire to clear away the mist of doctrinal error from the minds of his lapsed Galatian converts, and by familiar illustration to set forth the development of the purpose of God in the substitution of the covenant of Grace for the Law, shall we, therefore, speak softly of the conduct of Sarai and Abraham in this matter? I prefer to express frankly my disgust. To abstain from condemnation of their action would be to seem to charge God with approval of heartlessness and cruelty. The sacred

---

[32] A bar sinister is a black bar running from the top right to the lower left of a coat of arms, used to indicate illegitimacy.

writers never excuse, or call upon us to condone, what is wrong, immoral, or unjust in the life and conduct of the chosen servants of God, whose sins and errors he punishes and chastens, while he forgives. I am perplexed, in reading certain commentators, in noting a degree of—shall I call it complacency?—in their judgment of this story of Hagar, as if God himself had ordained each step in it, and Sarai had done well. It may be that an exclusive dwelling on the allegorical use made by St. Paul of the facts has encouraged this complacency, and so the cry "Cast out the bondwoman and her son" has, to some minds, lost its character of meanness and unmercifulness. But God is never, and can never be, the author or inspirer of any evil or selfish thought or deed. I continue to regard this and every part of Abraham's history from the human side, while trying to read it truly, as under the eye of God. My reading of it may only be a motherly, a womanly reading of it, and theologically worthless. Be it so! St. Paul was not a father, nor was the human heart of the man stirring in him at the moment when he wrote to the Galatians in the direction of pity for the outcast woman. In any case, the facts remain. There they are—the other side of the picture.

Irresistibly I am led on, in thought, through the ages, down to these later times, when the false principles underlying this conduct of the patriarch and his wife, as here recorded, had ripened and borne their natural fruit, when the world came to be filled with Hagars, and the line of demarcation between favoured womanhood and the outcast became more and more rigid and immovable, a "great gulf fixed" [Luke 16:26], so that no passing from the one side to the other was possible; and this became the accepted condition of things, the baser sort among men proclaiming it to be inevitable, and evolving from the depths of their own egotism the mighty falsehood that it is necessary for the preservation of the purity of family life.

Christ's teaching and action inaugurated a new era; but his professed followers have been, and still are, in a great measure, blind to the light of his new day, and unfaithful to his teaching. Virtuous womanhood, trained under the influence of the egotism of men, has consented for ages that the outcast should exist, and continue to be an outcast. But now, thanks be to God, the new era has, at last, indeed begun to dawn upon us!

After the birth of Isaac (Hagar having, in obedience to God, returned to the service of Sarah) we read that, on a certain day of festivity in honour of the son of the promise, Sarah (now no longer Sarai, but Sarah, the Princess) saw the son of Hagar the Egyptian mocking, and she called upon Abraham to "cast out the bondwoman and her son." The word "mocking" is given by some of the older interpreters as "playing," or "dancing gracefully." Perhaps we are mistaken in imputing spite or rudeness to Ishmael. He was at that time about thirteen years of age, and he might, in boyish fashion, have been only caressing or playing with the infant, but with a familiarity which Sarah, the Princess, did not deem suitable. That she considered Ishmael to be putting himself too much on an equality with Isaac seems expressed in her proud words—"For the son of this bondwoman *shall not be heir with my son*, even with Isaac." If Ishmael had been insulting or ill-treating the child, Sarah would scarcely have restrained herself so far as merely to repudiate the dreaded idea of any equality between the two boys. She would, I think, have used more denunciatory language against Ishmael.

"And the thing was very grievous in Abraham's sight, because of his son." Abraham appears to have spent a night of sorrow and of indecision as to the course of action he should adopt. Sarah had given her command, and, it may be, was sleeping peacefully; but Abraham's heart bled for Ishmael; and in the wakeful night hours God again spoke to him. The words which record this intervention reveal the wonderful loving-kindness of God towards his servant, and towards every member of his family. "Let it not be grievous in thy sight because of the lad, and" (not only because of the lad, but) "because of thy bondwoman." It is not stated that Abraham had felt much grief concerning the casting out of the mother of his child; only concerning his son is his grief mentioned. But God, more just, more tender, more "mindful of his own" than the best and holiest of men can be, supplies the omission. He names both the child and the mother; adding, "And also of the son of the bondwoman will I make a nation, because he is thy seed."

Sarah had acted cruelly, but God over-ruled her action for good. He bade Abraham not to oppose the advice of his imperious consort, but to act as she had decreed; for if Hagar and Ishmael had been retained in the family there never would have been peace or harmony there. God allowed the rejection of Hagar and her son, not that they should remain to the end forsaken, but that his own tender pity and grace might be extended to and manifested in them. They are to be his charge, and under his eye and protection, although driven from the sight of those who should have sheltered them. The heart of the father in Abraham saved him from the sin of initiating the cruelty enacted towards Hagar and her son; and in his sorrow God directed and reassured him.

Then the story proceeds. When the morning dawned, Abraham took some bread and a bottle of water—enough to keep the poor outcasts alive for half a day—and laid them on Hagar's shoulder, and sent her and her child away; and "*she departed*, and wandered in the wilderness of Beersheba." It makes one's heart ache, in picturing that desolate creature going forth with her deserted child, to recall how many millions of times that scene has been enacted since then, through all the ages. The prodigal son, whose misery is the nearest that a man's misery can be to that of the outcast woman, went forth from his fathers house of his own free will, and with more than a crust of bread and a bottle of water; for he had a sons "portion of goods" with him. His lot was wretched enough—in a "far country," lost, despairing, dire hunger driving him to feed with swine—until the vision of the home he had left arose in his mind, and he returned to it and his father [Luke 15:11-24]. There were no strong hands, no bars and bolts, to hinder his return, when once his own weak will was bent in the right direction. But the case of the lost daughter is sadder even than that of the lost son. It is the interest of every bad creature to *conceal her abode*. The son may be heard of, may, return, even from a far country; but all the cruelty, impurity, and avarice of earth combine to keep her hiding place unknown, to bar her return to the Fathers house, to hold her down, to the end that, once fallen, she may rise no more, but may "minister in dreadful promiscuity" to the vilest passions of the most ignoble of men. Even if this last agony be not in store for her, how forlorn is her state! If she be a mother, the burden of supporting her child—an outcast with herself—is thrown upon her, weak and poor, and still, perhaps, a mere child herself in character and understanding. It is her child only in the eyes of the world—not his—not the unknown father's; and happy is it for her if the struggle for life, her own and the child's, does not prove the beginning of the downward path which makes of her another "woman of the city who was a sinner" [Luke 7:37].

The most complete answer to any who might object to so purely human a reading of this story, or think the judgment expressed of Sarah too hard, is the evidence, so clear and so exquisitely consoling and sweet, of the mind and attitude of God towards this outcast mother and child. It is a great relief to turn from the earthly actors in the drama to the over-ruling God, the ever just, and ever merciful, and full of compassion.

Is it not a thought, a fact which should wake up the whole Christian world to a truer and clearer view of life as it is around us, that the first record of a direct communication from Jehovah to a woman is this of his meeting with the rejected Hagar, alone, in the wilderness? It was not with Sarah, the Princess, or any other woman, but with Hagar, the ill-used slave, that the God of heaven stooped to converse, and to whom he brought his supreme comfort and guidance. This fact has been to me a strength and consolation in confronting the most awful problem of earth, i.e., the setting apart for destruction, age after age, of a vast multitude of women—of those whom we dare to call lost—beyond all others lost—hopelessly lost. We ourselves, by our utmost efforts, have only so far been able to save a few, a mere handful among the multitude; and of the others, unreached by any divinely inspired *human* help, we are apt to think with dark and dismal foreboding. We forget that though they may be quite beyond the reach of our helping hands, they are never beyond the reach of his hand—his, who, "being put to death in the flesh," was "quickened by the Spirit, by which also he went and preached to the spirits in prison."* Into the vilest prison-houses of earth (I believe) he descends alone many a time, to save those souls buried out of the sight and ken of his servants and ministers, even as he—he alone, unaccompanied by any chosen ministers—descended into Hades and "preached the Gospel also to those that are dead," that they who have been "judged according to men in the flesh" may "live according to God in the Spirit."†

They say, in the creeds, that he was "crucified, dead, and buried, that he descended into hell (Hades), and rose again the third day."³³ The repentant malefactor on the cross, turning his dying eyes on Jesus, heard him speak to him these words of eternal assurance and joy, "*This day shalt thou be with Me in Paradise*" [Luke 23:43]. The hell, then, into which the Lord of Life descended was Paradise to the dying criminal. That very day the gate of this Paradise was thrown open to him. A dimly-lighted region as it has been fabled or believed by some, it was Paradise to him. Why? Because the Lord, his Saviour, was there; "Thou shalt be *with Me*," Jesus said. I thank God for this ray of heaven's light falling on the lot of those prisoners of Satan and of evil men, to whom no human voice has spoken of salvation, but who, "done to death" by the great enemy and his servants, have (I believe) many a time heard the words, as they stood on the brink, "This day shalt thou be *with Me*."

There were two occasions on which the Lord appeared to Hagar in the wilderness. The first was that on which, before the birth of her child, she fled in terror from her mistress; and "the angel of the Lord found her by a fountain of waters in the wilderness," and called her by her name, speaking tender and reverent words to the lonely, ill-used handmaiden of Sarah. "Whence comest thou," he asked, "And whither wilt thou go?" Hagar confessed that she had fled from her mistress. He then enjoined her to return to Sarah, and to bear patiently her treatment, adding words of sublime promise and blessing, even as he had done to Abraham. "Thou shalt bear a son, and shalt call his name Ishmael (or God shall hear), because the Lord hath heard thy affliction," and she called the name of the Lord that spake unto her, "Thou God seest me." Surprise, and gladness, and comfort filled the heart of the fugitive. She had thought herself alone and friendless, driven out to perish; and she discovered that God had been mindful of her, had followed her every step, and now, in her extremity, was speaking to her words of comfort, and guidance, and hope for the future. For some thirteen years after this she remained with Sarah, serving her in the spirit of submission of which God's angel had spoken. It is to be hoped that the heart of Sarah was softened by Hagar's humility, and that her treatment of her during those years was just and kind.

³³ The Apostles' Creed.

But Hagar's trial at the end of those years was severer than the first. The decree went forth that she must be cast out.

Once more, taking now her little son by the hand, she wandered forth into the wilderness, carrying her bottle of water and her loaf of bread, the "portion" given to her by the father of her child. As "the day increased from heat to heat," smiting upon the wide, dry desert, where no stream or pool reflected the sun's fierce rays, and the water in her bottle was exhausted, her heart sank within her. She laid her fainting boy under the shade of some of the desert brushwood, and retired to the distance of a bow-shot; for she said, "Let me not see the death of the child," and "she lifted up her voice and wept." *That weeping*, and the circumstances which caused it, are so often repeated in our own days as to have become quite familiar. We read in newspaper reports of deserted girl-mothers—without resources, and friendless—casting away their children, assisting their death, or slaying them outright. Scant pity is bestowed on such girl-mothers. The law lays its stern hand on them, they are hunted by police, condemned, and punished, their misery and shame published to the world; and even yet, although the new era has begun to dawn upon us, no one asks, "Where is the father?" or if a few ask the question, there is no following up of it—no answer. The law ignores him, and society (for the most part) is content that he should remain unknown and irresponsible. Had Hagar lived in our days, and had there been no divine interposition on behalf of her son, she would probably have been tried for his murder, and perhaps sentenced to imprisonment for life, as was a poor girl whose case excited some interest a few years ago, and who is now a prisoner, sentenced to remain one till death, because she, deserted and without resources, laid her child on the grass by the highway and left it, in the hope that some charitable passer-by would take it up and save it. Indeed, it might have gone hard, in our days, even with the mother of Moses, whom our law would have charged with exposing her child upon the water in order to get rid of it [Exod. 2:1-4]. Our law-makers would have seen in the one case the criminal act of a deserted mother, and in the other would have turned a sublime act of faith into evidence of intention to commit a deliberate and heartless act of desertion.

"And the angel of the Lord called to Hagar," and said to her, "What aileth thee, Hagar? Fear not, for God hath heard the voice of the lad where he is." Was it the voice of childish weeping only which God heard, or was it the voice of prayer? It matters not! "He hears the young ravens when they cry" in their hunger [Ps. 147:9]; and their cry is inarticulate enough. He did not even wait for Hagar's prayer. It is not said that she prayed. She only wept, wept aloud, and sobbed in the anguish of her soul, turning aside that she might not see the death struggles of her child.

"What aileth thee, Hagar?" Oh, the tenderness of this question asked by God of a woman—a deserted woman! If these words should meet the eyes of some sorrowing mother of an erring or ill-treated daughter, or of some seeker of souls in the vast mazes of Satan's infernal machinery for tracking and holding those whose footsteps have once slipped, I beg them to read again this story, in the light of God's presence, and to take to their hearts the comfort it is meant by him, I believe, to bring to us women in these latter days; for he knows our hearts are worn with sorrow in the contemplation of that world of woeful womanhood which the well-to-do, which even those who teach and preach in Christ's name, are still, in general, so content to leave where it is.

"Arise, lift up the lad, and hold him in thy hand;"—so spoke the angel; and at the same moment God opened Hagar's eyes, and she saw, close by, a well of water in the thirsty desert, which was life to her and to her son.

And so the God who had twice in these thirteen years spoken to her words of sweet and holy comfort, and twice granted to her just what she needed at the moment—guidance and sustenance—continued to support and to lead her; and the wilderness which became their home was no longer a wilderness to them, and Ishmael prospered, for God had given him his blessing.

Such is not, except in rare cases, the close of the career of Hagar's successors, the outcast women of the ages. Nevertheless, the record stands here for evermore of the undying pity and love of the Eternal Father for the myriads of those who, leaning on the stronger judgments of others, or trusting in human promises, have been brought into misfortune and misery, whose footsteps have slipped, and who have become the despised and rejected of men [Isa. 53:3].

In the dawn of the new era, the Sarahs are beginning to repent and to stretch forth their hands to the Hagars, and to bridge over the gulf which has so long separated them; and they will do so more and more; and in the doing it they have, and will have to the end, the powers of hell against them, together with the solid, passive opposition of the egotism of a portion of mankind, and even of the Church of Christ. But as they learn more and more of the truth, and of the mind of God in all these matters, less and less will their hearts fail them in regard to the end of all, though present seed sown may seem to yield scant harvest.

* I Peter, iii., 18, 19.
† I Peter, iv., 6, 7.

§47 Sarah Elizabeth Turnock
(fl. 1898–1907)

Not much is known about Sarah Turnock's life other than what she tells us in her published writings. Turnock went on a spiritual pilgrimage to Palestine in 1903 and wrote about her experience in *A Woman's Tour in Palestine*. From this account we learn that she was probably from Manchester. She travelled with a group led by the Rev. Dr. Leach of Cavendish Chapel. She obviously had enough money to afford this trip, though it was a Cook's tour,[34] and thus cheaper than travelling alone.

Turnock, like Butler, was interested in the stories of women in scripture, but, like Morgan, wrote specifically for women and applied the text to them. In the introduction to *Women of the Bible*, Turnock revealed her distinctly feminine point of view.

> Woman, I may add, should be given her just meed of praise, for we have not a single instance in the whole Bible of a woman insulting, deserting, betraying or persecuting Christ. She was first at the sepulchre, and last at the cross—she followed Him even to death; she was ever ready to minister to His wants—washed His feet with tears, and wiped them with the hairs of her head; anointed His head with oil, and whilst men spat upon Him, beat Him, nailed Him to the tree, women stood round in pity, weeping for the sorrow and pain they could not alleviate. Who can say that women had no part in writing the Bible, when it contains the glorious songs of Miriam, Deborah, and Mary. Looking backward, we may well be satisfied with the position women won for themselves in the early Church. Jewish traditions would have accorded them at best only an inferior place, but these converts to Christianity had lovingly accepted a creed whose Founder was cradled in the arms of a woman.[35]

Turnock brought her feminine lens to her very positive reading of the Hagar story. Turnock, like Butler, was very empathetic towards Hagar, who she viewed as a "typical outcast" and a typical woman for whom God cared. Again like Butler, Turnock noted that Hagar was the first woman to whom God spoke directly, and Turnock found it significant that God spoke to Hagar, not to Sarah.

---

[34] On Cook's tours, see Timothy Larsen, *Contested Christianity: The Political and Social Contexts of Victorian Theology* (Waco, Tex.: Baylor University Press, 2004), 29ff.

[35] Turnock, iii. The last sentence of this quote is an example of the kind of argument that Aguilar was trying to counter earlier in the century by writing for Jewish women.

Turnock filled in the emotional gaps in the story, though unlike M. G., she did not use other biblical texts to interpret the story. Like M. G., Turnock stressed the power of mothers for good and for evil. Turnock regarded Hagar as responsible for the banishment that she and Ishmael experienced. Hagar had power as a mother, but also responsibility and guilt for misuse of that power. Turnock like other women interpreters, exercised her own power and influence through her writing.

From Sarah Elizabeth Turnock, *Women of the Bible* (London: G. Burroughs, 1898), 6–7.

–Hagar–

THE story of Hagar's wanderings in the wilderness, her maternal sufferings and miraculous relief, is one of the most beautiful and touching, amongst the many interesting Bible narratives.

Hagar was not of Abraham's race, but one of a heathen and benighted nation. A bondwoman and a wanderer; a weak and lonely female, exiled from a home of love, overwhelmed with anxious fears for her child; perhaps, too, with self reproaches for the unguarded words she had encouraged her boy to utter, and which she regarded as the sole cause of her banishment. Yet this poor sufferer was the peculiar care of the Most High. He charged His angels to speak words of hope and comfort, and even for her human wants provided the necessary aid.

God did not guard her from sorrow; for not until the water was spent in the bottle, and the child cast under one of the shrubs, and the mother gone a long way off, (for she said "Let me not see the death of the child," then lifted up her voice and wept)—not until her trial was thus at its height did the angelic voice descend from heaven in such pitying and sympathizing accents. "What aileth thee, oh Hagar? Fear not, for God hath heard the voice of the lad whence he is. Arise, lift up the lad, and hold him in thine hand, for I will make him a great nation." And the promise was fulfilled.

How startling and significant it is, that the first record of a direct communication from Jehovah to a woman, is this of His meeting the rejected Hagar, alone in the wilderness. It was not with Sarah the princess, or any other woman, but with Hagar, the poor slave, the typical outcast, but still a woman possessing alike many engaging and faulty characteristics. Feeling and affectionate at one time; overbearing and insolent at another. Loving Ishmael with impetuous and clinging love which could not bear to see his supposed heritage become the property of another, though she knew it was the decree of God. Reverencing and loving Abraham, both as her master and the father of her child, but unable always to treat Sarah with respect and the submission due to her as mistress and indulgent friend. Still, with all these failings, God cared for her, and eventually permitted all these trials to give place to prosperity and joy.

The words of Hagar, "Thou God seest me," have been handed down from generation to generation and are amongst the first words we were taught to lisp in our childhood.

§48 Eloise Alberta Bibb
(1878–1927)

Eloise Alberta Bibb was a black American poet. We know very little about her life, but when she was seventeen she published a book of poetry, which included a poem on Hagar. This poem recounted a fictional conversation between Abraham and Hagar as Abraham sent Hagar and Ishmael away. In the poem Hagar loved Abraham, and Abraham was attached to her as well, but God told him to send her away. Bibb's characterization of Hagar's surprise at her banishment evokes deep sympathy from the reader. Bibb did not name Sarah in the poem, but implied Sarah's influence behind Hagar's character-ization of her years in Abraham's household as a "woeful night." Though Abraham told Hagar to pray to God, the poem ended not with prayer but with her bleak statement to Ishmael that "we are outcasts evermore."

Like Turnock, Bibb vividly imagined the emotions of the characters in this story. Both writers emphasized Hagar's love for Abraham and both down-played the importance of Sarah in the story. Like the other poets, Aguilar and Moise, Bibb only dealt with the second episode in Hagar's story. Also like Aguilar and Moise, Bibb was a member of an oppressed minority. Bibb wrote after American slavery had been outlawed, yet she depicted one of its ongoing effects in American society. She read Hagar as a black woman and Abraham as a white man and condemned Abraham's unjust behaviour toward Hagar and their son Ishmael.

From Eloise Bibb, *Poems* (Boston: Monthly Review Press, 1895), 92–94.

The Expulsion of Hagar

The morn hath risen clear and bright,
The sun displays his glorious light;
Through heaven's vault of azure dye,

Where peeps the glistening morning star,
And smiles the moon's great silver eye,
Ord'ring the dozing stars afar,
Give up their watch, withdraw from sight,
For now 'tis morn, no longer night.

A century's frost upon his brow,
Old Abraham arises now,
With hoary locks o'er shoulders bent,
And wasted form and withered cheek,
And faded eye to which is lent
A lurking sadness; it seems to seek
Poor Hagar there with Ishmael,
Who must bid him a long farewell.

"Hagar," he calls, "take thou the boy
And go, for thou wilt here destroy
My household's peace. Go thou, I say,
Depart in yonder wilderness;
Ne'er turn again thine eye this way,
God with thy son protect and bless.
Fear not. And now, take Ishmael,
I bid thee both a long farewell."

O Abraham! what dost thou say?—
That I depart? I must away
From out thy home, from out thy life!
What words are these? canst thou be mad,
Or do I dream? What means this strife?
Thy love alone hast made me glad;
O Abraham! thou hast been the light,
Within these years of woeful night.

"And now behold thee never more!
This woe has reached my bosom's core.
O Abraham! I kneel to thee,
Look thou upon thy Hagar now.
Thou art a paradise to me,
Let me but stay to smooth thy brow.

Let me but linger near thy side,
Thou ne'er before my wish denied.

"And mark thy son,—my Ishmael,
His beaut'ous face,—note thou it well;
In yonder wilderness, the sun
Will scorch that broad and noble brow,
And dark the cheek it shines upon.
My Abraham, O hear me now!
Oh! I would live in thy fond sight,
And dream in thine eye's softest light."

Low bowed the head on Abraham's breast,
And to his heart a hand he pressed,
And breathed a long and deep-drawn sigh.
At length he slowly raised his head,
And brushed a tear-drop from his eye,
He gazed, on Hagar, then he said,
"Begone! Though it should grieve my heart,
The Lord hath said that we must part."

"Take, thou, the water and the bread,
I mean the words that I have said.
Go thou into Beer-sheba there,
The Lord wilt guide thee and thy boy;
Lift, thou, thy heart to God in prayer,
And cease my soul thus to annoy.
Again, Hagar and Ishmael,
I bid to thee, once more, farewell."

"Alas! 'tis true, I see, I know,
Thou meanest what thou sayest, I go;
And Hagar ne'er shall smile again,
No rippling laughter leave her lips.
The saddest 'mongst the wives of men,
Will e'er be she, who sorrow sips.
My boy! my own! all, all is o'er,
And we are outcasts ever more."

§49 Mary L. T. Witter
(fl. 1870–1900)

Little is known about Mary L. T. Witter, a Canadian from Berwick, Nova Scotia, married to James S. Witter. Witter wrote three works, *A Book for the Young: being a history of the kings who ruled over God's Ancient people* (1870), *The Edomites* (1888), and *Angels* (1900).

This excerpt from *Angels* comes from the chapter called "The Angel of the Lord." Witter discussed the story of Hagar at the beginning of her book because the angel of the Lord first appeared to Hagar. Though this book was not specifically on women, Witter clearly read the text as a woman. Her retelling of the story was also influenced by her focus on the angel of the Lord. She compared the angel of the Lord to a "tender mother."

Like Turnock, Witter had a very high view of the responsibility of a mother for the behavior and character of her children (and husband), and so Witter placed responsibility for Ishmael's poor behaviour on Hagar. Witter smoothed over the more difficult questions raised by the text. She placed a very cheerful spin on the banishment of Hagar and Ishmael. Witter made Hagar appear much more pious than did most of the other authors.

From Mary L. T. Witter, *Angels* (Glasgow: William Asher, 1900), 2–6.

Was it not God the Son who in the beginning created the heaven and the earth? "All things were made by Him, and without Him was not anything made that hath been made" [John 1:3]. Was it not Christ who walked in the garden of Eden and clothed our first parents, thus prefiguring clothing man with His own righteousness? Was it not Christ who called Abraham out of Ur and bade him go to another country? But although it is presumable that all the manifestations of God recorded in the Old Testament were manifestations of the second subsistence of the Godhead, the Christ, yet I shall confine myself principally to those in which this Divine personage is designated the angel of the Lord.

We first meet with the term, "the angel of the Lord," about two thousand years before the incarnation. Abraham had been living several years in the land promised to his descendants, but as yet descendants he had none. Sarah, in this perplexity, gives her maid, according to the custom of the times, to her husband as secondary wife. The result is what might have been anticipated. Hagar, seeing she is likely to become a mother, treats her mistress with disrespect. This Sarah will not brook, but repays her maidservant's contempt with terrible interest. Hagar in her trouble flees, though she knows not whither. To be homeless appears to her to be preferable to remaining with her mistress. Having little if any food, her strength soon fails, and she sits down by a fountain in the wilderness. There seems no ray of light. Where can she procure food? Where can she find shelter? As far as she is known at all she is known as Sarah's maidservant, to whom all persons would think she was under obligation, to return; and she was resolved not to return even if she should die from hunger. She sobs with vexation. And does she not lift her heart Godward? Does she not feel that help can come thence, though not from elsewhere? Could she not have truthfully said, "My heart and my flesh crieth out for God?" [Ps. 84:2]. "Man's extremity is God's opportunity."[36] The angel of the Lord found Hagar. As a tender mother would seek for a wandering child, so the angel of the Lord sought her.[37] The inquiry is one of kind solicitude and well calculated to cause Hagar to reflect. He not only called her by name, but asked whence she came and whither she was going. Hagar's reply is humble and honest. She says nothing of the severity with which she has been treated by her mistress, and frankly confesses that she is endeavouring to flee from lawful authority. The Lord gave a command, perhaps the most unwelcome that to her could be given. She must return to her mistress and patiently endure whatever she pleases to inflict. And with this command the angel of the Lord gave Hagar far-reaching promises, which were very satisfactory in themselves and yet plainly indicated that she was not to be an ancestress of the promised seed in, whom all the families of the earth were to be blessed [Gen. 12:3; 28:14].

Hagar appears to have at once obeyed the command of the Lord; and, although of alien race, she was evidently a sharer in Abraham's faith. She called the name of the Lord that spake unto her "Thou art a God that seeth."

The next visit of the Lord to this earth to which I shall refer is that which occurred at the plains of Mamre. This visit is in some respects unique. The Lord is seen walking on the earth in human form, clothed as a man, and in company with two others who are apparently men. The Lord appears to have partaken of earthly food, and to have talked with Abraham as a man would talk with a friend. Yet there must have been something about Him which betokened His divinity; for Abraham believingly received promises from Him

---

[36] John Hamilton, Lord Belhaven in Scottish Parliament, Nov. 2, 1706.

[37] This feminine depiction of the angel is not atypical; it stands in continuity with a feminizing trend in depictions of angelic beings. According to Callum Brown, before 1800 angels were depicted as masculine; about that time, this depiction shifted and angels took on more feminine attributes (*The Death of Christian Britain* [London: Routledge, 2001], 58).

which none but God could fulfil, and with Him interceded for guilty Sodom, confident that He could save or could destroy.

Some three years have passed. Important changes have taken place in Abraham's family. Ishmael is no longer the only son. Isaac has been given, and a feast is in course of celebration in honour of his being no longer a nursling. This was not pleasing either to Hagar or to her son. There had been no feast when Ishmael was weaned. Why should there be a feast now?

Envy is not only one of the fruits of the flesh, but it is one of the bitterest of these fruits. It eats like canker into the soul of him who indulges in it. "Wrath is cruel, and anger is outrageous, but who is able to stand before envy?" [Prov. 27:4]. It is worse than cruel, worse than outrageous. Envy is the quality of a little mind. The truly great are incapable of envy.

Ishmael, with the connivance if not the encouragement of his mother, did much to disturb the peace of little Isaac, and interfered with the festivities of the occasion. This did not escape the notice of Sarah. When did wrong done to a child escape the notice of the mother? We are not told that Sarah said anything either to Hagar or Ishmael, but wife-like she went to Abraham and poured her complaints into his ear. Much depends on the manner in which words are spoken. At times as much as on the words themselves. The utterance of Sarah, "Cast out this bondwoman and her son, for the son of this bondwoman shall not be heir with my son, even with Isaac," sound like a peremptory command, but they probably were an humble entreaty. They may, have been in answer to the question—"What shall be done with Hagar and Ishmael?" or Sarah may have gone to Abraham and, with tremulous voice and streaming eyes, presented her petition. Abraham was in a dilemma. He wished to please Sarah for he loved her dearly, but his heart yearned over Ishmael. Even when Isaac was promised, the mind of Abraham at once reverted to the change the fulfilment of that promise would make in the condition of Ishmael, and he uttered the words so full of pathos, "O that Ishmael might live before thee," words in which we almost hear the throbbing of the father's heart. Abraham carried his cause to God; and this was the answer, probably with an audible voice, "Let it not be grievous in thy sight because of the lad and because of thy bondwoman; in all that Sarah hath said unto thee hearken to her voice."

The command of God was decisive. God was Abraham's friend [James 2:23], and with Him he had fellowship; his Father, and he loved and honoured Him; his God, and he adored and worshipped Him; his Lord, and to Him he rendered instant, implicit, unquestioning, cheerful obedience.

Preparations were at once made for the departure of Hagar and Ishmael; and on the morning of the next day, being provided with food and water, they set off.

If Ishmael must leave the parental roof Hagar would wish to go with him. He may have been the only person in the world whom she truly loved, and who in return loved her. Life without love is hardly worth living. Especially is this true of woman, for love is her element. When not loved she, like a plant removed from the sunny south to our climate, becomes stunted, if not mis-shapen.[38]

Abraham had, doubtless, advised these ejected members of his household where to go and what to do. And Ishmael, probably, with the love of adventure common to youth, would talk cheerfully of making new acquaintances and seeing new places. Hagar, too, would seem to be cheerful; but she was cheerful in seeming only, and her despondency would increase as she wandered farther and still farther from human habitation. Surely, thought she, I am travelling as my master directed, but what means this solitude! There are no flocks or herds or tilled fields to indicate proximity to any human dwelling. What can I do?

The bread is now nearly exhausted, and the last drop of water has been drained from the skin, and Ishmael complains of thirst. Hagar is thirsty too, far more thirsty than Ishmael, having for some time, for his sake, abstained from drinking; but of this she says nothing, and indeed cares little if Ishmael's wants can but be supplied. She searches all around for water, but to no avail. She ascends an eminence to see where the grass is of the richest green, hoping there to find some latent spring; but on going thither finds none. She returns to Ishmael but to confess her disappointment. She tenderly supports him for some time; but he so persistently asks for water that her feelings become unendurable; so she lays him down under a shrub, that being the best shelter the place affords. She cannot endure to behold the distress which it is not possible for her to relieve; and yet so intense is her love that she is constrained to remain near her boy. She had gone hither and thither though weary, hungry, and thirsty, and had shed no tear had heaved no sigh. She was buoyed up by hope. But now, being hopeless, she lifts up her voice and weeps. She well knows that no human ear can hear her cry. But did she not call to mind the former lovingkindness of the Lord when she was a voluntary fugitive from the home of her mistress? Would He who aided her then leave her uncared for now? Did not the promises made at that time imply that Ishmael would live? Would God fail to keep His promises? Could anything be too hard for Him [Gen. 18:14]? Could He not furnish water, or could He not preserve Ishmael alive without water? While, in the midst of these thoughts was not her cry changed into a prayer—her wail of woe into hopeful, trustful supplication?

[38] Witter is the only Canadian author included in this collection. Here, she alludes to the harshness of Canadian winters.

God heard the mother's voice, and the groans and moans of the lad. He had heard her prayer even before it was uttered, but had delayed the answer till she was prepared to receive it. The angel of the Lord, the eternal Word, now called to Hagar out of heaven. She had been crying aloud, now she ceases to cry and listens. Does she look upward whence the voice comes, or does she reverently bow down and worship? The words were as tender as were the words of the Man of Nazareth, and yet there was in them something of reproof. "What aileth thee, Hagar? Fear not, for God hath heard the voice of the lad where he is. Arise, lift up the lad and hold him in thine hand, for I will make of him a great nation." Hagar knows the speaker to be no other than God, and doubts not that He will fulfil His word. Though her lips are silent her heart says: "Thou art a God that seeth."

Hagar rises from the earth, and goes to Ishmael to fan the spark of life that still remains, and on her way God causes her to see a well of water for which she had previously looked in vain. She now lifts up the lad and, giving him water, he revives.

Before the mountains were settled, while as yet God had not made the earth, nor the fields, nor the beginning of the dust of the world [Prov. 8:25-26], the wants of these wanderers had been seen, and in the mind of God provided for. God is never taken by surprise. His children never have wants which were not foreseen. With God is one eternal now. And not only does He pity those who fear Him, as a tender father pities his child, but, unlike a human father, His power is always equal to His pity. His children can be in no difficulty beyond His power to relieve. Before man was created, God, seeing that man would fall, provided for his restoration; and when the believer enters the unseen world there will be a mansion prepared for him [John 14:1].

Conclusion

The women writing on Hagar interpreted and applied her story to their readers' devotional lives as well as to their roles in home and society. They emphasized three common devotional themes in their works and assessed Hagar as an example for their readers to either follow or avoid. The authors also dealt with the Woman Question, especially in terms of both women's oppression and women's power. These readings clearly show that nineteenth-century women read the biblical text in light of the world they knew; both their culture and gender influenced their interpretations of Hagar.

Three common devotional themes emerged in the selections on Hagar. One of the strongest themes was that God saw and heard the plight of the oppressed. The authors encouraged their readers to take hope from the story of Hagar: God would see, hear, and speak words of comfort and hope to any who were afflicted. A second theme highlighted by most authors was Hagar's forgetfulness of God's promises. Although Hagar forgot God, God did not forget her. Readers were encouraged to remember and trust in God's promises, unlike Hagar. The third theme evident through all the readings was one of duty and submission. The authors encouraged their readers to do their duty and submit to those in authority over them. Woosnam wrote that when in affliction, "we are generally put back into the path of duty. 'Go back and do better,' Christ seems to say. 'Return to thine own house and show (by a sweetened character, a consistent behaviour, a changed life, rather than by wordy profession) how great things God hath done unto thee.'" Readers were to be submissive as Hagar was after the angel visited her.

Many nineteenth-century women writers held up Hagar as an example for their readers. As a positive example, Aguilar showed Hagar telling Ishmael to thank God for providing water for them in the desert, and Beck portrayed her as a loving mother who sacrificed her own welfare and comfort for her son's benefit. As a negative example, Stowe described her as hot-headed and proud, and Witter depicted her as encouraging Ishmael's poor behaviour towards Isaac. Authors' assessments of Hagar's character varied and may have been influenced by their social location.

A woman's social location defined her role in a household. These readings on Hagar highlight the issue of who had power within a household. Sarah was given power over Hagar, while Abraham withdrew from the initial conflict between the women. Both Martyn and Stowe commended Abraham for avoiding the conflict between his wives. Martyn wrote, "With the dignity and wisdom which marked his character, Abram avoided entering into the merits of the case, simply assuring Sarah that Hagar was in her power and subject to her will." The women writers recognized that Hagar was oppressed, and most empathized with her plight. Behind their "God-cares-for-the-oppressed" devotional reading of the text was an acknowledgment of the oppression they and their readers experienced as women. At the same time, Sarah's power over Hagar reminded them that women were not always the oppressed—they could also be the oppressors.

The Hagar readings demonstrate that authors' cultural contexts influenced their interpretation of the Bible. The white Americans, Warner and Stowe, used language to describe Hagar that clearly indicates they read her as a black slave woman. Stowe called Hagar a "poor, fiery, impatient creature!—

moaning like a wounded leopardess." Warner wrote that Hagar "despised her former mistress, and would not take orders from her meekly, but carried her pretty black head high." Bibb, a black American, wrote poetry influenced by the memory of American slavery and its ongoing influence on society. She found no hope in the expulsion of Hagar and Ishmael, but put these words in Hagar's mouth, "My boy! my own! all, all is o'er, And we are outcasts ever more." On the other hand Morton, a British woman, defined slavery for her young readers without racial or emotional overtones. Morton wrote, "Those who are slaves belong altogether to their master or mistress; they may never go away from them, even if they are cruelly treated and are very unhappy." Aguilar and Moise both read this story of Hagar the outcast and wanderer through their experience as Jewish women doubly displaced from their homeland. In a further example of culturally influenced interpretation, most of the authors used the biblical text to reinforce the ideals of their dominant culture in their discussion of submission and duty, rather than as a tool to critique their culture. Butler stands out as a woman who did use this text prophetically to speak for change in British society.

The authors writing on Hagar also read the biblical text through the lens of their experience as women. They created and described scenes that men could not have written. For example, Martyn included details in her description of the birth of Isaac that were rooted in her own experience of motherhood. "The promise of God is fulfilled; a son has been given to Abraham, and Sarah, as she sheds happy tears on the soft cheek of her first-born, can hardly believe that all this bliss is a reality, that this precious gift of God is indeed her own, a part of herself, from which henceforth nothing can ever separate her affection." Similarly, Sarah Trimmer, a mother whose sons and daughters had to leave home to find employment, found comfort in the experience of Ishmael. She wrote, "Young people, in particular, who are obliged to leave their parents in order to get a livelihood, may take comfort from this part of Ishmael's history, as it proves that they may be under the protection and care of their heavenly Father in every place, and that GOD is ever ready to hear the prayer of those who call upon him in the time of their distress, and to help their necessities." It is clear that the gender of these interpreters shaped their reading and application of the biblical text. Butler named this type of reading a "motherly" or "womanly" reading.

Part 4

REBEKAH—MOTHER OF TWO NATIONS

Introduction

The story of Rebekah, the second of the matriarchs of Abraham's family described in Genesis, is found primarily in Genesis 24–27.[1] These chapters recount four major episodes in the life of Rebekah: her marriage to Isaac; the birth of her twin sons Esau and Jacob; the wife-sister story involving her husband Isaac, and Abimelech, king of Gerar; and her deception of Isaac so that he blessed Jacob rather than Esau. With the exception of the wife-sister episode, all of these narratives portray Rebekah as a more active and interesting character than her husband Isaac.

Genesis 24 recounts Rebekah and Isaac's arranged marriage. Abraham instructed his servant to find a wife for Isaac from among his relatives in Nahor. The servant traveled to Syria and on his arrival prayed for God's help in finding an appropriate wife. He met Rebekah at the well outside the city, discovered her relationship to Abraham, and negotiated a marriage arrangement. Rebekah consented to leave immediately and traveled with Abraham's servant and her nurse Deborah to Abraham's household in Canaan. On their arrival, Isaac took Rebekah into his mother's tent, loved her, and was comforted over the loss of his mother.

Like Sarah, her mother-in-law, Rebekah was barren. After twenty years of marriage, Isaac prayed to the Lord on behalf of his wife, and Rebekah conceived twins. During her difficult pregnancy she inquired of God, who spoke to her about the two nations struggling in her womb. God told Rebekah that

---

[1] Rebekah is also mentioned in Gen. 22:21; 28:5; 29:12; 35:8; and 49:31. Unlike Sarah, Rebekah was not mentioned as an example for Christians to follow in the New Testament; in fact, she is only mentioned there once, in Rom. 9:10, in the context of God's choice of one of her twin sons over the other.

her elder son would serve the younger. Isaac loved the elder twin, Esau, while Rebekah loved the younger, Jacob.

Like Abraham and Sarah, Isaac and Rebekah lied about their relationship. During a famine they went to Gerar and Isaac said Rebekah was his sister. Abimelech, king of Gerar, exposed this deception when he looked down from his window and saw Isaac caressing Rebekah. Only in this episode was Isaac active and Rebekah passive.

When Isaac thought he was going to die, he wanted to give Esau his blessing. Rebekah arranged that Jacob would gain his father's blessing instead of Esau. Trouble ensued when Esau planned to kill Jacob in retaliation for the stolen blessing. Rebekah arranged for Jacob to leave the country to stay with her relatives and find a wife. After Jacob left on his journey, Rebekah disappeared from the narrative. It appears that she never saw her son Jacob again. The circumstances of her death are not recorded, though details of the death of her nurse Deborah are. On his deathbed, Jacob noted that Rebekah was buried with Isaac, Abraham, and Sarah, in the cave of Machpelah (Gen. 49:31).

Nineteenth-century women were taught that their main spiritual responsibilities were for their husband and children. William Wilberforce[2] described women's spiritual responsibilities as follows.

> The female sex . . . seems, by the very constitution of its nature, to be more favourably disposed than ours to the feelings and offices of Religion; being thus fitted by the bounty of Providence, the better to execute the important task which devolves on it, of the education of our earliest youth. Doubtless, this more favourable disposition to Religion in the female sex, was graciously designed also to make women doubly valuable in the wedded state: . . . that when the husband should return to his family, worn and harassed by worldly cares of professional labours, the wife, habitually preserving a warmer and more unimpaired spirit of devotion than is perhaps consistent with being immersed in the bustle of life, might revive his languid piety that the religious impressions of both might derive new force and tenderness from the animating sympathies of conjugal affection.[3]

Women had spiritual power over their husbands and children in their homes; their influence as the angel of the house was widely acknowledged. This meant

---

[2] William Wilberforce (1759–1833), a member of parliament and prominent evangelical layperson, was primarily responsible for the legal abolition of the slave trade in the British Empire.

[3] William Wilberforce, *A Practical View of the Prevailing System of Professed Christians, in the Higher and Middle Classes in this Country, Contrasted with Real Christianity*, 2nd ed. (London: T. Cadell & W. Davies, 1799), 434–35. Cited in Sean Gill, *Women and the Church of England: From the Eighteenth Century to the Present* (London: SPCK, 1994), 29–30.

that women approached the story of Rebekah with a number of assumptions. First, the choice of a spouse was important, and God should be consulted about this decision. Second, it was a woman's responsibility to instruct her children in the faith; the behaviour of children reflected on their mother.

Given these assumptions, it is not surprising that the nineteenth-century writers chose to focus on the romantic and exotic story of Rebekah and Isaac's monogamous marriage, and Rebekah's influence on Jacob in the deception of Isaac. Women based their written "sermons" primarily on these two accounts, and taught moral and spiritual lessons about courtship, marriage, and parenting to their predominantly female audiences. Issues related to the Woman Question stood behind their discussion of the strong, independent, and courageous character of Rebekah.

The arranged marriage of Rebekah and Isaac provided an opportunity for women interpreters to discuss marriage and the proper behaviour of young women and wives. King expressed the emotional impact of this story on nineteenth-century women readers: "The inimitable beauty, interest, and simplicity of the 24th chapter in Genesis, which opens the history of Rebekah, must forcibly strike upon the heart of every reader of taste and feeling." The emotional connection to this story felt by King and others allowed them to enter the episode imaginatively, fill in details not given in the biblical text, and draw lessons from it. They used the geographical, cultural, and historical information available to them to enter the episode they reconstructed conversations, described physical details including the jewelry Rebekah was given by Abraham's servant, and described Rebekah's journey from her home to Isaac's mother's tent. The lessons women interpreters drew from the text included the importance of prayer, how to find an appropriate spouse, and the character qualities that young women and wives should possess. These character qualities were catalogues of qualities valued by nineteenth-century society. The women interpreters' contexts influenced the way they understood the biblical text.

The deception of Isaac by Rebekah and Jacob provided an opportunity for women interpreters to teach their readers about parenting, as well as to address theological and ethical issues. Isaac and Rebekah were both faulted for favouring one son over the other. Rebekah often received more blame than Isaac in the lessons taught from this story. She not only favoured Jacob but taught him to be deceitful. The women interpreters warned parents not to favour one child over another and cautioned them to teach their children good, not evil.

The deception of Isaac, however, had a positive outcome for salvation history: Jacob was blessed, as God had told Rebekah he would be. Many women writers wrestled with the problem of doing evil that good may result. Most often they concluded that the end did not justify the means and reminded their readers that faith involved patience and waiting for God to work. They argued that the separation of Rebekah and Jacob was a just consequence of their ill-advised use of deception to gain the promised blessing. Below the surface of this discussion of Rebekah and Jacob's deception of Isaac lingered the haunting question of women's power in a patriarchal world. Women were to be submissive wives, but they were considered spiritually superior to men. How should pious wives convince their husbands to follow God's way?

The women writers empathetically entered this episode in Rebekah's life. They imagined her feelings as Jacob departed. They imagined her sorrow over her separation from her favourite son. Some women were more sympathetic than others to Rebekah at this stage of her life. Most noticed her disappearance from the text after Jacob left Isaac's household, and many hoped that she repented of her sin in deceiving Isaac. By empathizing with Rebekah as only another woman could, nineteenth-century women produced gendered interpretations of the biblical text.

While most nineteenth-century women interpreters saw similar things in Rebekah, their works differ in detail and emphasis. The first selection, from King, is representative of the literal and narrative approach the majority of women used in interpreting the story of Rebekah. The final selection, from Ada Habershon, illustrates an entirely different spiritual or typological reading of the story of Rebekah.

§50 Frances Elizabeth King
(1757–1821)

Frances King, the wife of a Church of England clergyman, wrote extensively on social issues.[4] The title of King's book, *Female Scripture Characters: Exemplifying Female Virtues*, stated her purpose for writing. King upheld Rebekah as an example for nineteenth-century female readers. Rebekah's qualities, including kindness and civility to strangers, tenderness to animals, modesty, benevolence, useful industry for the good of others, and a religious and pious heart were to be developed by all women; Rebekah was the ideal nineteenth-century virtuous woman. King particularly addressed young women in her discussion of the marriage of Rebekah.

---

[4] For more details on King's life see part 2, "Sarah—The First Mother of Israel."

As Rebekah was the ideal woman, so Isaac was the ideal husband. King dwelt at length on how this ideal husband should be treated. An ideal marriage between these ideal partners was based upon the key elements of piety, reason, and discretion. In this ideal marriage, the wife was to be the moral guardian of the household.

Like many readers, King noted the similarities between Rebekah and Sarah: they were both barren, and they were both presented as their husband's sister to Abimelech of Gerar. Biblical scholars saw these parallels as evidence for separate sources standing behind the text of Genesis;[5] King, however, drew spiritual lessons from the differences between the parallel stories. For example, Sarah and Rebekah handled their barrenness in quite different ways, and King saw Rebekah as a better example in this case.

King's analysis of Rebekah's preferential treatment of Jacob was psychologically profound. Preference by both Isaac and Rebekah for one child over another led to consequences for their family. In this chapter, which reads mostly like a sermon, King advised all parents to learn from this negative example in Rebekah and Isaac.

From Frances Elizabeth King, *Female Scripture Characters; Exemplifying Female Virtues* (London, 1813). [This text from the 9th ed. (London: F. C. & J. Rivington, 1822), 34–50.]

–Rebekah–

The inimitable beauty, interest, and simplicity of the 24th chapter in Genesis, which opens the history of Rebekah, must forcibly strike upon the heart of every reader of taste and feeling.

We see the good and pious Abraham possessed by the common anxiety of a parent, the marriage of his only son; but possessed by it, not in the common way, to increase his riches, his splendour, and rank; though his own situation in society entitled him to seek the alliance of princes and potentates. His sole anxiety was, that his son should connect himself with a good and virtuous young woman; and be saved from any intercourse with idolatrous and profane people, however splendid their possessions and situation.

Let us pause an instant here, and apply this to ourselves, with the important question, Do we, in a similar case, "do likewise?"

---

[5] Beginning in the seventeenth and eighteenth centuries, scholars saw repetitions as evidence for multiple sources behind Genesis. Critics argued that two versions of the same story had been placed into the text from separate sources. For a helpful introduction to Old Testament source criticism, see John Barton, "Source Criticism: Old Testament," in *The Anchor Bible Dictionary*, ed. David Noel Freedman, vol. 6 (New York: Doubleday, 1992), 162–65.

The faithful old servant is summoned, and enjoined with an oath, to select for his darling son a wife from those of his friends and kindred, whom he knows to be attached to the worship of the true God. This good and pious servant proceeds on his errand, with the most anxious desire to fulfil his master's will; and, in order to be assisted in the performance of it, he fervently addresses his prayers to the Almighty, for blessings on his master, and divine directions in the important business in which he is engaged; humbly asking a sign as to the object he was in search of. This example suggests more than one useful reflection: first, on the duty of servants, their performing all the wishes and commands of their master, with diligence, zeal, and anxiety for his benefit and advantage: and next, the importance, in all our undertakings, of addressing ourselves to God for his blessing and direction; and this more especially in that most serious of all worldly concerns, chusing [sic] the companion and guide of our future life: in this important work, human wisdom and discretion would be a weak defence against the deceitfulness of human characters, without the guidance of that all-wise Providence, who will open the eyes of our understandings to search after and discover the only sign that can ensure our happiness and advantage—a religious and pious heart. The prayers of this good and faithful servant were answered, and the very sign given which he petitioned for. He asked not for a display of splendour, rank, or talents; but for a simple instance of kindness and benevolence in the character of his young master's future wife.

Rebekah's first appearance is truly amiable and interesting: she appears, amongst many others of her own age and sex, as a most lovely and beautiful young woman; employed in the habits of useful industry; and converting those habits to the good of others, by her courtesy and benevolence to a travelling stranger, and his thirsty camels. He petitions for a little water from her pitcher; she, with the most marked civility and respect to an unknown stranger, that she may not be deficient in giving him any title that may be his due, replies, "Drink, my lord;" and she hasted to let down her pitcher and gave him drink; and she said, "I will draw water for thy camels also, until they have done drinking;" a most laborious act of kindness, from the large quantity that camels drink.

Josephus, in addition to the Scripture History, relates, that many other damsels were with her, who were all asked for water in succession, and refused in a rude manner; and that it was reserved for the future wife of Isaac, as the sign prayed for, to show a benevolent and kind heart. All females, and indeed all human beings, have a very excellent example in this part of the history; all examples should produce in us self-examination, how far we imitate, or depart from, the pattern before us. Are we always anxious to shew kindness and civility to strangers? Do we even study to do so to our friends and neighbours? Are we constantly seeking occasion to assist and benefit all whom we meet with; *hasting* to employ the means in our power in supplying their wants, and contributing to their comfort; encountering any degree of labour we are capable of, and submitting to any inconvenience, where the necessities of our fellow-creatures, or even a poor animal may require it? If we have hitherto been deficient in these virtues, let us humbly beseech the Almighty to take from us "this heart of stone, and put his holy and benevolent Spirit within us."[6]

We next read of the wonder and joy of the good servant, at his prayers being thus miraculously answered; and his presenting her with the costly gifts sent by Abraham for the damsel he should select. She receives them with humility and gratitude; and modestly answers the enquiries as to who she is.

And here let it be remarked, that the first movement of the good man's heart, in having thus happily accomplished his errand, was pious gratitude to the Almighty, uttered in a thanksgiving for the blessings showered on his master and himself, in being thus miraculously, led to the object of his search.

Let us ask ourselves, Do our hearts daily rise in gratitude to the Giver of all good, for the many blessings we enjoy? Do we acknowledge his hand in all our miraculous escapes from danger, our recoveries from sickness, and our successes in life? And are we as grateful for a blessing given, as we were anxious for its attainment? If not, let us tremble, lest the blessing, thoughtlessly and ungratefully enjoyed, should, as a punishment, be withdrawn.

The history proceeds to relate the hospitable reception of the good servant and his cattle, at the house of Rebekah's brother; his eagerness to unfold the object of his journey; the satisfaction and confidence in God, with which it is received by the family; the anxiety of the servant not to keep his master in suspense; their reference to Rebekah for her consent; and the modest compliance she gives to accompany him back, and become the wife of a man, of whose worth she is assured. Again the pious servant bows his head and worships his Creator; and thus, feeling confidence in his protection, sets out to escort Rebekah to his master's house. And here I would call the attention of my younger readers to the foundation exemplified of a happy marriage: in this instance, it was formed on confidence in God, who seemed miraculously to point to it; on a conviction of the superior excellence of Isaac's character; and a rational deference to the opinions and wishes of those whose judgment and experience enabled them to point out the concomitants of happiness in the state. It was not a romantic attachment to person and manners, without conviction of internal worth, and against the remonstrances of kind and anxious

---

[6] Here King appears to refer to the image of the stony heart in Ezekiel 11:19 and 36:26. This is not an exact quote from either verse.

relatives. Ah! my young friends, reflect in time on the certain misery you bring on yourselves by allowing headstrong passions to lead you into a connection which can only be rendered happy by piety, reason, and discretion.

As Rebekah drew near to the end of her journey, she saw her future husband approaching; and, instead of advancing to meet him with a vain confidence in her own attractions, she alighted from her camel, and covered herself with a veil. The good servant presents her to his young master, and relates the interesting history we have reviewed; and it is said, "that he brought her into Sarah's tent; and she became his wife; and he loved her; and Isaac was comforted for the death of his mother."

In every point of view, Rebekah has hitherto appeared in a very interesting and amiable light; more especially as the comforter of her husband in the loss of a mother he so tenderly loved.

Isaac appears as a particularly excellent, domestic, and religious man; without any of the parade and eclat attached to great achievements; but as a dutiful, affectionate son; a good and kind husband; and a rare instance, in those times, of faithful attachment to one wife; no other female appearing in any way to have engaged his attention. Let all women who are blessed with such husbands, seriously ask themselves, Do they study to become their comforters in trouble, and their supports and example in affliction? Do they endeavour to supply to them every loss, and to assuage every sorrow? And do they, by their quietness, order, and regularity, increase the delights of that home, which is their principal seat of happiness? And are they grateful for the inestimable blessing they possess in such a friend and companion? Oh, let them bow their heads in devout gratitude for such a gift; a treasure far beyond all the splendid possessions this world can offer.

It appears that Isaac and Rebekah were, as might be expected, a very happy domestic couple; but a similar instance occurs, as in the case of Sarah and Abraham, in Isaac being induced, from the fear of Abimelech, to profess Rebekah to be his sister: a very unjustifiable deceit, which nearly brought a severe punishment on his head.

They had also a similar alloy to their happiness; Rebekah was twenty years married, without any prospect of a family. Isaac applied to the only source of redress in all earthly wants and disappointments; "he entreated the Lord for his wife, because she was barren; and the Lord was entreated of him; and Rebekah conceived." But even in the accomplishment of their only wish, much anxiety was ordained them both. In Josephus's history, she is recorded to have been in so singular a state, and so uncommonly large, "that her husband became apprehensive for her safety: under this depression of spirits, he addressed himself to God, praying that he would be graciously pleased to reveal the cause of Rebekah's unusual appearance. The Almighty condescended to inform him, that his wife would be delivered of twins, from whom two great and powerful nations would descend, and be distinguished under their names: adding, that in process of time, the youngest would become the most powerful."

The Scripture History relates, that Rebekah, in alarm for herself, "goes to enquire of the Lord," who gives her the same answer, nearly in the same words, that Isaac is recorded to have received in the above passage.

In due time, Rebekah produced twin sons, who grew up; Esau to be a cunning hunter; and Jacob a domestic, quiet man, living in his tent, and delighting in his home.

From the different characters of the two young men, probably arose two different causes of partiality, respectively shown by the two parents; and whose characters were also marked by their different distinctions. Isaac, excellent as his general character was, appears to have had a defect in the luxuriant indulgence of his appetite; he is said "to have loved Esau, because he did eat of his venison;" and this indulgence was the cause of that event, which fulfilled the prophecy, and decided the superiority of the younger brother over the elder. Rebekah's partiality to Jacob probably arose from his being a more domestic companion to herself; but it appears that the partiality of both parents was selfish, injudicious and unjust; and led to serious evils to themselves and their children.

Isaac's partiality to Esau blinded him to all the atrocious sins in his conduct: his contempt of his birth-right, which he sold to his brother for a sensual indulgence, and which was considered as a high privilege amongst the Jews; and his connecting himself, by marriage, with two Canaanitish women of the idolatrous and proscribed nations, "which was a great grief of mind to Isaac and Rebekah;" but still, while his father ate of his venison, he continued to love him.

Rebekah's partiality to Jacob led to a still greater evil, by plunging her into a crime of atrocious deceit and falsehood, in which she also involved her favourite son; and both, in their after life, suffered for the sin they had committed; though the Almighty saw fit to make it the instrument of accomplishing his wise purposes.

The history of the deception practised by Rebekah, is recorded in the 27th chapter of Genesis; and we read with regret and self-distrust, of a female, otherwise good, being so misled by parental partiality, as to commit a crime for the benefit of one child, that she foresaw would be the ruin of another.

What a lesson is here presented to us: first, on human corruption, which could produce such effects in an apparently good character; and. next, on the lamentable consequences of indulging a blind partiality in families. This is one of the many instances of otherwise good and pious persons being misled by evil passion and prejudice, and hurried by the strength of a sudden temptation, into vices the very opposite to their natures. Let these warnings increase our own humility and watchfulness over ourselves, and our compassion and forbearance towards others. . . .

Under this term [blind partiality in families], I mean not to include that just discrimination of merit, and marked censure of vice, which it is the duty of every parent to maintain in his family. It rarely happens that all are equally good; varieties of characters must produce various degrees of merit. Good conduct and sweet temper, must raise affection and esteem in the heart of every relative; but, most of all, in that of the tender and doating [sic] mother; and, if opposed to this, she smarts under the wayward temper and disrespect, or perhaps the profligate vice of another child; the latter could, neither in justice nor reason, be supposed to be an equal object of affection; but both should be equal objects of care and anxiety, and equal subjects of daily prayers to Heaven for their welfare. Alas! the very defects which the tender parent may have to lament, may make the wayward child a far greater object of care and anxiety, and a more incessant subject of her prayers, than the dear cherished blessing which already seems to her all she can wish. Parents may easily ascertain the correct state of their prejudices and partialities towards their children, by a few simple questions to themselves; Are they equally anxious for the welfare of all their children? Do they make the same efforts, and the same sacrifices for the benefit of all alike? Is the happiness of every one equally dear to them? And are they all constant objects of their care, and daily subjects of their prayers? And, if amongst the delinquents of the family, one repentant prodigal wishes to return to the parental arms, do they, like the tender father in the Gospel, meet the penitent half-way, and fold him to their hearts as if he had never offended? Let all parents carefully, examine themselves by these and similar queries; and avert from their families the sad effects of parental partiality exemplified in the history before us.

In the case of Isaac and Rebekah, it deprived them of the greatest of all earthly blessings, the union of a happy family; their two only children became inveterate enemies, aliens to each other, and wandering exiles from their paternal home; lost to their parents, their friends, and their country. . . .

Rebekah, who was the greatest sinner, was herself the greatest sufferer in the cause; summary justice seems to have instantly overtaken her, in the dread and apprehension that overwhelmed her mind for the safety of her darling son. Esau's revenge was bitter and rancorous; he even looked forward to his father's death, as the period of complete vengeance; when he threatened to murder his brother; dreadful scene for a mother to witness, and to consider herself as the principal cause of it. There was no safety for Jacob, but in flight; and bitter as such a separation was to Rebekah, it was the least [sic] of two dreadful evils. When separated from him, a fresh anxiety assailed her, in the fear of his marrying into one of those wicked families, which all true believers, at that time, shunned and abhorred. Rebekah's expression was miserably desponding; "If Jacob take a wife of the daughters of Heth, what good shall my life do me?" If we act wickedly, we forfeit the protection of heaven; and under this consciousness it is, that we dread the impending evils we know we have deserved. . . .

After the disgraceful event we have just reviewed, nothing more is said of Rebekah in the Sacred Writings; but, in Josephus, it is recorded, that her punishment for her deceit, was lasting in its effects; for she saw her darling son no more: she died a short time before his return to his native country.

Let all females reflect seriously on her character and example; and endeavour to imitate her domestic virtues and affectionate duty to her husband; and watch carefully over their own hearts, which are equally, perhaps more corrupt than her's, lest they also "fall into equal, perhaps greater condemnation."

§51 Lady Morgan
(c. 1783–1859)

Lady Sydney Morgan was born in Dublin, the elder of two daughters of Robert Owenson, an actor, and his wife, Jane Hill. Morgan was educated at home by her mother and later attended private schools, including a Huguenot academy and a Dublin finishing school. Following her schooling, Morgan worked as a governess and began to write poetry, publishing a volume of poems in 1801 and her first novel in 1802. She continued to write and publish through the next ten years. Her career as a writer of fiction and non-fiction continued after her marriage to Sir Thomas Morgan (c. 1780–1843).

In 1840, Morgan published her last major project, *Woman and Her Master*, a work of historical scholarship; however, she completed only the first two of four projected volumes. Morgan was a feminist, and this work was a history of women, particularly tracing the suffering of women as "the victim of man's physical superiority," and as "the subject of laws, in the enactment of which she has no voice."[7] Morgan used and acknowledged a wide variety of sources in this work.

Morgan's feminist agenda influenced her interpretation of Rebekah. She raised key issues for women in the story of Rebekah. She showed women's

---

[7] Sydney Morgan, *Women and Her Master*, vol. 1 (London: Henry Colburn, 1840), 17.

influence over their family through subtle contrivances. Morgan also assumed that Rebekah lived with "social inequality" and that this inequality was the origin of the "deep-felt wrongs" Morgan described.

Like King, Morgan drew parallels between the lives of Sarah and Rebekah. Morgan addressed the problematic ethical and moral issues surrounding the wife-sister stories, and the issue of the preferential treatment of children as both Abraham and Isaac preferred their elder son to the chosen son. Morgan claimed that both Sarah and Rebekah had to "combat and evade the passions and predilections of their husbands." But, unlike King, Morgan challenged the very patriarchal structure of marriage endorsed by King and other writers.

From Lady Morgan, *Woman and Her Master,* vol. 1 (London: Henry Colburn, 1840), 52–54.

The beautiful and pastoral story of Rebekah, full of graphic details of the domestic life of the Hebrew women, teems with fresh illustrations of their influence, their subtle contrivances, and of the social inequality inflicted on them, which originated their deep-felt wrongs.*

In maiden servitude, and in the bloom of her beautiful youth, Rebekah is first presented as coming forth among the daughters of the men of the city, "with her pitcher on her shoulder," meekly administering to the thirsty demand of Abraham's servant, and when she had "done giving him drink," "drawing water for his camels also." In the moral development of her matron maturity, and under her motherly and not unfounded partialities, she subsequently becomes the heroine of a stirring drama, full of energy and importance.

Rebekah was the chosen object of a glorious prophecy, and the agent, like her august mother-in-law, of the Divine Will. In a temporal point of view, she is also to be considered as the secondary cause of power to her husband and her family. Rebekah gained favour in the eyes of the king of the Philistines, (as Sarah had done with the king of Egypt)[8] to whose territories Isaac had deemed it expedient to resort (during a second famine). Isaac availed himself of the example of his father; but, the king, discovering that Rebekah was his wife, charged his people, saying:—"He that toucheth this man or his wife, shall surely be put to death." Isaac thus protected, "waxed great, and went forward," "for he had possessions of flocks, and possessions of herds, and great store of servants, and that which he sowed returned ten fold," and "when he removed to the valley of Gerar, he was visited by the king and the chief captain of his army," and he was sufficiently powerful to enter into a covenant of alliance with Abimelech himself.

[8] Here Morgan neglects to mention that Sarah also gained favour with Abimelech (Gen 20), the more obvious parallel to the Rebekah and Isaac wife-sister story.

Rebekah, too, was honoured beyond all human distinctions, by having been divinely pronounced to be the predestined mother "of two nations," whose founders "struggled in her womb." Yet, thus spiritually elevated, she was, humanly speaking, not the less wretched. Her partiality for her younger and superior son, who was predicted to be such by God himself,† originated those devices which perilled the lives of both, and extorted from the depths of her heart those pathetic exclamations:—"Why shall I be deprived also of you both," "I am weary of my life!" Still in the end, she was the cause of the fulfilment of the prophecy, and "secured to Jacob the blessing of Abraham to him and to his seed with him."

That the unhappy Rebekah, however, fell a victim to the morbid affections of maternity, and the perverted activity of her deviceful mind, may be inferred from the fact of the mysterious obscurity which hung upon her death and burial,—the more remarkable as the death and burial of her old Syrian nurse Deborah, who on her bridal day had accompanied her from her father's house, is recorded with graphic detail.⁺

It appears, then, that both Sarah and Rebekah were deeply interested, and energetically active in forwarding the ordinances of the all-ruling will, in favour of their sons Isaac and Jacob; and they had both to combat and evade the passions and predilections of their husbands, which had hurried Abraham and Isaac into preference for Ishmael and Esau, in contradiction of the divine promises.⁺⁺

* See the controversial writings on the character and conduct of Sarah and Abraham, from Origen, to the Augustin monk, Calmut, including Josephus, St. Ambrose, St. Chrysostom, St. Augustine, St. Victor, Calvin &c.

† Genesis, chap. xxv.

⁺ "But Deborah, Rebecca's nurse, died, and she was buried beneath Allon Bachath, under an oak, the 'oak of Weeping.'" The burial of the nurse of Eneas is similarly described by Virgil.

⁺⁺ "For the Lord's portion is his people, Jacob is the lot of his inheritance." "He found him in the desert land, and in the waste howling wilderness, He led him about. He instructed him! He kept him as the apple of his eye." "As an eagle stirreth up her nest, fluttereth over her young, spreading abroad her wings, taketh them, beareth them on her wings, so the Lord alone did lead him, and there was no strange face with him."—Deuteronomy, chap. xxxii., verse 9, 10, 11, 12. In this passage, the most poetical and sublime, the special intervention of the Deity in favour of Jacob is the justification of the conduct of Rebekah! It is remarkable, that when the women of the Patriarchs had become antiquity to the Jews, they were still referred to as the foundresses of "the house of Israel."—See Ruth, chap. iv.

§52 Grace Aguilar
(1816–1847)

Grace Aguilar[9] was a Jewish woman living in England. In her book *The Women of Israel* (1845) she wrote about Rebekah, her Hebrew foremother, for her intended audience of Victorian Jewish women. Aguilar called her audience to follow Rebekah's example, writing: "Let us ponder well upon these things, and, as daughters of Israel, make it our glory and our pride to do our simplest duty 'with all our might'; our pleasure, to scatter flowers on the path of all with whom we may be thrown; and dwelling with meek and loving contentment in our appointed sphere, remember that the cause of Israel is our own, and it is in our power to exalt or degrade it." Unlike Morgan, who urged change in women's position, role, and status, Aguilar looked for ways to empower women within their traditional spheres in society, family, and religion.

Aguilar saw Rebekah's conduct in the daily routine of domestic duties as exemplary for women of the nineteenth century. Rebekah drew water at the well as she did every day. When she was presented with an opportunity she showed kindness to Abraham's servant. This followed the spirit of the Old Testament law regarding receiving strangers. Aguilar suggested that while Jews living in Christian Britain were strangers in a strange land, they should still live out this same spirit of the law in kindness to others.

Aguilar used Rebekah's prayer to raise the question of woman's spiritual status within Judaism.[10] She reasoned that if their foremother Rebekah could pray without mediation, no one could deny her daughters the right to pray to God without the mediation of men or angels. Aguilar also argued that since God spoke to Rebekah, women must have sould and be able to hear God. She used strong, polemical language in discussing this issue; it was important to the whole argument of her book that Jewish women did not need Christianity to be able to pray directly to God.

Aguilar used the technique of comparison to draw lessons from the story of Rebekah. She compared Eve and Rebekah: the language of the fall highlighted parallels between Eve's and Rebekah's trials, their weaknesses, and their

---

[9] For more information on Aguilar see part 2, "Sarah—The First Mother of Israel."

[10] Traditionally, ten adult Jewish males make up a minyan for prayer. At the time Aguilar wrote, women were not counted toward a minyan.

children's actual or threatened death. Aguilar also found parallels between Rebekah's loss of Jacob and Abraham's test in sacrificing Isaac.

From Grace Aguilar, *The Women of Israel* (London, 1845). [Text from A New Edition (New York: Appleton, 1901), 75–95.]

–Rebekah–
[Aguilar retells the story of Rebekah from Gen. 24 in very elaborate detail]

To some dispositions, this sudden elevation in a social and domestic position [Rebekah's marriage to Isaac] would have been a dangerous ordeal; but neither presumption, arrogance, nor pride, appears to have marked the conduct of Rebekah. The same steady performance of household duty manifested in her girlhood, probably continued in her higher and more responsible station; and year after year found her calmly following the quiet routine of daily duty happily to herself and to her household. And here, for a brief while, we would pause to gather the sweet blossoms of instruction and guidance proffered by a Father's love, which Rebekah's history, thus far considered, can impart. We would linger a moment on the past ere we go forward, for the picture must be changed. Yet it is no marvellous or incomprehensible change, it is no history of woman in an era so long past that we wonder, and scarce believe—the picture is too perfect even now—it is woman *then*, and woman *now*, as we shall see hereafter.

Although from the wide distinction between patriarchal and modern times, our position and duties as daughters of Israel can never resemble those of Rebekah, we have, like her, domestic duties to perform, and a station not only to fulfil but to adorn, so as to excite toward us respect and love. The women of the Bible are forcibly portrayed, not for us to follow them exactly, for that we could not do, but from their conduct in their respective spheres to guide us in ours; from the approval or reproof bestowed directly or indirectly upon them, to teach their descendants what is acceptable in the sight of our heavenly Father and what is not; and of this we may rest assured there is no contradiction to puzzle us in the Word of God. The *precepts* of His law are proved by the *practice* of His servants. "Whatsoever thy hand findeth to do, do it with all thy might" [Eccl. 9:10], was said centuries after by the sage monarch, who, in obedience to the command of God relating to Kings, must have been acquainted with the whole of His law; and that precept was exemplified in Rebekah's conduct at the well. She had every temptation to turn aside a few moments in her simple task. Had she ever accustomed herself to encourage wandering thoughts in her different employments, to turn from them for every frivolous pretence, she would never have withstood the temptation of idling away her time with the goodly looking strangers, and thus demonstrated a character totally unfit to be the ancestress of God's chosen race. But as she went down to the well and filled her pitcher, and came up, "neither turning to the right nor to the left,"[11] so it behoves us to follow our daily duties, would we, like her, receive the blessing of the Lord. . . .

Nor is her steadiness the only portion of Rebekah's early character demanding our admiration. The winning and obliging gentleness with which she met the stranger's address proceeded from the genuine kindness, the real politeness of an utterly unselfish heart. The request was not only granted, but granted with such sweetness of manner and respectful words as threefold to enhance the kindness of the deed. The beautiful laws contained in the 32d, 33d, and 34th verses of the 19th chapter of Leviticus had not then been issued, yet the conduct of Rebekah was a practical illustration of the *spirit* which they teach. She paid respect to age, and did unto the stranger even as if he had been one born in the land; and this we may all do. . . .

On us more especially, aliens and exiles from our own land, is manner, as the mirror of the heart, incumbent. There was a time, but lately passed away, when to perform this duty was impossible, and therefore supposed to be unnecessary. When scorned, persecuted, condemned as the very scum of the earth, hated and reproached, it was as utterly impossible for us to manifest courtesy and kindness, as to receive them. Hatred begets hatred, as scorn begets scorn, more especially when neither emotion may be avowed. What did the cringing manner, the abject tone of the persecuted, tortured Jew conceal? Was it marvel it should be hatred as strong, if not stronger, because utterly powerless, than that of his cruel, his tyrannical oppressor? But now that in some enlightened and blessed realms these fearful times are past, and the right hand of fellowship extended to us, shall the exile and oppressed refuse to meet in amity and confidence, the sons of the land which gives them protection and home? We were commanded to show kindness to a stranger, as to one born among us. That blessed privilege is no longer ours, for we are strangers in a strange land; yet may we still obey the spirit of the law, and in the cultivation of a kindly heart, and manifestation of a kindly feeling, let us remember we have not only an individual, but a national character to support—that a brief half-hour's intercourse with a stranger is endowed with power to exalt or to lower the cause of Israel; and as Rebekah's kindly cordiality was blessed to her, by making her the wife of Isaac, and so revealing to her the glorious tidings of a God of love, so may the kindly manner of the youngest daughter of Israel be blessed to her, by making her the unconscious instrument, in God's hand, to exalt His holy faith, and proclaim His truth in the heart and mind of the Gentiles among whom she dwells.

[11] This is a common phrase in the Hebrew Bible used, for example, in Deut. 2:27, 17:11; 2 Sam. 2:19; etc.

Yet, Rebekah's courtesy to the steward demonstrates neither presumption nor forwardness incompatible with her age or sex. We find her, directly her brother Laban comes forth, retiring to her own modest station in her mother's tent, and claiming no further notice. We see, therefore, that to act kindly demands not the forsaking our natural sphere. We are not to look abroad for opportunities to act as Rebekah did; but, like her, we shall find them without leaving our home, in the domestic and social intercourse of daily life. Let us ponder well upon these things, and, as daughters of Israel, make it our glory and our pride to do our simplest duty "with all our might"; our pleasure, to scatter flowers on the path of all with whom we may be thrown; and dwelling with meek and loving contentment in our appointed sphere, remember that the cause of Israel is our own, and it is in our power to exalt or degrade it. . . .

Those twenty years saw Rebekah as we last beheld her, only matured in the graces of womanhood, and so grafted on the house of Abraham, as like him to worship and know the great God alone. She had had, as yet, no temptation to swerve aside from the straight path of duty. A beloved and cherished wife, daughter, and mistress, her life passed by so smoothly, her affection so devoted to one first object, and thence calmly emanating on all under her influence, that she was, as every other woman in a similar position must have been, still entirely ignorant of the shoals and quicksands in her heart, which might lead to sin, and end in sorrow.

Yet her first action, after proof was given of the Eternal's gracious answer to her husband's prayer, was one of such childlike simple confidence in the power and wisdom of the Lord to answer all of doubt and fear, that to reconcile her conduct afterward becomes more difficult. Unusual and incomprehensible suffering so oppressed her as to raise a doubt of the promise being then about to be fulfilled. "If it be so," she thought, "why am I thus?"—and without pause or hesitation, went directly "to inquire of the Lord." She asked no advice, demanded no human aid—but in heart-felt prayer—for in prayer only could she so inquire—laid before Him her every emotion, and from Him implored reply. We would humbly ask those, if indeed there can be such, who deny to woman an immortal soul, refuse her the blessed privilege of individual and secret commune with her Creator, and believe man's prayer alone omnipotent, how they would interpret this very simple narration? They may assert, as I believe some commentators do, that it was through Abraham she inquired of the Lord, and received reply—but, as we have no warrant whatever in Scripture, by direct word or implied inference, to confirm this assertion, we must reject it altogether. The long years which Rebekah had passed in the household of Abraham, had not flown by unused and spiritually unimproved. She had seen the Great and Invisible Being acknowledged and adored. She had been taught by example; and we may be scripturally certain, though the fact itself is not mentioned, by precept also. The natural impulse of humanity, under all difficulties and suffering, is to pray—and in the beautiful simplicity of the patriarchal ages, no artificial coldness, no appalling scepticism, no disheartening doubt, could have crowded round her, whispering that the prayer was vain, that the Creator of heaven and earth was a Being too far removed from woman's petty griefs to listen and give reply. In the simple trusting confidence of a child, she sought the Parent whose love was omnipotent not only to understand the doubt and pain, but to give relief, and her confidence was answered. How that gracious answer was vouchsafed, whether through Abraham, or directly to herself, is, I believe, an argument— but Scripture bids us believe, without hesitation, the latter—"And the Lord said *unto her*," clear simple words, banishing at once all necessity for mediation either of man or angel; words almost impossible, even wilfully to be misunderstood. The *how* she received this answer, whether through the medium of the ear, or by an impression on the mind—can be of very little consequence; and is one of those cavilling inquiries which we could wish banished, ere formed into words; tending as they do to fill up the mind with vain and idle speculations, instead of the pure simple truths of Scripture. It is enough, and a most blessed enough for us, that the "Lord said unto her," the direct answer to her inquiring prayer. The words were mysterious—that she was already the mother of two opposing nations, one of whom should be stronger than the other—"and the elder should serve the younger." Yet, mysterious as they must have been, they came from the Lord. He had graciously vouchsafed to explain the cause of her unusual sufferings, and Rebekah was satisfied; for we find not another word from her of either wonderment or complaint.

And oh! What a blessed incentive have we from this simple narrative, in all our griefs and sufferings, bodily or mental, to inquire of the Lord—to come to Him as our ancestress, in guileless faith and simple-minded prayer. He is our God as He was hers—yea, ours—exiles, wanderers, WOMEN as we are, and who, with the Holy Word of God within his hand, shall dare to refuse to us, as women, as Israelitish women, the power, the purity, the privilege of prayer? Who shall dare assert that we are powerless to pray, or need the mediation of man, to bear up our petitions to the throne of grace? Mothers, wives, daughters of Israel, you alone must prove the utter falsity of this charge! Before the law, under the law, during the captivity, we shall still find the Hebrew woman seeking her God in prayer, and receiving from Him direct reply. Oh! Shall we not thus prove that we have a soul immortal as that of man—that the very breath of our being, the light of our path, the support of strength, is prayer—that prayer which brings us daily, nay hourly, in commune with a loving Father, whose tender sympathy is endless as His love. Let us prove we need not Christianity either to teach, or direct us how to pray—but, turning to the blessed pages of our own Bible, make manifest that to look further is not needed. That there we have indeed sufficient for encouragement and hope; for confidence and faith. As Rebekah prayed, so too may we; and as our Father answered her, so will He us. Not indeed with word direct, but with that blessed calm, and hope, and faith, which prayer only can bestow; and with that heavenly patience which will enable us to "wait for the Lord," in the firm belief that whatever He may will is best. It is worthy of remark that Rebekah, is the first recorded instance of woman's immediate appeal to God, and the condescending reply.

At the appointed time Isaac and Rebekah became parents of twin sons, who grew and flourished; and in early youth displayed a contrariety of disposition and pursuits which must have appeared strange, in such nearly allied relations, had it not been rendered clearly intelligible, at least to their mother by the previous words of the Lord. But yet these words do not appear to me sufficient for Rebekah always to have regarded Jacob as the promised seed. The promise, or rather explanation, given in answer to her prayer, was simply, "the one people shall be stronger than the other, and the elder shall serve the younger"; not as was the case with Abraham, when the promised seed was specifically *named*. . . .

The Eternal expressly says "thy seed." Isaac might be justified in supposing that both his sons were concerned in the promises, until Esau's reckless disregard of his birth-right, and other spiritual blessings, in addition to his intermarrying with the daughters of Canaan, must have convinced his father that not from him could spring the chosen seed. The revelation that "the elder should serve the younger," must have occasioned Rebekah many mental inquiries; but even if she herself supposed that Jacob was the destined inheritor of Abraham's line, it is evident that she did not impart it to her Husband.

Isaac's love for the reckless and able hunter, Esau, is one of those contradictions of the heart, unaccountable indeed, but very often found. He loved Esau best, because in every respect he was completely his opposite. Isaac was meek, affectionate, faithful, quietly and contentedly dwelling in one spot, moving thence only at the command of the Lord: satisfied with the temporal blessings around him, and the spiritual blessings of promise. Esau, bold, enterprising, ever roving in search of active pursuit; heeding naught but the present; scorning his home and home ties; rude and rough, yet, when excited, deeply and warmly affectionate to his aged father. And Isaac loved him better than his younger son, who, more like himself, "was a plain or upright man dwelling in tents." But Rebekah loved Jacob. Sacred history does not say why—and we are therefore permitted to infer, that it was simply because it is in woman's nature to love him best who is least loved by his father. But Rebekah's favoritism, as we shall see in the sequel, was stronger and more culpable than that of Isaac. All such emotions are stronger in woman's heart than in man's—because, with the former, feeling is the most powerful, and with the latter, reason. Partiality must always occasion injustice, and more particularly in a parent; for no task demands more control and feeling, more complete conquest of self, than that of parental affection. The dispositions, the characters of the divers members of one family are so varied, that it is impossible to guide all by one and the same training. An impartial mother will know every light and shadow of every disposition, and guide and act accordingly. A partial mother sees but the virtues and qualities of one, and from want of sympathy and proper management of the other in early years, makes him in reality all that she believed him. Jacob was domestic, because a mother's doting love made his home one of enjoyment, and administered to every want.

It was not till after Sarah's death that Isaac even sought a wife, and not till he was parted from his mother that Jacob loved, proofs all convincing of the strength, the beauty, the fulness of the love which in those simple ages united the mother and the son.

To Esau this soothing and blessed love was not given as it was to Jacob; and while his hasty and inconsiderate marriage with the daughters of the Hittite was a grief of mind to Isaac and Rebekah, the latter's neglect might have been in part their cause. Esau had no kindly woman's heart to turn to, as had his brother, yet we have proof that his affections were as strong—perchance, from his ruder character, yet stronger—and the very want of female love at home might have first urged him to seek it from the stranger. Oh! It is sad when partiality and its concomitant, injustice, obtains entrance into a mother's heart. It steals in so silently, so disguisedly, that unless every avenue be guarded, its advances are utterly unknown, till it has gained a strength and substance which hold us chained. Mere human love, omnipotent as in a mother's breast it is, is not sufficient to guard us from such weakness—no, nor former strength and stability of character. Rebekah had all this, and yet as a mother she fell. It can only be that close communion with the universal Father, who alone knows and feels every secret throbbing of a mother's heart, and from whose hand alone can come the strength, not only to guide aright her treasures, but to feel aright herself.

During the growth of his sons, Isaac's temporal riches very greatly increased. Abraham's death did not take place till his grandsons were fifteen. He who had believed it next to impossible in his old age to have a son, lived not only to bless his son, but his son's seed. A famine had sent Isaac and his family, by direction of the Eternal, to Gerar, and there he dwelt until he became so rich and great that the "Philistines envied him"; and their king, Abimelech, said unto him, "Depart from us, for thou art much mightier than we." And he did so, and after some wanderings, fixed his tent at Beersheba; and there again the Lord appeared unto him, bidding him "fear not, for He was with him." Beersheba, therefore, appears to have been the scene of all the domestic events which followed—Esau selling his unvalued birthright—his subsequent marriage—the vexations thence proceeding to Isaac and Rebekah—and those bodily infirmities of the former, which occasioned his anxious desire to "bless his son before he died."

Rebekah heard the words of her husband. She had seen him call his firstborn to his couch, and bid him seek venison, and bring the savory meat that he loved, that his soul might bless him before he died; and her heart swelled tremblingly within her. Esau? Was Esau to have his father's blessing? He who had sold his birthright, and so spurned his privileges as heir; and if he had it, how could the Lord's word be fulfilled, and the "elder serve the younger"? Why could she not prevent it, and secure to him whom the Lord before his birth had chosen as the mightiest, the blessing of his father? It was easy to be accomplished; and surely, as the Lord had said it, she was justified in using any means to bring it to pass. Such was weak, finite reasoning—such the baneful whisper of our earthly nature, urged on by the rushing torrent of human affections. In that dread moment of temptation, how might she realize the unquestioning faith which would bid her feel, "The Lord hath spoken, and will He not do it?" That His will needed no human aid for its fulfilment; that He would do His pleasure in the very face of those contradictory events, which human will and finite wisdom might so weave as to render its fulfilment seemingly impossible. If Rebekah had but "inquired of the Lord" in this perplexity, as on a former one, the whole train of deceit and its subsequent suffering would have been averted. But she was still a woman, weak, wavering, a very reed in her mortal nature, and liable, as every child of Adam, to temptation and to sin.

Had she even waited but one brief hour, all would have been well—the evil impulse would have been conquered in her pious heart, by a train of thought as above, but there was no time either to wait or think again; and, acting on the impulse, she called Jacob, and after informing him of his father's directions to his brother, continued in a strain that would lead us to believe, that even at that moment she feared Jacob's upright nature would shrink from the task she imposed. "Now, therefore, my son, OBEY my voice, according to that which I command thee." She claimed his unquestioning obedience, ere imparting that which she desired, and then proceeded. Surely her heart must have reproached her, when her own son ventured to suggest, though guardedly and respectfully, that it was a fraud, and might bring upon him a curse instead of a blessing. Yet still she enforces the command, "Upon me be the curse, my son, only obey my voice." And he did obey her, weakly and mistakenly; for had he resisted, had he submissively, yet firmly braved her momentary wrath, the evil temptation must have been subdued, and the mother saved by the unscrupulous honesty of the son.

But this was not to be. To make manifest His ways, that suffering must attend deceit, however for the moment it may seem to succeed, the Eternal permitted the plans of finite forming uninterruptedly to proceed, working out indeed His will through them, but punishing even in success. . . . The inspired historian might not interrupt his brief, yet how deeply impressive detail, to dilate on a woman's feelings; yet we, her descendants, are surely justified in judging for a moment of Rebekah's emotions during this interview, by what our own would be. She could have had no support, no stay, for she had wilfully banished TRUTH, and how, then, might she PRAY? Her whole heart and mind must have been troubled and tossed by every trifling word; discovery and shame, perhaps the very loss or estrangement of her husband's love, were as likely as the longed-for success. How often, during that interim, must she have longed once more to tread the path of truth, for Rebekah was a mere novice in deceit! Her nature, as we have seen, was guileless and open as the day; the mere temptation of the moment, and its consequent anxious and impelling feelings, could not have so changed that nature, as to make her an unmoved witness of that which followed—the very falsehood repeated and insisted upon by those lips which she had taught from infancy to lisp forth truth. But when the blessing was obtained, when she saw her plan had in truth succeeded, we may suppose, judging still by human nature, that these agonizing doubts and fears were for the moment calmed in the triumph of success—conscience was hushed again, in the thought that she had compassed by stratagem that which she believed impossible to have been obtained else—that it must have been right and good so to have acted, or it would not have been permitted to succeed. Alas! how often do we so deceive ourselves! Could we but glance a little, a very little, further on, we should know, and feel (how bitterly!) that the very deceit we believed innocent, because it brought success, has been our first step in the paths of woe.

And so it was with Rebekah, though as yet she knew it not. Her feelings of triumph could not, however, have lasted long: "And it came to pass, as soon as Isaac had made an end of blessing Jacob, and Jacob was yet scarce gone out from the presence of his father, that Esau, his brother, came in from hunting"; and that interview followed, which, for simple and touching pathos, is not surpassed by any incident in the Bible.

Rebekah was a partial, but not a weak or unkind mother. She loved Jacob better than his brother, but Esau was still her son, her first-born, and oh! How painfully must her heart have yearned toward him, when she heard his "great and exceeding bitter cry!"—"Hast thou but one blessing, my father—bless

me, even me also, O my father—and Esau lifted up his voice and wept."
Esau, the rude, the careless hunter, who had seemed to care for naught but
his own pleasures; the chase, the field, the wild! He bowed down by his blind
father like an infant, and wept; beseeching the blessing of which a mother
and a brother's subtlety had deprived him. Could Rebekah have been a witness, or even hearer of this scene, without losing all the triumph of success, in
sympathy with the anguish of her first-born? It is impossible to ponder on her
previous character, without being convinced of this. It is not from one act,
one unresisted temptation, that we ought to pronounce judgment on a fel-
low-creature: yet, from our unhappy proneness to condemn, we generally do
so. The character of Rebekah is thus too often supposed to be evil alone, and
her unfortunate deception in favor of her best-beloved son is the only part of
her life brought strongly forward: whereas, if we look and think on all that
sacred history has recorded of her, that there is also perfect silence as to any
other fault (which, had she committed, we may be sure would have been told
for our warning)—it becomes evident that this guilty action proceeded, not
from forethought, which would have manifested a naturally evil disposition,
but from impulse; the thought, the temptation of a moment, overbalancing
by its force the rectitude of years. As forethought, we must condemn both the
sin and the sinner. As impulse, we must abhor the sin—but only grief and
trembling for the weakness of human nature must attend our reflections on
the sinner. Nor are we justified in denying her those emotions of grief and
doubt, which must have succeeded the triumphant success of her momen-
tarily formed plan.

But, self-accusation was not to be her only punishment. Did the blessed
Word of the All-Just relate the deception alone, we might well hesitate to
affirm that her conscience brought reproach, and believe that the deed was
not as guilty as it seems. But we are not thus left to our own imaginations.
The events which followed so prove, without doubt or question, the displeasure of the Eternal against the deed, that we can have no hesitation whatever
in believing that conscience, "the angel of the Lord," was busy within her, ere
the bolt of justice fell.

"And Esau hated Jacob, because of the blessing wherewith his father blessed
him. And Esau said in his heart, The days of mourning for my father are at
hand; then will I slay my brother Jacob. And these words of Esau her elder
son were told to Rebekah." What fearful tidings for a mother! How must her
thoughts have returned, with agonizing forebodings, to the *first death* which
had marred this beautiful world. Had not that been *fratricide*, and for envy,
the same feeling which now actuated Esau? And was not she, as Eve had been,
the cause? Still nearer cause; for she it was, who, by leading Jacob to deceive,
had armed a brother's hand against him. How Esau's intentions could have

been revealed to her, when the sacred historian expressly tells us that Esau but spake them in his heart, must remain unsolved, unless, as appears most probable, it was Rebekah's own fears which betrayed them; confirmed by the manner of Esau toward his brother, and by her own knowledge of his character. . . . Was it not her own fault, that in this wild wish for vengeance, the death of the offender, he thought not of the suffering which such a deed would inflict on her? That such thoughts were ascendant, and the voice of self-reproach more loud and thrilling than any anger against Esau for his fearful design, is proved by her counsel to Jacob—when calling him to her, she said, "Behold thy brother Esau, as touching thee, doth comfort himself, purposing to kill thee. Now, therefore, my son, obey my voice and arise, and flee thou to my brother Laban, in Haran. And tarry with him a few days, until thy brother's fury turn away, and he forget that which thou hast done to him; then I will send, and fetch thee from thence. Why should I also be deprived of you both in one day?"

. . . How affectingly do those simple words betray, not alone the love she bore to both her sons, but that her thoughts turned to the history of the past— foreboding Eve's awful trial for herself! There is no wailing, no complaint, but in those brief words, what a volume of woman's deepest feeling is revealed!

Her real emotions having thus had vent to Jacob, Rebekah was better able to control them before her husband; and she said unto him, "I am weary of my life, because of the daughters of Heth. If Jacob take a wife of the daughters of Heth, such as these which are of the daughters of the land, what good shall my life do me?"

It would have been the extreme of cruelty to have increased the grief of the infirm Isaac, by a narration of Esau's evil intentions toward his brother—when Esau himself had controlled his fierce passion for his father's sake. Nor could Rebekah's confession of her fault now in any way redeem it. It would but have excited against her the anger of her husband, as being the primary cause of the dissensions between his sons—and have occasioned him increased affliction. It was, in this instance, wiser and better to hide from Isaac the sad cause of Jacob's departure; and urge him to do that for his son of promise, which Abraham had done for him; and the mother's fearful anxiety was calmed by the paternal command, coupled with a reiterated blessing, for her younger son "to go to Padan-Aram, the house of Bethuel, thy mother's father, and take thee a wife from one of the daughters of Laban, thy mother's brother." "And Isaac sent away Jacob."

And thus was the mother parted from the son, for whose beloved sake she had been tempted to turn aside from the straight line of probity and truth which in such guilelessness and beauty she had trodden so changelessly before. . . .

With the departure of Jacob, the history of Rebekah concludes, for her name is no more mentioned.—Even on her death Holy Writ is silent. We only know that she was buried in the cave of Machpelah, by the words of Jacob in Gen. xlix. 31. And from there being no mention whatever of her on Jacob's return to Hebron, we must infer that she died before his arrival, and never had the happiness of folding him to her heart again. How sad and lonely must her declining years have seemed without him who had been so long her stay; . . .

Yet the death of Rebekah was in all probability one of peace, and calm holy reliance on the infinite mercy of her God. He had chastised, but in the midst of chastisement had mercy; the fury of Esau had been turned aside, Jacob been saved, and peace preserved in the household of Isaac. Her earthly idol removed from her sight, we may well believe that Rebekah returned to her domestic duties with that singleness of purpose and uprightness of heart which had marked her earlier years. . . .

Are we then, it may be asked, to give Rebekah the meed of unmixed admiration? To rest only on the good points of her character? No. Like all human nature, it was a blending of the good and evil. . . . Rebekah's fault was one, her virtues many; and therefore, while we abhor and pray against the sin, we can only grieve and lament that human weakness which triumphed in one moment of strong temptation over the virtuous strength of years. We dare not condemn and scorn that weakness; for did we so, we scorn, and condemn, and pronounce judgment on ourselves. How may we assert that, had we been placed as Rebekah in that dread moment, we too should not have done as she did? . . .

One point more, and we must conclude this memoir, already so much longer than we intended. It has been said, that as the Eternal ordained that Jacob was to receive the promised blessing, and that the "elder should serve the younger," it must have been obtained in some way; and therefore the means of its accomplishment were of little consequence, thus endeavoring to remove all that was reprehensible in the conduct of Jacob and his mother. Nay, some commentators try to make her conduct proceed from a belief that her course of "acting was in such conformity with the divine prediction, that she determined at all risks, and by any means, to secure the blessing for her younger and more worthy son."*

This species of reasoning appears as mistaken as the too violent condemnation of Rebekah, and so completely at variance with the simple, trusting piety of the patriarchs and their families, that we cannot at all suppose it actuating the mother's feelings. Besides which, to think thus, supposes a predetermination to deceive her husband, whereas the narrative of the Bible clearly marks it the impulse of the moment. . . .

As the command of the Lord to slay his son was the trial of Abraham's faith, so were the words of Isaac to Esau the trial of Rebekah's. . . . But her faith was not strong enough for that most difficult duty—to "wait for the Lord." Woman-like, feeling was her weakness, impulse her guide, faith succumbed before these, and so left her unguarded, when its invulnerable defence was more needed than it had ever been before.

Rebekah had perhaps some excuse for her momentary fancy that her course of acting was, from its *success*, acceptable to the Lord; but We have NONE. . . . It matters not how; it is enough to know that the ways of the Eternal are not our ways, and that His decrees require no aid of man. . . .

We are earnestly and heartily anxious to impress this important truth on the minds of our younger readers, who, in their early perusal of God's holy Word, may and will feel startled, that human weakness should not only be recorded, but its actions be permitted to succeed. Success is not always a proof of the Eternal's approbation. The history of both Rebekah and Jacob proves the displeasure of the Lord toward themselves individually, though their action was overruled to the accomplishment of His previous will. Rebekah never saw her son again; and Jacob, though spiritually blessed, was in his earthly career more unfortunate than any of his family before or after him.

* Philippson—See Notes to Mr. De Sola's Bible.

§53 Cecil Frances (Fanny) Alexander
(1818–1895)

Fanny Alexander, the wife of an Anglican Bishop, was a renowned Irish poet and hymn writer.[12] Like Aguilar, Alexander retold the story of the marriage of Isaac and Rebekah sentimentally. This poetic and imaginative retelling emphasized an exotic, patriarchal, and naïvely romantic setting for the story. The exotic nature of the setting accentuated the historical distance. Alexander highlighted some aspects of the narrative and elaborated on such details as how Rebekah looked and felt when Isaac took her into his mother's tent; here Alexander intimated that the wedding bed was to be feared by women. Like King, Alexander drew lessons of faith and trust for her readers from the story of Rebekah and Isaac. Alexander's version of the story, however, left out any problems and presented only a "tale so sweet and fair."

[12] For a more detailed account of Alexander's life, see part 1, "Eve—The Mother of Us All."

From Cecil Frances Alexander, "Isaac and Rebekah," in *Poems on Subjects in the Old Testament* (London: J. Masters, 1854). [Text is from 3rd ed. (London: J. Masters & Co., 1888), 20–22.]

–Isaac and Rebekah–

"And Isaac brought her into his mother Sarah's tent, and he took Rebekah, and she became his wife."—Gen. xxiv. 67

I READ in GOD'S great holy book
    The tale of Isaac's bridal tent;
And like the murmur of a brook,
    (That brings to "one in city pent"
Gleams of the country far away,
    Of blossomed orchards in their glory,
And clover fields, and scented hay,)
    Were thoughts that came with that sweet story;—

Till I was rapt into a dream
    Of olden days, and eastern clime,
Wherein I saw, (or so did seem)
    The men of Patriarchal time,
The pastoral chiefs who spake with GOD,
    The veiléd maid, the comely wife,
The rich flocks scattered o'er the sod,
    And all the charms of tented life.

The desert's burning breath I felt,
    I heard the camel's tinkling bell;
And when the faithful servant knelt
    At even by the city well,
I saw his young lord's destined bride—
    A damsel very fair, and young—
Come tripping to the water side,
    Her pitcher on her shoulder slung.

I marked his wonder, as the dew
    She scattered round the fountain's brink,
While in her courteous haste she drew
    And gave the weary camels drink.
I watched what blushes bright and warm
    To cheek and brow did instant spring,

When on the maiden's delicate arm
    He hung the heavy golden ring.

I saw the feast of welcome spread,
    While loud he praised his master's LORD;
I heard how well the wooing sped,
    How gentle was the kinsman's word,
Content—since GOD had willed it so,
    That hand and heart the maid hath given,
And when she whispered, "I will go,"
    They blessed her with the wealth of heaven.

Another eve—and Hebron lay
    All flooded with a tender light—
The last tints of a rosy ray
    That lingers somewhere out of sight,—
What time, the long day's labour done,
    Came Isaac from the green well-side
Out in the quiet fields alone
    To meditate at eventide.

He saw afar the dust uprise,
    The camel-driver's song he heard;
But who is she that lifts her eyes,
    Then hides them, like a frightened bird?
A trembling thing with covered face
    Into his mother's tent he led,
And set her there, in Sarah's place,
    And loved her, and was comforted.

Sure such a tale, so sweet, so fair,
    Around our hearts should linger long,
Familiar as a household air,
    And soothing as a cradle song.
And we may learn of their meek ways,
    Their trustful faith in heaven above,
Their calm of unambitious days,
    Their simple truth, and modest love.

§54 Sarah Hale
(1788–1879)

Sarah Hale was born in Newport, New Hampshire, the daughter of Captain Gordon Buell, a revolutionary soldier, and Martha Whittlesey. Hale was educated by her mother and learned Latin and philosophy from her brother who studied at Dartmouth. In 1813, she married Daniel Hale; the Hales had five children before Daniel died in 1822, leaving the family with little to live on. In order to provide for herself and her children, Hale began to write. After publishing a volume of poetry and a novel, she was offered the editorship of a monthly periodical for women, to be established in Boston. She edited the *Ladies' Magazine*, which was later renamed the *Ladies' Book*. She contributed heavily to these periodicals and also published thirty-six books. Hale was involved in many organizations, including societies to send women overseas in medical and missionary service.[13]

Hale's most ambitious undertaking was *Woman's Record: or, Sketches of All Distinguished Women From the Beginning Till A.D. 1850.* This project was one of many attempts by nineteenth-century women to recover the history of women who had been overshadowed or forgotten in histories written by men. For Hale, history began with the Bible, so she included many biblical women in her biographical dictionary of women. In her entry on Rebekah, Hale elevated Rebekah and called her morally superior to her husband, thus contradicting male commentators who censured Rebekah's deception of Isaac. Hale claimed that the Bible did not condemn Rebekah so neither should her readers.

> From Sarah Hale, *Woman's Record; or, Sketches of all Distinguished Women, from the Creation to A.D. 1854* (New York: Harper & Brothers, 1855), 54–55.

–Rebekah–

Daughter of Bethuel, and wife of Isaac the patriarch, is one of the most interesting female characters the Bible exhibits for the example and instruction of her sex. Her betrothal and marriage are graphic pictures of the simple

---

[13] "Hale, Sarah Josepha (Buell)," *American Authors 1600–1900: A Biographical Dictionary of American Literature*, ed. Stanley J. Kunitz and Howard Haycroft (New York: The H. W. Wilson Co., 1938), 326.

customs of her maiden life, and her own heart-devotion to the will of God. No wonder her beauty, modesty and piety, won the love and confidence of Isaac at once. She was his only wife, and thus highly favoured above those who were obliged to share the heart of a husband with hand-maidens and concubines. The plague-spot of polygamy which has polluted even the homes of the chosen of God did not fasten its curse on her bridal tent. So distinguished was this example, that ever since, the young married pair have been admonished to be, as "Isaac and Rebecca, faithful."

The first portion of her history, contained in Genesis, chap. xxiv (a synopsis would mar its beauty) has won for her unqualified approbation; while commentators and divines are almost as unanimous in censuring her later conduct. But is this censure deserved? Let us examine carefully before we venture to condemn what the Bible does not.

This pious couple, who inherited the promises of God, and in whom centred the hopes of the world, were childless for twenty years; when Rebekah's twin sons were born. Before their birth, it had, in some mysterious manner, been revealed to the mother that these sons would be the progenitors of two nations, different from each other, and that the *elder* should serve the *younger*. From their birth the boys were as unlike as though they were of different races. Esau is represented as red, rough, reckless, rebellious; Jacob was fair, gentle, home-loving and obedient; such a son as must have gladdened his mother's heart. But there was a higher and holier motive for her devoted love to this, her youngest son,—*she knew he was the chosen of God.*

"Isaac loved Esau, because he did eat of his venison; but Rebekah loved Jacob;"—that is, she loved him with the holy, disinterested affection which her faith that he was born for a high destiny would inspire. She kept him with her and instructed him in this faith, making him thus aware of the value of the birthright; while Esau, like a young heathen, was passing his life in the hunting-field, caring nothing for the promises made to Abraham; probably scoffing at the mention of such superstitions, he "despised his birthright," and sold it for a mess of pottage.

Next occurs a scene reflecting great honour on the character of Rebekah, as it shows she had the heart-purity which is ever under the holy guardianship of heaven;—we allude to what passed at Gerar. Isaac was there guilty of a cowardly falsehood, and seems to have been forgiven, and great privileges allowed him solely on account of the reverence and admiration felt for his wife. Thus the patriarch prospered exceedingly in consequence of Rebekah's beauty, virtue, and piety; while Esau's perverse disposition manifested itself more and more. And yet, though he grieved the hearts of his parents by uniting himself with idolaters, (marrying two Hittite wives,) still the father's heart clung to this unworthy son—*because he furnished him savoury food!*

Isaac had grown older in constitution than in years; "his eyes were dim so that he could not see;" fearing he might die suddenly, he called Esau, and said to him—"Take, I pray thee, thy weapons, thy quiver and thy bow, and go out to the field, and take me venison; and make me savoury food, such as I love, and bring it to me, that I may eat; that my soul may bless thee before I die." It is worthy of note that Isaac did not allude to any blessing the Lord had promised to his eldest son, nor to any motive, save indulging his own appetite. If Isaac knew that Jacob the younger son had been by God preferred before the elder, did he not purpose committing a great sin, in thus attempting to give the blessing to Esau? And if Isaac did not know the promise made to Rebekah concerning the destiny of her sons, then we must allow the spiritual insight conferred on her devolved also the duty of preventing, if possible, the sin her husband would bring on his own soul by attempting to bless him whom the Lord had not blessed. It is manifest that Rebekah felt the time had come for her to act. If she had entreated her husband to bless the youngest born, he had not listened to her counsel, as Abraham was directed to do when Sarah advised him. We may say Rebekah should have had faith that God would bring to pass what he had ordained; but we cannot know her convictions of the duty devolving on herself. She certainly did not wait the event; but overhearing the directions of Isaac, she immediately took such measures as deceived him, and obtained his blessing for Jacob.

Rebekah must have been either perfectly assured she was working under the righteous inspiration of God, or she was willing to bear the punishment of deceiving her husband rather than allow him to sin by attempting to give the blessing where God had withheld it. That the result was right is certain, because Isaac acknowledged it, when after the deception was made manifest, he said of Jacob—"yea, and he shall be blessed."

When, to avoid the murderous hatred of Esau, Jacob fled from his home, the Lord met him in a wondrous vision, where the promise made to Abraham and to Isaac was expressly confirmed to this cherished son of Rebekah; thus sealing the truth of her belief and the importance of her perseverance; and not a word of reproof appears on the holy page which records her history. She did not live to see her son's triumphant return, nor is the date of her decease given; but she was buried in the family sepulchre at Macpelah; and as Isaac had no second wife, she was doubtless mourned. It has been urged that because her death was not recorded, therefore she had sinned in regard to her son. No mention is made of the death of Deborah, or Ruth, or Esther,—had they sinned?

There are no perfect examples among mankind; but in the comparison of Isaac and Rebekah, the wife is, morally superior to her husband; and appears to have been especially entrusted by God with the agency of changing the succession of her sons, and thus building up the house of Israel. See Genesis, chapters xxvi, xxvii, xxviii.

§55 Susan Warner
(1819–1885)

Susan Warner[14] lived with her sister near West Point and socialized with the American army officers and cadets from that institution. In *Walks from Eden* (1866) she used a family conversation between an uncle and his nieces and nephews to teach her young readers about the opening chapters of Genesis.

Warner paid close attention to geographical, historical and cultural settings, portraying the character of Uncle Sam as an expert in Middle Eastern geography and languages. Uncle Sam described in great detail the exotic people and places he had seen in his travels. He repeatedly described the women of the Middle East as "black-eyed" women; this was likely a coded reference to the race of Rebekah.[15] Warner used Uncle Sam to critique contemporary female culture, using Rebekah's veil as a way into the Woman Question. Warner clearly articulated a prosperity gospel using the authoritative voice of Uncle Sam to affirm that good people always get on in the world. Warner painted a very positive picture of Rebekah as a business woman.

The grandmother's matriarchal voice brought spiritual wisdom and insight to the conversation. She discussed the prayer of Abraham's steward. Warner argued for the authority of the text and faith over reason; the facts recorded in the Bible must be acknowledged to be true even if they do not appear reasonable.

This book was written for children; the voices of the children and young teens in the book allowed younger readers to feel as though they had a voice in the retelling of Rebekah's story. Like Morgan, Warner raised the question of women's roles. Like Alexander, Warner emphasized the historical distance of the story.

From Susan Warner, *Walks from Eden* (New York: Hurst & Co., 1866), 386–410.

---

[14] For more information about Warner see part 1, "Eve—The Mother of Us All."

[15] Mary DeJong, "Dark-Eyed Daughters: Nineteenth-Century Popular Portrayals of Biblical Women," *Women's Studies* 19, no. 314 (1991): 286.

Sep. 20. Isaac's Wife

"We have the twenty-fourth chapter of Genesis to talk about to-day," said Priscilla. "We are getting on."

"We are not getting on very fast," said Liph.

"Fast enough," said Dan.

"There are different ways of getting on," said uncle Sam. "But to-day we have to take a wedding journey. The first wedding we are told of in history. Abraham was growing to be a very old man—towards a hundred and forty years old—and he and his son were left alone by Sarah's death. Isaac took it hard; the loss of his mother was grievous to him; and as soon as time enough had passed, Abraham bethought him to make arrangements for his son's marriage."

"I should think Isaac would have been the one to make the arrangements himself," Liph said.

"Yes, that is American fashion; but we are talking of a very different day and place. And Isaac was very unlike you, Liph. He was not so eager for having his rights. A gentle, docile, affectionate nature his seems to have been; perhaps not very energetic about anything; and just then, it may be, his thoughts were too tenderly full of his lost mother for him to cast up any schemes of happiness for himself. Abraham took the matter in hand, as the custom was.

"Abraham was now in a condition of great prosperity. The Lord had blessed him in all things. He was a mighty man among his fellows. And so it is written, children, 'Blessed is the man that feareth the Lord, that delighteth greatly in his commandments. His seed shall be mighty upon earth; the generation of the upright shall be blessed. Wealth and riches shall be in his house; and his righteousness endureth for ever'" [Ps. 112:1-3].

"But sir," said Liph, "do good people always get on in the world?"

"Always—" said uncle Sam.

"But I am sure they are very poor, often," said Liph.

"'I have been young, and now am old; yet have I not seen the righteous forsaken, nor his seed begging bread'" [Ps. 37:25.]

"Yes, sir; but you were speaking of *prosperity*."

"Liph, remember in the first place the conditions. Then see the promise. The righteous have often troubles—when there is a need for it—but the word will stand. 'Seek ye *first* the kingdom of God and his righteousness, and all these things shall be added unto you' [Matt. 6:33]. That is, provided you do not seek these things first, but the kingdom."

"Godliness hath the promise of the life that now is [1 Tim. 4:8]," my grandmother put in, "as well as of that which is to come."

Liph looked unsatisfied, but my uncle went on.

"Abraham at any rate had prospered. And now he summoned his chief servant, his steward and man of business, and charged him with the matter he had at heart. He was to go and fetch a wife for Isaac. What is more, he was to go all the way to Mesopotamia for her; something as if in these days he had been sent over beyond the Rocky Mountains. And he was ordered to take a most solemn oath that he would not play false in his charge; would not bring to Isaac a girl from one of the Canaanitish nations, which were so much nearer hand and easier to get at; but that he would verily go to Mesopotamia and bring one from among Abraham's own kindred there."

"Why he did not know there was a woman among them that would do," said Priscilla.

"He thought there was," said uncle Sam.

"And I don't see why he wanted one of his own kindred," said Dan. "They were idolaters and Abraham was separated from them."

"It is just like the Arab prejudice and practice now," said my uncle. "Great families especially are very particular about marrying only with their kindred; and even among the common Arabs it is an established rule that a girl's cousin has the first right to her. He may waive it, and she may take another husband; but in that case, or in the other, he will be apt to say scornfully, 'She was my slipper; I have cast her off.'"

"What horrid people!" said Priscilla.

"So you see Abraham was acting precisely as a distinguished sheikh of the present day would act, when he sent his steward into Mesopotamia to choose a wife for his son Isaac. The man made one very sensible objection. 'Peradventure the woman will not be willing to follow me into this land.' It seemed a very possible case. Here was a long, dangerous journey to be taken, and an unknown home to be invited to; and the only person to invite her, an old man of business of her proposed father-in-law; very respectable, no doubt, and even dignified, as I dare say he was; but still nobody that could guaranty her what sort of a husband or what sort of a fortune in life she was coming to."

"Isaac ought to have gone himself," said Liph.

"The old servant thought that would be more promising. But Abraham forbade. 'Beware that thou bring not my son thither again.' Isaac might be enticed to stay there, and then what would become of his birthright. And now came out another instance of Abraham's beautiful, simple, trustful faith. 'The Lord God of heaven, which took me from my father's house, and from the land of my kindred, and which spake unto me, and that sware unto me, saying, Unto thy seed will I give this land; he shall send his angel before thee, and thou shalt take a wife to my son from thence.' Children, there is no way of doing business like that, which those know who in all their dealings serve the Lord!—in all their ways acknowledge him. Look how sure Abraham was. He knew Isaac must not go back into that land; knew too that he must not take a wife of the wicked and cursed Cannanitish nations; so to his servant's objection he answers quietly—'the Lord will send his angel before thee, and it will be all right. If it is not, then you are quit of your oath.'"

"But, uncle Sam, do you think the Lord sends an angel before people now?"

"Tiny, do you remember that Jesus Christ is the same yesterday, to-day, and forever? That means, that he does not change. 'The angel of the Lord encampeth round about them that fear him, and delivereth them' [Ps. 34:7]. What do you think of that? '*Encampeth round about them*.' And then, 'He shall give his angels charge over thee, to keep thee in all thy ways' [Ps. 91:11]. That is, of course, if you trust God as Abraham trusted. 'In all thy ways acknowledge him, and *he shall direct thy paths*'" [Prov. 3:6].

"Abraham's servant seems to have had faith too," said Dan.

"Yes. And well he might. He was satisfied now; he took the oath required of him, and set about the preparations for his journey."

"It seems odd, to leave all that to a servant," said Priscilla.

"Not a servant like a footman or a butler, Prissy. Great men in those times were accustomed to have a trusted steward or overseer, in whose care their whole business was left. Joseph was such a servant to Potiphar; his master knew nothing about his affairs, beyond the meals that he ate every day. Joseph afterwards had such a steward of his own. Now this man, Eliezer,[16] if it was Eliezer, had all Abraham's goods in his hand; he did what he thought right; and he knew what to do. It was necessary to go with such an outfit as should prove what kind of a man Abraham was in the world's estimation; it was needful to show tokens of his master's prosperity and carry what would honour his own mission. He took ten camels for the journey; some of them were for riding, for his own and his servants' use and to bring back the wished-for lady and her attendants; the others were laden with provisions and with rare and costly things for presents; ornaments of gold and silver; rich dresses; and probably spices and southern fruits. Less than ten camels would not be taken for such an expedition now, in such a family."

"I should think ten would not have been enough," said Liph. "Why the provisions would have been a great deal."

"And I should think they might have taken horses or mules for riding," said Priscilla. "I thought camels were so disagreeable to ride."

"In the first place, Liph, a fine camel will carry a load of three or four hundred pounds. A good deal of value, do you see, in gold and spices, might go

---

[16] Many women assumed that Abraham's steward Eliezer (see Gen.15:2) was the servant Abraham entrusted with finding a wife for Isaac.

on the back of a single one. And secondly, it was not needful to take much in the way of food for the journey, for that might be had in great part by the way. No; ten camels were enough. And my dear Prissy, in the desert tract between Aleppo and Haran camels were the most convenient animals for the journey, if not the only ones. Horses must have plenty of water and plenty of grass or corn; and it would be far less easy to provide them with both during those nine days. Nobody would go from Hebron now upon the same expedition with any other beasts but camels."

"Horses would not carry much," said Liph; "and they would want camels to take along food enough for them. Horses would not do."

"Well, with his camels and goods the servant departed, 'and arose and went to Mesopotamia, unto the city of Nahor.' The Bible tells it in few words. But let us look at the line of travel he and his ten camels followed. First up through Palestine, round by the west side of the lakes, and then into this beautiful valley called the Bukaa. Look here, children; on this side of Palestine, following the range of the coast, is the long mountain line of Lebanon—*Jebel Libnan*, the Arabs call it. A little east, you see here is another mountain line; this is Anti-Lebanon; or as the Arabs have it, *Jebel-esh-Shurley*—the east mountain. Hermon is the southernmost peak of this line. Between the two, do you see, there is a long valley, stretching northeast and southwest. This is what used to be called Coele-Syria. It is the corn field of northern Palestine. Through the lower portion of it runs the Litany, the largest river of Syria; and through the upper lies the bed of the Orontes. The one runs to the south and the other to the north; and this upper portion watered by the Orontes is the old kingdom of Hamath. The Hamathite, you know, was one of the descendants of Canaan. Up through this rich valley the ten camels would have an easy time; then through Hamath onto Aleppo; from thence across to the Euphrates; and then they would be in Mesopotamia, and two days from the city of Nahor. Abraham's brother was so considerable a man that the place was known as his place. And we do not know much more about it."

"Don't you know anything about it, uncle Sam?"

"Very little. It was a famous place too in olden time; famous down into Roman times, as a city devoted to the worship of the Moon goddess. The defeat of Crassus happened there too, boys. Yet we know nothing about it, except its wells. The caravan routes fork off from it, or used to do so, towards the different fords of the Tigris on the east and the Euphrates on the west; so it must have been a place of business and importance as a meeting point for them. But when we think of Haran, we do not think of that, nor of Crassus, nor of the worship of the moon; but we remember that well of water outside the city beside which Abraham's servant made his camels kneel down. It was evening when they got there; the day was drawing to a close; they stopped at the well; and there in something like Abraham's faith, Abraham's servant made his camels kneel down, and prayed for direction and that the Lord would give him good speed."

"Why did the camels kneel down?" Priscilla asked.

"Don't you know any more about camels than that?" said Liph.

"Why did they, then?" said uncle Sam.

"Why sir, they have callous places on their knees and breast, just where they touch the ground in kneeling."

"And therefore they kneel?" said my uncle. "Well Liph—that is not very clear; but the fact is, that kneeling is the natural posture of repose for the camel; and as you say, he has special provision made for taking it with comfort." . . .

"Well, we don't get on with our wedding journey," said Priscilla. "The ten camels were kneeling around the well. How little Rebecca thought what she was coming to, when she came out that night."

"Most true," said my uncle. "It was the time when the women who draw water go forth, as the Hebrew reads; so Rebecca was on her way from the city as usual, with her pitcher on her shoulder. The whole story is perfectly Eastern. Among the Arabs, as I have told you, it is only the women that draw the water. I have seen them myself hundreds of times at the wells and fountains near the villages in Syria, coming with their jars or water-skins and bearing them away on their heads or their shoulders. Where flocks were watered, I have seen men helping them."

". . . To the fountain all the women of the village come forth at eventide; and Eliezer, if it was he, knew what he was about when he halted his camels there."

"And still better he knew what he was about," said my grandmother, "when he made his prayer. 'O Lord God of my master Abraham, I pray thee, shew me good speed this day, and shew kindness unto my master Abraham. Behold, I stand here by the well of water; and the daughters of the men of the city come out to draw water: and let it come to pass, that the damsel to whom I shall say, Let down thy pitcher, I pray thee, that I may drink; and she shall say, Drink, and I will give thy camels drink also; let the same be she that thou hast appointed for thy servant Isaac.'"

"And before he had done speaking," my uncle went on, "a very fair and beautiful girl came out from the city towards the well, with her pitcher upon her shoulder; she was nobody else but Nahor's granddaughter, coming like others for water, though she belonged to the greatest family in the city. And no doubt the old servant watched her, and noted her beauty and grace, and the superior quality of her dress and appearance, as she went down to the well and filled her pitcher; and I dare say it was with a good wish in his heart that he ran to meet her—perhaps he had forgotten himself looking and thinking—and asked her to give him a little water out of her pitcher—a 'sip,' he asked for."

"Then he knew," said Dan.

"Quickly the polite answer came—'Drink, my lord'—and the pitcher was let down on the hand; and then as the old man put his lips to the water, the damsel's black eye noted his stranger's dress and his following of men and camels, and in the true spirit of hospitality she added, 'I will draw water for thy camels also, until they have done drinking.' She was an energetic little lady that, no sooner said than done, she emptied her pitcher into the trough, and ran to the well and filled it again, and filled it and emptied it until the camels had done. And the man wondering at her held his peace, till he should know whether he had got indeed the sign that he had asked for from the Lord."

"But I have got a question to ask," said Priscilla.

"And so have I," said Liph.

"Come on," said my uncle. "Let us have them."

"Why did she go *down* to the well?" said Priscilla. "How could she?"

"The only way to got her pitcher filled," said my uncle. "There were steps at the side or at the corner of the well, leading down to the water; Rebecca went down the steps, dipped in her pitcher, or dropped it in with a piece of rope, and so filled it. Where the water is far down and cannot be reached in that way, there are no steps, but a rope is let down from the top with a bucket, often a skin bucket, and drawn up over the curb stone. Round the mouth of the well, I should have told you, is built a low wall or parapet, to prevent accidents; and in some old wells the stone coping of this wall is worn into grooves—fluted—by the long wear of ropes drawn back and forth over it. At Beersheba it is so. In some places an ass or ox is employed to pull up the rope; and sometimes a pulley or a wheel is used to help."

"But I have another question," said Priscilla, "Eliezer prayed that the damsel that gave him that sign—now the boys will laugh at me if I go on."

"Never mind," said my uncle. "Let them laugh."

"The words are: 'Let the same be she that thou hast appointed.' Uncle Sam, do you think it is *appointed* who people shall marry?"

The boys did laugh, and uncle Sam too a little. But he answered soberly enough.

"I have no sort of doubt of it, Prissy, my dear. But very often indeed, not the individuals they do marry. I mean this, my dear. In this matter, as in every other, if we will humbly seek and follow the Lord's guidance, we shall have it. 'In all thy ways acknowledge him, and *he shall direct thy paths*' [Prov. 3:6]. For want of doing that, people miss the good that is really appointed for them, in various lines, and get into great scrapes."

"Uncle Sam," put in Liph, "What I want to know is how Rebecca came to say that?"

"What, 'drink, my lord, and I will give thy camels drink also?' How came she to say it? Out of her own free wit and will. Then how was it the Lord's sign to his servant? I do not know, Liph, any more than you do. Only we must take the facts of the Bible just as we find them; and in this matter submit to be children together before the Lord. If we do not, depend upon it we shall become fools."

"Uncle Sam, how do you know that Rebecca had black eyes?"

"That's a nice question, Tiny! Why, my dear, they all have. Big, handsome, black eyes, and keen too; and Rebecca was not the least sharp of her family. She was a woman of business, that was!"

"Eliezer was not a lord," Priscilla remarked.

"No, but Rebecca's calling him so was merely politeness. Her very words are the same that are used now in those regions to any respectable traveller that makes the same request that Eliezer did. '*Ishrub ya seedy.*' That is it."

"Will they be as hospitable now as Rebecca was, and water your camels too?" Dan asked.

"Never, within my knowledge. I have found it hard enough to get that service done for my horse when I was willing to pay for it. That was the Lord's sign. Yet Eliezer did not feel quite sure that he had found what he sought, till he heard something further. As the camels had done drinking, he took out of his packages some fine golden ornaments, far richer than were usually seen, and putting them on the girl's hands, asked whose daughter she was, and whether he and his troop could be accommodated at her father's house for the night. And then came the answer he wanted—'I am the daughter of Bethuel, the son of Milcah, which she bare unto Nahor.' 'And the man bowed down his head and worshipped the Lord. And he said, Blessed be the Lord God of my master Abraham. . . . I being in the way, the Lord led me to the house of my master's brethren.'"

"Why didn't he give her two earrings?" said Priscilla.

"Because, I fancy, he did not give her one. The word should be translated 'nose-ring,' as only one is spoken of. The Bedouin women wear all sorts of rings, and in their noses as well as on their fingers sometimes little, sometimes big. There is one kind three inches in diameter. You must imagine such a gold ring depending beneath Rebecca's black eyes, and just showing her pretty mouth within its circle."

"Uncle Sam, that is very ugly."

"She did not think so, nor Isaac neither. The Bedouins care little about dress in their own persons, but they like to have the ladies of their family make a good appearance. They think it is an honour to themselves."

"But, Uncle Sam," said I, "that was a queer time for her to put on such ornaments, when she was going with her pitcher from the well."

"Little Tiny, that is another of your American notions. An Arab woman thinks there is no reason why she should not be handsomely dressed at one time as well as at another; and really I do not know what reason there is." . . .

"Uncle Sam," said Priscilla, "why does it say that Rebecca ran and told them of her mother's house? why not her father's house?"

"Eastern again, Prissy. Her mother's children were all of her father's house that she cared particularly about, or that cared particularly about her; Bethuel might have other wives and other families of children, you know. Rebecca went to her own; and her careful brother Laban took up the matter. It was very plain to him, from the richness of the jewels that Eliezer had adorned his sister with, that this stranger was a man to be honoured. He ran out to find him where Rebecca had left him by the well. 'Come in, thou blessed of the Lord; wherefore standest thou without? for I have prepared the house, and room for the camels.' So he brought him in."

"But it sounds as if the camels came in too, I think. We should prepare the barn," said Daniel.

"I presume the camels did come in. Barns are a Western institution. It is usual enough to lodge in the same room with the camels, in those regions; and children are often put to sleep in a manger, after it has been cleaned and whitewashed. Yes, they all came in; and Laban engirded the camels and gave them straw, with barley or some other grain mixed with it. At least that is the way cattle are fed there now; hay is not known. And the usual kindness was shewn to Eliezer and the men that were with him, in washing their feet and preparing food for them; but he was a faithful servant. 'I will not eat,' he said, 'until I have told mine errand.' Laban was all expectation; and Eliezer went on to declare the whole story, what he was there for and how he had been led. 'Then Laban and Bethuel answered and said, The thing proceedeth from the Lord: we cannot speak unto thee bad or good. Behold, Rebecca is before thee, take her, and go.'"

"I should think they might have asked Rebecca what she thought about it," Priscilla said.

"That is not the way things are done. The lady's friends settle the matter for her; the father, if he is living, or the brother, if she have no father. Her consent may possibly be asked, but it is not at all needful. In like manner, it is not always the bridegroom who chooses the bride; his parents or some friend whom he appoints may manage even that matter for him; and at any rate conduct the arrangements after the bride has been fixed upon. So Hagar, you remember, took a wife for her son out of Egypt [Gen. 21:21]; and here Abraham sends Eliezer. However, after the lady is found and her friends have consented, the next thing is the espousal; that is a formal engagement, made with presents to the bride and her friends. Presents are a necessary part of the ceremony; so much so, that the word which means 'to betroth,' means literally, 'to make a present.' Eliezer understood all that, you see; as soon as Bethuel and his forward son Laban had given their consent, he brought out his gifts; rich and costly dresses and ornaments of gold and silver for the bride, and for her mother and brother other precious things; what, we do not know. The word may mean a great variety of things, rare fruits and plants, or delicacies; or dresses and jewels, somewhat less valuable than those given to the bride herself."

"Is that the purchase-money of the lady?" my grandmother asked.

"Not in those old times. The women were not bought and sold then. Now they are, in Syria, by Turks, Jews and Christians; bought and paid for according to the rank of the lady's father. But the Bedouins would think it a disgrace if a man were to take a price for his daughter. In one tribe it is customary for the father to receive the gifts made to the bride—the 'five articles,' as they are called; but they go to her and are her property. The 'five articles' mean, a large nose-ring of silver, a silver chain for the neck, silver bracelets, a carpet, and a camel-bag of Bagdad carpet work."

"Rebecca had a great deal more than that," said Priscilla.

"Everybody was satisfied. So then Eliezer was feasted, and Rebecca and her mother, we may suppose, in the women's apartments, were very busy over her dower—that is, these wedding gifts—and her proposed journey and her prospects. It was usual to let a little time go by between the day of the espousals and the day of the wedding. But when the morning was come, Abraham's servant demanded to be let go, that he might return to his master; he and Rebecca. Laban and her mother pleaded for ten days at least; perhaps the crafty fellow meditated some trick or cheatery to get more advantage to himself; but Eliezer was firm to his demand. 'Hinder me not, seeing the Lord hath prospered my way.' Then they called Rebecca. Would she start off, at one day's notice, and leave her old home for a new one? But Rebecca was never wanting in pluck; and she had made up her mind upon those gold bracelets and things, and that gold jewel banging over her upper lip. So she said, 'I will go.' The thing was done. They sent her away with her nurse, on the camels provided for her. Now children, the Bible tells us nothing about the journey; how they went and where they stopped, and what they did by the way. We can only imagine how the little caravan went back by the road it had come, across the desert to Aleppo; [here Warner describes the journey]. A wonderful journey it must have been to the Mesopotamian girl, who had never been far from the plains of Haran before. And we know without being told, what good care Eliezer took of his charge, and how he provided all things for her comfort by day and by night; and what nice stopping places he arranged."

"It must have been a terrible long journey for her," said Priscilla.

"Down through the whole length of Palestine; . . .. And past Beersheba too, further south; for Isaac dwelt at the well Lahai-roi, the same where Hagar had rested on her flight into Egypt and had been turned back. Isaac's home was there now. And this we know; it was getting towards evening when the camels were at last coming near home. The sunlight was slanting in long beams over the grass and the flowers of those rolling downs; lighting up herds of camels and flocks of sheep coming to be watered. The tents of the encampment would be seen from a distance, spotting a large space with their black curtains. Rebecca could look from afar and see what sort of a home she was coming to; and she was enough of a business woman to count the flocks and measure the herds with her eye, and guess what a rich man her husband was. Then, before they got quite home, she spied a solitary man, not busy with the cattle or anything else, but seemingly walking out for his pleasure, and then walking towards the camels. 'What man is this that walketh in the field to meet us?' she asked Eliezer. And he answered, 'It is my master.' Would you have done then what she did, Prissy? She lighted down from off her camel."

"What for?"

"To shew respect to Isaac."

"I think she was very particular," said Prissy.

"No doubt, and Isaac liked her for it. She covered herself with a veil too."

"What was that for?" Dan asked.

"A veil was part of the Eastern wedding attire, and has been for ages. Perhaps it was so then, and I suppose it was. She had been unveiled before; now, you see, she covered herself. The great veil, covering not only the face but the whole figure, was said to be a token of the wife's subjection to her husband. Nobody else; had a right to even look at her, unless he pleased."

"I think that would be a very poor custom," said Priscilla.

"I should not like our ladies to go veiled," said uncle Sam; "but a little of the principle I think would not be out of place. 'That women adorn themselves in modest apparel, with shame-facedness and sobriety.' [1 Tim. 2:9] But neither were the ladies in those times veiled all the while, as they are in the streets of Syria now; the veil was a wedding veil. 'And the servant told Isaac all things that he had done;' and Rebecca stood by, I suppose, in her veil, while the story was told. Then Isaac led her to his mother's tent; the tent which had stood empty for three years; he gave her the chief place, and she became his wife; the lady of the encampment. After that, it says, Isaac was comforted for the loss of his mother. And there you see what a deep, gentle, affectionate nature belonged to him; and also, Prissy, that there must have been some good in Sarah. Three years, and Isaac had mourned for her yet, and was not comforted. Until now at last he gave his love to his pretty young wife."

§56 Etty Woosnam
(1849–c.1883)

Etty Woosnam[17] was a member of a British family with ties to India. She wrote to prepare young women for their future vocations as Christian women, wives, and mothers. Woosnam's interpretation of Rebekah testified to the tensions among women regarding changes in women's education and in their own understanding of their place and behavior in society. Unlike Morgan, who saw Rebekah as an oppressed woman, Woosnam held up Rebekah as an example for her readers. Like King, she used the story as a platform for teaching moral and religious lessons. In a unique interpretive move that reflected her high view of women's responsibility for the spiritual and moral climate in a family, Woosnam blamed the wife-sister incidents on women rather than on men.

From the story of Rebekah, Woosnam developed ideas about divine guidance and the need for both faith and reason in making decisions, especially for young women whose lives she viewed as being more uncertain than those of men. She was ambivalent about the key hermeneutical question around divine guidance in the life of Rebekah. Woosnam argued that it was possible that Rebekah was led by God to deceive her husband, but it was not clear. Woosnam did not dwell on negative aspects of the story. She minimized both the problem of Rebekah's partiality and the distance between her readers and the world of the text.

Woosnam also used a typological approach to find a deeper spiritual meaning in this story. She shifted the traditional understanding of Isaac and Rebekah as a type of Christ and the Church to a more individualized understanding of Christ and the individual believer.

From Etty Woosnam, *The Woman of the Bible: Old Testament* (London: S. W. Partridge, 1881), 52–64.

–Rebekah: Divine Guidance–

In studying the inspired sketches of women, there is one thing very clear—we must not wait to learn lessons from them until we can find faultless models. Just as, in our observation of our fellow-creatures, we see much that we may

---

[17] For more information on Woosnam see part 1, "Eve—The Mother Of Us All."

copy and admire in those who in other respects are far from perfect. By all means let us glean profit wherever we can; and after we have tried to imitate the salient good point in each of our friends and acquaintances, we shall still see much that is amiss in our own lives. We can take no Scripture character, man or woman, for a perfect pattern, except our Blessed Lord Himself. But some feminine virtue we often find very beautifully exemplified and illustrated by the very woman whose faults surprise us; as in Rebekah's case.

In the twenty-fourth chapter of Genesis, at her meeting with Isaac's servant at the well, her ready kindliness and maiden grace are worthy of all honour: so also the modesty with which she first met Isaac. He was meditating in the field at eventide. She was told who it was, and "she lighted off the camel and took a veil and covered herself." It is a most becoming virtue in women—this modesty, and in all ages of the world appears to have been much admired by men. Strange it is that in the present advanced state of the world—in which women have more liberty than they ever possessed before and more educational advantages—in which they are altogether placed on a higher footing—strange that they should try early in life to throw off their natural sensitiveness, and to conceal as far as they can the shyness and modesty which they really do feel, till they have soon got rid of the sensation and the virtue together. A great many, too many young English women have loud voices and noisy manners, and are quite willing to be considered independent and uncontrolled, and are at no pains to conceal their emotions. . . . What a grievous pity it is that the very words "The Girl of the Period"[18] present to our minds so very unattractive and unwomanly a picture! Does it seem out of place to speak of these faults of the age to thoughtful young women anxious to follow Christ and to please God? It may be useful even to Christian girls to remind them to be vigilant in this respect, and to exercise carefully both the inward reality as well as the outward show of modesty and decorum. . . .

Rebekah, then, was modest. But she was deceitful. The first occasion was when in Gerar she pretended to be Isaac's sister (Genesis xxvi. 7) just as Sarah had pretended to be Abraham's and for the same supposed purpose of preserving her husband's life. The second occasion was when she not only recommended but urged Jacob to supplant his elder brother Esau and to get the father's blessing. To us it seems base treachery to Isaac in his old age, when rendered helpless by his blindness and infirmities. It may be that God disapproved of the trick and showed His displeasure by permitting Jacob afterwards to be himself deceived by Laban, then by his ten sons, till their cruel artifices crushed his tender heart and brought down his grey hairs with sorrow to the grave. God has often dealt in this way, punishing people with

[18] See E. L. Linton, *The Girl of the Period* (Bristol: R. W. Bingham, 1868).

the very weapons which they had used against others. Some commentators think, however, that she had had God's will respecting her two sons specially revealed to her, and that she was only doing His bidding and carrying out His unalterable purposes in bestowing the birthright on the younger. It may be so. But whether she pleased God by her action or not, she certainly was the instrument used by Him in furtherance of His great designs, and she probably understood the future destiny of Jacob and his descendants in some sense in which others did not. It may be that this comprehension was given to her as a special favour. In all other respects she implicitly followed God's leading, and it is written: "The secret of the Lord is with them that fear Him and He will show them His covenant" [Ps. 25:14]. . . .

The character of Rebekah is not very fully explained. What is most astonishing is that the seeking for a bride for Isaac should be related so minutely and at such length. This is an incident of Eastern pastoral life as poetical as it is true to nature, and we cannot but be touched with its details and their simplicity. Can anything be more graphic than the whole scene? A fresh and beautiful maiden—modest yet free from self-consciousness—not coming forward to push her services and yet obliging and courteous to an unknown servant—bounding with alacrity, good humour, and the graceful ease of youth and physical health—hospitable and dignified—going down to the well and drawing water as usual without particularly noticing the stranger. Then his asking her for "a little water out of her pitcher," and her ready willingness to minister to him. "She hasted and let down her pitcher upon her hand and gave him to drink." It costs us no effort to picture the attitude of the girl, and we can almost hear the respectful, girlish tones of her voice saying, "Drink my lord;" and when he had finished a refreshing draught: "I will draw water for thy camels also until they have done drinking."—And backwards and forwards she ran filling her pitcher down in the well and emptying it into the drinking trough to water the camels. She intent on doing the business that her hand had found to do, and the man sitting there "wondering at her," thinking not so much of admiring the fair face and form of the young girl before him, nor of the womanly enthusiasm she showed in making herself useful, as he thought of his errand. . . .

All that Rebekah was every young woman ought to be, no matter of what country or born in what station of life—modest, courteous, accustomed to domestic work and manual labour, willing to oblige and befriend any one standing in need of assistance, thankful to do all the good she can in any way she can, a pure mind in a pure body, active, strong, and self-forgetful. . . .

It seems as if this page were specially written for the benefit of young women, to whom in a definite and marked manner God's dispensations generally come.

For women have less to do with shaping their own education, their own career, or determining their own work and destiny, than young men. They often have little or no idea what their occupation will be, and are in some perplexity in girlhood as to the best use to make of their time to fit them for the unknown exigencies they will have to meet, the unknown burdens they will have to bear, the unknown interests and duties in which they will be engaged. A man commonly has some difficult vocation to prepare for, or he ought to have: and though he too must wait upon the Lord for instruction as to what course to take, yet there is more special need for the patient looking unto God for guidance in "those pale virgin lives that wait and pray." It is a happy circumstance for a girl when she is shown early in life the work God would have her to do—whether she is to earn her own livelihood, or to be the comfort of the old home, or to teach children, or to marry, or to spend her days in kindly ministrations to friends and relations. There is something about the very uncertainty of a woman's life which gives it a strange fascination, but which is extremely trying to some dispositions. Think, in the first place, that God knows it all and sends it all. He who permitted His servant Moses to dwell so fully on the minute details of Rebekah's story and Sarah's story, enters into every feeling and want we have, and has pledged Himself to provide for our spiritual, intellectual, and moral necessities as amply as for our bodily ones. "My God shall supply all your need" [Phil. 4:19].

How suddenly the change comes into some lives! One evening Rebekah goes out as she has done every day for months, perhaps years past, to draw water. . . . At the next sunset she is preparing to set out on a journey to the "south country" where Isaac dwelt—to a strange place and an unknown husband. But God had opened "a plain path" [Ps. 27:11] before her and guided her to believe in the protection and love offered to her, and when they had asked her, "Wilt thou go with this man?" she had said, "I will go." There would be more happy marriages than there are if God's leading and choice were thought of in all cases, and as earnestly sought as in this of Isaac's servant.

But every circumstance of life is of vast importance; the school to which we are sent, the bosom friend we make there, the accomplishment for which we develop a taste, the acquaintances with whom we go to stay, the church and ministry we attend—all these seem trivial things, but the results to us are of great moment. For they mould the character which is to mark us, and individualize us through this world and into the life beyond. . . .

When you really want to do what is God's will and not to be led by your own inclination or prejudiced understanding at all—first kneel down and ask God to fulfil the promise "I will instruct thee and teach thee in the way which thou shalt go, I will guide thee with Mine eye" [Ps. 32:8]. Then sit down quietly alone and consider. God has given you judgment and reasoning powers, and these talents are not to be laid up in a napkin, but used; and you have asked the Holy Spirit to influence you. After weighing the matter come to a decision and straightway follow your judgment and your conscience. . . .

If a man cannot direct his steps, I am sure a woman, who is a doubly dependent being, needs all the more a guide to protect her through the world. Though the road is narrow that leads to everlasting life, it is not too narrow for Jesus Christ to walk with us and lead us by His right hand "In all thy ways acknowledge Him and, He shall direct thy paths" [Prov. 3:6].

The marriage of Isaac and Rebekah has always been regarded as a type of the spiritual union of Christ and His bride the Church. How far it falls short of being a complete one! Each of the Old Testament foreshadowings serves only to allegorize one or two points connected with the glorious scheme of Redemption. All the sacrifices and offerings together but faintly typify the Cross. We read that Rebekah became Isaac's wife and "he loved her." But Christ loved the Church and gave Himself for it.

When Abraham's servant said: "Peradventure the woman will not be willing to follow me," and asked if his young master should go and fetch her, he was told that Isaac could on no account go. What a feeble symbol of the mighty love and pity which led the Lord of glory to come into this world to save the Church and exalt her to His own right hand, that she through His poverty might be rich [2 Cor. 8:9].

The Church is not sought collectively. To each individual sinner Christ calls: "Come unto Me all ye that labour and are heavy laden, and I will give you rest," [Matt. 11:28] To each disciple He said: "Follow Me."[19] Have we replied with readiness, "I will go," as Rebekah did?

"He calleth His own sheep by name." [John 10:3]

As to Rebekah were given bracelets and earrings, so Christ has many pledges of His love to us here—sweet peace in trusting in Him, and joy in serving Him, as an earnest of the fuller blessedness we shall taste beyond if we follow Him. Hearken, O daughter, and consider and incline thine ear; forget also thine own people and thy father's house. So shall the King greatly desire thy beauty, for He is thy Lord, and worship thou Him [Ps. 45:10-11]. Jesus does desire our heart, and He will clothe us with the garments of salvation and cover us with the robe of righteousness [Isa. 61:10]. He will provide our fitness as well as our title. He will lead us safely through this life, through the valley of the shadow of death [Ps. 23:4], and into the golden gates of His

---

[19] "Follow Me" occurs often in the gospels, including Matthew 4:9, Matthew 9:9, Mark 8:34, and many other places.

Heavenly Kingdom, and then we shall follow the Lamb whithersoever He goeth [Rev. 14:4].

§57 Elizabeth Julia Hasell
(1830–1887)

Elizabeth Julia Hasell was the second daughter of Edward Williams Hasell (1796–1872) and his wife, Dorothea King. The Hasells were a wealthy family with large estates. Hasell was educated at home and taught herself Latin, Greek, Italian, German, Spanish, and Portuguese. She published numerous essays and reviews, demonstrating her expertise in classical and contemporary literature. She was also well read in theology and wrote a number of devotional works including *The Rock; and other short lectures on passages of Holy Scripture* (1867); *Bible Partings* (1883); *Short Family Prayers* (1884); *Via Crucis; or, Meditations for passion and Easter tide* (1884). In addition to her studies and writing, Hasell promoted education and worked for the welfare of those on her family's estates and in the district. She walked long distances to teach, often giving extempore addresses.[20]

Hasell's book *Bible Partings* consisted of essays that were originally published in the *Day of Rest* between 1845 and 1847. These essays focus on the theme of parting; the separation of Rebekah and Jacob narrated in Genesis 27 provided the focus for the selection reproduced here. Hasell struggled with the deceitful means Rebekah used to gain the promised end of Isaac's blessing on Jacob, invoking the notion of progressive morality to account for differences in the ethical standards between what she read in the text and her nineteenth-century context. Hasell examined two cases of Rebekah using the wrong means to gain a good end: the deception of Isaac so that he blessed Jacob, and the argument that Jacob needed to leave home to find a wife rather than admitting he needed protection from his angry brother. As well, Hasell noted that Rebekah did not pray or bless Jacob on their parting as Isaac did, inferring from this that Rebekah was out of favor with God.

Like Aguilar, Hasell drew parallels between Eve and Rebekah. The curse both women received was most fully realized in their children. The happiness or unhappiness of both women as mothers was found in the happiness or unhappiness of their children. This idea assumed women's power and responsi-

[20] Source: Norman Moore, "Hasell, Elizabeth Julia," in *The Oxford Dictionary of National Biography*, ed. H. C. G. Matthew and Brian Harrison, vol. 25 (Oxford: Oxford University Press, 2004), 703.

bility in their family. At the same time it placed guilt for the failure of children on the heads of mothers. Hasell also compared the relationship of Rebekah and Jacob with that of Mary and Jesus. Jesus was Hasell's final example for her readers, rather than Jacob.

From E. J. Hasell, *Bible Partings* (Edinburgh: W. Blackwood & Sons, 1883), 10–20.

–Rebekah and Jacob–
(Genesis xxvii)

NEVER did the failure of any design cause greater sorrow than that which was brought to Rebekah by the success of her clever plan to secure her husband's blessing for her favourite son Jacob. Nor can this surprise us when we consider that her plan, clever as it might be, was a sinful one. Not that Rebekah (in the main, doubtless, a holy woman) sinned in desiring Isaac's blessing for Jacob; for she knew, from God's word of promise before his birth, that her younger son had a greater destiny than his elder brother. She knew, likewise, that Esau's thoughtless sale of his birthright to Jacob had given the latter a right to receive the blessing of the first-born from his father. Thus the end which she had in view was in itself a lawful one: it was in the means by which she gained that end that she transgressed. The right course would have been to bid Jacob claim the blessing for himself, with a frank and truthful statement of his grounds for expecting it; while his mother prayed earnestly to God to direct her husband aright in the matter. But, alas! Rebekah allowed herself to choose a crooked path, which looked smoother at the outset than the straight-forward road of truthfulness. No doubt she thought that she was acting for the best; that it was both kind and prudent to avoid grieving her husband, as he lay on what seemed his deathbed, by pointing out the injustice which his love for Esau was leading him to commit; and that, after all, there could be no great harm in avoiding a family quarrel by sending Jacob to steal what in point of fact belonged to himself. So she got Jacob to personate Esau to his blind father,—a false part, the acting of which could only be carried on by the utterance of lie upon lie; and so small were her misgivings as to using all her authority as a mother in order to make her son take this wrong course, that she did not hesitate to offer to let any harm it might bring come upon her own head.

Now in thus accepting the devil's help in order to obtain an end which she ought to have trusted God to accomplish for her in His own good time, Rebekah unquestionably showed a sad want of faith, and incurred the condemnation pronounced in after-times by an apostle upon those who say, "Let us do evil that good may come" [Rom. 3:8]. Her offence may indeed have been of less deep a dye than would mark the like sin if committed now in days of light far exceeding that by which men dimly discerned right and wrong in the early patriarchal times; but the thing which she did evidently displeased the Lord, and she suffered (in this life) the penalty of distrusting His goodness and dishonouring His truth.

And this punishment befell her by means of the very success of her own scheme. Jacob indeed obtained the blessing, which was his by right. Esau, punished by means of another's sin for his own earlier sin in "despising his birthright," "lifted up his voice and wept" in vain; while Isaac, even though his heart was wrung by his favourite son's "great and exceeding bitter cry," owned God's overruling hand, declined to reverse his words to Jacob, and solemnly pronounced, "I have blessed him; yea, and he shall be blessed." But what joy could all this bring Rebekah, when she found herself, as she soon did, obliged in consequence to part with her beloved Jacob for an uncertain period? For Esau threatened to kill him; and his mother saw no safety for him except in her far-distant brother's house.

True to her character, she once more gains her end by indirect means. Her fear of Jacob's marrying a heathen wife, as his brother had done, is the only reason which she mentions to her husband for sending their son away. To Isaac it seems a sufficient one; and, with a solemnly repeated blessing, he dismisses Jacob to find a bride in his uncle Laban's house. But with her favourite child himself Rebekah uses no such concealment. To him she discloses the anguish of her spirit, and owns the full extent of the mischief which her fatal device has wrought. Rashly had Rebekah spoken when, in her eagerness to persuade Jacob to do her bidding, she had exclaimed, "Upon me be thy curse, my son: only obey my voice;" and now she sees that she has been taken at her word, and that the curse has indeed come upon her. Her children hopelessly estranged—one son a murderer in intention, the other banished from the home he loved so well for a time of which the end could not be foreseen,—what bitter fruits were these to gather off the tree which Rebekah had so rejoiced to plant!

It does not seem that Jacob added to her grief by upbraiding his mother with the bad effects of her evil counsel. Doubtless he felt that equal blame rested on himself for following it. And so they parted in sorrow,—and a sorrow uncheered by a good conscience, for it was one which they had brought upon themselves; unalleviated by trust in a heavenly Father's favour, for both were oppressed by a sense of guilt. And thus (so far as the sacred record tells us) Rebekah dared not commend the son whom she had led into sin to the mercy of the God whom they had jointly offended. The sacred name does not pass her lips in her parting words to Jacob. . . .

Jacob's punishment, and its good effects upon himself, have often formed the theme of useful discourses and meditations. Rebekah's punishment is inferred from, not described in, Scripture—neither are its effects; but from the severity of her chastisement, we are warranted in hoping that to her, as to her son, according to God's merciful purpose, "it afterwards yielded the peaceable fruit of righteousness" [Heb. 12:11]. For hers would seem to have been the heart-sickness of "hope deferred" [Prov. 13:12]—the longing for a face she was never again to see in this life. Whether so long as she lived Esau's wrath never abated, so as to make it safe to send for Jacob,—or whether (her desire overcoming her prudence) she sent, but her messenger failed to reach him, we know not. But in whatever way it happened, Rebekah seems to have died before Jacob's long exile ended. Her life must have closed prematurely, according to the usual standard of the patriarchal times; for Isaac, who was much older than herself, outlived her many years. That it was shortened by pining for her absent son, and by her remorse for the sin which had driven him from her side, seems very likely.

Thus when Jacob and his family reached Canaan, there was no fond mother there to welcome him back, to kiss his children, and see her son's childhood and youth pictured to her in their goodly faces. Only her aged nurse Deborah survived to tell him of his mother's last moments,—to tell him, perhaps, how, as she listened (as she had done for near twenty years) for the sound of his returning footstep, and still listened in vain, she owned God's judgment to be just, yet died hoping in His mercy. Dear to Jacob for his mother's sake, to his children for her own, this good old woman received from them, when she died, those solemn lamentations and funeral rites which God did not suffer them to give to Rebekah. It was her grave, not Rebekah's, which gave to the oak at Bethel its name of "the oak of weeping;" yet the chief of the mourners who stood round it must have wept comparatively few tears for Deborah, but many, under her name, for her long-buried mistress. Thus, if not expressly mentioned in the Book of God, yet distinctly to be discovered in it by the diligent searcher, stands God's sentence against Rebekah of separation from the son whom she led into sin—a sentence unrepealed down to the moment when that son, in extreme old age, in the far-distant land of Egypt, gave orders how his bones were to be laid beside her who had loved him "not wisely but too well," "in the cave that is in the field of Machpelah," where "they buried Isaac, and Rebekah his wife:" a sentence unrepealed indeed till then,—but who will doubt that in the heavenly Canaan that penitent son and mother will meet to part no more? that God's merciful severity *here* has fitted them to love one another in Him *there* for ever.

Now it is precisely because the two who thus sinned and thus suffered were, in the main, servants of God, that their story conveys a useful warning to all. That insincerity which is the bane of modern life, and which women especially, from their natural weakness, are so often tempted to have recourse to, stands here branded with God's strong displeasure. Strange to say, it is a fault to which religious persons in the early stages of their spiritual progress have more temptations than other people. Alas! they sometimes yield to those temptations, and by so doing dishonour their Saviour and bring discredit on their profession. They are often tempted to dissemble their own convictions, especially while they fear that they will not have strength to act up to them. Again, rightly dreading the quarrels which some around them rush into without fear, anxious to live in charity with all men, they are frequently inclined to sacrifice truthfulness to peace—forgetting that the God whom they serve is the God of both Truth and Peace alike. Can they wonder if, when they have trod the paths of deceit, and so sought help from their Master's enemy instead of from Himself, He has made them to feel that "the way of transgressors is hard" [Prov. 13:15]? Is it not well for them if He has done so, and if bitter experience has taught them to observe the much-needed apostolic injunction, "Wherefore, putting away lying, speak every man truth with his neighbour: for we are members one of another" [Eph. 4:25]?

And if thus history speaks to all, it has a word of especial admonition to parents and to children. It tells mothers that if God has given them the first place in their children's hearts in their childhood and youth, it is that they may lead them to Him; and that in proportion to the holiness of the bond by which He has knit them together, will be His displeasure if He ever sees it used as one of the "cords of sin," [Prov. 5:22]. The mother who, in advising her son in his choice of profession, or her daughter as to marriage, bids them sacrifice higher aims to worldly considerations, will be made, sooner or later, to feel that she has done wrong; very likely by this, that she will see her children's affection to herself dying away, strangled by the growth of the selfishness which she has herself fostered. And who can tell what sorrowful partings, or yet more sorrowful meetings, for eternity, may be the result of a mother's influence habitually misused, as Rebekah's was once, and not repented of, as we believe her fault to have been? For "if the righteous scarcely be saved, where shall the ungodly and the sinner appear?" [1 Pet. 4:18].

And what should children learn from this history? Surely to remember Christ's saying, "He that loveth father or mother more than me, is not worthy of me" [Matt. 10:37]; and respectfully but firmly to reject advice, even coming from dearest lips, which would draw them from their Saviour. So may they follow the example of that holiest and most loving of sons, whose tender affection to His mother never made Him forget for a single moment the superior claims of His heavenly Father to His obedience. So may the blessing of Jacob's God rest upon them, without those sharp thorns, planted by an early transgression, which made "the days of his pilgrimage so evil" [Gen. 47:9].

§58 Mary L. T. Witter
(fl. 1870–1900)

Mary Witter was a Canadian writer who wrote several books on the Bible.[21] The book cited below, *The Edomites: Their History as Gathered from the Holy Scriptures* (1888), was written for the young. Witter attempted to write a connected history of the Edomites from the fragmentary references to them in twenty-four books of the Bible. In her preface, she warned her readers not to use her book as a substitute for studying the Bible, but as an aid to its study.[22] Witter used a number of standard Bible reference works. In her preface she listed the following as particularly helpful: "Josephus, Smith's Bible Dictionary, Bush's Notes on Genesis, and Barnes' Notes on the Acts of the Apostles."[23]

Like Warner, Witter enhanced the story of Rebekah by giving a detailed account of the geography of Rebekah's and Eliezer's journey from Haran to Abraham's household near Lahai-roi. Also like Warner, Witter used places along the journey as prompts for Eliezer to tell the story of Abraham's family to Rebekah. Witter presented these discussions on the journey as catechistic: readers overhear the lessons Eliezer taught Rebekah about the history of salvation.

Witter read the story of Rebekah in light of the larger history of salvation. Like Hasell, she noted a parallel between Rebekah and Mary—Rebekah and Mary both privately pondered promises given to them about their children. Witter also assumed Rebekah knew the promise made to Eve and desired to be the ancestress of the promised seed.

Witter's understanding of women's roles and character was traditional. She reinforced the Christian message of sacrificial ministry, but for her, like many

---

[21] For more information about Witter see part 3, "Hagar—The Wanderer."

[22] Mary L. T. Witter, *The Edomites: Their History as Gathered from the Holy Scriptures* (Halifax, NS: S. Sheldon, 1888), 3.

[23] Witter, *The Edomites*, 3. Many editions of Josephus's works were available in the nineteenth century. William Smith, *A Concise Dictionary of the Bible* (first published 1865). George Bush, *Notes on Genesis* (New York, 1852). Albert Barnes, *Notes Explanatory and Practical, on the Acts of the Apostles* (London, 1841).

nineteenth-century interpreters, self-sacrifice was gender specific. Women's piety was displayed through their sacrificial service of others.[24]

From Mary L. T. Witter, *The Edomites: Their History as Gathered from the Holy Scriptures* (Halifax, NS: S. Seldon, 1888), 25–42.

Rebekah's Journey

THIS journey, which was a distance of about five hundred miles, must have been rather a formidable undertaking. Now a journey of that length can be performed in two or three days, then it occupied long, weary months. The first great difficulty would probably be the crossing of the Euphrates, the largest and longest and most important river in western Asia, and, even where most shallow, of very considerable depth. There were no bridges at this early date, hence the manner in which Rebekah and her nurse and maids were conveyed over the river must remain a matter of conjecture. As there is not even a hint relative to their route there can be no certainty as to the tract of country through which they passed, but one may presume that after crossing the Euphrates they traversed the fertile plains of Damascus, through districts familiar to Eliezer, and through the plateau of Bashan, afterwards the kingdom of Og, and then entered Gilead. Travellers have described the scenery from this elevated tract of country as very fine, at times almost enchanting, its plains being covered with a fertile soil and its hills with forests, and presenting at every turn new and varied features of the landscape. The caravan, for thus may this company of travellers be designated, crossed, one may presume, the swiftly flowing Jabbok and the muddy, circuitous Jordan both of which are now rich in historic interest; the former for a mysterious contest between God and man, and the latter for having been thrice miraculously divided, and more especially for having been the baptismal font of the Son of God. Having reached the western side of the Jordan we may imagine them travelling south-westerly till they come to Luz, and thence nearly south till they reach Salem, the capital of the kingdom of Melchizedec. The origin of this king is so obscure that he is described "as being without father, without mother, without descent" [Heb. 7:3], and although he was living in the midst of an idolatrous people he was a priest of the most high God—the first priest of which there is a record. The sight of Salem would naturally remind Eliezer of events which had occurred some fifty years previously, and one imagines him telling the story to Rebekah as follows [here Witter has Eliezer recount the stories of Lot and his family being captured and their rescue.] . . .

---

[24] Elizabeth Rundle Charles's poem "Ministry" claimed woman was created for service. The poem serves as a preface to *Sketches of the Women of Christendom* (New York: Dodd, Mead & Co., n.d.), iii–iv.

The heart of Rebekah was, no doubt, pained as she from time to time met with evidences of idolatry even in its most revolting forms. It is quite possible that it might have so occurred that as she was passing the ravine, afterwards known as the valley of the son of Hinnon [sic], the welkin rang with the sound of the toph and cymbal, intermingled with shrieks of agony; and if Rebekah asked what it meant she would be told that a babe had just been offered to the idol Moloch. She would be further told that, although the mother was a devotee to that horrid idol, and had voluntarily given her first-born for the sin of her soul, yet when she heard the cries of her babe her mother nature so triumphed over her religious prejudices as to cause her to utter the fearful shrieks which had been heard, and that in this country such scenes were not unfrequent, for mothers were taught that the sacrifice of a child, especially if that child be the first-born, was the most meritorious of all acts. "Though the religious element," Eliezer would say, "is a component part of the very soul of woman, yet in sacrificing her female children she may not be actuated wholly by religious motives, for life here among this idolatrous people is to woman, for the most part, barren of enjoyment. In nothing else does the household of my master contrast more strongly with the households by which we are surrounded. In his family females are loved, protected, honored, and the life of the weakest infant or the most decrepit old woman is guarded as carefully as his own life."

As they came within sight of Mount Moriah Eliezer would naturally recall the tragedy which occurred there some fifteen years previously, and almost as naturally he would relate the strange story to Rebekah, especially as he whom she was to marry was the designed victim of that tragedy. Eliezer would tell Rebekah that Isaac was from his infancy the object of his father's tenderest and deepest affection, and that he was not less surprised than pained when, after the boy had risen to manhood he received the command. "Take now thy son, thine only son Isaac, whom thou lovest, and get thee into the land of Moriah, and offer him there for a burnt offering upon one of the mountains I will tell thee of" [Gen. 22:2]. Eliezer would, no doubt, also tell Rebekah that his master knew that no such command had been given in the whole history of man, and that the great God had said: "Whoso sheddeth man's blood by man should his blood be shed" [Gen. 9:6]. And besides, to take the life of Isaac would seemingly render the fulfilment of the promise impossible, but so strong was his master's faith that he accounted that God was able to raise Isaac up even from the dead.[25] If Rebekah expressed astonishment that such a sacrifice should be commanded by God, or would be at all acceptable to him, she would be told that it is quite possible that the great God had a special

[25] See Heb. 11:19

object in view, namely the trial of Abraham's faith, love and obedience, and the teaching of the doctrine of substitution. These remarks were probably followed by a number of questions by Rebekah as to how Isaac was affected by the command. Did he believe that God had so ordered? Was he willing that his life should be thus cut short, or did he determine to resist? Did he resist, or how did it happen that the command was not executed? These questions or such as these, would very likely follow each other in such quick succession that Eliezer would make no attempt to reply, but when her excitement subsided so far as to render an answer possible he, perhaps, told her that, with her permission he would relate the story to her just as Isaac had told it to him, and would proceed about as follows . . . [here Witter retells the story of the binding of Isaac very dramatically from Isaac's perspective, see Gen. 22:1-14].

Rebekah, one imagines, had listened almost breathlessly to the narrative, and when Eliezer ceased to speak she asked, "Was the ram slain in Isaac's stead? Do the animals sacrificed die in our place? Can there be efficacy in their blood? Sacrifices must point to something in the future, but to what, to whom? All seems to me mysterious, so mysterious! More is known, I think, of God in your master's household than in my paternal home. About all I know of God is that he is an independent Being, and a holy Being, and, knowing that I am both sinful and dependent, I am never quite easy, as I fail to understand how I can become reconciled to him."

The return journey from Haran to Lahai-roi was quite unlike that from Lahai-roi to Haran. Then the travellers were all men, now they were a mixed company. Then there was some uncertainty as to the result of their enterprise, now that enterprise had been brought to a successful issue, and they were conducting a bride to her husband. Eliezer and Deborah were doubtless happy, but they could not have been merry; they were carrying too heavy responsibilities for that. The other travellers were among the merriest of the merry. Those connected with Abraham's household would never weary telling of his silver and gold, camels and asses, men-servants and maid-servants, and Rebekah's maids would be as eager listeners as they were speakers; but while they listened eagerly to a careful observer it would have been apparent that they were anxious to make it appear that Bethuel was no less important a personage than Abraham. But there was one in this company for whom this long journey, with its consequent toil and privations had been undertaken, who was shielded from every danger, relieved from every care, whose every wish was anticipated, but who must have been very far from being merry. Indeed her reticence might have been, by some, mistaken for sadness. Rebekah, no doubt, had learned that God had promised Abraham that all nations should be blessed in him [Gen. 12:1-3], and that it was in the line of Isaac that the Deliverer was to come; and like Mary, the mother of that Deliverer, she pondered these things in her heart, so pondered them as to be at times oblivious of what was passing around her. She thought on the seemingly strange promise, and, one may presume, questioned within herself whether it could be possible that she should be the ancestress of that wonderful personage who was to exercise so powerful an influence on all generations. All mankind blessed in an individual! How blessed? Wherefore blessed?

Rebekah's mind would also at times be occupied with the lesser but not unimportant question whether or not her husband would be pleased with her. Might it not so happen that while she bore the name, and enjoyed the amenities of a wife, some other woman would have the chief place in Isaac's affections?

Eliezer had, no doubt, despatched a messenger on a swift dromedary to Abraham, informing him of the success of the undertaking, of the manner in which Rebekah was employed, and of her conduct through the whole affair; and, if he was a close observer of human nature, he would be able to form a pretty correct opinion of his prospective daughter-in-law. That she was obliging, industrious, and courteous he could infer from her readiness to give water to a stranger, and from her drawing water for ten camels. That she possessed a large share of modesty might be pretty safely predicated from her spending no unnecessary time with the travellers ere she informed her parents of their coming, and her decision of character would be learned from her prompt "I will go."

As with Rebekah so with Isaac, though in an inferior degree, the period of time occupied by the journey could not have failed to be one of anxiety. A woman depends vastly more for happiness on her husband than does a man on his wife. Indeed it may be said that she is happy or miserable as is his will. Not so with a man. Many sources of enjoyment are open to him, even though his home be not a happy one. But as Isaac was to be the husband of one whom he had never seen, and of whose tastes and inclinations he was necessarily in a great measure ignorant, he would naturally question within himself whether she would be a true help-meet; soothing his cares and anxieties, sharing his toils, alleviating his sorrows, and in the hour of pain and sickness be the tender, affectionate, self-sacrificing nurse, or would she be one of the too numerous class of women who consider their own ease and comfort of paramount importance, and think themselves injured if anything is allowed to cross their plans or interfere with their wishes.

At eventide Isaac went out to pray or meditate in the fields. Was it his custom to spend the hour of twilight in intercourse with heaven, or did he retire to pray, on this occasion, because his anxieties were too heavy to endure unaided? Either view exhibits his piety in a favorable light, for, in a season of absorbing worldly interests he is found seeking communion with God. . . .

The solitary man walking in the field was not less noticed by those who composed the caravan than they were by him. Rebekah seems to have been the first who observed Isaac, and, on learning who he was, she at once dismounted and caused herself to be covered with the bridal veil; by the former act she avoided treating Isaac as an inferior, and by the latter she showed her subjection to him as her husband. I can scarcely avoid remarking in this connection that every true woman shuns every act that could be construed as implying that her husband is her inferior. Though in this enlightened Christian land a conventional superiority is acceded to woman, she is far from arrogating to herself that superiority.

When Rebekah dismounted, her attendants doubtless dismounted too, and walked in procession till she was presented to her husband. Isaac conducted Rebekah to his late mother's tent, and, as Deborah raised the veil, he would look for the first time on the face of his bride. Rebekah possessed personal charms of a very high character, and the respect and admiration which the report of Eliezer had elicited, as we have supposed, now culminated in love. The sacred historian exhibits the conjugal happiness of the newly-married pair in an equally pleasing and impressive manner by the following words: "He loved her; and Isaac was comforted after his mother's death."

§59 Mary Elizabeth Beck
(fl. 1872–1908)

Mary Beck was a member of the Society of Friends in England. She was a prolific writer, publishing books on the Bible and on Quaker principles. She also wrote devotionally for Mothers' Meetings.[26] She focused this study for mothers primarily on the problem of parental partiality. Unlike Woosnam and Witter, Beck had little good to say about Rebekah. She viewed her as a poor parent and wife who paid the price for loving one child more than the other. Her readers could similarly expect to reap what they had sown. Beck reinforced the prevalent ideology regarding the importance of mothers in the lives of their children, but thought partiality to one child was very dangerous. Beck concluded her meditation on Rebekah with a reference to Galatians 6:7-9, verses on reaping what one sows.

[26] For more information on Beck, see part 3, "Hagar—The Wanderer."

From Mary E. Beck, *Bible Readings on Bible Women: Illustrated from Incidents in Daily Life* (London: S. W. Partridge, & Co., 1892), 21–24.

The Story of Rebekah: Deceit and Its Consequences

"Beware of little sins; the gallant ship may sink
Though only drop by drop the watery tide she drink."

Read aloud, Genesis xxv. 28, and Genesis xxvii.

IF you have read the beautiful history of Rebekah's marriage in Genesis xxiv, I am sure you will feel sorry that she was not on all occasions a helpmeet to Isaac. One especial virtue of the Bible is that it does not hide people's faults. It tells us the good side and the bad side, and some of its lessons are intended as a warning to us. The fault in Rebekah's case began with her showing favour to her younger son. I think Isaac was partly to blame, too, for he loved Esau best.

Parents should be very careful to make no difference between their children. If one is known to be a favourite, jealousy creeps in; the other children think it is unfair, and they often dislike the favoured one. It brings bitterness into the family, and it is very bad, too, for the poor spoiled child, who gets his own way, and is not punished when he deserves it. Such children always have to suffer in after-life from the effects of selfishness, for other people will not be indulgent to their faults. The kindest parents are those who early train their children to habits of obedience and of thinking of the happiness of their brothers and sisters equally with their own.

Now we will go back to Rebekah. She was very desirous that Jacob should have his father's blessing, instead of Esau,* and as she could not get her way by fair means, she was determined to do so by deceit and cunning, and she did not hesitate to instruct her son to act a lie! What a sorrowful and fearful thing it is when a mother, either by her own example or by her encouragement, puts sin before her child! She cannot escape suffering from it sooner or later. So it was with Rebekah. She obtained her purpose, but her darling son had to flee for his life, to spend twenty years in exile under a selfish uncle, to be in his turn deceived, to give up a large part of his possessions to appease his injured brother; and though at last he returned in peace to his father, his mother, so far as we can learn, never saw him again. This was the price she paid to get that by guile which doubtless, had she waited for it, God would have given to her some other way, with His blessing; for though He carries out His purposes in spite of our sins, our sin is a hindrance, and never a help. It is most important that the truth should always be spoken to children. If once they find out that mother has deceived them, or if they hear her saying what is not true to someone else, their confidence is gone. Some children have been frightened out of their senses by a cruel and wicked threat, which was only meant to keep them quiet. Mothers are always by their example sowing a little seed in the heart of their children. If they can tell a lie when it suits their purpose, their child will very soon tell one too, and the mother who begins by deceiving her little boy or girl is very likely to be deceived herself by that son or daughter when they grow older. There is a hymn you often sing, called "What shall the harvest be?"[27] The harvest is just the same kind of plant that you sow—only in much larger quantity. Thus we are told that if we sow the wind, we shall reap the whirlwind. And Christ said that the good seed brought forth "some thirty, some sixty, some an hundred-fold," [Mark 4:8]. If you sow in your child's mind a seed of truth or a seed of falsehood, you will reap the same. If you say "Don't tell father," they will soon begin to say, "Don't tell mother." If you are vexed and angry and speak sharply to your child, you must not wonder if he shows a bad temper; but if you are gentle as well as firm, your children will love and obey you, and when they grow up you will most likely have comfort in them.

Let us repeat together what the Apostle Paul teaches us about sowing, in Galatians vi. 7-9.

* This blessing belonged of right to the eldest son, and bestowed special privileges.

§60 M. G.
(fl. 1893)

Like Beck, the British author M. G. wrote for Mothers' Meetings.[28] Unlike Beck, however, M.G. focused on the courtship and marriage of Rebekah and Isaac, as well as on issues related to parenting and character. Like Woosnam, M. G. told her readers/hearers that prayer and the counsel of parents and others were important as young people considered the subject of marriage. M. G. stressed the significance of God's blessing on a marriage and the value of a Christian wedding in a church. The ceremony in a church was critical, not just as a form, but because it was there that God really blessed the marriage union.

On the issue of parental partiality, M. G.'s views are unlike all the other women. She allowed that parents might feel partiality, but argued that they

[27] "What Shall the Harvest Be?" by Emily Oakley, 1870.
[28] For more information about M. G. see part 3, "Hagar—The Wanderer."

cannot show it. However, like other interpreters, she acknowledged that partiality had consequences; Rebekah's partiality led to her separation from Jacob.

M. G. presented Rebekah as a "charming example" of Christian maiden-hood. She included a comprehensive list of nineteenth-century female virtues that maidens needed who wished to be "numbered amongst the Lilies whose perfume fills the Garden of the Lord." In this list, written at the end of the century, M. G. stressed traditional characteristics also valued by King and other earlier women writers. Though women's legal status with respect to owning property and divorce had changed by the time M. G. wrote, tradi-tional values were deep-seated and remained influential.

From M. G. *Women Like Ourselves: Short Addresses for Mothers' Meetings, Bible Classes, etc.* (London: SPCK, 1893), 29–35.

–Rebekah–

OUR Bible lesson to-day is founded upon the story of a Courtship.

What! does God give us a story and an example about such a matter as this? Yes, indeed. No matter is too small or trifling for God to care about; and Courtship and Marriage are not trifling matters, affecting as they do the hap-piness of at least two lives. Therefore our Bible stories would not be complete without pictures like these of the wooing of Rebekah and of Rachel.

The details of the marriage customs and the circumstances of the court-ship must vary in different countries and individual cases; but the great prin-ciple remains the same. "A good wife is from the Lord" [Prov. 18:22], and it is to the Lord therefore that we should look in these matters. [Here M.G. retells the story of Rebekah and Isaac] . . .

Dear friends, if we would have God's blessing rest upon us, as it did upon Isaac and Rebekah, we too must seek it at the outset. Can we expect it to be given where it is never sought? A marriage performed before the registrar may be perfectly legal in the eyes of the law; but if God's Blessing is not asked upon the union, in His House, from the hands of His authorized Priests, we cannot look for the protection and comfort from God which Sarah and Rebekah and thousands upon thousands of married couples have found in the "honourable estate" of holy matrimony "after God's holy ordinance."

Are there some here to whom it seems too late, why have already entered into that estate without thinking of the God that liveth and seeth? Oh, do not say it is too late. Even now you can have the Church's blessing if you wish. Many couples who have begun by going to the registrar have come afterwards to have the ceremony quietly performed in God's House.

Or perhaps you looked upon the Marriage Service as a mere form, and thought little, as you knelt together in His presence, of the Father Who was watching you all the time as tenderly as He watched over Hagar by the well, and over the courtship of Isaac and Rebekah. Then turn to Him and look to Him now; He will overlook the mistakes of the past, if you humbly own them. Ask Him not to withhold His Blessing because you have been careless in seeking it; and God grant that each wife among us may be a true comforter to her husband, even as Rebekah comforted Isaac after his mother's death (ver. 67).

So far the character of Rebekah has appeared one of fair beauty. But unfortunately it would not be a truthfully-drawn character if we had no faults shown us. It is only in story-books that we meet with people who are either perfectly good or hopelessly bad. But one perfect Being has ever walked this earth. All others, in real life, have the good and bad qualities so intermixed that, though in some the good and in others the bad seem to come upper-most, we can, as we saw in the case of Sarah, scarcely judge whether they deserve most praise or blame. The men and women of the Bible are no excep-tional cases. They are set before us as real men and real women, such as we see moving around us every day, such indeed as we are ourselves with faults as well as virtues for us to see.

So, later in life, Rebekah's failings come to light. The first is that of a fool-ish mother; she loved one son better than another (chap. xxv. 28). In itself, perhaps, this could hardly be called a fault; the fault lay rather in her show-ing it. Whatever partiality a mother may feel in her heart, she should be very careful not to let it be suspected by her children, and still less should she show it by any injustice or want of fairness. How often it happens that one fault leads to another! Rebekah's partiality for Jacob led her to act unjustly towards her elder son, in trying to get the blessing, that belonged by right to Esau, for her favourite. The fact that God had hinted that Jacob should be the greater of the two was no excuse, for it never can be right to do evil that good may come, nor to try to hurry the accomplishment of God's purposes by unfair means. And these two faults, her avowed partiality for the younger son, and the grasping injustice by which she wanted for his sake to deprive the elder brother of his rights, led to a third sin. See how one sin leads on to another! She was tempted to practise a wicked deception upon her husband, and to make her son sin with her.

. . . But we see this: that the outward rite thus obtained by stratagem brought no inward happiness along with it. Jacob was forced to fly from his brother's wrath, and was deceived by others even as he had deceived at home. Rebekah lived on many years, more estranged from her elder son than ever;

but she never saw her darling Jacob again, probably knew nothing of his wanderings nor whether he lived or died.

Thus we see that the sin brought its own punishment. We may fairly hope that it wrought the fruit of true repentance in this life, and that Rebekah is now re-united to her long-lost son, and to the husband with whom she lived so faithfully. To Christian maidens she will ever remain a charming example of what their own maidenhood should be. Frank and courteous, ready to help where needed with her own hands in acts of kindness to both men and animals, yet retiring into the background as soon as no longer required; dutiful and wise in confiding at once to her parents all the advances that had been made to her; firm and true towards her betrothed in not shilly-shallying, or playing fast and loose, when once a favourable answer had been given; trustful, in leaving her own home and country for his sake; modest in veiling herself, with maidenly reserve, in the presence of her lover, as though to check any undue liberties; such as this every maiden amongst us should be, must be, if she would be numbered amongst the Lilies whose perfume fills the Garden of the Lord.

§61 Ada Ruth Habershon
(1861–1918)

Ada Habershon was the youngest daughter of Dr. S. O. Habershon and his wife, Grace. Raised in a pious Christian home, Habershon devoted her life to God's service. She wrote extensively on the Bible, attacking biblical criticism and teaching a typological reading of Scripture. She also wrote poetry and hymns. Habershon was associated with a variety of figures in the evangelical world of the late nineteenth century including Sir Robert Anderson,[29] and the Americans, Dwight L. Moody (1837–1899) and Ira D. Sankey (1840–1908).[30]

Habershon's *The Study of the Types* introduced readers to Old Testament types. She read the Old Testament narratives as illustrations of New Testament

---

[29] Sir Robert Anderson (1841–1918) worked in Scotland Yard and wrote a number of books on the end times; he was particularly interested in the book of Daniel. See B. J. Porter, "Anderson, Sir Robert," in *The Oxford Dictionary of National Biography* 2:71–72.

[30] For a summary of Moody's and Sankey's evangelistic work in Britain, see D. W. Bebbington, *Evangelicalism in Modern Britain: A History from the 1730s to the 1980s* (London: Unwin Hyman, 1989), 162–64.

theology. With Augustine she argued that "The New is in the Old contained: the Old is by the New explained."[31] The final chapter of this work was entitled "Types of the Holy Spirit." In this chapter she explained several Old Testament types of the Holy Spirit. Abraham's servant, for example, was understood as a type of the Holy Spirit in the story of the arranged marriage of Isaac and Rebekah. Like Woosnam, Habershon saw Isaac as a type of Christ and Rebekah as a type of the individual believer. Habershon expanded this brief treatment of the story of Rebekah and Isaac into a chapter in her later work, *Hidden Pictures: Or, how the New Testament is concealed in the Old Testament* (1916).

From Ada R. Habershon, *The Study of the Types* (London: Morgan & Scott, 1898), 143–47.

A beautiful picture is given in the twenty-fourth of Genesis of the work of the Holy Spirit. Isaac is, as we know, a type of Christ. The promises to Abraham concerning his seed are shown in Galatians to have referred to the Lord Himself, though they had their first fulfilment in Isaac. He was the only begotten son of the father, his well-beloved; and we have seen how the scene on Mount Moriah foreshadowed the love of Him who "spared not His own Son, but delivered Him up for us all," and thus became Jehovah-Jireh, for with Him He freely gives us all things [Rom. 8:32]. In this chapter we have an account of the father sending *his servant* to find a wife for his son—the one who in figure has already passed through death and resurrection; and this servant is a wonderful type of the Holy Ghost, who is now calling out a people for His name. First we have the charge to the servant. The bride of Isaac is to be brought right up out of the land in which she dwells. There is no mistake about the directions. The servant suggests that perhaps she will want to remain in her own home, and will not come to Isaac; is he then to bring Isaac down to her? But Abraham is very decided—Isaac's place is not there. As Mr. Spurgeon[32] has said on this verse, "The Lord Jesus Christ heads that grand emigration party which has come right out of the world."

In the tenth verse we are told that the servant does not go empty-handed, but takes with him samples of the riches of Abraham and Isaac—"all the goods of his master were in his hand." When the Holy Spirit came down, He,

---

[31] This rhyme summarizes Augustine's interpretive philosophy. This rhyme is cited by others as representing Augustine. See, for example H. A. Ironside, *A Historical Sketch of the Brethren Movement* (Grand Rapids.: Zondervan, 1942; reprint, Neptune, NJ: Loizeaux Brothers, 1985), 27.

[32] Charles Haddon Spurgeon (1834–1892), a well-known Baptist preacher. Spurgeon's sermons have been widely published.

too, brought with Him an earnest of the inheritance which they who listen to His message would receive, for He Himself is the earnest.

In the beautiful Eastern picture of the scene at the well we have the servant, having been led to the one whom God had appointed for Isaac, asking if there is room for him in her father's house. Had she refused, he would never have been able to tell her about Isaac. When he is admitted, his first thought is of his errand: "I will not eat until I have told mine errand." He never forgets it; and his object, like that of Him whom he foreshadows, is to speak of the one who sent him. "When the Comforter is come, whom I will send unto you from the Father, even the Spirit of truth, which proceedeth from the Father, He shall testify of Me" [John 15:36]. "He shall not speak of Himself" [John 16:13].

So Abraham's steward tells about his master, his master's son, and all his possessions; and gives to Rebekah some of the precious things which he has brought. "The Lord has blessed my master greatly, and he is become great": and unto his son "hath he given all that he hath." In John we read, "The Father loveth the Son, and hath given all things into his hand" [John 3:35]; and again, "All things that the Father hath are Mine" [John 16:15]. But there was one more thing that Isaac needed: he could not enjoy these things alone; as God had said of Adam, "It is not good that the man should be alone: I will make him an helpmeet for him" [Gen. 2:18], and the servant's business was to fetch Rebekah. He therefore took that which was Isaac's and showed it unto Rebekah, to prove the truth of his words about his riches. "He shall receive of Mine, and shall show it unto you" [John 16:14]. He also promised blessing to her in Isaac, and he showed her things to come.

Her friends would have detained her, but there must be no delay—"Hinder me not," he says to them, when they suggest her waiting at least ten days. "The Holy Ghost saith, To-day" (Heb. iii. 7). "Behold, now is the accepted time" [2 Cor. 6:2]. The question is put to Rebekah. Does she believe what she has heard? Is she satisfied that Isaac really wants her to him? Is she willing to trust herself to the guidance of the one who has come to fetch her? "Wilt thou go?" she is asked; and her answer is, "I will go."

She believes the report he has brought her; and forgetting the things which are behind, and reaching forth unto those things which are before, she presses toward the mark for the prize of the high calling [Phil. 3:13-14]—which is, that she shall be the bride of Isaac.

She leaves the old home, and forgetting also her own people and her father's house (Psa. xlv. 10), she commences the desert journey under the guidance of the servant. We read in Genesis xxiv. 61 that she "followed the man; and the servant took Rebekah and went his way." It was the right way, we may be sure, for he knew just the best road to take, having travelled that way before; and it was not likely that Rebekah tried to choose her own path—she was satisfied to be guided. Thus we also are being led by the Spirit of God.

We can imagine that during the journey, and at various stopping places, she would question him about Isaac, and would want to learn more about the one to whom she was going. We are not told anything about those conversations, only one question and answer are given; but they are characteristic of the whole. "What man is this?" asks Rebekah. "My master," is the answer. From first to last this is the servant's one theme. He does not speak of himself; but only speaks well of Isaac, and at last is able to bring her right into his presence. The type is so plain that none can fail to see its beauty. We, too, who have believed this message are being led by the faithful Guide through the desert journey, till by and by we shall see Him face to face.

> Oh, the blessed joy of meeting—
> All the desert past!
> Oh, the wondrous words of greeting
> He shall speak at last![33]

Isaac, meanwhile, was waiting for his bride; and we are told two things about him: the one, that he came to meet her from the well Lahai-roi, where was his dwelling place (Gen xxiv. 62; xxv. 11), "the well of Him that liveth and seeth me" (Gen. xvi. 14, *margin*); the other, that as she journeyed he went out into the field at evening to meditate, or to pray (*margin*).

The words of Isaac's prayer are not given; but we have the record of another prayer offered by One who ever dwelt in the presence of God, and who pleads for those who are journeying to Him through the wilderness. "Holy Father, keep through Thine own name those whom Thou hast given Me." "The glory which Thou gavest Me I have given them." "Father, I will that they also, whom Thou has given Me, be with Me where I am, that they may behold My glory" [John 17:11; 17:22; 17:24].

The chapter ends with the assurance of Isaac's satisfaction and love—"He loved her." The story falls far short of the Antitype, for Isaac did not have to bear anything in order to win her for his bride; but He whom He foreshadows "shall see of the travail of His soul and shall be satisfied" [Is. 53:11]. The very expression in Revelation, "the bride, the Lamb's wife" [Rev. 21:9], tells us of the Lamb that had to be slain, that He might have her for Himself.

---

[33] From a hymn called "The Bride" by P. G. (Possibly Paul Gerhardt [1607–1676]), translated from German into English by Emma Frances Bevan (1827–1909).

Conclusion

Nineteenth-century female authors loved "the beautiful and pastoral story of Rebekah." They approached this narrative looking for lessons and applications for their own lives and the lives of their readers. King's exhortation to her readers encapsulated this interpretive approach: "Let us pause an instant here, and apply this to ourselves, with the important question, Do we, in a similar case, 'do likewise?'" Most of these authors would agree with King that all readers could find points at which Rebekah's story resonated with their lives:

> All females, and indeed all human beings, have a very excellent example in this part of the history; all examples should produce in us self-examination, how far we imitate, or depart from, the pattern before us. Are we always anxious to shew kindness and civility to strangers? Do we even study to do so to our friends and neighbours? Are we constantly seeking occasion to assist and benefit all whom we meet with; *hasting* to employ the means in our power in supplying their wants, and contributing to their comfort; encountering any degree of labour we are capable of, and submitting to any inconvenience, where the necessities of our fellow-creatures, or even a poor animal may require it? If we have hitherto been deficient in these virtues, let us humbly beseech the Almighty to take from us "this heart of stone, and put his holy and benevolent Spirit within us."

Although the lessons women authors drew from Rebekah's story varied, a number of common themes emerged. First, Rebekah's virtuous qualities (modesty, industry, generosity, hospitality) made her a positive model for women called to take up their appointed domestic duties. Second, Rebekah's negative qualities (preferential parenting and deception) allowed women to address issues related to parenting and family life and forced them to wrestle with such theological questions as divine guidance and providence, and the relationship of ends and means. Their teaching and preaching of the Rebekah story revealed their high view of "the pure simple truths of Scripture." They used the Bible to authorize their applications of the story to the present, especially in their conclusions. They knew the Bible very well, and many authors felt free to cite verses out of context if they proved their point. But since the writers who did this viewed all Scripture as true, they regarded its principles as true regardless of context.

These selections also show that women used a number of different interpretive strategies in their approach to the text. Most women drew on the resources of academy and church to help them with difficult interpretive issues. Some women knew Hebrew, or had access to several translations and Bibles with marginal notes; many used commentaries, general reference works, including Josephus, and travel journals. Many authors felt it was important to interpret the biblical narratives within a historical framework and with reference to their physical or geographical settings.[34] Some, like Warner and Alexander, stressed cultural and historical differences and highlighted the exotic nature of the story. King and other authors minimized difference, stressing commonalities; they read the text and found the stories resonated with their lives. In these cases, the text was tamed to their culture instead of confronting their culture.

The authors read the story of Rebekah within the larger framework of salvation history and often drew parallels between various stories. Parallels drawn between Rebekah and Eve, Rebekah and Sarah, and Rebekah and Mary, opened up fruitful comparisons and applications. Writers also drew on their own experiences as wives and mothers to help them interpret the story. Because the authors lived in a patriarchal culture and because many of them had servants, they were attentive to details in the story that modern readers often miss.

Even in the most traditional selections the Woman Question stood in the background, at times pushing its way forward. The Woman Question was front and centre in Morgan's discussion of Rebekah: "The beautiful and pastoral story of Rebekah, full of graphic details of the domestic life of the Hebrew women, teems with fresh illustrations of their influence, their subtle contrivances, and of the social inequality inflicted on them, which originated their deep-felt wrongs." Other writers addressed Morgan's categories of social inequality, contrivance, and influence, though in more subtle ways.

The women writers had a variety of opinions on the nature of gender equality. Aguilar and others assumed spiritual equality between men and women. Some writers, like Hale, intimated the spiritual superiority of women over men. Most women, however, consistently held the social inequality of women: they were to be submissive, do their duty, and live lives of self-sacrifice. Women exercised power and influence in the private sphere, but were not considered equal to men. These selections provide a window into life in the nineteenth century, especially women's culture and women's views on marriage and marriage preparation.

---

[34] This concern for historical, cultural, and geographical settings seems odd given the authors' propensity to cite other verses of Scripture out of context. The context of narrative accounts concerned these writers, whereas biblical principles and their supporting prooftexts could be applied in any situation.

The nineteenth-century women wrestled with Rebekah's deception of Isaac. They dealt with Rebekah's "subtle contrivances" in a variety of ways. Alexander ignored the deception of Isaac entirely. M. G. judged Rebekah, calling her action a "wicked deception." Hale praised Rebekah's action, calling her "morally superior to her husband." Rebekah gained power through her use of subtle contrivances; nineteenth-century women were divided on whether her actions were appropriate.[35]

All of the women writers assumed the importance of women's influence. They encouraged it, they preached it, and they lived it. These authors were women committed to influencing others through their ministry of writing; their writing pushed the boundaries of their influence beyond their own households and placed these women in the public sphere. Warner subtley emphasized women's power and ability to interpret Scripture by portraying the grandmother's voice as wisdom. By contrast, Witter and Woosnam call women to influence others through a life of self-sacrifice and service. Nineteenth-century writers clearly did not all agree on women's roles, nature, and character; women's culture was not monolithic.

[35] For one discussion of women's use of manipulation in the nineteenth century, see Henrietta Twycross-Martin, "The Drunkard, the Brute, and the Paterfamilias: the Temperance Fiction of the Early Victorian Writer Sarah Stickney Ellis," in *Women of Faith in Victorian Culture: Reassessing the Angel in the House*, ed. Anne Hogan and Andrew Bradstock (London: Macmillan, 1998), 6–30.

Part 5

Leah and Rachel—
Founders of the House of Israel

Introduction

The matriarchs, Leah and Rachel,[1] with their two maids Zilpah and Bilhah, were the mothers of the twelve sons of Jacob who became the twelve tribes of Israel. Their story is found in Genesis 29–35. Leah and Rachel were the daughters of Laban, the brother of Rebekah. "Leah was tender eyed; but Rachel was beautiful and well favored" (Gen. 29:17). Jacob fell in love with Rachel, the younger daughter, and agreed to work for seven years for her hand in marriage. On the wedding day, Laban switched his daughters, and Jacob inadvertently married the older, Leah. Jacob agreed to work for seven more years for the hand of Rachel. Leah had four sons, filling the childless Rachel with envy. Her words to Jacob, "Give me children or I die!," foreshadowed her death years later following the birth of a second son. Like Sarah, Rachel tried to solve her infertility problem by giving her maid, Bilhah, to Jacob. Leah similarly gave her maid Zilpah to Jacob. Jacob's four wives bore twelve sons and a daughter, Dinah.

Jacob asked Laban for permission to leave for his own country with his wives and children but Laban resisted, acknowledging that he had been blessed because of Jacob's presence. Jacob set up a scheme to increase his flocks and became exceedingly prosperous. The Lord directed Jacob to return to the Promised Land. His wives agreed to leave their father's household. Laban pursued them and searched unsuccessfully for the household gods, which Rachel had stolen. The family stopped for a while near Shechem, where

---

[1] Rachel and Leah are mentioned in Ruth 4:11 as the two women who founded the house of Israel.

325

Leah's daughter, Dinah, was raped. The family then left that area and moved toward Isaac's household. Onroute, Rachel died giving birth to Benjamin and was buried on the way to Ephrath (Bethlehem). Jacob set up a pillar over her tomb to perpetuate her memory. Leah's death is not recorded, but her burial site was the Cave of Machpelah, where Jacob was also buried (Gen. 49:31).[2]

In writing on Leah and Rachel, women interpreters confronted a long and complex narrative that focused on Jacob. Leah and Rachel and their maids were relatively flat, or undeveloped characters.[3] Rachel's character was more complex than the others, though, and as Northrop Frye observed, Rachel became "the typical wife of Jacob or Israel and hence . . . the symbolic mother of Israel (Matthew 2:18)."[4] Harriet Beecher Stowe wrote, "The characteristics of these two sisters, Leah and Rachel, are less vividly given than those of any of the patriarchal women. Sarah, Hagar, and Rebekah are all sharply defined characters, in and of themselves; but of Leah and Rachel almost all that can be said is that they were Jacob's wives, and mothers of the twelve tribes of Israel." Because the text did not present Leah and Rachel as fully developed figures, the women interpreters looked for other ways to flesh out the personalities of Leah and Rachel. They searched for hints in the text and behind the text. Then they drew upon their imaginations and experiences as daughters and wives, and as readers and (in some cases) writers of romantic literature. Their commitment to the importance of families, especially mothers, for character development led them to look for clues about the sisters' personalities in the character and names of their children. They found further information on the personalities of Leah and Rachel in Jacob's relationship with his wives, the two women's prayers, and even in their obituaries, as Rachel's death was recorded and Leah's was not. Their culturally conditioned assumptions about the qualities women were expected to display (piety, purity, submissiveness, and domesticity) provided a further set of interpretive guidelines for understanding and evaluating the wives of Jacob. Assumptions about the nature of scripture as inspired, or in the case of Stanton and Colby, 'uninspired,' also

[2] Rachel is mentioned in Jeremiah 31:15: "A voice is heard in Ramah, mourning and great weeping, Rachel weeping for her children and refusing to be comforted because her children are no more." This image of Rachel weeping is applied in Matthew 2:18 to Herod's slaughter of the innocent children of Bethlehem.

[3] Literary critics usually distinguish between flat and round characters. "Flat characters, or types, are built around a single quality or trait. They do not stand out as individuals. Round characters, on the other hand, are much more complex, manifesting a multitude of traits, and appearing as 'real people.'" Adele Berlin argues for three categories: full-fledged character (round); type (flat) and the agent who serves as a functionary (*Poetics and Interpretation of Biblical Narrative* [Winona Lake, Ind.: Eisenbrauns, 1994], 23).

[4] Northrop Frye, *The Great Code: The Bible and Literature* (Toronto: Academic Press Canada, 1982), 140.

affected their approach to the female figures in the story. Stanton challenged the common use of this story to reinforce the importance of wifehood and motherhood and instead argued that "the woman trained to self-protection, self-independence, and self-support holds the vantage ground against all theories on the home sphere."[5]

Nineteenth-century women writers evaluated the characters of Leah and Rachel differently. Neither sister exemplified all the virtues a nineteenth-century woman looked for in the holy women from the past (1 Pet 3: 5). Most interpreters compared the two sisters and many preferred one to the other. Not all women preferred the same sister, however, and the reasons for their choice varied.

The complex narratives involving Leah and Rachel also raised issues about women's roles and functions. Women loved the idyllic story of Rachel's romance with Jacob, but it was complicated by the switch of the sisters on the wedding day. Colby wrote "the love which Jacob bore for Rachel has been through all time the symbol of constancy."[6] Some interpreters ignored the complex issues surrounding the nature of Jacob's two marriages, but most entered into the debate about their legality. Sarah Hall's character, Mother, gave a sermon on the nature of marriage in answer to a child's question about the legality of marrying two sisters. Many authors argued that Jacob's dysfunctional family provided a clear picture of the problems resulting from having multiple wives. Cornwallis suggested that polygamous marriages set aside "the friendship, the confidence, the honourable and refined delicacies of conjugal love" for "intestine broils, jealousies, mean suspicions, undermining plots, envy, all that can poison domestic comfort."[7] Cornwallis and others presented a clear Christian theology of monogamous marriage as a contrast to the ills of polygamy.

Looming behind most discussions of marriage was the larger Woman Question. What was a woman's role in marriage? Was she an object to be purchased? Was she simply a vehicle for producing sons? Rachel said, "Give me children or else I die!" What was a daughter's duty to parents after marriage? Was marriage for convenience or companionship? Did women have to stay in loveless marriages? These questions continue to be discussed in the twenty-first century.

Nineteenth-century women tended to ignore scenes in the Leah and Rachel story involving sexuality. They did not comment on Rachel's refusal

---

[5] Elizabeth Cady Stanton, *The Woman's Bible Commentary* (New York: European Publishing, 1895), 63–64.

[6] Colby in *The Woman's Bible*, ed. Stanton, 58.

[7] Mary Cornwallis, *Observations, Critical, Explanatory, and Practical on the Canonical Scriptures*, vol. 1 (London: Baldwin, Cradock, & Joy, 1820), 73–74.

to rise before her father, since "the custom of women" was upon her.[8] Most women closed their eyes to the very dark stories of the rape of Dinah and the affair between Reuben and Bilhah, which raised many questions about the boundaries of female sexuality.[9] Few women writing on Genesis explored the implications of these stories of abuse. Colby alone noted "the chief lesson taught by history is danger for violating, physically, mentally, or spiritually the personal integrity of woman."[10] In other contexts, women like British moral reformer and Christian feminist, Josephine Butler (1828–1906), spoke about women's vulnerability to sexual servitude as a cause of women's oppression, which they traced to the sexual double standard inherent in patriarchal culture.[11]

The themes of deception and lying in these stories further challenged these women writers, as their society extolled women's piety and virtue. In the last chapter we saw that many authors regarded Rebekah's separation from Jacob as the just consequence of her deception of Isaac. In this chapter, many regarded Laban's deception of Jacob as the just consequence for Jacob's involvement in deceiving his father. Hall's character Charles commented: "Then the imposition that Jacob had practiced on his father, was now returned on his own head."[12] A number of authors noted the family propensity for fraudulent behaviour. Both Leah and Rachel were seen as carrying on this tradition: Leah in her possible role in deceiving Jacob into marrying her, and Rachel in stealing her father's household gods. Cornwallis reasoned that if Rachel stole the gods for idolatrous reasons "we may consider her being snatched away by death before Jacob settled in Canaan, both as punishment of her crime, and a necessary intervention of Providence to prevent her from corrupting others."[13]

The genres of writing represented in this chapter are varied. The chapter begins with an excerpt from a romantic novel based on the biblical story written by Adelaide O'Keeffe in the late eighteenth century, though not published until 1811. The chapter ends with the critical comments of Elizabeth Cady Stanton and Clara Bewick Colby found in *The Woman's Bible*, compiled at the end of the nineteenth century.

---

[8] That is, she was having her period.

[9] See also the section on Dinah in part 6, "The Other Women of Genesis."

[10] Stanton, *The Woman's Bible*, 57.

[11] Lucretia A Flammang, "'And Your Sons and Daughters Will Prophesy': The Voice and Vision of Josephine Butler," in *Women's Theology in Nineteenth-Century Britain*, ed. Julie Melnyk (New York; London: Garland, 1998), 151.

[12] Sarah Hall, *Conversations on the Bible* (Philadelphia: Harrison Hall, 1827), 50.

[13] Cornwallis, *Observations*, vol. 1, 76.

§62 Adelaide O'Keeffe
(1776–c.1855)

Adelaide O'Keeffe was the only daughter and third child of Irish parents, the Roman Catholic dramatist and actor John O'Keeffe (1747–1833) and the Protestant actress Mary Heaphy (1757–1813). Because of difficulties in her parents' marriage, Adelaide was raised by a nurse and sent to school in London and a convent school in France. When she was twelve, she became her blind father's amanuensis. She launched her own successful writing career with the publication of her first novel in 1799, though the poetry she published in Ann and Jane Taylor's *Original Poems for Infant Minds* (1804) was her best-known work. She is recognized today as a significant Irish writer of children's literature. In 1798 she wrote a fictional adaptation of Genesis 21:8–46:29 entitled *Patriarchal Times, or, The Land of Canaan*, but it was not published until 1811. It became a critical and commercial success and was republished several times in Britain, and translated into German and French. An American edition, sponsored by a Jewish publisher, was released in 1822.[14] In 1898 O'Keeffe's father, who had written over fifty popular comic operas, left the stage, and his daughter dutifully cared for him and supported him through her writing and later as a governess.

Patriarchal Times is a 600-page novel telling the story of Abraham's family and descendants, beginning with Isaac's weaning feast and ending with Israel's arrival in Egypt. O'Keeffe followed the main narrative line of the biblical story, but embellished the account by adding characters and scenes, inventing dialogue, and making use of elaborate descriptions. The seven chapters of the work are entitled "Abraham," "Ishmael," "Isaac," "Jacob," "Esau," "Joseph," and "Benjamin." Despite the male focus of the chapter titles, O'Keeffe gave female characters a prominent place in her work.

---

[14] In e-mail correspondence Dr. Donelle Ruwe (Department of English, Northern Arizona University) described a Jewish republication of O'Keeffe's novel in America (in a series called "The Jewish Miscellany," entitled *Patriarchal Times, or, The Land of Canaan; in Seven Books; Comprising Interesting Events, Incidents, and Characters, founded on the Holy Scriptures,* by Miss O'Keeffe (Philadelphia: Jewish Publication Society, 1848). The society published books that portrayed Jews positively. O'Keeffe's *Patriarch Times* was the first book the Jewish Publication Society published written by a non-Jew. The preface to the American edition notes that O'Keeffe's version of the Old Testament focuses a bit too much on Christian ideas of predestination.

The selection below describes Jacob's arrival in Haran. O'Keeffe set up the meeting between Jacob and Rachel by introducing the characters Ashbel and his wife Taphanes, who were discussing their old friend Rebekah as Jacob approached and asked them if they knew Laban. The old couple provided Jacob with information about Laban's family, foreshadowing the marriage of Jacob to both Laban's daughters in the conversation. O'Keeffe described Rachel and her meeting with Jacob very elaborately and sensually. Rachel was portrayed as a righteous woman, showing concern for the poor by instructing her father's labourers to leave grain for gleaners, and to let the birds go free. At the same time, Rachel used her feminine wiles to manipulate her father who was not as interested in helping others.

From Miss O'Keeffe, *Patriarchal Times, or, The Land of Canaan: A Figurative History: in seven books: Founded on the Holy Scriptures: In Two Volumes* (London, 1811). [Text from the 3rd ed. (London: Rivington, 1820). Two volumes in one, 300–312.]

Soft, said Ashbel, who comes yonder? he quits the highway and advances,— he stops, as doubtful of his path, and leans on his staff, seemingly wearied. The youth they descried, approached, and looking upon the sheep lying in separate flocks around the well, addressed Ashbel, saying, Tell me, I pray thee, whence art thou?—I am of Haran, replied the shepherd, but thou art spent with fatigue, young man: Thy voice is faint, thy limbs tremble—come this way, and sit thee down beside my wife and me.

Know ye Laban, the son of Bethuel? demanded Jacob, bowing thankfully, and placing himself between the aged pair. We do, answered Ashbel, and if thou tarriest here, thou mayest ere long behold him, for he has been all the morning to and fro among his shepherds and herdsmen, but if he comes not soon, I will guide thee to his habitation. The heart of Jacob fluttered with doubt and hope, he sighed deeply, and was raising his eyes to examine the different objects around him, when his attention was suddenly attracted by an object advancing at a distance, down a green slope.

A lovely Iris, heavy with the dews of night, droops on its delicate stalk lamenting, until the sun-beams bursting through the morning vapours, penetrates its tender bosom, dries its tears, and cheers it with friendly warmth, when it looks up smiling with brilliant tints, breathing delicious fragrance. Thus revived the fainting youth at sight of the beauteous shape before him.

Her short white garment was confined to her waist by a girdle out blushing the carnation, and of the same bright hue were her sandals; her temples were encircled by a simple branch of jessamin, intended to confine her light brown hair, but a few ringlets, disdaining even such sweet thralldom, wantoned in careless negligence over her neck and shoulders, the fair luster of which she was not aware might be tarnished by the sun; her round and polished arms were likewise uncovered, and with a striped willow rod, she drove her bleating flock before her.

The children of the shepherds, on distinguishing the maiden, rose from the ground with loud acclamations, and ran towards her in full speed; some hung upon her raiment, others seized her hands, and the little ones, who had been left behind in the race, stretched out her arms, intreating the first kiss.

Ashbel and Taphanes looked upon Jacob; they read his youthful heart, and smiled at each other. This lovely damsel, said the shepherd, is Rachel, the daughter of Laban, who comes to water her father's sheep. Jacob, in a low voice, asked, was this his only daughter?

No, replied Taphanes; he has an elder, named Leah, whose mind is fairer than her face, being renowned among us for mildness, economy, and marvelous skill in such works as best become a woman. Even Rachel, this young one, although a child in appearance, has arrived at excellency in many things. She spun flax, and wove the apparel in which she is clad, and with juices extracted from the flowers of her garden, dyed her sandals and her girdle the dazzling crimson thou seest. She milks the ewes, prepares the milk into butter, and presses the curds: at sun-rise she is seen either standing at the kneading-troughs, gathering the sweet orange-dew, washing the garments in the river, or leading her sheep to pasture. To her is left salting the bitter olive, drying the grape in the sun, setting those birds whose eggs are food, and preserving the date. Though diligent in all duties, yet is she skilled in music, ever mirthful, rejoicing every eye, and chasing every sorrow. But Laban comes this way, and seemingly much displeased.

The maiden had reached the well, surrounded by the children and her sheep, when she was met by her father. Rachel, said he, is it thou who ordered the pheasants and the partridges to be spared? I mark the slowness of my hirelings, and they reply, that thou hadst them reap with caution, and even examine the corn ere they put in the sickle; thus hast thou lost to me many hours of their labour, they having abused thy command, and thrown away that time which is so valuable at this season.

My father, replied the maiden, bending her lovely head at every pretended apology, the sweet birds will be saved to beautify the land; the men will escape the danger of over-heat from excess of toil; and the corn my father, will stand until to-morow.

Stay, said Laban, I have more to say to thee. I see the ground scattered with wheat, and reprove the negligence of the binders; they answer that thou hast been in the field since morning, and that when the sheaves swelled fuller than seemed proper in thy wisdom, thou drewest away the ears, and scattered them again among the stubble, saying, 'Leave thus much for the gleaner.'

And what is wheat or barley harvest without the joyful gleaner, my father? demanded Rachel; they must have their share. Last autumn the poor of Haran murmured against thee, saying, 'Of what service is it to visit the fields of Laban? he leaves not an ear to glean.' I love not to hear thee murmured at, my father. This harvest I spake thus to them: 'Touch not the sheaves, but gather ye what ye shall find scattered, for I will provide for ye all.' They did so, and blessed thee—I love to hear thee blessed, my father.

Laban strove to supprese [sic] a smile, and attempted, but in vain, to avoid the kiss she gave when springing on his neck. Were I not fearful of being reproved, as usual, by my mother Zarapha, for chiding thee, I would not let these things pass. In the vintage season thou givest away my grapes to the right and to the left; thou wilt not suffer those who beat my olive-trees to clear them of fruit; and thou encouragest strangers to milk my kine, and ewes, and camels. The produce of my orchards, distributed to all the neighbouring little ones, was never blown down by the wind; many of these children are clothed with my unbought wool; and if my overseer, even for a moment, orders the muzzle to be put on the ox treading out the corn, thou straightway orderest it to be taken off. When I think of thy unsparing hand, I wonder my possessions diminish not, rather than increase.

My father, she replied, the increase of thy possessions is owing to my unsparing hand; those who feed the poor always prosper—therefore I am thrifty of thy success, and give away but to increase they wealth.—O thou art well skilled in computation! answered Laban; so was my sister Rebekah— with her, loss was ever gain. But I say no more—water thy flock; omit none, of thou hast still the number I gave thee in charge—each day I look to see it diminish, if not wholly disappear.

When Laban turned away, Rachel, looking after him, archly remarked, If my father rebuke me, he always smiles, thereby turning anger into approbation.

O spotless beauty! enchanting mildness! exclaimed Jacob. Here is not the scornful air of Judith, neither the languishing softness of Selemiah,[15] but captivating gaiety, and winning sweetness; all life, spirit, and vivacity—treasures at her age, which in time promise the perfections of maturer years—diffidence and retiring modesty. Neither studied, nor careless in her raiment, but pure and delicate in her own innocent bosom.

Fairest Rachel, said Ashbel, come this way; I have tidings to impart with which thou wilt be pleased.—No, no, replied the damsel, laughing, and shaking her bright locks over her cherub face. No, no, good Ashbel; believe me

---

[15] Judith and Selemiah are the fictionalized names O'Keeffe gives to the wives of Jacob's brother, Esau.

now I know full well what are these tidings. For these five years past I have daily heard the tale of thy youth repeated, and were I to hear it ten years to come, I could not love my aunt Rebekah, or despise old Zibeon,[16] or honor thy constancy to Taphanes more than I do now; but yet, if it will please thee, I will listen to the often-told story once again.

The aged Ashbel and his wife, delighted with her cheerfulness, opened their arms to receive her as she ran towards them; but they were disappointed of the expected embrace for on perceiving a stranger, she suddenly stopped, and gazed upon him. Jacob arose abashed, and on meeting her eyes, his were cast upon the ground. New-born passion rendered him timid, but Rachel knew not yet even the name of passion.

Taking a white rose from her breast, she stood rapidly plucking it in pieces, regardless of the shepherds, who reminded her that they were preparing to water their flocks. A favorite sheep rubbed its head against her knee, and looking up into her face, bleated, as if reproaching her delay, but wholly occupied by the presence of the youth, still with bewitching simplicity, she remained gazing on his interesting countenance, when Jacob approached her. With graceful dexterity he put back the men, and laying his hand upon the stone at the mouth of the well, rolled it away; then softly taking the willow branch from Rachel, he drove her sheep forward, and watered them at the spring, which act of courtesy pleased more than surprised the maiden, for it was the emulation of every youth of Haran daily to pay her the like token of respect.

Returning the rod to her hand, he perceived that her eyes were once again fixed on his; she withdrew them, but once more looked with earnest attention.—Thou hast been weeping, young man, she said; thine eyes are heavy and inflamed. Then, turning to Taphanes, I could also weep, for how afflicting is the sight of sorrow!—Young man, thy cheeks are pale, and I should think thou didst hunger but that thy dress is fair and comely: thou art young, and my father Laban is in years, and yet thou resemblest him—O how strong is now the resemblance! wert thou aged, indeed I would call thee father.

Tears gushed from Jacob's eyes: stooping, he folded his arm round her neck, saying, And if thou wert not young as new-fallen snow, I would call thee mother; for in voice, in form, and look, thou resemblest my mother Rebekah, who is sister to thy father Laban. I am Jacob, Rebekah's younger son, and am even now come from the house of my father Isaac, who dwell [sic] in Canaan. Suffer me then, O most lovely Rachel, to claim kindred with thee, by impressing this holy kiss upon thy virgin cheek.

---

[16] Zibeon is another character O'Keeffe adds to the story.

Rachel, with an exclamation of joy, sprang from his embrace to meet her father, leaving Jacob in the arms of Ashbel and Taphanes, who, with transport, pressed the child of their beloved Rebekah to their bosoms.

My sister's son! cried Laban, then looked upon him. Thou art indeed, for in thy features I trace those of Rebekah. Come to my arms, my kinsman, and tell me—but why this languor, why these downcast looks? and why art thou alone? why came not thy brother Esau with thee? But thou wilt open to me thy heart when beneath my roof. Thou hast need of repose, and if I may judge by thy countenance, of consolation also: with me thou shalt find both.

Jacob sighed his thanks, and suffered himself to be conducted in silence, between Laban and the enraptured Rachel, who held his trembling hand. Ashbel and Taphanes accompanied them to hear tidings of the friend of their youth; and the children, trailing Jacob's staff, and carrying his scrip, followed to the dwelling of Laban, around which were now assembled the shepherds, the reapers, and the neighbours, with their families, among whom the rumour had spread—all eager to behold the son of the dearly-remembered Rebekah—all anxious to welcome the youthful traveler to Padan-aran [sic].

§63 Mary Cornwallis
(1758–1836)

Mary Cornwallis was married to Rev. William Cornwallis, who served as the Anglican priest to the parish of Elham and Wittersham in Kent, England for more than fifty years.[17] The Cornwallises had two daughters. The elder married James Trimmer, the son of author and educator Sarah Trimmer,[18] but she died in 1803, shortly after giving birth to a son, James Cornwallis Trimmer, who died at the age of twelve. The younger daughter, Caroline Frances Cornwallis (1786–1858), became a well-known writer, scholar, feminist, and social advocate.[19]

Cornwallis wrote a four-volume commentary on the Bible, entitled *Observations, Critical, Explanatory, and Practical on the Canonical Scriptures.* This work was first published in 1817, and a second edition was published in

---

[17] A sketch of Cornwallis's life is found in the introduction to her *Observations, Critical, Explanatory, and Practical on the Canonical Scriptures* (London: Baldwin, Cradock, & Joy, 1820).

[18] See Trimmer's biography in part 2, "Sarah—The First Mother of Israel."

[19] See the entry on Caroline Frances Cornwallis in *The Oxford Dictionary of National Biography.*

1820. Cornwallis's commentary was written over a long period of time. She initially wrote study notes for her own use, then found these notes useful for teaching her daughters, and later still reworked them for teaching her grandson, James Trimmer. When her grandson tragically died, she published her work and used the proceeds to endow a free primary school in his memory.[20]

The following excerpts are from Cornwallis's comments on Genesis 29–31 and 35. Unlike O'Keeffe's novel, Cornwallis's book is a reference work. Cornwallis paid careful attention to details in the text. She noted, for example, the difference in age between Jacob and Rachel, a difference that O'Keeffe glossed over when she portrayed the couple as being about the same age. Cornwallis relativized Jacob's age based on life expectancies in patriarchal times and in the present. She was very aware of cultural and historical distances between biblical times and the present. She betrayed her own cultural classism and racism in the way she described the women of patriarchal times. Cornwallis was sympathetic to Leah, calling her a pious woman. Rachel, by contrast, was an impious woman, as Cornwallis showed in her remarks on the matter of the stolen household gods. Cornwallis mentioned the texts in Jeremiah and Matthew, which describe Rachel weeping for her children, but did not expand on their meaning. She passed judgment on the affair between Bilhah and Jacob's son Reuben, calling it "horrid."

From Mary Cornwallis, *Observations, Critical, Explanatory, and Practical on the Canonical Scriptures,* vol. 2 (London: Baldwin, Cradock, & Joy, 1817). [Text from 2nd ed. (1820), 71–76, 82.]

Why Jacob should leave his father's house alone, and so unprovided, is not to be explained; but it furnished occasion for a more particular Providence to be exerted in his behalf; it might be, in consequence of his own choice, or it might be that his mother sent him away secretly, lest Esau should pursue him. It is likely that he had resolved to rest his destiny upon some such test as that, on which the faithful Eliezer depended, when he went in search of a wife for Isaac his father, and that God was pleased to direct events to the same issue. The meeting of Jacob with Rachel and her family affords a pleasing and interesting picture. She was probably younger than Jacob, who, being born when Isaac was threescore, must have been above that age when he set out for Mesopotamia. This seems to have been more than the third part of man's life in those days, therefore not exceeding four or five and twenty at this time. The refusal to open the well probably arose from the fear of its being choked by the sand, should a sudden gust of wind arise: it is a common practice still

---

[20] See the "advertisement" or preface to the second edition of Cornwallis's work.

in the East to assemble all the flocks before the stone is removed from the well's mouth, from the frequency of this accident.

It is difficult to imagine a more cruel injury than that which Jacob sustained in the substitution of Leah for Rachel; the practice of veiling the bride furthered the deceit. Commentators usually consider this as an instance of the retributive justice of Providence; and if Jacob had been actuated by self-interested or fraudulent motives, he would certainly have deserved his present misfortune: but throughout his subsequent history we find the Almighty still operating for his advantage; and counteracting the unjust proceedings of Laban, which leads to establish the opinion already advanced, that he was the oppressed character, and that if he had erred in judgment he had not an intention. Had not a plurality of wives been in those times permitted, the injury would have been still more severely felt; but the consequences appear to have been such as Laban ought to have expected, domestic misery. Rachel appears to have been given to Jacob at the end of the seven days' festival, which usually accompanied eastern weddings, but another seven years' servitude was the condition. What intercourse took place during this period between him and his family in Canaan is not mentioned; but if Rebekah sent for her son as she said she would do, he was by this engagement prevented from complying with the summons. The situation of Leah was distressing; she appears to have been a pious woman, as we may collect from her constantly giving glory to God for every child she bare. Her first-born she called Reuben, that is, *see a son*. The second Simeon, or *hearing*, because she thought his birth an evidence that God had heard that she was not beloved, and had taken pity on her. The third she named Levi, or *joined*, because she hoped he might bind the heart of her husband to her. The fourth Judah, or *praise*; for she said, "Now will I praise the Lord." Judah being the head of the tribe in which our Lord came, Leah had indeed cause to praise the Lord, and to rejoice, though she might not be sensible of the great honour conferred upon her.

. . . 'It is difficult,' observes Bishop Patrick[21] 'to account for the struggle between Jacob's wives for his company, and at the same time bestowing their maids upon him, or for Moses being so particular in relating circumstances not in themselves being worthy of notice, unless we conclude that they had always in view the Blessed Seed, and each hoped to become by herself or maid, whose children she esteemed to be her own, the mother of the Messiah.' This appears plainly to be the case; and as their children were ordained of God to be the heads of the *twelve* tribes of Israel, every thing concerning them became important.

---

[21] Biship Symon Patrick, *A Commentary upon the First Book of Moses, called Genesis* (London: R. Chiswell, 1695). This work was republished numerous times. Patrick (1626–1707) was the Anglican Bishop of Ely.

In perusing the present chapter we must keep in view the times of which it treats, and the customs of the country. Literature appears to have been unknown to the common mass of mankind; whose occupations were agricultural, and manners uncultivated. The women carried their thoughts no higher than to rear their children, and provide for their households, and were far less refined in their ideas and manners than European servants. We have before us, probably, a very exact picture of the interior of every family in which polygamy exists. The friendship, the confidence, the honourable and refined delicacies of conjugal love, and the tender ties of fraternal affection, must ever be unknown to it; and intestine broils, jealousies, mean suspicions, undermining plots, envy, all that can poison domestic comfort, will be seen in their place; while the children of mothers, each contending for their own interest, must grow up in hatred. How thankful ought we to be, who live under that pure dispensation which has put a check to vagrant desires, and compelled men to seek their own felicity in wedded life, by confining them to one wife. Concubines were considered as subordinate wives, entitled to protection and provision: they stood therefore on a respectable footing in society according to their station, and were women of as much virtue as the superior wife, whom they seem to have attended as servants. The impatience of Rachel because she had no child was justly displeasing to Jacob: it could only be excusable from a wish to bear the Promised Seed. The birth of Dan and afterwards of Naphtali appears to have been highly gratifying to her, though born by her handmaid; and the names were likewise appropriate, Dan signifying *judging* and Naphtali, *my wrestling*. Gad and Asher were next born by the handmaid of Leah, who seems to have been fearful that she should not preserve her pre-eminence: Gad signified *a troop* or *company*; Asher, *happy*. Issachar and Zebulon were afterwards born of Leah, the name of the first signifying *hire*, that of the second *dwelling*; and she was also the mother of Dinah, whose name means *judgment*. At length it pleased God to listen to the desire of Rachel, and to give her a child of singular qualities, whom she called Joseph, or adding, because God had added another son to those she had adopted.

. . . There is a variety of opinion respecting the images, or teraphim, stolen by Rachel, and her motive in taking them. Some imagine that they were only pictures or statues of Rachel's ancestors, abused by Laban to purposes of idolatry; others that they were household gods held in superstitious reverence by the family, and that she removed them to prevent her father from discovering, through their means, the route her husband had taken. The Scriptures are silent on the subject; but at all events Rachel may be suspected of wrong motives, by her concealment of the act from Jacob: she excelled her sister in beauty, but she did not equal her in piety; and if she stole these images for idolatrous purposes, we may consider her being snatched away by death before Jacob settled in Canaan, both as punishment of her crime, and a necessary intervention of Providence to prevent her from corrupting others.

. . . He [Jacob] seems to have been on the road to Mamre, the residence of his father Isaac when two misfortunes overtook him, as great as could well be experienced: the death of his beloved Rachel in childbed, and the horrid connexion of Bilhah with his own son. If the death of his father followed close upon these events, it must be allowed that he stands as a strong evidence, that "whom the Lord loveth he chasteneth, and scourgeth every son whom he receiveth."* It is remarkable that Rachel died by the accomplishment of her desires; this shows the danger of taking ourselves out of God's hand, who, knowing the future, is alone competent to direct the present to advantage. The place at which she was buried was that where Jesus was born, and the babes slain by Herod's order. She is represented by the prophet Jeremiah as mourning and lamenting for them; and St Matthew quotes the passage in his relation of the barbarous deed.† Her sepulchre is mentioned as existing in the reign of Saul.⁺

* Heb. xii.6
† Matt. ii, 17, &c.
⁺See I Sam. x.2.

§64 Sarah Hall
(1788–1879)

Sarah Hall was an American writing for children and youth.[22] Her book *Conversations on the Bible* featured the characters of Mother, Catherine, Charles, and Fanny who discussed the main story of the Old Testament. Mother told the story while her children asked questions. Hall placed very pointed comments and questions in these characters' mouths and through the Mother character she addressed some difficult interpretive issues.

This excerpt on Leah and Rachel begins with Jacob's arrival at the well outside Haran and his meeting with Rachel there. It concludes with a discussion of the deaths of Rachel, Isaac, and Rebekah. Hall's purpose in retelling the biblical stories was to recount the main thread of salvation history, so she emphasized the actions of Jacob. She did fill in some details of the story, so that Rachel and Leah become more rounded characters. Like O'Keeffe, she

[22] See Sarah Hall's fuller biography in part 2, "Sarah—The First Mother of Israel."

romanticized the story and imagined the emotional responses of the characters. However, Hall did not use the sensual language that O'Keeffe did. Unlike Cornwallis, who portrayed Jacob as an oppressed character, Hall implied that Jacob got what he deserved when Laban deceived him.

Hall raised good questions about Leah and Rachel that any reader might have asked. For example, Fanny asked about the legality of Jacob's marrying two sisters. Her mother's answer was a brief summary of a Christian theology of marriage. Cornwallis and Hall had similar theologies of marriage. Like Cornwallis, Hall was sensitive to cultural differences, as seen both in the answer on marriage and in the discussion of the relative ease of moving a household in patriarchal times compared with the present.

From Sarah Hall, *Conversations on the Bible* (Philadelphia: Harrison Hall, 1818). [Text from the 4th ed. (1828), 49–54.]

Laban, the brother of Rebekah, had two daughters. Leah, the elder, was not handsome, but Rachel, the younger, was beautiful! Overpowered by her unexpected appearance—his spirits exhausted by a long journey, of nearly five hundred miles, and recollecting his forlorn situation, an exile from his father's house, Jacob could not restrain his tears, while he told her he was her relative—the son of her father's sister! Then courteously removing the stone, he drew water for her flock, while she ran to carry the news of his arrival to her father. Laban himself came out to receive him, and the fugitive was conducted to the house with the tenderest expressions of joy and affection!

Consoled now by the caresses of his new friends, Jacob found himself at home in his uncle's family. He took an interest in their affairs, and a share in their labours. Days and weeks rolled pleasantly away, but he said nothing of the purpose of his visit, until Laban observing his capacity for business, proposed to give him salary, for his services, because, 'it was unreasonable,' he said, 'that they should be received without a compensation.' He bid him therefore, to fix his own terms, and Jacob required no time to deliberate. The charms of Rachel had captivated his affections, the voice of avarice was silent, and love alone preferred her claim: for Rachel—the beautiful shepherdess, was all he desired! Seven years would he serve were she the reward! Unwilling to part with his nephew, or to alienate his family from that of Isaac, Laban accepted the offer.

Time now moved on silken wings—years were but days in the estimation of Jacob; he kept the herds of his kinsman, and felt neither the noon-day sun, nor the midnight dew; for in the society of Rachel, every toil was delightful! Seven years were completed, and he claimed his reward. Laban prepared for the wedding. The neighbours were invited, and the banquet was spread. But a cruel disappointment awaited the lover; for the deceitful Laban, favoured by the eastern custom of covering the bride with a long veil, united him to Leah, instead of Rachel!

CHARLES. Then the imposition that Jacob had practiced on his father, was now returned on his own head.

MOTHER. Yes. But we do not choose that others should do unto us as we do unto them; and Jacob accordingly, grieved and indignant, complained of the cheat. He had served for Rachel; why then was Leah, the disagreeable Leah, imposed upon him? They who commit injustice are seldom without an excuse, and the crafty Syrian had one at hand. It was not their custom, he said, to give away the younger daughter, before the elder; but seeing that poor Jacob had given his heart wholly to Rachel, another seven years' servitude might obtain her also. No price was too great to obtain the object of his affection, and another period of bondage was readily undertaken by the devoted lover.

It is not, however, understood by commentators that the reward of his constancy was withheld until the stipulated service was rendered. The circumstances of their subsequent history require that Rachel should have been given to Jacob immediately upon his agreeing to serve another seven years and acknowledging Leah publicly by "fulfilling her week," which is supposed to mean, the celebration of the marriage festivities, for a week.

FANNY. Was it lawful for Jacob to marry two sisters?

MOTHER. It was never lawful for any man to have more than one wife at a time. The will of the Creator is unequivocally declared in the formation of one man and one woman at the first. Reason easily deduces the same, and the testimony of the Messiah is to us conclusive. But the patriarchs, were not so clear in the knowledge of their duty as we are: besides, they were unhappily surrounded by Heathens, into whose vicious practices they were sometimes betrayed. Their deviations are faithfully recorded, to show us, that the best of men were imperfect. Jacob was certainly a pious man, yet he committed several actions that cannot be justified. He not only married both sisters, but while they yet lived, he took two other wives.

Jacob seems to have remained contentedly with Laban many years after his marriage; for we have no intimation of a desire to return to his country, till he was the father of eleven sons and one daughter. He then began to think of settling his family in the land which was ultimately to be their inheritance. But when he communicated his intention to his father-in-law, the latter would not consent to his desire. Experience, he said, had taught him, that the blessing of heaven attended the labours of Jacob. The cattle had increased to a multitude under his careful hand; and now if he would yet remain in his service, whatsoever he required should be his. Persuaded by this tempting offer, Jacob proposed to receive for his wages a certain share of the flocks committed to his charge. The terms were accepted, and he removed with his family several days' journey from the dwelling of his father-in-law, and attended his charge with assiduity. As wealth accumulated around him, the jealousy of Laban's sons was proportionably excited. They saw a stranger growing rich on their patrimony, and forgetting the long and faithful service by which he had purchased his right, they instigated their father to treat him with coldness.

About the same time, in a dream he was commanded to return to his native country; a step which he knew would be opposed by Laban, who had manifested, so repeatedly, his anxious desire to convert to his own advantage the temporal blessings so abundantly bestowed upon Jacob. To compel his continuance in Mesopotamia, violent measures might perhaps be adopted— even the seizure of his wives and their children, should his intention to depart be communicated to his father-in-law. A secret removal would prevent inconvenient collisions—and to obtain the acquiescence of Leah and Rachel, when he informed them of the mandate he had received, he expatiated on the services he had rendered to their family, and the ingratitude and treachery he had experienced. The sisters had been made sadly sensible of the avaricious disposition of their father; they now saw the alienation of his affections, and declared their readiness to submit to the divine command.

CATHERINE. Their simple mode of life was favourable to the execution of their plan; they were not encumbered, with the multifarious articles of household furniture indispensable with us.

MOTHER. A very few utensils, and those of primary necessity, supplied the wants of Jacob's family. Their wealth consisting chiefly in cattle and servants, was easily put in motion; so that the Euphrates was passed, and three days journey performed, without interruption. But the march of so large a cavalcade could not be concealed; Laban heard of it, and immediately pursuing, he overtook them encamped on Mount Gilead, and warmly expostulated with Jacob for having carried off his daughters, and his grandchildren without allowing him to dismiss them with paternal embraces, and with feasting and music, agreeably to their customs. It was still in his power, he said, to injure him, but he would abstain, because he had been warned by God, not to touch his servant.

Although Laban had affected to mingle kindness with his censures, this last acknowledgment was to Jacob a conviction, that he did not owe his safety to the voluntary forbearance of his father-in-law: he therefore recited the labors and sufferings he had endured, the unjust treatment he had received, and declared plainly that he had departed in silence because he had apprehended the loss of his family, had he permitted them to take leave. The acrimony of their mutual upbraidings, however, at length gave way to tender recollections; and, after they had agreed to separate in peace, they built a pillar of stones on the Mount, as a memorial of their friendship.

CHARLES. I am impatient to know how his brother Esau received him. I hope he had forgiven him during his long absence.

MOTHER. Jacob had now been twenty years in exile, and seems to have held no correspondence with his father's house: for he was ignorant of any change in his brother's disposition towards him, and still dreaded his presence. To appease him, therefore, and to signify his own penitence and submission, he sent messengers before him to Mount Seir, the dwelling of Esau, to apprise him respectfully of his approach; and was greatly distressed when returning, they told him that his brother was coming to meet him with four hundred men. Uncertain of his fate, yet fearing the worst, even the sacri¬fice of his wives and his children, he prepared to defend them: he divided his company into two bands; that if one should perish, the other might escape. Then solemnly, calling upon the God of his fathers to deliver him from his enemies, he acknowledged his guilt and unworthiness of all the mercies he had received—he, who had gone out with "his staff in his hand," and was now returning with abundant possessions!

The next morning he took from his flocks a munificent present for Esau, and sent it before him commanding his servants to deliver his gift in the lowliest language, and to say, "*thy servant* Jacob is behind us." The night following, his Almighty Benefactor again appeared to him —again renewed his promise of protection—and gave him a new name, that of *Israel**—a word which imports peculiar honour. Still suffering in his reproving conscience the just punishment of his former duplicity, when he came in sight of Esau, he arranged his family in order, to meet the hostile company, as he supposed; placing his beloved Rachel and her only son Joseph, behind the rest—and then advanced bowing himself seven times to the ground. But how great was his joy and surprise to find himself in the arms of a reconciled brother, shedding tears of love and pardon on his neck! His Leah and his Rachel were now introduced—the little ones were presented—and the gift which Esau had considerately declined, because he already possessed more than enough, was again pressed, and finally accepted. The now happy Jacob, in his turn, declined the offer of his brother's attendance on his journey. His servants were then offered to assist the more delicate of the train, and wait upon the children. But the friendship of his brother was all that Jacob required, and he civilly refused to put him to any further trouble. So they parted in perfect amity. Esau returned to his dwelling at Mount Seir, and Jacob at length arrived in safety in the land of his nativity.

FANNY. It is a little strange that Jacob was so willing to dispense with his brother's company on his journey, considering his own anxiety and Esau's kindness.

MOTHER. In this interview, although the behaviour of Esau was kind, his brother was perhaps not satisfied of its sincerity, and did not therefore feel very easy in the presence of his four hundred attendants. Under this impression, he might naturally wish for an immediate separation.

At a place called Shalem, a city of Sichem, Jacob first erected his tents. Some time afterwards he was commanded to remove to Bethel, (the sacred spot where God had appeared to him when he fled from Esau,) to build an altar and to dwell there. At Ephrath (afterwards Bethlehem,) on this sorrowful journey, he buried Rachel, (after she had given birth to Benjamin, her second son,) and gratified his steady affection by erecting a monument to her memory.

Before he left Shalem, he called on his wives and his servants to deliver up all the household gods, they had brought with them from Mesopotamia, and there he buried them, resolving to perform the vow he had made, that the "Lord should be his god."

CHARLES. What do you mean by household gods?

MOTHER. A sort of tutelary idol retained by the heathens in their houses, under the vain imagination, that they derived protection and prosperity from their presence.

FANNY. You tell us, mother, no more of the venerable Isaac, or of Rebekah. Did they not live to receive the fugitive?

MOTHER. Isaac saw him return; his death is recorded soon after, (B. C. 1716) at the age of an hundred and fourscore years. Of Rebekah we hear no more, although the death and burial of Deborah her nurse, one of the females who attended her from her father's house, is mentioned about this time.

*Israel, one who prevails with God.

§65 Grace Aguilar
(1816–1847)

Aguilar was a Jewish woman living in England.[23] She wrote for other Jewish women to show them that the Hebrew scriptures portrayed women in a posi-

---

[23] For more details on Aguilar's life, see part 2, "Sarah—The First Mother of Israel."

tive light, and so argued that they did not need to convert to Christianity to gain equality with men. In her book *The Women of Israel* (1845), Aguilar wrestled at length with the interpretive difficulties found in the Leah and Rachel story.

Like other interpreters, Aguilar compared the characters of the two sisters. She found them very different and marveled that they came from the same family. Aguilar portrayed Leah as a pious woman, whom readers should pity because she was unloved. Rachel was impatient and rebellious and suffered the consequences of her poor attitude. Aguilar also discussed the positive qualities of Rachel: she drew a lesson for readers from the fact that God answered Rachel's prayer for children, and thought that Joseph's positive qualities reflected well upon his mother. In the conclusion of the chapter, Aguilar noted that both Leah's and Rachel's children were equally represented in the two remaining tribes of Israel, Judah and Benjamin.

Aguilar drew attention to details that O'Keeffe and Hall also noticed. Like O'Keeffe, Aguilar noted the detail of Jacob's tears when he met Rachel. Like Hall, Aguilar mentioned the speed with which Jacob's family was able to pack up and move. Unlike the two previous writers, Aguilar was concerned to explicitly apply lessons from the story of Leah and Rachel to her readers. She preached sermons to her assumed audience of Jewish women, exhorting them to learn from and be comforted by the stories of their foremothers.

From Grace Aguilar, *The Women of Israel* (London, 1845). [Text from New York: D. Appleton (1901), 96–121.]

–Leah and Rachel–

. . . Lonely and sad the exiled Jacob had turned from the home of his childhood and the parents of his love. The child of promise and of prayer—the inheritor of God's especial blessing—the ancestor of kings—was compelled to make his bed on the cold earth, with nothing but stones for his pillow. How must his thoughts have clung to his mother and his home! That his heart was once more fitted for the reception and comprehension of holy things, is proved by the dream which Infinite Wisdom vouchsafed, to strengthen and encourage him. The promise would not have been revealed to one unworthy to receive it. Though human weakness may sully and darken even the choicest servants of the Lord, yet not unto the impure, the unholy, the unrepentant, would the Holy One impart the blessing of His spirit and His guidance. Acknowledgment of his fault must have brought Jacob once more to the feet of his Heavenly Father, or the confirmation of the blessed promise would have still been delayed. . . .

As Jacob was subject to all the inconveniences, fatigue, and suffering of travelling through a strange and often hostile country, as any other wanderer—his feelings, on nearing the abode of his uncle, may more easily be imagined than described. In his conversation with the shepherds, and then in his actively rolling aside the stone and watering the sheep, we may read the manly effort to restrain emotion, which, however, spurned all control when, in the simple and beau¬tiful affection of the patriarchal age, "he kissed Rachel, and lifted up his voice and wept." Wept, that God had in His loving mercy guided him thus far, and seemed to promise that newly known, yet instinctively loved, relations should fill up the aching void in his heart, which the sudden separation from his mother must have caused.

"And it came to pass, when Laban heard the tidings of Jacob, his sister's son, that he ran to meet him, and em¬braced him, and kissed him, and brought him to his house. And he told Laban all these things. And Laban said, Surely thou art my bone and my flesh. And he abode with him the space of a month." Again is family affection vividly brought before us.

If the reckoning of some commentators be true, and Jacob was seventy-six when he entered the household of Laban, nearly one hundred years must have elapsed since Rebekah had quitted her maiden home. Yet how closely and fondly must her memory have been enshrined in the heart of her brother, and through him cherished by his children, that Jacob was thus so warmly and delightedly welcomed, simply because he was "Rebekah's son.". . .

Two daughters blessed the house of Laban; the elder Leah, the younger Rachel. Now "Leah was tender-eyed, and Rachel beautiful and well-favored." As the sacred historian disdains not to mention this, we may be permitted to pause one moment upon the characteristics of the two sisters. That Leah was much less beautiful than her sister is evident from the words of the text, but it does not appear that she was as plain and homely as some commentators declare her. The Hebrew word translated "tender," "And the eyes of Leah were tender (וְעֵינֵי לֵאָה רַכּוֹת)," does not signify weak only, as is generally supposed, but soft and delicate, and leads me to suppose that the soft and tender eyes of Leah were her only good feature, whereas her younger sister was "very beautiful and of exceeding beauty," which is the literal meaning of the Hebrew expression וְרָחֵל הָיְתָה יְפַת־תֹּאַר וִיפַת מַרְאֶה, though even such translation is far from possessing the force of the original. This difference of appearance occasioned, as would appear by the sequel, a complete difference of character.

One month Jacob abode with his uncle, evidently doing him active service in return for the hospitality which he had received. That he did so, tells well for the real character of the wanderer; for in his father's house Jacob had never been accustomed to active service, and it must have demanded some little exertion of will over inclination, to have permitted its steady and active performance. Laban, however, at this period of their intimacy, felt too kindly and generously toward his nephew to permit him to work without wages. "And he said unto him, Because thou art my brother, shouldst thou therefore serve me for naught? Tell me what shall thy wages be? And Jacob loved Rachel, and said, I will serve thee seven years for Rachel thy younger daughter. And Laban said, It is better I give her unto thee than to another man. Abide with me. And Jacob served seven years for Rachel; *and they seemed unto him but a few days, for the love he had to her.*"

We think much of those tales of chivalry where man per¬forms some great and striking deed—conquers his own pas¬sions—becomes a voluntary wanderer—all to win the smile and love of woman. And we do right, for the motive is pure and the moral good. But such high-wrought volumes should not blind our hearts and eyes to this exquisite narration, wherein the same truth, the same moral is impressed, with equal force and beauty, only in the simple language of the Bible. Jacob's servitude was a more convincing proof of his love and constancy than those exciting deeds of heroism which chivalry records. His was no service to call upon distant lands and far-off ages to admire. Nothing for FAME, that brilliant meteor, which, equally with love, divided the warrior's heart in the middle ages. Nothing to vary the routine of seven years' domestic duty, the wearisome nature of which we find in the 38th and 39th verses of chapter xxxi. Yet these "seven years seemed but *as a few days for the love he had to her.*" A brief yet most emphatic sentence, revealing the purest, the holiest, the most unselfish love, unrestrained by one fleeting thought of worldly aggrandizement, or a hope beyond making that beloved one his own. "Consumed by the draught by day, chilled by the frost at night," still he never wavered. Love was his upholder—his sustainer. And it was for this end love was so mercifully given. . . .

Something more than Rachel's beauty, marvellous as that was, must have so retained Jacob's love for her in those seven years of domestic intercourse, as to make the time appear but a few days. Beauty may attract and win if the time of courtship be too brief to require no other charm, but it is not sufficient of itself to *retain* affection. Gift from God, as it is, how may it be abused, and how may it be wasted in caring only for the lovely shape *without*, and leaving the rich invisible gems within uncared for and unused! Oh! if there be one among my youthful readers, of beauty exceeding as that of Rachel, who holdeth in her possession this rich gift of God, let her remember that He will demand of her how she hath used it—that its abuse, its *pretended* neglect, yet in reality proud value, will pass not unnoticed by its beneficent Giver. It has been granted for some end—for if to look on a beautiful flower will excite emotions of admiration and love, and consequently enjoyment, how much more deeply would such feelings be called forth by a beautiful face, could we but behold it as the hands of God had formed it, unshaded by the impress of those emotions of pride, contempt, or self-sufficiency, or that utter void of intellect, which are but too often its concomitants, from the mistaken notion that outward beauty is omnipotent, and needs no help within.

To hide from a young girl that she is beautiful is the extreme of folly, for her mirror will tell her that she is being deceived, and the influence of such informers will be lost at once. No—let the real value and consequent *responsibility* of beauty be inculcated, and there will be no fear of its abuse.

That Rachel had many most endearing qualities we may quite infer from Jacob's devoted love to her even to her death. The spirit most impatient under contradiction, and loving its own will, is often united to a manner so engaging, and qualities so calculated to win regard, that trivial faults of temper and will are literally engendered from the difficulty it is to reprove a being so beautiful and so beloved; and this would seem the case with Rachel. Young, joyous, and loving, we may fancy her the very star of her father's home, valuing her beauty as it gave her power to obtain whatever she willed uncontradicted, but using it only in the sphere of home.

But though Jacob's affections were devoted to one alone, those seven years of intimate association must have been fraught with suffering and sadness to Laban's elder daughter, whose strong affection for Jacob the sequel will reveal. Her compelled agency in her father's fraud must have been fraught with absolute horror to a heart that loved secretly and unreturned, as herself, and heightened the trial of unrequited affection in no ordinary degree.

We will not linger on the affairs narrated in Genesis xxix., from the 21st to the 30th verse, because they belong so strictly to the manners and customs of the Eastern nations: that it is quite impossible to comment upon them with any justice, prejudiced, as birth and education cannot fail to make us, in favor of the manners and customs of modern Europe. Yet the customs of the East have undergone little or no change; and repeatedly we find that which in the narratives of the Bible may startle our modern European notions, as strange and improbable, confirmed by events passing in the East at this very day, so that those very narratives would there be scarcely considered a history of the past.

Though beguiled into another seven years' servitude for his much-loved Rachel, it is evident that she had become his wife *first*, Jacob honorably performing the word he had pledged, *after* the wished-for prize had been obtained; and not till those seven years were completed, do we hear him utter one word of complaint or one wish to provide for "his own house also."

"And when the Lord saw that Leah was hated (lit. less loved), He gave her children, but Rachel had none. And she called the name of her eldest son Reuben: for, she said, "Surely the Lord hath looked upon my affliction; now therefore my husband will love me." What a volume of woman's deepest feelings and the compassionating love of the Eternal do these brief lines reveal! He who had, in His inscrutable wisdom, ordained that Leah should be tried in the fiery ordeal of woman's saddest loneliness, unrequited affection, yet deigned to grant a compensating blessing in all the sweet, pure feelings of a mother's love. Who that reads but this one verse can uphold that woman is less an object of tender love and compassion to her God than *man*? Who can say that the Mosaic records are silent on this head? The words of man to point out the proper station and value of woman we need not, for the children of Israel have the WORD of THEIR GOD. And do we not still recognize the God of Leah? His ear has not become heavy that it cannot hear, nor His arm shortened that it cannot save. And though He may not bestow on us a *visible* and audible manifestation of His tender compassion as on Leah, yet we may be certain that He will grant us some compensating blessing for every joy of which he may think fit to deprive us. And even for those bitter griefs, which from their nature, their seeming selfishness, woman shrinks in trembling from bringing before her God, and buries them in her own heart till it bleeds at every pore—Leah's history proves that He will grant peace and healing. It may be that a wiser and kinder will than her own has flung an insuperable barrier between woman's heart and its dearest object; and impelled her by all that is refined and delicate in her character, to hide deep from every eye the anguish which is her burden. How blessed then that even for such a grief there is the fount of healing waters still in the Word of God—that she may come there and read, not only the abundance, the fulness of his love, but that He has especial tenderness for those by earth unloved! And as He gave Leah children because she was not loved, so will He grant such sufferers a peace, and calm, and joy in the consciousness of His unfailing tenderness, far surpassing even the rich and glowing, but too transient happiness of sympathy on earth.

Leah must have known and loved the Lord long before the event recorded, else she had not thus welcomed the birth of her first child. Eight years of Jacob's sojourn in her father's household would scarcely have been sufficient for her to know and love her cousin's invisible God, had she not had some vague yet true notions of Him before.

That Jacob should often have alluded to the God of his fathers, and narrated the wonderful manifestations of His providence, and that such solemn themes should have fallen with peculiar impressiveness on the heart of Leah, and but lightly on the buoyant impetuous Rachel, may be inferred from the history of both. After the gods of her father, Leah has no hankering whatever; her reference, in both her griefs and joys, is to Jacob's God alone.

By her exclamation at the birth of her second son, we may suppose that the fond hope expressed the year previous, "Now therefore my husband will love me," was still not realized. "Because the Lord hath heard that I am not loved, He hath therefore given me this son also." To many the repetition of a blessing renders it invaluable, and, in the imperfection of our earthly nature, the continued disappointment of our dearest wishes would have rendered the heart callous, perhaps repining, at the very blessing which had before brought joy. But not thus was it with Leah: gratefully she received a second little treasure from the hand of her God; and, bearing again the pang of ever-blighted hope, she utters no wish of an earthly kind, but simply feels she has still the love of God. Another year, and another son is granted; and we may trace a ray beaming even through her earthly darkness, in the new upspringing of buoyant hope—"Now will my husband be joined unto me, for I have borne him three sons."

Whether, indeed, the fond wish was realized, and Jacob's heart was softened toward her, must be but conjecture; yet it would almost appear so, for, at the birth of her fourth son, her pious heart is satisfied with the fervent ejaculation, "Now will I praise the Lord." Drawn closer and closer unto her God, with His every precious gift, she, who gave her first-born a name signifying "the son of affliction," gave her fourth the beautiful appellation of "praise unto the Lord." It was not only a gift of children, then, His love bestowed. He had brought light from darkness, He had turned her mourning into praise, and returned with tenfold blessing her meek enduring confidence in Him. Shall we then, who may be in the darkness of sorrow and heavy care, shrink from walking in her steps, and dwell only on the *affliction* which is ours? Shall we not also look and strive for some blessing which can bid us too "praise the Lord," and lead us to behold *light* where all was heaviness? There is no lot so desolate which, if we seek Him, the Lord will not bless: not, perhaps, by the removal of our present sorrow, but by some compensating mercy. We must not suppose that seeking Him and loving Him will exempt us from affliction. No, for, if it did, where would be that heavenly exercise which alone can fit us for heaven? Nor are we, as some enthusiasts would urge, to regard *trials* as *joys*, and welcome them with gladness. When a tender loving parent chastises a beloved child to keep him from the paths of sin, would he feel that the chastisement had done its work if the little being received it with smiles and rejoicing? Surely the parent would be more hopeful if the child were serious, and even sad. And is it not so with the afflictions sent from our eternal and most tender Father? We may think that we surely need them not; and our lives may even be, in the sight of man, as we ourselves suppose them. Nay, they may be numbered among those whom the Bible gives us promise shall be accounted the righteous in the sight of God; yet how know we what we might have been *without* such affliction? How know we but those very sorrows, lasting but a *time*, are preparing us to be of those whom the Lord writeth in His book for eternity, who shall be His when He maketh up His jewels? Of this only are we certain, that the Lord *loveth* whom He correcteth. Then, while like Leah we *feel* affliction, let us hope on, pray on, with undoubting faith, that one day we too shall cry aloud, "Now will I praise the Lord."

Very different to the meek submissiveness and gentle disposition of her elder sister, is the impetuous temper and sinful feeling of envy which urged Rachel angrily to exclaim, even to her doting husband, "Give me children, or else I die." And Jacob's anger was kindled against Rachel and he said, Am I in God's stead, who hath withheld children from thee?

We have been previously told—"And when Rachel saw that she bare Jacob no children, she envied her sister." Envied whom? even the homely, the unloved Leah. It was not enough that God had endowed her with most surpassing beauty; and given her the perfect love of a husband who had proved, was still proving his devoted attachment to herself alone, by fourteen years' hard servitude. It signified little that Leah *had but her children*, and that her own cup of blessings was filled to flowing over.

In glancing over the history of the two sisters, must we not feel that Rachel *ought* to be the happier, as she was the more blessed? Yet it was not so. Leah, with her heavy burden of affliction, was the happier, for she neither envied nor complained, but leaned upon her God—and in consequence, from Him received consolation. Rachel could have had no such stay. "Give me children, or else I die!" was the exclamation of a querulous, self-willed spirit, looking only to man, and depending upon him. Yet the knowledge of the Lord must have been equally revealed to Rachel as to her sister. Daughters of the same household, cousins of the same witness of God—Jacob's religious education and experience must have been imparted to her also. She may have even listened during the time for Jacob's sake, banishing its recollection entirely afterward, as a theme much too solemn and grave for her present joyous days. And are there not such even now, deeming religion and her rich train of holy and blessed thoughts, quite incompatible with youth and beauty, and who believe age is time enough to think of such serious things?

That her feeling and its expression were both wrong we perceive by Jacob's anger and reproof. Loving Rachel as he did, it must have been something very blamable to call severity from his lips. Ignorance may excite our pity, but not our blame. Had Rachel been ignorant who had blessed her sister with children, Jacob would have answered differently—but her impatient words caused his "anger to be kindled against her," because he felt and knew that

they must have come from a spirit as impatient as rebellious, and were therefore likely to excite the displeasure of the Lord. "Am I in God's stead?" meaning, can I give you children if God hath withheld them. Words brief, but
impressively proving Jacob's individual dependence on and trust in his God,
and which ought to have subdued and humbled the discontent and envy of
his wife. But though they checked the querulous *words*, they had no power to
change the inward *feelings*, and determined at all risks, all sacrifices, to obtain
children also, she followed the example of Sarah, and forced her husband, by
increasing the number of his wives, to undergo all the miseries of a divided
household.

Yet when Bilhah had a son, we find Rachel welcoming him with such a
joyful thanksgiving, and as a gift from God—that we might wonder at her
former impatience did we not know, that there are many who trace the hand
of the Lord, and think they love and serve Him, when all of life is smooth
and smiling, yet act, at the first trial, for the first cross, as if they knew Him
not at all, and denied His power to help and save. "God hath judged me; and
hath also heard my voice, and hath given me a son." Had she then prayed—
and did she recognize in thoughtfulness the answer *to her prayer?* Or was
her exclamation at the birth of Dan but a presumptuous supposition from a
presumptuous spirit—believing without due authority that she had prevailed
with God? We have not sufficient authority in Scripture, to pronounce judgment one way or the other on this point, and must therefore leave it to the
consideration of our readers.

Once only do words of sorrowing reproach escape Leah's lips toward her
sister. "Is it a small matter that thou hast taken my husband?" Words simply expressive of the natural pang which must sometimes have entered her
heart—when year after year passed, and still beheld her deep affections less
valued than the lighter love of Rachel.

Two other sons were born unto the elder sister; and one daughter, a
blessing which had never before been vouchsafed the patriarchs. Then it
was, "that God remembered Rachel; and God hearkened to her and gave
her children." "God remembered Rachel." Had He forgotten? no, neither
forgetfulness nor memory dwelleth with God—for He is omniscient as
omnipotent, knowing and perceiving all. But when speaking of Him, His
dealings with His children must be expressed in language, and by images
suited to their finite conception—not according to the adorable and glorious, but unfathomable infinity surrounding Him. He *thought* upon and
hearkened to her—for such is, equally with *remember*, the meaning of the
term—וַיִּזְכֹּר אֱלֹהִים אֶת־רָחֵל וַיִּשְׁמַע אֵלֶיהָ אֱלֹהִים—words, how full
of consolation and encouragement to Rachel's female descendants! Man
would have condemned, and sentenced her to a chastisement of perpetual

childlessness—for the tenderest mercies of humanity are cruel compared to the tender mercies of the Most High, but He whom she had offended by mistrust, forgetfulness, impatience, angry emotions toward her sister, had compassion, and not only "remembered" that she was a weak and yearning woman, but "hearkened" to her supplications, and gave reply.

"God hath taken away my reproach," Rachel gratefully exclaimed. "And she called his name Joseph, and said, "the Lord shall add unto her another son." Could she have penetrated futurity well indeed might she have felt that God had removed her reproach; for who that reflects on the angelic beauty and faultlessness of Joseph, can recall his mother without bestowing on her a portion of the love and veneration we lavish on her son.

It is when bowed down by inward remorse for a consciousness of innate sinfulness, by the impossibility of realizing that perfect holiness which would guard us from approach to wrong either in act and thought toward our fellow-creatures, or in mistrust and forgetfulness of God, that we should remember the history of Rachel and take comfort. There are some, who, unable to bear the sting of an awakened conscience, drown it altogether, by fleeing from every holy exercise of prayer and self-examination, and believe that as in this life we must be liable to occasional faults, it is perfectly useless striving, much less praying against them, as such prayer can be of no service, and is but a mockery before God. Some minds may bear this awful state to others, the young, the deeper feeling, and more yearning hearts, it is a period of absolute anguish which, without some spiritual help, is impossible to be sustained; and so religion is cast off as a subject of terror, of suffering, and the world and the world's panaceas substituted in its place. To such, more especially if they be women, we would say, Come but to the Word of God—and even for such griefs there is all we need. There the Eternal not only proclaims "Himself a God full of compassion, long suffering, abundant in goodness and mercy, forgiving iniquity, transgression, and sin," but *proves* these consoling and most blessed attributes, not only *after*, but *before* they were proclaimed. Rachel was more faulty than many of her sex, yet her prayers were heard, her affliction compassionated, her wish fulfilled. How may we then despair, or think that the infirmities of our mortal frame and the sinfulness they bring, can throw a barrier between us and our God? It is not to the righteous alone He awardeth mercy and love, but to the contrite and humble spirit, with whom the "High and Holy One who inhabiteth eternity delighteth to dwell." With such proofs we may not despair, we *dare not* doubt, but we are called to Him as little children sorrowing to be *forgiven*, in the full consciousness how deeply we are *loved*. . . .

Increasing exceedingly in much cattle, and maidservants and men-ser-vants, and camels, and asses, the wrath and envy of Laban's sons were excited toward him [Jacob]. And he saw that Laban's own countenance was not toward him as before—circumstances which must have excited much human anxiety and fear. And then it was the Lord said unto him, "Return unto the land of thy fathers and thy kindred, and I will be with thee."

"And Jacob sent and called Rachel and Leah to the field unto his flock." And in the perfect confidence of love and respect, imparted all to them. "I see your father's countenance is not toward us as before; but the God of my fathers has been with me. And ye know that with all my power I have served your father; and your father has deceived me, and changed my wages ten times; but God suffered him not to hurt me. If he said thus, The speckled shall be thy wages, then all the cattle bare speckled; and if he said thus, The ring-straked shall be thy hire, then all the cattle bare ring-straked. *Thus God hath taken away the cattle of your father, and given them to me.*"

There is something to me peculiarly beautiful in this simple address of Jacob, spoken as it is to his wives. Not a word of reproach on their father, but the simple truth infinitely more expressive of the wrong he has suffered than any violence or invective. All that has blessed him, he traces unfailingly to God. The whole of his address, from the 5th to the 13th verse of Gen. xxxi., demands attention from its revealing so much more concerning Laban's real conduct to his nephew, and in what manner that conduct was regarded and overruled by the Eternal, than we can learn by the bare narration of the previous chapter. Our present subject forbids our lingering on it, except to say, it completely absolves Jacob from all fraudulent dealings with his uncle, while it reveals that he himself was the victim of deceit.

The mandate of God was in Jacob's ear, and every emotion of humanity was urging him to tarry not, but to flee at once. He had dominion over all his household, yet he waits to impart his wishes and his fears to his wives: he will make no step in advance without their concurrence; thus at once proving his love and their equality. And, without a moment's hesitation, Rachel and Leah answered and said unto him, "Is there yet any portion or inheritance for us in our father's house? Are we not accounted of him as strangers? for he hath sold us, and has quite devoured our money. For all the riches which God has taken from our father, that is *ours* and *our* children's. Now then, whatsoever God hath said unto thee do."

Different as the sisters were in disposition, and placed in a situation most likely to create discord and disunion, yet when the interests of a beloved husband are at stake, they act in perfect unity and love. There is no "mine and thine"—words how often fraught with discord—but simply "ours and our children's." Seeking even to reconcile him yet more to his flight—enriched as he was—by stating the simple fact, that Laban had failed in his duty toward them, by giving them neither portion nor inheritance; and by having *sold* them to Jacob for fourteen years of labor. That which God then had marked as Jacob's share of the flocks and herds, was but their right and their children's.

Yet it must have been a trial to both sisters to remove so hastily and unexpectedly with their young children from the home of their earliest years, without even bidding farewell to the parent they had loved so long, to their brothers and their friends, to venture on a strange and dangerous track to a land they knew not, save that it was far away from their childhood's home. We already know where Leah's affliction always led her, and are, therefore, justified in believing that now, as before, prayer was the soother of her natural sorrows, and her confidence, that even if her father pursued them, he would not be permitted to work them harm. But Rachel could not thus realize the ever-present, ever-protecting arm of the Eternal; and, as before she had sought human means to further her impatient wishes, so now does she bear away with her secretly "the images which were her father's"; superstitiously believing, according to some commentators, that by consulting them, Laban would discover their route, and so be enabled to follow and arrest them. It is scarcely possible to peruse the history of these two sisters without being struck with the beautiful unity and harmony displayed in their two characters distinct from first to last, and each preserving her individual peculiarities. Thrown back upon herself, from wanting the attractions of beauty and vivacity granted to her younger sister, Leah's graces expanded inwardly and spiritually; her yearning affections always strongest from never finding vent by being called for and appreciated by man. Rejoicingly and gratefully acknowledging and believing the blessed religion which told her of an unchanging Friend and most tender loving Father, she found in such belief enough, and could realize content in the midst of trial, happiness in the midst of grief. Such a character as Leah's, from the time she is revealed to us, so perfectly free from all wrong feelings in a situation so likely to excite them, is not natural to woman; and we may, therefore, infer that her youth had had its trials, which the grace of God had blessed, in making her rise from them the gentle, enduring, lovable being which His Word reveals.

The faults of Rachel originated in the very cause which had been a chastening to her sister. Her own surpassing loveliness, while ever the theme of admiration to her fellows, so raised her in her own estimation, that it was difficult to look beyond this world, where she reigned pre-eminent, to another, where she, in all her beauty, was but an atom—a creature of the dust. What to her was the love and protection of an Invisible Being, when she was so surrounded by the love and care of man? What to her needed the tale of future happiness? Was she not joyous and laughter-loving the livelong day? With power in herself to bend all hearts, and direct all circumstances to the furtherance of her own impetuous will? Such we must believe the youth of Rachel, when we see her repining that children were granted to her sister and not to her. We behold her secretly bearing away the gods of her father whether from the reason mentioned above, or from her own lingering belief in their efficacy and power, still equally reprehensible in the wife of Jacob.

If, indeed, Rachel supposed that in removing the images she prevented her father from discovering their route, she very speedily found herself mistaken. Jacob had stolen "away unawares from Laban the Syrian, in that he told him not that he fled; so he fled with all that he had, and he rose up, and passed over the river, and set his face toward the mount Gilead." And there, seven days after their hasty flight, Laban overtook him with all his kindred, and sufficient followers "to do them hurt," "Had not the God of your father," he said, "spake unto me yesternight, saying, Take thou heed that thou speak not to Jacob good or bad."

Anxiously and fearfully, according to their different characters, must Leah and Rachel have awaited the issue of the conference. The number of followers argued ill; yet the words of Laban were at first but mild reproach. "Wherefore didst thou flee away secretly, and steal away from me, and didst not tell me, that I might have sent thee away with mirth and with songs, with tabret and with harp: and hast not suffered me to kiss my sons and daughters? Thou hast done foolishly in so doing."

We may well suppose words as these, being fraught with self-reproach to affectionate daughters, that they had indeed so left their father. To Leah his next words, alluding to the "God of thy father," must have been particularly and gratefully soothing. He to whom she prayed was indeed ever around them, turning aside the wrath of men, forbidding him to arouse wrath by "speaking either bad or good." Holy Writ does not indeed tell us, that Leah prayed in this instance; but she who welcomed the birth of every child with prayer and thanksgiving—who in no instance had recourse to her father's gods—was not likely to forget her husband's God when his protection was so needed. We may be permitted to believe she prayed; and can we not imagine the fervor of her grateful thanksgiving when she heard such words from her father? And we may all experience this. There is not one who has addressed the Lord in prayer—the daily prayer for all things, who can say he has had no answer. And oh! who would not realize the glowing of the heart—the burst of thanksgiving which fills it—when we trace his hand in the daily events of life, and feel that that which we have asked for He has given? But to realize this, we must come to Him in all things. We must pray to Him in our hearts as well as with our lips; we must *think* individual prayer as well as those public petitions framed for us. We must be in the constant habit of tracing all things to His almighty hand, and believe that his love is as deep, as pitying, for us individually, as his bounty is shown throughout the world. We must so commune with Him, that the hours of prayer will feel but the *continuation*, not the commencement and end of devotion. Did we but do this—bring before Him every care, and thought, and grief, and joy, and doubt, and thankfulness—how many, many instances of answered prayer would the briefest life recall. Then, oh! how can we keep Him far from us, by withholding from Him the wishes which He alone has power to grant, the sorrows which He alone has compassion sufficient to heal?

On Rachel's ear, the words which filled her sister's heart with deepest thankfulness must have fallen little heeded, while those which followed them, utterly meaningless to Leah, must have been fraught to her with wildest terror, fearfully increased by the instant answer of her husband: "And now, though thou wouldst needs be gone, because thou sore longest after thy father's house, yet wherefore hast thou stolen my gods? And Jacob answered and said (in reply to Laban's previous words of reproach), Because I was afraid, for I said, peradventure thou wouldst take by force thy daughters from me." And then, with regard to the last accusation: "With whomsoever thou findest thy gods let him not live. Before our brethren discover what is thine, and take it to thee. For Jacob knew not that Rachel had stolen them."

That she had concealed the theft from her husband proves at once that she knew the feelings dictating it were wrong, yet had not sufficient moral courage to resist them. And now what must have been her terrors? Not only was the plan which she had adopted to prevent a hostile meeting between her father and husband, apparently about to be the very means of dissension, but if discovered, Jacob's own lips had pronounced her death-doom. We know not if in the patriarchal times death was usually the punishment awarded to criminals convicted of theft; but it is evident that Jacob fully intended the criminal in his household to suffer even death for his offence, by the sacred historian so expressly declaring that "Jacob knew not that Rachel had stolen them." How could he suspect the wife of his bosom—his best beloved—of such theft as might almost convict her of idolatry?

Little did he dream whom he was condemning, or the misery he would have drawn upon himself, had not the God who had promised to bring him to his father's home in peace, here interposed, and saved both him, and for his sake, and the sake of His own great name, the faulty Rachel.

Yet during the period of Laban's search for the images, till the danger of discovery was quite past, how terrible must have been her alarm, and how painful her emotions! How different from the meek quietude of a holy spirit, at peace with itself and its God, which throughout this interview was Leah's! Yet no doubt, true to the contrarieties of imperfect humanity, when discovery was averted, and Laban found not the gods, Rachel only felt penetrated with pious gratitude, and resolved to keep her fault more strictly secret from her husband than ever. Some commentators, I believe, accuse her of an inclination to, if not of direct, idolatry; but we do not think that Holy Writ sufficiently authorizes such a charge. Superstition, the remains of childhood's tales, which urged her to the course of acting with regard to the images already dilated upon, is not in the least incompatible with her recognition of, and belief in, Jacob's God, even though the images remained with her until Jacob bade them "put away the strange gods that were among them," nearly seven years afterward. As his household consisted only of those who had lived with Laban he might easily have supposed the strange gods theirs, and Rachel had thus an opportunity of resigning them, without causing her husband the suffering it would have been, to suspect her of having either stolen them at first, or harbored them so long.

There is something very beautiful in Laban's parting care of his daughters, when the somewhat warm recrimination between himself and Jacob was at an end. The heap of stones was raised by all who had met in wrath, proving their reunion by their united labor, and the feast which all shared in harmony when the work was concluded. "And Laban said, This heap is a witness between thee and me. Therefore was the name of it called Gilead and Mizpah, for he said, the Lord watch between me and thee when we are absent one from another. *If thou shalt afflict my daughters, or if thou shalt take wives beside my daughters* (though no man is with us), see God is witness betwixt thee and me. This heap be my witness, and this pillar be my witness, that I will not pass over this heap to thee, and thou shalt not pass over this heap and this pillar unto me for harm. The God of Abraham, and the God of Nahor, and the God of thy father judge betwixt us. And Jacob swore by the fear of his father Isaac. And Jacob offered sacrifices on the mount, and called his brethren to eat bread; and they did eat bread, and tarried all night in the mount. And early in the morning Laban rose up, and kissed his sons (i. e. grandsons) and daughters, and blessed them; and Laban departed, and returned unto his place."

Thus were angry feelings calmed and soothed by a mutual covenant of love. While to the wives of the one, and the daughters of the other, how thrice blessed must have been the reconciliation which gave them again the dear privilege of a father's loving kiss and parting blessing! We learn too, from this simple narrative, that even in the East, a multiplicity of wives was decidedly not lawful, and that Laban considered the rights of his daughters would be infringed, and so call upon him to come forward in their defence, even to break the covenant of peace, did Jacob take any other wives. Human nature is indeed the same in all ages—for as Laban spake to Jacob thousands and thousands of years ago, so would a father now. As truly as the Bible reveals the truth, the beneficence, the tenderness of God—so truly does it reveal and answer every emotion of the human heart.

As our task is a record only of Leah the wife of Jacob, we must pass lightly over the events of the xxxii. and xxxiii. chapters of Genesis, which belong exclusively to the history of the patriarch himself. The wrath of man was again turned aside, and the blessing of the Lord made Jacob at peace even with his brother Esau. His doubts and fears, which must have extended painfully to the weaker nature of his wives, at news of Esau's armed approach, were subdued by the influence of his prayer, and the long separated brothers met in mutual tenderness and love. They did not, however, long remain together. Jacob and his family proceeded to Succoth, and then to Shechem, where he "bought a parcel of a field," after erecting his tents, and "built there an altar," and there remained, till commanded by the Lord to "arise and go to Bethel."

The period of these sojournings between his departure from Padan-Aram, to his proceeding to Bethel, must have been full seven years. The then tender ages of his younger children, and the number of his flocks and herds, in all probability prompted him to settle his residence in the first convenient spot in the land of Canaan. It appears strange that he did not pursue his way without any pause to his father's house; but it is one of those subjects on which the Word of God gives us no information, and therefore may be dismissed without wasting time and thought on what can be only speculation. At Shechem, Leah must have encountered indeed a fiery trial in the insult offered to her daughter, and the guilty conduct of her sons—Simeon and Levi. Here, as elsewhere, Jacob was punished by *deception*, causing fear and trouble, as he justly says: "Ye have troubled me to make me to stink among the inhabitants of the land, among the Canaanites and Perizzites, and I being few in number, they shall gather themselves against me, and slay me, and I shall be destroyed, I and my household." . . .

Ephrah was nearly reached, when the sudden illness of Rachel compelled the whole cavalcade to halt—and Jacob must have beheld with inexpressible anguish his best beloved wife torn from him, at the very moment she had increased his joy and her own by giving birth to a second son. When in the midst of bodily and mental anguish, she called his name Benoni, son of my sorrow, did she think of her own impatient words— "Give me children, or else I die!" and feel that it would have been better for her to have waited for the Lord? How may we answer? Enough for us to benefit by the record vouchsafed, and feel His will is better than our own—and in impatient restless longings for blessings granted to another, we may know, that even in the very fulfilment of the wish, the punishment may fall.

Rachel committed no fault in wishing for a child—her fault had been envy and its subsequent discontent. Years had passed, the very recollection of her restless discontent may have faded from her mind, but not from His whom she had by want of faith and gratitude offended. In His infinite mercy He forgave, He blessed, for He called her to Himself ere the evil days came, and her beloved one was sold by his brethren, and reported for long, long years as dead. He saved the mother this deep suffering, but, in His justice toward her and love to her descendants, He chastised by an early and painful death, the most trying separation of soul and body which human nature (so to speak) may know. Her husband, her Joseph—her new-born—suddenly and fearfully the silver links of love, binding her to all of these, were snapt asunder, and she might know her place on earth no more. "Give me children, or else I die." Alas! the too impatient cry was heard and answered; children were bestowed, and with them death. How little knew she what she asked! In all her surpassing loveliness, in the full possession of most faithful love, the destroying angel came and snatched her from this world. Oh! will not this teach us to be content with what God has given, and restrain us from looking with secret envy on the richer (in seeming) blessings of another? Will it not bid us beware of seeking aught of good only because it belongs to a companion, or because we fancy we have equal right to its possession, by the lesson that, even were it ours, we might have no power to enjoy it? Death, indeed, may not come between us and its enjoyment; but that which we have coveted loses its value the moment we possess it. Will not the warm young heart shrink from the very anticipation of the sin toward God and man which discontent may bring? Let us think more of our sorrowing and afflicted fellow-creatures, and less of those more blessed in outward seeming. Did we think on the bereaved, the physically afflicted, the poor, how could we still retain discontent of our own lot, or envy of our fellow-creatures? And oh! if no other reasoning will avail, let us remember, our God is not only a merciful, tender Father, but a just and jealous God, who will one day, we know not when or how, call upon us to render an account of the blessings He has given; and if we know them not, how may we answer? Long years had passed since Rachel's offence, yet He who slumbereth not nor sleepeth, chastised it in the very hour that the wish which caused it was fulfilled.

It may be asked (as in similar cases of bereavement it, alas! too often is), Why, granting that the lot of the departed is blessedness, does the God of love so afflict the survivors? Why did He cause such deep grief to His favored servant Jacob? Because God loved him; because His omniscience had seen that Rachel might come between Jacob's heart and his God; because He would demonstrate to futurity that, to possess His favor, His blessing, does not in any manner emancipate us from trial and suffering in this world; because He would lift up our affections from the narrow limits of this world, He would make His heaven a dearer home than our earth, He would people it with the immortal spirits of those we have loved on earth, that we may look upon it no longer as a strange land; but as the beautiful country where our beloved are gone, and where we shall follow. This is wherefore He bereaves, and therefore even in the bereavement there is love. . . .

The death of Leah is not recorded; we only know that she did not accompany the patriarch and his family to Egypt, and that she was buried with Abraham and Sarah, Isaac and Rebekah, in the cave of Machpelah. Left dependent on her tenderness and love, the extent of which we know, Jacob no doubt lavished warmer affection upon her, after the death of Rachel than before. How gratefully her pious heart must have traced this tranquil calm, which probably closed her days, to her God, we may infer from the thanksgiving with which every previous blessing had been received. But, as her future life can only be suggestion, much as imagination may love to dwell upon it, our present task must be concluded. We have dilated already at so much length upon the characters of the sisters, and the instruction and consolation therein developed, that we need add little further now, except to notice what has always appeared a remarkable manifestation of the perfect equality of the sisters in their position as mothers of that race which is to last forever. Ten tribes are lost—not to be discovered till the day which will behold the glorious and stupendous miracle of our restoration. The two which remain to bear witness to the mercy and justice of the Eternal, and the truth of His word, are JUDAH, the descendants of LEAH, and BENJAMIN, the descendants of RACHEL, from one or other of which every Israelite (except the representatives of the Levites, who were accounted the priests of the Lord, not of the twelve tribes) traces his descent.

Shall we then dismiss the beautiful record of Leah and Rachel, which the Word of God contains, as a mere relation, concerning an age so long past as to appear almost fabulous and obsolete? Shall we not rather take it to our hearts, and, as women of Israel, feel it is of our own ancestry we read? Shall we not emulate the much enduring piety of Leah; and in all our afflictions—even in that of a lone and unloved heart—turn to her God, and emulate her rejoicing acknowledgment of blessings at His hand? Shall we not take warning of the loved and lovely Rachel, and feel that neither beauty nor love—the dearest love of man—can afford us happiness and joy, unless both are traced to, and held from the grace of God? That not in outward attraction—not even in human love—can blessedness exist, unless the vital spark, to give them rest and life and continuance, hath dwelling *within*, to lift up the whole soul to God. O better—far better—homeliness of form and face, with a guileless contented heart. Better—far better—a heart desolate of earthly sympathy, with the love of our Father in heaven, than beauty and grace and human love, the fullest, dearest, combined with every worldly blessing—if these be sufficient for our need, and we pass through life without one thought of God.

§66 Clara Lucas Balfour
(1808–1878)

Clara Lucas Balfour (née Lyddell) married James Balfour at age 15. Balfour educated herself by reading extensively. She was raised in the Church of England but became a Baptist at age 32. The Balfours had six children. Balfour supported the family by public speaking and writing because her husband was unable to hold down a job due to his drinking problem. He later signed the temperance pledge and gave up drinking entirely.

Balfour joined the Baptist church at the same time she joined the temperance movement. Temperance, social justice, and feminism were important themes in her writing and speaking. These themes influenced her reading of scripture. Balfour wrote over seventy works (novels, journal articles, stories) on temperance over a forty-year period. She also wrote four books on women: *Women of Scripture* (1847); *Working Women of the Last Half Century: the Lessons of Their Lives* (1854); *The Bible Patterns of a Good Woman* (1867); and *Women Worth Emulating* (1877).

This selection on Leah and Rachel is taken from *Women of Scripture* (1847). Balfour's interpretation of the story was similar to other women's readings. Like O'Keeffe, she used descriptive language to bring the story to life. Like Hall and Aguilar, she gave the reason for Jacob's tears when he first met Rachel. Balfour addressed the issue of parental favoritism raised by Jacob's treatment of Rachel's sons, Joseph and Benjamin. Balfour suggested this was not favoritism but the "compensating tenderness" of a father who had to be both mother and father to his sons. Balfour recognized the historical distance of the patriarchal times; she used developmental language in referring to that era as "the infancy of civilization." Like both Aguilar and Cornwallis, Balfour compared Leah and Rachel. Balfour requested readers to interpret using their judgment rather than their sympathies and feelings so they could see the lesson provided for them in the contrast between the two sisters.

Like Aguilar, Balfour addressed the Woman Question in this chapter. Balfour, however, was more direct in her approach to the question: she noted that both sons and daughters needed to obey their parents, so this was not unjust to women. Balfour also noted the strong influence of mothers on their children and used that influence to argue for woman's place. She concluded her chapter with an extended argument on the Bible's recognition of women's "spiritual and intellectual privileges, and her social influence, authority, and rights."

From Clara Lucas Balfour, *The Women of Scripture* (London, 1847). [Text from the 2nd ed. London: Houlston & Stonemann (1850), 53–67.]

–Leah and Rachel–

THE sun, though not in noontide splendour, was still high in the heavens when the youthful fugitive from his father's house drew near his journey's end, and approached the well of Haran. Notwithstanding his fatigue, his step was light and firm, for he felt the sweet consciousness of sin forgiven; and the cheering remembrance of his gorgeous vision assured him that he walked in the light of God's reconciled countenance. The fields were fresh with verdure, and the peaceful flocks whitened all the plain. The kindly shepherds answered his anxious inquiries relative to the household of Bethuel, and pointed to a young shepherdess approaching to water her flock, who was of their family. Kindred ties are never felt to be so dear as when we have known what it is to have them rudely severed. The loneliness, self-communion, visions and prayers, of the preceding days, had softened the heart and elevated the character of Jacob. Doubtless many a time, during his happy boyhood, he had heard, from his mother's lips, of that meeting with the messenger of Abraham, on the plains of Haran, which had ended in her coming as a bride to his father's house. Jacob, gazing around, beheld scenery often described, and in that sense familiar: he runs to meet his cousin, the fair shepherdess pointed out to him, and, anxious to ingratiate himself by some act of kindly courtesy, before disclosing himself, he rolls away the stone from the mouth of the well, and waters the flocks for her. We recognise the son of the prompt and benevolent Rebekah, in this act. The mother's characteristics in this, as in most cases, had influenced the disposition and habits of her son: this is a fact of general application and great importance. When Jacob had watered the flock, his full heart could hold out no longer. In the beautiful language of Scripture, "Jacob kissed Rachel, and lifted up his voice and wept." How mingled were the sources of those tears! Recollections of his father's house, of his mother's tenderness, his brother's just displeasure, the varied emotions of his journey, gratitude that he had been guided safe, and that kindred and friends would yet be his, even in a strange land; these and a multitude of new and conflicting feelings, welled up and overflowed, in that flood of tears.

We are delighted to read of the ready sympathy of the gentle maiden—the generous hospitality of her father Laban and his household. How the family crowded around, to welcome the son of their long absent Rebekah; and what warm entreaties they uttered that he would tarry awhile with them! A month passed happily away; a brief space in the calendar of time—a long and important period in the records of the heart. In that time, Jacob had formed his estimate of his newly-found kindred; friendship and kindness he evidently felt for all, but a sentiment far stronger for one Rachel, the first seen, the best beloved.

It is a forcible instance of the sympathy felt for those who entertain an affection at once pure and ardent, that most readers lose themselves so completely in the interest they feel in the sweet narrative of Jacob's love for Rachel, that they adopt his partiality and preference, and scarcely one reader can be found who, in judging of the two sisters, Leah and Rachel, does not feel all their sympathies enlisted for the latter. The homely unloved Leah is generally treated by the reader as if her misfortunes were faults. Every incident respecting Rachel is noted with kind interest, or extenuating indulgence, while Leah's trials are passed over without notice or sympathy. If, however, we exercised our judgment, instead of yielding to our feelings, we should perceive that the characters of the sisters afford a fine contrast, and convey a useful lesson.

Leah, coming before us as a wife grieved in spirit and neglected, would doubtless create a more immediate interest for so painful a situation; but we remember that Jacob had made an honourable and distinct avowal of his love for Rachel, in the early days of his sojourn in his uncle Laban's house. Rachel was his chosen wife—for her he had consented to serve seven years. Laban found means to deceive Jacob; the marriage ceremonies of the East affording him facilities for substituting Leah, his eldest daughter, for Rachel. He alleged afterwards, in reply to Jacob's indignant remonstrance, that the customs of the country did not permit the younger sister to be married before the elder. Jacob having professed no love for Leah, not voluntarily espousing her, affection not only could not be expected, but aversion or indifference was the natural result.

From the thoughtful character which it is evident Jacob possessed, there can be little doubt that this cruel act of domestic treachery, which gave to him an unloved and unsought bride instead of his fair Rachel, must have recalled the sin he had practised towards his father; and this remembrance probably softened Jacob's resentment towards his unjust kinsman; while his fervent love for Rachel urged him to add another seven long years of servitude to the term already promised, in order to obtain her as his wife. And how eloquent is the statement of Scripture, "They seemed to him but a few days for the love he bore to her!"

The devotedness of this affection throws a charm around the object of it, which her own character does not appear to warrant. In reality, the only merits we can discover in Rachel are personal beauty and great affection towards her husband; the first, a merely adventitious gift, the second deteriorated by something of impatience.

It is evident that piety was a leading characteristic of Leah, and in being substituted for her sister Rachel by the fraud of her father, doubtless she only yielded that implicit obedience to paternal authority which was required in that state of society; an authority equally as binding on the sons as on the daughters of a family, and, therefore, not unjust to woman. For we have already read of Abraham sending for a wife for Isaac; and it was evidently considered an act of filial disobedience in Esau, that he chose a wife of the daughters of Heth. Therefore we must remember the customs of the patriarchal times, and not condemn Leah for the act her father compelled. It is manifest that the Lord compassionated Leah, for when he saw that "she was hated," (less loved, the Hebrew language having no comparative to qualify the term,) he conferred upon her the honour of maternity—an honour especially prized among the women of that race to whom the Messiah had been promised in the emphatic announcement, "In thy seed shall all the nations of the earth be blessed." Leah's piety is shown, as well as her affection for her husband, in her remarks on the birth of each of her sons, and the names she bestowed on them. Her first son she called Reuben, "for she said, the Lord hath looked upon my affliction; now therefore my husband will love me." Her second son she welcomed with the words, "Because the Lord hath heard that I was hated, he hath therefore given me this son also." And again, her heart yearning for sympathy, she exclaims, on the birth of her third son, "Now, this time will my husband be joined unto me;" and when her fourth son, Judah, was given to her, she exclaimed, with pious gratitude, "Now will I praise the Lord."

These exclamations are the history of a heart that had known affliction, and had learned that best of lessons, where to look for consolation. A grateful recognition of God's love comforted her in her trials, and enabled her to endure them with a gentle spirit, that gave serenity and dignity to her character. Leah—the unloved Leah!—as a happy mother, was an object of envy to the beautiful and well-beloved Rachel. It is expressly said, "she envied her sister;" and, under the influence of this malignant feeling, she broke forth into impatient impetuous complaints at her childless condition. "Wrath is cruel, and anger is outrageous, but who is able to stand before envy?" Of all the evil feelings that degrade the human heart, this is the meanest; and it preys so completely on its possessor, it so embitters the spirit, it is so torturing and futile, that it is as foolish as it is wicked. The individual who cherishes an envious spirit, inflicts a greater injury on his own happiness than the cruellest enemy could possibly invent or perpetrate. Even the deep affection of Jacob for Rachel was shaken by her envious complaints: we read that "his anger was kindled against her" for her impatient repinings after offspring. We have reason to conclude that Rachel ultimately attained a better frame of mind, for we hear that "God remembered Rachel, and God hearkened to her." And Joseph was given in answer to her prayers.

At length, after twenty years' servitude of Jacob to Laban—"fourteen for his daughters and six for cattle,"—Jacob's heart yearned towards his father's house; and therefore he consulted Rachel and Leah in reference to his departure. They consented to accompany him; and from circumstances of mutual distrust between Jacob and Laban the departure was secret. Another act of Rachel's in reference to this journey displays her character unfavourably,—she dishonestly carried off her father's gods,—an act wrong in itself, but especially culpable in her, as it would seem to imply, that, with all her privileges as the wife of Jacob, and with her previous acknowledgments of God in the dispensation of events, yet some remnants of pagan superstition clung to her.

Before, however, we condemn too harshly a woman living at a time that may be called the infancy of civilization, let us ask whether weak and silly superstitions are unknown to women who are living in all the light of Christian institutions and knowledge? Alas! remnants of superstition, in reference to omens, lucky days, dreams, and other puerilities, cling to many even in the present day, and are the stolen and secret objects of foolish, infatuated attention and reverence.

The patriarch, and his numerous family of children, retainers, and servants, lived an unsettled life for a considerable time after leaving the country of Laban; and though the narrative of the journeying of the company is full of incident and interest in reference to Jacob, as it records his wrestling with the Angel, his receiving a new name, Israel, his reconciliation with Esau,—yet of Rachel and Leah we hear nothing of importance until we come to the record of the mournful death of Rachel, under circumstances of peculiar sorrow. She who had once exclaimed so rashly, "Give me children, or I die," perished in giving birth to her second son. "And it came to pass, as her soul was departing (for she died), that she called his name, Ben-oni." Son of my sorrow, is the mournful signification of the name bestowed by the dying mother. And thus it is with human requests and desires. How many an ardent wish has been denied in mercy by an all-wise Providence! how often have our requests been granted to our own sorrow! Ill does it become weak, short-sighted children of the dust, to repine at the appointments of Providence, or seek to direct the counsels of Omnipotence.

It is an affecting testimony of Jacob's love for Rachel, that he changed the mournful name she gave her infant, and called the child, Benjamin (Son of my right hand). He could not bear to hear the epithet which would bring the death scene of his beloved wife continually before his mind. He preferred to designate the motherless babe by a name implying affectionate reliance in, and constant affinity to, the child of his old age. And it is evident his heart reposed the fullest affection on the two pledges of love that Rachel left him. Though Jacob was not free from the error of favouritism, which had been so fatal in his own case early in life, yet when we remember that many of his sons were arrived at man's estate, and several of them had troubled him sorely by their crimes and disobedience, it was only natural that he should feel most deeply interested in his innocent young motherless boys: and it is fair to infer, that his partiality to Joseph and Benjamin was not so much favouritism, as the compensating tenderness of one who felt he had the duties of both parents to discharge.

The place of the beloved Rachel's burial is memorable; it was near to Ephrath, after known as Bethlehem, the birth-place of our Saviour. Jacob set up a pillar over her remains,—"That is the pillar of Rachel's grave unto this day." The practice of commemorating events in remote times was by piling heaps of stones, planting a grove of trees, or setting up a pillar. There were so many landmarks, stretching out into the vast sea of time, tradition relating their purport for ages; and thus the reputed tomb of Rachel is yet found by the traveller in the East. Mr. Carne, in his Recollections of the East, beautifully says—"The spot is as wild and as solitary as can well be conceived: no palms or cypresses give their shelter from the blast; not a single tree spreads its shade where the ashes of the beautiful mother of Israel rest. Yet there is something in this sepulchre in the wilderness that excites a deeper interest than more splendid and revered ones. The tombs of Zacharias and Absalom, in the Valley of Jehoshaphat, or that of the kings, in the Plain of Jeremiah, the traveller looks at with careless indifference; beside that of Rachel his fancy wanders to the land of the people of the East, to the power of beauty that could so long make banishment sweet, to the devoted companion of the wanderer who deemed all troubles light for her sake."[24]

Mr. Buckingham gives a particular description of this tomb, which has been enclosed with a building by the Turks. "We entered it," says he, "on the south side, by an aperture through which it was difficult to crawl, as it has no door-way, and found on the inside a square mass of masonry in the centre, built up from the floor nearly to the roof, and of such a size as to leave barely a narrow passage for walking round it. It is plastered with white stucco on

[24] John Carne, Recollections of Travels in the East (London, 1830).

the outer surface, and is sufficiently large and high to enclose within if any ancient pillar that might have been found on the grave of Rachel."[25]

Notwithstanding the honours which the patriarch bestowed on the last resting-place of the beloved companion of his life, she occupied a lonely grave. And of the descendants of the two sisters, we find the tribe of Judah, the son of Leah, most honoured in being the progenitors of our Lord, and Joseph the son of Rachel, distinguished by becoming the preserver of his father's house, and his tribe being long the most prosperous in Israel. The dispersion of the ten tribes has also equalized the claims of these sisters as the mothers of Israel; for though their number of children was so dissimilar, yet of the two tribes of that ancient people now left, dispersed and scattered from Judah, the son of Leah, the other from Benjamin, the son of Rachel.

Before closing this chapter of the eminent women of the patriarchal times it is worthy of remark, that though the patriarchal form of government is manifestly least likely to promote human freedom, yet, in the instances recorded in the Bible, we do not find that woman was in any sense degraded under that system. The Supreme, at that time, condescended to hold intercourse with man, and especially provided for the adequate consideration, dignity, and happiness of the female members of the patriarch's household. Abraham hearkens to Sarah's counsel. Rebekah demands implicit obedience from her son—a man of mature age; and Leah and Rachel are summoned to hear Jacob's reasons for desiring to quit the service and country of their father, and their counsel and consent are obtained to this important act. Thus we evidently perceive that Sacred History, even of the most remote times, recognises woman's spiritual and intellectual privileges, and her social influence, authority, and rights.

§67 Sarah Hale
(1788–1879)

Sarah Hale was a well-educated American widow who wrote to provide for herself and her children.[26] She edited and contributed to the *Ladies' Magazine*

---

[25] James Silk Buckingham was a renowned traveler, who lectured on his journeys to the Near East, India and America. See for example his *Notes of the Buckingham Lectures: embracing sketches of the geography, antiquities and present condition of Egypt and Palestine: compiled from the oral discourses of the Hon. J. S. Buckingham, Together with a Sketch of His Life* (New York: Leavitt, Lord & Co., 1838).

[26] For more information about Sarah Hale see part 4, "Rebekah—Mother of Two Nations."

and published thirty-six books. Hale's most ambitious undertaking was *Woman's Record: or, Sketches of All Distinguished Women From the Beginning Till A.D. 1850* (1855). This biographical dictionary of women contained short selections on Leah and Rachel. The two entries on Leah and Rachel are printed separately in the alphabetically-arranged dictionary. Placing them together here emphasizes the comparisons Hale made between the two sisters. Unlike Balfour and Aguilar, Hale preferred Rachel to Leah. She condemned Leah for her part in Laban's deception of Jacob. On the other hand, Hale claimed that Rachel's good character was reflected in the good character of her two sons.

> From Sarah Hale, *Woman's Record; or, Sketches of all Distinguished Women, from the Creation to A.D. 1854* (New York: Harper & Brothers, 1855), 45–46, 53–54.

–Leah–

ELDEST daughter of Laban, the Syrian, who deceived Jacob into an inter-course, then termed marriage, with this unsought, unloved woman. She became mother of six sons, named as heads of six of the tribes of Israel. Among these was Levi, whose posterity inherited the priesthood, and Judah, the law-giver, from whom descended "Shiloh," or the Messiah. These were great privileges; yet dearly did Leah pay the penalty of her high estate, obtained by selfish artifice, in which modesty, truth, and sisterly affection, were all violated. Jacob, her husband, "hated her," and she knew it; knew, too, his heart was wholly given to his other wife, her beautiful, virtuous sister; what earthly punishment could have been so intensely grievous to Leah? As her name implies, "tender-eyed," she was probably affectionate, but unprincipled and of a weak mind, or she would never have taken the place of her sister, whom she knew Jacob had served seven years to gain. Leah loved her husband devotedly; but though she was submissive and tender, and bore him many sons, a great claim on his favour, yet he never appeared to have felt for her either esteem or affection.

Jacob had sought to unite himself with Rachel in the holy union of one man with one woman, which only is true marriage; but the artifice of Laban, and the passion of Leah, desecrated this union, and by introducing polygamy into the family of the chosen Founder of the house of Israel, opened the way for the worst of evils to that nation, the voluptuousness and idolatry which finally destroyed it. A treacherous sister, a forward woman, an unloved wife, Leah has left a name unhonoured and unsung. She was married about B. C. 1763.

–Rachel–

The youngest daughter of Laban, the Syrian, the beloved wife of Jacob, the patriarch, mother of Joseph and Benjamin;—how many beautiful traits of character, how many touching incidents of her husband's life, are connected with her name! Rachel was the true wife of Jacob, the wife of his choice, his first and only love. For her, "he served Laban seven years, and they seemed to him but a few days, for the love he bore her." At the close of this term, the crafty father, who wished to retain Jacob in his service, practised the gross deception of giving Leah instead of Rachel, and then permitting Jacob to have the beloved one as another wife, provided he would serve another seven years! Thus Rachel really cost her husband fourteen years' servitude.

She was "beautiful and well-favoured," Moses tells us; yet surely it was not her personal charms which gained such entire ascendancy over the wise son of Isaac. Jacob must have been nearly sixty years old at the time of his marriage; and if Rachel had been deficient in those noble qualities of mind and soul, which could understand and harmonize with his lofty aspirations to fulfil the great duties God had imposed on him, as the chosen Founder of the house of Israel, she never would have been his confidant, counsellor, friend, as well as his lovely, and loving wife. That she was this all in all to her husband, seems certain by the grief, the utter desolation of spirit, which overwhelmed him for her loss. He cherished her memory in his heart, loved her in the passionate love he lavished on her children till his dying day. Her two sons were, in moral character, far superior to the other sons of Jacob; and this is true testimony of her great and good qualities. She died in giving birth to Benjamin, while Jacob, with all his family, was on his way from Syria to his own land. She was buried near Bethlehem, in Judea, and Jacob erected a monument over her grave. Her precious dust was thus left, as though to keep possession of the land sure, to hers and her husband's posterity, during the long centuries of absence and bondage. And, as if to mark that this ground was hallowed, the Messiah was born near the place of Rachel's grave. She died B.C. 1732.

§68 Constance and Annie de Rothschild
(1843–1931) and (1844–1926)

Baroness Constance de Rothschild (1843–1931) and her sister, Baroness Annie Henrietta de Rothschild (1844–1926), were the daughters of Sir Anthony Nathan de Rothschild (1810–1876), baronet, banker and landowner, and

Louisa Montefiore (1821–1910), a philanthropist. The girls received a fine education from private tutors in mathematics, English literature, philosophy, drawing, music, French, and Hebrew. Their mother educated them in their Jewish faith and taught them about the New Testament. As teenagers, their mother also encouraged them to visit the poor and teach in a Jewish Free School in a poor East London Jewish community. Their teaching experience undoubtedly inspired their impressive two-volume work, *The History and Literature of the Israelites*, published in 1871. Though this work was ostensibly for children, it often assumes a sophisticated readership. The authors were clearly educated readers of the Old Testament and critically engaged with contemporary Old Testament scholarship. They introduced readers to the idea of the dual authorship of Isaiah, a notion that was not popularized in Britain until the last decade of the century.[27]

Constance de Rothschild later questioned the Jewish faith she promoted in her book. She searched relentlessly for spiritual meaning in various expressions of the Christian faith. She was drawn to a life of good works and asceticism. In 1877, she married Cyril Flower (1843–1907), an Anglican, with the condition that she and her mother would promote his political career. Her refusal to move to New South Wales in 1893 when her husband was offered the governorship caused marriage problems. Constance Flower developed a significant public life through her involvement in prison ministry, the National Union of Women Workers (NUWW), the temperance movement, and various other public causes.

Annie de Rothschild married the Honorable Eliot Yorke (1843–1878) in 1873. Little is known about her married life, although she continued to work with her sister in various philanthropic enterprises.

In *The History and Literature of the Israelites,* the de Rothschilds followed the biblical account closely. In their retelling of the story, they interpreted the situations and characters in similar ways to their contemporaries: for example, like Aguilar they called Jacob's act of watering the sheep chivalrous. They did not compare the two sisters, Leah and Rachel (perhaps because they were sisters themselves) but, like O'Keeffe, compared Rachel with her aunt Rebekah. Whereas other writers compared Jacob's and Laban's deceit, the de Rothschilds compared Laban's deceit to that of his sister Rebekah. They depicted Rachel as deceitful, "the true daughter of a crafty father, the true wife of a crafty husband." The de Rothschilds did not make explicit applications of the story for their readers; their goal in writing was to retell the biblical stories to teach the history of Israel.

[27] See S. R. Driver, *An Introduction to the History of the Old Testament* (New York: Charles Scribner, 1891).

From C. and A. de Rothschild, *The History and Literature of the Israelites*, vol. 1 (London: Longmans, Green & Co., 1870), 65–79. [Text from the 2nd ed., 1871.]

Jacob's Sojourn With Laban, His Marriage and Children
[Genes. XXIX.–XXX. 34.]

Jacob departed from the solitary field, and traversing the desert tracts in the east of the Jordan, he at last drew near to the town of Nahor. A well, surrounded by herdsmen with their cattle, showed him that he was approaching the dwelling-place of man. The shepherds came from Haran, and were of course acquainted with the wealthy Laban. Whilst they were answering the questions of Jacob, they saw advancing towards them Rachel, the daughter of Laban, driving her flock of sheep before her. Like Rebekah, her occupations led her out into the field; like Rebekah, she was respectful and courteous towards the stranger. Now, the shepherds were obliged to delay the watering of their flocks until all the herdsmen of the neighbourhood had assembled, for it was only by their united efforts that the heavy stone, which covered the mouth of the well, could be rolled away. Jacob, however, was determined to show by an act of attention his friendship for his kinswoman. When, therefore, Rachel approached, he went to the well, and with his own unaided strength performed the feat of removing the ponderous stone. Filled with tenderness for the child of his mother's brother, Jacob kissed Rachel, and lifted up his voice and wept. Then he told her that he was the son of Rebekah, her father's sister. Placing full reliance in the stranger, she at once hastened home to inform her father of his arrival. Laban, the cordial and hospitable Laban of old, came forth to the well to meet his kinsman, and to bring him back as the honoured and loved guest of his house. He was delighted with his young relative, and exclaimed, 'Surely thou art my bone and my flesh.' But Jacob, full of strength and activity, could not bear to eat the bread of idleness; he took part in all the occupations of the house and the field, and Laban felt that, in all justice, his kinsman should not serve him without a reward.

Laban had, besides Rachel, another and older daughter, Leah. But Rachel was very beautiful, while the eyes of her sister were weak and dim. Jacob loved Rachel, and he offered to Laban to work for him during seven years, if, at the end of that time, he might receive Rachel for his wife. Laban apparently assented to the proposal, and replied, 'It is better that I give her to thee, than that I should give her to another man; abide with me.' So Jacob served seven years for Rachel, and 'they seemed to him but a few days for the love he bore to her.' The time for the marriage had approached; but Laban felt vexed and disappointed that the younger sister should marry before the elder. With the deceit worthy of his sister Rebekah, Laban bethought himself of a scheme by which he might substitute Leah for Rachel. Taking advantage of the long and thick veil worn by the eastern maiden on her marriage-day, he brought Leah, thus closely shrouded, to the unsuspecting Jacob, who learnt the dishonesty of Laban too late. As he had deceived his father, so his own kinsman now deceived him. When he upbraided Laban, the latter sheltered himself under vain excuses, 'It is not done so in our place, to give the younger before the elder.' But he proposed that Jacob should celebrate his marriage-week, and that he might then take Rachel as a second wife, and work for her another seven years. Jacob, unwilling to renounce the maiden whom he had loved so long, agreed to this unjust demand, and in seven days he married Rachel also. In accordance with the eastern custom, each daughter received her maidservant; Zilpah was given to Leah, and Bilhah to Rachel.

Jacob's love for Rachel was true and strong; he never could quite forgive the deception of Laban, and although Leah blessed him with offspring, and Rachel remained childless, still he clung to the younger sister with greater fondness than to the elder. Leah felt bitterly the indifference of her husband; so bitterly indeed, that at the birth of her firstborn son, Reuben, she exclaimed, 'Surely the Lord has looked upon my affliction, for now my husband will love me.' But that love was still denied her; and when a second son, Simeon, was born to her, she said again, 'Surely the Lord has heard that I am hated, and He has given me this son also.' But the affection she so longed for was even now withheld; for when she became the mother of a third son, Levi, she gave utterance to her deep attachment in the words, 'Now this time will my husband be joined to me, for I have born him three sons.' Jacob's heart must have been touched at last, for Leah was full of joy and gratitude when she exclaimed at the birth of her fourth son, Judah, 'This time I will praise the Lord.' After a long interval she had two more sons, Issachar and Zebulun, and last of all a daughter, Dinah. Moreover, the two maids, Bilhah and Zilpah, bore children to Jacob; the sons of Bilhah were named Dan and Naphtali, those of Zilpah, Gad and Asher. Rachel had envied her sister Leah, and full of sorrow and vexation, she vented her disappointment in words of anger. God remembered her at last, and when she became the mother of a son, she called him Joseph, exclaiming in gladness, 'God has taken away my reproach; may the Lord add to me another son!'

Jacob had served Laban long and faithfully. During the fourteen years he had lived with his kinsman, the house of the latter had been blessed and had prospered, and his wealth and possessions had vastly increased. Jacob now felt that the time had come for him to return to Beersheba; he had never received from Rebekah the message which, at his departure, she had promised to send him. He was ninety years of age, and still an exile and a servant. So he entreated of Laban to let him depart. Laban, fully appreciating the advantage of Jacob's services, could not bear the thought of losing them. Therefore, he offered him any reward he might propose. Jacob bethought himself of a stratagem by which he hoped to secure the finest portions of Laban's flocks. He succeeded so well that in six years he found himself the master of very considerable wealth. The Bible, after detailing the scheme of Jacob, which is another stain upon his character, tells us that 'he increased exceedingly, and possessed much cattle, and maidservants, and menservants, and camels, and asses.'

Jacob's Flight, and his Treaty With Laban
[Genes. XXXI.]

The unprecedented increase of Jacob's property, and the corresponding diminution of his own, must have opened Laban's eyes with regard to the fraud of which he had been the victim, and he naturally regarded Jacob with suspicion and distrust. Indeed the latter felt that he could no longer dwell in Padanaram with safety. The voice of the Lord bade him at once return to his native country. So he sent for Leah and Rachel to meet him in the fields where he was tending his flocks. There he told them that they must prepare for immediate departure. 'I see,' he said, 'your father's countenance that it is not towards me as in former days; but the God of my father has been with me, and you know that with all my power I have served your father.' Then accusing Laban of deceit and injustice, he spoke of the Divine protection which was granted to him, and through which, in spite of the stratagems and frauds of Laban and his sons, he had obtained great wealth. Quite unconscious of the deep-laid schemes of their husband, Leah and Rachel readily agreed to follow him to the land of his birth, and spoke of their father with harshness: 'Are we not regarded by him as strangers? for he has sold us, and has also entirely eaten up our money. Indeed, all the wealth which God has taken from our father it belongs to us and to our children: and now whatever God has said to thee, do.' Jacob proceeded forthwith to carry out his departure, or rather, his flight. The time was peculiarly favourable.

Laban had gone forth to shear his sheep. Rachel, who still clung to the superstitious idolatry of her youth, took with her as a protection the Teraphim or house-gods which belonged to her father, and which she knew he valued highly. Secretly and in precipitate haste the caravan passed out of the city; first Leah and Rachel with their children; next their handmaids and their children, all sitting upon camels: and then followed Jacob with his train of servants, driving his vast herds and flocks before them. As their road lay westwards, they crossed the Euphrates, and turned their steps toward the range of the mountains of Gilead. On these rich pastures Jacob's herds and flocks grazed for a time, whilst he pitched his tents and rested on the mountain.

In the meantime Laban had been informed of the flight: he at once set out in pursuit, and after a seven days' precipitate journey, he found Jacob and his companions in the region of Gilead. Here he halted for the night at the foot of the mountain, and was visited by an awe-inspiring vision. The Lord warned him that he should take care not to harm Jacob in any way. With this solemn bidding still ringing in his ears, Laban appeared before his son-in-law. He was full of indignation and anger, and could with difficulty govern his passion. He burst forth directly into accusations, which were indeed well merited by Jacob's cunning conduct: 'What hast thou done, that thou hast deceived my heart, and carried away my daughters, like captives taken with the sword.' He then upbraided him for having fled secretly and deceitfully; he said that Jacob had acted foolishly in not telling him his intentions, whereas he would willingly have sent him away with song and music; he had not even permitted him to kiss his children and grand-children before they left him, perhaps for ever. He added, with ill-repressed anger, that it would be in his power to do him injury; yet he refrained from revenge, because the God of Abraham had spoken to him in the night and had warned him against violence. And he concluded by urging that if Jacob had departed, because he longed for his father's home, it was certainly inexcusable that be had stolen his gods. Jacob, with a self-possession that never forsook him, was resolved not to humble himself before Laban. He knew that he had acted wrongly, but he pleaded falsely: 'Indeed, I was afraid; for I said, perhaps thou wouldst take by force thy daughters from me;' and then, conscious of his innocence with regard to the theft of the Teraphim, which Rachel had taken without his knowledge, he vehemently and with uncalled-for exaggeration demanded justice of Laban— 'With whomsoever,' he said, 'thou findest thy gods, let him not live: before our kindred, search what is with me and take it to thee.' Laban's investigation for the treasured Teraphim was fruitless. Rachel had hidden away the image in the litter of her camel; and the true daughter of a crafty father, the true wife of a crafty husband, had seated herself on the litter, and remained there sitting during the search. Now Jacob believed he had a right to burst forth into angry invectives against Laban: he had been wrongfully accused; his innocence was clear; had he not been a good and faithful servant to Laban for twenty years? had he not increased the wealth of his kinsman by working for him incessantly and unweariedly? 'Thus I was,' he exclaimed; 'in the day the drought consumed me, and the frost by night, and my sleep departed from my eyes; and thou hast changed my wages ten times: had not the God of my father, the God of Abraham and the fear of Isaac, been with me, indeed thou wouldst now have sent me away empty; God has seen the affliction and the labour of my hands, and rebuked thee yesternight.' These last words of Jacob must have powerfully impressed Laban; they probably brought before him the solemn vision of the night, and he felt that he must bow before the will of the Lord, even if the agent of that Divine will was unworthy of the love and protection he enjoyed. With a sudden generosity and good-will, which would else be inexplicable, Laban answered: 'The daughters are my daughters, and the children are my children, and the cattle are my cattle, and all that thou seest is mine: and what can I do this day to these my daughters, or to their children whom they have born? And now come, let us make a covenant, I and thou; and let it be for a witness between me and thee.'

The proposed reconciliation was effected, and the altar was raised by the two kinsmen. Laban gave it the Chaldee name Jegar-sahadutha, and Jacob the Hebrew appellation Galeed, both meaning Pile of Witness. Here a feast was prepared, and here Laban and Jacob swore to each other friendship and peace. Leah and Rachel were to remain the only wives of the patriarch, and never was Jacob to invade the territory of the Aramaens. The proceedings were ratified by the invocation of the name of the Lord and by a sacrificial meal.

Early on the following morning Laban bid farewell to his children and grand-children, blessed them, and departed to return to his home. The name of Laban now disappears from the sacred narrative, and the country of Mesopotamia falls into the background, as Jacob proceeds to the land of Palestine.

. . . But a sight more heartstirring, more touching to Jacob than that glimpse of the land of Palestine, must have been the advance of Esau, as he came to meet him at the head of his four hundred men. Still trembling before the anger and power of his brother, he judiciously divided his household into groups: first he placed the handmaids with their children, then Leah with her children, and last of all the beloved Rachel with her son Joseph-thus trying to expose those he loved most to the least danger. He himself took his position in front, and humbly prostrated himself seven times to the ground before his brother. But Esau, his heart overflowing with affection at the sight of Jacob, forgetful of the past, seeing in him only the exiled brother, the companion of his youth, ran to meet him, and fell on his neck, and kissed him. The two brothers wept for gladness. Seeing the groups of women and children standing awe-struck and trembling behind Jacob, Esau asked, 'Who are those with thee?' Jacob answered, 'The children whom God has graciously given to thy servant.' Then the women and children came near, and they all prostrated themselves before Esau.

Jacob in Schechem, Beth-el, and Hebron
[Genes. XXXIV–XXXV.]

Jacob sojourned at Shechem about six or eight years, when a sin occasioned by his daughter Dinah, and accompanied by violent and wrathful actions on the part of her brothers Simeon and Levi, put an end to the peace and happiness which the family had enjoyed in that abode. The voice of the Lord commanded Jacob to leave his newly-bought field, and to depart again until he should come to Beth-el. There, where he had seen the angels of God descending from heaven, he was to stay and to build an altar to the Lord. But he felt that he ought not to approach the holy spot where he had made his solemn vow, before all his followers had given up the idolatrous images and emblems which still tainted their worship. Therefore, he assembled his household and said, 'Remove the strange gods that are among you, and clean yourselves and change your garments.' With prompt alacrity his command was obeyed; and he buried all the objects of superstition under an oak near Shechem: among them were the earrings worn by men and women not merely as ornaments, but as amulets or charms against evil, and generally covered with allegorical figures or mysterious words; they belonged indeed to the 'enchantments' strictly forbidden in a later age.

. . . At Beth-el, Deborah had died, the nurse of Rebekah, who had accompanied her mistress from Mesopotamia. She had been buried under the spreading branches of an oak, which was called the Oak of Weeping in commemoration of the event. Probably Jacob's caravan passed by the oak on their journey southward, and doubtless some herdsmen or other wanderers may have told them of the faithful and well-beloved servant resting beneath its shade. . . .

He departed from Beth-el, and journeyed on southward, hoping soon to arrive at Hebron, the abode of his youth. But Rachel was not to see that old home, consecrated by the faith of Abraham and the piety of Isaac. Bethlehem, where the caravan halted, standing high on the narrow ridge of long grey hills, was the birthplace of Benjamin and the grave of Rachel. The dying mother called the new-born child Benoni (son of my grief); but Jacob, bent down indeed by the loss of his beloved wife, yet glorying in his twelfth son, gave him the name Benjamin (son of happiness). Rachel was buried on the heights of Bethlehem, where the purple vine grows in most luxuriant beauty. The mourning Jacob raised a pillar over her sepulchre. The fond love with which he had ever cherished her was perpetuated in his affection for the two sons she had left him; they were to him the dearest of his children.

And now at last he arrived at Hebron, and stood once again in the presence of the aged Isaac. The Bible gives us no detail of this meeting, and Rebekah is not mentioned again. We are only told that Isaac died when he was a hundred and eighty years old, and that he was buried by his two sons Esau and Jacob.

§69 Harriet Beecher Stowe
(1811–1896)

Stowe was an American novelist.[28] Her book, *Women in Sacred History* (1873) contained interpretations of the women of scripture. Stowe's husband, an Old Testament scholar, and her brother, Henry Ward Beecher (1813–1887) (a well-known preacher who was interested in evolution and later wrote a book called *Evolution and Religion* [1885]), influenced Stowe's thinking and writing. Her use of developmental and evolutionary language to discuss the choice of the line of promise in Genesis reflects these influences.

Stowe sensitively interpreted the biblical text. The Genesis stories focused on Jacob, not on Leah and Rachel, so in this chapter of her book on women, Stowe followed the text and discussed Jacob more than Leah and Rachel. She specifically noted that Rachel and Leah were flat characters and looked for clues to their personalities in the nature of their home and father. Stowe did not favour one sister over the other but presented both as flawed. She noted that "the sacred narrative is a daguerreotype [or photograph] of character; it reflects every trait and every imperfection without comment."

From Harriet Beecher Stowe, *Women in Sacred History* (New York: Fords, Howard, & Hulbert, 1873), 51–58.

–Leah and Rachel–

IN the earlier portions of the Old Testament we have, very curiously, the history of the deliberate formation of an influential race, to which was given a most important mission in the world's history. The principle of selection, much talked of now in science, is the principle which is represented in the patriarchal history as operating under a direct Divine guidance. From the calling of Abraham, there seems to have been this continued watchfulness in selecting the party through whom the chosen race was to be continued. Every marriage thus far is divinely appointed and guided. While the Fatherly providence and nurture is not withdrawn from the rejected ones, still the greatest care is exercised to separate from them the chosen. The latter are selected apparently not so much for moral excellence in itself considered, as for excellence in relation to stock. The peaceable, domestic, prudent, and

[28] For more on Stowe, see part 2, "Sarah—The First Mother of Israel."

conservative elements are uniformly chosen, in preference to the warlike and violent characteristics of the age.

The marriage of Isaac and Rebekah was more like the type of a Christian marriage than any other on record. No other wife shared a place in his heart and home: and, even to old age, Isaac knew no other than the bride of his youth. From this union sprang twin boys; between whom, as is often the case, there was a remarkable difference. The physical energy and fire all seemed to go to one, the gentler and more quiet traits to the other. Esau was the wild huntsman, the ranger of the mountains, delighting in force,—precisely adapted to become the chief of a predatory tribe. Jacob, the patient, the prudent, the submissive, was the home child, the darling of his mother. Now, with every constitutional excellency and virtue is inevitably connected, in our imperfect humanity, the liability to a fault. The peace-loving and prudent, averse to strife, are liable to sins of artifice and deception, as stronger natures are to those of force and violence. Probably, in the calm eye of Him who sees things just as they are, the one kind of fault is no worse than the other. At all events, the sacred narrative is a daguerreotype of character; it reflects every trait and every imperfection without comment. The mild and dreamy Isaac, to save his wife from a rapacious king, undertakes to practice the same artifice that his father used before him, saying, "She is my sister"; and the same evil consequence ensues. The lesson of artifice once taught in the family, the evil spreads. Rebekah, when Isaac is old and doting, commands Jacob to personate his older brother, and thus gain the patriarchal blessing, which in those days had the force of a last will and testament in our times. Yet, through all the faults and errors of the mere human actors runs the thread of a Divine guidance. Before the birth of Jacob it was predicted that he should be the chosen head of the forming nation; and by his mother's artifice, and his own participation in it, that prediction is fulfilled. Yet the natural punishment of the action follows. Esau is alienated, and meditates murder in his heart; and Jacob, though the mother's darling, is driven out from his home a hunted fugitive, parted from her for life. He starts on foot to find his way to Padan-Aram, to his father's kindred, there to seek and meet and woo the wife appointed for him.

It is here that the history of the patriarch Jacob becomes immediately helpful to all men in all ages. And its usefulness consists in just this, that Jacob, at this time in his life, was no saint or hero. He was not a person distinguished either by intellect or by high moral attainment, but simply such a raw, unformed lad as life is constantly casting adrift from the shelter of homes. He is no better and no worse than the multitude of boys, partly good and partly bad, who, for one reason or another, are forced to leave their mothers and their fathers; to take staff in hand and start out on the great life journey alone. He had been religiously brought up; he knew that his father and his mother had a God,—the Invisible God of Abraham and Isaac; but then, other gods and lords many were worshiped in the tribes around him, and how did he know, after all, which was the right one? He wanders on over the wide, lonesome Syrian plains, till dark night comes on, and he finds himself all alone, an atom in the great silent creation,—alone, as many a sailor-boy has found himself on the deck of his ship, or hunter, in the deep recesses of the forest. The desolate lad gathers a heap of stones for a pillow and lies down to sleep. Nothing could be more sorrowfully helpless than this picture; the representative portrait of many a mother's boy to-day, and in all days. We cannot suppose that he prayed or commended his soul to God. We are told distinctly that he did not even remember that God was in that place. He lies down, helpless and forlorn, on his cold stone pillow, and sinks, overcome with fatigue, to prayerless slumber. And now, in his dreams, a glorious light appears; a luminous path opens upward to the skies,—angels are passing to and fro upon it, and above, in bright benignity, stands a visible form, and says: "I am the LORD God of Abraham thy father, and the God of Isaac: the land whereon thou liest, to thee will I give it, and to thy seed; and thy seed shall be as the dust of the earth; and thou shalt spread abroad to the west, and to the east, and to the north, and to the south; and in thee and in thy seed shall all the families of the earth be blessed. And, behold, I am with thee, and will keep thee in all places whither thou goest, and will bring thee again unto this land; for I will not leave thee, until I have done that which I have spoken to thee of. And Jacob awaked out of his sleep, and he said, Surely the Lord is in this place; and I knew it not. And he was afraid, and said, How dreadful is this place! This is none other but the house of God, and this is the gate of heaven. And Jacob arose up early in the morning, and took the stone that he had put for his pillow, and set it up for a pillar, and poured oil upon the top of it. And Jacob vowed a vow, saying, If God will be with me, and will keep me in this way that I go, and will give me bread to eat, and raiment to put on, so that I come again to my father's house in peace, then shall the LORD be my God: and this stone, which I have set for a pillar, shall be God's house: and of all that Thou shalt give me I will surely give the tenth unto thee."

In one night how much is born in that soul! The sentiment of reverence, awe of the Divine,—a conviction of the reality of God and an invisible world,—and the beginning of that great experiment by which man learns practically that God is his father. For, in the outset, every human being's consciousness of God must be just of this sort. Have I a Father in heaven? Does he care for me? Will he help me? Questions that each man can only answer as Jacob did, by casting himself upon God in a matter-of-fact, practical way in the exigencies of this present life. And this history is the more valuable because it takes man in his earlier stages of imperfection. We are apt to feel that it might be safe for Paul, or Isaiah, or other great saints, to expect God to befriend them; but here a poor, untaught shepherd boy, who is not religious, avows that, up to this time, he has had no sense of God; and yet between him and heaven there is a pathway, and about him in his loneliness are ministering spirits; and the God of Abraham and of Isaac is ready to become his friend. In an important sense, this night dream, this gracious promise of God to Jacob, are not merely for him, but for all erring, helpless, suffering sons of men. In the fatherly God thus revealed to the patriarch, we see the first fruits of the promise that through him all nations should be blessed.

The next step of the drama shows us a scene of sylvan simplicity. About the old well in Haran, shepherds are waiting with their flocks, when the stripling approaches: "And Jacob said unto them, My brethren, whence be ye? And they said, Of Haran are we. And he said unto them, Know ye Laban the son of Nahor? And they said, We know him. And he said unto them, Is he well? And they said, He is well: and, behold, Rachel his daughter cometh with the sheep. And he said, Lo, it is yet high day, neither is it time that the cattle should be gathered together. Water ye the sheep, and go and feed them. And they said, We cannot, until all the flocks be gathered together, and till they roll the stone from the well's mouth; then we water the sheep. And while he yet spake with them Rachel came with her father's sheep; for she kept them. And it came to pass, when Jacob saw Rachel, the daughter of Laban, his mother's brother, and the sheep of Laban, his mother's brother, that Jacob went near, and rolled the stone from the well's mouth, and watered the flock of Laban, his mother's brother. And Jacob kissed Rachel, and lifted up his voice, and wept; and Jacob told Rachel that he was her father's brother, and that he was Rebekah's son: and she ran and told her father. And it came to pass, when Laban heard the tidings of Jacob, his sister's son, that he ran to meet him, and embraced him, and kissed him, and brought him to his house."

In the story of Isaac, we have the bridegroom who is simply the submissive recipient of a wife at his father's hands; in that of Jacob, we have the story of love at first sight. The wanderer, exiled from home, gives up his heart at once to the keeping of his beautiful shepherdess cousin, and so, when the terms of service are fixed with the uncle, the narrative says: "And Laban had two daughters; the name of the elder was Leah, and the name of the younger was Rachel. Leah was tender-eyed; but Rachel was beautiful and well-favored. And Jacob loved Rachel, and said, I will serve thee seven years for Rachel, thy younger daughter. And Jacob served seven years for Rachel, and they seemed unto him but a few days, for the love he had to her."

But when the wedding comes, in the darkness and secrecy of the night a false bride is imposed on the lover. And Jacob awoke, and behold it was Leah.

Not the last man was he who has awakened, after the bridal, to find his wife was not the woman he had taken her to be. But the beloved one is given as a second choice, and seven years more of service are imposed as her price.

The characteristics of these two sisters, Leah and Rachel, are less vividly given than those of any of the patriarchal women. Sarah, Hagar, and Rebekah are all sharply defined characters, in and of themselves; but of Leah and Rachel almost all that can be said is that they were Jacob's wives, and mothers of the twelve tribes of Israel.

The character of their father Laban was narrow, shrewd, and hard, devoid of any generous or interesting trait, and the daughters appear to have grown up under a narrowing and repressing influence. What we learn of them in the story shows the envies, the jealousies, the bickerings and heart-burnings of poorly developed natures. Leah, the less beloved one, exults over her handsomer and more favored sister because she has been made a fruitful mother, while to Rachel the gift of children is denied. Rachel murmurs and pines, and says to her husband, "Give me children, or I die." The desire for offspring in those days seemed to be an agony. To be childless, was disgrace and misery unspeakable. At last, however, Rachel becomes a mother and gives birth to Joseph, the best-beloved of his father. The narrative somehow suggests that charm of personal beauty and manner which makes Rachel the beloved one, and her child dearer than all the rest. How many such women there are, pretty and charming, and holding men's hearts like a fortress, of whom a biographer could say nothing only that they were much beloved!

When Jacob flees from Laban with his family, we find Rachel secretly taking away the images which her father had kept as household gods. The art by which she takes them, the effrontery with which she denies the possession of them, when her father comes to search for them, shows that she had little moral elevation. The belief in the God of her husband probably was mixed up confusedly in her childish mind with the gods of her father. Not unfrequently in those dim ages, people seemed to alternate from one to the other, as occasions varied. Yet she seems to have held her husband's affections to the last; and when, in giving birth to her last son, she died, this son became the darling of his father's old age. The sacred poet has made the name of this beloved wife a proverb, to express the strength of the motherly instinct, and "Rachel weeping for her children" is a line that immortalizes her name to all time.

Whatever be the faults of these patriarchal women, it must be confessed that the ardent desire of motherhood which inspired them is far nobler than the selfish, unwomanly spirit of modern times, which regards children only as an encumbrance and a burden. The motherly yearning and motherly spirit give a certain dignity to these women of primitive ages, which atones for many faults of imperfect development.

Twenty-one years elapse, and Jacob, a man of substance, father of a family of twelve children, with flocks and herds to form a numerous caravan, leaves the service of his hard master to go back to his father. The story shows the same traits in the man as in the lad. He is the gentle, affectionate, prudent, kindly, care-taking family-man, faithful in duty, and evading oppression by quiet skill rather than meeting it with active opposition. He has become rich, in spite of every effort of an aggressive master to prevent it.

When leaving Laban's service, he thus appeals to him: "These twenty years have I been with thee: thy ewes and thy she-goats have not cast their young, and the rams of thy flock have I not eaten. That which was torn of beasts I brought not unto thee; I bare the loss of it. Thus was I: in the day the drought consumed me, and the frost by night, and my sleep departed from mine eyes. Thus have I been twenty years in thy house. I served thee fourteen years for thy two daughters, and six years for thy cattle; and thou hast changed my wages ten times. Except the God of my father, the God of Abraham, and the fear of Isaac, had been with me, surely thou hadst sent me away now empty. God hath seen my affliction and the labor of my hands, and rebuked thee yesternight."

To the last of the history of Jacob, we see the same man,—careful, patient, faithful, somewhat despondent, wrapped up in family ties and cares, and needing at every step to lean on a superior power. And the Father on whom he seeks to lean is never wanting to him, as he will never be to any of us, however weak, or faulty, or blind. As the caravan nears home, news is brought that Esau, with an army of horsemen, is galloping to meet him. Then says the record: "Jacob was greatly afraid and distressed: and Jacob said, O God of my father Abraham, the God of my father Isaac, the Lord which saidst unto me, Return unto thy country and to thy kindred, and I will deal well with thee: I am not worthy of the least of all the mercies and of all the truth which thou hast showed unto thy servant: for with my staff I passed over this Jordan; and now I am become two bands. Deliver me, I pray thee, from the hand of my brother, from the hand of Esau; for I fear him, lest he will come and smite me, and the mother with the children. And thou saidst, I will surely do thee good, and make thy seed as the sand of the sea, which cannot be numbered for multitude." The prayer is not in vain. That night a mysterious stranger meets Jacob in the twilight shadows of morning. He seeks to detain him; but, as afterwards, when the disciples met an unknown Friend on the way to Emmaus, he made as though he would go farther. So now this stranger struggles in the embrace of the patriarch. Who, then, is this?—is it the Divine One? The thought thrills through the soul as Jacob strives to detain him. There is something wildly poetic in the legend, "And he said, Let me go, for the day breaketh. And he said, I will not let thee go, except thou bless me.

And he said unto him, What is thy name? And he said, Jacob. And he said, Thy name shall be called no more Jacob, but Israel: for as a prince hast thou power with God and with men, and hast pre¬vailed. And Jacob asked him: Tell me, I pray thee, thy name. And he said, Wherefore dost thou ask after my name? And he blessed him there. And Jacob called the name of the place Peniel, for he said, I have seen God face to face, and my life is preserved." God's love to man, the power of man's weakness and sorrow over the Father-heart, were never more beautifully shown than in this sacred idyl. The God of Abraham, Isaac, and Jacob; the God of the weak, the sinful, the despondent, the defenceless; the helper of the helpless,—He is the God of this sacred story; and so long as man is erring, and consciously frail, so long as he needs an ever-present and ever-loving Friend and Helper, so long will this story of Jacob be dear to the human heart.

§70 Leigh Norval
(fl. 1889)

Nothing is known about Leigh Norval except her church affiliation and what can be drawn from the contents of her book. The book was published by the Methodist Episcopal Church, South, Sunday-School Department, a denominational publishing house which opened in 1854. Norval's book was written for children. She used simple language and sentences and explained details and cultural differences for her readers.

Norval noted that Dinah, as Jacob's only daughter, was probably badly spoiled. Using the technique of comparison as a tool to evaluate various characters, she compared not only Leah and Rachel, but the characters of their children, as well. Norval wrote that Joseph's good character should not be used to judge Rachel, as history showed she sometimes trusted in God and sometimes did not. Norval also raised the issue of polygamy.

> From Leigh Norval, *Women of the Bible: Sketches of All the Prominent Female Characters in the Old and the New Testament* (Nashville, Tenn.: Publishing House of the M.E. Church, South, Sunday-School Department, 1889), 47–53.

–Jacob's Wives, Rachel and Leah–

JACOB fled from the murderous anger of his brother Esau back to the country east of the Euphrates. The Euphrates is a river eighteen hundred miles long, and Jacob went to the neighborhood of the city of Haran, where his mother had lived, near the upper part of the great river. Water is often scarce in the East, and if you read the Bible with care you will observe that wells were the occasion of various meetings. A noted preacher called attention in a sermon to another fact: the men and women in the Bible were usually engaged in diligent every-day work when God raised them to great honors. Doing daily duties is a good way to get ready to be great and famous. Jacob stopped at a well near Haran, and there met his beautiful cousin, Rachel. She was attending to her work, which was to take care of a flock of sheep.

Rachel was the daughter of Laban, Jacob's uncle, and Jacob had parted from his family under sorrowful circumstances, and came a long distance alone on foot. When he met her, "Jacob kissed Rachel, and lifted up his voice, and wept." She ran to tell her father, Laban, who came and received Jacob most affectionately as the son of his beloved sister, Rebekah. At the end of a month Jacob was so in love with the bewitching Rachel that he said to Laban: "I will serve thee seven years for Rachel, thy younger daughter." Laban had offered to pay him for his work, and accepted Jacob's proposal. Rachel proved so agreeable that the seven years "seemed unto Jacob but a few days for the love he had to her." Somehow girls do not make themselves quite that charming now. Perhaps they stay too closely indoors, and are too artificial.

Laban had an elder daughter, Leah, who does not seem to have been pretty. Laban deceived Jacob, and married him to Leah instead of Rachel. He excused himself by saying it was the custom of his country for the older daughter to marry. Following another bad custom, he gave Rachel also to Jacob after he had been married a week to Leah. Jacob had to serve seven more years for Rachel—fourteen years in all. Laban gave Zilpah to Leah for a handmaid, and Bilhah to Rachel. After awhile, according to a third very wrong fashion, Leah and Rachel gave Zilpah and Bilhah to Jacob for wives. Lots of trouble came from this.

Leah seems to have been a good woman, and to have prayed to God. She loved Jacob, and was very unhappy at times because he loved the pretty Rachel so much more than he did her. The Lord pitied her, and made her heart glad by giving her six sons—Reuben, Simeon, Levi, Judah, Issachar, and Zebulon. She had a daughter also, named Dinah. Dinah was Jacob's only daughter, and it is to be suspected was badly spoiled. Rachel had but two sons, Joseph and Benjamin. Bilhah had two, Dan and Naphtali; and Zilpah likewise had two, Gad and Asher. The third son of Leah, Levi, was honored in being the father of those set aside to conduct the worship of God. From Levi, Moses, the mighty law-giver and the meekest of men, was descended, and Aaron, the high-priest. Leah is made still more illustrious by her fourth son, Judah. He was the ancestor of David, and through Mary of Christ; and if Leah knew this, she might well exult in her motherhood. Jacob apparently foresaw it in his blessing upon Judah, and possibly she had been informed of the prediction. She was very proud of her sons, but they were occasionally rough and wicked. Zilpah and Bilhah are scarcely more than mentioned. Jacob appears to have treated them as belonging to Leah and Rachel.

After Jacob had remained twenty years with his father-in-law, Laban, and had grown rich in cattle, he called a family council. Leah and Rachel came to the field to see him at his summons. They had, it seems, ceased to be shepherdesses after their marriage. Jacob complained to them of Laban's fickle and unjust treatment in changing his wages ten times, and he said God commanded him to return to Canaan. The two wives agreed with their husband in his views, and reasonably answered him: "Whatever God has said unto thee, do." Rachel, however, in her superstition, stole her father's images when they started away. She took good care not to let Jacob know she had Laban's gods with her, and cunningly hid them under the camel's furniture. When Laban pursued Jacob, and by Jacob's consent made search for the images, Rachel sat on them, and they were so covered up with her skirts and the camel furniture that they were not found.

Jacob went on his way to the city of Shalem, in the land of Canaan, some thirty miles north of Jerusalem. Before he crossed the Jordan his brother Esau came to meet him with a band of four hundred armed men. Jacob and his wives no doubt were in a great panic, as Esau had vowed vengeance on Jacob for cheating him of his birthright. Jacob showed his tender affection for Rachel by placing her and her boy, Joseph, the farthest possible from the danger he dreaded, but Esau gave him a kind, brotherly welcome. The whole party with Jacob stopped awhile at Succoth, and there the wives and children rested in a house built for them ere they proceeded to Shalem, where a tent was pitched before the city for their home.

If Rachel is judged by her great and noble son, Joseph, it would be supposed she had a purer and more loving character than Leah; but her history does not show this. She sometimes prayed and trusted in God, and sometimes did wrong, but was always exceedingly loved by her husband. Her beauty may account for his devotion, but she had probably the winning ways that make even homeliness attractive. In one of the family journeys, as they neared Bethlehem, Rachel died. She left a little baby she called Benoni, "son of my sorrow"; but Jacob found consolation in the sweetness of his child, and changed his name to Benjamin, "the son of my right-hand."

Rachel was buried not far from Bethlehem, and her husband set a pillar over her grave. Perhaps Leah outlived Rachel, but her death is not noticed.

§71 M. G.
(fl. 1893)

M. G. was an Anglican woman, who was involved in mothers' meetings.[29] Her book, *Women Like Ourselves*, consisted of lectures given in these meetings, written down so that others could use them in their own mothers' meetings. Like the de Rothschilds and O'Keeffe, M. G. compared Rachel to Rebekah, and suggested that Jacob was attracted to her because she resembled his mother. M. G. called Rachel and Jacob's youthful love the last remnant of the happiness that Adam and Eve knew in Eden. M. G., like other women writers, noted that marriage between one man and one woman was the biblical ideal. Unlike other writers, however, she drew lessons for monogamous marriage both from the relationship of Leah and Jacob, and the relationship of Rachel and Jacob. M. G. also raised the question of women's nature and role by noting that Laban treated his daughters like property, but she argued that his poor parenting did not excuse his daughters from obeying him.

From M. G. *Women Like Ourselves* (London: SPCK, 1893), 35–41.

–Rachel and Leah–

IN the early part of Rachel's history we have a beautiful love-story, another pure and honourable courtship, undertaken, like that of her aunt Rebekah, in the fear and under the guidance of Almighty God (see Gen. xxviii. 1-5, 20-22). Around such pure and holy love-scenes the angels delight to hover, for the Father Who made the sunshine and the flowers, the birds and the butterflies, rejoices in the happiness of His creatures, and He sends these golden hours into our lives to be a treasured possession all through the weary days to come, as well as to make present misfortunes sit lightly. The blissful days of youthful love are all that we have left now of the perfect happiness which our first parents enjoyed in the Garden of Eden. How often, still, that perfect happiness is ruthlessly destroyed by disobedience to the restrictions which God's law has placed upon it!

Rachel reminds us in many ways of her aunt Rebekah. Perhaps it was this resemblance to his mother which won the heart of Jacob, when he first saw her. Lonely and weary, he was sitting by the well in the noonday heat, when he learned that he was near to his uncle's house, and that the beautiful girl

[29] For more information on M. G., see part 3, "Hagar—The Wanderer."

whom he saw in the distance was his uncle's daughter (see Gen. xxix. 1-7). It seems to have been a case of love at first sight. Jacob had been driven away from his home and his mother by his own sin and his brother's anger, and had been wandering among strangers for many days, with none to care for him or show him kindness. Now to come suddenly face to face with one so near of kin to himself, the daughter of that Laban of whom he had so often heard his mother speak, and to find her such a lovely, attractive girl, almost overpowered Jacob, and we cannot be surprised that he gave the shepherds a strong hint to go away (ver. 7), that he might meet her without being watched by inquisitive strangers.

With that inborn courtesy which he had inherited from Rebekah, Jacob rolled away the stone for her from the well's mouth, which the shepherds were too idle to do more than once a day, and watered her sheep for her; and then, unable to restrain his sobs, he told her who he was, and pressed the first warm kiss of love upon her lips (vers. 8-13).

What was the first impulse of Rachel when she was released from his embrace? (see vers. 12, 13). "She ran and told her father." Like Rebekah on a similar occasion, she never thought of concealing anything from her parents. If Jacob was, as she hoped, an honourable man, why need she be ashamed of his attentions? If, on the other hand, they should prove objectionable, it was well that her father should know at once what had passed, that she might have the benefit of his experience and protection. Jacob was evidently of the same mind, for he too told Laban frankly "all these things" at once, and very shortly after, since each day spent in her company only increased his affection for her, he made a distinct avowal of his love, and a formal proposal for her hand. And this, although Laban was no ideal father. His thoughts and aims and desires were wholly centred in himself. He seemed to have no affection for either of his daughters (chap. xxxi. 14, 15), looking upon them only as so much property, with which, if judiciously bestowed, he could further his own interests. Honour is due, then, we learn from this, not only to loving and considerate parents, but also to the bad and selfish.

The strength of Rachel's character, and her fidelity to her promised husband, is shown in her case by her faithful waiting, as that of Rebekah was seen in her ready decision to go. Perhaps it was almost harder to have to wait seven long years for the fulfilment of her desires, than if she had not been allowed to wait at all. Seven years is a long time in a maiden's life. To Jacob they did not seem long. His work in the fields kept his hands and mind busy during the day, and he could see his Rachel morning and evening. But it is harder for the girl to sit and wait at home while her lover is working for her sake. . . . Jacob was not breaking any known commandment in marrying his wife's sister. Until the time of Moses, men intermarried freely among their own relations without any scruple. Thus Abraham was brother to Sarah, on the father's side. By degrees, as they were able to understand and to hear it, God taught His people that such marriages must be avoided, and that a man must regard the relations of his wife exactly as if they were his own. It was still longer before they came to see, as all these stories might have taught them, that matrimony in its highest form was the union of one man with one woman.

Under the circumstances, Leah and Rachel seem to have got on well together, excepting for a little jealousy, which we see in chapter xxx., on the part of each—with Leah for her husband's love, with Rachel for the children which were filling her sister's tent so quickly, whilst her own remained empty. With bitter and unreasoning envy she vents her annoyance upon Jacob, as many a woman has done since upon her unoffending husband, when something has vexed or disappointed her. And in thus speaking she sinned not only against her affectionate and sympathizing husband, but against God, Who alone could give or withhold the coveted blessing. Oh, beware of using such rash words before God. " I shall die if I do not have children more than one," Rachel had said (chap. xxx. 1). Many years passed; she had probably quite forgotten her sinful words, and she had learnt to turn to God in earnest prayer for the desired gift, and God heard her and gave her a son at last (ver. 22.) But in her temper Rachel had demanded not only one child, but children. The second child came, but in giving birth to him the life which Rachel had despised was taken from her. Once more, then, this story warns us against grasping too covetously after those gifts and blessings which God seems to will that we should not have, lest they turn to ashes when we obtain them.

It is pleasing to find that the love which Jacob felt for Rachel when he first met her as a fair young girl, lasted all through their married life, making his fourteen years of labour and Laban's meanness and over-reachings seem but light trifles for the love he bare her; and that not only to her death in Bethlehem, and to the setting-up of a handsome monument over her grave (chap. xxxv. 21), but that Jacob's love lived on beyond the grave, to the end of his own life ; so that on his deathbed, in extreme old age, Jacob in looking back upon the blessing and promises of God, and looking forward to prophesy great things for the children of Rachel's son, Joseph, could only say in speaking of himself, "As for me, Rachel died" (chap. xlviii. 7), as though with her all earthly hopes and joys had perished also.

A good man's love is the greatest earthly gift which God can give to us women. May those amongst us who have been blessed with it, treasure it, preserve it, and return it, that it may be as true and as lasting as that of Jacob and Rachel! And where this full deep love is wanting, as, alas! it is unfortunately wanting in many married lives, let there be at least the unfailing courtesy and consideration, in spite of all faults on both sides, that existed between Jacob and Leah, with constant prayers, like those of Leah in her loneliness, that the Lord would look upon her affliction and join her husband unto her.

§72 Elizabeth Baxter
(1837–1926)

Elizabeth Baxter was an Anglican author who wrote a number of books on scripture.[30] Her book, *The Woman in the Word* (1897), discussed the women of scripture with lessons for her readers. Baxter had high expectations of women. She considered them a powerful influence on others and expected them to use this influence for good.

In this selection on Leah and Rachel, Baxter, unlike Hale, argued that only Leah's marriage to Jacob was legal. Baxter emphasized the problems of polygamy and the trouble this brought on Jacob's family; she used Galatians 6:7 as a text to show that Jacob reaped what he had sown. She also used the idea of marriage as a type of Christ and the church to argue for monogamy.

> From Elizabeth Baxter, *The Woman in the Word*, 2nd ed. (London, 1897), 42–47.

Jacob left home, and on his journey he had the wondrous vision of Christ as God's ladder, connecting heaven and earth, and so became REALLY AQUAINTED WITH HIS GOD.

Proceeding to Haran, he made the acquaintance of some Syrian shepherds who were watering their flocks, and inquired about the family of Laban. He learnt from them that he was living and well, and that Rachel, his daughter was at hand with the sheep.

The first sight of Rachel, recalling to mind Jacob's home-loving mind the family of his mother, touched a tender chord in his heart. He immediately became her servant, and rolled the stone from the well's mouth, and watered the flock; and he "kissed Rachel, and lifted up his voice and wept," telling her his near relationship, that he was Rebekah's son. A real affection sprang up between the two, and when Laban, who was a sharp-eyed man of business, suggested to Jacob some reward for his work,—for Jacob could not be an idle man,—Jacob suggested that he should serve him seven years for Rachel, his younger daughter.

---

[30] For more information on Baxter, see part 1, "Eve—The Mother of Us All."

"And Jacob served seven years for Rachel; and they seemed unto him but a few days, for the love he had to her." But after all, this was human love. He admired the beautiful girl: there was perhaps much which accorded in their dispositions, but he had not received her from the hand of God as his father had received Rebekah. It accorded more with the character of Jacob to toil for his wife. His whole spirit was servile, and all his religion took its tone from this characteristic.

When his seven years' betrothal came to an end, the wedding day was fixed; but Laban deceived him, and gave him his elder daughter instead. And when Jacob remonstrated with him:

"What is this thou hast done to me? did not I serve with thee for Rachel? Wherefore, then, hast thou beguiled me?" Laban answered, and, perhaps, there was something of irony in the reply:

"It must not be so done in our country, to give the younger before the firstborn."

Was it an allusion to his dealings with Esau?

Jacob was legally married to Leah. In God's order, man was to have one wife, and He had never reversed this order, nor given His blessing to polygamy in any sense. What should Jacob do? He had served for Rachel; his heart was united to her; but just as cleverly as he had deceived his father, Laban had deceived him. "Be not deceived; God is not mocked; for WHATSOEVER A MAN SOWETH that shall he also reap." (Gal. vi. 7.) Jacob had sown deception, and he was reaping it now.

Laban proposed that Jacob should serve seven other years for Rachel, but that he should marry both the sisters at this time. And Jacob, without consulting his God, hearkened to the half-heathen Laban, who, while he feared God, yet had idols in his house. (xxxi. 19.)

God could not bless this arrangement. Jacob loved Rachel more than Leah. The Lord executeth judgment for the oppressed (Ps. ciii. 6), and He gave Leah a son, whom she named Reuben—"See a son"—for she said: "Surely the Lord hath looked upon my affliction; now therefore my husband will love me (Gen. xxix. 32)." Poor despised Leah! she was plain, and Rachel was beautiful. There was something attractive in her younger sister; there was little attraction about Leah; but God made compensation in giving her to be a happy mother. O, how this misery in the family shows the terrible mistake of reversing God's order of things! Marriage is the type of Christ and His Church. A man shall leave father and mother and cleave to his *wife*, not his wives.

God gave Leah another son, and she called him Simeon, and said: "Because the Lord hath heard that I was hated, He hath therefore given me this son also." And then a third son also, whom she called Levi—"joined"—and then a fourth son, whom she called Judah, and said: "Now will I praise the Lord."

It was a great compensation to this woman, lonely in her own home, that she should have the little ones around her and the consciousness that each child came as a direct gift from God.

But as Leah grew happier in her surroundings, Rachel became more dissatisfied. She "envied her sister, and said unto Jacob:"

"Give me children, or else I die." (Gen. xxx. 1.)

Jacob bitterly retaliated, and said: "Am I in God's stead, who hath withheld from thee the fruit of the womb." Then, following the example of Sarah, and probably the custom among the heathen, she gave her maid to her husband, that in case she should bear children, Rachel might reckon them her own, and Bilhah bore Jacob two sons. Leah followed her example, and gave her maid to her husband, and Zilpah also bore him two sons. But the complications in the family only grew greater by this multiplication: it was not God's divine order.

At last God heard Rachel's prayer; and after her sister's family had numbered seven, and four children were born to the handmaids, God gave Rachel also a child, "and she called his name Joseph, and said: The Lord shall add to me another son." Oh how this history shows us the misery there is in the ways of man, and how much of the evil of human nature comes out when the strict lines which God has laid down are not followed by His children! The family of Jacob must have been a hot bed of jealousy, strife, contention, evil-speaking, pride, and bitterness; and the chief contention was between two sisters! If Jacob had trusted God to give him Rachel, or had given up his will and been satisfied with Leah, all these complications would not have arisen.

Meanwhile, business matters brought other difficulties. Laban was a selfish and self-seeking man. God blessed Jacob according to His promise, and Laban envied him; and, at last, "Jacob beheld the countenance of Laban, and, behold, it was not toward him as before." (xxxi. 2.) And now the Lord visited Jacob, and told him to return to the land of his fathers and to his kindred, and promised, "I WILL BE WITH THEE."

Jacob must break to Leah and Rachel the news that he was about to take them from their father's house and from their home. Both the sisters, when they found that God had spoken to him, sided with their husband against their father, and were ready to depart. But Jacob, instead of trusting God and doing the thing openly, "stole away unawares to Laban the Syrian, in that he told him not that he fled." (xxxi. 20.)

His mother's example had told only too strongly upon Jacob, and instead of raising Leah by uprightness and integrity, he persuaded them to share his deceit, and help him in his flight. It is a precious thing when a man watches over the faults in his wife with a godly jealousy, seeking in every way to warn her, that she may be purified and kept pure in the sight of God. And it is a blessed thing when a wife watches over her husband in the same way, each watching over the other's soul. God has meant that husband and wife should be "heirs together of the grace of life." (1 Pet. iii. 7.) If two people who have agreed to spend their lives together are not made a blessing to each other, they must naturally be a curse. It is easier for one to do wrong if he sees his partner in life doing the same.

From this time we hear little of importance about the wives of Jacob, except when Rachel's youngest son was born, and the mother died, calling the little babe: "The son of my sorrow," whereas his father called him "The son of the right hand." His life was his mother's death.

Neither of these wives was, as God would have had her, a true and unselfish helpmeet for her husband.

§73 Elizabeth Cady Stanton and Clara Bewick Colby
(1815–1902) and (1846–1916)

Elizabeth Cady Stanton was born in Johnstown, New York, the daughter of Judge Daniel Cady and Margaret Cady. She was educated in a local academy and at Emma Willard's female seminary. Following her schooling, she read law in her father's office and became interested in women's legal status. She married Henry Brewer Stanton in 1840; the Stantons had seven children. With Lucretia Mott, Stanton convened the first women's rights convention in 1848 in Seneca Falls, New York, and throughout her life, she worked tirelessly for women's rights in the United States. In 1895, she published *The Woman's Bible*, a work containing selected parts of the Pentateuch, with comments on the selections. Stanton and her revising committee excluded texts which upheld patriarchy.[31]

Stanton wrote most of the comments on Leah and Rachel excerpted below. She did not include all of the Jacob cycle in *The Woman's Bible* and only offered comments on the included sections. Like M. G., Stanton noted that women were treated like property, though her comparison of marriage to the purchase of a lamb goes further than M. G. While Stanton's comments are similar in theme to those of other women writers, the tone of her writing has an edge not found in the other authors included in this chapter. The Bible did not have the same authority for her that it had for the other women writers.

---

[31] For more information on *The Woman's Bible* see part 1, "Eve—The Mother of Us All."

Clara Bewick Colby, a University of Wisconsin graduate, was active in the woman's suffrage movement.[32] In addition to publishing the *Woman's Tribune*, the official publication of the Woman's Suffrage movement, Colby was a contributor to Stanton's *Woman's Bible* project. Her comments on part of the story of Leah and Rachel below, including remarks on the Dinah incident, clearly show that she was a feminist, and so read and understood the Bible in this light. She was also interested in spirituality and spiritual experiences, as seen in her remark on Jacob's visions of God.

From Elizabeth Cady Stanton, ed. *The Woman's Bible* (New York: European Publishing Co., 1895), 55–58, 59–61.

Comments on Genesis 29:1-21.

JACOB'S journey to the land of Canaan in search of a wife, and the details of his courtship, have a passing interest with the ordinary reader, interested in his happiness and success. The classic ground for the cultivation of the tender emotions in these early days, seems to have been near a well, where the daughters of those who were rich in flocks and herds found opportunities to exhibit their fine points in drawing water for men and cattle. From the records of these interesting events, the girls seemed ready to accept the slightest advances from passing strangers, and to give their hands and hearts as readily as they gave a drink of water to the thirsty. Marriage was as simple a contract as the purchase of a lamb, the lamb and the woman having about an equal voice in the purchase, though the lamb was not quite as ready to leave his accustomed grazing ground. . . .

E. C. S.

. . . When one or another people sinned against a Jewish woman the men of the family were the avengers, as when the sons of Jacob slew a whole city to avenge an outrage committed against their sister. Polygamy and concubinage wove a thread of disaster and complications throughout the whole lives of families and its dire effects are directly traceable in the feuds and degeneration of their descendants. The chief lesson taught by history is danger of violating, physically, mentally, or spiritually the personal integrity of woman. Customs of the country and the cupidity of Laban, forced polygamy on Jacob, and all the shadows in his life, and he had no end of trouble in after years, are due to this. Perhaps nothing but telling their stories in this brutally frank way would make the lesson so plain.

If we search this narrative ever so closely it gives us no hint of Divinely intended subordination of woman. Jacob had to buy his wives with service

[32] For more information on Colby, see part 2, "Sarah—The First Mother of Israel."

which indicates that a high value was placed upon them. Now-a-days in high life men demand instead of give. The degradation of woman involved in being sold to a husband, to put it in the most humiliating way, is not comparable to the degradation of having to buy a husband. Euripides made Medea say: "We women are the most unfortunate of all creatures since we have to buy our masters at so dear a price," and the degradation of Grecian women is repeated all flower-garlanded and disguised by show in the marriage sentiments of our own civilization. Jacob was dominated by his wives as Abraham and Isaac had been and there is no hint of their subjection. Rachel's refusal to move when the goods were being searched for, showed that her will was supreme, nobody tried to force her to rise against her own desire.

The love which Jacob bore for Rachel has been through all time the symbol of constancy. Seven years he served for her, and so great was his love, so pure his delight in her presence that the time seemed but as a day. Had this simple, absorbing affection not been interfered with by Laban, how different would have been the tranquil life of Jacob and Rachel, developing undisturbed by the inevitable jealousies and vexations connected with the double marriage. Still this love was the solace of Jacob's troubled life and remained unabated until Rachel died and then found expression in tenderness for Benjamin, "the son of my right hand." It was no accident, but has a great significance, that this most ardent and faithful of Jewish lovers should have deeper spiritual experiences than any of his predecessors.

C.B.C.

Comments on Genesis 29:18-28, 30:25-26, 31:17-23

. . . The parting of Jacob and Laban was not amicable, although they did not come to an open rupture. Rachel's character for theft and deception is still further illustrated. Having stolen her father's images and hidden them under the camel's saddles and furniture, and sat thereon, when her father came to search for the images, which he valued highly, she said she was too ill to rise, so she calmly kept her seat, while the tent was searched and nothing found, thus by act as well as word, deceiving her father.

Jacob and his wives alike seemed to think Laban fair game for fraud and deception. As Laban knew his images were gone, he was left to suspect that Jacob knew where they were, so little regard had Rachel for the reputation of her husband. In making a God after their own image, who approved of whatever they did, the Jews did not differ much from ourselves; the men of our day talk too as if they reflected the opinions of Jehovah on the vital questions of the hour. . . .

To criticise the peccadilloes of Sarah, Rebekah and Rachel does not shadow the virtues of Deborah, Huldah and Vashti; to condemn the laws and customs of the Jews as recorded in the book of Genesis, does not destroy the force of the golden rule and the ten commandments. Parts of the Bible are so true, so grand, so beautiful, that it is a pity it should have been bound in the same volume with sentiments and descriptions so gross and immoral.

E.C.S.

Comments on Genesis 35:8-20

Jacob was evidently a man of but little sentiment. The dying wife gasps a name for her son, but the father pays no heed to her request, and chooses one to suit himself. Though we must admit that Benjamin is more dignified than Ben-oni; the former more suited to a public officer, the latter to a household pet. And now Rachel is gone, and her race with Leah for children is ended.

The latter with her maids is the victor, for she can reckon eight sons, while Rachel with hers can muster only four. One may smile at this ambition of the women for children, but a man's wealth was estimated at that time by the number of his children and cattle; women who had no children were objects of pity and dislike among the Jewish tribes. The Jews of to-day have much of the same feeling. They believe in the home sphere for all women, that wifehood and motherhood are the most exalted offices. If they are really so considered, why does every Jew on each returning Holy Day say in reading the service, "I thank thee, oh Lord! that I was not born a woman!"? And if Gentiles are of the same opinion, why do they consider the education of boys more important than that of girls? Surely those who are to fill the most responsible offices should have the most thorough and liberal education.

The home sphere has so many attractions that most women prefer it to all others. A strong right arm on which to lean, a safe harbor where adverse winds never blow, nor rough seas roll, makes a most inviting picture. But alas! even good husbands sometime die, and the family drifts out on the great ocean of life, without chart or compass, or the least knowledge of the science of navigation. In such emergencies the woman trained to self-protection, self-independence, and self-support holds the vantage ground against all theories on the home sphere.

E.C.S.

Conclusion

Nineteenth-century women authors using several literary genres retold and interpreted the story of Leah and Rachel for readers of various ages and religious and social locations. They dealt with the numerous interpretive challenges posed by the Genesis story with considerable confidence, drawing on the expertise of male commentators and historians, on their own experiences as readers and writers of various types of literature, and perhaps most importantly, on their experiences as women. They empathized with the many deep personal, marital, maternal, and spiritual struggles of Leah and Rachel (rivalry and jealousy between sisters, barrenness, a loveless marriage, unanswered prayer, sexual improprieties in families, wayward husbands and children, and risks of childbirth). At the same time, the differences in ethics, customs, standards of behavior, and even religious practices, made them aware that they needed to use a number of different reading strategies to bridge the gap between the world of the text and the world of the reader. Cornwallis was not alone when she wrote: "In perusing the present chapter we must keep in view the times of which it treats, and the customs of the country."[33]

The key issue that women authors agonized over was polygamy. Most women writers denounced the evils of polygamy. However, some authors, like Stowe, used developmental language to excuse the multiple marriages of Jacob, while others noted the differences in customs, and ignorance of God's plan for marriage. Sometimes the practice of polygamy was described as "heathen." Some authors used the difficulties of Jacob's polygamous marriages as a reason to discuss the virtues of monogamous Christian marriage.

A second issue relating to differences between the world of the text and the world of the women writers involved the issue of moral and religious values. Authors were especially troubled by the use of deception and its consequences. While women authors identified with the theme of deception that continued on from the story of Leah and Rachel's aunt Rebekah, they judged the act of deception harshly. They stressed its consequences and wrestled with the way God seemed to work through human sin to bring about his will. Similarly, they regarded Rachel's demand for children from her husband as improper and thoughtless, and wondered whether Rachel's early death may have been precipitated by this demand. Despite Rachel's questionable behaviour, many authors thought she must have had some redeeming qualities

[33] Cornwallis, *Observations*, 73.

because of Jacob's love for her and the stellar character of her son Joseph. Most writers saw Leah as a pious woman because of the names she gave her children, and they encouraged readers to follow Leah's piety and constancy even in unhappy marriages.

The differences between the world of the text and the world of the reader gave some writers a platform for discussing the Woman Question, though not all of them explicitly addressed it. Balfour, Colby, and Stanton looked for evidence of equality in the distant world of the text. They viewed such things as Jacob's consultation with his wives when he decided to move back to the land of promise as evidence that women were not subordinate in this story. Similarly, the fact that obedience to both mothers and fathers was required of both daughters and sons suggested the equality of men and women. Rachel and Leah's influence and power over their children, and in the case of Rachel over her father and her husband, was assumed by most authors, again suggesting the importance of women's influence. Later tradition which named the sisters as foundresses of Israel similarly recognized Leah and Rachel's power and importance. The only issue some authors used as arguing against equality was the fact that Leah and Rachel were treated as property and sold by Laban. Colby, however, turned this into an argument for the value of women: they were not taken for granted but assigned a large monetary value.

Although the nineteenth-century authors recognized many of the differences between the world of the story and their own world, they also emphasized similarities. They effectively and imaginatively entered into the world of Leah and Rachel. Their common experiences as women allowed them to feel with the characters and to learn with them the hard lessons of the life of faith. Their empathy enabled them to draw many practical and spiritual lessons from this story. Aguilar's passionate sermon on spiritual equality shows how the Woman Question intersected with the spiritual life:

> And when the Lord saw that Leah was hated (lit. less loved), He gave her children, but Rachel had none. And she called the name of her eldest son Reuben: for, she said, 'Surely the Lord hath looked upon my affliction; now therefore my husband will love me.' What a volume of woman's deepest feelings and the compassionating love of the Eternal do these brief lines reveal! He who had, in His inscrutable wisdom, ordained that Leah should be tried in the fiery ordeal of woman's saddest loneliness, unrequited affection, yet deigned to grant a compensating blessing in all the sweet, pure feelings of a mother's love. Who that reads but this one verse can uphold that woman is less an object of tender love and compassion to her God than man? Who can say that the Mosaic records are silent on this head? The words of *man* to point

out the proper station and value of woman we need not, for the children of Israel have the WORD OF THEIR GOD. And do we not still recognize the God of Leah?[34]

Many other women went on to push the spiritual equality advocated by Aguilar into full equality between men and women.

---

[34] Aguilar, "Leah and Rachel," *The Women of Israel*, 103.

Part 6

Lot's Wife and Daughters, Dinah, Tamar, and Potiphar's Wife—The Other Women of Genesis

Introduction

Nineteenth-century women looked to Eve, Sarah, Hagar, Rebekah, Leah, and Rachel for inspiration and self-understanding. They overlooked many of the less prominent and more controversial female figures like Lot's wife and daughters, as well as Dinah, Tamar, and Potiphar's wife. Elizabeth Cady Stanton wrote: "The texts on Lot's daughters and Tamar we omit altogether, as unworthy a place in the 'Woman's Bible.'"[1] Other women writers shared Stanton's opinion of the accounts of women involved in "unspeakable" acts. Many authors omitted these stories entirely from their writings; others referred to them briefly, with disdain; others used the negative examples of these women to admonish and preach to their readers. Only a few writers moved beyond judgment to empathize with the plight of marginalized women like the rejected Tamar and the abused Dinah.

The reaction of the nineteenth-century writers to the stories involving sexuality reflected the sensibilities of their culture. Women craved and cultivated "delicacy," or an inner intuition that allowed them to distinguish between good and evil. Delicate women were supposed to be shocked at every encounter with evil; to maintain this sensibility, women avoided frequent contact with immoral behavior, so they did not write about these questionable stories in Genesis.[2]

---

[1] Elizabeth Cady Stanton, *The Woman's Bible* (New York: European Publishing Co., 1895), 67.

[2] For a more detailed discussion of the sensibility of delicacy in the nineteenth century, see Noel Perrin, *Dr. Bowdler's Legacy: A History of Expurgated Books in England and America* (New York: Atheneum, 1969), 7–15.

The sensibilities, prejudices, and presuppositions that nineteenth-century women brought to their reading of the stories of "other" women in Genesis prevented them from recognizing the potential of these stories as resources in the ongoing debate over woman's nature, role, and place in society. Some women of faith did raise the sexual issues in debates over the woman's question. Josephine Butler worked with prostitutes and then worked to change the laws of England to eliminate sexual double standards for men and women.[3] Butler had a theological basis for her work; some of the stories discussed in this chapter might also have been helpful resources for her.[4] It took another century for biblical scholars such as Phyllis Trible (b. 1932) to begin to see the value of stories involving female sexuality for addressing ongoing issues of abuse.[5]

Lot's Wife and Daughters

Lot's unnamed wife is mentioned briefly in Genesis 19:26. While Lot's family was fleeing from the destruction of Sodom, she looked back and was turned into a pillar of salt. She is also mentioned in another cryptic verse in Luke 17:32 in which Jesus told hearers, "Remember Lot's wife." The eschatological context of the verse in the gospel, the mystery surrounding Lot's wife's metamorphosis, and the brevity of both these accounts all provide interpreters with an opportunity for amplification and elucidation of this narrative.

Many Christian interpreters began with the New Testament citation and preached to their readers. They saw Lot's wife as typical of sinners of their own day and admonished their readers to learn from her negative example. Most of the women who wrote on Lot's wife also engaged the issue of the historicity of this story. They used historical sources and travel books in their discussions.

---

[3] For more information on Butler's life, see Judith R. Walkowitz, "Butler, Josephine Elizabeth," in *Oxford Dictionary of National Biography*, ed. H. C. G. Matthew and Brian Harrison, vol. 9 (Oxford: Oxford University Press, 2004), 180–86.

[4] See Lucretia A. Flammang, "And Your Sons and Daughters Will Prophesy," "The Voice and Vision of Josephine Butler," in *Women's Theology in Nineteenth-Century Britain: Transfiguring the Faith of their Fathers*, ed. Julie Melnyk (New York: Garland, 1998), 151–64.

[5] Phyllis Trible, *Texts of Terror: Literary-Feminist Readings of Biblical Narratives* (Philadelphia: Fortress Press, 1984). Also see: Anne Michele Tapp, "An Ideology of Expendability: Virgin Daughter Sacrifice in Genesis 19:1-11, Judges 11:30-39 and 19:22-26," in *Anti-Covenant: Counter-Reading Women's Lives in the Hebrew Bible*, ed. Mieke Bal (Sheffield: Almond Press, 1989), 157–74; Illona N. Rashkow, "The Rape of Dinah," in *Upon Dark Places: Anti-Semitism and Sexism in English Renaissance Biblical Translation*, Bible and Literature Series 28 (Sheffield: Almond Press, 1990) 75–96; Alice Bach, "Breaking Free of the Biblical Frame-Up: Uncovering the Woman in Genesis 39," in *A Feminist Companion to Genesis*, ed. Athalya Brenner (Sheffield: Sheffield Academic, 1993), 318–42.

The story of Lot and his daughters is found in Genesis 19: 8, 30-38. Lot initially offered his virgin daughters to satisfy the lust of the men of Sodom who wanted to rape his male guests. After the death of Lot's wife and the destruction of Sodom, Lot and his daughters lived in the mountains. The two young women decided to get their father drunk and have children by him to preserve the family line. Some women who wrote about Lot's wife included the story of her daughters in their discussion, though none mention the earlier scene involving their father's offer of them as victims of gang rape.

Surprisingly, 2 Peter 2:7 describes Lot as a just or righteous man, an example supporting the argument that "The Lord knoweth how to deliver the godly out of temptations, and to reserve the unjust unto the day of judgment to be punished." This positive assessment of Lot's character provided a striking contrast to the character of his wife and daughters, and lent further weight to using the story of Lot's wife in an exemplary fashion.

§74 Sarah Trimmer
(1741–1810)

Sarah Trimmer was an Anglican author and educator.[6] Her book *A Help to the Unlearned* (1805) was written as an aid to Bible reading for those who could not afford more expensive study guide. Trimmer's aim was to explain what readers found difficult so that "Christians in general" could understand what was necessary for right faith and practice.[7]

In the extracts from her comments on Genesis 19, Trimmer briefly remarked on Lot's wife and daughters. She did not elaborate on the characters themselves, but drew brief lessons from the episodes. Trimmer referred to the Gospel text on Lot's wife and interpreted it in an end-time context for her readers.

> From Sarah Trimmer, *A Help to the Unlearned in the Study of the Holy Scriptures* (London: F. C. & J. Rivington, 1805), 23, 24.

. . . Observe the punishment of Lot's wife, who looked behind her either with a wish to return contrary to the will of God, or because she did not believe

---

[6] For further biographical information on Sarah Trimmer, see part 2, "Sarah—First Mother of Israel."

[7] Sarah Trimmer, *A Help to the Unlearned* (London: F.C. & J. Rivington, 1805), i.

the cities would be destroyed. Our Saviour, speaking of the destruction of the world at the last day said, *Remember Lot's wife, Luke* xvii. 32. . . .

What is related of Lot and his daughters at the end of this chapter [Genesis 19], should teach us at all times to be upon our guard, and to avoid all temptation to sin, especially those of drunkenness and intemperance, which generally lead to other vices.

§75 Mary Cornwallis
(1758–1836)

Mary Cornwallis, wife of the rector of an Anglican Parish in Wittersham, Kent, authored a four-volume commentary on the entire Bible.[8] Her commentary included quotations and paraphrases of others' work, as well as her own reflections on the text. She included comments on Lot's wife and his daughters in her remarks on Genesis 19.

Cornwallis, included the New Testament's positive assessment of Lot as a righteous man as an interpretive issue in Genesis 19. However, she wrestled deeply with the issue of the apparent disconnect between the portrayal of Lot in the Genesis stories and his designation as "righteous" in 2 Peter 2:6. Cornwallis cautiously raised the issue of the reason Lot's wife turned back. Cornwallis admitted that it was conjecture to determine why Lot's wife disobeyed, but reasoned that her action must have been motivated by a serious "wrong affection of the heart" because she was "so signally punished and made a monument of disobedience and ingratitude to succeeding ages." Cornwallis cited a deutero-canonical wisdom saying for evidence that Lot's wife was an example of unbelief.[9]

Cornwallis set out her theology of scripture, stressing its importance for teaching, using Jesus' reference to Lot's wife combined with 2 Timothy

---

[8] For a fuller biography of Mary Cornwallis, see part 5, "Leah and Rachel—Founders of the House of Israel."

[9] Wisdom of Solomon 10:7. "Evidence of their wickedness still remains: a continually smoking wasteland, plants bearing fruit that does not ripen, and a pillar of salt standing as a monument to an unbelieving soul." A long-standing interpretive tradition stood behind Cornwallis's understanding of Lot's wife's motives, though she does not cite any further references. For example, I Clement 11:3 suggests that Lot's wife "being of a different mind from himself and not continuing in agreement with him" was punished "that all might know that those who are of a double mind, and who distrust the power of God, bring down judgment on themselves and become a sign to all succeeding generations."

3:16 as proof texts.[10] Cornwallis stressed the issue of the story's historicity. By including an exhaustive account of ancient and modern testimonies to the destruction of Sodom and Gomorrah to corroborate Moses' testimony, Cornwallis showed her concern for apologetics and education.

Cornwallis was one of few nineteenth-century women to comment on Lot's daughters. She challenged commentators who attributed religious motives to the daughters. Instead, she suggested that the story was included to account for the origin of the Moabites and Ammonites.

Cornwallis was very aware of the interpretive problem of reading meaning into the text, and so she set out clear principles of interpretation for her readers. She acknowledged the challenges interpreting presented: "the Scriptures seldom comment upon the events they record; it is for us to judge of them by the revealed law, and with that before our eyes, we can be at no loss to determine right and wrong."

From Mary Cornwallis, *Observations, Critical, Explanatory, and Practical on the Canonical Scriptures*, vol. 1 (London: Baldwin, Cradock, & Joy, 1817). [Text from the 2nd ed. (1820), 54–56.]

Lot is styled *righteous** in the New Testament; but the righteousness imputed to him was either confined to a certain period, or regarded his adherence to the worship of the true God; his moral character *after he left Sodom* cannot be supported, and it is impossible to excuse his continuing to dwell and form connexions with so corrupt a people. It seems as if his principles and those of his family had been tainted by such an intercourse, since we find his wife looking back to the devoted[11] city with desire, as may be fairly conjectured; because without some very wrong affection of the heart, we may be assured that she would not have been so signally punished, and made a *monument*†of disobedience and ingratitude to succeeding ages. What the substance was into which she was changed is *immaterial*;+ it was certainly not common salt, because it remained visible for a length of time. Josephus speaks of it as still existing when he wrote, and says that he had seen it himself.[12]

It may not be uninteresting here to collect what various ancient authors and travellers have recorded, to corroborate the testimony of Moses respecting the destruction of Sodom and Gomorrah, by a judicial shower of fire and brimstone. Diodorus Siculus mentions that the lake which covered the

[10] 2 Tim. 3:16: "All scripture is given by inspiration of God, and is profitable for doctrine, for reproof, for correction, for instruction in righteousness."

[11] A devoted thing, called "an accursed thing" in the KJV, was set apart for God. See the story of Achan whose sin of taking devoted things was considered more serious than mere stealing in Josh. 6:17-19.

[12] Josephus, *Jewish Antiquities* 1.11.23.

country where these cities stood 'is bitter and fetid to the last degree; inso-much, that neither fish nor any other aquatic animal is able to live in it.'[13] Tacitus relates that a tradition still prevailed in his days of certain powerful cities having been destroyed by thunder and lightning, and of the plain in which they were situated being burnt up. He adds, that 'evident traces of such a catastrophe remained; the earth was parched, and had lost its natural pow-ers; and whatever sprung, up, either spontaneously or in consequence of being planted, gradually withered away and crumbled into dust.'[14] Thévenot, in his Travels, says, 'there is no sort of fish in this sea by reason of its extraordinary saltness; and when the fish of the river Jordan come down so low, they imme-diately die. The land within three leagues is not cultivated, but is white and mingled with salt and ashes.'[15] Josephus bears the same testimony.[16]

We are told by St. Paul that the Scriptures are designed for the purposes of *doctrine*, of *reproof, for correction, for instruction in righteousness*;++ and we may observe that our Lord himself made such use of them: when he was declaring to the disciples the destruction that should fall upon Jerusalem, and warning them to flee for their lives, he says, "Remember Lot's wife" [Luke 17:32]. And the apostles refer continually to the examples of Abraham, Noah, and others whose lives are recorded in this history.

In the preceding part of Lot's history there is much to deplore. Whether he was tempted to presumption by the signal deliverance he had experienced, and was in consequence permitted to fall thus dreadfully, cannot be known; but he stands a caution to all, not to consider their warfare over till their eyes are sealed in death. Some commentators endeavour to justify the conduct of Lot's daughters, under the idea that they were influenced by a desire to bear the Promised Seed, and apprehended that their father was the only man that had escaped the flames. Had they, however, been actuated by religious motives, it is more natural to suppose that they would have confided their thoughts to their parent, and consulted him upon a subject of such impor-tance. The Scriptures seldom comment upon the events they record; it is for us to judge of them by the revealed law, and, with that before our eyes, we can be at no loss to determine right and wrong. It is probable that this dread-ful relation is only given to show the origin of the Moabites and Ammonites,

[13] Diodorus Siculus was a Greek historian, born in Sicily, who flourished in 49 B.C. He relied on the works of others to put together his voluminous work, *Bibliotheca Historia*, which consisted of forty volumes.

[14] Tacitus (c. 56–c. 117), one of antiquity's greatest historians, wrote about the history of the Roman Empire in the first century A.D. in the *Annals* and the *Histories*.

[15] [Jean de Thévenot], *The Travels of Monsieur de Thévenot into the Levant*. Part I: *Turkey*. Part II: *Persia*. Part III: *The East-Indies* (London, 1687).

[16] Josephus, *Jewish Antiquities* 1.11.23.

nations most corrupt and idolatrous, but who make a very important figure in the Jewish history. Lot and his family are from this time no where mentioned in the sacred writings.

* 2 Pet. ii.8.

† See Wisdom of Solomon, x.7. [Evidence of their wickedness still remains: a continually smoking wasteland, plants bearing fruit that does not ripen, and a pillar of salt standing as a monument to an unbelieving soul.]

+ Mr. Bruce, in his Travels, mentions a kind of salt so hard that it is used as money, and passes from hand to hand no more injured than a stone would be. [Cornwallis is referring to James Bruce (1730–1794), a renowned traveler. His book, *Travels between the years 1768 and 1773, through part of Africa, Syria, Egypt and Arabia, into Abyssinia, to discover the source of the Nile, comprehending an interesting narrative of the author's adventures in Abyssinia* (London: James Cundee, Albion P., 1805), was very popular and republished numerous times.]

++ See 2 Tim iii.16.

§76 Sarah Ewing Hall
(1761–1830)

Sarah Hall was an educator writing in the United States for young people.[17] Her book, *Conversations on the Bible* (1818), retold and commented upon the Old Testament story of salvation history. The book was written in the form of a conversation between a mother and her three children. In this selection on Lot's wife, Mother told the story, and Charles and Catherine asked pointed questions that allowed Hall to discuss the issue of the historicity of the story and its literal and spiritual sense. By portraying Lot positively, Hall contrasted his behaviour with that of his wife who disobeyed "an express command, 'not to look back.'" To a large extent Hall resisted the temptation felt by most interpreters to explain at length why Lot's unnamed wife looked back; rather, she showed empathy for Lot's wife, suggesting that perhaps she was "bewailing" her unworthy city and friends and forgot the divine injunction. Hall included a brief discussion of the debate over the pillar of salt by inserting a child's question on whether the "metamorphosis is to be literally true." Hall's Mother character was ambiguous about the historicity of the story; this underscored one of the character's (and thus Hall's) stated purposes in teaching, to encourage her children to examine scriptures themselves as they matured.[18]

[17] For further biographical information on Sarah Hall see part 2, "Sarah—First Mother of Israel."

[18] Sarah Hall, *Conversations on the Bible* (Philadelphia: Harrison Hall, 1827), 16.

From Sarah Hall, *Conversations on the Bible* (Philadelphia: Harrison Hall, 1818). [Text is from the 4th ed. (1827), 30–32.]

The same year, after the famine had ceased, Abram with his wife, and his nephew, returned to their former residence near Bethel. But their flocks were become so numerous, that they could no longer remain together. The ground they occupied was insufficient for their support, and disputes frequently arose between their herdsmen. That they might not themselves be involved in contention, these primeval shepherds agreed to separate. Lot accordingly, journeyed on towards the river Jordan and pitched his tents on a fertile plain, watered by that celebrated stream.

Lot was still in the territory of the Canaanites, the descendants of Ham, who, as I hinted just now, were by this time abandoned to vices of every description. Exemplary judgments had been denounced against them, and the Sovereign Avenger began now to execute them. But the virtue of Lot was regarded with singular favour. Two angels, in the character of travellers, were commissioned to tell him, that Sodom, the city of his residence, would be consumed by fire from heaven; and to direct him to repair with his family to the mountains! He obeyed; and thus with his two daughters, was preserved; whilst his wife, heedless of an express command, "not to look back," lingered. Bewailing perhaps, her unworthy city and friends, she forgot the injunction, and "was turned into a pillar of salt."

CHARLES. Is that metamorphosis supposed to be literally true?

MOTHER. The words of Moses are often metaphorically understood by infidels to serve their own impious ends, but as his history was written for the instruction of the common people, and all classes were commanded to teach it to their children, we can seldom admit of figures beyond their comprehension. In this case, however, commentators have found several interpretations to explain the difficulty. It is enough for us to know, that she was punished for *disobedience*; and let us remember the example of Lot's wife, whenever we are tempted to transgress a known command!

Five populous cities with all their inhabitants were utterly destroyed by this judgment, and a remarkable lake, now covers the soil where once they flourished—the lasting monument of that tremendous event!

CATHERINE. You mean, I suppose, the lake Asphaltites; or in more modern language, the Dead Sea.[19] But why do you call it a remarkable lake?

---

[19] Asphaltitis is the Greek name for the Dead Sea. In scripture, it is referred to as the Salt Sea (Gen. 14:3; Num. 34:12; etc.), the Sea of the Arabah (Deut. 3:17; 4:49; etc.), and the Eastern Sea (Ezek. 47:18; Joel 2:20; Zech. 14:8). Josephus and other early writers called the Dead Sea Lake Asphaltitis.

MOTHER. Because its appearance and properties are really so, independently of the fables to which it has given rise. It has been called the Dead sea, for example, because its waters were supposed to have a fatal influence on animal and vegetable life. Modern travellers have detected the fallacy of this opinion.

CATHERINE. How is it ascertained that it flows where Sodom once stood?

MOTHER. The site is described with sufficient precision by Moses; the Arabs who dwell on its borders acknowledge it, and, according to some writers, call it "the sea of Lot." Mr. *Maundrel*, who has written an account of *A Journey to Aleppo*, was even told by two aged persons of probity, that they had actually seen pillars, and other fragments of buildings in the water near the shore, but he could not discover them.[20]

§77 Eliza Smith
(fl. 1850–1852)

Eliza Smith, writing as "A Clergyman's Daughter," wrote *The Battles of the Bible* (1852) and *Chapters on the Shorter Catechism* (1850). In the preface to *The Battles of the Bible*, she wrote that it was her desire "to lead the young, and those who assist them in studying the Holy Book, to study it with a purpose,—with regard to every passage of Sacred Writ to ask themselves, What may I learn from this?" Four characters, Grandfather, George, Johnnie, and Marianne (the narrator), discussed battles of the Bible. They began their discussion after Grandfather learned that George did not appreciate the chapters in the Bible he read every day at home. George claimed that he knew all about the battles of the Bible, but did not realize there were battles before the time of David and the kings. Grandfather then began to tell them about all the battles of the Bible. Marianne was reluctant to hear about the battles and asked, "Does it do us any good to hear about battles? for I do not like to hear of people killing one another." Grandfather then told her to listen and see what she could learn. The lessons to be learned were very specifically

---

[20] Henry Maundrell toured Palestine in 1697 and wrote of his travels in his very popular book, *A Journey from Aleppo to Jerusalem, at Easter, A.D. 1697*. This book was reprinted many times in the eighteenth and nineteenth centuries. The 1810 edition of the book was reprinted in 1963 by David Howell.

spelled out, as seen in the excerpt below. Grandfather began with Abraham's battle with the five kings in Genesis 14. This battle story was followed by the story of the destruction of Sodom and Gomorrah (Gen. 18 and 19) as the children wanted to hear what became of Lot and his family. Smith's treatment of the fate of Lot's wife shows similarities to Hall's in terms of genre and content. Unique, though, is her suggestion that Lot's wife cared more about her husband's approval than about God's approval.

> From Eliza Smith (writing as "A Clergyman's Daughter"), *The Battles of the Bible* (Edinburgh: Paton & Ritchie, 1852), 11–12.

(Grandfather is speaking to George, Johnnie, and Marianne, the narrator. They have just heard about Abraham's defeat of the 5 kings, and now Grandfather tells what became of Lot and his family in Sodom.)

. . . "The angels—for Lot's visitors were not mortals—told him now to collect his family and flee from this place, for the Lord had sent them to destroy it. Lot told his sons-in-law, but they did not heed; it seemed a jest to them.

"The morning dawned. 'Arise, take thy wife and thy two daughters which are here,' the angels said to Lot. He lingered, unwilling it may be, to leave all his riches behind him. They kindly took his hand and led him away.

"'Escape,' they said, 'to the mountain; stay not in all the plain, lest thou be consumed.' Lot entreated leave to go into the city of Bela, which was near, thinking himself not able to go to the mountain, as if the God who had saved him out of Sodom could not give him strength for the journey he had commanded him to take. But God was merciful; his petition was granted; for his sake the city was spared; and because he had pleaded its being little, as a reason for its not being destroyed, it was called Zoar, which means a little one. On the way, Lot's wife looked back from behind him, and for that she died. Some of the fiery particles that were in the air fell on her, and crusted over her body, so that she became like a pillar of salt."

"There was not very much harm in only looking back, grandfather," I said, "why was she punished so very much?"

"In looking back she disobeyed a positive command of God, and in looking back from behind Lot she shewed that she had more regard to her husband's approbation than to the approbation of God. She did not wish Lot to know that she was doing wrong; she did not care though God knew it. The fate which befel [sic] her teaches us to obey God rather than man.

"Then the Lord rained fire and brimstone upon Sodom and Gomorrah, so that fertile plain, where many people and cattle had dwelt, was changed into a place where nothing could live."

"What is the place like now, grandfather?" George asked.

"It is a lake called the Dead Sea, a large lake about forty miles in length and eighteen in breadth. The waters of it are very salty, as some one says they taste like fire. Nothing that lives or breathes is to be found in them, and they are the only waters of the world of which that can be said. Travellers have told that they could see pillars and fragments of buildings under the clear waters, but that is not necessary to prove the truth of the story I have told you." . . .

§78 S. G. Ashton
(1819–1872)

Sophia Goodrich Ashton, the American author of *Mothers of the Bible* and *Women of Worth*, used her pen to preach to women.[21] Her sermon on Lot's wife is filled with guilt-inducing rhetoric and a view of God as a harsh judge. She imagined that her audience had the same faults as Lot's wife and made an evangelistic appeal to them.

Ashton interpreted the story of Lot's wife and her daughters through the lens of Jesus' injunction to remember Lot's wife. Lot's wife was a type of an unbelieving and disobedient woman. Ashton drew parallels between the life in Sodom that Lot's family were called to leave and the contemporary world that Christians were called to leave. She called her readers to prepare for the future by fleeing the wrath to come. Like Hall and Cornwallis, Ashton wondered why Lot's wife turned back. She confidently gave an answer and built her sermon on the issues of unbelief and disobedience to God's command. Ashton's own sense of power as a preacher and her message about mothers' power and responsibility for their daughters' future inadvertently raised the woman's issue.

From S. G. Ashton, *The Mothers of the Bible* (New York: The World Publishing House, 1877), 60–64.

–The Wife of Lot–
"Remember Lot's wife."

THIS was our Saviour's injunction, and in obedience to it we here take occasion to address some, who, though not generally interested in the study of

---

[21] For more biographic information on Ashton, see part 1, "Eve—Mother of Us All."

the Bible, nor in such volumes as this, may nevertheless glance over its pages, either accidentally or at the suggestion of a friend.

Do not be offended that we charge you with the same faults as she possessed, who was made a perpetual monument of folly, and whom you have ever been accustomed to regard with dislike, and whom you think you do not in any particular resemble.

Have you ever seriously considered the nature of the sin which Lot's wife committed? Are you quite sure that you are not chargeable with like foolishness? Lot and his family dwelt in Sodom, a place where not a single righteous man or worshipper of the true God could be found, save himself. The cry of the wickedness of that wicked city rose up to heaven, and God determined to destroy it. He sent an angel, who warned Lot to flee, with all his household, to the mountains, and to go in such haste as not to cast a single glance behind, lest the scorching heat of the fearful flame should devour them before they reached a place of safety. They went; but the wife and mother, not believing the message of the angel, and grieved at leaving her home and worldly possessions, turned a lingering, longing look back on the doomed city, and was instantly destroyed. Her sin was unbelief,—its fruit was disobedience to the direct command of God.

You, dear friends, live in a world in which like sentence has gone forth. "The earth, and the works that are therein, shall be burned up," [2 Pet. 3:10]. Do you believe this word of God? Perhaps you will answer that it is of little consequence whether you do believe or not, as the day is far distant, and will affect you little. But there is another word of God which is addressed to you. "It is appointed unto men once to die," [Heb. 9:27]. Do you believe this? You will say it is preposterous to ask such a question. We know that we shall die; we must believe that. But do you act as if you believed it? Are you prepared for it? Are you so training your children that they shall be prepared for it? When the summons comes, will it find you willing to leave this world, and all its pleasures, and enter at God's command on untried scenes? There is yet another message which God is even now speaking in your ears: "Flee from the wrath to come," [Matt. 3:7]. "He that believeth on the Son hath everlasting life; he that believeth not the Son shall not see life, but the wrath of God abideth on him," [John 3:36]. Is this message any more acceptable to you than was that of the angel to Lot's wife? Do you credit it at all? Are you taking any means to avoid the wrath or gain the faith of which it speaks? Are you daily instructing your children, those who are so precious to you that you would shield them with your life from harm, to flee from this fearful wrath? When you lie down at night and when you wake, do you earnestly pray for mercy for them and yourself? Do you lead their young affections to the Saviour, as the one most worthy of their love? Do you teach them to bend the knee and fold the little hands in prayer? Is there anything in your daily life to convince them that you fully believe this truth of God's word? Do you not rather so live as to prove yourselves participators in the very sins of Lot's wife,—unbelief and disobedience?

We beg you, by your peace of mind, by your own eternal welfare, by your love for the immortal beings committed to your care, by the death and atoning sacrifice of your Lord and Saviour Jesus Christ, to *"think on these things"* [Phil. 4:8].

Perhaps you are devising plans and cherishing expectations for your loved ones, which such views as these would disturb and destroy. In this, also, your circumstances are not unlike those of the mother of Lot's children. She had two daughters who were affianced to two men of that gay but devoted city. Doubtless she rejoiced in what she considered their good fortune and excellent prospects. Have you ever inquired after the fate of those daughters, and the result of their early training? Seek the history in the book of God, and do not turn away with disgust because we have directed you to it, and with entire assurance that your daughters will walk the path of life clear of all such dangers. The *worldly-minded, ungodly* mother has no security for the upright conduct of her children, even according to the low standard of the world's morality.

The only security for ourselves, and those to whom we have given being, is a firm faith in the words of God, and an obedient spirit to his commands. Failing of these, we may any of us be as lasting monuments of his displeasure as Lot's wife; and our children may sink to a degradation even worse than that of hers.

§79 Charlotte Mary Yonge
(1823–1901)

Charlotte Yonge was the only daughter and eldest child of William Crawley Yonge, a magistrate, and Frances Mary Bargus. Her parents were both from clerical families and very involved in the educational mission of the church. At the age of seven Charlotte Yonge became a teacher in the Sunday school her mother started in a school built by her father. She continued to teach Sunday School for the next seventy-one years. John Keble, a leader in the Oxford movement in the Anglican Church,[22] was her parish priest, and later

---

[22] The Oxford movement began as a renewal movement in the Anglican Church in 1833. John Henry Newman, one of its founders, wrote a series of "Tracts for the Times," which gave

became her spiritual mentor, confessor, teacher, and editor. A wreath placed at the foot of the Keble memorial cross read, "In Reverent Memory of John Keble, Master and Inspirer of Charlotte Mary Yonge."

Yonge was a popular and prolific writer of over 200 works of fiction and non-fiction. Additionally, she wrote articles, both for her own magazine, *The Monthly Packet*, and other magazines. The proceeds from her writing funded many educational, mission, and church building projects. Elisabeth Jay suggests that Yonge was "the Tractarian movement's most important lay voice as well as its most comprehensive chronicler."[23]

Yonge's popular book for children, *Aunt Charlotte's Stories of Bible History* (1875), was republished many times; *Young Folks' Bible History* is derived from this work. Yonge's dramatic retelling of the story of Lot for young children shows empathy towards Lot's family. She stayed closer to the Genesis story itself than other women like Ashton who filled in the gaps in their retelling of the story. Like Hall, who also wrote for young children, Yonge was concerned to explain the "metamorphosis" of Lot's wife and rationalized that "the deadly storm overtook her." Similarly, she suggested that the physical geography of the area of the Dead Sea shows God's curse on the place. Further, like many interpreters, Yonge used the New Testament as a lens for interpretation and read the story typologically. She drew parallels between the world of Sodom and this world, and emphasized God's anger.

From Charlotte Yonge, *Young Folks' Bible History* (New York: Eaton & Mains, 1880), 35–37.

Those strangers [the angels] told him [Lot] the place was to be destroyed, with all that were in it, because it was so wicked! Though the fields looked so quiet, the walls so strong, and the sun had gone down as usual, all would be ruined in a few hours' time! Then the strangers took hold of him, and his wife and daughters, and led them almost by force away from their home in the dawn of morning, bidding them escape for their lives to the mountain, and not look back. They were frightened, and begged not to have to go so far as the wild mountain. Might they not go to the little city near at hand? And their wish was granted. Just as the sun had risen they entered the little city for which they had begged; and as soon as they were safe the four towns, that had seemed so strong and firm, were all burning with fire and brimstone; and all

the movement its well-known name the "Tractarian movement." John Keble, Richard Hurrell Froude, Charles Marriott, and later Edward Bouverie Pusey and Richard William Church were also important leaders in this movement to bring certain Roman Catholic doctrines and rituals back into the Anglican church.

[23] Elisabeth Jay, "Yonge, Charlotte Mary," in *Oxford Dictionary of National Biography* 60:808–10.

the sinners who had mocked at warning were soon lying dead under God's awful anger. Four alone had been led out of the city by the strangers, but even of these only three came into the city of refuge. The wife did not heed the warning not to linger nor look back, the deadly storm overtook her, and she remained rooted to the spot—a pillar of salt!

The names of those cities were Sodom and Gomorrah, and the one good man who was saved by the mercy of God was named Lot. And now a strange gloomy lake called the Dead Sea covers that valley with its heavy waters, and the bare rocky hills, crusted with salt, show that the curse of God is on the place.

Let us try to carry home one thought from this terrible history. This world will one day be burnt up like those cities, and its looking safe and prosperous now does not make it safe. But God sends messengers to lead us out of it. If we attend to them, and follow their advice, we shall through all our lives be getting out of danger, and going on to a safe home in heaven; but if we care only for pleasant things here, it is like looking back, and our souls will perish with what they love. That is why our Saviour bade us "Remember Lot's wife." We should remember her when we are tempted to think it hard to give up anything pleasant, because we are told that it is wrong, and may put us in danger of God's anger.

§80 Etty Woosnam
(1849–c. 1883)

Etty Woosnam was part of a British family with ties to India.[24] In her topical studies on women in the Bible written for teenage girls, published in two volumes, Woosnam presented examples from the biblical stories for her readers to follow.

Woosnam's reading of Lot's wife is remarkable in many ways. Her retelling provides another example of female preaching and, more importantly, an example of gendered exegesis as Woosnam read the story through a distinctively female lens. Like Ashton, Woosnam preached in a heavy-handed way to her readers. She emphasized "the vengeance of Almighty God" in the events recorded in Genesis 19 and, like many women, she drew parallels with God's workings in the modern world. Lot's wife was a type for the unconverted, lukewarm, or worldly-minded Christian who was suddenly struck down.

[24] For a fuller biography of Woosnam, see part 1, "Eve—Mother of Us All."

Rereading the story from a woman's point of view, Woosnam fabricated Lot's wife's choice to live in the plain of Jordan (Gen. 13:10), and her arrangement of marriages for her daughters (Gen. 19:14). Woosnam attributed great power to women for good and evil; she recalled Eve's story and held Lot's helpmeet accountable for family problems, and, by extension, the destruction of the four cities. Woosnam's method of reading women back into the biblical story could be viewed as embryonic of a methodology modern feminists develop much further.[25] Like Hall, she proposed that Lot's wife's forgetfulness contributed to her downfall. Woosnam likened the Christian life of discipleship to a journey and used a scene from *Pilgrim's Progress* to illustrate her point about the folly of being too absorbed in "our little daily concerns." Woosnam's use of sacramental language to describe the pillar of salt,[26] included language echoing the Anglican service of Evening Prayer,[27] and a verse from one of Charles Wesley's hymns[28] reflected her evangelical Anglican piety.

In an unusual group of metaphors, Woosnam consistently used vision and scientific instruments of vision as an illustration. She described the "telescope of faith" and "Satan's microscope." She called God the Great Oculist who can help the faithful with their spiritual myopia. It is not clear why Woosnam chose this illustration, but it shows her skill as a writer and teacher.

From Etty Woosnam, *The Women of the Bible: Old Testament* (London: S.W. Partridge, 1881), 42–51. [Text fro the 4th ed., n.d.]

Lot's Wife: Worldly-mindedness
(GENESIS xiii. 5 to 13. GENESIS xix. 1 to 3, and 12 to 26)

"BUT his wife looked back from behind him and she became a pillar of salt." And there that pillar of salt remained in the valley of Sodom an everlasting

---

[25] See for example, Phyllis Trible, "Bringing Miriam out of the Shadows," *Bible Review* 5 (1989): 14–25, 34. Trible assumes that the full story of Miriam has been suppressed by patriarchal storytellers. She attempts to reconstruct Miriam's story from fragments "buried within Scripture," understanding her task to be "unearthing fragments, assembling them, pondering the gaps and constructing a text." Woosnam did not express her motives for looking for Lot's wife in the text and probably did not make the same assumptions about patriarchal storytellers and editors that Trible did.

[26] The word *sacrament* is defined as "an outward and visible sign of an inward and spiritual grace, given to us by Christ himself, as a means whereby we receive this grace, and a pledge to assure us thereof" (*The Book of Common Prayer* [Toronto: Anglican Book Centre, 1962], 550).

[27] A prayer in the Anglican service of Evening Prayer reads: "We have left undone those things which we ought to have done, And we have done those things which we ought not to have done." *The Book of Common Prayer*, 19.

[28] Charles Wesley (1707–1788), one of the founders of Methodism, wrote thousands of hymns.

memorial of the vengeance of Almighty God; and every one that passed it must have hurried on with a shudder and a very vivid impression of the power and presence of Jehovah. No doubt all over the country it was rumoured about, and men held their breath with awe when first they heard of it. It *was* a terrible thing! but not more terrible than the sudden deaths by illness and accident of unconverted sinners that occur in our midst every day. People live around us, making their way in the world, and getting through life somehow, with a little show of religion and church-going to fill up parts of Sunday and intervals of spare time, and they seem to flourish like the green bay tree. And lo! suddenly they are struck down as Lot's wife was. At the death of a lady of precisely the type that Lot's wife was, no suspicion is felt sometimes that it was not all right with her at the last. Look at the godly family she belonged to. Her uncle Abraham, the most pious and highly respected man living, her husband a man "who vexed his righteous soul from day to day with the ungodly, deeds" of his neighbours. She herself had been what is called "an excellent mother" with an eye to business in choosing such a "garden of the Lord" to settle her family down in; bent on her sons bettering themselves and her daughters making comfortable marriages. If God had *not* turned her into a pillar of salt for our warning, I daresay all would have supposed that she had been one of God's saints. Oh, thank God that her history was written for our admonition; and let us learn what wordly-minded Christians *won't do*. You may be a member of the most religious family in the world, and pass muster admirably as a highly thought of person, but the lukewarm God spues out of His mouth. First, consider how nearly she was saved! It is said that nine-tenths of the ships that are lost at sea are wrecked in harbours close to shore; and Christ emphatically explains that God's worst judgments are for those who have heard the gospel constantly and know all about it, without knowing Jesus and being known of Him. She had a special call from God. Two angels came to warn her. Have you ever had any one sent to speak to you individually about your soul? Did you receive him or her as a messenger from God? Lot's wife was frightened—aroused. I have no doubt she trembled when she heard the doom of Sodom, and wanted to get to heaven, to be saved from hell. Do not mistake these sensations for conversion. They often lead a soul to Christ the Saviour from sin; but many are alarmed, and awakened to a sense of their danger, who are never saved. Felix trembled but was not converted [Acts 24:25]. The jailer at Philippi trembled, and followed on to know the Lord [Acts 16:30-31]. The fear of death will make *everybody* shudder—except the Christian. It did not make Ignatius shudder when, in the persecution under Trajan he heard, good old man, that he was to be devoured by wild beasts in the amphitheatre, and he cheerfully endured this horrible martyrdom. His death was short and easy. He said just before it: "It is better for me to die for Jesus Christ than to reign over the ends of the earth."[29] A Christian is not afraid of death, but of sin. An unconverted man is not afraid of sin, but he is a very coward at the thought of dying.

Do you think that punishment to Lot's wife was severe in proportion to the one little offence of looking back? Consider what opportunities she had had. Consider, too, that that turning of her head was not an exceptional sin, but the result of months and years past of worldly mindedness. It was all in keeping with her choosing the plain of Jordan because it was well watered and a garden of the Lord (Gen. xiii. 10), though "the men were wicked and sinners before the Lord exceedingly" (verse 13). It was all of a piece with the marriages she had made for her daughters. She had approved of men who mocked when Lot told them of their danger and entreated of them to flee from ruin—men who never pretended to mind that God's anger had waxed great against them (Gen. xix. 14). No, it was not an isolated act. That pillar of salt in the vale of Sodom was an outward and visible sign of an inward and spiritual falling away from grace, and a warning to us women of the nineteenth century that we cannot serve God and mammon. We must love Christ with all our heart and forsake all that we have, or we cannot be His disciple. To be a Christian means to have one supreme object in life, and that to be Christ-like. To be His disciple is to be unselfish, and never look back or repent of it. When He was coming to live in this ungrateful world, He did not look back to the glories of Heaven and hesitate to leave them. When the time was come for Him to die by the hands of wicked men, He "steadfastly set His face to go to Jerusalem" [Luke 9:51]. If we are Christians, we delight to do God's will as Christ did it.

We *know* all these things so well. The difficulty is to *remember* them. We need to be constantly thinking of how to please God; to live in prayer. Otherwise we are too apt to be absorbed in our little daily concerns, the friends we have lately made, the duties we have to do, the plans we are going to carry out. Do you remember in the "Pilgrim's Progress"[30] the scene Christian saw at the Interpreter's house of the man eagerly scraping away with the muck rake, his eyes fixed on the ground while an angel held a crown of glory over his head? So do we often keep on clasping our rake, and hope in the rubbish of earth to find some good and forget to raise our heads to see the incorruptible crown that might be ours. We know as well as anyone can tell us, that the value of earthly things is of no importance compared with the salvation of our souls; but when we have to decide on some little question of daily life,

---

[29] From *The Epistle of Ignatius to the Romans*, ch. 6. "By death I shall attain true life."
[30] John Bunyan, *Pilgrim's Progress*, 1678. Reprinted many times.

we forget that our soul is in the balance, and this is why Christ charged His hearers to "Remember Lot's wife."

This is a busy age. Our acquaintance is large. There are numbers of people going out and coming in, and we have much to talk over and to plan with them. Besides, a notion seems to prevail generally that everyone must have a change of air occasionally, and so all our work is interrupted by railway journeys. We may lead an utterly useless, unprofitable life, and yet appear to be very hard worked, and so we need constantly to be *reminded* of the real purpose of our existence:

> A charge to keep I have;
> A God to glorify;
> A never-dying soul to save,
> And fit it for the sky.[31]

When Sir Isaac Newton[32] was asked how he managed to make his wonderful discoveries, he said, "By always thinking about them." There was once an order of nuns who made it a rule of their convent to cross themselves and pray every time the clock struck. Their crossing themselves may have been a mere form, and their prayer oftentimes meaningless; but the intention of the rule was right, and no doubt there were some who sincerely raised to God a contrite look and a desire to be holy and good. Let us imitate them in this—in fixing some circumstances or hours of the day, as points at which to stop short, as it were, to pause for a minute or two, and raise the heart to God.

And make haste away out of Sodom. Do not linger there. There is danger about everywhere. There are germs of infectious disease floating in the air which may settle on us at any time, sparks of the great burning which may set us all on fire. Nothing but living in the Spirit—being led by God's Spirit, watching unto prayer—can make us proof against them. Have you got a worldly connection? Friends whom you cannot look upon as spiritually-minded, but yet those whose blame or ridicule you would greatly dislike? Do you try to conceal your aspirations after goodness on purpose not to annoy them? Remember Lot's wife. Do you mix with some careless pleasure-seeking companions because you feel so sincere in your wish to do them good that you are confident they will never lead you in their ways? Remember the argument. "Disease is infectious, but health is not."* Remember Lot's wife. She could not persuade her sons-in-law to go the right way, and she was lost herself at last.

---

[31]This is the first verse of Charles Wesley's hymn, "A Charge to Keep I Have."

[32] Sir Isaac Newton (1642–1727) was a mathematician and physicist who developed calculus and the theory of universal gravitation.

Another question let me earnestly put before you. Are you running as a man runs in a race, trying to outstrip all the others in devotion to Christ and zeal in His service; looking neither to the right hand nor to the left, but straight on to the goal? Or are you a straggler behind the rest of your religious friends, just looking out for what they will do, saying Amen to what they think right? When a large army is crossing through a hostile country, it is best not to be in the *rear guard*. The enemy always harasses the stragglers in the rear; and if the weather is cold, and difficulties are great, as in Napoleon's retreat from Moscow, the hindmost travellers of the party perish in the snow as the rear guard of the grand army did. In Genesis xix. 26, we read, "Lot's wife looked back *from behind him*." She was the last of the party.

I have sometimes thought that worldly-mindedness is spiritual shortsightedness. The revised version of the New Testament makes me think so still more. (See II Epistle St. Peter i. 9.) The secret of worldly-mindedness is that what we see we believe in most readily and firmly, and what is out of sight is out of mind. Mammon worshippers cannot see afar off. "They see only *the near* things." They see that one situation brings in £1000 and the other £500. There is a clear profit here. They see *that*! There is a more influential connection to be gained by settling down in one place than in another; they see *that*! There are certain inconveniences attending a certain course which after all may be an over-scrupulous one; and difficulty and inconvenience are disagreeable things—that is quite evident! But when it comes to the necessity for holiness, for abstaining from fleshly lusts—when the invisible things of the world to come, the hope of eternal life, are in question, "they cannot see afar off." And this is a shortsightedness which does not improve with advancing age, but which Satan makes feebler and dimmer year by year. As God's angels who came to Lot smote the wicked men outside his house with blindness so that they wearied themselves to find the door, so also the devil seems to delight in spoiling correct eyesight. We need the telescope of faith to bring heavenly things within the range of our vision. What an imperfect idea we get of the number of stars with the naked eye! and though the number is marvellously multiplied to our gaze by the telescope, yet even those thousands probably bear only the same proportion to the number which are really there, that the heavenly glories revealed to the eye of faith here, bear to the full fruition beyond.

People get very magnified and distorted views, too, out of Satan's microscope. He makes grains of dust and sand look like precious gems worth toiling and struggling for; and no matter how often people are disappointed in the real effect of what seemed so bright and tempting to them, they will still go on judging of things by earth's false electric light, and buy dearly the baits which they have seen in the microscope. The instrument has also a great power of magnifying as well as multiplying difficulties in the Christian life, and makes mountains of molehills.

One of the most certain signs of being in bondage to sin is impaired vision; and this defect is the more dangerous in that we are unconscious of it. We are altogether misled by it. We think we must bow down ourselves in the house of Rimmon as Naaman asked to do [2 Kgs. 5:11] because otherwise we should lose our position and spoil our career. We think we must at least ensure for ourselves the necessaries of life, as the poor man in court who thought to excuse himself for stealing by saying, "You see, Sir, I was starving, and a man must *live*." The judge's reply was perfectly just, though it seemed hard, "I do not see the necessity."

No, there never is any necessity to sin. Oh, if only we could turn out the fear of pecuniary loss, of inconvenience, of pain, or even of death, and learn to fear sin instead! If only we could get rid of the fear of man and walk in the fear of God all the day long!

Observe, that Lot's wife had separated from the world. She had got out of Sodom. We can give up worldly amusements, novels, friends, much more easily and long before we can give up worldly mindedness. Nothing can turn it out but the entrance of God's Spirit and heavenly mindedness. We can only lose our shortsightedness, our constitutional myopy, by going to the Great Oculist; for if we say "We see" our sin remaineth, but if we pray "Lord, that I may receive my sight," He will open our eyes, for "He came that they which see not might see."

In Eve's story we dwelt on the influence of women. See how great a hindrance to goodness, true happiness, and safety a worldly wife and mother is Lot must have found his wife a terrible thorn in his side. There are many family circles in England where a believing husband has his righteous soul vexed from day to day by a frivolous or half-hearted wife. If Lot's wife had been a proper helpmeet for him and brought up their children in the right way, it is possible that their united piety and consistency might have led ten Sodomites to worship the God of Israel, and the cities of the plain would have been saved. The destruction of those four cities seems to have been the terrible consequence of that Hebrew family's having left undone what they ought to have done as regards example and soul winning. The words: "the Lord being merciful unto *him*" look as if we were distinctly led to understand that this special warning and visit of the angels were sent for Lot's sake to his whole family, because he was approved unto God; and the sin of the compromising life they had led was charged to *her*, as she was made such a terrible example. Whenever we are inclined to sacrifice principle to expediency, and duty to pleasure or earthly profit—when we have an opportunity of letting our light shine and we hide it under a bushel—when we look back upon past days, inclined to be dissatisfied with what God holds out to us forgiveness, life, and glory—then let us remember Lot's wife.

* J. C. Ryle, Bishop of Liverpool.

§81 Mrs. Donaldson
(fl. 1882)

Little is know about Mrs. Donaldson; her name, like that of Lot's wife, has been lost to history. Mrs. Donaldson led mothers' meetings for poor women in her husband's parish of St. Stephen's, Spitalfields, in East London. She was commended for her work by William Walsham How (1823–1897), who was the assistant bishop for East London at the time the book was published. He was also the author of a number of commentaries, books of practical theology and devotion, and almost sixty hymns. While How was in East London, he took a keen interest in the spiritual renewal of his diocese and established the East London Church Fund, for which he raised large sums. Bishop How's preface to Donaldson's book suggests that he was supportive of her teaching and evangelistic ministry to women. Indeed, he claimed this book was "just what one wants," for use in mothers' meetings. "Poor weary women, in such a population as East London, want very plain teaching, and very kind loving words."[33]

Donaldson's approach to Lot's wife was very similar to Ashton's. They both used Luke 17:32 as the interpretive key for reading, applying, and preaching the story of the "sad tragedy of Lot's wife." Donaldson imaginatively and romantically fleshed out the reasons for Lot's wife's demise. Unlike other women who used historical records to make the events of the story seem more plausible, Donaldson suggested that she could "fill up" the story further "to make the event appear even more real and solemn." She applied the story to the lives of her audience using an allegory. Like Lot's wife, her readers had to flee from the wrath that was about to come upon the City of Destruction (moral Sodom), to the mountain (likened to the Rock of Ages), to take shelter in God. Donaldson used the metaphor of a journey to describe the Christian life. She emphasized the power that women had, and, even more powerfully than Ashton, Donaldson employed guilt and fear tactics to motivate women

[33] Mrs. Donaldson, *Home Duties for Wives and Mothers, Illustrated by Women of Scripture* (London: William Hunt, 1882), vi.

to take their influential roles as mothers and wives seriously. Like Ashton, she emphasized the wrath and vengeance of God.

From Mrs. Donaldson, *Home Duties for Wives and Mothers, Illustrated by Women of Scripture* (London: William Hunt, 1882), 1–12.

LOT'S WIFE; Disobedience to God's Command in Looking Back
Luke xvii. 32

A VERY short injunction, yet one full of meaning and importance. The reason for keeping this woman in mind is not that we may admire and praise her, but, on the contrary, by recalling her wilful disobedience, and her deplorable fate we may learn to avoid her sin, and not to waver on our heavenward journey.

Let us consider briefly the outline of her history. We are told (Gen. xix. 16) that when the two angels came to Sodom to rescue Lot and his family, at the intercession of Abraham, before the wicked cities of the plain should be destroyed, that they laid hold of them each by the hand, and led them out of the city. Not only did they bring them forth before the work of destruction began, but bade them all to flee to the mountain for safety, adding with deep meaning and affectionate caution, "Look not behind thee, neither stay thou in all the plain; escape to the mountain, lest thou be consumed."

Onward they sped to the city of Zoar, which was to be their refuge, when the wrath of the Almighty was to descend in awful vengeance on the inhabitants of those wicked towns. One short verse tells us, in thrilling distinctness, the sad tragedy that was enacted by the way: "But his wife looked back from behind him, and she became a pillar of salt."

Still in the neighbourhood of the dismal Dead Sea stands a rocky stone of salt, which, among the inhabitants of those regions, is known by the name of "Lot's wife." And as the passer-by looks at it he can almost fancy he can trace the outline of her veiled form as she seems to stand hesitatingly and timidly glancing round, to cast one longing look back at the scenes she has left. And there, in the very act of disobedience, that wrath from which she might have fled, strikes her on the spot. There she stands a monument to all future generations.

And as we look at the picture before us, we shall do well, my dear friends, to gather a few important lessons from this woman's sad end.

She had been rescued, singled out, as it were, from among a multitude of sinners, being distinctly told what was going to be the fate of all in the city. Nevertheless, we find that she lingered by the way; her heart wandered back, it may be, to some of the things she had left behind. Perhaps she had other friends of whom she was thinking, or some possessions which she valued highly. We are not told what was the special cause of it; but that she first began to falter, to linger on the road longer,—then at last she paused as her husband and daughters hastened on, and once fallen back she lost the tones of their voices; and then her last fatal act was done. It may be that she wished or even intended to return, or, perhaps, she did not believe the word of the angels that the city was in danger. She obeyed not the command, but *did* look back from behind him, and she became a pillar of salt.

Such, then, dear friends, is the brief outline of this sad scene. We might fill it up in various ways, to endeavour to make the event appear even more real and solemn. But *this* is ample and plain enough for us at the present moment.

We feel, perhaps, surprised that the wife of such a man as Lot—righteous Lot, as he is called—should have erred in such a way [2 Pet. 2:7]. And some of us may be inclined to say, "I am sure that I should not have looked behind, nor lingered on the road." But stop, I pray you, before you make this assertion. Let us not speak too hastily of our own strength of character. "Let him that thinketh he standeth take heed lest he fall" [1 Cor. 10:12].

Now, we are all dwelling in the city of destruction,—a moral Sodom: nay, more, we are under sentence of destruction ourselves, unless we, too, flee from the wrath to come,—yes, flee to the mountain, to the Rock of Ages, and take shelter in the city of refuge, even the Lord Jehovah Himself.

Perhaps too, like Lot and his family, we have required much urging by Christian friends to depart from the danger so near at hand. The Gospel has been preached and read to us, over and over again; God's servants have spoken most earnestly and faithfully to us concerning our souls, and pointed out a loving and waiting Saviour. Or God has sent His own angels to speak to us the same message. He has laid us low on beds of sickness, and in the stillness of the chamber of death He bade us flee from the wrath due to our sins. In sickness, in losses, and in afflictions, His still small voice has spoken the same words, and at last, perhaps,—I trust it is so,—we have obeyed the call. And though we may have needed even to be led forth, yet we have at length fairly left it all behind. Past sins, former friends, old pleasures, ill-gotten possessions,—all are given up, and, better still, if in the company of those we love dearest upon earth, we have all started together on the narrow path, with our faces Zionward.

So far all is well; but wait awhile. The road is long and dull, the path is straight and narrow, our feet begin to ache with the burning sand of the desert. Or, to speak more plainly, we find that the road to heaven is less easy than we anticipated. The danger which we thought so great seems less as our fears grow calmer; our ardour and zeal slacken, and Christian duties and privileges become less joyous, nay, almost irksome.

And sure I am, dear friends, if there be one here present who has over reached this stage of the journey, that these same duties and privileges will soon be dropped; the company of God's people will be avoided, and thus the help to be obtained by the advice, the experience, and spiritual converse of fellow-Christians will be lost.

When once we come to this point of the journey, and find ourselves alone, as it were, we not only lose the help of Christian communion in making progress in the right path, but the good influence is also lost which hitherto kept us from yielding to our old sins and temptations. We have hesitated, we have lingered, we have stopped behind like Lot's wife, and we shall soon be in the condition of the man described in the Gospel, "The last state of that man is worse than the first" [Luke 11:26; Matt. 12:45]. If we are beginning to feel a vacancy within, we shall soon yearn for something to take the place of those good companions we have relinquished, and those blessed privileges which we have given up, and we shall without fail turn round to look back to the world which we had once so determinedly forsaken at the time of our first good impression.

And think how dreadful such it position must necessarily be! What a fearful state of peril it involves! "No man, having put his hand to the plough, and looking back, is fit for the kingdom of God" [Luke 9:62]. To have our faces towards the world is to have turned our backs upon heaven. To be looking and longing for the pleasures of sin, and to believe the deceitful, fair promises of the devil, is to leave behind us the joys of Zion and to disbelieve the gracious promises of a God who cannot lie. And, oh, how terrible to contemplate the state of such an one, if the dread vengeance of an offended God, of an angry Judge, should be launched forth, in the midst of such wilful sin and disobedience!

Now I would like to ask each of you here, dear mothers, Are you in this danger? Have you once set forth in the right path? It may have been in your youth, perhaps at your confirmation, or at some special season of trouble or of affliction; or perhaps it was later, when you married a godly partner, and in the first joy of the new life you were commencing, you both resolved to dedicate yourselves to God, and to live henceforth for Him. And, oh, how happy might you have been had you remained firm to your good resolves! You can call to mind how regularly you attended all the means of grace. You honoured God's day, you read His Word, you never missed attendance at His house; nay, perhaps you even knelt at His Holy Table. But, one by one, all this was given up: Bible classes and mothers' meetings were no longer attended; gradually all the outward signs of open profession were forsaken, and the companionship of those whom you once so highly respected was lost, and you were left in loneliness and well-nigh despair. They had not given you up, but you had lingered behind.

Perhaps the loved husband with whom you had started so hopefully has been removed by death; or else the sweet children of your love have outstripped you in the race, and reached the goal long before.

But, sad to relate, in many cases, I fear, the bad example of the mother influences these loved ones, and causes them to follow in her steps. How fearful to think of the awful responsibility of a wife and mother!

I firmly believe that, in nine cases out of ten, where a husband turns out badly, it may be traced in some measure to the bad influence, or at least to the lack of a good influence of the wife. If her neglect has not driven him away, in the greater number of cases, I believe that the wife might have saved him and drawn him back, if she had used her influence aright.

And if the influence of a wife be thus great, how much greater even must be that of a mother! You know it is. Think, O mothers! is *your* influence over your children such as it ought to be? Do your authority and your example tally? Do you teach them what is right,—to serve God and keep His commandments, to attend His house, to study His Word? And do you do the same yourselves; or do they see you gradually neglecting these things, and therefore think there is no need for *them* to observe them? Ponder these things well, my dear friends: examine your own lives, and see whether you are in the right road yourselves, or whether you are beginning to linger behind; nay, even "looking back from behind." If so, turn again, turn again with us, I entreat you, and "we will do thee good" [Num. 10:29].

But, before I close, I would most earnestly urge those of you who have never yet set out at all on the road to Zion to do so without delay. To remain behind is certain death: destruction is at hand, even at the door. Jesus has died; nay, is risen again, and bids all come to Him that they may find pardon for all their sins in His precious blood. He asks nothing of you: no goodness of your own; but simply to cast yourself on His mercy, and He will pardon and bless you. And while you look to Him in all dangers and difficulties, He will keep you safe in this world, and bring you at last to His eternal home in the world to come.

To all, then, I would say, "Escape for your life: look not behind thee, neither stay thou in all the plain; escape to the mountain, lest thou be consumed;" for "remember Lot's wife" [Luke 17:32].

–Dinah–

The story of Dinah, the only daughter of Leah and Jacob (Gen 30:21), is recorded in Genesis 34. Dinah "went out to visit the women of the land" near

Shechem, where her father had bought land, and was raped by Shechem, son of
the ruler of the area. Shechem loved her and asked his father to make arrangements for them to get married. Jacob heard that Dinah had been defiled and
said nothing until her brothers came home from the fields. Shechem's father
approached Jacob and proposed that Jacob give Dinah to his son in marriage
and that his family settle down with the people of Shechem. Jacob's sons
consented to the marriage on the condition that the males of the city were
circumcised. Three days later, two of Jacob's sons killed the unsuspecting men
of the city and the brothers looted the city and carried off all their wealth,
women, and children. Though Jacob chastened his sons, they justified their
actions with a rhetorical question, "should he have treated our sister like a
prostitute?"

The story of Dinah's rape was not discussed by many nineteenth-century
women. We have chose four. The first two selections, written by Trimmer and
Cornwallis early in the century, come from commentaries on the whole Bible;
thus the authors could not easily avoid commenting on the story. The final
selection by M.G., from late in the century used the story as an entry point to
a discussion of courtship and sexuality with young women.

§82 Sarah Trimmer
(1741–1810)

Trimmer's[34] remarks on Genesis 34 do not use Dinah's name. Trimmer's brief
comments are characteristic of her unwillingness to engage issues in the text
which may have been considered improper. Trimmer expected that her readers use her book along with the Bible and so did not need to be reminded of
the content of the biblical story. She simply commented on the nature of the
story and the lessons, which she thought should be drawn from it.

> From Sarah Trimmer, *A Help to the Unlearned in the Study of the Holy
> Scriptures* (London, F. C. & J. Rivington, 1805), 35.

The shocking things related in this chapter [Gen. 34] show that it is dangerous for young women to go about by themselves, and make acquaintance
with strangers; and that those people who give way to revenge often commit

---

[34] For a biography of Sarah Trimmer, see part 2, "Sarah—First Mother of Israel."

cruel and unjust actions. Jacob by no means approved of what Simeon and Levi had done; his wish was rather to gain a good reputation among the people of the land by fair and upright dealing.

§83 Mary Cornwallis
(1758–1836)

Cornwallis's[35] treatment of Dinah was part of her commentary on Genesis 34. She introduced the story with a remark about the violence of the culture in which the story took place. Cornwallis explained Dinah's actions as typical of a young girl of about fifteen, "an age at which the mind is open, frank, and unsuspicious, and, neither knowing nor meditating evil, apprehends none." She put considerable weight on Josephus' idea of Dinah's going to a great festival. Cornwallis assumed it must have been an idolatrous festival, and that Dinah went without her parents' knowledge. The descriptive words Cornwallis used of the rape of Dinah (violence, misfortune, injury, and disgrace) betrayed her own feelings regarding the act. She also read the story through the lens of her experience as a mother of two daughters and noted the "disrespectful and undutiful" response of Jacob's sons to his admonition. The lessons Cornwallis drew from Dinah's rape were similar to Trimmer's.

> From Mary Cornwallis, *Observations, Critical, Explanatory, and Practical on the Canonical Scriptures* (London: Baldwin, Cradock, & Joy, 1817). [Text is from 2nd ed. (1820), 80–81.]

The violence offered to Dinah shows that both Abraham and Isaac had cause for their distrust when they were driven by famine into idolatrous countries. Her conduct was undoubtedly indiscreet; but she is thought to have been only about fifteen, an age at which the mind is open, frank, and unsuspicious, and, neither knowing nor meditating evil, apprehends none. Josephus says that she went to see a great festival.[36] If so, it must have been an idolatrous one, and her going thither was probably unknown to her parents. Her misfortune is not without instruction, and teaches young women the necessity of circumspection in the choice of companions, as well as the danger of giving way to indiscreet curiosity. It was very natural that her brothers should keenly

---

[35] For a biography of Mary Cornwallis, see part 5, "Leah and Rachel—Founders of the House of Israel."

[36] Josephus, *Antiquities of the Jews*, 1:21.

feel the injury; and the disgrace brought upon the family; but intemperate rage generally leads to unlawful revenge; and nothing could excuse the making a holy rite instrumental to it, or the cutting off a whole city for the offence of one individual. The whole transaction appears to have been unknown to Jacob, and to have caused him extreme displeasure when it reached his ears. Indeed, had not God preserved them, there was every reason to expect that they would in turn be exterminated by the surrounding heathen nations. The reply of Jacob's sons to the admonitions of their parent shows that right and wrong may be easily confounded. The sentiment of indignation expressed in it was in itself laudable, but, viewed as a reply to their parent's admonition, it was disrespectful and undutiful; as the subsequent history shows that the whole transaction was registered on high, and entailed upon those concerned in it a lasting curse.

§84 Sarah Hale
(1788–1879)

Sarah Hale's[37] brief account of Dinah's life focused on the lessons to be learned from her life. Hale's interpretive approach was that "every character in the Bible has its mission as an example or a warning." Unlike Cornwallis, Hale showed no sympathy for Dinah. Nor did she portray her as a victim of violence. She thought Dinah's mission was to be "the beacon to warn the young of her sex against levity of manners and eagerness for society." She imputed to Dinah the qualities of "idle curiosity and weak vanity" and warned all women against "seeking excitement and amusement," as these could lead to a potentially fatal end for themselves and their families.

From Sarah Hale, *Woman's Record; or, Sketches of all Distinguished Women, from the Creation to A.D. 1854* (New York: Harper & Brothers, 1855).

–Dinah–

The only daughter of the patriarch Jacob. Her seduction by prince Shechem; his honourable proposal of repairing the injury by marriage, and the prevention of the fulfilment of this just intention by the treachery and barbarity of

---

[37] For a biography of Sarah Hale, see part 5, "Leah and Rachel—Founders of the House of Israel."

her bloody brethren Simeon and Levi, are recorded in Gen. xxxiv. But every character in the Bible has its mission as an example or a warning, and Dinah's should be the beacon to warn the young of her sex against levity of manners and eagerness for society. "She went out to see the daughters of the land"; the result of her visit was her own ruin, and involving two of her brothers in such deeds of revenge as brought a curse upon them and their posterity. And thus the idle curiosity or weak vanity of those women who are always seeking excitement and amusement, may end most fatally for themselves and those nearest connected and best beloved. Dinah lived B.C. 1732.

§85 M. G.
(fl. 1893)

M. G. is a forgotten woman, a British Anglo-Catholic author, who published studies on women in the Bible. M. G. prepared these studies primarily for mothers' meetings, although this particular lesson was for a class of teenage girls. Unlike most of her female peers, who passed over the story of Dinah quickly, M. G. saw in it an opportunity to raise issues about sexuality with her young female audience.

Like Cornwallis, M. G. felt the tragedy in the narrative. She likened Dinah to an abused butterfly, a soiled lily, a broken rose. Like Cornwallis, she used Josephus as a source for further information on the story and embellished the story considerably. Like Hale, she laid the blame for Dinah's ravishment on her own folly. M. G. drew several lessons from this story about relationships with young men, courtship, and pre-marital sex. She advised her "dear girls," to "watch and pray" that they might keep their chastity until God "comes to transplant" them to "bloom in Paradise."

From M. G., *Women Like Ourselves* (London: SPCK, 1893), 42–48.

–Dinah–
(Originally intended for a class of girls)

Our story to-day is a terribly sad one, so sad that I could have wished to have left it out of our series. But the fact that God the Holy Spirit has written it for us in the first book of the Bible, shows us that there are lessons which He would have us learn from it, lessons for us girls more than for any one else.

Let us pray to Him to cleanse the thoughts of our hearts,[38] that while I speak to you very plainly, we may consider this sad subject with pure and guarded minds. (*Pause for silent prayer.*)

Have you sometimes noticed a gay butterfly, that a few minutes ago was dancing in the sunshine, now dashed to the ground by some rude boy, and crawling painfully along with the bright colour gone from its wings? Have you seen a fair white lily broken on its stalk, and lying soiled in the mud? or a sweet climbing rose, which has started away from the supports that held it to the wall, and now trails its sweetness in the dust? Such a wounded butterfly, such a soiled lily, such a broken rose became Dinah, whose story is written for our warning in Genesis xxxiv. Alas! alas! there are Dinahs in every town and village now; many a fair young girl, made to be the sweetest flower in the shelter of a happy home, but through her own folly spoiled, trampled, and defiled.

And yet they meant no harm. They never thought it would come to this, they only wanted to amuse themselves, as Dinah wanted to do; and then when they were least on their guard, Satan sprang upon them, as a roaring lion sometimes rushes out of the jungle when people venture too far, and wrought their ruin.

Dinah's life at home had been somewhat lonely, for she was the only daughter, and though her eleven brothers loved her dearly and made much of her, they could not quite make up for the want of a sister, and they were often absent for long together in the fields with their flocks. Dinah was young and pretty, and she wanted to share in the games and amusements which were going on among the young people who lived near; she wanted to see and be seen, feeling that both in beauty and in wealth she was at least the equal of any of the girls round about. What was the use of being rich, she thought, if she might never appear in those splendid ornaments and handsome clothes to be admired?

The home in which Dinah had been brought up was somewhat strict. Jacob and Leah put all their trust in God, and both walked in His laws themselves and tried to train their children to do the same. Wherever they went they built an altar for the worship of the true God, and avoided the heathen customs of the nations among whom they dwelt. Therefore they would not encourage their young people to mix more than was necessary with their neighbours, and though the sons were often obliged to do so in their out-door occupations, they did not give their pretty daughter many opportuni-

---

[38] "Cleanse the thoughts of our hearts," is a phrase taken from the Collect for Purity used in the sacrament of Holy Communion in *The Book of Common Prayer*.

ties of making acquaintances, knowing, as older people know too well, what dangers would arise from companionship with friends, however pleasant and charming, whose customs and opinions and religious views were so different from their own. We some of us know what it is to be kept in check in this way, don't we? And we too perhaps have chafed against it, and wondered how it is that parents and mistresses are so strict, as if they did not want us to have any pleasure. I fancy that we can none of us appreciate their reasons at the time. We only see the bright side of society and gaiety while we are young, and cannot understand the dangers that lurk underneath till we learn them by experience. Our best safe¬guard lies in trusting those whom God has placed over us to judge best, remembering that if they are in no other ways wiser than ourselves, they have at least the benefit of longer experience and knowl-edge of the world. The name "Dinah" means "judgment," and it was through thinking herself able to judge for herself that she fell.

So "Dinah went out to see the daughters of the land," without asking her parents' advice or permission, without taking a brother or a servant to protect her, thinking, as so many a maiden has thought since, with a toss of her pretty head, " I am quite able to take care of myself."

As she had perhaps half hoped, she met, not only the daughters, but also the sons of the land, and the richest and highest of them all took notice of the new-comer. For the time Dinah's triumph would be complete, to be thus singled out for attention and evident admiration by the young prince, whom we may be sure all the daughters of the land had longed to win. Readily she listened to his honied words of love, without once thinking of telling her father, like Rachel, or asking her mother's advice, as Rebekah had done. She rather kept Shechem's attentions secret from them, fearing lest Jacob and Leah might object to the intimacy, and thinking to herself that they were a par-ticular, prejudiced, bigoted old couple, whilst her noble lover, who was above her in station, was all that was honourable and charming. And so instead of bidding Shechem come and woo her openly in her father's house, she stole out secretly to him. It was so tempting to the lonely girl to have somebody to pet her and flatter her, and " speak kindly to her" (ver. 3). Dinah had never had any one to speak heart to heart with her before, and Shechem's devotion to her was so real, and his promises of eternal unchanging affection so sincere, that she doubtless clave to him as much as he clave to Dinah. I do not sup-pose Dinah forgot herself so far as to fall at her first meeting with Shechem. Probably she went out to see him again and again, " meaning no harm," and forgetting that a courtship carried on without her parents' knowledge, and without God's blessing being sought, was sure to lead to no good.

So there came a day when Dinah yielded to temptation. Had any one warned her beforehand what might happen, she would have answered indignantly, that it was impossible (like Hazael in 2 Kings viii. 13, who asked, " Is thy servant a dog, that he should do this great thing?"). Therefore it is, dear girls, that I want you to lay to heart this sad story, lest any of you should some day be surprised into sin when you are off your guard. You shrink from the thought of it now, as you would shrink from any loathsome beast that crossed your path in the woods; but some day that loathsome thing may suddenly take the form of a handsome lover, even as the ugly bear in the fairy tale of "Beauty and the Beast" was changed all at once into a prince, and the temptation to yield to his entreaties may come upon you with terrible force, and then nothing but God's grace will enable you to resist it.

If then you have already had the good fortune to gain some good man's love, do not trust too implicitly in his honour (Shechem, we are told, ver. 19, was considered a very honourable man), nor yet in your own virtue, but pray daily, "Lead us not into temptation, but deliver us from the evil one" [Matt. 6:13]; for Satan is very cunning, and he will be sure to be very near you.

And from the first, when any man speaks words of love to you, which sound sweet in your ears, ask yourselves these two simple questions before you allow the courtship to go on—Am I willing to tell my father and mother all about it, as Rachel did; should I mind their knowing all that he has said to me? And next—Is it a connection upon which I can ask God's blessing; can I hope that God will approve it and further it, as He did in the case of Rebekah? If we feel ashamed and afraid to ask for our parents' consent and for God's approval, we may be sure that there is something wrong, and that the acquaintance will bring us no good. In that case, even though the love may have twined itself round our heart until to put it from us would be as hard as to cut off a hand, or to pluck out an eye, we must be brave and do it; for surely it will be better to enter into life with a broken heart bound up by a loving Saviour, than to enjoy the pleasures of sin here for a little while and then to be cast into hell fire (S. Matt. xviii. 8, 9).

Shechem was ready and desirous to marry Dinah as soon as might be afterwards, and I am afraid that many people among us think that no harm is done if marriage follows. Jacob and his sons thought very differently. If in some ways they were allowed greater freedom in the marriages that they might make, yet impurity was never permitted, not even between engaged lovers. It was "folly," which really means wickedness, not only an injury to the damsel, but an insult to the whole body of God's people, which no subsequent marriage could wipe out, and therefore a thing which, as Dinah's brothers emphatically declared, "ought not to be done." And if it ought not to have been done in those early ages, when so little of God's purposes for us were known, what excuse can be made for Christian men and maidens, whose bodies have been made in Baptism members of Christ? Those of us who

have been confirmed have moreover been made thereby temples of the Holy
Ghost, and in the Holy Communion we have been made one with Christ
by eating His Flesh. Read carefully what S. Paul says in 1 Cor. vi.15 to end,
and then again Ephesians v.3-13. Would it not be terrible to be cut off from
membership with Christ, to he forbidden to inherit the kingdom of God? I
think that many girls cannot understand that that word "fornication," which
is spoken of with such awful warnings again and again in Scripture, is nothing
else than this sin of Dinah's. Girls nowadays call it "getting into trouble," and
the results of it "having a misfortune"; but God calls it by this strong word,
and gives many terrible warnings that He will not judge it at the last Day so
lightly. Reuben and Simeon had no right to take vengeance for it themselves;
"Vengeance is Mine, saith the Lord" [Rom. 12:19]; but nothing but a most
deep and true repentance can atone for thus defiling the bodies which have
been consecrated to Christ, and should be kept pure for Him.

Oh, dear girls, watch and pray that you may keep that chastity, which is
your most precious jewel, pure and spotless in His sight, that when He, the
Bridegroom of Souls, shall come, you may go out to meet Him, either among
the chaste virgins or the holy matrons, with your lamps trimmed and burning [Matt. 25:1-3]. "As a lily among thorns, so is My love," says He, "among
the daughters" (Canticles ii. 2). You are His Lilies, if you will remain true to
Him. He has placed you, as He placed Dinah, among thorns, in the midst
of temptation among the careless and godless companions you meet in the
world. Dinah ran in among the thorns, and was bruised and defiled; but if
you follow His guidance He will keep you spotless as a lily, until He Himself
comes to transplant you to bloom in Paradise, where the pure in heart shall
see God [Matt. 5:8].

–Tamar–

The story of Tamar is found in Genesis 38. After the death of Tamar's husband,
Er, her father-in-law, Judah, directed Onan, Er's brother, to lie with Tamar in
order to produce children to continue his dead brother's line. Judah's request
was in line with the ancient practice of levirate marriage, which mandated
that a deceased man's brother, or nearest male relative, marry his brother's
widow and raise up descendants in his brother's name (Deut. 25:5-10). Onan
"spilled his seed" so that he would not produce heirs for his brother and he
died. Judah sent Tamar back to live in her father's house as a widow until his
youngest son was grown, but he feared for his youngest son's life and never
intended to have Tamar return to his house. Years passed and Tamar heard
that her father-in-law was in the neighbourhood. She took off her widow's
clothes and disguised herself as a prostitute. Judah slept with Tamar and left

her his seal, cord, and staff as a pledge for payment. She became pregnant and Judah commanded that she be burned to death. When Tamar revealed that Judah was the father of the unborn child, he declared her more righteous than he, because he refused to give her his third son. Twins were born of this union, Perez and Zerah. Tamar is remembered in Ruth 4:12, in the genealogy of 1 Chronicles 2:4, and in Matthew 1:3, where she is named in the genealogy of Jesus.

The story of Tamar raises many interesting interpretive questions, which troubled nineteenth-century interpreters. Their sensibilities about issues related to sexuality made them reluctant to write about this story in any detail. In his dictionary entry on Tamar, Sir William Smith (1813–1893) described Tamar more fully than most women who wrote about her, suggesting "she resorted to the desperate expedient of entrapping the father himself into the union which he feared for his son."[39] But comments on this chapter in a commentary by Robert Jamieson, *et al.,* show that male commentators also were uncomfortable with this story:

> This chapter contains details, which probably would never have obtained a place in the inspired record, had it not been to exhibit the full links of the chain that connects the genealogy of the Saviour with Abraham; and in the disreputable character of the ancestry who figure in this passage, we have a remarkable proof that "He made himself of no reputation." [Phil. 2:7][40]

Unlike modern interpreters, both male and female nineteenth-century interpreters seemed reluctant to discuss Tamar's bold tactics of deception or appreciate her initiative, courage, and importance in the sacred line.[41]

---

[39] "Tamar," in *A Dictionary of the Bible, Comprising its Antiquities, Biography, Geography and Natural History,* vol. 4, ed. Sir William Smith (London: 1860–1863), 3171. Also published as *A Concise Dictionary of the Bible for the Use of Families and Students,* ed. William Smith (London: J. Murray, 1865).

[40] Robert Jamieson, A. R. Fausset, and David Brown, *A Commentary, Critical and Explanatory, on the Old and New Testaments,* vol. 1 (New York: S. S. Scranton, 1873), 39.

[41] See Phyllis Bird's helpful discussion of Tamar's role as prostitute in "The Harlot as Heroine: Narrative Art and Social Presupposition in Three Old Testament Texts," in *Women in the Hebrew Bible: A Reader,* ed. Alice Bach (New York: Routledge, 1999), 99–117. See also Susan Niditch, "The Wronged Woman Righted: An Analysis of Genesis 38," *Harvard Theological Review* 72 (1979): 143–49.

§86 Sarah Trimmer
(1741–1810)

Sarah Trimmer[42] wrote even less on the story of Tamar in Genesis 38 than on the story of Dinah in Genesis 34. In her comments on this chapter, she wrote as little as possible, dismissing the details surrounding Tamar's story as abhorrent to Christians and contrary to the gospel.

> From Sarah Trimmer, *A Help to the Unlearned in the Study of the Holy Scriptures* (London: F. C. & J. Rivington, 1805), 38.

This chapter relates to some very irregular conduct in Jacob's sons, which every true Christian must abhor, as contrary to the pure laws of the gospel.

§87 Mary Cornwallis
(1758–1836)

Cornwallis,[43] the English commentary writer, dealt with the story of Tamar in her interpretation of Genesis 38. She left out many details in her retelling, while underlining the sin of Judah and his sons. Her comments suggest that she had reserved sympathy towards Tamar. She attributed to Tamar an honourable motive for her ruse of wanting to bear "a child to one of that family, out of which the Messiah was to spring."

> From Mary Cornwallis, *Observations, Critical, Explanatory, and Practical on the Canonical Scriptures*, vol. 1 (London: Baldwin, Cradock, & Joy, 1817). [Text from 2nd ed. (1820), 86–87.]

THE present chapter forms an interruption to the history of Joseph, and may therefore be passed over, but, if read, the observations made in the introduc-

---

[42] For further biographical information on Sarah Trimmer, see part 2, "Sarah—First Mother of Israel."

[43] For a biography of Mary Cornwallis, see part 5, "Leah and Rachel—Founders of the House of Israel."

tion should be recollected.[44] As Er and Onan died by the hand of God, their offence was probably contempt of the Divine laws, and disregard of the blessing that was promised to the seed of Abraham. The sin of Judah was rendered instrumental to one important end, which accounts for the introduction of this chapter: it proved beyond a doubt that he was the father of Pharez, from whom Christ is traced in his genealogy, Matt. i .3. Tamar was probably actuated to the measures she took, by the desire of bearing a child to one of that family, out of which the Messiah was to spring. The forms of marriage in the patriarchal times are not known; but, by the demands she made of Judah's ring, his bracelets, and his staff, we may conjecture that she considered them as matrimonial pledges; and they seem to have been so esteemed when the transaction became public, as her name is mentioned in St. Matthew's genealogy with that of Judah.

§88 Sarah Hale
(1788–1879)

Sarah Hale's[45] brief biographical entry on Tamar suggests that she, like Cornwallis, is uncomfortable writing about this story. She emphasized the differences between cultures: "this history displays the gross manners of those old times, and how false are all representations of the purity of pastoral life." She showed little sympathy for Tamar.

From Sarah Hale, *Woman's Record; or, Sketches of all Distinguished Women, from the Creation to A.D. 1854* (New York: Harper & Brothers, 1855).

–Tamar–

Was daughter-in-law to the patriarch Judah, wife of Er and Onan. After Onan's death, Tamar lived with her father-in-law, expecting to marry his son Shelah, as had been promised her, and was the custom of the time. But the

---

[44] Cornwallis writes, "If there are expressions which may offend persons of fastidious nicety, they ought to recollect that, at the time the translation was published, they were used in the most polite circles, and were consequently deemed decorous. Custom determines opinion on this score; but there is a purity, a chastity, and a sobriety of thought, dependent on no custom; and this the Bible, under the present translation, possesses" (*Observations*, xv).

[45] For a biography of Sarah Hale, see part 5, "Leah and Rachel—Founders of the House of Israel."

marriage not having taken place, some years after, when Judah went to a sheep-shearing feast, Tamar disguised herself as a harlot and sat in a place where Judah would pass—and this old man yielded at once to the temptation. When it was told Judah that his daughter-in-law had been guilty, he immediately condemned her to be brought forth and burned alive; never remembering his own sin. But when he found that he was the father of the child she would soon bear, his conscience was awakened, and he made that remarkable admission that "she was more just than he had been."

This history displays the gross manners of those old times, and how false are all representations of the purity of pastoral life. Tamar had twins, sons—and from one of these, Pharez, the line of Judah is descended. These events occurred B.C. 1727.

–Potiphar's Wife–

Potiphar, an official of the Egyptian pharaoh, purchased Joseph (Rachel and Jacob's son) from the Ishmaelites,[46] who had bought Joseph from his brothers (Genesis 37:28, 36). With God's help, Joseph prospered in Potiphar's house and Potiphar placed Joseph in charge of his household. Potiphar's wife tried to seduce the well-built and handsome Joseph; but Joseph refused her advances. Potiphar's wife did not give up; one day when they were alone in the house, she caught him by his cloak and said, "Come to bed with me!" Joseph ran out of the house and Potiphar's wife falsely charged him with rape. Joseph was imprisoned (Gen. 39).

§89 Mary Cornwallis
(1758–1836)

Cornwallis was one of few nineteenth-century women to write about Potiphar's wife. She saw value in the story as a teaching tool. She may have had her daughters or, more likely, her young grandson in mind as readers of her work, as she vilified the conduct of Potiphar's wife, a woman Cornwallis described in terms recollecting the portrait of the adulterous woman in Proverbs 5–7. At the same time, Cornwallis praised the nobility of Joseph's actions.

---

[46] In Gen. 37:36, Joseph is sold to the Midianites.

From Mary Cornwallis, *Observations, Critical, Explanatory, and Practical on the Canonical Scriptures*, vol. 1 (London: Baldwin, Cradock, & Joy, 1817). [Text from 2nd ed (1820), 87–88.]

We gladly trace the steps of Joseph into a respectable family, and find him placed in an office of trust; for we are apt to consider all adversity evil, and every increase of prosperity an accession of happiness: in these opinions however, we often err; and, in the history of this youth, we find that the very circumstance which appeared so desirable was but a prelude to a still greater trial than he had already experienced, because, though innocent, he incurred all the disgrace of guilt, heightened by the basest ingratitude. Joseph had not the Gospel before him, but God was with him, and assuredly the same Spirit spake peace and encouragement to him in his dreary and shameful confinement, which dictated, "If ye suffer for righteousness' sake, happy are ye: and be not afraid of their terror, neither be troubled." "For it is better, if the will of God be so, that ye suffer for well doing than for evil doing."* His chaste and noble conduct affords a fine example to all young men, showing them that those who serve and fear God are not left to the mercy of their passions. Had Joseph yielded to the blandishments of this artful woman, his error might, according to the laxity of worldly opinion, have been deemed venial: but God passes a very different judgment; and Joseph, young as he was, could discern that sensuality debases the character; that lewdness is a sin of the deepest dye, and ingratitude to a kind benefactor, the greatest baseness. A woman, without modesty or goodness, was probably to him an object of disgust, and would be so to all men, did they not corrupt their own hearts. In the conduct of Potiphar's wife, a very just picture is drawn of vicious women throughout all ages; for, having broken through the restraints of religion and virtue, they commonly plunge deep in sin; their love is sensual, their hate vindictive; they are selfish, cruel, treacherous; and, so far from seeking the advantage of the unhappy wretch whom they have ensnared, they appear to delight in bringing him to shame, to poverty, or even to destruction. Besides, who shall foresee all the entanglements of sin. Had Joseph engaged in an illicit connexion with his mistress, what would have been his feelings every time he beheld his generous protector? to what mean arts must he have had recourse to conceal the guilty intercourse? what perplexities, what anxieties, what shame, would have filled his bosom? chains and imprisonment, with a clear conscience, may be deemed bliss compared with such a state. Oh! The happiness of innocence, the delight of being able to look up to heaven, in the hour of affliction, and to say, I have not brought it upon myself! The noble reply of Joseph "How then can I do this great wickedness, and sin against God," should be indelibly engraven on the memory; for every temptation would vanish, were we at its approach to set the Deity before us, with the sword of justice in his hand; or, for a moment weigh the pleasures of sin, if pleasures they may be called, against the miseries of eternal punishment. The kindness Joseph experienced at the hands of his keeper, and the trust reposed in him, while it bettered his condition, must have been to him an evidence that he was not forsaken of Heaven; but it is in the school of adversity that God's most favoured children are trained for the skies. "Whom the Lord loveth he chasteneth, and scourgeth every son whom he receiveth."†

* 1 Pet. iii.14, 17.

† Heb. xii. 6.

§90 Elizabeth Cady Stanton and Lillie Devereux Blake
(1815–1902) and (1833–1913)

Elizabeth Cady Stanton[47] was a prominent advocate for women's legal, social, and spiritual equality. Lillie D. Blake[48] was a suffragist, writer, women's rights activist, and president of New York City Woman's Suffrage League. She was a contributor to Stanton's *Woman's Bible* project.

Elizabeth Cady Stanton and Lillie Blake both commented briefly on Potiphar's wife. Stanton's comments are of interest in that she agrees with Cornwallis's negative assessment of the character of Potiphar's wife.[49] After criticizing Potiphar's wife's character, Stanton expressed a wish for a female counterpart to the "noble, high-minded, virtuous" Joseph.

Blake's interesting comments offer a more empathetic interpretation of Potiphar's wife, who, she claimed, was a wife in name only. Blake's claim was based on a literal translation of Potiphar's title; most translators call

[47] For more biographical information about Stanton, see part 5, "Leah and Rachel—Founders of the House of Israel."

[48] For a fuller biography of Blake, see part 1, "Eve—Mother of Us All."

[49] More positive interpretations of Potiphar's wife existed in nineteenth-century commentaries. Jamieson, Fausset, and Brown's *A Commentary Critical and Explanatory on the Old and New Testaments*, citing John G. Wilkinson, *Topography of Thebes and General View of Egypt* (London: J. Murry, 1835), portrayed Potiphar's wife as "not worse than many of the same rank, and her infamous advances made to Joseph arose from her superiority of station" (40). Egyptian literature often portrayed women much more negatively than the biblical portrayal of Potiphar's wife. See for example the *Egyptian Tale of Two Brothers*. One critical edition of this story can be found in Susan T. Hollis, *The Ancient Egyptian "Tale of Two Brothers": The Oldest Fairy Tale in the World* (Norman: University of Oklahoma Press, 1990).

him 'Pharaoh's officer' but this phrase could be translated, in some contexts, 'Pharaoh's eunuch.' Blake based her comments on the literal translation of the Bible by Julia Evelina Smith (1792–1886) who translated the entire Bible from the original languages numerous times during her life.[50]

> From Elizabeth Cady Stanton, ed. *The Woman's Bible* (New York: European Publishing Co., 1895), 65–66.

POTIPHAR'S wife surpasses all the women yet mentioned in perfidy and dishonor.

Joseph' s virtues, his dignity, his honor, go far to redeem the reputation of his ancestors, and the customs of his times. It would have been generous, at least, if the editor of these pages could have given us one woman the counterpart of Joseph, a noble, high-minded, virtuous type. Thus far those of all the different nationalities have been of an ordinary low type. Historians usually dwell on the virtues of the people, the heroism of their deeds, the wisdom of their words, but the sacred fabulist dwells on the most questionable behavior of the Jewish race, and much in character and language that we can neither print nor answer. . . .

E.C.S.

The literal translation of the first verse of chapter xxxix of Genesis is as follows:

"And Joseph was brought down to Egypt, and Potiphar, Pharaoh's eunuch, chief of the cooks, an Egyptian bought him of the Ishmaelites who brought him down."

These facts which are given in Julia Smith's translation of the Bible throw a new light on the story of Joseph and the woman who was Potiphar's wife only in name.

L.D.B.

Conclusion

Mary Cornwallis noted that stories like Lot's wife and daughters presented a hermeneutical challenge to readers, as the biblical text does not always comment on the events recorded. She wrote, "it is for us to judge them by the

---

[50] For more information on Smith, see Blake's work in part 1, "Eve—The Mother of Us All."

revealed law, and with that before our eyes, we can be at no loss to determine right or wrong."[51] The authors who wrote on Lot's wife and daughters, as well as Dinah, Tamar, and Potiphar's wife did judge these women as women who had "broken through the restraints of religion and virtue."[52] Their judgments were based on the revealed law and precepts of both the Old and New Testaments, traditional interpretations of the stories, as well as the values of their own societies.

Nineteenth-century women described these stories in Genesis as shocking, unworthy, abhorrent, deplorable, disgusting, degrading, and terrible. They regarded the characters in the stories as indiscrete, disrespectful, undutiful, treacherous, barbarous, perfidious, dishonourable, vicious, and having gross manners. Such descriptors demonstrate that many of the authors were uncomfortable with the content of these stories.

Given their level of discomfort with the sexual content in the stories, it is not unexpected that few nineteenth-century women wrote on the stories discussed in this chapter. The women who chose to write on them in detail used them as the basis for sermons and moral lessons. The biblical characters were examples or warnings for their audience; Hale described this as the biblical characters' "mission." These distasteful Bible stories were used as a resource for moral advice on subjects like courtship and marriage, motherhood, friendship, and sexuality.

The women writers used the entire biblical canon as well as deuterocanonical literature, academic resources, assumptions about woman's nature, role and place, and their imaginations as interpretive resources. The works on Lot's wife referred to the gospel mention of her as well as the mention of her in the Wisdom of Solomon. Details on the story of Dinah from Josephus provided new data for explanations and embellishments of the story. The undeveloped characters and ambiguous nature of these narratives allowed room for imaginative retellings of the stories. The authors' desire to make a particular point with their audience may have motivated this gap filling. Woosnam, in particular, had a very high view of women's power and assumed Lot's wife's influence over her husband throughout his life, though she is not specifically mentioned in other stories of Lot'. Woosnam's desire to recover more of the story of Lot's wife is shared by later feminist interpreters who use a plethora of resources drawn from a wide range of disciplines (including sociology, anthropology, archaeology, comparative literature, and biblical studies) to unearth and reconstruct the lost voices of women in the Bible.

---

[51] Cornwallis, *Observations*, 56; see above pp. 403–5.
[52] Cornwallis, *Observations*, 88; see above pp. 437–38.

These nineteenth-century women interpreters understood the biblical text to have both historical and spiritual meanings. The historical sense of the text was important to these women. Especially in the retellings of the story of Lot's wife, the interpreters showed apologetic concern to ground the story in history. Further, in the case of Potiphar's wife, a new, literal translation of the Bible opened up new possibilities for understanding the story. The authors were concerned to understand the spiritual and moral sense of the text, but in these stories, the moral sense was firmly grounded in the literal sense—their audiences could learn from the historical example of these women. The writers used analogies to draw parallels between the world of the text and their contemporary world and so make applications to their readers. Some also used the traditional methods of typology and allegory to connect the world of the text to the world of the reader.

The interpretations of these negatively described and understood stories have several themes in common: the judgment of God, the nature of salvation, and the nature of the Christian life. God was often portrayed as a judge. For example, authors described God as the Sovereign Avenger, the Angry Judge, and the God who cannot lie. Readers were reminded of God's awful anger, and this led some writers to then preach the message of salvation using what many today would judge to be "heavy-handed" and "guilt-inducing" sermons. If readers were already Christians, they were admonished to beware of the influence of sin in their lives.

Many nineteenth-century women used the rhetoric and tone of sermons in their works. They preached with their pens to other women and children. At least two of these women, M. G. and Mrs. Donaldson, delivered sermons to mothers' meetings or girls' classes, then transcribed and published them as a guide for other classes. These are prime examples of sermons by women who found a way to preach despite being officially barred from the pulpit.

Nineteenth-century women writing on the marginal female figures in Genesis revealed more about themselves and their world than they did about the women in Genesis. Their acts of interpretation were cultural events, and so they provide an important window into women's lives in the nineteenth century. Their writings unveil their attitudes to the authority of the Bible, to theology, and to the task of interpretation or hermeneutics. Their interpretive acts demonstrate women interpreting, applying, preaching, and teaching Scripture; they show women as purveyors, and, on occasion, as critics of culture.

Perhaps most importantly, these women's writings disclose their own attitudes towards human sexuality and, in particular, the female person. Most women were unwilling to explore issues related to female sexuality and face the issues of the victimization and abuse of women by fathers (Lot) and by men of power (Shechem). At the same time, these women failed to name or recognize women's power in sexual relationships (Potiphar's wife and Tamar). Some nineteenth-century women who avoided these difficult stories may have been trying to live up to an ideal of "the protected and refined ladies who are not only to be good, but who are, if possible to know nothing except what is good."[53] Nineteenth-century women writers did not speak with one voice on the Woman Question. The authors writing on the marginal women in Genesis did not use these stories as resources to call for substantial changes in education, politics, religion, and law; however, women used other biblical texts as resources to call for these changes.

---

[53] Josephine Butler, as cited in Flammang, "'And Your Sons and Daughters Will Prophesy', The Voice and Vision of Josephine Butler," 154.

CONCLUSION

In *The Women of Israel*, Grace Aguilar called Jewish women to rediscover their foremothers, the matriarchs of their faith. We have now heard Aguilar's voice along with the voices of forty-nine other women who wrote in the nineteenth century. These women have spoken. We need to listen to them and acknowledge them as our foremothers in biblical interpretation. Their diverse voices need to be heard and included in scholarly discussions of the history of biblical interpretation[1] and the history of feminist biblical scholarship in particular,[2] as well as in other scholarly discussions, such as the intellectual and social histories of the nineteenth century, the history of religious education,[3] and women's studies. Some of these voices (Crocker, Grimké, Weld, and Stanton) have already been acknowledged as important in any reexaminations of traditional interpretations of biblical texts related

[1] D. K. McKim, in *Historical Handbook of Major Biblical Interpreters* (Downers Grove: InterVarsity, 1998), focuses on major figures and only includes the work of two modern feminists interpreters in his book. Timothy Larsen speaks of the importance of listening to other voices in his work, *Contested Christianity: The Political and Social Contexts of Victorian Theology* (Waco, Tex: Baylor University Press, 2004).

[2] Dorothy C. Bass, "Women's Studies and Biblical Studies: An Historical Perspective," *Journal for the Study of the Old Testament* 22 (1982): 6–12; and Dorothy C. Bass, "Women with a Past: A New Look at the History of Theological Education," *Theological Education* 8 (1972): 213–24. Bass focuses on the modern period when women began to be involved in the academy.

[3] Women's contributions to religious education are widely recognized. Contributions of twentieth-century women are recognized in works like Barbara Anne Keely, ed. *Faith of our Foremothers: Women Changing Religious Education* (Louisville: John Knox, 1997). Also see James E. Reed and Ronnie Prevost, *A History of Christian Education* (Nashville: Broadman & Holman, 1993). Reed and Prevost carefully include a chapter on women in each period of history they present; however, women are often presented as recipients of education, are seldom named, and their written contributions before the twentieth century are not acknowledged.

to women.[4] However, the whole range of women's voices, from traditional to feminist must be heard for a complete picture of nineteenth-century women as interpreters of scripture to emerge, and indeed for a complete understanding of the other fields of study listed.

Reading these writings both inspires and humbles us.[5] It inspires us to find women who engaged the biblical text, interpreted the text, and wrote and published their thinking for the benefit of others. It humbles us to realize that women working in biblical studies in the twentieth and twenty-first centuries are not the first women to work in this field; others have interpreted the Bible, working in much more difficult social contexts. These recovered writings reveal the complexity of the history of biblical interpretation. We are only beginning to understand women's contributions to this history; the selections in the book represent only a small part of women's writings in the nineteenth century. Many more women interpreters remain to be recovered.

As we have listened to the voices of these women writing about the women in Genesis, we have heard many things. These writings show plainly that biblical interpretation is itself a cultural event. Nineteenth-century women interpreters make no claims about being objective and scientific in their interpretive work. They read scripture through the distinctive lens of their time. Reading their interpretations of scripture draws us quickly into the complex world of women in the nineteenth century. Further, while the women interpreters represented here primarily wrote at the popular level, they were influenced by the academic world. They employed and sometimes criticized the tools used by biblical scholars. Their experiences as women also shaped how they interpreted and applied the stories of women in Genesis. These women interpreters brought their understanding of the Bible to faith communities and influenced many through their work. We need to listen to these women's voices and allow them to influence our assessment of their times, and our

---

[4] Carolyn De Swarte Gifford, "American Women and the Bible: The Nature of Woman as a Hermeneutical Issue," in *Feminist Perspectives on Biblical Scholarship*, ed. Adela Yarbro Collins (Atlanta: Scholars Press, 1985): 11–33. Gifford highlights American women's work on the hermeneutical problem of the nature of woman. She discusses the contributions of Judith Sargent Murray, Angelina and Sarah Grimké, Abby Kelley Foster, Lucy Stone, Frances Willard, Phoebe Palmer, Elizabeth Cady Stanton and Matilda Joslyn Gage. In *The Woman's Bible. Feminist Interpretation: The Bible in Women's Perspective* (Minneapolis: Fortress Press, 1998), Luise Schottroff, Silva Schroer, and Marie-Theres Wacker begin their discussion of feminist biblical interpretation with the publication in 1895 of Stanton's. See also Marla Selvidge's important work that recovers the voices of many feminists, *Notorious Voices: Feminist Biblical Interpretation, 1550–1920* (London: SCM, 1996).

[5] Their writings also elicit other emotional responses such as anger, dismay, surprise, and amazement.

times. Their writings inspire, warn, and challenge us to rethink how we read, teach, and use the Bible in our own day.

Cultural Influences on Interpretation

The stories of women in Genesis centered on family life. Thus women interpreting these biblical stories used them as entry points into the great debates about the Woman Question in the nineteenth century: what was women's nature, their character, and their roles in marriage and society? In addition, women used the stories of their foremothers as a starting point for reflection on women's problems related to sexuality—barrenness, abuse, rape, and rejection—as well as issues related to motherhood, work, class, race, and religion. Nineteenth-century culture exalted woman as the angel and priest of the home; she was a domestic goddess but at the same time an evil temptress in an older, still remembered metanarrative.[6] Women of faith recognized the power of women for both good and evil. They found examples of both the good and the bad in the women of Genesis and encouraged their women readers to exercise their power and influence for good. Their writing often revealed more about nineteenth-century attitudes toward sexuality and gender than about the biblical stories themselves.

Nineteenth-century women reflected, reinforced, and challenged the values of their culture. We have heard voices which challenged British and American men and women to see gender equality in Genesis. Grimké, Weld, Balfour, and Stanton argued that women and men are equal before God, and so society should change to reflect that reality. Other voices upheld the patriarchal culture in word, but not always in deed. Even the most traditional voices, like Baxter and Baillie, challenged their culture in various ways.[7] The very act of writing and publishing their works set these fifty women apart as not entirely conforming to the cultural or societal norms for the containment of women in a separate sphere. This was especially true for these women, who were involved in theological discourse and teaching and preaching from scripture.

---

[6] Sean Gill writes of this tension: "the new emphasis on female virtue did not in fact obliterate the older image of the sexually rampant woman; instead it was projected on to the fallen women whose existence in the form of organized prostitution was in one sense the guarantee of bourgeois family values and property rights" (*Women and the Church of England: From the Eighteenth Century to the Present* [London: SPCK, 1994]), 28).

[7] Baxter helped her husband manage the *Christian Herald* publishing enterprise; her parachurch ministries moved her outside of the boundaries of the domestic sphere. Baillie seemed to exempt herself from the need to conform to the standards she set up for others.

We have also heard classism and racism in women's interpretations of Genesis. The British women read about Old Testament women of wealth, privilege, and status in light of their own experience of British society. American women's experience of the institution of slavery provided them with a different set of cultural lenses for reading stories that involved assumed differences in race and status. Many British and American women also expressed Anti-Arab sentiments.

We must acknowledge that these fifty women are not representative of all women in North America or Great Britain. They were literate, educated, and had access to theological libraries, whether through male relatives or through collecting books themselves. They do not represent the working class—factory workers and labourers—and in fact, many of them had servants and taught working-class women in mothers' meetings and poor children in Sunday Schools. Their lives were not always easy, and some of them wrote to make money to support their families, but to earn money through writing was a privilege not available to many.

The fifty women represented in this book interpreted the Bible within their cultural context. We also face the task of interpretation within our cultural context. Listening to their voices and working to understand their context can make us more sensitive to the ways that our own context influences our interpretation. We can easily identify the cultural assumptions that allowed these women who themselves experienced patriarchy, to read the stories enmeshed in the patriarchal world of the ancient Near East with particular clarity. At the same time, immersion in their own culture prevented them from reading the stories in fresh and even prophetic ways. We also live with these tensions: listening to women's voices from the nineteenth century can clarify the discontinuities between the ideal and real in our own life and work, and differences between what we read in the text and what we read into the text—the difference between exegesis and eisegesis.

Traditional and Academic Influences on Interpretation

Women writing on female figures in Genesis interpreted the biblical texts using approaches and methods of study and analysis that interpreters through the centuries also used. Most authors came to the task of interpreting the Bible with the assumption that it was inspired by God. Sarah Ashton expressed her effusive devotion to the sacred texts:

> My Bible! my precious, blessed Bible! what were life without thee? Guide of my otherwise wandering feet, solace of all my cares! Only competent instructor of my ignorance—truest, safest counselor in difficulty—most cheerful compan-

ion in hours of darkness! Rich treasure house, in which are stored the thoughts of my God, his purposes of mercy toward a ruined world! Inexhaustible fountain of pure and sweet waters, from which I daily drink and am refreshed![8]

Women may have differed on the exact definition of inspiration, but they would have at least agreed that scripture was to be read as more than, and as different from, other texts.[9] As Clara Balfour advised her readers, scripture was a source-book for all truth, including truth about the subject of women and her influence: "On all great moral questions, that involve the well being of any large section of the human race, thoughtful persons are in the habit of appealing 'to the law and the testimony,' in the unerring oracles of sacred Truth—and to confirm or correct their opinions from that investigation."[10] Because scripture was sacred, some women, like Ellet, read the Bible stories differently than they read other historical texts. The sacred nature of the text became a justification for the use of allegory, typology, analogy, and intertextual associations to draw out the spiritual, or hidden and devotional, meaning of the scriptures. The characters themselves often functioned as examples for both the authors and their readers to learn from. Sarah Hale spoke for many when she said: "Every character in the Bible has its mission as an example or a warning."[11] Because these women read the Bible as scripture, they believed that it spoke to them; its message was God's word to them, and they were called to share or teach or preach God's word to their readers.

Women's devotional reading of the Bible fit with their culture's traditional understanding of how women should read scripture. Popular conduct books for women written by men in the eighteenth century encouraged "a purely affective and devotional approach to scripture."[12] James Fordyce[13] advised women to acquire "religious Knowledge, reading the scriptures throughout,

[8] S. G. Ashton, *The Mothers of the Bible* (New York: World Publishing, 1855), 5.

[9] See the introduction for a discussion of Jowett's enlightenment dictum: "Read the Bible like any other book." For an alternative female voice critical of the Bible, see Elmina Drake Slenker, *Studying the Bible: or, Brief Criticisms on Some of the Principal Scripture Texts* (Boston: Josiah P. Mendum, 1870).

[10] Clara Lucas Balfour, *The Women of Scripture* (London: Houlston & Stoneman, 1847), iv.

[11] Sarah Hale, *Woman's Record; or, Sketches of all Distinguished Women, from the Creation to A.D. 1854* (New York: Harper & Brothers, 1855), 37.

[12] Julie Straight, "Religious Controversy in Hester Chapone's *Letters on the Improvement of the Mind.*" *Nineteenth-Century Contexts* 27, no. 4 (2005): 320.

[13] James Fordyce, D.D. (1720–1796) was an eloquent Scottish preacher. Many of his sermons and addresses were published. His conduct books were especially influential. See *Sermons to Young Women*, 2 vols. (London, 1760) and *The Character and Conduct of the Female Sex, and the Advantages to be Derived by Young Men from the Society of Virtuous Young Women; a Discourse in Three Parts, Delivered in Monkwell Street Chapel, 1st January, 1776* (London: Printed for T. Cadell, 1776).

and often large portions at a time."[14] Women should then go on to peruse and ponder "at leisure, first without any commentary at all, and so indeed for the most part, except where there is a manifest difficulty; in doing which, you [they] should with awful reverence and child-like simplicity lay your [their] minds open to the native impressions of the truth, and to the secret teachings of its Author."[15] Fordyce cautions women against reading many books in divinity and against reading all books of "religious controversy."[16] In *Letters on the Improvement of the Mind, Addressed to a Young Lady*, Hester Chapone[17] encouraged a devotional reading of scripture, but also challenged women to go deeper into the text, and even to consult various translations and marginal notes and commentaries.[18] In contrast to Fordyce, she encouraged women to use their minds to explore their faith.

The nineteenth-century women we have read developed an approach to the scriptures that incorporated the learning of experts and their own devotional reflection, similar to the approach suggested by Chapone. Some women specifically differentiated their method from that of male interpreters of scripture.[19] They used traditional female genres of writing like instructional literature and poetry, but they also adopted and adapted such traditional male genres as commentary, and used many of the techniques employed by novelists to retell the women's stories in order to transport readers into a distant world of conflict, love and romance, and heroics.

---

[14] James Fordyce, *Sermons to Young Women*, 3rd ed., vol. 2 (London: 1766), 232.

[15] Fordyce, *Sermons to Young Women*, 233.

[16] Fordyce, *Sermons to Young Women*, 237.

[17] Hester Chapone (1727–1801), English essayist and Bluestocking.

[18] Mrs. (Hester) Chapone, *Letters on the Improvement of the Mind, Addressed to a Young Lady* (London, 1777). Julie Straight writes: "Chapone offered women an alternative Christianity to that advocated by Fordyce and Gregory: one that encouraged them to acknowledge reason's limits, but also to have confidence in their own ability to study and understand scripture for themselves. Such confidence may in turn have contributed to the rise of women's religious writing in the nineteenth century, and possibly to the rise of women's writing more broadly: a woman deciding her own stand on religious questions would necessarily recognize her own intellectual and spiritual autonomy more fully than she would otherwise, . . . if a woman took on the responsibility to formulate her own views in matters that she believed had eternal consequences, she was more likely to recognize her own agency and choice in other matters also" (317).

[19] A very prolific exegetical writer of dozens of books, Gracilla Boddington, defended herself against those who might think it presumptuous of her to write a commentary on such a difficult book as Revelation. She distinguished her book from the works of "learned men" who study to "find out, as far as possible, what was foretold to St. John concerning the events about to arise." Instead, she wrote for "the unlearned," so they might gain "a deep impression on their minds by the awful nature of the subjects it contains." Boddington was aware that her approach was distinct from that of many "learned men." Her purpose was not historical reconstruction but life-giving teaching. (*The Revelation of St. John the Divine: Practically Considered in Simple and Familiar Language* [London: James Nisbet, 1881], vi.)

Nineteenth-century women read the Bible as history and so used all available resources to set the Genesis narratives in their historical and geographical context. As travel to the Middle East became more accessible, many travelers, including Elizabeth Rundle Charles and E. C. C. Baillie,[20] published journals describing the land and culture. These publications changed how many of these women read and understood the Bible. For example, descriptions of pillars of salt near the Dead Sea influenced discussions of Lot's wife. The biblical world was exotic, and for many of these authors a tension existed between recognizing that the women of Genesis were part of this distant, exotic world, and making them behave more like nineteenth-century women so that the text could be easily applied to the interpreter's audience.

In addition to reading about the culture and lands of the Middle East, actual artifacts were brought back to Britain and displayed in the British Museum. During the nineteenth century, women who lived in or near London could visit the Museum and view the artifacts for themselves.[21] Women often incorporated drawings, maps, and portraits into their work, including their own or commissioned sketches of the artifacts displayed at the British Museum, or traveler's drawings or photographs from the Holy Land.[22] The illustrations in some books portrayed the women in Genesis as eastern women, though in other cases, famous paintings of female figures (often with an exotic and sensuous element) were used to illustrate the literary portraits of biblical women. Stowe, for example, illustrated her *Women in Sacred History* with twenty-five chromo-lithographs after paintings by such artists as Raphael, Batoni, and Horace Vernet.[23]

While most women were aware of the historical and cultural distance between their world and the world of the biblical text, they did not read Genesis only as history. They subtly opened up the question of the genre of Genesis, thus allowing the possibility of reading the text as more than history. Some, like Stowe, were open to the possibility of the stories not being history at all—they could be a fiction, parable, or allegory. Ada R. Habershon criticized the movement toward viewing the Old Testament "as a collection of historical

---

[20] See part 1, "Eve—The Mother of us All" for biographies of Charles and Baillie.

[21] The Museum was established in 1753 and opened to the public in January 1759. Admission tickets were abolished in 1810 so that anyone could view the collection. From "The History of the British Museum" accessed online at http://www.thebritishmuseum.ac.uk/visit/datelist.html (last accessed August 24, 2005).

[22] For example, see Mrs. John Stewart Oliphant, *Jerusalem the Holy City Its History and Hope* (London: Macmillan, 1893). Also see Henrietta Lee Palmer, *Home Life in the Bible* (Columbus, Ohio: T. P. Ballard & Co., 1885).

[23] Stowe was very interested in art and wrote a book on the subject. See "Toward an Ecumenical Art," in Gail Smith, "Reading the Word: Harriet Beecher Stowe and Interpretation" (Ph.D. diss., University of Virginia, 1993), 209–81.

tales, giving the origin of the Jewish people, and illustrating Oriental manners and customs; useful in supplying Sunday stories for the children, but of very little practical importance as to spiritual teaching." Instead she compared the Bible to a beautifully illustrated volume of engravings "followed by chapters of letter-press describing them, giving their history, or telling something of the life of the artist. We can scarcely conceive of any one trying to understand such descriptions without referring to the pictures themselves; yet this is how the Bible is often treated."[24] In Habershon's view, the Old Testament provided the illustrations and the New Testament the explanations of these pictures.

Many nineteenth-century women accessed the same resources for understanding the biblical text as men did. Many women writers were well educated and knew several languages. A surprising number of British women, who had a long tradition of learning languages, knew Hebrew and Greek. For example, Elizabeth Carter, who corresponded with Sarah Trimmer, knew Greek and published a translation of Epictetus' extant works in 1758.[25] Mary Cornwallis's daughter, Caroline Frances Cornwallis (1786–1858), who was involved in her mother's massive commentary project, knew many languages, including Hebrew and Greek. Helen Spurrell published her translation of the Old Testament from an unpointed Hebrew text;[26] Julia Greswell published a grammar of the Hebrew of the Psalter.[27] Elizabeth Baxter read the New Testament in Greek and preached from the Greek text. American women also recognized the importance of knowing the original languages of scripture for the interpretive task. Julia Evelina Smith (1792–1886) translated the entire Bible numerous times during her life.[28]

While not all women knew the biblical languages, most were aware of translation issues, and so made use of multiple translations, Bibles with marginal notes, and scholarly commentaries which often contained the commentator's

---

[24] Ada R. Habershon, *The Study of the Types* (London: Morgan & Scott, 1898), 9. "But although teaching spiritual lessons, the incidents really took place. Some who are giving up their belief in the inspiration of the Bible would try and make us believe that though there is spiritual meaning in these old stories they are only traditions and fables; not records of real events, but merely allegorical, and no more to be taken literally than Bunyan's 'Pilgrim's Progress.' It is enough for us that the Lord Himself and the writers of the New Testament looked up on them as truthful records of actual events" (11–12). Sarah Hall put into the mouths of one of the children the question of the historicity of the story of Lot's wife changing into a pillar of salt.

[25] Epictetus, *All the Works of Epictetus which are now Extant; Consisting of his Discourses, preserved by Arrian, in Four Books, the Enchiridion, and Fragments, translated from the original Greek with an introduction and notes by Elizabeth Carter* (London: S. Richardson, 1758).

[26] Helen Spurrell, *A Translation of the Old Testament Scriptures from the Original Hebrew* (London: James Nisbet, 1885).

[27] Julia Greswell, *Grammatical Analysis of the Hebrew Psalter* (Oxford, 1873).

[28] See part 1, "Eve—The Mother of Us All" for more information on Julia Smith.

own translation. They used the best academic resources available to them. These women took reading and interpreting the Bible very seriously. They valued learning; if they were denied a formal education, then they learned from brothers and fathers, or stayed up at night reading and studying.

A few women, such as the DeRothschilds and Julia Wedgwood, used the results of source criticism in their work. Wedgwood in particular found this critical approach useful as a new tool to challenge traditional values.[29]

Women were also influenced by other ideas of the time; evolutionary development is one example. Many authors invoked the idea of "primitive" morality to excuse the questionable behaviour of biblical heroes like Sarah. Harriet Beecher Stowe appropriated the idea of natural selection in her discussion of the "chosen race." Stowe also spoke of sacred history as "the purest naturalism":

> We have been so long in the habit of hearing the Bible read in solemn, measured tones, in the hush of churches, that we are apt to forget that these men and women were really flesh and blood, of the same human nature with ourselves. A factitious solemnity invests a Bible name, and some good people seem to feel embarrassed by the obligation to justify all the proceedings of patriarchs and prophets by the advanced rules of Christian morality. In this respect, the modern fashion of treating the personages of sacred story with the same freedom of inquiry as the characters of any other history has its advantages. It takes them out of a false, unnatural light, where they lose all hold on our sympathies, and brings them before us as real human beings. Read in this way, the ancient sacred history is the purest naturalism, under the benevolent guidance of the watchful Father of Nations.[30]

While many women embraced methods and tools traditionally restricted to those with special training and authority in the church and academy, some voiced concerns about the inadequacies of reading scripture only with the intellect rather than also with the soul.[31] In her work on the Ten Commandments, Rossetti offered an extended critique of the work of historical critics, and on their focus on the historical details of the text. In her view, contemporary

---

[29] See Carolyn De Swarte Gifford, "American Women and the Bible: The Nature of Woman as a Hermeneutical Issue," in *Feminist Perspectives on Biblical Scholarship*, ed. Adela Yarbro Collins (Atlanta: Scholars Press, 1985): 11–33, and Dorothy C. Bass, "Women's Studies and Biblical Studies: An Historical Perspective," *Journal for the Study of the Old Testament* 22 (1982): 6–12; and idem, "Women with a Past: A New Look at the History of Theological Education," *Theological Education* 8 (1972): 213–24.

[30] Harriet Beecher Stowe, *Women in Sacred History* (New York: Fords, Howard, & Hulbert, 1873. Republished, New York: Portland House, 1990), 12.

[31] Harriet Beecher Stowe uses the image of reading with the soul and not the eye or intellect in *Uncle Tom's Cabin*. See Gail Smith, "Reading the Word," 43.

biblical scholars paid too much attention to such details that have nothing to do with the spiritual, theological, or moral meaning of the text.

> It is, I suppose, a genuine though not a glaring breach of the Second Commandment, when instead of learning the lesson plainly set down for us in Holy Writ we protrude mental feelers in all directions above, beneath, around it, grasping, clinging to every imaginable particular except the main point.
>
> Take the history of the Fall. The questions of mortal sin shrinks into the background while we moot such points as the primitive status of the serpent: did he stand somehow upright? did he fly? what did he originally eat? how did he articulate? Or again, man's overwhelming loss ceases to be the chief concern, when at the gate of Paradise our eye lights upon the flaming sword. How about that sword? was it a sword as we understand a sword? was it a blade flashing and swaying towards each point of the compass, or was it rather a blazing disk to be flung with rotary motion against the foe? . . . At every turn such questions arise.[32]

Grace Aguilar also reflected upon the inadequacy of an approach to the study of the scriptures that neglected the soul:

> To desert the Bible for its commentators; never to peruse its pages without notes of explanation: to regard it as a work which of itself is incomprehensible, is, indeed, a practice as hurtful as injudicious. Sent as a message of love to our own souls, as written and addressed, not to nations alone, but as the voice of God to individuals—whispering to each of us that which we most need; thus it is we should first regard and venerate it. This accomplished, works tending to elucidate its glorious and consoling truths, to make manifest its simple lessons of character, as well as precept; to bring yet closer to the youthful and aspiring heart, the poetry, the eloquence, the appealing tenderness of its sacred pages, may prove of essential service. In this hope, to bring clearly before the women of Israel all that they owe to the Word of God, all that it may still be to them, the present task is undertaken.[33]

The voices we have heard present a wide variety of approaches, often blending an academic and devotional approach. However, when the pieces are viewed chronologically, it becomes clear that almost all later interpreters both show an awareness of changing ideas about the nature of the Bible and history, and appropriate newly available data about the ancient world into their work.

---

[32] Christina G. Rossetti, *Letter and Spirit: Notes on the Commandments* (London: SPCK, 1883), 85–87.

[33] Grace Aguilar, *The Women of Israel* (New York: Appleton, 1901. Originally published, London, 1845), 1.

Influence of Women's Experience on Interpretation

Nineteenth-century men and women read and interpreted the same Bible and published many of the same types of popular works on the Bible for similar audiences. However, men's and women's experiences, which functioned as a hermeneutical guide, were different. Nineteenth-century culture recognized and valued differences between women and men and between the private world of women and the public world of men;[34] however, not all were agreed on exactly what these differences entailed. Clara Balfour wrote of "those peculiar principles of piety, feminine excellence, moral conduct, and mental power, which the sacred heroines individually exhibited."[35] Sarah Hale argued for women's moral superiority, but inferiority in physical strength and worldly knowledge.

> The Bible history of woman clearly illustrates these important truths; showing that when the faith and resources of men have been utterly overwhelmed, then the salvation of the *cause* of improvement has been her work. Thus maternal love, faith and energy, preserved Moses to be the Law-Giver for the world; made Samuel the High Priest of the Lord; seated Solomon on the throne of David. Each one of these events was of great and momentous import, not only to the destiny of the Hebrew nation, but to the progress of mankind. Deborah was the Deliverer of Israel when not a Hebrew man dared lift his hand in defence of his country till she led the way. Esther saved the Jews when no man could have stayed the decree of death. In short, from the time when the promised seed was reaffirmed to the descendants of Sarah, "a mother of nations," the Hebrew women kept the hope of "Shiloh" ever in their race. This divine faith, like a living light, passing from hand to hand, shines out in the characters of the Hebrew women from Sarah to Huldah the prophetess, who had the light of God's law when the high priest was in darkness. It is worthy, too, of note, that the Bible furnishes no record of an apostate Hebrew woman; while the Hebrew men could not be restrained from licentiousness, idolatry and apostasy.[36]

[34] In a letter written to Mary Gladstone, 27 November 1888, Lucy Cavendish, British anti-suffragist and promoter of women's higher education, wrote: "It is not weakness either that differentiates between men and women. They have their own special strengths for their own special duties which men are quite devoid of . . . if women will undertake men's work their own must suffer" (Cited by Julia Bush in "'Special Strengths for the Own Special Duties': Women, Higher Education and Gender Conservatism in Late Victorian Britain," *History of Education* 34.4 [2005]: 388).

[35] Clara Lucas Balfour, *The Women of Scripture* (London: Houlston & Stoneman, 1847), v.

[36] Sarah Hale, *Woman's Record; or, Sketches of all Distinguished Women, from the Creation to A.D. 1854* (New York: Harper & Brothers, 1855), 18. See also Barbara Kellison, *The Rights of Women in the Church* (Dayton, Ohio: The Herald & Banner Office, 1862).

Nineteenth-century interpreters brought their assumptions about differences between women and men and their respective worlds to the interpretive task. The writings on the women of Genesis collected here suggest that women writers' self-understanding and experience functioned as an interpretive guide. Even Sarah Trimmer and Mary Cornwallis who used the male genre of commentary and wrote for mixed audiences sometimes revealed their distinctive female voice and approach. Cornwallis's experiences as a mother of teenaged daughters gave her insights into the character of Dinah. Cornwallis's concerns as the moral guardian of her children and grandchildren similarly pushed her to read and apply the text through her female eyes.

When women read the stories of women in Genesis, they read them in light of their own experiences as women. The biblical characters, as M.G. suggested, "were not impossible beings of a stained-glass window type, but real men and women of ordinary flesh and blood, with trials and temptations extremely like our own, who acted for the most part exactly as we ourselves would be likely to act under the same circumstances."[37] Women read the stories about marriage in light of their own experiences of marriage: from first love to the marriage bed, from marriage by choice to marriage by coercion, from helpmeet to victim, from beloved wife to wife in a loveless marriage, from first wife to mistress, from death and burial to remarriage.

Women felt a particular bond with the mothers in Genesis. Ashton focused her entire book on the mothers in scripture. She explained her purpose in writing on mothers:

> In the Bible, however, there are the names of those [mothers] concerning whom God has spoken. It [the study of these mothers] will, perhaps, enable us to understand better how the heart of our heavenly Father is affected toward the mothers of the earth—with what feelings he regards them, as they toil on amid their cares and anxieties. It will bind us to him in new bonds. It will elevate our views. It will refine and purify our affections. It will make the relations we sustain appear more sacred and solemn in our eyes, as we shall see them taking hold on eternity. It will lead us to more earnest prayer—to more cheerful, hopeful efforts for the best welfare of our precious ones. It will endear us to the holy Scriptures, the invaluable communications of sovereign wisdom and love to us who are ignorant and erring.[38]

Like the women of Genesis, nineteenth-century women experienced infertility, difficult pregnancies, childbirth, breastfeeding, the death of children,

---

[37] M. G., *Women Like Ourselves* (London: SPCK, 1893), iv. Even the title of her book shows her hermeneutical approach to the characters in scripture.

[38] S. G. Ashton, *The Mothers of the Bible* (New York: World Publishing, 1855), 8–9.

sibling rivalry, disagreements over styles of parenting, and the pain of separation from children when they left home.

Women writers of the nineteenth century also related to the stories of biblical women managing domestic help, selflessly working to serve others, and having to move households quickly. The authors' experiences of women's power and powerlessness, women's goodness and women's sin, allowed them to see both the good and bad in their foremothers.

Women's experiences of living in a culture that undervalued their voices and feelings many have motivated them to invest value in the voices and feelings of the biblical characters. More negatively, their experiences blinded these women writers from reading and understanding the stories. In particular, social assumptions about sexuality made them reticent to comment on the stories of rape and abuse. Nineteenth-century women's experience, culture, and social location allowed them insights into the stories of women in Genesis that male readers of the nineteenth century missed, and male and female modern readers may miss.

The nineteenth-century novelists Charlotte Lennox, Jane Austen, Margaret Fuller, and Harriet Beecher Stowe raised hermeneutical questions about the relationship between reading and gender: could the gender of a reader alter the effect of a text, that is, change what a text is or what it does; are texts constant if the character of a reader changes?[39] In her novel, *Dred*, Stowe explores how race and gender influence reading. She suggested that by listening to those who read differently because of sex or race, a more complete understanding of what is read can be achieved, and so readers "grow in humanity and morality as a result."[40]

The nineteenth-century women represented in this book provide clear examples of gendered interpretation. They challenge us to reconsider the place of "difference" in how we read, interpret, and teach scripture. Stowe calls us to learn from the readings of those of different gender, race, and culture than our own. The implications of this call are far-reaching for academics who aspire to an "objective" reading of the biblical text. The place of experience in the interpretive process must be considered; other voices, including popular voices, must be heard in our teaching.

---

[39] See Gail Smith, "Reading the Word." See also Gail K. Smith, "Reading with the Other: Hermeneutics and the Politics of Difference in Stowe's *Dred*," *American Literature* 69. 2 (1997): 289–315.

[40] Smith, "Reading the Word," 144, 198. Smith also suggests that Stowe's idea that men learn to read with the eyes of women, free men and women with the eyes of a slave, and privileged readers with the eyes of the oppressed, raises the possibility of there being no "authorized" reading.

Roles of Women Interpreters in the Faith Community

The nineteenth-century interpreters of Genesis represented in this book had a variety of roles in their faith communities: they acted as teachers, preachers, evangelists, missionaries, apologists, and theologians. In each of these roles, they speak into our contemporary discussions of what it means to fulfill these responsibilities in our own communities of faith.

Educating the young was a widely accepted and encouraged role for women in the home; they were held to be responsible for teaching faith and morality to their children and also to their servants. It is not surprising, then, that women wrote to teach. Their lessons covered all ages and subjects: they wrote to teach children, teens, young older adults, and adults about issues of faith. Faith touched all aspects of their life, so they taught about all aspects of life in a very practical way. Most of this instructional literature was based on the authors' experiences in actually teaching the material to children, teens, or adults, whether in their own home to their own children, or in parish ministries such as Sunday Schools and Mothers' Meetings.

Lessons for young children were written with simplified language and grammar; Mortimer and Barton wrote simple lessons to teach children the basics of the Christian faith. They left out aspects of the stories of Genesis thought to be inappropriate for their young audience. Hall, Witter, Warner, Woosnam, and Copley wrote to instruct older children and youth, and used a variety of genres to do this. These authors were concerned that young men and (especially) young women knew and practiced their faith; Woosnam and Copley gave practical advice to young people from their readings of Genesis.

Ashton, Balfour, M. G., Donaldson, and Baxter directed their instruction at adult women. M. G., Donaldson, and Baxter wrote lessons for Mothers' Meetings; their applications drawn from the stories of the women of Genesis were intended for working-class mothers. Balfour wrote for her peers, with "a sincere desire to deepen the conviction of the religious and social responsibilities of her own sex, by calling attention to the testimony and illustrations of Scripture."[41] Ashton addressed mothers in her work, intending to "gather together, in as interesting a manner as we may, such instruction and encouragement as [the Bible] will afford mothers in their important work."[42]

Women were denied official pulpits for most of the nineteenth century,[43] yet many preached in alternative locations, like classes for mothers or young

---

[41] Clara Lucas Balfour, *The Women of Scripture* (London: Houlston & Stoneman, 1847), iv.

[42] Ashton, *Mothers of the Bible*, 7.

[43] Of course there were exceptions to this general rule, and women worked toward ordination to gain official pulpits. Antoinette L. Brown (Blackwell) is honoured as the first American

women. The fifty women collected here who wrote on Genesis preached eloquently with their pens. Many used the language and form of sermons to
make their points to their listening or reading audiences.[44] King admitted
that she was preaching; in her introduction, she noted that she needed to
learn the lessons she had written as much as, and probably more than her
readers, lest she find that "while she presumes to 'preach to others, she may
herself a cast-away.'"[45] Here King quoted 1 Corinthians 9:27, using these
apostolic words of her own writing. As a preacher she identified herself with
Paul the apostle.

Women preached the gospel and so acted as evangelists. Ashton and
Donaldson appealed for repentance using the story of Lot's wife. Some women
writers were also involved in foreign missions: Tucker spent the last years of
her life working in India; Charles wrote for the women of India; Yonge supported missions financially with the proceeds from her work; Baxter started a
training school for missionaries.

Grace Aguilar was an apologist for her Jewish faith. She resisted calls to
convert to Christianity and wrote *The Women of Israel* to assist Jewish women
in understanding and embracing their faith. Stowe was also an apologist: her
book *Footsteps of the Master* was intended to counter the influence of modern
skepticism. Many other writers showed an interest in apologetics in their
writings; they used reasoned arguments and archeological discoveries to argue
for the truth of the Bible and their faith.

As women examined the text of scripture and interpreted it for others,
they did theology; they asked and answered questions about the nature of
God, the nature of humans, and the interaction between the human and
divine. M. G. consciously taught sacramental theology in her lessons for
mothers' meetings:

> An endeavour has also been made to bring out as far as could be done at
> the same time the Sacramental teaching which underlies so many of the Old
> Testament histories. . . . It is by fearlessly and lovingly explaining in simple
> language the value and necessity of all the means of grace which Christ in His

---

woman to be ordained. See Nancy A. Hardesty, *Women called to Witness: Evangelical Feminism
in the Nineteenth Century,* 2nd ed. (Knoxville: University of Tennessee Press, 1999), 78–79.
Also see Barbara Brown Zikmund, "Women and Ordination," in *In Our Own Voices: Four
Centuries of American Women's Religious Writing,* ed. Rosemary Skinner Keller and Rosemary
Radford Ruether (Louisville: Westminster John Knox, 1995), 291–340. For an examination
of women as preachers in America, see Catherine A. Brekus, *Strangers & Pilgrims: Female
Preaching in America, 1740–1845* (Chapel Hill: University of North Carolina Press, 1998).

[44] For example, in her lessons to young women, Woosnam used illustrations that would
have been at home in any sermon.

[45] Frances Elizabeth King, *Female Scripture Characters; Exemplifying Female Virtues*
(London: F. C. & J. Rivington, 1822), xii.

mercy has given us in His Church, in order to enable us to draw nearer to Him, that we shall be best able to win "the masses" back to the visible Fold, and to bring souls to Jesus.[46]

Nineteenth-century women wrote specifically on theological topics:[47] E. C. C. Baillie's *The Protoplast* contained theological essays about firsts, which began with the first scripture reference to a topic, then continued with theological reflection.[48] Women who studied, interpreted, and applied the biblical text for others could not avoid theological reflection in their work; thus female biblical interpreters often became popular theologians.

From their defined role as teachers of faith and morality to children, youth, and adults, nineteenth-century women became preachers, evangelists and missionaries, apologists, and theologians. They carefully read and interpreted the Bible using a variety of methods and tools,[49] then wrote and published their thought for the benefit of others.

Unfortunately, the works these women wrote were not considered important enough to be remembered, and so were lost. The reasons for this loss are many and complex: popular works, whether authored by men or women, have not been valued and studied by academic guilds; some of these works were not widely distributed, and thus easy to ignore; at the same time, the books were written and marketed to particular audiences, so new trends in publishing or shifts in culture meant they became dated. Fortunately, the loss of these works was not permanent. Copies were preserved, and these women's voices can be heard again.

Many factors led to the loss of these works, and, as they are recovered, we need to ensure the voices represented by these works are not lost again. The memory of women interpreters must be integrated into courses on the Bible; women worked on all books of the Bible and should be included in these discussions. If we separate these women into special optional courses on "women in the Bible" or "women interpreters of the Bible," they will remain ghettoized, and "lost" as far as most students and scholars are concerned. They need to be brought into conversation with their male contemporaries, with feminist scholars of the twentieth and twenty-first century, with women and men who interpreted before them, and with the women and men who will interpret the Bible in the next generation.

[46] M. G., *Women Like Ourselves*, iv.

[47] For example, see Caroline Fry, *The Table of the Lord* (London: Howe & Co., nd.).

[48] The extract from Baillie's essay on the first women, reproduced in part 1, "Eve: The Mother of Us All," precedes a lengthy theological reflection on women.

[49] Some women wrote books on hermeneutics, for example, see Mary L. G. Carus-Wilson, *Unseal the Book: Practical Words for Plain Readers of Holy Scripture* (London : Religious Tract Society, 1899).

BIBLIOGRAPHY

Pre-20th-Century Sources

Aguilar, Grace. *The Women of Israel.* London, 1845; New York: Appleton, 1901.

———. "The Wanderers (1838)." *The Occident and American Jewish Advocate* 3.7 (1845).

Aikin, Lucy. *Epistles on Women, Exemplifying their Character and Condition in Various Ages and Nations.* London: J. Johnson, 1810.

Alexander, Mrs. Cecil. F. "The Temptation," and "Isaac and Rebekah." In *Poems on Subjects in the Old Testament.* London: 1854; 3rd ed. London: J. Masters, 1888.

Ashton, S. G. *Mothers of the Bible,* Boston: J. P. Jewett, 1855.

Baillie, E. C. C. *The Protoplast: A Series of Papers.* London: Wertheim & MacIntosh, 1853.

Balfour, Clara Lucas (née Lyddell). *The Bible Patterns of a Good Woman.* London: S.W. Partridge, 1867.

———. *Women of Scripture.* London, 1847. 2nd ed. London: Houlston & Stonemann, 1850.

———. *Women Worth Emulating.* London: Sunday School Union, 1877.

———. *Working Women of the Last Half Century: The Lessons of Their Lives.* London: W. & F. G. Cash, 1854.

Barnes, Albert. *Notes Explanatory and Practical, on the Acts of the Apostles.* London: T. Ward, 1841.

Barton, Lucy. *Bible Letters for Children.* London: John Souter, 1831.

Baxter, Elizabeth. *The Women in the Word.* 2nd ed. London: Christian Herald, 1897.

Bayley, Dr. *The Magnificent Scenes in the Book of Revelation.* London: Gratton, Marshall & Co. 1878.

———. *Observations made during a Tour through Norway, Sweden, Finland, and Russia in the summer of 1866.* London: Alvey, 1867.

———. *Religion: its influence on the working man, as a lover, husband, and father: a lecture delivered in the Concert Hall, Liverpool, on Sunday, September 19th, 1852.* Liverpool: Egerton Smith, 1852.

Beck, Mary E. *Bible Readings on Bible Women: Illustrated by Incidents in Daily Life*. London: S.W. Partridge, 1892.

Besant, Annie. *God's Views on Marriage as Revealed in the Old Testament*. London: Freethought Publishing, 1881.

Bibb, Eloise. *Poems*. Boston: Monthly Review Press, 1895.

Blackwell, Antoinette Brown. "Exegesis of 1 Corinthians XIV. 34, 35; and I Timothy II. 11, 12." *Oberlin Quarterly Review* 4 (1849): 358–73.

Blake, Lillie Devereaux. *Fettered for Life, or Lord and Master*. New York: Sheldon, 1874.

———. *Woman's Place To-Day: Four Lectures, in Reply to the Lenten Lectures on "Woman" by the Rev. Morgan Dix*. New York: J.W. Lovell, 1883.

Boddington, Gracilla. *The Revelation of St. John the Divine: Practically Considered in Simple and Familiar Language*. London: James Nisbet, 1881.

Buckingham, James Silk. *Notes of the Buckingham Lectures: Embracing Sketches of the Geography, Antiquities and Present Condition of Egypt and Palestine: Compiled from the Oral Discourses of the Hon. J. S. Buckingham. Together with a Sketch of his Life*. New York: Leavitt, Lord 1838.

Bunyan, John. *The Pilgrim's Progress*. Edited with an introduction by Roger Sharrock. London: Penguin, 1987.

Bush, George. *Notes on Genesis*. New York: Newman & Ivison, 1852.

Butler, Josephine E. *The Lady of Shunem*. London: H. Marshall, 1894.

———. *Social Purity*. 3rd ed. London: Dyer Brothers, 1882.

Carne, John. *Recollections of Travels in the East*. London: Henry Colburn & Richard Bentley, 1830.

Carus-Wilson, Mary L. G. *Unseal the Book: Practical Words for Plain Readers of Holy Scripture*. London: Religious Tract Society, 1899.

Chapone, Hester. *Letters on the Improvement of the Mind, Addressed to a Young Lady*. London: H. Hughes, 1773.

Charles, Elizabeth Rundle. *Sketches of the Women of Christendom*. New York: Dodd, Mead & Co., 1880.

Christian, Ernst Wilhelm. *Sartorius, The Doctrine of Divine Love: Or, Outlines of the Moral Theology of the Evangelical Church*. Translated by Sophia Taylor. Edinburgh: T&T Clark, 1884.

Clarke, Adam. *The Holy Bible, Containing the Old and New Testaments, according to the Authorized Translation; with all the parallel texts and marginal readings: to which are added, notes, and practical observations, designed as a help to a correct understanding to the sacred writings*. Liverpool: Nuttall, Fisher, & Dixon, 1813.

Copley, Esther Hewlett. *Scripture Biography: Comprehending all the Names Mentioned in the Old and New Testaments*. London: Fisher, Fisher, & Jackson, 1835.

———. *Scripture History for Youth*. London: H. Fisher, Son & P. Jackson, 1833.

Corbaux, Fanny. "The Rephaim, and their Connexion with Egyptian History." *Journal of Scared Literature* NS, vol. 1 (1851): 151–72.

Cornwallis, Mary. *Observations, Critical, Explanatory, and Practical, on the Canonical Scriptures*. vol. 1, 2nd ed. London: Baldwin, Cradock, & Joy, 1820.

Crocker, Hannah Mather. *Observations on the Real Rights of Women, with their Appropriate Duties, Agreeable to Scripture, Reason and Common Sense.* Boston, 1818.

Delitzsch, Franz. *A New Commentary on Genesis.* Translated by Sophia Taylor. 5th ed. Vol. 2 of *Clark's Foreign Theological Library.* Edinburgh: T&T Clark, 1888–1894.

Donaldson, Mrs. *Home Duties for Wives and Mothers, Illustrated by Women of Scripture.* London: William Hunt, 1882.

Dorner, Isaac August. *History of Protestant Theology: Particularly in Germany: Viewed According to Its Fundamental Movement: And in Connection with the Religious, Moral, and Intellectual Life.* Translated by George Robson and Sophia Taylor. 2 vols. Edinburgh: T&T Clark, 1871.

Driver, S. R. *An Introduction to the Literature of the Old Testament.* New York: Charles Scribner, 1891.

Ellet, Mrs. Elizabeth. *Family Pictures from the Bible.* New York: G.P. Putnam, 1849.

Epictetus. *All the Works of Epictetus which are now Extant; Consisting of his Discourses, preserved by Arrian, in Four Books, the Enchiridion, and Fragments.* Translated from the original Greek with an introduction and notes by Elizabeth Carter. London: S. Richardson, 1758.

Fordyce, James. *The Character and Conduct of the Female Sex, and the Advantages to be Derived by Young Men from the Society of Virtuous Young Women; a Discourse in Three Parts, Delivered in Monkwell Street Chapel, 1st January, 1776.* London: Printed for T. Cadell, 1776.

———. *Sermons to Young Women.* 2 vols. London, 1766.

Frank, Henrietta G. "Jewish Women of Modern Days." In *Papers of the Jewish Women's Congress.* Philadelphia: The Jewish Publication Society of America, 1894.

Frank, Ray. "Women in the Synagogue." In *Papers of the Jewish Women's Conference.* Philadelphia: The Jewish Publication Society of America, 1894.

Fry, Caroline. *The Table of the Lord.* London: Howe, n.d.

Ginzberg, Louis. *The Legends of the Jews.* Philadelphia: The Jewish Publication Society of America, 1909.

Gresswell, Julia. *Grammatical Analysis of the Hebrew Psalter.* Oxford: James Parker, 1873.

Grimké, Angelina E. *Letters to Catherine Beecher.* Boston: I. Knapp, 1838.

Grimké, Sarah. *Letters on the Equality of the Sexes, and the Condition of Woman.* Boston: I. Knapp, 1839.

Habershon, Ada R. *The Study of the Types.* London: Morgan & Scott, 1898.

———. *Hidden Pictures: or, How the New Testament is Concealed in the Old Testament.* London: Oliphant, 1916.

Hale, Sarah. *Woman's Record; or, Sketches of all Distinguished Women, from the Creation to A.D. 1854.* New York: Harper & Brothers, 1855.

Hall, Sarah. *Conversations on the Bible.* Philadelphia: Harrison Hall, 1827. Originally published, 1818.

Hasell, Elizabeth Julia. *Bible Partings.* Edinburgh: W. Blackwood & Sons, 1883.

———. *The Rock; and other short lectures on passages of Holy Scripture.* London, 1867.

Hasell, Elizabeth Julia. *Short Family Prayers*. London: W. Hunt, 1879.

Hasell, Elizabeth Julia. *Via Crucis; or, Meditations for Passion and Easter Tide*. London, 1884.

Henry, Matthew. *Commentary on the Whole Bible*. 6 vols. London, 1706–1721.

Hyneman, Rebekah. "Sarah." *The Occident and American Jewish Advocate* 4.4 (1846).

Jamieson, Robert, A. R. Fausset, and David Brown. *A Commentary, Critical and Explanatory, on the Old and New Testaments*. New York: S.S. Scranton, 1873.

Jowett, Benjamin. "On the Interpretation of Scripture." In *Essays and Reviews*. Edited by Frederick Temple. London: Parker & Sons, 1860.

Keil, C. F. *Bible Commentary on the Old Testament: The Books of Ezra, Nehemiah, and Esther*. Translated by Sophia Taylor. Edinburgh: T&T Clark, 1873.

Kellison, Barbara. *The Rights of Women in the Church*. Dayton, Ohio: The Herald & Banner Office, 1862.

King, Frances Elizabeth. *Female Scripture Characters; Exemplifying Female Virtues*. 9th ed. London: F.C.&J. Rivington, 1822. Originally published, 1813.

Laurie, Charlotte L. *On the Study of the Bible*. London: SPCK, 1899.

Lewis, Agnes Smith. *In the Shadow of Sinai: a Story of Travel and Research from 1895 to 1897*. Cambridge: Macmillan & Bowes, 1898.

Linton, E. L. *The Girl of the Period*. Bristol: R. W. Bingham, 1868.

M.G. *Women Like Ourselves: Short Addresses for Mother's Meetings, Bible Classes, Etc*. London: SPCK, 1893.

Martyn, S. T. *Women of the Bible*. New York: American Tract Society, 1868.

Maundrell, Henry. *A Journey from Aleppo to Jerusalem, at Easter, A.D. 1697*. Oxford, 1703.

Moise, Penina. *The Secular and Religious Works of Penina Moise*. Charleston: Nicholas G. Duff, 1911.

More, Hannah. *Strictures on the Modern System of Female Education*. London: T. Cadell & W. Davies, 1799.

Morgan, Sydney Lady. *Woman and Her Master*. Vol. 1. London: Henry Colburn, 1840.

Mortimer, Favell Lee. *The Peep of Day*. London: J. Hatchard & Son, 1833.

Morton, Mrs. G. E. *From the Beginning or Stories from Genesis*. London: Thomas Nelson & Sons, 1893.

Norval, Leigh. *Women of the Bible: Sketches of All the Prominent Female Characters in the Old and the New Testament*. Nashville: Publishing House of the M. E. Church, South, Sunday-School Department, 1889.

O'Keeffe, Adelaide. *Patriarchal Times, or, The Land of Canaan: A Figurative History: in Seven Books: Founded on the Holy Scriptures: In Two Volumes*. 3rd ed. London: Rivington, 1820. Originally published, 1811.

Oehler, Gustav Friedrich. *Theology of the Old Testament*. Translated by E. D. Smith and Sophia Taylor. 2 vols. Edinburgh: T&T Clark, 1880.

Oliphant, Mrs. John Stewart. *Jerusalem the Holy City Its History and Hope*. London: Macmillan, 1893.

Palmer, Henrietta Lee. *Home Life in the Bible.* Columbus, Ohio: T. P. Ballard, 1885.

Patrick, Bishop Symon. *A Commentary upon the First Book of Moses, Called Genesis.* London: Printed for R. Chiswell, 1695.

Petrie, Mary L. G. *Clews to Holy Writ or, The Chronological Scripture Cycle.* London: Hodder & Stoughton, 1894.

———. *Unseal the Book: Practical Words for Plain Readers of Scripture.* London: The Religious Tract Society, 1899.

Putnam, Catherine H. *The Gospel by Moses, in the Book of Genesis; or, the Old Testament Unveiled.* New York: Edward H. Fletcher, 1854.

Robinson, Thomas. *Scripture Characters, or a Practical Improvement of the Principal Histories in the Old and New Testament.* 3rd ed. London: J. Matthews, 1793.

Rossetti, Christina G. *The Face of the Deep: A Devotional Commentary on the Apocalypse.* London: SPCK, 1893.

———. *Letter and Spirit. Notes on the Commandments.* London: SPCK, 1883.

de Rothschild, Baroness Constance, and Baroness Annie Henrietta de Rothschild. *The History and Literature of the Israelites.* 2 vols. London: Longmans, Green, 1870.

Shadwell, Mrs. Lucas. *Bible Exercises, for the Family Reading, for the Cottage Meeting, and the Temperance Bible Class. [Exodus 1-12].* London: W. Tweedie, 1869–1872.

[Sherwood, Mrs.]. *Eyes and No Eyes; or, How to Read the Bible Aright.* New York: American Tract Society, n.d.

Slenker, Elmina Drake. *Studying the Bible: or, Brief Criticisms on Some of the Principal Scripture Texts.* Boston: Josiah P. Mendum, 1870.

Smith, Eliza. ("A Clergyman's Daughter"). *The Battles of the Bible.* Edinburgh: Paton & Ritchie, 1852.

———. *Chapters on the Shorter Catechism.* Edinburgh: Paton & Ritchie, 1850.

Smith, Elizabeth. *A Vocabulary, Hebrew, Arabic, and Persian.* London: W. H. Lunn, 1814.

Smith, Julia E. *The Holy Bible Containing the Old and New Testaments. Translated Literally from the Original Tongues.* Hartford, Conn.: American Publishing, 1885.

Smith, Sir William, ed. *A Dictionary of the Bible, Comprising its Antiquities, Biography, Geography and Natural History.* London: 1860–1863.

de Sola, D.A., I. L. Lindenthal, and the Rev. Morris. *The Sacred Scriptures in Hebrew and English: A New Translation with Notes Critical and Explanatory.* J. Raphall. London: Samuel Bagster & Son, 1844.

Spurrell, Helen. *A Translation of the Old Testament Scriptures from the Original Hebrew.* London: James Nisbet, 1885.

Stanton, Elizabeth Cady. *The Slave's Appeal.* Albany: Weed, Parsons, 1860.

———, ed. *The Woman's Bible Commentary.* New York: European Publishing, 1895.

Stowe, Calvin E. *Origin and History of the Books of the Bible, Both the Canonical and the Apocryphal, Designed to Show What the Bible Is Not, What It Is, and How to Use It.* Hartford: Hartford Connecticut Publishing, 1867.

Stowe, Harriet Beecher. *Footsteps of the Master.* New York: J.B. Ford, 1877.

———— *Women in Sacred History.* New York: Fords, Howard, & Hulbert, 1873.

Stickney, Sarah (Ellis). *The Women of England, Their Social Duties, and Domestic Habits.* 2nd ed. London, 1839.

[de Thévenot, Jean]. *The Travels of Monsieur de Thévenot into the Levant.* Part I: *Turkey.* Part II: *Persia.* Part III: *The East-Indies.* London, 1687.

Trimmer, Mrs. Sarah. *A Help to the Unlearned in the Study of the Holy Scriptures: Being an Attempt to Explain the Bible in a Familiar Way.* London: F. C.&J. Rivington, 1805.

————. *Some Account of the Life and Writings of Mrs. Trimmer.* London: F.C.&J. Rivington, 1814. [Trimmer's son Henry may have authored this unsigned memoir of his mother's life.]

Tucker, Charlotte (A.L.O.E.). *A.L.O.E.'s Sunday Picture Book: Illustrating the Life of the Lord Christ: In a Series of Short Poems.* 1871.

————. *House Beautiful; or, The Bible Museum.* London: T. Nelson & Sons, 1868.

————. *Pride and his Prisoners.* London: Nelson, 1876.

————. *The Young Pilgrim: A Tale Illustrative of "The Pilgrim's Progress."* London: T. Nelson & Sons, 1860.

Turnock, Sarah Elizabeth. *Women of the Bible.* London: G. Burroughs, 1898.

Verney, Lady Eliza. *Practical Thoughts on the First Forty Chapters of the Book of the Prophet, Isaiah.* London: James Nisbet, 1858.

Ward, Mrs. Humphrey. *Robert Elsmere.* London: Smith, Elder, 1888.

Wardle, Mary. *The Law: Moral, Ceremonial and Judicial. [Explanation of Chapters of the Books of Genesis, Exodus and Deuteronomy].* London, 1879.

Warner, Susan. *Walks from Eden.* New York: Hurst, 1866.

Wedgwood, Julia. *The Message of Israel in the Light of Modern Criticism.* London: Isbister, 1894.

————. *The Moral Idea: A Historic Study.* London: Trübner, 1888.

Weld, Rev. H. Hastings, ed. *The Women of the Old and New Testaments.* Philadelphia: Lindsay & Blakiston, 1848.

Wellhausen, Julius. *Geschicthe Israels.* Berlin: G. Reimer, 1878.

Wilberforce, William. *A Practical View of the Prevailing System of Professed Christians, in the Higher and Middle Classes in this Country, Contrasted with Real Christianity.* 2nd ed. London: T. Cadell & W. Davies, 1799.

Witter, Mary L. T. *Angels.* Glasgow: William Asher, 1900.

————. *A Book for the Young: Being a History of the Kings Who Ruled over God's Ancient People.* Halifax: A. & W. Mackinlay, 1870.

————. *The Edomites: Their History as Gathered from the Holy Scriptures.* Halifax: S. Seldon, 1888.

Wollstonecraft, Mary. *Vindication on the Rights of Woman.* London, 1792.

Woosnam, Etty. *The Woman of the Bible: Old Testament.* London: S.W. Partridge, 1881.

Wordsworth, Elizabeth. *Psalms for the Christian Festivals.* London: Longmans, Green, 1906.

Yonge, Charlotte. *Young Folks' Bible History.* New York: Eaton & Mains, 1880.

Twentieth-Century and Contemporary Sources

Anderson, Gary A. *The Genesis of Perfection: Adam and Eve in Jewish and Christian Imagination.* Louisville: Westminster John Knox, 2001.

Atwood, Margaret. *Negotiating with the Dead: A Writer on Writing.* Cambridge: Cambridge University Press, 2002.

Bach, Alice. "Breaking Free of the Biblical Frame-Up: Uncovering the Woman in Genesis 39." In *A Feminist Companion to Genesis.* Edited by Athalya Brenner, 318–42. Sheffield: Sheffield Academic, 1993.

Bailey, Warner M. "William Robertson Smith and American Biblical Studies." *Journal of Presbyterian History* 51 (1973): 285–308.

Baker-Fletcher, Karen. "Anna Julia Cooper and Sojourner Truth: Two Nineteenth-Century Black Feminist Interpreters of Scripture." In *Searching the Scriptures* Vol. 1. Edited by Elizabeth Schüssler Fiorenza, 41–51. New York: Crossroad, 1993.

Bass, Dorothy C. "'In Christian Firmness and Christian Meekness': Feminism and Pacifism in Antebellum America." In *Immaculate & Powerful: The Female in Sacred Image and Social Reality.* Edited by Clarissa W. Atkinson, Constance H. Buchanan, and Margaret R. Miles, 201–25. Boston, Mass.: Beacon Press, 1985.

———. "Women's Studies and Biblical Studies: An Historical Perspective." *Journal for the Study of the Old Testament* 22 (1982): 6–12.

———. "Women with a Past: A New Look at the History of Theological Education." *Theological Education* 8 (1972): 213–24.

Bebbington, D. W. *Evangelicalism in Modern Britain: A History from the 1730s to the 1980s.* London: Unwin Hyman, 1989.

Benbow-Pfalzgraf, Taryn, ed. *American Women Writers.* Vol. 1. 2nd ed. Detroit: St. James Press, 2000.

Berlin, Adele. *Poetics and Interpretation of Biblical Narrative.* Winona Lake: Eisenbrauns, 1994.

Bird, Phyllis. "The Harlot as Heroine: Narrative Art and Social Presupposition in Three Old Testament Texts." In *Women in the Hebrew Bible: A Reader.* Edited by Alice Bach, 99–117. New York: Routledge, 1999.

Bray, Gerald. *Biblical Interpretation: Past and Present.* Downers Grove, Ill.: InterVarsity, 1996.

Brekus, Catherine A. *Strangers & Pilgrims: Female Preaching in America 1740–1845.* Chapel Hill: University of North Carolina Press, 1998.

Brown, Callum G. *The Death of Christian Britain: Understanding Secularization 1800–2000.* London: Routledge, 2001.

Brown, Ira V. "The Higher Criticism Comes to America, 1880–1900." *Journal of the Presbyterian Historical Society* 38.4 (1960): 193–212.

Bush, Julia. "'Special Strengths for Their Own Special Duties': Women, Higher Education and Gender Conservatism in Late Victorian Britain." *History of Education* 34.4 (2005): 387–405.

Caskey, Marie. *Chariot of Fire: Religion and the Beecher Family.* New Haven: Yale University Press, 1978.

Clark, Elizabeth A., and Herbert Richardson. *Women and Religion.* 2nd ed. San Francisco: Harper Collins, 1996.

Curle, Richard, ed. *Robert Browning and Julia Wedgwood: A Broken Friendship as Revealed in their Letters.* London: John Murray & Jonathan Cape, 1937.

D'Amico, Diane. *Christina Rossetti: Faith Gender and Time.* Baton Rouge: Louisiana State University Press, 1999.

———. "Christina Rossetti's Helpmeet." *Victorian Newsletter* 88 (1994): 25–29.

D'Amico, Diane, and David A. Kent. "Christina Rossetti's Notes on Genesis and Exodus." *Journal of Pre-Raphaelite Studies* 13 (2004): 49–98.

DeJong, Mary. "Dark-Eyed Daughters: Nineteenth-Century Popular Portrayals of Biblical Women." *Women's Studies* 19 (1991): 283–308.

Dunlop, John. *Autobiography of John Dunlop.* London: Spottiswoode, Ballantyne, 1931.

Flamming, Lucretia A. "'And Your Sons and Daughters Will Prophesy': The Voice and Vision of Josephine Butler." In *Women's Theology in Nineteenth-Century Britain: Transfiguring the Faith of their Fathers.* Edited by Julie Melnyk, 151–64. New York: Garland Publishing, 1998.

Freedman, David Noel, ed. *The Anchor Bible Dictionary.* 6 vols. New York: Doubleday, 1992.

Frye, Northrop. *The Great Code: The Bible and Literature.* Toronto: Academic Press, 1982.

Garraty, John A., and Mark C. Carnes, eds. *American National Biography.* Vol. 5. New York: Oxford University Press, 1999.

Gifford, Carolyn De Swarte. "American Women and the Bible: The Nature of Woman as a Hermeneutical Issue." In *Feminist Perspectives on Biblical Scholarship.* Edited by Adela Yarbro Collins, 11–33. Atlanta: Scholars Press, 1985.

Gill, Sean. *Women and the Church of England: From the Eighteenth Century to the Present.* London: SPCK, 1994.

Giltner, John H. *Moses Stuart: The Father of Biblical Science in America.* Atlanta: Scholars Press, 1988.

Glover, W. *Evangelical Nonconformists and Higher Criticism in the Nineteenth Century.* London: Independent Press, 1954.

Hardesty, Nancy A. *Women called to Witness: Evangelical Feminism in the Nineteenth Century.* 2nd ed. Knoxville: University of Tennessee Press, 1999.

Harris, Daniel A. "Hagar in Christian Britain: Grace Aguilar's 'The Wanderers.'" *Victorian Literature and Culture* 27 (1999): 143–69.

Hatch, Nathan O. *The Democratization of American Christianity.* New Haven: Yale University Press, 1989.

Hollis, Susan T. *The Ancient Egyptian "Tale of Two Brothers": The Oldest Fairy Tale in the World.* Norman: University of Oklahoma Press, 1990.

James, Edward T., Janet Wilson James, and Paul S. Boyer, eds. *Notable American Women 1607–1950: A Biographical Dictionary.* Vol. 2. Cambridge, Mass.: Harvard University Press, 1971.

Karp, Abraham J. *From the Ends of the Earth: Judaic Treasures of the Library of Congress.* Washington, D.C.: Library of Congress, 1991.

Keely, Barbara Anne, ed. *Faith of Our Foremothers: Women Changing Religious Education.* Louisville: John Knox Press, 1997.

Kelley, Mary. *Private Woman, Public Stage: Literary Domesticity in Nineteenth-Century America.* New York: Oxford University Press, 1984.

Kerfoot, Donna. "Etty Woosnam: A Woman of Wisdom and Conviction." Term Paper, Wycliffe College, 2004.

Kimball, Gayle. *The Religious Ideas of Harriet Beecher Stowe: Her Gospel of Womanhood.* New York: Mellon Press, 1982.

Krueger, Christine L. *The Reader's Repentance: Women Preachers, Women Writers, and Nineteenth-Century Social Discourse.* Chicago: University of Chicago Press, 1992.

Kunitz, Stanley J., and Howard Haycroft, eds. *American Authors 1600–1900: A Biographical Dictionary of American Literature.* New York: H.W. Wilson, 1938.

Larsen, Timothy. *Contested Christianity: The Political and Social Contexts of Victorian Theology.* Waco, Tex.: Baylor University Press, 2004.

Larsen, Timothy, David Bebbington, and Mark A. Noll, eds. *Biographical Dictionary of Evangelicals.* Downers Grove, Ill.: InterVarsity, 2003.

Lerner, Gerda. *The Creation of Feminist Consciousness: From the Middle Ages to Eighteen-Seventy.* New York: Oxford University Press, 1993.

McKim, D. K., ed. *Historical Handbook of Major Biblical Interpreters.* Downers Grove, Ill., InterVarsity, 1998.

Matthew, H. C. G., and Brian Harrison, eds. *The Oxford Dictionary of National Biography.* Oxford: Oxford University Press, 2004.

Myers, Sylvia Harstock. *The Bluestocking Circle: Women, Friendship, and the Life of the Mind in Eighteenth-Century England.* Oxford: Clarendon, 1990.

Neil, W. "The Criticism and Theological Use of the Bible, 1700–1950." In *The Cambridge History of the Bible: The West from the Reformation to the Present Day.* Edited by S. L. Greenslade, 238–93. Cambridge: Cambridge University Press, 1963.

Niditch, Susan. "The Wronged Woman Righted: An Analysis of Genesis 38." *Harvard Theological Review* 72 (1979): 143–49.

Nightingale, Florence. *Florence Nightingale's Spiritual Journey: Biblical Annotations, Sermons and Journal Notes.* Vol. 2 of *The Collected Works of Florence Nightingale.* Edited by Lynn McDonald. Waterloo, ON: Wilfred Laurier University Press, 2001.

Perrin, Noel. *Dr. Bowdler's Legacy: A History of Expurgated Books in England and America.* New York: Atheneum, 1969.

Raser, Harold E. *Phoebe Palmer: Her Thought and Life.* Lewiston: Mellen Press, 1987.

Rashkow, Illona N. "The Rape of Dinah." In *Upon Dark Places: Anti-Semitism and Sexism in English Renaissance Biblical Translation.* Bible and Literature Series 28, 75–96. Sheffield: Almond Press, 1990.

Reed, James E., and Ronnie Prevost. *A History of Christian Education*. Nashville: Broadman & Holman, 1993.

Riesen, Richard Allan. *Criticism and Faith in Late Victorian Scotland: A.B. Davidson, William Robertson Smith and George Adam Smith*. Lanham, Md.: University Press of America, 1985.

Robertson, Darrel M. "The Feminization of American Religion: An Examination of Recent Interpretations of Women and Religion in Victorian America." *Christian Scholars' Review* 8.3 (1978): 238–46.

Sage, Lorna, ed. *The Cambridge Guide to Women's Writing in English*. Cambridge: Cambridge University Press, 1999.

Selvidge, Marla J. *Notorious Voices: Feminist Biblical Interpretation 1500–1920*. New York: Continuum, 1996.

Shaw, Susan J. *A Religious History of Julia Evelina Smith's 1876 Translation of the Holy Bible: Doing More Than Any Man Has Ever Done*. San Francisco: Mellen Press, 1993.

Smith, Gail. "Reading the Word: Harriet Beecher Stowe and Interpretation." Ph.D. Diss., University of Virginia, 1993.

———. "Reading with the Other: Hermeneutics and the Politics of Difference in Stowe's *Dred*." *American Literature* 69.2 (1997): 289–315.

Stevens, L. Robert. "Intertextual Construction of Faith: Julia Wedgwood (1833–1913)." In *Women's Theology in Nineteenth-Century Britain*. Edited by Julie Melnyk, 83–93. New York: Garland, 1998.

Straight, Julie. "Religious Controversy in Hester Chapone's Letters on the Improvement of the Mind." *Nineteenth-Century Contexts* 27.4 (2005): 315–34.

Summers, Anne. "Ministering Angels." *History Today* 39 (1989): 31–37.

Tapp, Anne Michele. "An Ideology of Expendability: Virgin Daughter Sacrifice in Genesis 19:1-11, Judges 11.30-39 and 19:22-26." In *Anti-Covenant: Counter-Reading Women Lives in the Hebrew Bibl*. Edited by Mieke Bal, 157–74. Sheffield: Almond Press, 1989.

Trible, Phyllis. "Bringing Miriam Out of the Shadows." *Bible Review* 5 (1989): 14–25.

———. "Genesis 22: The Sacrifice of Sarah." In *"Not in Heaven." Coherence and Complexity in Biblical Narrative*. Edited by Jason Rosenblatt and Joseph Sitterson. Indiana Studies in Biblical Literature, 170–91. Bloomington: Indiana University Press, 1991.

———. *Texts of Terror: Literary-Feminist Readings of Biblical Narratives*. Philadelphia: Fortress, 1984.

Tweed, Thomas A. "An American Pioneer in the Study of Religion: Hannah Adams (1755–1831) and Her Dictionary of All Religions." *Journal of the American Academy of Religion* 60.3 (1992): 437–64.

Twycross-Martin, Henrietta. "The Drunkard, the Brute, and the *Paterfamilias:* The Temperance Fiction of the Early Victorian Writer Sarah Stickney Ellis." In *Women of Faith in Victorian Culture: Reassessing the Angel in the House*. Edited by Anne Hogan and Andrew Bradstock, 6–30. London: Macmillan, 1998.

Wagenknecht, Edward. *Harriet Beecher Stowe: The Known and the Unknown.* New York: Oxford University Press, 1965.

Washington, Margaret, ed. *Narrative of Sojourner Truth.* New York: Random House, 1993.

Welter, Barbara. "The Cult of True Womanhood: 1820–1860." *American Quarterly* 18 (1966): 151–74.

———. "The Feminization of American Religion: 1800–1860." In *Clio's Consciousness Raised: New Perspectives on the History of Women.* Edited by Mary S. Hartman and Lois Banner, 137–57. New York: Harper & Row, 1974.

———. "She Hath Done What She Could: Protestant Women's Missionary Careers in Nineteenth-Century America." *American Quarterly* 30 (1978): 624–38.

Wiseman, Nathaniel. *Elizabeth Baxter: Saint, Evangelist, Preacher, Teacher and Expositor.* London: The Christian Herald, 1928.

———. *Michael Paget Baxter: Clergyman, Evangelist, Editor and Philanthropist.* London: The Christian Herald, 1923.

Zikmund, Barbara Brown. "Women and Ordination." In *In Our Own Voices: Four Centuries of American Women's Religious Writing.* Edited by Rosemary Skinner Keller and Rosemary Radford Ruether, 291–340. Louisville: Westminster John Knox, 1995.

Zink-Sawyer, Beverly. *From Preachers to Suffragists: Women's Rights and Religious Conviction in the Lives of Three Nineteenth-Century American Clergywomen.* Louisville: Westminster John Knox, 2003.

Subject Index

Abel, 22, 37, 45, 76–77, 104; death of, 66–67

Abimelech, King of Gerar: gift of veil to Sarah, 122, 132, 154; relationship with Abraham and Sarah, 107, 110–11, 138–39, 180; relationship with Isaac and Rebekah, 255–56, 259, 262, 266, 274

abolition, 4, 7, 32, 42, 46–47, 71, 207, 211, 234. *See also* slavery.

Abraham (also Abram), 12, 16, 107, 108, 110–17, 119–21, 123–34, 136, 138– 57, 159, 160–64, 166, 167, 170, 172–81, 183, 185–92, 194, 197–200, 202–4, 207, 209–12, 214, 215, 218, 220– 23, 225–29, 231, 233, 235–38, 240, 244–51, 253–57, 259, 261, 262, 266–269, 271–74, 278, 280, 284–91, 293–95, 298, 301, 307, 310, 311, 318, 319, 329, 357, 360, 362, 364, 367, 374, 376, 377, 379, 380, 382, 383, 387, 394, 404, 406, 408, 421, 426, 433, 435

Abram. *See* Abraham

Absalom, David's son, 156–57, 366

abuse: interpretation of, 328, 399–400; by men, 230, 328, 393, 428, 442, 445, 455; of servants, 187; and women's influence, 37, 87, 114,

346–47. *See also* alcohol; women, oppression of

Adam, 21, 22, 23, 24, 25, 26, 27, 28, 30, 31, 33, 35, 36, 37, 38, 39, 40, 41, 42, 43, 45, 46, 48, 52, 53, 54, 55, 56, 57, 58, 59, 60, 61, 65, 66, 67, 69, 70, 71, 72, 73, 74, 75, 76, 77, 78, 79, 80, 82, 83, 84, 85, 93, 95, 97, 98, 99, 100, 101, 102, 103, 105, 146, 166n, 226, 275, 319, 386, 465

adultery, 115, 436

Aguilar, Emanuel, 121

Aguilar, Grace, 10, 443, 452, 457; on Hagar, 191–94; on Leah and Rachel, 343–61; on Rebekah, 268–80

Aikin, Lucy, 27n

alcohol, 86, 89, 206; abuse of, 4, 32–33; women and, 171. *See also* temperance

Alexander, Cecil (Fanny) Frances: on Eve, 61–63; on Rebekah, 280–82

Alexander, Rev. William, 61–62

allegory, 12n, 15, 23, 213, 220, 235, 237, 376, 420, 441, 447, 449–50; of "the two covenants," 174, 220, 235–36. *See also* figure/figurative reading; spiritual sense; type/typology

SCRIPTURE INDEX